MW00715662

R. Gupta's®

Popular Master Guide

IBPS Specialist Officer

Institute of Banking Personnel Selection

HR/Personnel Officer (Scale-I)

Preliminary & Main Exams

by
RPH Editorial Board

2020
EDITION

RAMESH PUBLISHING HOUSE, New Delhi

Published by
O.P. Gupta *for* Ramesh Publishing House

Admin. Office
12-H, New Daryaganj Road, Opp. Officers' Mess,
New Delhi-110002 ① 23261567, 23275224, 23275124

E-mail: info@rameshpublishinghouse.com
Website: www.rameshpublishinghouse.com

Showroom
● Balaji Market, Nai Sarak, Delhi-6 ① 23253720, 23282525
● 4457, Nai Sarak, Delhi-6, ① 23918938

Book Code: R-1799

ISBN: 978-93-86845-79-5

HSN Code: 49011010

SCHEME OF ONLINE EXAMINATIONS

The structure of the Examinations which will be conducted online are as follows:

A. PRELIMINARY EXAMINATION

Sr. No.	Name of Tests	No. of Questions	Maximum Marks	Medium of Exam	Duration
1.	English Language	50	25	English	40 minutes
2.	Reasoning	50	50	English & Hindi	40 minutes
3.	Quantitative Aptitude	50	50	English & Hindi	40 minutes
	Total	150	125		

Candidates have to qualify in each of the three tests by securing minimum cut-off marks to be decided by IBPS. Adequate number of candidates in each category as decided by IBPS depending upon requirements will be shortlisted for Online Main Examination.

B. MAIN EXAMINATION

Name of Tests	No. of Questions	Maximum Marks	Medium of Exam	Duration
Professional Knowledge (HR/Personnel)	60	60	English & Hindi	45 minutes

Note:

- **Penalty for Wrong Answers (Applicable to both – Preliminary and Main Examinations):** There will be penalty for wrong answers marked in the Objective Tests. For each question for which a wrong answer has been given by the candidate one fourth or 0.25 of the marks assigned to that question will be deducted as penalty to arrive at corrected score. If a question is left blank, i.e. no answer is marked by the candidate, there will be no penalty for that question.

- **Interview:** Candidates who have been shortlisted in the Main examination will be called for an Interview to be conducted by the Participating Organisations and coordinated by the Nodal Banks in each State/UT with the help of IBPS.

- The total marks allotted for Interview are 100. The weightage (ratio) of Online (Main Exam) and interview will be 80:20 respectively.

Contents

Personnel Management; Human Resource Development (HRD); Organizational Behaviour; Industrial Relations; Trade Unions; Labour Legislation and Administration; Settlements of Industrial Disputes and Wage Legislation; Labour Administration

Numbers; HCF and LCM; Simplification; Surds and Indices; Ratio and Proportion; Partnership; Average; Profit and Loss; Simple and Compound Interest; Time and Work; Area and Perimeter; Volume and Surface Area; Data Interpretation.

Comprehension Passages; Synonyms & Antonyms; Fill in the Blanks; Spotting Errors; Sentence Correction; Cloze Test; Idioms & Phrases; Reordering Sentences; Spelling Errors.

Series; Coding-Decoding; Symbol Substitution; Blood Relation; Direction Sense; Statement Analysis; Sitting Arrangement; Data Sufficiency; Coded Inequalities; Input Interpretations; Drawing Inference; Syllogism; Cause & Effect; Course of Action; Distinguishing Argument; Drawing Conclusions; Statement Assumptions; Cubes and Dice; Figure Series; Analogies or Relationships; Classification or Odd-One Out.

Institute of Banking Personnel Selection (IBPS) Specialist (HR/Personnel) Officer Scale-I Online Preliminary Exam 2018*

REASONING

Directions (Qs. No. 1-5): *Read the following information carefully to answer the following questions.*

Twelve friends P, Q, R, S, T, U, A, B, C, D, E and F are sitting in a straight line facing north but not necessarily in the same order. F sits third to the right of S. B sits fourth to the right of P, who is not the immediate neighbour of U. C and D are not immediate neighbours of F, who sits second to the right of E. There are two persons between U and A. There are two persons between D and Q. S is not an immediate neighbour of A. E sits at the fifth position from the right end. F is sixth to the right of T. C is not an immediate neighbour of D and Q.

1. Who among the following sit at the extreme ends of the line?
   A. B, C
   B. P, D
   C. T, C
   D. R, F
   E. None of these

2. Who among the following sits third to the right of the fourth to the left of Q?
   A. R
   B. C
   C. A
   D. E
   E. None of these

3. How many persons are there between C and the one who sits on the immediate left of S?
   A. Two
   B. Three
   C. Four
   D. One
   E. None of these

4. Who among the following are immediate neighbours of R?
   A. F and D
   B. E and T
   C. A and C
   D. F and Q
   E. None of these

5. Which of the following statements is/are true?
   A. There are three friends between F and R
   B. T and B are immediate neighbours
   C. C sits at one of the ends of the line
   D. P is on the immediate left of D
   E. None of these

Directions (Qs. No. 6-10): *Study the following information carefully and answer the given questions:*

Twelve persons are sitting in two parallel rows containing six persons each, in such a way that there is an equal distance between adjacent persons. In row-1, J, K, L, M, N and O are seated (but not necessarily in the same order) and all of them are facing south. In row-2, C, D, E, F, G and H are seated (but not necessarily in the same order) and all of them are facing north. Therefore, in the given seating arrangement each person seated in a row faces another person of the other row.

M sits third to the left of J. The person facing M sits second to the left of H. Two persons are sitting between H and E. L and K are immediate neighbours. L and K do not sit at any of the extreme ends of the line. Only one person sits between N and L. The person facing K is an immediate neighbour of C. G is not an immediate neighbour of E. D does not face M.

6. Who amongst the following sits seconds to the right of the person who faces F?
   A. L   B. K
   C. N   D. J
   E. Cannot be determined

7. Which of the following statements regarding N is true?
   A. N sits second to the left of L
   B. M sits to immediate left of N
   C. H faces N
   D. K is an immediate neighbour of N
   E. The person who faces N is an immediate neighbour of D

8. Who amongst the following faces E?
   A. M   B. K
   C. L   D. J
   E. Cannot he determined

9. Who amongst the following sits exactly between H and F?
   A. G   B. C
   C. D   D. E
   E. Cannot be dctermined

10. Four of the following live are alike in a certain way based on the given seating arrangement and thus form a group. Which is the one that does not belong to the group?
   A. O   B. C
   C. H   D. L
   E. J

Directions (Qs. No. 11-15): *Study the information given below and answer the questions based on it.*

Some persons were born in the same year but in different months *i.e.* from January to December. Only two persons were born before A. R is the youngest person. The number of person born before Q is same as after R. Two months gap between R and C. P is the 2nd eldest person. S was born in May. M is elder to C but younger to S. K was born in a month which was having 31 days. The number of persons born before A is same as after C. The number of month gap between Q and S is same as M and R. P was not born in March and C was not born in July. R was not born in December. The number of month gap between A and M is same as M and K.

11. Who among the following was born in October?
   A. No one   B. R
   C. K   D. S
   E. M

12. What is the total number of person?
   A. 6   B. 7
   C. 8   D. 9
   E. 5

13. Who among the following is the eldest?
   A. Q   B. A
   C. C   D. R
   E. K

14. Which of the following is TRUE?
   A. Q was born in February
   B. Only one person was born after R
   C. M was born in March
   D. A was born in a month which was having 30 days
   E. C was born in October

15. Who among the following is the youngest?
   A. Q   B. A
   C. C   D. R
   E. K

Directions (Qs. No. 16-20): *Study the information given below and answer the questions based on it.*

A, B, C, D, E, F, G and H are eight students of a school. They study in standards VI, VII, and VIII with not more than three in any standard. Each of them has a favorite subject from Physics, Geography, English, Marathi, Mathematics, Chemistry, Biology and Economics but not necessarily in the same order.

D likes Chemistry and studies in standard VIII with only H. B does not study in standard VII. E and A study in the same standard but not with B. C and F study in the same standard. Those who study in standard VI do not like Mathematics or Biology. F likes Physics. The one who studies in standard VIII likes English. C does not like Geography. A's favorite subject is Marathi and G does not like Biology.

16. Which of the following groups of students studied in VII standard?
   A. DHA   B. EAG
   C. BCF   D. ABC
   E. Cannot be determined

17. Which of the following combinations of student-standard-subject is correct?
   A. D-VIII-Biology   B. A-VI-Marathi
   C. G-VII-Math   D. F-VIII-Economics
   E. None of these

18. What is C's favorite subject?
   A. Chemistry   B. English
   C. Biology   D. Economics
   E. Geography

19. In which standard does C study?
   A. VI   B. VII
   C. VIII   D. Either VI or VIII
   E. None of these

20. Which subject does H like?
   A. Marathi   B. Physics
   C. English   D. Geography
   E. None of these

Directions (Qs. No. 21-25): *Study the information given below and answer the questions based on it.*

Nine boys Vikash, Kamal, Sunil, Saurabh, Rohit, Sanjay, Amit, Anit and Sushil stays in a nine floor building and all of them stays on different floors. Each of them likes different girls namely—Sanjana, Surabhi, Amita, Anita, Komal, Suhana, Kumkum, Saroj and Susheela. Each boys belongs to different cities *i.e.* Patna, Lucknow, Chennai, Varanasi, Mirzapur, Allahabad, Mathura, Noida and Agra but necessarily in the same order. The topmost floor is numbered 9, the floor below it is numbered 8 and so on, and the ground floor is numbered 1.

The one who likes Surabhi stays on an even numbered floor. Sanjay does not belong to Allahabad. The one who belongs to Lucknow stays on the topmost floor. The one who likes Sanjana stays immediately below the one who likes Amita. Sanjay likes Anita and does not stay on the ground floor. Vikash belongs to Chennai and stays on an even numbered floor and he likes Sanjana. Saurabh stays on the second floor and belongs to Mirzapur. There are three boys between the one who likes

Suhana and the one who likes Komal. The one who likes Suhana stays below the boy who likes Komal. The one who belongs to Allahabad stays on the third floor. The one who likes Saroj does not stay on sixth floor. There is one floor between the floors in which the one who likes Susheela and the one who likes Kumkum stay. Kamal stays on an even numbered floor below the floor on which Vikash stays. There are two floors between the floors on which the boys who are from Mathura and Chennai. The boy who likes Komal is from Mathura. Sushil belongs to Patna. The one who belongs to Noida stays on the fourth floor. Kamal does not belong to Varanasi and does not like Anita and Komal. There are three floors between the floors on which Sushil and Amit stay. Sunil stays on a floor immediately above the Anit's floor. The one who likes Kumkum stays immediately above Sushil. There is one floor between the floors on which Sanjay and Amit stay.

21. Which among the following boys likes Anita?
   A. Sanjay   B. Amit
   C. Anit   D. Rohit
   E. Vikash

22. Who among the following stays between the floor of Sunil and Saurabh?
   A. Anit   B. Amit
   C. Kamal   D. Vikash
   E. Rohit

23. Which of the following combinations is true?
   A. Sanjay – Suhana – Varanasi
   B. Amit – Amita – Allahabad
   C. Rohit – Saroj – Varanasi
   D. Sunil – Susheela – Noida
   E. Kamal – Surabhi – Chennai

24. If 'Sanjay' is related to 'Mathura', 'Vikash' is related to 'Agra', in the same way 'Kamal' is related to?
   A. Allahabad   B. Patna
   C. Chennai   D. Noida
   E. Varanasi

25. How many boys stay between the one who likes Amita and the one who likes Kumkum?
   A. Five   B. Two
   C. One   D. Six
   E. Four

Directions (Qs. No. 26-30): *In these questions, a relationship between different elements is shown in the statements. The statements are followed by two conclusions.*

26. **Statements** : A ≥ P = S > T, V < B = T > X
    Conclusions : I. A > X   II. P < B
    A. only conclusion I is true
    B. only conclusion II is true
    C. either conclusion I or II is true
    D. neither conclusion I nor II is true
    E. both conclusions I and II are true

27. **Statements** : S > U > V, Y < U < Z,
    Z < X > W
    Conclusions : I. S < Z   II. X > Y
    A. only conclusion I is true
    B. only conclusion II is true
    C. either conclusion I or II is true
    D. neither conclusion I nor II is true
    E. both conclusions I and II are true

28. **Statements** : P < X < Y < Q, S > Y < T,
    P = V > R
    Conclusions : I. V < S   II. T > R
    A. only conclusion I is true
    B. only conclusion II is true
    C. either conclusion I or II is true
    D. neither conclusion I nor II is true
    E. both conclusions I and II are true

29. **Statements** : A ≥ B > C, D ≥ E = F ≥ G,
    H ≥ I = E
    Conclusions : I. H < C   II. H > D
    A. only conclusion I is true
    B. only conclusion II is true
    C. either conclusion I or II is true
    D. neither conclusion I nor II is true
    E. both conclusions I and II are true

30. **Statements** : A ≥ B > C, D ≥ E ≥ F > B,
    P ≥ Q > E = S
    Conclusions : I. P < B   II. S > A
    A. only conclusion I is true
    B. only conclusion II is true
    C. either conclusion I or II is true
    D. neither conclusion I nor II is true
    E. both conclusions I and II are true

Directions (Qs. No. 31-35): *In each of the questions below are given four statements followed by four conclusions numbered I, II, III and IV. You have to take the given statements to be true even if they seem to be at variance from commonly known facts. Read all the conclusions and then decide which of the given conclusions logically follows from the given statements disregarding commonly known facts.*

31. **Statements** : All lotus are beautiful.
    All beautiful are Rose.
    No Rose are stinky.
    All sky are Rose.
    Conclusions : I. All stinky are beautiful is a possibility.
    II. Some stinky are lotus.
    III. Some Rose are Stinky is a possibility.
    IV. All beautiful can never be Sky.
    A. None follows
    B. Only I and IV follow
    C. Only II follows
    D. Only II and III follow
    E. None of these

32. **Statements** : Some planes are waters.
    Some waters are doors.
    All doors are guitars.
    No guitar is a flat.
    Conclusion : I. At least some guitars are Planes.
    II. All doors are flat is a possibility.
    III. Some planes are both waters and doors.
    IV. At least some flat is a door.
    A. Only IV follows
    B. Only either II or III follow
    C. Only III follows
    D. Only I follows
    E. None follows

33. **Statements** : Some red are blue.
    Some blue are grey.
    All grey are white.
    No white is black.

Conclusion : I. No black is grey.
                   II. Some blue are white.
                   III. Some black are red.
                   IV. No black is red.
A. Only I and II follow
B. Only either III or IV follows
C. Only I and either III or IV follow
D. Only I, II and either III or IV follow
E. None of these

34. **Statements :** All red are white.
                  Some white are pink.
                  Some pink are yellow.
                  No yellow is blue.

Conclusion : I. No blue is pink.
                   II. Some pink are red.
                   III. Some blue are red.
                   IV. Some blue are pink.
A. None follows
B. Only either I or IV follows
C. Only I follows
D. Only III & IV follow
E. All follow

35. **Statements :** All green are pink.
                  Some pink are black.
                  Some black are blue.
                  All blue are white.

Conclusions : I. Some black are white.
                    II. Some blue are pink.
                    III. Some pink are green.
                    IV. No green is white.
A. None follows
B. Only I and III follows
C. Only III follows
D. Only either I or II follows
E. None of these

Directions (Qs. No. 36-40): *In each question below is given a statement followed by two courses of action numbered I and II. You have to assume everything in the statement to be true and on the basis of the information given in the statement. Decide which of the suggested courses of action logically follow(s) for pursuing. Give answer:*

36. **Statement :** The government of India has launched a new scheme known as "Digital India" to help promote Digital Banking.

Course of action:
I. Traditional Banks should embrace the new scheme as it relates to the modern trend of digitalized banking.
II. Traditional Banks should do nothing as a bunch of money transaction apps cannot replace the traditional banking system, and hail it as a useless scheme.
A. If only course of action I follows
B. If only course of action II follows
C. If both I and II follow
D. If neither I nor II follows
E. If either I or II follows

37. **Statement :** A student was caught cheating in a class-test.

Course of action:
I. The teacher should report him to the principal.
II. Teacher should accept his test answer sheet and leave him with a final warning.
A. Only course of action I follows
B. Only course of action II follows
C. Both I and II follow
D. Neither I nor II follows
E. Either I or II follows

38. **Statement :** IT companies have stated that a large number of Engineers employed in their firms are not suitable for employment as they lack basic programming skills.

Course of action:
I. They should fire all unskilled and unproductive employees.
II. They should not fire the employees.
A. Only course of action I follows
B. Only course of action II follows
C. Both I and II follow
D. Neither I nor II follows
E. Either I or II follows

39. **Statement :** State police of Bihar came under the cloud with recent news that 9 lakh liters of liquor has been missing from the police station after the declaration of Bihar a

dry state. The police department claimed that the whole of the liquor had been drunk by rats.

Course of Actions:

I. A thorough investigation should be ordered and those who are liable if any then they must have to be punished.

II. Suspension of those police officers who claim that rats drunk the liquor.

A. If only course of action I follow

B. If only course of action II follows

C. If both the course of action follows

D. If neither course of action fallows

E. Data inadequate

40. Statement : There has been an allegation on some of army officers that they had been involved in illegal arms trade with a few arms smuggler.

Course of Actions:

I. An investigation should be ordered by the Indian government to reveal the actual culprits.

II. They should be punished with court marshal.

A. Only course of action I follows

B. Only course of action II follows

C. Both I and II follow

D. Neither I nor II follows

E. Either I or II follows

Directions (Qs. No. 41-45): *The question below, there is a statement followed by two conclusions/ assumptions numbered I and II. You have to assume everything in the statement to be true. Then consider the two conclusion/assumption together and decide which of them follows/implicit beyond a reasonable doubt from the information given in the statement.*

41. Statement : High pressure boilers are hazardous pieces of equipment, which are strictly regulated with special laws.

Conclusions:

I. If not regulated, high pressure boilers will be easily available in the market

II. High pressure boilers are rare.

A. Only conclusion I follows

B. Only conclusion II follows

C. Both conclusion I and II follows

D. Neither conclusion I nor II follows

E. Either conclusion I or II follows

42. Statement : The principal announced that students who score more than 95% will get special prize and medal. Kevin scored 96% but was found to have cheated in some of the exams.

Conclusions:

I. Kevin is going to get special prize and medal.

II. Kevin might not get any prize.

A. Only conclusion I follows

B. Only conclusion II follows

C. Both conclusion I and II follows

D. Neither conclusion I nor II follows

E. Either conclusion I or II follows.

43. Statement : Using calculator for simpler calculations adversely affects mathematical abilities of children.

Assumptions:

I. Using calculator for complex calculations may not affect mathematical abilities adversely.

II. Complex calculations cannot be done manually without the help of a calculator.

A. Only I is implicit

B. Only II is implicit

C. Either I or II is implicit

D. Neither I or II is implicit

E. Both I and II are implicit

44. Statement : An advertisement by Easy Air, a private airliner reads: 'Travel to Meerut by our airlines and get a chance to win an all-expenses-paid holiday to Bangkok'.

Assumptions:

I. Easy Air flights are available for Bangkok.

II. The city of Meerut has an airport.

A. Only I is implicit

B. Only II is implicit

C. Either I or II is implicit

D. Neither I or II is implicit

E. Both I and II are implicit

45. **Statement :** Ms. Suu Kyi, a recipient of the Nobel Peace Prize, has found it pragmatic not to challenge the official rhetoric in Myanmar, which suggests the military's actions were aimed at tackling "terror" in Rakhine.

Conclusions:

I. Ms. Suu Kyi does not want to upset the fragile balance of power.

II. Ms. Suu Kyi's action shows lack of empathy for the Rohingya in a country.

A. only conclusion I follows

B. only conclusion II follows

C. both conclusion I and II follow

D. neither conclusion I nor II follows

E. either conclusion I or II follows

Directions (Qs. No. 46-50): *Each of the question below consists of a question and three statements numbered I, II and III given below it. You have to decide whether the data provided in three statement are sufficient to answer the question.*

46. How many daughters does W have?

I. B and D are the sister of M.

II. M's father T is the husband of W.

III. Out of the three children which T has, only one is a boy.

A. I and III are sufficient to answer the question

B. All I, II and III are required to answer the question

C. I and II are sufficient to answer the question

D. Question cannot be answered even with all I, II and III

E. II and III are sufficient to answer the question

47. Among A, B, C, D, E, F and G, is B greater than F?

I. A is either greater or equal to B which is lesser than C which is equal to D which is greater than E which is either greater or equal to F which is equal to G.

II. A is lesser or equal to B which is equal to C which is greater to D which is greater to E which is lesser to F which is lesser to G.

III. A is greater to B which is greater to C which is equal to D which is greater or equal to E which is greater to F which is lesser to G.

A. I and II

B. II and III

C. III

D. Any Two

E. All of the above

48. In which direction is M with respect to N?

I. M is to the south of G, which is to the west of H. G is to the east of T.

II. N is between G and H.

III. N is to the north-west of T.

A. Only I and II

B. Only I

C. Only II and III

D. Only I and III

E. Only I and either II or III

49. Are writers not words?

I. Some writers are covers. No cover is a page.

II. All writers are books. Some books are covers.

III. No book is a word. Some words are pens.

A. Only I

B. Only II and III

C. Only I and III

D. I, II and III together are not sufficient

E. Only I and II

50. Who among Nitesh, Mahi, Rita, Priya, Neha and Rahul, each having different heights, is the tallest?

I. Mahi is taller than Nitesh but shorter than Neha.

II. Only two of them are shorter than Rita.

III. Priya is taller than only Rahul.

A. Only I and III

B. Only I and II

C. Only II and III

D. All I, II and III together

E. None of these

GENERAL ENGLISH

Directions (Qs. No. 51-55): *Read the following passage carefully and answer the questions that follow. Certain words/phrases are printed in bold to help you locate them while answering some of the questions.*

The Cabinet decision to allow spectrum trading will give a huge **impetus** to the on-going efforts for making broadband available in even the remotest parts of the country under the Digital India campaign. There are many compelling reasons why the time is ripe for the introduction of spectrum trading. One of the objectives of the new National Telecom Policy is to achieve a base of 600 million broadband users, with a minimum access speed of 2 Mbps by 2020. The Centre wants to create digital infrastructure to provide utility services like banking, education and healthcare to every Indian citizen. These ambitious targets can be achieved only if every operator in the country has access to adequate spectrum. The more spectrums an operator holds, the more data traffic it can carry over its network. Despite several rounds of auctions in the last two years, the quantum of airwaves with Indian telecom companies is less than that of their global counterparts. Mobile companies in the US and Japan, for instance, are able to offer high speed video services because they have 30-40 MHz of spectrum. In contrast, a 3G operator in India has only 5 MHz. Spectrum trading will allow the operators to get access to a larger pool of air waves, in turn ensuring that spectrum does not lie fallow. The option to trade spectrum also introduces an element of liquidity to its value. Interest in future auctions will increase because operators can bid with the knowledge that they can get returns by further leasing the airwaves. For smaller operators who are looking for an exit, trading gives them the opportunity to monetize their key asset without going through complex merger or acquisition deals.

However, the guidelines approved by the Cabinet have some concern areas which, if not addressed, could make it difficult for operators to trade spectrum. For example, the spectrum seller will have to pay 11 to 13 per cent of the proceeds to the government in the form of licence fee and spectrum usage charge. This could be a major **deterrent** if the operator is debt-laden or in an exit mode. The other big concern is the rule asking operators who bought spectrum in the 800 MHz band in the 2013 auctions, to first pay the price arrived at in the 2015 auction if they want to enter into a trading deal. Though the prices arrived at in the 2013 auctions were significantly lower than in 2015, both were market-driven processes. Thus the Centre's view that it did not receive the full price then is misplaced.

The benefits of sharing resources can be seen in the telecom tower business where operators were able to drive down costs and improve efficiencies by sharing space on towers. Similar sharing is now happening in the optical fibre cable infrastructure. Spectrum trading will benefit consumers, since at least those operators with adequate spectrum will be able to offer better quality of service. That said, quality improvement across the board will be achieved only when more spectrum is made available.

51. According to the given passage, which among the following is TRUE?
   A. Mobile companies in the US and Japan are able to offer high speed video services.
   B. Mobile companies in US and Japan have 30-40 MHz of spectrum.
   C. A 3G operator in India has only 5 MHz Spectrum trading.
   D. All are true
   E. Only A and B are true.

52. According to the passage, how will Spectrum trading benefit the consumers in India?
   A. Quality of services will improve.
   B. Broad spectrum will be made available.
   C. The cost of telecom companies will rise.
   D. All the above
   E. Only A and B

53. Which of the following concerns in the guidelines approved by the Cabinet needs to be addressed by the Government?
  A. The spectrum seller will have to pay license fee and spectrum usage charge to the government.
  B. The cost was higher for the bidders in the auction of 2013.
  C. The rule asking operators who bought spectrum in the 2013 auctions, to first pay the price arrived at in the 2015 auction if they want to enter into a trading deal.
  D. All of the above
  E. Only A and C

54. Which of the following is the MOST SIMILAR in meaning to "impetus"?
  A. Momentum   B. Block
  C. Check   D. Hindrance
  E. Incentive

55. Which of the following is the MOST OPPOSITE in meaning to "deterrent"?
  A. Disincentive   B. Encouragement
  C. Damper   D. Curb
  E. Restraint

Directions (Qs. No. 56-65): *Read the following passage carefully and answer the questions that follow. Certain words are printed in bold to help you locate them while answering some of these.*

With half the fiscal year nearly complete, it is not surprising that the government is beginning to **fret** over the slow progress of the disinvestment programme. Of the budgeted ₹ 69,500 crore from PSU stake sales, only ₹ 12,700 crore has been raised so far. Reports that the Centre wants the EPFO to park part of the money that it has been allowed to invest in equity market in the CPSE ETF, highlights this desperation. Almost half the stocks in this ETF are companies that have been hard hit by the crash in commodity prices. This is not an asset the EPFO should be investing in now. The Centre, staring at yet another failure to meet its divestment target, appears ready to use any means to inch towards the target set for this year.

The urgency stems from the tight fiscal condition that the country is currently in. The fiscal deficit for the April to June period has already covered 69.3 per cent of the current year's target. This is despite a 36 per cent increase in indirect tax collection in the first five months of the current fiscal, thanks to the steep hike in excise duty on petrol and diesel, and the higher rate of service tax. A slowdown in income tax collection, along with a wide shortfall in the money raised through selling stakes in public sector companies, can make it a challenge for the Centre to meet this fiscal year's targeted deficit of 3.9 per cent of GDP. The increase in pension pay-outs for defence personnel is expected to add pressure on this goal. Inability to raise sufficient revenue can result in the government cutting back on investments, **pegging** back growth.

But the Centre has only itself to blame for this **predicament.** That the divestment department has gone about its task in a very **lackadaisical** manner in recent times is borne out by the fact that the gap between proceeds from stake sales and the budgeted target has been between 20 and 65 per cent since 2011-12. Given the decision to almost double its target for this fiscal, the Centre could have shown more **alacrity** in front-loading the sales this fiscal year, when the equity market was buoyant. The success of the REC's offer for sale in April highlights investor willingness to subscribe when the outlook for stocks is rosy. The divestment department needs to employ professionals to advise it on the timing of the sales better. Anyone who was tuned in to the stock market would have known that the second half of the year was expected to be rocky for stocks, given the impending monetary policy normalisation by the Fed. The offer for sale mechanism being employed for these stake sales also needs a rethink. With a retail discount of 5 per cent and the almost immediate availability of allotted shares, many investors have taken to short-term speculation through these offers.

56. What is the author of the above passage trying to suggest through it?
  A. The tardiness in PSU stake sales will pressure the fiscal deficit.

B. The offer for sale mechanism for stake sales of companies must be remodelled.

C. The disinvestment programme is not furthering with a desired pace.

D. Only A and C

E. All of the above

57. Why the author believes that it is a challenge for the Centre to meet this fiscal year's targeted deficit of 3.9 per cent of GDP?

A. The fiscal deficit for the April to June period has already covered 69.3 per cent of the current year's target.

B. Slowdown in income tax collection.

C. Wide shortfall in the money collected through selling stakes in public sector companies.

D. All of the above

E. None of the above

58. Which among the following statements is **TRUE** according to the passage given above?

A. ₹ 12,500 crore has been raised so far through PSU stake sales.

B. In the first five months of the current fiscal there has been a 36 per cent increase in indirect tax collection.

C. The difference in proceeds from stake sales and the budgeted target is around 20 and 55 per cent since 2011-12.

D. Only A and C

E. Only B and C

59. What could be the results of the Centre's inability to raise sufficient revenues?

A. Government might cut back its invest-ments.

B. The growth of the country could be pegged back.

C. Steep hike in excise duty on petrol and diesel may take place.

D. Only A and B

E. All A, B and C

60. Which among the following is **NOT TRUE** according to the passage given above?

A. A person who knows about stock market would have known that the second half of the year would be unhealthy for stock sales.

B. Many investors have bought the shares of the disinvestment portfolio just because of the 5% retail discount and immediate availability of stocks.

C. The targeted deficit of fiscal year 2011-12 is 3.9% of the GDP.

D. Only B and C

E. All are correct

61. Which among the following express the opposite meaning of the word "Fret" as given in the passage?

A. Affront   B. Calm

C. Anguish   D. Brood

E. Chafe

62. Which among the following express the opposite meaning of the word "Pegging" as given in the passage?

A. Clinch   B. Fasten

C. Remove   D. Tighten

E. Pin

63. Which among the following express the similar meaning of the word "Predicament" as given in the passage?

A. Fix   B. Fortune

C. Solution   D. Quandary

E. Ease

64. Which among the following express the SIMILAR meaning of the word "Lackadaisical" as given in the passage?

A. Abstracted   B. Careful

C. Active   D. Hard-working

E. Caring

65. Which among the following express the similar meaning of the word "Alacrity" as given in the passage?

A. Avidity   B. Cessation

C. Idleness   D. Repose

E. Inaction

Directions (Qs. No. 66-71): *In the following passage there are blanks each of which has been numbered. These numbers are printed below the passage and against each, five words/phrases are suggested, one of which fits the blank appropriately.*

Citing intensifying regulatory uncertainty, Wells Fargo is ___**66**___ roughly 200 agreements with builders, brokers and other real estate firms that the bank uses to bolster its mortgage business. One of the nation's largest mortgage lenders, Wells Fargo ___**67**___ that it was ending all mortgage marketing services and desk rental agreements with builders and real estate brokers. These arrangements are widespread throughout the highly competitive mortgage industry, where lenders scrap to find ___**68**___ borrowers. Such arrangements involve, for example, Wells renting desk space from a home builder in an effort to more easily sell mortgages to the home buyers passing through the sales office. "The decision was made as a result of increasing ___**69**___ surrounding regulatory oversight of these types of arrangements," the bank said in a statement. A bank spokesman said the move was not related to a specific regulatory problem or investigation. Rather, he said, the bank was responding to broader regulatory scrutiny of such arrangements, which are ___**70**___ by the Real Estate Settlement Procedures Act. The federal law is meant to ___**71**___ mortgage lenders, real estate brokers, builders and any other party involved in the home buying process from handing out or receiving kickbacks in exchange for referrals.

66. Find out the appropriate word in each case.
  A. serving   B. giving
  C. signed   D. having
  E. proclaiming

67. Find out the appropriate word in each case.
  A. noticed   B. say
  C. announced   D. given
  E. established

68. Find out the appropriate word in each case.
  A. good   B. eligible
  C. sustainable   D. amiable
  E. passable

69. Find out the appropriate word in each case.
  A. confusion   B. burden
  C. pressures   D. uncertainty
  E. curiosity

70. Find out the appropriate word in each case.
  A. held   B. told
  C. acclaimed   D. given
  E. governed

71. Find out the appropriate word in each case.
  A. provide   B. prevent
  C. allow   D. accept
  E. pause

Directions (Qs. No. 72-77): *In the given question, select the sentence which should follow the given statement in a grammatically and conceptually appropriate manner.*

72. Even though the school premises had a lot of space _____.
  A. there were plenty of play areas for the children
  B. there was no playground for the children
  C. yet it remain underutilized
  D. there was no shortage of classrooms
  E. none of the above

73. Political power is just as permanent as today's newspaper. Ten years down the line, _____ the most powerful man in any state today.
  A. Political power shall have shifted weight into the hands of
  B. New political parties shall have emerged
  C. Few shall know, or care about
  D. A new party may have absorbed into its ranks
  E. None of these

74. Evolving in the mid-eighteenth century, from the pleasure houses of Japan where courtesans who would entertain the samurai, _____
  A. would discuss the state matters secretly.
  B. would hold plays which would entertain the crowd.
  C. the first geisha was actually men.
  D. the first geisha were actually men, who entertained the guests with drums and music.
  E. the first geisha will be actually men, who entertained the guests with drums and music and were all warriors.

12

75. The media's relationship with democracy has allowed people _____.
   A. As well as the conviction that media should be democratic itself and media ownership concentration is not democratic
   B. The right to participate in media and share the information they found and want to contribute to the people through the media.
   C. To be seen as a theater in modern societies in which political participation is enacted through a medium of talk and a realm of social life which public opinion can be formed
   D. To communicate with one another through digital media and share the information they want to
   E. None of the above

76. The influences in our lives—family, school, church, work environment, friends _____
   A. all have made their silent unconscious impact on us and help shape our frame of reference, our paradigms, our maps.
   B. try to change outward attitudes and behaviours which does very little good in the long run
   C. shows how powerfully our paradigms affect the way we interact with other people.
   D. begin to realize that others see them differently from their own apparently equally clear and objective point of view
   E. None of the above

77. To enjoy good health, to bring true happiness to one's family, to bring peace to all, one must first discipline _____.
   A. to clear a good place for man's dwelling
   B. and control one's own mind
   C. to create a hindrance in the music that is in nature
   D. to know the vast world outside
   E. None of the above

Directions (Qs. No. 78-82): *Select the phrase/connector from the given three options which can be used to form a single sentence from the two sentences given below, implying the same meaning as expressed in the statement sentences. Pick out the option which when used to start a sentence combines both the above sentences in one.*

78. Flagging off partnerships in a host of economic and development projects through a Memorandum of Understanding has been done. The two Prime Ministers have set the stage for long-term collaboration in spheres ranging from energy and infrastructure to special economic zones.
   I. Since
   II. While
   III. The reason behind the
   A. Only I   B. Only II
   C. Only III   D. All of the above
   E. None of these

79. New Delhi's anxiety over Chinese presence might be justified. It should avoid using the China lens to view Sri Lanka, respecting the country's autonomy to engage with any willing partner.
   I. While   II. Awhile
   III. Among
   A. Only I   B. Only II
   C. Only III   D. Both I and III
   E. None of these

80. The Modi government's fiscal deficit bumped to 3.5% of GDP in 2017-18, a slippage from the figure targeted in the budget. 3% of the GDP was envisaged in the fiscal consolidation unveiled earlier.
   I. In the first place   II. Although
   III. As a result
   A. Only I   B. Only III
   C. Only II   D. Both II and III
   E. All of these

81. The partition was enforced by the ruling government. People started rushing towards their side of the town before the riots began.
   I. Nevertheless   II. As soon as
   III. In place of
   A. Only I   B. Only III
   C. Only I and III D. Only II and III
   E. None of these

82. The U.S. Administration announced its intent to withdraw from the Paris Agreement on climate change against a backdrop of rising carbon emissions, extreme weather events that devastated homes; and one of the top three hottest years on record. The momentum continued as other countries held firm in their determination to honour national and international commitments under Paris, in the face of the U.S. announcement.

I. Additionally

II. By comparison

III. Yet

A. Only I

B. Only II

C. Both I and III

D. Only III

E. All of these

Directions (Qs. No. 83-87): *In the given question, there are five sentences numbered 1,2,3,4 and 5. Read the sentences and find out which of the combinations is correct and mark the respective option.*

83. 1. Goa has so much for the fun-loving tourists.

2. Goa is always ready to welcome its guests.

3. No place can beat Goa in India.

4. Thus tourists receive a very warm treatment in Goa.

5. Whenever we think of a beach holiday,

A. 12453 B. 15324

C. 15432 D. 12543

E. 12345

84. 1. Safdar, Ajay and I dashed out of the classroom as the bell rang.

2. He was our leader.

3. It was the lunch break and we had a whole hour to play.

4. Safdar was the tallest, also the strongest amongst us.

5. Ajay and I followed him meekly like lambs.

A. 14523 B. 15423

C. 12345 D. 13524

E. 13425

85. 1. When you infuse creativity into your writing, you try to

2. You can paint it with your words thus selection of words is important

3. Stoke the emotions of your readers by narrating a story

4. In this way you can make a story that they can relate to easily

5. Thus creative writing classes are getting popular these days

A. 13425 B. 13245

C. 14523 D. 13254

E. 12543

86. 1. Online bingo or Internet bingo sites are virtual in nature.

2. It includes online blackjack, slots, roulette and poker.

3. The odds are undoubtedly better online.

4. These sites allow users to place bets on bingo games.

5. There are several benefits of playing online.

A. 14253 B. 12345

C. 12435 D. 14325

E. 15432

87. 1. Hospitals require one centralized software

2. Since all the functions and working of the hospital will depend on it

3. System which smartly manages a lot of functions

4. It should be able to manage a huge crowd and Should not crash easily

5. The entire hospital can then be easily managed by one software solution

A. 12345 B. 13245

C. 12354 D. 13425

E. 14325

Directions (Qs. No. 88-92): *In the following question, a part of the sentence is printed in bold. Below the sentence alternatives to the bold part are given at (A), (B), (C) and (D) which may help improve the sentence. Choose the correct alternative. In case the given sentence is correct, your answer is (E) i.e. No correction required.*

88. Many subsequent attempts at human **self-definition has faced similar problems** in relation to exceptionality.

A. self-defining has faced similar problems

B. self-definition have faced similar problems

C. self-definition has faced similar problem

D. self-definition has faced similarity problems

E. No correction required

89. They wanted to show how desire interacts with the material world, and to **examine how it were entwined with politics.**

A. examination how it were entwined with politics

B. examine how it were entwine with politically

C. examine how it was entwined with politics

D. examine why it were entwined at politics

E. No correction required

90. That all meaningful experience **requires tapping in to a divine realm** will trigger a severe frown in any non-believer.

A. required tapping in to a divine realm

B. requires tapping into a divine realm

C. requires tapping in to at divine realm

D. required tapped in to a divine realms

E. No correction required

91. Although China has recognized India's sovereignty over Sikkim and had initiated the trade at Nathu La pass, the Doklam fiasco **could mean trouble at all** ends.

A. could mean trouble by all

B. could mean trouble for all

C. could meant trouble at all

D. can mean trouble by all

E. No correction required

92. For centuries, caste dictated almost every aspect of Hindu religious and social life, **with every group occupying** a specific place in this complex hierarchy.

A. by every group occupying

B. with each group occupying

C. by each group occupying

D. through every group occupying

E. No correction required

Directions (Qs. No. 93-97): *Rearrange the following six sentences (a), (b), (c), (d), (e) and (f) in the proper sequence to form a meaningful paragraph: then answer the questions given below them.*

(*a*) Having a bank account for the purpose of savings and remittances has always been the central objective behind banking.

(*b*) Keeping in mind the goal of financial inclusion and extending finance to small businesses and low-income households, under-serviced by traditional commercial banks.

(*c*) The Reserve Bank of India's decision to allow 10 players to set up small finance banks out of the 72 applicants may seem conservative.

(*d*) The need for institutions with greater penetration and wide distribution models has, to some extent, been met with the issue of payments banks licences.

(*e*) With more than half the population in India still unable to access such basic services,

(*f*) But by permitting eight microfinance institutions (MFIs) to set up small banks, the RBI has chosen wisely.

93. Which of the following will be the **Fourth** sentence?

A. (*a*)   B. (*b*)

C. (*f*)   D. (*d*)

E. (*c*)

94. Which of the following will be the **First** sentence?

A. (*a*)   B. (*f*)

C. (*c*)   D. (*d*)

E. (*e*)

95. Which of the following will be the **Last** sentence?

A. (*f*)   B. (*d*)

C. (*c*)   D. (*e*)

E. (*a*)

96. Which of the following will be the **Third** sentence?

A. (*a*)   B. (*b*)

C. (c)   D. (d)
E. (e)

97. Which of the following will be the **Fifth** sentence?
A. (a)   B. (f)
C. (c)   D. (d)
E. (e)

Directions (Qs. No. 98-100): *In each question below, a sentence is broken into four parts which are marked as (A), (B), (C) and (D). One of them may be grammatically or structurally wrong in the context of the sentence. The letter of that word is the answer. If there is no wrong word or group of words, your answer will be (E), i.e., 'No error'. (Ignore the errors of punctuation, if any).*

98. (A) There is just not enough/(B) timing in my job to sit around/(C) talking about how we feel/(D) about each other./(E) No error.

99. (A) Reasonable ambition, if supported/(B) at persistent efforts,/(C) is likely to yield/(D) the desired results./(E) No error.

100. (A) Even after worked in the office/(B) for as many as fifteen years,/(C) he still does not understand/(D) the basic objectives of the work./(E) No error.

QUANTITATIVE APTITUDE

Directions (Qs. No. 101-105): *What will come in place of the question mark (?) in the following number series?*

101. 51, 60, 42, 78, ?, 150
A. 96   B. 108
C. 6   D. 144
E. None of these

102. 82, ?, 286, 373, 436, 451
A. 155   B. 175
C. 139   D. 145
E. 187

103. 20, 32, 30, ?, 105, 360, 577.5
A. 85   B. 90
C. 80   D. 75
E. 70

104. 49, 193, 766, 3055, 12208, ?
A. 47062   B. 49643
C. 48105   D. 48817
E. 46611

105. 21, 27, 64, 204, ?, 4150
A. 828   B. 700
C. 510   D. 705
E. 599

Directions (Qs. No. 106-110): *Given below is the table shows five types of mobile phones sold by two sellers (X and Y). Table shows cost price, profit percentage and market price of the phones.*

Table

Brand	X			Y		
	C.P.	Profit%	M.P.	C.P.	Profit%	M.P.
MI	-	-	-	-	25%	-
Lenovo	-	20%	25000	-	12%	-
Vivo	-	-	-	-	-	28000
Apple	-	20%	-	-	-	-
Oppo	-	35%	-	-	30%	-

106. How much percentage C.P. of Lenovo phones sold by seller X is less than M.P. of Oppo sold by seller Y. If X gave 10% discount on Lenovo phone while seller Y gave 20% discount on Oppo phone on M.P.?
A. 23.33%   B. 24.43%
C. 27.88%   D. 25.59%
E. 29%

107. What is the ratio between C.P. of Apple phone sold by seller X to C.P. of MI phone sold by seller Y, if M.P. of Lenovo sold by X and M.P. of MI sold by Y is 56.25% more than the M.P. of Oppo sold by Y. (take S.P. equals to M.P.)
A. 15/13   B. 12/11
C. 13/12   D. 10/13
E. 18/7

108. If seller Y sells Vivo phone at 20% discount, he got ₹ 2400 as profit and if he give 30% discount, he losses ₹ 400. Then what will be the profit percentage if a total 8 phones sold by seller Y, 2 phones at 20% discount and 6 phones at 30% discount.
  A. 1.4% B. 1.2%
  C. 1.7% D. 1.5%
  E. 1.9%

109. If the ratio between S.P. of lenovo and M.P. of Vivo sold by Y is 3 : 4 then what is the average of cost price of 2 phones of lenovo bought by X and 6 phones of Lenovo bought by Y if X gave 10% discount of M.P.
  A. 10000 B. 18750
  C. 18710 D. 14750
  E. 15000

110. If the average C.P. of Apple and Oppo bought by 'X' is 14000 and average S.P. of Apple and Oppo by 'X' is 18000 then what will be the difference between the C.P. of Apple and Oppo laptop bought by seller 'X'?
  A. 4000 B. 5000
  C. 6000 D. 7000
  E. 9000

Directions (Qs. No. 111-115): *In the following questions two equations are given. You have to solve both the equations and give answers:*

111. $2x^2 - 31x + 84 = 0$
  $3y^2 + y - 2 = 0$
  A. If $x > y$ B. If $x \geq y$
  C. If $x < y$ D. If $x \leq y$
  E. If $x = y$ or no relation can be established between x and y.

112. $6x^2 + 14x - 12 = 0$
  $6y^2 + 11y + 4 = 0$
  A. If $x > y$ B. If $x \geq y$
  C. If $x < y$ D. If $x \leq y$
  E. If $x = y$ or no relation can be established between x and y.

113. $x^2 - 30x + 216 = 0$
  $y^2 - 21x + 108 = 0$
  A. If $x > y$ B. If $x \geq y$

  C. If $x < y$ D. If $x \leq y$
  E. If $x = y$ or no relation can be established between x and y.

114. $8x^2 + 21x - 9 = 0$
  $3y^2 + 28y + 25 = 0$
  A. If $x > y$ B. If $x \geq y$
  C. If $x < y$ D. If $x \leq y$
  E. If $x = y$ or no relation can be established between x and y.

115. $4x^2 - 15x + 14 = 0$
  $3x^2 - 6x + 3 = 0$
  A. If $x > y$ B. If $x \geq y$
  C. If $x < y$ D. If $x \leq y$
  E. If $x = y$ or no relation can be established between x and y.

116. A man invested certain sum on money of ₹ 10000 in three different schemes P, Q and R in such a way that he will get simple interest as 20%, 39% and 13%. If amount invested in scheme Q is 30% of amount invested in scheme R, he earned an interest of ₹ 4000 in 2 years. Find the amount invested in scheme P.
  A. ₹ 5000 B. ₹ 4000
  C. ₹ 3000 D. ₹ 1000
  E. ₹ 6000

117. According to a new plan rolled out by bank, the rate of simple interest on a sum of money is 10% p.a. for the first 2 years, 12% p.a. for the next three years, and 4% p.a. for the period beyond the first five years. The simple interest accrued on a sum for a period of 9 years is ₹ 11,520. A person invested P amount of sum in this new plan and also invested same P amount of sum for 2 years on the other scheme which offers 10% compound interest. Find the compound interest he got on the sum after 2 years?
  A. ₹ 3360 B. ₹ 3450
  C. ₹ 3120 D. ₹ 3250
  E. None of these

118. Three cooks have to make 80 cakes, they are known to make 20 cakes every minute working together. The first cook began working alone and made 20 cakes having worked for sometime more than 2 minutes. The remaining part of the work was done by the second and the third cook working together. It took a total of 8 minutes to complete 80 cakes. How many minutes would it take the first cook alone to bake 160 cakes for birthday party next day?

A. 30 minutes   B. 32 minutes
C. 40 minutes   D. 45 minutes
E. None of these

119. Two trains of lengths 200 m and 300 m pass each other with constant and same speeds on parallel tracks in opposite directions. The drivers and guards are at the extremities of the trains. The time gap between the drivers passing each other and first driver-guard pair passing each other is 30 s. How much later will the other driver-guard pair pass by?

A. 20 sec   B. 30 sec
C. 15 sec   D. 15 sec
E. Can't be determined

120. In a school, there are 76 students. In an examination, the difference between the highest and the least marks is 33. When the average of their marks was taken without considering the highest marks then the average was reduced by 2% but when the average of their marks was taken without considering the least marks then the average of the marks was increased by 3%. Find the original average of the marks of all the candidates?

A. 8.8   B. 9.8
C. 11   D. 19
E. Can't be determined

Directions (Qs. No. 121-125): *What approximate value will come in place of the question mark (?) in the following questions? (You are not expected to calculate the exact value).*

121. 62.5% of 18920 + ? % of 5325 = 16827
A. 86   B. 102
C. 77   D. 82
E. 94

122. $(14.989)^2 + (121.012)^3 + 2090 = ?$
A. 1239219
B. 1119391
C. 1669319
D. 1773876
E. None of these

123. 61.99% of 2004.85+ 69.99% of 1706.03 = ?
A. 2445   B. 2497
C. 2437   D. 2520
E. 2350

124. $(9000)^{1/3} * (10/9) / (40\%$ of $120) = ? / 8\%$ of 600 $* (100/81)^{1/2}$
A. 28   B. 21
C. 44   D. 57
E. 69

125. $(15.98)^2 + (19.09)^2 - 29.92\%$ of $799.87 = ?$
A. 354   B. 377
C. 254   D. 294
E. 315

Directions (Qs. No. 126-130): *Study the following information carefully and answer the questions given below:*

The given information briefs about the percentage of work done by five sanitation workers in Municipal Corporation of Delhi and also the number of hours taken by sanitation workers to complete the respective percentage of same work.

Five workers Mahendra, Rampal, Vijay, Ramesh and Suresh do the sanitation work together. Mahendra did 37.5% of the work in 9 hours while Rampal does 20% of the work in 3.2 hours. Vijay took 35 hours to finish 125% of the work while Ramesh took 9 hours to complete 25% of the work. Suresh takes 27 hours to finish 150% of the work.

126. Out of the given five sanitation workers, who has the highest efficiency?
A. Mahendra   B. Rampal
C. Vijay   D. Ramesh
E. Suresh

127. Out of the given pairs, who will complete the work in the minimum time if they are working together?
A. Mahendra and Ramesh
B. Ramesh and Suresh

C. Rampal and Mahendra

D. Suresh and Mahendra

E. Rampal and Vijay

128. Find the number of hours taken by Mahendra, Ramesh and Suresh for the completion of work if they work together.

A. 6 hours   B. 8 hours

C. 12 hours   D. 16 hours

E. None of these

129. Mahendra, Rampal and some other sanitation worker named Ajay can complete the work in 8 hours. They are paid ₹ 12000 and the amount is divided between them on the basis of their work done. What is the share of Ajay?

A. ₹ 2000   B. ₹ 3000

C. ₹ 4000   D. ₹ 5000

E. ₹ 6000

130. If Rampal is x% more efficient than Vijay, then find the value of x.

A. 20   B. 25

C. 40   D. 50

E. 75

131. The distance between two stations A and B is 180 km. From a station C, which is between A and B, two cars x and y started simultaneously with speeds of 11 kmph and 13 kmph towards A and B respectively. After reaching their respective destinations, they reverse their direction and continue travelling. When X crosses C and travels an additional 5 km, it crosses y. What is the distance AC?

A. 120 km   B. 150 km

C. 80 km   D. 70 km

E. None of these

132. Menka, Nishu and Ojasvi entered into a partnership in a partnership company. Ojasvi got retired and her sons Dev and Eshan are taken as partners in the firm. The ratio of share in the profit of Dev and Eshan is 3 : 5. Menka's share is double than Eshan's share and Nishu receives ₹ 10500 out of the total profit of ₹ 37500. In what ratio the profit will be shared among Menka, Nishu, Dev and Eshan?

A. 7 : 10 : 3 : 5

B. 10 : 3 : 7 : 5

C. 10 : 7 : 3 : 5

D. 5 : 3 : 7 : 10

E. None of the above

133. Pipes A, B and C are attached to a cuboidal pool which empty it at the rate of 12 litres/hour, 15 litres/hour and 25 litres/hour, respectively. The length, breadth and height of the pool are in the ratio of 7 : 2 : 1 respectively. The sum of the length, breadth and height is 40 m. If pipe A and B are open in the 1st hour and pipe B and C are open in the 2nd hour and this pattern continues, then how long will it take to completely empty (1/500)th of the pool? [Round off to the nearest decimal]

A. 55 hours   B. 54 hours

C. 56 hours   D. 50 hours

E. 53 hours

134. Three vessels contain alcoholic solutions with the concentrations of alcohol as 0.25, 0.5 and 0.75 respectively. 4 litres from the first, 6 litres from the second and 8 litres from the third are mixed. What is the ratio of alcohol and water in the resultant mixture?

A. 1 : 2   B. 1 : 3

C. 1 : 1   D. 5 : 9

E. 5 : 4

135. The speed of boat A in still water and speed of stream B are 40 km/hr and 20 km/hr respectively. The speed of boat B in still water and speed of stream A are 'x' km/hr and 'y' km/hr respectively. The sum of time taken by boat A to cover 450 km upstream and the same distance downstream in stream A is 24 hours and the sum of the time taken by boat B to cover 320 km upstream and 320 km downstream in stream B is 12 hours. Find $x + y$.

A. 90 km/hr

B. 70 km/hr

C. 20 km/hr

D. 15 km/hr

E. None of these

Directions (Qs. No. 136-140): *The question given is followed by the information in statements. You have to decide the information in which of the statements is necessary and sufficient to answer the question and mark answer accordingly.*

136. Every man in a certain class either belongs to group A, belongs to group B, or belongs to both groups. 20% of group A consists of men and 65% of group B consists of men. What percentage of the two groups together is made up of men?
(1) Group A contains 50 people.
(2) Group B contains 100 people.
A. Statement (1) ALONE is sufficient, but statement (2) alone is not sufficient to answer the question asked
B. Statement (2) ALONE is sufficient, but statement (1) alone is not sufficient to answer the question asked
C. BOTH statements (1) and (2) TOGETHER are sufficient to answer the question asked, but NEITHER statement ALONE is sufficient
D. EACH statement ALONE is sufficient to answer the question asked
E. Statements (1) and (2) TOGETHER are NOT sufficient to answer the question asked, and additional data are needed

137. A 40 m long wire is cut into three pieces. What is the length of the largest piece?
I. Two pieces are each 2 m shorter than the longest piece.
II. Two pieces of the wire are of the same length.
A. I alone
B. II alone
C. Either I alone or II alone
D. Both I and II
E. Both I and II are not sufficient

138. What is the weighted average of marks obtained by Ankur?
I. History, English and Hindi have weights 7, 10, 13 respectively
II. Simple arithmetic mean of History and English is 150, which is twice the average of English and Hindi

A. I alone
B. II alone
C. Either I alone or II alone
D. Both I and II
E. Both I and II are not sufficient

139. If each of the 20 bolts of fabric on a shelf is either 100 per cent cotton, 100 per cent wool, or a mixture of cotton and wool, how many bolts contain both cotton and wool?
(1) Of the 20 bolts, 18 contain some wool and 14 contain some cotton.
(2) Of the 20 bolts, 6 are 100 per cent wool.
A. Statement (1) ALONE is sufficient, but statement (2) alone is not sufficient to answer the question asked
B. Statement (2) ALONE is sufficient, but statement (1) alone is not sufficient to answer the question asked
C. BOTH statements (1) and (2) TOGETHER are sufficient to answer the question asked, but NEITHER statement ALONE is sufficient
D. EACH statement ALONE is sufficient to answer the question asked
E. Statements (1) and (2) TOGETHER are NOT sufficient to answer the question asked, and additional data are needed

140. A farmer has a total of 60 pigs, cows, and horses on his farm. How many pigs does he have?
(1) The ratio of horses to cows is 2 : 9.
(2) He has more than 36 cows.
A. Statement (1) ALONE is sufficient, but statement (2) alone is not sufficient to answer the question asked
B. Statement (2) ALONE is sufficient, but statement (1) alone is not sufficient to answer the question asked
C. BOTH statements (1) and (2) TOGETHER are sufficient to answer the question asked, but NEITHER statement ALONE is sufficient
D. EACH statement ALONE is sufficient to answer the question asked
E. Statements (1) and (2) TOGETHER are NOT sufficient to answer the question asked, and additional data are needed

141. Piyush went to buy an article. The shopkeeper sold the article at the marked price but told him to pay 20% tax on the marked price if he asked for the bill. Piyush manages to get the discount of 5% on the actual marked price of the article. Besides he manages to avoid paying 20% tax on the already discounted price. He paid the shopkeeper ₹ 2280 without tax after the discount. What is the amount of discount he got?

A. 500   B. 550
C. 600   D. 650
E. 700

142. One container contains a mixture of spirit and water in the ratio 2 : 3 and another contains the mixture of spirit and water in the ratio 3 : 2. How much quantity from the second should be mixed with 10 litres of the first so that the resultant mixture has ratio of 4 : 5?

A. 2.86 litres   B. 3.45 litres
C. 4.31 litres   D. 5.67 litres
E. 8.94 litres

143. The average age of a class of 30 students and a teacher reduced by 0.5 years if we exclude the teacher. If the initial average age is 14 years and then the age of the teacher is

A. 29 years   B. 30 years
C. 35 years   D. 32 years
E. 33 years

144. 3 bell ring at an interval of 48, 72, 108 second. If they ring at 6 : 00 am then after this at what time they will ring together?

A. 6 : 07 : 12
B. 6 : 08
C. 6 : 05 : 13
D. 6 : 10
E. 6 : 12

145. When one-fifth of a number x, is added to 118, it becomes equal to y^2. If one-eighth of y is equal to 2.5, what is the value of x?

A. 1420   B. 1310
C. 1410   D. 1460
E. 1470

Directions (Qs. No. 146-148): *Study the following data carefully and answer the questions:*

Percentage of women opted different specialization

Number of men opted different specialization

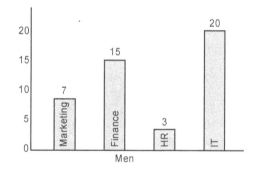

The pie charts shows the distribution of no. women preferring different specialization where the total number of women = 50.

146. If an audit is being conducted by a 10 member finance team, what is the probability that it can accommodate maximum of women?

A. 0.6   B. 0.8
C. 0.7   D. 0.9
E. 0.5

147. A prefectural board is selected comprising of 8 men or 8 women. What is the probability that equal number of men or women is selected from each department?

A. 0.001   B. 0.003
C. 0.005   D. 0.007
E. 0.009

148. What is the probability that number of women in a 20 member dancing club will have no women taking part from HR department?
- A. 0.133
- B. 0.833
- C. 0.633
- D. 0.338
- E. None of these

Directions (Qs. No. 149 and 150): *In the following number series, only one number is incorrect. Find out the wrong number in the series.*

149. 25, 21, 30, 14, 139, 3
- A. 103
- B. 30
- C. 25
- D. 20
- E. 139

150. 1000, 500, 271, 153.5, 97.75, 72.875
- A. 271
- B. 500
- C. 153.5
- D. 97.75
- E. 72.875

ANSWERS

1	2	3	4	5	6	7	8	9	10
B	D	B	A	B	B	A	C	A	D

11	12	13	14	15	16	17	18	19	20
C	C	A	D	D	B	C	D	A	C

21	22	23	24	25	26	27	28	29	30
A	A	D	D	D	A	B	E	D	D

31	32	33	34	35	36	37	38	39	40
A	E	D	B	B	A	B	B	A	A

41	42	43	44	45	46	47	48	49	50
D	B	D	E	C	E	C	E	B	B

51	52	53	54	55	56	57	58	59	60
D	E	E	A	B	E	D	B	D	E

61	62	63	64	65	66	67	68	69	70
B	C	D	A	A	A	C	B	D	E

71	72	73	74	75	76	77	78	79	80
B	B	C	D	B	A	B	C	A	C

81	82	83	84	85	86	87	88	89	90
A	D	B	E	B	A	D	B	C	B

91	92	93	94	95	96	97	98	99	100
A	B	A	C	B	B	E	B	B	A

101	102	103	104	105	106	107	108	109	110
C	E	C	D	A	C	A	D	B	A

111	112	113	114	115	116	117	118	119	120
A	E	B	E	A	A	A	B	B	A

121	122	123	124	125	126	127	128	129	130
E	D	C	B	B	B	C	B	A	E

131	132	133	134	135	136	137	138	139	140
C	C	B	E	B	E	A	E	A	C

141	142	143	144	145	146	147	148	149	150
C	A	A	A	C	B	D	B	E	B

EXPLANATORY ANSWERS

For Qs. 1-5:

- F sits third to the right of S.
- F is sixth to the right of T.
- C and D are not immediate neighbours of F, who sits second to the right of E.
- E sits at the fifth position from the right end.
- B sits fourth to the right of P, who is not the immediate neighbour of U.
- There are two persons between U and A.
- There are two persons between D and Q.
- S is not an immediate neighbour of A.
- C is not an immediate neighbour of D and Q.

From the above statement, we conclude:

Facing North:

P	C	A	T	B	U	S	E	Q	F	R	D

For Qs. 6-10:

In row-1, J, K, L, M, N and O are seated and all of them are facing south. In row-2, C, D, E, F, G and H are seated and all of them are facing north

- M sits third to the left of J.
- The person facing M sits second to the left of H.
- Two persons are sitting between H and E.
- G is not an immediate neighbour of E.
- D does not face M.
- L and K are immediate neighbours.
- L and K do not sit at any of the extreme ends of the line.
- Only one person sits between N and L.
- The person facing K is an immediate neighbour of C.

According to above statement, we conclude:

```
 ┌─┬─┬─┬─┬─┬─┐ Row 1 (Facing South)
 │J│K│L│M│N│O│
 │C│D│E│F│G│H│
 └─┴─┴─┴─┴─┴─┘ Row 2 (Facing North)
```

For Qs. 11-15:

Month	Person
January (31)	Q
February (28/29)	P
March (31)	-
April (30)	A
May (31)	S
June (30)	-
July (31)	M
August (31)	C
September (30)	-
October (31)	K
November (30)	R
December (31)	-

For Qs. 16-20:

Students	Subjects	Standard
D	Chemistry	VIII
H	English	VIII
E	Biology	VII
A	Marathi	VII
G	Math	VII
C	Economics	VI
F	Physics	VI
B	Geography	VI

For Qs. 21-25:

Floor	Boy	Girl	City
9	Rohit	Amita	Lucknow
8	Vikash	Sanjana	Chennai
7	Sanjay	Anita	Varanasi
6	Kamal	Surabhi	Agra
5	Amit	Komal	Mathura
4	Sunil	Susheela	Noida
3	Anit	Saroj	Allahabad
2	Saurabh	Kumkum	Mirzapur
1	Sushil	Suhana	Patna

26. I. A > X → True (as A ≥ P = S > T > X)

II. P < B → False

Hence, only conclusion I follows.

27. I. S < Z → False (as S > U < Z)

II. X > Y → True (as Y < U < Z < X)

Hence, only conclusion II follows.

28. I. V < S → True (as V = P < X < Y < S)

II. T > R → True (as T > Y > X > P = V > R)

Hence, both conclusions follow.

29. I. H < C → False (as there is no relation between H and C)

II. H > D → False (as H ≥ I = E ≤ D)

Hence, no conclusion follows.

30. I. P < B → False (as P ≥ Q > E ≥ F > B)

II. S > A → False (as P ≥ Q > E = S ≥ F > B ≤ A)

Hence, no conclusion follows.

31.

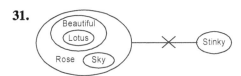

32.

33.

34.

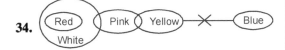

35.

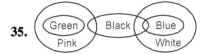

47. From I, A ≥ B < C = D > E ≥ F = G

We can't compare B and F.

From II, A ≤ B = C > D > E < F < G

We can't compare B and F.

From III, A > B > C = D ≥ E > F < G

Clearly B is greater to F.

So, Only III is sufficient. Hence, option C.

48. From I,

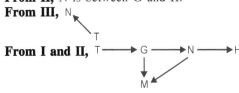

From II, N is between G and H.

From III,

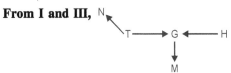

From I and II,

Hence, M is to the south-west of N.

From I and III,

Thus, M is to the south-east of N.

So answer can be found by using I and either II or III.

49. From I,

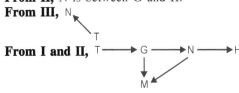

In this only 'writer' is given nothing information about 'word'.

From II,

In this only 'writer' is given nothing information about 'word'.

From III,

No information about 'writer'

From II and III,

If we combine both II and III we can get that 'no writer is word'.

So, both II and III will be answer.

50. From I. Neha > Mahi > Nitesh

From II. – > – > – > Rita > – > –

Now combining all the statements, we have

Neha > Mahi > Nitesh > Rita > – > –

Thus, Neha is the tallest.

101.

$$51 \quad 60 \quad 42 \quad 78 \quad \boxed{6} \quad 150$$
$$+9 \quad -18 \quad +36 \quad -72 \quad +144$$

102.

$$82 \quad \boxed{187} \quad 286 \quad 373 \quad 436 \quad 451$$
$$+105 \quad +99 \quad +87 \quad +63 \quad +15$$
$$-6 \quad -12 \quad -24 \quad -48$$

103.

$$\times 1.5 \qquad \times 3.5 \qquad \times 5.5$$
$$20 \quad 32 \quad 30 \quad \boxed{80} \quad 105 \quad 360 \quad 577.5$$
$$\times 2.5 \qquad \times 4.5$$

104.

$$49 \quad 193 \quad 766 \quad 3055 \quad 12208 \quad \boxed{48817}$$
$$\times 4 - 3 \quad \times 4 - 6 \quad \times 4 - 9 \quad \times 4 - 12 \quad \times 4 - 15$$

105.

$$21 \quad 27 \quad 64 \quad 204 \quad \boxed{828} \quad 4150$$
$$\times 1 + (1 \times 6) \quad \times 2 + (2 \times 5) \quad \times 3 + (3 \times 4) \quad \times 4 + (4 \times 3) \quad \times 5 + (5 \times 2)$$

106. S.P. of Lenovo sold by X

$$= 25000\left(1 - \frac{10}{100}\right) = 22500$$

$$\text{S.P.} = 22500 = \left(1 + \frac{20}{100}\right) \times (\text{CP})_{\text{Lenovo}}$$

$\Rightarrow$ C.P. of Lenovo = 18750

S.P. of Oppo sold by Y

$$= 16000\left(1 + \frac{30}{100}\right) = 20800$$

$$\text{M.P. (Oppo)} \times \left(1 - \frac{20}{100}\right) = 28000$$

$$\text{M.P. (Oppo)} = 26000$$

$$\text{Desired } \% = \frac{(26000 - 18750)}{26000} \times 100$$
$$= 27.88\%.$$

107. Desired ratio $= \dfrac{\text{C.P. of Apple phone by X}}{\text{C.P. of MI by Y}}$

$$\text{M.P. of Apple phone} = \left(1 + \frac{44}{100}\right) \times 25000$$
$$= 36000$$

$$\text{C.P. of Apple phone} = 36000 \times \frac{100}{120}$$
$$= 30000$$

M.P. of MI phone

$$= 16000\left(1 + \frac{30}{100}\right) \times \left(1 + \frac{56.25}{100}\right)$$

$$= 16000 \times \frac{130}{100} \times \frac{156.35}{100} = 32500$$

$$\text{C.P. of MI} = 32500 \times \frac{100}{125} = 26000$$

$$\text{Desired ratio} = \frac{30000}{26000} = \frac{15}{13}.$$

108. M.P. after 20% discount

$$= 28000\left(1 - \frac{20}{100}\right) = 22400$$

$$\text{C.P.} = 22400 - 2400 = 20000$$

or, M.P. after 30% discount

$$= 28000\left(1 - \frac{30}{100}\right) = 19600$$

$$\text{C.P.} = 19600 + 400 = 20000$$

$$\text{Net profit} = 2 \times 2400 - 6 \times 400 = 2400$$

$$\text{Profit } \% = \frac{2400}{(8 \times 20000)} \times 100 = 1.5\%.$$

109. S.P. of Lenovo by Y $= 28000 \times \dfrac{3}{4} = 21000$

C.P. of Lenovo bought by X

$$= 25000 \times \frac{90}{100} \times \frac{100}{120} = 18750$$

C.P. of Lenovo bought by

$$= 21000 \times \frac{100}{112} = 18750$$

Desired average

$$= \frac{(2 \times 18750 + 6 \times 18750)}{8} = 18750.$$

110. Let, C.P. of Apple phone $= x$

C.P. of Oppo $= y$

According to question,

$$\frac{(x + y)}{2} = 14000$$
$$x + y = 28000 \qquad \dots(i)$$

$$\frac{x * 1.2 + y * 1.35}{2} = 18000$$

$$1.2x + 1.35y = 36000 \quad ...(ii)$$

On solving (i) and (ii) $y = 16000$; $x = 12000$

Desired difference = $16000 - 12000$

$$= 4000.$$

111. (i)
$$2x^2 - 31x + 84 = 0$$
$$2x^2 - 24x - 7x + 84 = 0$$
$$2x(x - 12) - 7(x - 12) = 0$$
$$(x - 12)(2x - 7) = 0$$
$$x = 12, \frac{7}{2}$$

(ii)
$$3y^2 + y - 2 = 0$$
$$3y^2 + 3y - 2y - 2 = 0$$
$$3y(y + 1) - 2(y + 1) = 0$$
$$(y + 1)(3y - 2) = 0$$
$$y = -1, \frac{2}{3}$$
$$x > y.$$

112. (i)
$$6x^2 + 14x - 12 = 0$$
$$6x^2 + 18x - 4x - 12 = 0$$
$$6x(x + 3) - 4(x + 3) = 0$$
$$(x + 3)(6x - 4) = 0$$
$$x = -3, \frac{2}{3}$$

(ii)
$$6y^2 + 11y + 4 = 0$$
$$6y^2 + 8y + 3y + 4 = 0$$
$$2y(3y + 4) + 1(3y + 4) = 0$$
$$y = -\frac{4}{3}, -\frac{1}{2}$$

No relation.

113. (i)
$$x^2 - 30x + 216 = 0$$
$$x(x - 12) - 18(x - 12) = 0$$
$$(x - 18)(x - 12) = 0$$
$$x = 18, 12$$

(ii)
$$y^2 - 21y + 108 = 0$$
$$y^2 - 12y - 9y + 108 = 0$$
$$y(y - 12) - 9(y - 12) = 0$$
$$(y - 9)(y - 12) = 0$$
$$y = 9, 12$$
$$x \geq y.$$

114. (i)
$$8x^2 + 21x - 9 = 0$$
$$8x^2 + 24x - 3x - 9 = 0$$
$$8x(x + 3) - 3(x + 3) = 0$$
$$x = 3/8, -3$$

(ii)
$$3y^2 + 28y + 25 = 0$$
$$3y^2 + 3y + 25y + 25 = 0$$
$$3y(y + 1) + 25(y + 1) = 0$$
$$y = -1, -\frac{25}{3} \Rightarrow \text{No relation.}$$

115. (i)
$$4x^2 - 15x + 14 = 0$$
$$4x^2 - 8x - 7x + 14 = 0$$
$$4x(x - 2) - 7(x - 2) = 0$$
$$(x - 2)(4x - 7) = 0$$
$$x = 2, 7/4$$

(ii)
$$3y^2 - 6y + 3 = 0$$
$$3y^2 - 3y - 3y + 3 = 0$$
$$3y(y - 1) - 3(y - 1) = 0$$
$$(y - 1)(3y - 3) = 0$$
$$y = 1, 1 \Rightarrow x > y.$$

116. Amount invested in scheme Q is 30% of Amount invested in scheme R.

$$Q = \left(\frac{30}{100}\right) \times R \Rightarrow \frac{Q}{R} = \frac{3}{10}$$

Let the amount invested in scheme P = P

Ratio = P : Q : R = P : 3 : 10

Let, P = Px, Q = 3x, R = 10x

Rate in scheme P = 21%

Rate in scheme Q = 39%

Rate in scheme R = 13%

Rate in scheme Q and R

$$= \left(\frac{3}{13}\right) \times 39\% + \left(\frac{10}{13}\right) \times 13\% = 19\%$$

Time = 2 years

Simple interest in 2 years = 4000

Simple interest in 1 year = 2000

Principal = 10000

$$\text{Rate in 3 schemes} = 2000 \times \frac{100}{10000}$$

Now, By allegation method:

P	Q + R
21%	19%
	20%
1	1

Amount invested by $P = \dfrac{(10000 \times 1)}{2}$

$\qquad\qquad = ₹\ 5000.$

117. Rate of interest for a period of 9 years

$= (10 \times 2 + 12 \times 3 + 4 \times 4)\% = 72\%$

Hence, the amount is returning 72% in the form of S.I. according to the new plan of bank.

Now, 72% of P = 11520

$\Rightarrow \qquad\qquad P = ₹\ 16000$

Now the person invested same amount in 2nd scheme which offers C.I.,

Effective rate $= 10 + 10 + 10 \times \dfrac{10}{100} = 21\%$

C.I. $= 21\%$ of $16000 = ₹\ 3360.$

118. Let three cooks are x, y and z. And they bake number of cakes in 1 minute $\dfrac{1}{x}, \dfrac{1}{y}, \dfrac{1}{z}$ respectively.

Now, it is given that they can bake 20 cakes in a minute when they work together.

$\left(\dfrac{1}{x} + \dfrac{1}{y} + \dfrac{1}{z}\right) = 20 \qquad \ldots(i)$

Now let cook x works for K minutes and K > 2

So, $\qquad K\left(\dfrac{1}{x}\right) = 20 \qquad \ldots(ii)$

And y and z complete remaining work.

They complete the whole work in 8 minutes.

$(8 - K)\left(\dfrac{1}{y} + \dfrac{1}{z}\right) = 60 \qquad \ldots(iii)$

By equation (i), (ii) and (iii),

$\qquad\qquad x = \dfrac{1}{5}, \dfrac{1}{10}$

If we take $x = \dfrac{1}{10}$ then K = 2 and is equal to 2

So, we will take $x = \dfrac{1}{5}$

Now x bakes 1 cake in $= \dfrac{1}{5}$ minute.

160 cake in $= \dfrac{1}{5} \times 160$

$\qquad\qquad = 32$ minutes.

119.

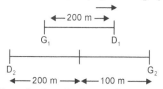

Time gap passing D_1D_2 and D_2G_1 = 30 sec

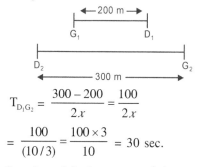

Let Speed of train is x m/s

$T_{D_1D_2} = \dfrac{200 + 200}{x + x} = \dfrac{400}{2x}$

$T_{D_2G_1} = \dfrac{500}{2x}$

$\therefore \qquad T_{D_2G_1} - T_{D_1G_2} = 30$ sec

$\dfrac{500}{2x} - \dfrac{400}{2x} = 30$

$\dfrac{100}{2x} = 30 \Rightarrow x = \dfrac{100}{60}$

$2x = \dfrac{10}{3}$ m/s

$\because$ Speed of both the train is same

$T_{D_1G_2} = \dfrac{300 - 200}{2x} = \dfrac{100}{2x}$

$= \dfrac{100}{(10/3)} = \dfrac{100 \times 3}{10} = 30$ sec.

120. Let the original average of the marks of all the candidates = x

The highest marks = a

The least marks = b

Then, according to the question,

98% of $x = \dfrac{76x - a}{75}$

98% of $75x + a = 76x \qquad \ldots(i)$

And 103% of $x = \dfrac{76x - b}{75}$

103% of $75x + b = 76x \qquad \ldots(ii)$

From equation (*i*) and equation (*ii*),

$$98\% \text{ of } 75x + a = 103\% \text{ of } 75x + b$$
$$5\% \text{ of } 75x = a - b$$

According to the question,

$$a - b = 33$$

So,

$$5\% \text{ of } 75x = 33$$
$$5 \times \frac{75x}{100} = 33$$

By solving, $x = 8.8$

121. 62.5% of $18920 + ?\%$ of $5325 = 16827$

$\Rightarrow \quad 11825 + ?\%$ of $5325 = 16827$

$\Rightarrow \quad ? \times \dfrac{5325}{100} = 5002$

$\Rightarrow \quad ? = 94\%.$

122. $(14.989)^2 + (121.012)^3 + 2090 = ?$

$$225 + 1771561 + 2090 = 1773876.$$

123. 61.99% of $2004.85 + 69.99\%$ of $1706.03 = ?$

$$\frac{(2005 \times 62)}{100} + \frac{(1706 \times 70)}{100} = ?$$

$$1243 + 1194 \text{ (Approx)} = 2437.$$

124. $\dfrac{(9000)^{1/3} \times (10/9)}{(40\% \text{ of } 120)} = \dfrac{?}{8\% \text{ of } 600} \times \left(\dfrac{100}{81}\right)^{1/2}$

$$? = 20.80 = 21.$$

125. $16^2 + 19^2 - \dfrac{29}{100} \times 800$

$$= 256 + 361 - \frac{30}{100} \times 800 = 617 - 240 = 377.$$

For Qs. No. 126-130:

Workers	Percentage of Word Done	Time taken (hours)
Mahendra	37.5%	9
Rampal	20%	3.2
Vijay	125%	35
Ramesh	25%	9
Suresh	150%	27

Time taken by Mahendra to complete 37.5% of the work = 9 hours

Time taken by Mahendra to complete the whole work = $\dfrac{9}{37.5} \times 100 = 24$ hours

Time taken by Rampal to complete 20% of the work = 3.2 hours

Time taken by Rampal to complete the whole work = $\dfrac{3.2}{20} \times 100 = 16$ hours

Time taken by Vijay to complete 125% of the work = 35 hours

Time taken by Vijay to complete the whole work = $\dfrac{35}{125} \times 100 = 28$ hours

Time taken by Ramesh to complete 25% of the work = 9 hours

Time taken by Ramesh to complete the whole work = $\dfrac{9}{25} \times 100 = 36$ hours

Time taken by Suresh to complete 150% of the work = 27 hours

Time taken by Suresh to complete the whole work = $\dfrac{27}{150} \times 100 = 18$ hours.

126. As, Rampal takes the minimum number of hours to complete the work, therefore, he has the highest efficiency.

127. So, time taken by Mahendra and Ramesh to complete the work if they are working together

$$= \frac{24 \times 36}{24 + 36} = \frac{72}{5} \text{ hours}$$

So, time taken by Ramesh and Suresh to complete the work if they are working together

$$= \frac{18 \times 36}{18 + 36} = 12 \text{ hours}$$

So, time taken by Mahendra and Rampal to complete the work if they are working together

$$= \frac{24 \times 16}{24 + 16} = \frac{48}{5} \text{ hours}$$

So, time taken by Mahendra and Suresh to complete the work if they are working together

$$= \frac{24 \times 18}{24 + 18} = \frac{72}{7} \text{ hours}$$

So, time taken by Vijay and Rampal to complete the work if they are working together

$$= \frac{28 \times 16}{28 + 16} = \frac{112}{11} \text{ hours.}$$

128. So, one hour work done by Mahendra, Ramesh and Suresh if working together

$$= \frac{1}{24} + \frac{1}{36} + \frac{1}{18} = \frac{1}{8}$$

Therefore, number of hours taken by Mahendra, Ramesh and Suresh if working together = 8 hours.

129. Let the time taken by Ajay to complete the work = x days

Therefore, $\quad \frac{1}{24} + \frac{1}{16} + \frac{1}{x} = \frac{1}{8}$

On solving, we get, $\quad x = 48$ hours

Therefore, ratio of their efficiency

$$= \frac{1}{24} : \frac{1}{16} : \frac{2}{48} = 2 : 3 : 1$$

Therefore, share of Ajay

$$= \frac{1}{2+3+1} \times 12000 = ₹\ 2000.$$

130. So, $\quad \dfrac{16 \times (100 + x)}{100} = 28$

On solving, we get, $\quad x = 75$.

131.

$$\frac{2x+5}{11} = \frac{2(180 - x) - 5}{13}$$

$$26x + 65 = 22\ (180) - 22x - 55$$

$$48x = 3840$$

$$\therefore \qquad x = \frac{3840}{48} = 80 \text{ km}$$

Distance between A and C = 80 km.

132. The ratio of share in the profit of Dev and Eshan is 3 : 5

Menka's share is double than Eshan's share and Nishu receives ₹ 10500 out of the total profit of ₹ 37500

Let Eshan's share be x,

So Menka's would be $2x$ and Dev's share would be $\dfrac{3x}{5}$

$$\text{Nishu's share} = \frac{10500}{37500} = \frac{7}{25}$$

So, the share of Menka, Dev and Eshan would be

$$= 1 - \frac{7}{25} = \frac{18}{25}$$

So, $\qquad x + 2x + \dfrac{3x}{5} = \dfrac{18}{25}$

On solving, we get, $\quad x = \dfrac{1}{5}$

So, $\qquad$ Eshan's share $= \dfrac{1}{5}$

$$\text{Menka's share} = \frac{2}{5}$$

$$\text{Dev's share} = \frac{3}{25}$$

So the required ratio $= \dfrac{2}{5} : \dfrac{7}{25} : \dfrac{3}{25} : \dfrac{1}{5}$

So, the ratio in which the profit will be shared among Menka, Nishu, Dev and Eshan

$$= 10 : 7 : 3 : 5.$$

133. Length of the pool $= \dfrac{7}{10} \times 40 = 28$ m

Breadth of the pool $= \dfrac{2}{10} \times 40 = 8$ m

Height of the pool $= \dfrac{1}{10} \times 40 = 4$ m

Volume of the pool $= l \times b \times h$

$$= 28 \times 8 \times 4 = 896000 \text{ litres}$$

Quantity needed to be emptied

$$= \left(\frac{1}{500}\right) \times 896000 = 1792 \text{ litres}$$

Portion emptied in the 1st 2 hours

$$= (12 + 15) + (15 + 25)$$
$$= 27 + 40 = 67 \text{ litres}$$

So, portion emptied in the 1st 53 hours

$$= 26 \times 67 + (12 + 15)$$
$$= 1742 + 27 = 1769 \text{ litres}$$

Remaining quantity to be emptied

$$= 1792 - 1769 = 23 \text{ litres}$$

This can be emptied by A and B in (23/40) hours = 0.575 hours

So, total time taken = 53.575 hours = 54 hours.

134. The concentration of alcohol in the resulting mixture

$$= \frac{4 \times 0.25 + 6 \times 0.5 + 8 \times 0.75}{4 + 6 + 8} = \frac{10}{18} = \frac{5}{9}$$

Ratio of Alcohol : Water = 5 : 4.

135. According to the question,

$$\frac{450}{40 + y} + \frac{450}{40 - y} = 24$$

$$\frac{80}{1600 - y^2} = \frac{24}{450}$$

$$1600 - y^2 = 1500$$

$$100 = y^2$$

$$y = 10 \text{ km/hr}$$

$$\frac{320}{x + 20} + \frac{320}{x - 20} = 12$$

$$\frac{2x}{x^2 - 400} = \frac{12}{320}$$

$$3x^2 - 160x - 1200 = 0$$

On solving, we get $x = 60$ km/hr

So, $x + y = 60 + 10 = 70$ km/hr.

137. Let the length of the largest piece be x

From statement I:

$$x + x - 2 + x - 2 = 40$$

$$3x - 4 = 40$$

$$3x = 44$$

$$x = \frac{44}{3} \text{ m}$$

From statement II:

Let the length of shorter piece be y m

$$y + y + x = 40$$

Here the value of y is unknown. Hence, statement I alone is sufficient to answer this question.

138. From statement I:

Only weights are given, H = 7 (history)

E = 10 (english)

Hn = 13 (hindi)

From statement II: $\frac{(H + E)}{2} = 150$

$$H + E = 300$$

$$\frac{(E + Hn)}{2} = \frac{150}{2}$$

$$E + Hn = 150$$

Weighted average $= \frac{(7H + 10E + 13Hn)}{(7 + 10 + 13)}$

Here the individual marks are unknown. Hence, Both the statements together are not sufficient.

141. Let the marked price of an article be 100

Then, selling price with tax

$$= 100 + 20\% \text{ of } 100 = 120$$

New selling price = 100 − 5 = 95

Effective discount = 120 − 95 = 25

At selling price of ₹ 95, he get discount of ₹ 25

At selling price of ₹ 1, he get discount of

$$\left(\frac{25}{95}\right)$$

At selling price of ₹ 2280, he get discount of

$$\left(\frac{25}{95}\right) \times 2280 = 600.$$

142. Ratio of mixture of spirit and water in Container 1 = 2 : 3

Amount of mixture taken = 10 litres

$$\text{Amount of spirit} = \frac{2}{5} \times 10 = 4 \text{ litres}$$

$$\text{Amount of water} = \frac{3}{5} \times 10 = 6 \text{ litres}$$

Ratio of mixture of spirit and water in Container 2 = 3 : 2

Amount of mixture taken = x litres

$$\text{Amount of spirit} = \frac{3}{5} \times x = \frac{3x}{5} \text{ litres}$$

$$\text{Amount of water} = \frac{2}{5} \times x = \frac{2x}{5} \text{ litres}$$

Ratio of mixture of spirit and water in resultant mixture = 4 : 5

Therefore, $\dfrac{\left(4 + \dfrac{3x}{5}\right)}{\left(6 + \dfrac{2x}{5}\right)} = \dfrac{4}{5}$

$$\frac{\left(\dfrac{20}{5}+\dfrac{3x}{5}\right)}{\left(\dfrac{30}{5}+\dfrac{2x}{5}\right)}=\frac{4}{5}$$

$$\frac{(20+3x)}{(30+2x)}=\frac{4}{5}$$

$$100 + 15x = 120 + 8x$$

$$7x = 20$$

$$x = 2.86 \text{ litres.}$$

143. Age of teacher = Total age of (students + teacher) – Total age of students

= 31 × 14 – 30 × 13.5

= 434 – 405 = 29 years.

144. If they all have to ring together then the number must be multiple of 48, 72, 108.

So, in this case just take the LCM of these numbers and add those seconds in 6:00 am.

145. First condition: $\dfrac{x}{5}+118 = y^2$ ...(i)

Second condition: $\dfrac{y}{8} = 2.5$

$$y = 2.5 \times 8$$

$$y = 20$$

Put value of y in equation (i)

$$\frac{x}{5}+118 = (20)^2 = 400$$

$$\frac{x}{5} = 400 - 118$$

$$\frac{x}{5} = 282$$

$$x = 282 \times 5 = 1410.$$

For Qs. No. 146-148.

Gender	Specialization			
	Marketing	Finance	HR	IT
Women (50)	13	8	26	3
Men (45)	7	15	3	20

146. Probability of getting maximum women from finance department = $\dfrac{8}{10}$

So, the total probability = $\dfrac{8}{10}$ = 0.8.

147. If the 8 members selected are women then each department can accommodate maximum of 2 women

Probability of getting 2 women from each department

$$= \frac{2}{13}\times\frac{2}{8}\times\frac{2}{26}\times\frac{2}{3} = 0.0019$$

If the 8 members selected are men then each department can accommodate maximum of 2 men

Probability of getting 2 men from each department

$$= \frac{2}{7}\times\frac{2}{15}\times\frac{2}{3}\times\frac{2}{20} = 0.0050$$

So, the total probability of getting equal number of men or women from each department

= 0.0019 + 0.0050 = 0.0069 = 0.007.

148. Total women = 50

Number of women from HR department = 26

Number of women other than HR department = 24

So, 20 women is to be selected from 24 women non – HR department

Probability of getting 20 women from department other than HR

$$= \frac{20}{24} = \frac{10}{12} = \frac{5}{6} = 0.8333.$$

149. The pattern is:

Thus, the incorrect number is 139.

150. The pattern is:

Thus, the incorrect number is 500.

Previous Paper (Solved)

Institute of Banking Personnel Selection (IBPS) Specialist (HR/Personnel) Officer Scale-I Online Main Exam 2018*

PROFESSIONAL KNOWLEDGE (HR/PERSONNEL)

1. Recruitment means
   A. Total number of inquiries made
   B. Total number of applications received
   C. Total number of persons short listed
   D. Total number of selections made
   E. None of these

2. A small voluntary group of employees doing similar or related work who meet regularly to identify, analyse and solve product quality problems and to improve general operations is known as
   A. Task Group   B. Kaizen Groups
   C. Quality Circles   D. Informal Groups
   E. Formal Groups

3. 'First come last go and last come first go' is the principle of
   A. Lay-off   B. Closure
   C. Retrenchment   D. Dismissal
   E. None of these

4. "A place for everything and everything in its place" is the principle that governs
   A. Placement   B. Housekeeping
   C. Officekeeping   D. Floor Management
   E. Forming

5. Which of the following theories of wages was propounded by Karl Marx?
   A. Subsistence Theory
   B. Surplus Value Theory
   C. Wage Fund Theory
   D. Residual Claimant Theory
   E. All of these

6. Which of the following is *not* a semantic barrier of communication?
   A. Faulty translation
   B. Ambiguous words
   C. Specialist's language
   D. Inattention
   E. Translation

7. Fish bone analysis as a tool of quality circle was advanced by
   A. Edward Deming   B. Joseph Juran
   C. Kouru Ishikawa   D. Phillip Crosby
   E. Ivan Pavlov

8. According to Fiedler's Contingency Model of Leadership, which one of the following is a situational variable?
   A. Leader – Member relationship
   B. Organisational System
   C. Degree of task structure
   D. Leader's position power
   E. T-Group Training

9. Who coined the term 'informal sector'?
   A. Keith Davis   B. Amartya Sen
   C. Mahabub Ul Haq   D. Keith Hart
   E. Alan Price

10. Which of the following is not a method of social security?
   A. Social Assistance
   B. Social Action
   C. Social Insurance
   D. Mutual Assistance
   E. Social & Cultural Insurance

11. Which of the following statements about I.L.O. is *not* true ?
    A. I.L.O. is a tripartite body.
    B. I.L.O. was established in 1919.
    C. I.L.O. passes only recommendations.
    D. I.L.O. conventions are mandatory for those countries which ratify them.
    E. I.L.O. was established in 1909

12. Which of the following organizations are world oriented?
    A. Geocentric   B. Polycentric
    C. Regiocentric   D. Ethnocentric
    E. Procedure

13. A system of industrial relations where social and labour issues are discussed between trade unions and management at enterprise level is:
    A. Bipartism
    B. Tripartism
    C. Social dialogue
    D. Bilateral Dialogue
    E. None of the above

14. OCTAPACE culture means
    A. Openness-cooperation-Truth-Authenticity-Proaction-Autonomy-Collaboration-Experimentation
    B. Openness-Confrontation-Trust-Autonomy-Proaction-Authority-Collaboration-Experimentation
    C. Openness-Confrontation-Trust-Authority-Proaction-Autonomy Cooperation Experimentation
    D. Openness-Confrontation-Trust-Authenticity-Proaction-Autonomy-Collaboration-Experimentation
    E. None of these

15. Which one of the following is not an interpersonal role identified by Henry Mintzberg?
    A. The Figure head role
    B. The Leader role
    C. The Liaison role
    D. The Resource – allocator role
    E. Laissez-faire

16. 'Red hot stove' rule of disciplinary action was suggested by
    A. Douglas McGregor
    B. Dale Yader
    C. Richard P. Calhoon
    D. Fred Luthans
    E. Albert Bandure

17. A manager may delegate any of the following except
    A. Authority
    B. Work load
    C. Responsibility
    D. Coordination
    E. None of these

18. The article in Indian Constitution that imposes prohibition on traffic in human beings, beggar and other similar forms of forced labour is
    A. Article 19
    B. Article 23
    C. Article 32
    D. Article 45
    E. Article 21

19. Workers' facilitation centres shall be set up by the facilitating agency under the
    A. Payment of Bonus Act, 1965
    B. Equal Remuneration Act, 1976
    C. Factories Act, 1948
    D. The unorganized sector workers' Social Security Act, 2005
    E. None of these

20. The first factory commission was appointed in
    A. 1875   B. 1881
    C. 1885   D. 1895
    E. 1899

21. Which Act provides for the appointment of conciliation officers and adjudication authorities?
    A. The Factories Act, 1948
    B. The Industrial Disputes Act, 1947
    C. The Trade Unions Act, 1926
    D. The Minimum wages Act, 1948
    E. The Employees' State Insurance Act, 1948

22. The first to introduce the term collective bargaining:
- A. Sidney and Beatrice Webb
- B. Samuel Gompers
- C. Clark Kerr
- D. Robert Hoxie
- E. Havold Koontz

23. Which of the following is the outcome of job satisfaction?
- A. High employee turnover
- B. High productivity
- C. Absenteeism
- D. Low Productivity
- E. None of these

24. Which is not a structure of Trade Union of Industrial Organisation?
- A. Craft union
- B. General union
- C. Industrial union
- D. Consumers' union
- E. All of these

25. The founder of Ahmedabad Textile Labour Association was
- A. V.V. Giri
- B. M.K. Gandhi
- C. B.P. Wadia
- D. N.M. Lokhande
- E. J.L. Nehru

26. Which of the following statements about labour market is *not* true?
- A. Labour market like commodity market is analyzed by supply, demand and price equilibrium.
- B. Labour Market is relatively more local than commodity market.
- C. Unlike a commodity market, the relation-ship between a buyer and seller in a labour market is not temporary.
- D. Monopoly in the labour market is high.
- E. None of these

27. Money Wage is otherwise called as:
- A. Real wage
- B. Living wage
- C. Nominal wage
- D. Fair wage
- E. All of these

28. Sensitivity training is also known as:
- A. X-group training
- B. Y-group training
- C. t-group training
- D. Core group training
- E. Z-group training

29. Statutory Minimum wage is fixed under
- A. Payment of Wages Act, 1936
- B. Equal Remuneration Act, 1976
- C. Workmen's Compensation Act, 1923
- D. Minimum Wages Act, 1948
- E. The Mines Act, 1952

30. The Employee State Insurance Act was enacted the basis of which committee's report?
- A. B.R. Ambedkar Committee
- B. B.P. Adarkar Committee
- C. Royal Commission on Labour
- D. Labour Investigation Committee
- E. None of these

31. In which company 'Six Sigma' was first experimented?
- A. Toyota
- B. Motorola
- C. Sony
- D. Ford
- E. Nokia

32. Who has given the 'Balance Score Card' as a measurement based performance management strategy?
- A. Robert S. Kaplan and David P. Norton
- B. Hammel and Prahallad
- C. Stablein and Nord
- D. Pascale and Athos
- E. Pascale & Hammel

33. Who are not the actors according to Dunlop's framework of industrial relations system?
- A. Managers and their representatives
- B. Workers and their organisations
- C. Specialized government agencies
- D. Communities and their associations
- E. None of these

34. The concept/theory of industrial capitalism/ dialectical materialism was developed by:
A. Karl Marx
B. Mahatma Gandhi
C. Dunlop J.T.
D. Thakur C.P.
E. Henery Fayol

35. The International Organization of Employer's (I.O.E.) with headquarters in Geneva was formulated in:
A. 1910   B. 1920
C. 1930   D. 1940
E. 1915

36. Off the job training does not include:
A. Role playing
B. Lecture method
C. Coaching
D. Conference or discussion
E. None of these

37. Which one is not of Michael Porters five force model of industry analysis?
A. Threat of new entrants
B. Substitutes
C. Intensity of rivalry among existing players
D. Cost leadership
E. None of these

38. Under the Equal Remuneration Act, 1976 remuneration means
A. Basic wage only
B. Basic wage and dearness allowance
C. Basic wage and emoluments whatsoever payable
D. None of the above
E. All of these

39. Which of the following is not a function of human resource management?
A. Planning   B. Organising
C. Directing   D. Accounting
E. Reporting

40. Moonlighting means
A. Working simultaneously in two organisations.
B. Working under moonlight.
C. Working in the night.
D. Encouraging employee to improve productivity.
E. None of these

41. Which of the following is not a content theory of motivation?
A. Maslow's Need Hierarchy Theory
B. Alderfer's ERG Theory
C. Vroom's Expectancy Theory
D. Herzberg's Two Factor Theory
E. Fiedler's Contingency theory

42. _____ means willingness to exert high levels of effort on behalf of the organisation.
A. Organisational Commitment
B. Organisation Effectiveness
C. Organisational Control
D. Organisational Coordination
E. None of the above

43. The Chairman of the Second National Commission on Labour was
A. Gajendra Gadkar   B. Ravindra Verma
C. George Fernandes   D. Vallabhbhai Patel
E. None of these

44. Match the following:

Trade Union		*Year of establishment*
(a) INTUC	(i)	1970
(b) AITUC	(ii)	1955
(c) BMS	(iii)	1947
(d) CITU	(iv)	1920

Codes:

	(a)	(b)	(c)	(d)
A.	(iii)	(ii)	(i)	(iv)
B.	(iii)	(iv)	(ii)	(i)
C.	(iii)	(iv)	(i)	(ii)
D.	(iv)	(iii)	(i)	(ii)
E.	(i)	(ii)	(iii)	(iv)

45. The terms 'arising out of employment' and 'during and in the course of employment' have been used in
A. Maternity Benefit Act, 1961
B. Payment of Gratuity Act, 1972
C. Workmen's Compensation Act, 1923 (Employees' Compensation Act, 1923)

D. Employees' Provident Fund (and Miscellaneous Provisions) Act, 1952

E. None of these

46. Which of the following is not an intra-mural labour welfare measure?

A. Canteen

B. Créche

C. Rest room, shelter and lunch room

D. Housing and hospital facility

E. Housing and Educational facility

47. The principle of 'Unity of Command' is violated in

A. Functional Organization

B. Informal Organization

C. Matrix Organization

D. Formal Organization

E. All of the above

48. In Vroom's theory, motivation is expressed as

A. Valence + Expectancy

B. Valence − Expectancy

C. Valence × Expectancy

D. Valence ÷ Expectancy

E. Valence = Expectancy

49. Which of the following benefits is not found under the Employees' State Insurance Act, 1948?

A. Sickness Benefit

B. Maternity Benefit

C. Children's Allowance

D. Dependent's Benefit

E. None of these

50. Employment Exchanges (Compulsory Notification of Vacancies) Act, 1959 and Apprenticeship Act, 1961 represent which of the following types of labour legislations?

A. Protective Legislation

B. Regulative Legislation

C. Social Security Legislation

D. None of the above

E. All of these

51. Which approach emerged from the findings of Hawthorne experiments?

A. Systems Approach

B. Human Behaviour Approach

C. Human Relations Approach

D. Process Approach

E. None of these

52. 'Grapevine' is a type of

A. Written communication

B. Formal communication

C. Informal communication

D. Lateral communication

E. Horizontal communication

53. Job description provides information about

A. Nature and characteristics of the job.

B. Characteristics of the person performing the job.

C. Characteristics of the organisation.

D. Characteristics of the management.

E. None of these

54. Which of the following is not a method of Performance Appraisal?

A. Behaviourally Anchored Rating Scales

B. Critical Incidence Method

C. Grading Method

D. Weighted Check List Method

E. Self-Assessment Method

55. Which of the following countries is said to be the home of collective bargaining?

A. United Kingdom

B. United States of America

C. Sweden

D. France

E. Japan

56. Which of the following is not regarded as a wage legislation?

A. Payment of Wages Act, 1936

B. Minimum Wages Act, 1948

C. Payment of Bonus Act, 1965

D. Equal Remuneration Act, 1976

E. Maximum Wages Act, 1949

57. Welfare is considered as

A. Total Concept

B. Social Concept

C. Relative Concept

D. All of the above

E. None of these

58. The internal wage differentials and relative worth of the job for the organization are determined by
A. Job Analysis
B. Job Design
C. Job Enrichment
D. Job Evaluation
E. Job Satisfaction

59. In ERG theory of motivation, the words E, R and G respectively stand for
A. Existence, Resources and Growth
B. Existence, Relatedness and Growth
C. Effectiveness, Risk and Groups
D. Efficiency, Responsiveness and Grid
E. None of these

60. Which of the following is not a tripartite body?
A. Indian Labour Conference
B. Joint Management Councils
C. Standing Labour Committee
D. Wage Boards
E. All of these

ANSWERS

1	2	3	4	5	6	7	8	9	10
B	C	C	B	B	D	C	B	D	B

11	12	13	14	15	16	17	18	19	20
C	A	A	D	D	A	C	B	D	A

21	22	23	24	25	26	27	28	29	30
B	A	B	D	B	D	C	C	D	B

31	32	33	34	35	36	37	38	39	40
B	A	D	A	B	C	D	C	D	A

41	42	43	44	45	46	47	48	49	50
C	A	B	C	C	D	C	C	C	C

51	52	53	54	55	56	57	58	59	60
C	C	A	C	A	D	B	D	B	B

Institute of Banking Personnel Selection (IBPS) Specialist (HR/Personnel) Officer Scale-I Online Preliminary Exam 2017*

REASONING

1. In the past, consumers would rarely walk into an ice cream store and order low-fat ice cream. But that isn't the case today. An increasing health conscious-ness combined with a much bigger selection of tasty low-fat foods in all categories has made low-fat ice cream a very profitable item for ice cream store owners. Which of the following best support the statement?
   A. low-fat ice cream produces more revenue than other low-fat foods.
   B. ice cream store owners would be better off carrying only low-fat ice cream.
   C. ice cream store owners no longer think that low-fat ice cream is an unpopular item.
   D. low-fat ice cream is more popular than other kinds of ice cream.
   E. consumers are fickle and it is impossible to please them.

2. **Cause:** All the major rivers in the state have been flowing way over the danger level for the past few weeks.
   Which of the following is/are possible effect(s) of the above cause?
   (a) Many villages situated near the river banks are submerged forcing residents to flee.
   (b) Government has decided to provide alternate shelter to all the affected villagers residing near the river banks.
   (c) The entire state has been put on high flood alert.

   A. Only (a)
   B. Only (a) and (b)
   C. Only (b) and (c)
   D. All (a), (b) and (c)
   E. None of these

Directions (Qs. Nos. 3-6): *In these questions, relationship between different elements is shown in the statements. These statements are followed by two conclusions. Study the conclusions based on the given statement and select appropriate answer.*

Give answer—
   A. If either conclusion I or II follows
   B. If neither conclusion I nor II follows
   C. If only conclusion II follows
   D. If both conclusions I and II follow
   E. If only conclusion I follows

3. **Statements :** $C \geq V \leq R = N \geq T > Q;$ $Y \geq N < A$
   Conclusions : I. $Q > V$ II. $Q < Y$

4. **Statements :** $C \geq V \leq R = N \geq T > Q;$ $Y \geq N < A$
   Conclusions : I. $Q \geq Y$ II. $A > Q$

5. **Statements :** $P \geq R < U \leq M < V;$ $T \leq U; L < M$
   Conclusions : I. $T < L$ II. $L > V$

6. **Statements :** $P \geq R < U \leq M < V;$ $T \leq U; L < M$
   Conclusions : I. $V > T$ II. $T \leq P$

Direction (Qs. No. 7): *Study the given information carefully and answer the given question.*

Following are the observations of an experiment on 'sleep and memory' conducted on 18 healthy young adults (ages 18 to 25) and 18 healthy older adults (ages 61 to 81).

(*a*) The recall after 8 hours of sleep in younger adults was 65% more than that in the older adults.

(*b*) Night-sleep had higher negative impact on all of the participants as compared to that of day-sleep of equal duration.

(*c*) If a given set of words is memorised immediately before going to sleep, its recall after waking up was found to be better in younger adults than in the older adults.

7. Which of the following can be concluded from the given findings of the research?
   I. As per the experiment, there is some correlation between sleep and memory.
   II. The part of brain involved in memory is more active during the day as compared to that during the night.
   III. A sleep of more than 8 hours can improve the memory in older adults.
   IV. Memorising something immediately after waking up from an 8-hour long sleep will yield better results than memorising before sleep.
   A. Only IV
   B. All the given statements can be concluded from the given findings of the research.
   C. Both I and III
   D. Both II and IV
   E. Only II

8. In this question, two statements I and II are given. These statements may be either independent causes or may be effects of independent causes or a common cause. One of those statements may be the effect of the other statement. Read both the statements and decide which of the given answer choice correctly depicts the relationship between these two statements.

Statements :
I. Company ABC, a leading automobile company in country G has decided to merge all its subsidiary companies into the parent company last week.
II. Company XYZ, a subsidiary of automobile company ABC, has opened five new branches in country F in the previous financial year.
A. Both the statements I and II are effects of some common cause.
B. Both the statements I and II are independent causes.
C. Statement II is the cause, and statement I is its effect.
D. Statement I is the cause and Statement II is its effect.
E. Both the statements I and II are effects of independent causes.

9. If all the letters in the word 'REGULATION' are arranged in English alphabetical order from left to right and then all the vowels are changed to the next alphabet in the English alphabetical series and all the consonants are changed to the previous alphabet in English alphabetical series, how will the word be written?
   A. BFFJKOQQSV   B. ZFFJKONSSV
   C. ZDHHMONSUT   D. BFHUKMPORV
   E. BFFJKMPQSV

10. In Country A, it is mandatory for all government organizations to provide transportation facilities (home pick-up and drop) to employees if 75% or more number of total employees working in the organization reside more than 15 km away from office. The same, however, does not apply to XY enterprises as only 1500 of their employees travel more than 15 km to work.

Which of the following can be inferred from the given statement?
(*a*) The total number of employees in XY enterprises is definitely more than 2000.
(*b*) Only 25% employees of XY enterprises travel less than 15 km to office.

(c) If 25 new recruits who travel more than 15 km join XY enterprises, the XY enterprises will be definitely have to provide transportation facilities.

(d) XY enterprises is definitely not a government enterprise

A. Only (a)
B. Only (c)
C. Both (b) and (d)
D. Only (d)
E. (a), (b) and (c)

Directions (Qs. Nos. 11-15) : *Study the given information carefully to answer the given questions.*

Seven people — J, K, L, M, N, O and P have an interview on seven different days of the same week, starting from Monday and ending on Sunday, but not necessarily in the same order. Each one of them also likes different subjects namely — Statistics, Zoology, Sociology, English, Mathematics, Psychology and Economics, but not necessarily in the same order.

Only four people have their interview between N and the one who likes Zoology. Neither N nor the one who likes Zoology has an interview on Sunday. P has an interview immediately after the one who likes Zoology. Only two people have their interviews between P and J. The one who likes Psychology has an interview on one of the days before J but not on Wednesday. Neither N nor P likes Psychology. Only two people have their interviews between the one who likes Psychology and the one who likes Statistics. The one who likes Economics has an interview immediately before the one who likes Statistics. The number of people having interview between P and the one who likes Economics is same as that of the number of people between J and the one who likes English. N does not like English. Only one person has an interview between the one who likes English and K. The one who likes Sociology has an interview immediately after O. L has an interview on one of the days after M.

11. Four of the following five are alike in a certain way based on the given arrangement and hence form a group. Which of the following does not belong to the group?
    A. K-English

B. Wednesday-K
C. Mathematics-Wednesday
D. Sociology-Statistics
E. Friday-L

12. How many people have their interviews between L and M?
    A. Two
    B. Three
    C. None
    D. One
    E. More than three

13. Which of the following statements is TRUE as per the given arrangement?
    A. None of the given statements is true
    B. Only one person has an interview between K and J.
    C. O likes Psychology.
    D. M has an interview on Friday.
    E. The one who likes Zoology has an interview on one of the day after M.

14. Who has an interview immediately after K?
    A. M
    B. The one who likes Zoology
    C. The one who likes Statistics
    D. J
    E. P

15. How many people have their interview before the one who likes Mathematics?
    A. One
    B. More than three
    C. None
    D. Two
    E. Three

Directions (Qs. Nos. 16-20) : *Study the following information and answer the given questions.*

Seven people namely, J, K, L, M, N, O and P like seven different movies namely, Twilight, Gladiator, Wanted, Dread, Hero, Jumanji and Signs but not necessarily in the same order. Each person also works in the same office but in a different department (on the basis of experience) namely Administration, Production, Marketing, HR, Finance, R & D and Client relations (CR), not necessarily in the same order.

(Please Note: Each person has been allocated to a department as per increasing order of experience with the one in Administration being the least experienced whilst the one in Client Relations (CR) being the most experienced).

Only two persons have less experience than K. P works in R & D. The one who likes Wanted has more experience than K but less than one who likes Jumanji. P neither likes Wanted nor Jumanji. The one who likes Wanted does not work in Finance.

J, who is more experienced than K, likes Twilight. The person who works in Production is less experienced than the person who likes Hero. K does not like Hero. The person who works in HR is more experienced than both L and N. N is not the least experienced person. The one who likes Signs has more experience than N. M is more experienced than J. L does not like Dread.

16. Four of the following five are alike in a certain way based on the given arrangement and so form a group. Which is the one that does not belong to that group?
    A. MO
    B. NK
    C. PK
    D. NJ
    E. LO

17. Which combination represents the department in which O works and the movie he likes?
    A. CR-Signs
    B. CR-Gladiator
    C. HR-Gladiator
    D. Marketing-Wanted
    E. HR-Wanted

18. Which of the following movies does M like?
    A. Jumanji
    B. Hero
    C. Gladiator
    D. Signs
    E. Dread

19. As per the given arrangement, HR is related to Signs and CR is related to Hero in a certain way. To which of the following is Production related to in the same way?
    A. Dread
    B. Jumanji
    C. Wanted
    D. Gladiator
    E. Twilight

20. Which of the following pairs represent the respective people who have more experience than J and less experience than K?

A. M, N
B. P, O
C. O, J
D. L, N
E. P, M

21. *Read the given information and answer the question.*

'Despite spending huge amount of money, we have not yet been able to find life on other planets. I am personally of the opinion that such research should stop with immediate effect as it is a waste of time and money as no good will ever come out of it. Instead it would be better to use this money to research other elements in space' Statement by a Scientist from Space Institute of Country X.

Which of the following does not weaken the statement of the scientist of space institute of country X?
A. Although life on other planets has not been discovered yet, such research has widened our knowledge and under-standing about other planets and has led to growth and development in science.
B. According to space scientists, if such efforts are continued, the probability of finding life in at least one other planet is much higher as compared to not finding life at all.
C. Various other research projects taken up by the said institute in the past have also failed despite spending huge amount of time as well as money on them.
D. With the amount of time and money that has already been invested in this research, shutting it now would lead to a greater loss than continuing the search.
E. None of the above

22. This question consists of information and two statements numbered I and II given below it. You have to decide which of the given statements weaken(s) or strengthen(s) the information and decide the appropriate answer. In order to discourage crowd built-up at railway station X, the platform ticket (charged to all such priced at ₹ 10 should be increased to ₹ 20.

I. The price of ticket from X to nearest railway station is ₹ 12.

II. On an average, every railway station generates ₹ 24 lacs revenue by charging ₹ 10 for platform ticket while X generates ₹ 28 lacs.

A. Both statement I and statement II weaken the information.

B. Statement I weakens the information while Statement II is a neutral statement.

C. Statement I strengthens the information while statement II weakens the information.

D. Statement I weakens the information while Statement II strengthens the information.

E. Both statements I and II strengthen the information

23. Which of the following expressions will be definitely false if the given expression 'G > H = I ≥ V ≤ Y ≤ Z ≤ T is definitely true?
A. I < G 　　　　　　B. T < V
C. Y ≤ T 　　　　　　D. Z ≥ V
E. V < G

Directions (Qs. Nos. 24-28) : *A word and number arrangement machine when given an input line of words and numbers rearranges them following a particular rule in each step. The following is an illustration of input and rearrangement. (All the numbers are two-digit numbers.)*

Input: 42 prey burn 78 21 melt gulp 96 83 head

Step I : ban 23 42 prey 78 melt gulp 96 83 head

Step II : gap 44 ban 23 prey 78 melt 96 83 head

Step III : had 80 gap 44 ban 23 prey melt 96 83

Step IV : mat 85 had 80 gap 44 ban 23 prey 96

Step V : pay 98 mat 85 had 80 gap 44 ban 23

Step V is the last step of the above arrangement as the intended output of arrangement is obtained.

As per the rules followed in the given steps, find the appropriate steps for the given input.

Input: 61 rust 33 colt 86 four torn 28 49 leap

24. Which of the following is the fourth to the left of the eighth element from the left end of step II?
A. cat 　　　　　　B. far
C. 35 　　　　　　D. rust
E. 30

25. Which of the following represents the element that is fifth to the right of 'cat' in step III?
A. torn 　　　　　　B. 63
C. lap 　　　　　　D. far
E. 86

26. In step III, how many elements are there between '86' and the third element from the left end?
A. More than three 　　B. One
C. Three 　　　　　　D. None
E. Two

27. What is the difference between the third element from the right end in step V and the fifth element from the left end in step II?
A. 31 　　　　　　B. 55
C. 26 　　　　　　D. 5
E. 16

28. 'torn' is related to 'rust' in step I in the same way as 'lap' is related to 'tan' in step V. Following the same pattern to which element is '86' related to in step IV?
A. cat 　　　　　　B. 51
C. 35 　　　　　　D. far
E. 30

29. The question consists of a statement followed by two courses of action numbered I and II given below it. A course of action is an administrative decision to be taken for improvement, follow-up or further action in regard to the problem, policy etc. You have to assume everything in the statement to be true and then decide which of the suggested courses of action logically follow(s) from the given statement.

Statement: Most of the people looking for buying/renting properties these days complain of being taken to the same property by more than 6-7 brokers. So, even after contracting multiple agents, they end up having usually the same options.

Courses of action :

I. All the owners should strictly give the responsibility of their properties to only one.

II. The brokers should be instructed to mandatorily disclose the list of all the properties they will be showing the customers on a particular day before taking them to the actual site.

A. Both I and II follow
B. Only II follows
C. Only I follows
D. Neither I nor II follows
E. Either I or II follows

Directions (Qs. Nos. 30-34) : *Study the following information to answer the given questions.*

In a certain code language,

'economy and work related' is written as 'oj my bx st'

'work and employment today' is written as 'pk bx oj dy'

'employment for growth only' is written as 'el pk fd zn'

'growth is related today' is written as 'el dy gm my'

(All codes are two letter codes only)

30. If the code for 'related people only' is 'ld my xd' then what may be the code for 'people for decision' in the given code language?
    A. to xd my   B. zn xd fd
    C. zn xd dy   D. zn kz xd
    E. kz fd xd

31. What does the code 'pk' stand for in the given code language?
    A. growth   B. employment
    C. only   D. economy
    E. today

32. What may be the code for 'economy is boosting' in the given code language?
    A. gm rc st   B. zn gm st
    C. ye st el   D. cp st rc
    E. st bx gm

33. Which of the following additional statements is required to definitely find the code of 'and' in the given code language?
    A. 'work and prosper now' is written as 'bx yp jn oj'

B. 'work today also important' is written as 'iv en oj dy'
C. No additional statement is required to find the code
D. 'and more work today' is written as 'zl oj dy bx'
E. 'related only for employment' is written as 'mv zn fd pk'

34. What is the code for 'growth today' in the given code language?
    A. fd el   B. dy fd
    C. pk dy   D. dy el
    E. an fd

Directions (Qs. Nos. 35-39) : *Study the following information carefully to answer the given question:*

Ten persons from different companies viz Samsung, Bata, Microsoft, Google, Apple, HCL, ITC, Reliance, Airtel and Vodafone are sitting in two parallel rows containing five people each, in such a way that there is an equal distance between adjacent persons. In row 1-B, C, D, E and F are seated and all of them are facing south. In row-2 R, S, T, U and V are seated and all of them are facing north. Therefore, in the given seating arrangement, each member seated in a row faces another member of the other row. (All the information given above does not the order of seating as in give the final arrangement.)

- There people sit between R and the person from Apple. The person from Reliance is an immediate neighbour of the one who faces the person from Apple. V sits to the immediate left of the one who faces the person from Reliance.

- Only one person sits between V and T. The person from Bata sits second to the right of the one who faces T. F sits second to the left of the person from Google. The person from Google does not sit at an extreme end of the line.

- Only two people sit between F and D. The person from Samsung faces an immediate neighbour of D. U is an immediate neighbour of the person from Microsoft. V is not from Microsoft. B sits second to the left of C.

- The person from ITC is an immediate neighbour of the person from Vodafone. Neither V nor F is from ITC. The person from ITC faces the person from HCL.

35. F is related to ITC in the same way as T is related to HCL, based on the given arrangement. To who amongst the following is D related to following the same pattern?
   A. Microsoft   B. Samsung
   C. Apple   D. Bata
   E. Reliance

36. Which of the following is true regarding E?
   A. E is from ITC.
   B. E is an immediate neighbour of the person from Samsung.
   C. E sits at an extreme end of the line.
   D. The person from Airtel faces E.
   E. None of the given options is true.

37. Who amongst the following sit at extreme end of the rows?
   A. The person from Apple and F.
   B. V, E
   C. The person from Samsung and C.
   D. The person from HCL and Bata
   E. R and the person from Reliance.

38. Four of the following five are alike in a certain way based on the given arrangement and so form a group. Which is the one that does not belong to that group.
   A. R   B. V
   C. C   D. F
   E. B

39. Who amongst the following faces the person from Airtel?
   A. The person from Google
   B. B
   C. The person from Reliance
   D. E
   E. The person from Bata

40. Which of the following symbols should replace the question mark (?) in the given expression in order to make the expressions 'H < R' as well as 'D ≥ M' definitely true ?

$D \geq I \geq H = S ? M < P \leq R$
A. $\geq$ B. $\leq$
C. $<$ D. $>$
E. $=$

41. T is the father of M and P. P is the only daughter of V. M is married to N. A and B are children of M. How is V related to B?
   A. Grandmother   B. Uncle
   C. Aunt   D. Sister
   E. Grandfather

42. A severe cyclonic storm hit the Eastern coastline last month resulting in huge loss of life and property on the entire east coast and the Government had to disburse a considerable amount for relief activities through the district administration machineries.

   Which of the following may possibly be a follow up measure to be taken by the Government?
   A. The Government may set up a task force to review the post relief scenario in all districts and also to confirm proper end user receipt of the relief supplies.
   B. The Government may set up a committee for proper disbursement' of relief supplies in future.
   C. The Government may empower the District magistrates to make all future disbursements of relief.
   D. The Government may send relief supplies to the affected, people in future only after proper assessment of the damage caused by such calamities.
   E. The government may need not to activate any follow up measure.

Directions (Qs. Nos. 43-47) : *These questions consist of a question and two statements numbered I and II given below it. You have to decide whether the data provided in the statements are sufficient to answer the question. Read both the statements and mark the appropriate answer.*

Give answer:
   A. The data even in both statements I and II together are not sufficient to answer the question.

B. The data in statement I alone are sufficient to answer the question while the data in statement II alone are not sufficient to answer the question.

C. The data either in statement I alone or in statement II alone are sufficient to answer the question.

D. The data in both statements I and II together are necessary to answer the question.

E. The data in statement II alone are sufficient to answer the question while the data in statement I are not sufficient to answer the question.

43. In a building, the ground floor is numbered one, first floor is numbered two and so on till the topmost floor is numbered five. Amongst five people—M, N, O, P and Q, each living on a different floor, but not necessarily in the same order, on which floor does Q live?
   I. O lives on an odd numbered floor. M lives immediately below O. Only two people live between M and P. N lives neither immediately below M nor immediately below P.
   II. N lives on an even numbered floor. Only two people live between N and O. Only one person lives between O and Q.

44. Among people A, B, C, D, E and F, each having a different height, who is the second shortest?
   I. Only two people are taller than A. E is taller than both B and C. F is shorter than E. F is taller than C.
   II. Only two people are shorter than D. A is taller than D but shorter than E. F is neither the tallest nor the shortest. B is taller than C.

45. How many people are standing between A and D (Note: All are standing in a straight line facing north)?
   I. K stands second from the left end of the line. Only four people stand between K and T. Y is an immediate neighbour of T. A stands second to the right of Y. As many people stand between K and D as between A and D.
   II. A stands second from the right end of the line. Z stands third from the left end of the line. D stands exactly in the centre of the line. As many people stand between A and T as between D and Z.

46. How far and in which direction is Point M from Point S?
   I. Point E is 2 m to the east of Point S. Point B is 4 m to the south of Point E. Point L is 10 m to the east of Point B. Point L forms a midpoint of the vertical straight line of 8 m formed by joining points Q and D. Point M is 5 m to the west of Point Q.
   II. Point M is 8 m to the north of Point A. Point M forms the midpoint of the horizontal straight line formed by joining points O and F. Point F is 8 m to the west of Point O. Point S is 4 m to the west of Point F.

47. Amongst six people—P, Q R, S, T and U standing around a circle, some facing the centre while some facing outside (*i.e.,* opposite to the centre) but not necessarily in the same order, what is the position of T with respect to U ?
   I. P stands second to the right of R. R faces the centre. Q stands second to the left of P. Q is an immediate neighbour of both U and T. U and P face opposite directions (*i.e.,* if U faces the centre then P faces outside and vice-versa.) Only two people stand between P and T.
   II. Only two people stand between R and U. P stands to the immediate left of U. P faces outside. R is an immediate neighbour of T.

Directions (Qs. Nos. 48-50) : In these questions, two/three statements followed by two conclusions numbered I and II are given. You have to take the given statements to be true even if they seem to be at variance from commonly known facts and then decide which of the given conclusions logically follows from the given statements disregarding commonly known facts.

Give answer:
   A. If either conclusion I or II follows
   B. If neither conclusion I nor II follows
   C. If only conclusion II follows

D. If both conclusions I and II follow

E. If only conclusion I follows

48. **Statements :** Some coffee is tea. All tea is water. All water is milk.
   Conclusions :
   I. All coffee being water is a possibility.
   II. All milk is tea.

49. **Statements :** No sea is a sky. Some skies are kites. All kites are balloons.

Conclusions :
I. Some balloons are seas.
II. All balloons being skies is a possibility.

50. **Statements :** Some stars are planets. Some planets are galaxies. Some galaxies are suns.
   Conclusions :
   I. All suns being galaxies is a possibility.
   II. Some galaxies are stars.

QUANTITATIVE APTITUDE

51. A can complete a project in 20 days and B can complete the same project in 30 days. If A and B start working on the project together and A quits 10 days before the project is completed, in how many days will the project be completed?
   A. 18 days   B. 27 days
   C. 26.67 days   D. 16 days
   E. 12 days

52. A runs 25% faster than B and is able to allow B a lead of 7 metres to end a race in dead heat. What is the length of the race?
   A. 10 metres   B. 25 metres
   C. 45 metres   D. 15 metres
   E. 35 metres

53. A train travelling at 100 kmph overtakes a motorbike travelling at 64 kmph in 40 seconds. What is the length of the train in metres?
   A. 1777 metres   B. 1822 metres
   C. 400 metres   D. 1111 metres
   E. 520 metres

Directions (Qs. Nos. 54-58): *Study the following graph and table to answer the given questions.*

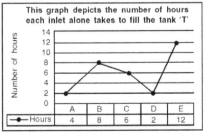

This table depicts the number of hours taken by each outlet alone to empty the full tank 'T'

Outlets	Number of hours
W	–
X	34
Y	–
Z	30

54. The time taken to fill the empty tank completely when inlet A and outlet X were opened together was 6 hours 40 minutes less than that taken by inlet B and outlet W together. How much time will outlet W alone take to completely empty the full tank? (in hours)
   A. 26   B. 28
   C. 20   D. 48
   E. 24

55. When the tank was completely full, outlets X and Y were opened together for 8 hours 30 minutes. Both were then closed and inlet A was opened which filled the tank completely in 3 hours 30 minutes. In how much time (in hours) will outlet Y alone empty the full tank?
   A. 15 hours   B. 13.6 hours
   C. 13 hours   D. 14 hours
   E. 15.5 hours

56. When the tank was completely full, outlets X and Z were opened together for 'H' hours. Had outlet Z been open alone, it would have taken 'H + 10' hours to empty the same quantity of water from the tank. What is the value of 'H'?

A. 10

B. 18

C. $11\frac{1}{3}$

D. $18\frac{1}{3}$

E. $10\frac{2}{3}$

57. Inlet E was open for 2 hours and then closed. If the remaining tank was filled by inlets B and C together, what was the total time (in hours) taken to fill the tank completely?

A. $5\frac{1}{7}$

B. $5\frac{4}{7}$

C. $4\frac{3}{7}$

D. $4\frac{6}{7}$

E. $5\frac{6}{7}$

58. When the tank was completely empty, inlets A, D and E were opened for one hour each and then closed. If after that outlet Z was opened, how much time (in hours) will it take to empty the tank completely?

A. $15\frac{2}{5}$

B. 18

C. 17

D. 20

E. 25

59. A boat running upstream takes 8 hours 48 minutes to cover a certain distance, while it takes 4 hours to cover the same distance running downstream. What is the ratio between the speed of the boat in still water and speed of the water current respectively?

A. 2 : 1

B. 3 : 2

C. 8 : 3

D. 3 : 5

E. 8 : 2

60. A, B and C jointly thought of engaging themselves in a business venture. It was agreed that A would invest ₹ 6,500 for 6 months, B, ₹ 8,400 for 5 months and C, ₹ 10,000 for 3 months. A wants to be the working member for which, he was to receive 5% of the profits. The profit earned was ₹ 7,400. What is the share of B in the profit?

A. ₹ 1,900

B. ₹ 2,660

C. ₹ 2,800

D. ₹ 2,840

E. ₹ 2,900

61. How much time will it take for an amount of ₹ 900 to yield ₹ 81 as interest at 4.5% per annum of simple interest?

A. 2 years

B. 3 years

C. 1 year

D. 4 years

E. 5 years

62. Mr. Thomas invested an amount of ₹ 13,900 divided in two different schemes A and B at the simple interest rate of 14% per annum and 11% per annum respectively. If the total amount of simple interest earned in 2 years be ₹ 3,508, what was the amount invested in scheme B?

A. ₹ 6,400

B. ₹ 7,200

C. ₹ 6,500

D. ₹ 7,500

E. ₹ 7,000

63. A bag contains 2 red, 3 green and 2 blue balls. Two balls are drawn at random. What is the probability that none of the balls drawn is blue?

A. $\frac{10}{21}$

B. $\frac{11}{21}$

C. $\frac{2}{7}$

D. $\frac{5}{7}$

E. $\frac{3}{7}$

64. A can contains a mixture of two liquids A and B in the ratio 7 : 5. When 9 litres of mixture is drawn off and the can is filled with B, the ratio of A and B becomes 7 : 9. How many litres of liquid A were contained by the can initially?

A. 10

B. 20

C. 21

D. 25

E. 29

65. A circular swimming pool is surrounded by a concrete wall 4 ft. wide. If the area of the concrete wall surrounding the pool is $\frac{11}{25}$ that of the pool, then the radius of the pool is:

A. 8 ft

B. 16 ft

C. 20 ft

D. 30 ft

E. None of these

Directions (Qs. Nos. 66-70): *In the given questions, two quantities are given, one as Quantity I and another as Quantity II. You have to determine relationship between two quantities and choose the appropriate option.*

    A. If Quantity I ≥ Quantity II

    B. If Quantity I > Quantity II

    C. If Quantity I < Quantity II

    D. If Quantity I = Quantity II or the relationship cannot be established from the information that is given.

    E. If Quantity I ≤ Quantity II

66. The boat takes total time of 4 hours to travel 14 km upstream and 36 km downstream together. The boat takes total time of 5 hours to travel 20 km upstream and 24 km downstream together?

    Quantity I : Speed of the boat in still water (in km/h).

    Quantity II : 16 km/h.

67. M is an integer selected at random from the set.

    (7, 14, 25, 27, 33, 29 and 30)

    Quantity I : Probability that the average of 12, 9 and M is at least 17.

    Quantity II : $\dfrac{1}{3}$.

68. $\left(\dfrac{x^2}{5}\right) + x + \left(\dfrac{4}{5}\right) = 0$

    $3y^2 + 4y + 1 = 0$

    Quantity I : x

    Quantity II : y

69. $mn \neq 0$

    Quantity I : $m = n$

    Quantity II : m/n.

70. A and B can together finish a piece of work in 20 days. If B starts working and after 15 days is replaced by A, A can finish the remaining work in 24 days.

    Quantity I : Number of days taken by B alone to finish the same piece of work.

    Quantity II : Number of days taken by A alone to finish the same piece of work.

Directions (Qs. Nos. 71-75): *Study the given information carefully and answer the given questions.*

The revenue of a given railway zone was collected from 4 primary sources—Offline Ticket Sales, Online Ticket Sales, Freight, Fines–during 3 Financial Years (FY 2013-14, FY 2014-15, FY 2015-16).

FY 2013-14 : Total revenue collected was ₹ 3,500 crore. Fines (₹ x crore) comprised $7\dfrac{6}{7}\%$ of the total revenue and revenue from online ticket sales was ₹ 'x + 300' crore. Revenue from freight was 12% more than that from offline ticket sales.

FY 2014-15 : Revenue from online ticket sales increased by ₹ 25 crore over FY 2013-14. Revenue from Offline ticket sales was 40% of the total revenue in FY 2014-15. Revenue from Freight and Fines was in the respective ratio of 5 : 1.

FY 2015-16 : Revenue from fines in FY 2013-14 was $\dfrac{11}{16}$th of that in FY 2015-16. Revenue from online ticket sales increased by 50% over that in FY 2014-15 and that from offline ticket sales was the average of that in FY 2013-14 and 2014-15. Revenue from freight has been and will continue to increase steadily by ₹ 250 crore every financial year.

71. Revenue from fines comprised two sources—vendors and passengers. Fines from passengers (₹ y crore) remained constant in FY 2013-14 and FY 2014-15. If the fine from vendors in FY 2013-14 was 55% of that in FY 2014-15, what was the value of y?

A. 180   B. 200
C. 218   D. 208
E. 220

72. If the railway profit in FY 2014-15 was 12.5% of the total expense, what was the total expense for FY 2014-15? (in ₹ crore)
A. 2900   B. 2400
C. 3200   D. 3000
E. 3822

73. In FY 2017-18, if the revenue from fines increases by 20% over FY 2015-16, what would be the ratio between the revenues from fines and freight in FY 2017-18?
A. 2 : 3   B. 1 : 5
C. 2 : 5   D. 3 : 4
E. 4 : 5

74. If the average revenue from online ticket sales in FY 2014-15, FY 2015-16 and FY 2016-17 was ₹ 1150 crore, by what per cent did the revenue from online ticket sales increase in FY 2016-17 as compared to that in 2014-15?
A. 250   B. 150
C. 300   D. 225
E. 230

75. If the average cost of a railway ticket was ₹ 300 in FY 2014-15, how many passengers (approx) travelled by railways in FY 2014-15? (in ₹ crore)
A. 4.8   B. 6.4
C. 6.2   D. 5.4
E. 7.73

Directions (Qs. Nos. 76-80): *Refer to the pie-charts to answer the given questions.*

Data regarding five villages—A, B, C, D and E—in a district in 2015.

Total village population = 18000

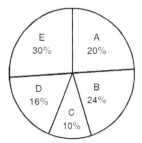

Total number of illiterates = 40% of Total village population

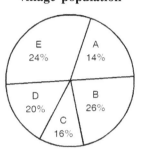

Total village population = Number of literates + Number of illiterates

76. In 2017, the population of village C remained the same as that in 2015, but the number of literates increased by '*x*'. As a result, the total number of literates became 70% of that of illiterates. What is the approximate value of '*x*'?
A. 620   B. 440
C. 680   D. 485
E. 430

77. The difference between the number of illiterates in villages D and E is approximately what per cent of that of literates in villages D and E?
A. 30%   B. 20%
C. 35%   D. 13%
E. 15%

78. In village D, the male to female ratio among the illiterates is 5 : 3 respectively. Out of the illiterates, if '*x*' females and '1.25*x*' males work as farmers and the ratio between males and females who do not work as farmers is 5 : 2 respectively, what is the value of '*x*'?
A. 240   B. 300
C. 360   D. 380
E. 280

79. The average number of illiterates in villages D, F and G is 1910. 40% and 30% of the population of villages F and G respectively are illiterates. If the ratio of the population of villages F and G is 4 : 5 respectively, what is the total population of villages F and G together?
A. 10000   B. 12000
C. 12456   D. 13000
E. 14000

80. In village A, if the respective ratio between number of males and females is 17 : 13 and there are 1000 male literates, what is the number of male illiterates in village A?
A. 480   B. 540
C. 940   D. 1040
E. 1140

Directions (Qs. Nos. 81-85) : *In this question, a number series is given. Only one number is wrong which doesn't fit in the series. Find out the wrong number?*

81. 6   4   5   8.5   18   48   139
A. 8.5   B. 4
C. 5   D. 18
E. 48

82. 10080   1440   240   48   12   3   2
A. 240   B. 3
C. 1440   D. 48
E. 12

83. 1   2   6   21   88   505   2676
A. 21   B. 6
C. 2   D. 505
E. 88

84. 18   21   25   35   52   78   115
A. 25   B. 21
C. 28   D. 35
E. 52

85. 120   137   178   222   290   375   477
A. 178   B. 137
C. 290   D. 375
E. 222

86. Area of a rectangle is 150 metre sq. When the breadth of the same rectangle is increased by 2 meter and the length decreased by 5 metre, the area of the rectangle decreases by 30 metre square. What is the perimeter of the square whose sides are equal to the length of the rectangle?
A. 76 m   B. 72 m
C. 120 m   D. 80 m
E. 60 m

87. A, B and C started a business with investments of ₹ 4200, ₹ 3600 and ₹ 2400 respectively. After 4 months from the start of the business, A invested ₹ 1000 more. After 6 months from the start of the business, B and C invested additional amounts in the respective ratio of 1 : 2. If at the end of 10 months they received a profit of ₹ 2820 and it's share in the profit was ₹ 1200, What was the additional amount that B invested?
A. ₹ 800   B. ₹ 200
C. ₹ 500   D. ₹ 600
E. ₹ 400

88. A vessel contains a mixture of milk and water in the respective ratio of 5 : 1. 24 litres of mixture was taken out and replaced with the same quantity of milk so that the resultant ratio between the quantities of milk and water in the mixture was 13 : 2 respectively. If 15 litres of the mixture is again taken out from the vessel, what is the resultant quantity of milk in the mixture? (in litres)
A. 97   B. 89
C. 91   D. 99
E. 84

Directions (Qs. Nos. 89-93) : *Refer to the table and answer the given question.* Data related to performance of 6 batsmen in a tournament:

Name of the batsman	Number of matches played in the tournament	Average runs scored in the tournament	Total balls faced in the tournament	Strike rate
A	8	-	-	129.6
B	20	81	-	-
C	-	38	400	114
D	-	-	-	72
E	28	55	1280	-
F	-	-	-	66

Note:

(*i*) Strike rate = (Total runs scored/Total balls faced) * 100

(*ii*) All the given batsmen could bat in all the given matches played by them.

(*iii*) Few values are missing in the table (indicated by –). A candidate is expected to calculate the missing value, if it is required to answer the given question, on the basis of the given data and information.

89. The respective ratio between total number of balls faced by D and that by F in the tournament is 3 : 4. Total number of runs scored by F in the tournament is what per cent more than the total runs scored by D in the tournament?

A. $22\frac{2}{9}$ B. $32\frac{4}{9}$

C. $18\frac{8}{9}$ D. $24\frac{4}{9}$

E. $28\frac{2}{9}$

90. If the runs scored by E in last 3 matches of the tournament are not considered, his average runs scored in the tournament will decrease by 9. If the runs scored by E in the 26th and 27th match are below 128 and no two scores among these 3 scores are equal, what are the minimum possible runs scored by E in the 28th match?

A. 137   B. 135
C. 141   D. 133
E. 139

91. In the tournament, the total number of balls faced by batsman A is 74 less than the total number of runs scored by him. What is the average run scored by batsman A in the tournament?

A. 42.5   B. 39.5
C. 38   D. 44
E. 40.5

92. Batsman B faced equal number of balls in first 10 matches he played in the tournament and last 10 matches he played in the tournament. If his strike rate in first 10 matches and last 10 matches of the tournament are 120 and 158 respectively, what is the total number of balls faced by him in the tournament?

A. 1150   B. 1400
C. 1200   D. 1000
E. 1500

93. What is the number of matches played by batsman C in the tournament?

A. 10   B. 16
C. 12   D. 18
E. 8

94. 10 men can complete a project in 12 days, 12 children can complete the same project in 16 days and 8 women can complete the same project in 20 days. 5 men and 12 children started working on the project. If after 4 days, 8 children were replaced by 4 women. In how many days the remaining project was completed?

A. $4\frac{2}{5}$ B. $5\frac{1}{2}$

C. $7\frac{1}{2}$ D. $3\frac{5}{9}$

E. $6\frac{2}{3}$

95. In a village, 60% registered voters cast their votes in the election. Only two candidates (A & B) were contesting the election. A won the election by 600 votes. Had B received 40% more votes, the result would have been a tie. How many registered voters are there in the village?

A. 4000   B. 3500
C. 3000   D. 3250
E. 3750

96. Eight years ago, Poorvi's age was equal to the sum of the present ages of her one son and one daughter. Five years hence, the respective ratio between the ages of her daughter and her son that time will be 7 : 6. If Poorvi's husband is 7 years elder to her and his present age is three times the present age of their son, what is the present age of the daughter? (in years)

A. 15 years   B. 23 years
C. 19 years   D. 27 years
E. 13 years

97. Boat A travels downstream from Point X to Point Y in 3 hours less than the time taken by Boat B to travel upstream from Point Y to Point Z. The distance between X and Y is 20 km, which is half of the distance between Y and Z. The speed of Boat B in still water is 10 km/h and the speed of Boat A in still water is equal to the speed of Boat B upstream. What is the speed of Boat A in still water? Consider the speed of the current to be the same?

A. 10 km/h   B. 16 km/h
C. 12 km/h   D. 8 km/h
E. 15 km/h

Directions (Qs. Nos. 98-100) : *Study the following information carefully and answer the given question.*

Data regarding number of applications received for various courses in University A and that in University B in the year 2001.

(Note : Universities A and B offer courses in six courses only, namely, Commerce, Science, Engineering, Arts, Management and Law.)

- In University A, applications received for Commerce, Science and Engineering together constituted 70% of the total number of applications received (for all the given courses together). Applications received for Arts, Management and Law were 800, 750 and 400 respectively. Applications received for management were 40% less than that for engineering. Applications received for Commerce were 20% more than that for Science.

- In University B, applications received for Science were 20% less than that for Science in University A.

- In University B, applications received for Arts were 780 and they constituted 15% of the total number of applications received (for all the given courses together). Also the applications received for arts were 40% less than that received for Commerce. Total number of applications received for engineering and management together, were double the total number of applications received for arts and law together. Applications received for engineering were equal to that for management.

98. What is the respective ratio between the total number of applications received for Engineering and Science together in University A and that for the same courses together in University B?

A. 50 : 47   B. 65 : 53
C. 52 : 37   D. 55 : 42
E. 43 : 36

99. Number of applications received for only Commerce in University B is what per cent less than that in University A?

A. 30   B. $27\frac{7}{9}$
C. 20   D. 15
E. $15\frac{5}{8}$

100. $\frac{5}{8}$th of the number of applications for Arts in University A were by female students. If the number of female applicants for the same course in University B is less than that in University A by 120, what is the number of male applications for Arts in University B?

A. 500   B. 420
C. 450   D. 360
E. 400

GENERAL ENGLISH

Directions (Qs. Nos. 101-110) : *Read the following passage carefully and answer the questions based on it. Some words have been printed in **bold** to help you locate them while answering some of the questions.*

Gross Domestic Savings (GDS) play a vital role in the economic growth of a country since it facilitates to provide requisite financial resources to undertake various developmental and welfare programs. A high level of savings helps the economy to progress on a continuous growth path as investment is mainly financed out of savings. GDS is one of the important economic indicators to measure financial regulation and soundness of the country. Absence of required savings rate may lead to external dependence, which may **jeopardize** the interests of the Nation.

Savings habit is an in-built culture of the Indian system and it has been growing consistently over the years. The GDS percentage to GDP has shown considerable improvement from 10% in 1950 to 33.70% in 2010, which is one of the highest globally. It is interesting to note that while the share of corporate sector increased from 10% to 24% during 1950 to 2010, the share of public sector has come down to 6% from 18% during the said period. The buoyancy of corporate sector in post reform era could be one of the reasons for increased share of corporates in GDS. While there is increasing trend in saving rate, marginal decline is observed under household sector *i.e.,* 72% to 70%.

Notwithstanding the fact that the share of household savings to GDS is showing decline, still this segment is the significant contributor to GDS with 70% share. Indian households are among the most frugal in the world. However, **commensurate** capital formation has not been taking place as a lion's share of household savings are being parked in physical assets compared to financial assets.

The pattern of disposition of saving is an important factor in determining how the saved amount is utilized for productive purposes. The proportion of household saving in financial assets determines the channelisation of saving for investment in other sectors of the economy. However, the volume of investment of saving in physical assets determines the productivity and generation of income in that sector itself.

Post independence era has witnessed a significant shift in deployment of household savings especially the share of financial assets increased from 26.39% in 1950 to 54.05% in 1990 may be on account of increased bank branch network across the country coupled with improved awareness of investors on various financial/banking products. However, contrast to common expectations, the share of financial assets in total household savings has come down from 54.05% to 50.21% especially in post-reform period *i.e.,* 1990 to 2010 despite providing easy access and availability of banking facilities compared to earlier years. The increased share of physical assets over financial assets (around 4%) during the last two decades is a cause of concern requires focused attention to arrest the trend.

Traditionally, the Indians are risk-averse and prefer to invest surplus funds in physical assets such as Gold, Silver and lands. Nevertheless, considerable share of savings also flowing to financial assets, which includes, Currency, Bank Deposits, Claims on Government, **Contractual** Savings, Equities.

The composition of household financial savings shows that the bank deposits (44%) continue to remain the major contributor along with the rise in the Contractual Savings, Claims on Government and Currency.

Though there was gradual decline in currency holdings by the households *i.e.,* 13.79% in 1970s to 9.30% in 2007, still the present currency holding level with households appears to be on high side compared to other countries. The primary reasons for higher currency holdings could be absence of banking facilities in majority villages (5.70 lakh villages) as well as hoarding of unaccounted money in the form of cash to circumvent tax laws. Though, cash is treated as financial asset, in reality, a major portion of currency is blocked and become unproductive.

Bank deposits seemed to be the preferred choice mainly on account of its inbuilt features such as Safety, Security and Liquidity. Traditionally, the Household sector has been playing a leading role in the landscape of bank deposits followed by the Government sector. However, the last two decades has witnessed significant shift in ownership of Bank deposits. While there was improvement in Corporate and Government sectors' share by 8.30% and 7.20% respectively during the period 1999 to 2009, household sector lost a share of 13.30% in the post reform period.

In the post-independence era, Indian financial system was characterized by poor infrastructure and low level of financial deepening. Savings in physical assets constituted the largest portion of the savings compared to the financial assets in the initial years of the planning periods. While rural households were keen on acquiring farm assets, the portfolio of urban households constituted consumer durables, gold, jewellry and house property.

Despite the fact that the household savings have been gradually moving from physical assets to financial assets over the years, still 49.79% of household savings are wrapped in unproductive physical assets, which is a cause of concern as the share of physical assets to total savings are very high in the recent years compared to emerging economies. This trend needs to be arrested as scarce funds are being diverted into unproductive segments.

Of course, investment in Real estate sector can be treated as productive provided construction activity is commenced within reasonable time, but it is regrettably note that many investors just buy and hold it for speculation leading to unproductive investments.

India has probably the largest fascination with gold than any other country in the world with a share of 9.50% of the world's total gold holdings. The World Gold Council believes that they are over 18000 tonnes of gold holding in the country. More impressive is the fact that current demand from India alone consumes 25% of the world's annual gold output. Large amount of capital is blocked in gold which resides in bank lockers and remain unproductive.

Indian economy would grow faster if the capital markets could attract more of the nation's savings and channel them into more productive areas, especially infrastructure. If the Indian market can develop and evolve into a more mature financial system, which persuades the middle class to put more of its money into equities, the potential is **mind-boggling.**

101. Which of the following statement (s) is/are correct tn the context of the given passage?
  I. The GDS percentage GDP has shown considerable improvement from 10% in 1950 to 33.7% in 2010. which is one of the highest globally.
  II. The saving rate however shows an increasing trend, marginal decline is observed under household sector.
  III. The share of financial assets in total household savings have come down from 54.05% to 50.21% especially in post-reform era.
  A. Only I   B. Only I and II
  C. Only II and III   D. All I, II and III
  E. None of these

102. Post-independence era has witnessed a significant shift in deployment of household savings especially the share of financial assets increased to 54.05% in 1990. Which of the following is/are supposed to be the prime cause of this shift?
  A. It is due to bank branch network across the country
  B. Government has made arrangements to aware the people
  C. It is due to increase in bank branch network and awareness among investors on various banking products
  D. Indian economy is growing at 8% and people are saving more than earlier
  E. None of these

103. India has probably the largest fascination with gold than any other country in the world. Which of the following is incorrect in regard to this fascination as mentioned in the passage?

A. India shares 9.50% of the total gold holdings

B. According to the World Gold Council estimates, there are over 18000 tonnes of gold holding in India

C. The current demand from India alone consumes 25% of the world's annual gold output

D. A small amount of capital is blocked in gold in banks but is however productive

E. None of these

104. Which of the following are the primary reasons, cited in the passage, for higher currency holdings?

A. It is due to large banking network that stashes money.

B. It is due to absence of banking facilities in majority of villages and tendency to circumvent tax laws for unaccounted money.

C. People do not believe in banks and fear that government may take their money.

D. There is lack of awareness among people about savings in banks

E. None of these

105. Despite the fact that the household savings have been gradually moving from physical assets to financial assets over the years. What percentage of household savings is wrapped in unproductive physical assets?

A. 45%   B. 46.79%

C. 58%   D. 49.79%

E. None of these

106. Which of the following should be a suitable title of the passage?

A. Importance of Gross Domestic Savings

B. Growth of Indian economy

C. Fascination for Gold

D. Physical assets versus financial assets

E. None of these

Directions (Qs. Nos. 107 and 108) : *Choose the word/group of words which is **most nearly the same** in meaning to the word/group of words printed in bold.*

107. Contractual

A. promising   B. agreeing

C. promissory   D. agreeable

E. concord

108. Commensurate

A. matching   B. commensal

C. commemorative   D. unmatching

E. comfortable

Directions (Qs. Nos. 109 and 110) : *Choose the word(s) which is **most opposite** in meaning of the word printed in bold, as used in the passage.*

109. Jeopardize

A. severe   B. endanger

C. saddle   D. safeguard

E. saturate

110. Mind-bogging

A. conscious   B. inclined

C. very difficult   D. surprising

E. unsurprising

Directions (Qs. Nos. 111-115) : *In the following questions, a passage is given with a blank space in the beginning. Three statements are given following the passage. You are required to select which of the statement(s) may be the starter?*

111. .... It is so pleasant a profession that it is not surprising if a vast number of persons adopt it who have no qualifications for it. The writer is free to work in what he believes.

I.   I am a writer.

II. I am a writer as I might have been a doctor or a lawyer.

III. I was a writer as I might have been a doctor.

A. Only I   B. Only II

C. Only III   D. Both I & II

E. Both II & III

112. .... It grew faster in year 2010. The conditions were favourable which helped in economic boom. The agriculture, tourism, export and mining helped in the growth of the economy.

I. Indian economy is not growing well.

II. The Indian economy grew fast as 10 per cent in 2008.

III. Due to economic reforms, economic growth of India was 8 per cent in 2009.

A. Only I   B. Only II

C. Only III   D. Both I & II

E. Both II & III

113. .... So, Anti Corruption campaign occupied centre stage during election season. Corruption prevailing in the high and mighty adversely impacts our nation and its global image.

I. Corruption is a big evil in India.

II. Corruption is not a big evil in India as propagated.

III. Anti corruption is a big challenge in India.

A. Only I   B. Only II

C. Only III   D. Both I & II

E. Both II & III

114. .... Roads are unsafe because of shortcomings in road and traffic engineer, old and non standard codes of traffic control devices, poor driver training and assessment, out dated legislations and a poor enforcement system.

I. Road safety is not a stand-along pheno-menon.

II. Indian roads are unsafe not due to a single factor.

III. Road safety is a stand-along phenomenon.

A. Only I   B. Only II

C. Only III   D. Both I & II

E. Both II & III

115. .... Such an initiative was long overdue. India has been characterized as one of the most over regulated countries in the world. No central data base of all laws and regulations exists in the country.

I. The government was considering to prepare database.

II. The government is considering to prepare a database of all laws and regulations.

III. The government has considered to prepare a database.

A. Only I   B. Only II

C. Only III   D. Both I & II

E. Both II & III

Directions (Qs. Nos. 116-120) : *Rearrange the following six sentences (a), (b), (c), (d), (e) and (f) in the proper sequence to form a meaningful para-graph; then answer the questions given below them.*

(*a*) Arctic sea ice has been melting at break-neck speeds in the past few decades, driven by warming air temperature, warming air temperature, warming ocean water temperature, all of which are caused by or accelerated by man-made climate change.

(*b*) But there are other factors at play in the decline of ice in the Arctic Ocean.

(*c*) Sea ice is generally moderated by sunlight.

(*d*) Warm ocean currents travel north from the equator and usher in warmer and warmer water, making sea ice growth difficult.

(*e*) It grows in the winter and melts in the summer.

(*f*) Weather patterns over the high mid-latitudes and the Arctic can also affect sea ice growth.

116. Which of the following should be the **fourth** sentence after rearrangement?

A. (*e*)   B. (*d*)

C. (*c*)   D. (*b*)

E. (*a*)

117. Which of the following should be the **sixth** sentence after rearrangement?

A. (*a*)   B. (*b*)

C. (*c*)   D. (*d*)

E. (*e*)

118. Which of the following should be the **Second** sentence afer rearrangement?

A. (*e*)   B. (*d*)

C. (*c*)   D. (*b*)

E. (*a*)

119. Which of the following should be the **first** sentence afer rearrangement?

A. (*a*)   B. (*b*)

C. (*c*)   D. (*d*)

E. (*e*)

120. Which of the following should be the **third** sentence afer rearrangement?
  A. (*a*)   B. (*b*)
  C. (*c*)   D. (*d*)
  E. (*f*)

Directions (Qs. Nos. 121-130) : *In the following passage there are blanks, each of which has been numbered. These numbers are printed below the passage and against each, five words are suggested, one of which fits the blank appropriately. Find out the appropriate word in each case.*

The rise of Asian manufacturers in the 1990s hit African firms hard; many were wiped out Northern Nigeria, which once had a ...(121)... garments industry, was unable to ...(122)... with low cost imports. South Africa has similar problems; its manufacturing failed to grow last year ...(123)... the continental boom.

This is partly the ...(124)... of governments. Buoyed by commodity income, they have neglected industry's needs, ...(125)... for roads and electricity. But that, too, may at last be changing. Wolfgang Fengler, a World Bank economist says, "Africa is now in a good position to industrialise with the right mix of ingredients." This includes ...(126)... demography, urbanisation, an emerging middle class and strong services. "For this to happen," he adds, "the continent will need to scale up its infrastructure ...(127)... and improve the business climate and many [African] countries have started to ...(128)... these challenges in recent years."

Kenya is not about to become ...(129)... next South Korea. African countries are likely to follow a more diverse path, benefiting from the growth of countless small and medium-sized businesses, as well as some big ones. For the next decade or so, services will still generate more jobs and wealth in Africa than manufacturing, which is fine. India has ...(130)... for more than two decades on the back of services, while steadily building a manufacturing sector from a very low base. Do not bet against Africa doing the same.

121. A. thriving   B. flourish
      C. detractive   D. dooming
      E. repulsive

122. A. competed   B. compete
      C. complete   D. surrender
      E. commensurate

123. A. inspite   B. additional
      C. in addition   D. despite
      E. despite of

124. A. fact   B. quality
      C. fault   D. default
      E. fiction

125. A. specific   B. especially
      C. particular   D. partially
      E. generally

126. A. favourable   B. favourably
      C. ferrocious   D. special
      E. contrast

127. A. expenditures   B. disinvestment
      C. investments   D. development
      E. developing

128. A. tackle   B. tackling
      C. decrease   D. increase
      E. improve

129. A. a   B. an
      C. the   D. such
      E. for

130. A. boomed   B. booming
      C. boom   D. expand
      E. plummeted

Directions (Qs. Nos. 131-135) : *In each of the question below, a sentence is broken into four parts. One of them may be grammatically or structurally wrong in the context of the sentence. The letter of that word is answer. If there is no wrong word or group of words, year answer will be "No error".*

131. Birthmarks on the back/could be signs of Tethered Spinal Cord Syndrome (TCS)/a neurological disorder/caused by tissue attachments.
  A. Birthmarks on the back
  B. could be signs of Tethered Spinal Cord Syndrome (TCS)

C. a neurological disorder
D. caused by tissue attachments
E. No error

132. As a part of the new survey,/if you says you
are/unhappy, the city police may/call to ask
you that reason.
A. As a part of the new survey,
B. if you says you are
C. unhappy, the city police may
D. call to ask you that reason.
E. No error

133. By keeping the brain/engaged, anyone can/
become learn to/control immediate cravings.
A. By keeping the brain
B. engaged, anyone can
C. become learn to
D. control immediate cravings.
E. No error

134. Foodies have realised/that there is more to
eating out/than switch restaurants that has/
predictable menus and sterile decors.
A. Foodies have realised
B. that there is more to eating out
C. than switch restaurants that has
D. predictable menus and sterile decors.
E. No error

135. The doctors are been worried/that the ace
cricketer will/suffer from a heart ailment/for
the rest of his life.
A. The doctors are been worried
B. that the ace cricketer will
C. suffer from a heart ailment
D. for the rest of his life.
E. No error

Directions (Qs. Nos. 136-140) : *Rearrange the
following seven sentences (a), (b), (c), (d), (e), (f)
and (g) in the proper sequence to form a meaningful
paragraph, then answer the given question.*

(a) These companies have long seen the US
market as the scene of a battle for
distribution, where they must secure
placement for their products in the fastest
growing retail channels just to maintain
their share of a pie that's not getting bigger.

(b) Companies can thus generate above-
average growth in the United States by not
only taking market share from competitors,
but also making targeted investments in
these specific product categories.

(c) Somewhat surprisingly, a number of cities
in developed markets, including the United
States and Western Europe, are growing as
rapidly as those in emerging markets.

(d) Our analysis forecasts that between 2014
and 2025, certain product categories will
grow at almost twice the rate of overall US
consumer spending.

(e) But this no-growth, or, at best, low-growth,
picture isn't entirely accurate.

(f) Most CPG companies have had very low
expectations for growth in the US market.

(g) Companies that ignore these cities could
be missing out on opportunities, very close
to home.

136. Which of the following should be the
SECOND sentence after the rearrangement?
A. (g)   B. (a)
C. (e)   D. (b)
E. (c)

137. Which of the following should be the FIRST
sentence after the rearrangement?
A. (a)   B. (b)
C. (f)   D. (d)
E. (g)

138. Which of the following should be the
FOURTH sentence after the rearrangement?
A. (g)   B. (f)
C. (e)   D. (d)
E. (c)

139. Which of the following should be the THIRD
sentence after the rearrangement?
A. (a)   B. (b)
C. (c)   D. (d)
E. (e)

140. Which of the following should be the LAST
(SEVENTH) sentence after the rearrangement?
A. (b)   B. (g)
C. (d)   D. (c)
E. (f)

Directions (Qs. Nos. 141-150) : *In the following passage, there are blanks, each of which has been numbered. Against each, five words are suggested, one of which fits the blank appropriately. Find out the appropriate word in each case.*

Poverty is a perception–it is a status which is ...(141)... on people who have relatively little-even in societies of plenty. That is why we ...(142)... can never really ever "end" poverty. To see a world in which so many people have less than you and to want them to have more is, to many of us, human ...(143).... It is why poverty in the UK matters as much as poverty elsewhere, despite the material differences. Relative poverty will always ...(144)... and it should always be at the forefront of efforts to improve our world because it ...(145)... more than the bare minimum solution. ...(146)... this, the aid industry currently has quite a few eggs in the end poverty basket. We risk assuming that the public ...(147)... between absolute and relative poverty. It probably doesn't especially not in austere times. Just look at the ...(148)... political view on and to the middle income countries that contain hundreds of millions of desperately poor people. Too much negatively and we are ...(149)... of not making any progress with aid money, too much task of progress and aid is no longer necessary. It shouldn't be a Catch 22 situation but in ...(150)..., for some, it is.

141. A. subjected   B. apprehended
     C. bestowed   D. lifted
     E. labelled

142. A. spritely   B. objectionably
     C. fatally   D. continually
     E. probably

143. A. problem   B. nature
     C. face   D. being
     E. population

144. A. remainder   B. leave
     C. allow   D. exist
     E. touch

145. A. seek   B. asks
     C. insists   D. ensure
     E. demands

146. A. Along   B. Added
     C. Despite   D. Favouring
     E. Siding

147. A. understands   B. distinguishes
     C. grasps   D. separates
     E. draws

148. A. prevailing   B. currently
     C. aimed   D. lost
     E. multiple

149. A. accused   B. alleged
     C. suspicion   D. remarked
     E. stationed

150. A. actual   B. now
     C. place   D. reality
     E. form

ANSWERS

1	2	3	4	5	6	7	8	9	10
D	D	C	C	C	E	E	E	E	A
11	**12**	**13**	**14**	**15**	**16**	**17**	**18**	**19**	**20**
E	A	C	B	C	D	A	A	E	C
21	**22**	**23**	**24**	**25**	**26**	**27**	**28**	**29**	**30**
C	C	C	E	A	A	C	D	A	D
31	**32**	**33**	**34**	**35**	**36**	**37**	**38**	**39**	**40**
B	A	B	D	B	E	A	D	A	E
41	**42**	**43**	**44**	**45**	**46**	**47**	**48**	**49**	**50**
A	B	C	A	E	E	D	E	C	E

51	52	53	54	55	56	57	58	59	60
A	E	C	B	B	C	D	E	C	B
61	62	63	64	65	66	67	68	69	70
A	A	A	C	C	B	C	E	D	B
71	72	73	74	75	76	77	78	79	80
D	E	C	D	E	D	D	C	C	D
81	82	83	84	85	86	87	88	89	90
E	B	D	B	A	E	E	C	A	A
91	92	93	94	95	96	97	98	99	100
E	A	C	E	C	B	D	D	B	E
101	102	103	104	105	106	107	108	109	110
D	C	D	B	D	A	C	A	D	E
111	112	113	114	115	116	117	118	119	120
D	E	A	D	B	B	A	A	C	B
121	122	123	124	125	126	127	128	129	130
A	B	D	C	B	A	C	A	C	A
131	132	133	134	135	136	137	138	139	140
B	B	C	C	A	C	C	A	C	A
141	142	143	144	145	146	147	148	149	150
E	E	B	D	E	C	B	A	A	D

EXPLANATORY ANSWERS

51. Let the work be finished in x days

Then A's $(x - 10)$ day's work + B's x day's work = 1

$$\frac{x-10}{20} + \frac{x}{30} = 1$$

$\Rightarrow \quad \dfrac{3(x-10)+2x}{60} = 1$

$\Rightarrow \quad 3x - 30 + 2x = 60$

$\Rightarrow \quad 5x = 90 \Rightarrow x = 18$

Hence, the project will be completed in 18 days.

52. Let B runs 100 m then A runs 125 m

Ratio of speed $= \dfrac{125}{100} = \dfrac{5}{4}$

Length of the race $= \dfrac{7 \times 1}{\left(1 - \dfrac{4}{5}\right)} = 7 \times 5 = 35$ m

53. Let length of the train = x m

Relative speed = $(100 - 64) = 36$ km/hr

$$= 36 \times \frac{5}{18} \text{ m/s} = 10 \text{ m/s}$$

length of the train = speed × time

$$= 10 \times 40 = 400 \text{ m}.$$

54. A's 1 hour work $= \dfrac{1}{4}$

X's 1 hour work $= \dfrac{1}{34}$

(A + X)'s 1 hour work

$$= \frac{1}{4} - \frac{1}{34} = \frac{17-2}{68} = \frac{15}{68}$$

∴ Tank will fill in $\dfrac{68}{15}$ hours

Now, B's 1 hour work = $\dfrac{1}{8}$

W's 1 hour work = $\dfrac{1}{x}$

(B + W)'s 1 hour work = $\dfrac{1}{8} - \dfrac{1}{x} = \dfrac{x-8}{8x}$

∴ Tank will fill in $\dfrac{8x}{x-8}$ hours

But $\dfrac{8x}{x-8} = \dfrac{68}{15} + \dfrac{20}{3}$

$\Rightarrow \dfrac{8x}{x-8} = \dfrac{68+100}{15} = \dfrac{168}{15} = \dfrac{56}{5}$

$\Rightarrow \quad 56x - 448 = 40x$

$\Rightarrow \quad 56x - 40x = 448$

$\Rightarrow \quad 16x = 448$

$\Rightarrow \quad x = \dfrac{448}{16} = 28$

Hence, outlet W alone empty the full tank in 28 hours.

55. A's 1 hour work = $\dfrac{1}{4}$

A's $\dfrac{1}{2}$ hour work = $\dfrac{1}{4 \times 2} = \dfrac{1}{8}$ part

$1 - \dfrac{1}{8} = \dfrac{7}{8}$ part

∵ $\dfrac{7}{8}$ part empty $(x + w)$ in $\dfrac{17}{2}$ hours

∴ 1 part can empty = $\dfrac{7}{8} \times \dfrac{2}{17} = \dfrac{7}{68}$ hours

∴ y can alone empty 1 part

$= \dfrac{7}{68} - \dfrac{1}{34} = \dfrac{7-2}{68} = \dfrac{5}{68}$

Hence, y can alone empty full tank in $\dfrac{68}{5}$ hours

$= 13\dfrac{3}{5}$ hours = 13.6 hours.

56. (X + Z)'s 1 hour work

$= \dfrac{1}{34} + \dfrac{1}{30} = \dfrac{15+17}{510} = \dfrac{32}{510}$

(X + Z)'s H hour work = $\dfrac{32\,H}{510}$

Z's 1 hour work = $\dfrac{1}{30}$

Z's (H + 10) hour work = $\dfrac{(H+10)}{30}$

$\dfrac{32\,H}{510} = \dfrac{H+10}{30}$

$32H = 17H + 170$

$15H = 170$

$H = \dfrac{170}{15} = \dfrac{34}{3} = 11\dfrac{1}{3}$

Hence, value of H = $11\dfrac{1}{3}$ hours.

57. E's 1 hour work = $\dfrac{1}{12}$

E's 2 hours work = $\dfrac{1}{12} \times 2 = \dfrac{1}{6}$

Remaining work = $1 - \dfrac{1}{6} = \dfrac{5}{6}$

(B + C)'s 1 hour work

$= \dfrac{1}{8} + \dfrac{1}{6} = \dfrac{3+4}{24} = \dfrac{7}{24}$

∵ $\dfrac{7}{24}$ part is filled in 1 hour

∴ $\dfrac{5}{6}$ part is filled in $\dfrac{1}{\dfrac{7}{24}} \times \dfrac{5}{6}$ hours

$= \dfrac{24}{7} \times \dfrac{5}{6} = \dfrac{20}{7}$ hours

∴ Total time taken to fill the tank completely

$= 2 + \dfrac{20}{7} = \dfrac{34}{7} = 4\dfrac{6}{7}$ hours.

58. (A + D + E)'s 1 hour work

$$= \frac{1}{4} + \frac{1}{2} + \frac{1}{12} = \frac{3+6+1}{12} = \frac{10}{12} = \frac{5}{6}$$

Z's 1 hour work $= \frac{1}{30}$

$\because \frac{1}{30}$ part can empty in 1 hour

$\therefore$ 1 part can empty in $\frac{30}{1}$ hour

$\therefore \frac{5}{6}$ part can empty $= 30 \times \frac{5}{6}$ hours = 25 hr

Outlet Z can empty the tank completely in 25 hours.

59. Let the speed of the boat $= x$ km/hr and speed of stream $= y$ km/hr

Let distance $= d$ km

$$\frac{d}{x+y} = 4$$

$\Rightarrow \qquad d = 4(x + y)$ ...(i)

$$\frac{d}{x-y} = \frac{44}{5}$$

$\Rightarrow \qquad d = \frac{44(x-y)}{5}$ ...(ii)

From (i) and (ii)

$$4(x+y) = \frac{44(x-y)}{5}$$

$\Rightarrow \quad 20x + 20y = 44x - 44y$

$\Rightarrow \qquad 24x = 64y$

$\Rightarrow \qquad \frac{x}{y} = \frac{64}{24} = \frac{8}{3}$

$\therefore \dfrac{\text{Speed of boat}}{\text{Speed of stream}} = 8 : 3.$

60. A : B : C $= 6500 \times 6 : 8400 \times 5 : 10000 \times 3$

$= 39000 : 42000 : 30000$

$= 39 : 42 : 30$

$= 13 : 14 : 10$

$\because$ A is working member

$\therefore \qquad \frac{5}{100} \times 7400 = ₹ 370$

Profit $= 7400 - 370$

$= ₹ 7030$

Share of B in the profit

$= \frac{14}{37} \times 7030$

$= ₹ 14 \times 190$

$= ₹ 2660.$

61. Time $= \dfrac{\text{S.I.} \times 100}{\text{P} \times r} = \dfrac{81 \times 100 \times 2}{900 \times 9} = 2$ years.

62. Let Amount deposited in scheme A $= ₹ x$

$\therefore$ Amount deposited in scheme B

$= ₹ 13900 - x$

According to the question,

$$\frac{x \times 14 \times 2}{100} + \frac{(13900 - x) \times 11 \times 2}{100} = 3508$$

$\Rightarrow 28x + 13900 \times 22 - 22x = 3508 \times 100$

$\Rightarrow \qquad 6x = 350800 - 305800$

$\Rightarrow \qquad 6x = 45000$

$\Rightarrow \qquad x = 7500$

Hence, amount deposited in scheme B

$= 13900 - 7500$

$= ₹ 6400.$

63. Required probability $= \dfrac{10}{21}.$

64. Suppose the two liquids A and B are $7x$ litres and $5x$ litres respectively.

Now, when 9 litres of mixture are taken out,

A remains $= 7x - 9\left(\dfrac{7}{7+5}\right)$

$= 7x - \dfrac{63}{12} = \left(7x - \dfrac{21}{4}\right) l$

and B remains $= 5x - 9\left(\dfrac{5}{7+5}\right)$

$= 5x - \dfrac{45}{12} = \left(5x - \dfrac{15}{4}\right) l$

When 9 litres of liquid B are added

$\left(7x - \dfrac{21}{4}\right) : \left(5x - \dfrac{15}{4} + 9\right) = 7 : 9$

$$\Rightarrow \quad \frac{7x - \dfrac{21}{4}}{5x - \dfrac{15}{4} + 9} = \frac{7}{9}$$

$$\Rightarrow \quad 63x - \frac{189}{4} = 35x - \frac{105}{4} + 63$$

$$\Rightarrow \quad 28x = \frac{189}{4} - \frac{105}{4} + 63$$
$$= 21 + 63 = 84$$

$$\Rightarrow \quad x = \frac{84}{28} = 3$$

$$\therefore \quad 7x = 7 \times 3$$
$$= 21 \text{ litres.}$$

65. $$\pi(r + 4)^2 - \pi r^2 = \frac{11}{25}\pi r^2$$

$$\Rightarrow \quad \pi(r^2 + 8r + 16 - r^2) = \frac{11}{25}\pi r^2$$

$$\Rightarrow \quad 8r + 16 = \frac{11}{25}r^2$$
$$\Rightarrow \quad 200r + 400 = 11r^2$$
$$\Rightarrow \quad 11r^2 - 200r - 400 = 0$$
$$\Rightarrow 11r^2 - 220r + 20r - 400 = 0$$
$$\Rightarrow 11r(r - 20) + 20(r - 20) = 0$$
$$(r - 20)(11r + 20) = 0$$
$$\Rightarrow \quad r = 20$$

or $$\quad r = \frac{-20}{11}$$

Hence, radius of the swimming pool
$$= 20 \text{ feet.}$$

66. $$\frac{14}{x - y} + \frac{36}{x + y} = 4$$

$$\frac{20}{x - y} + \frac{24}{x + y} = 5$$

$$36a + 14b = 4 \qquad] \times 2$$
$$24a + 20b = 5 \qquad] \times 3$$
$$72a + 28b = 8$$
$$72a + 60b = 15$$
$$\underline{- \quad - \qquad -}$$

$$32b = 7 \Rightarrow b = \frac{7}{32}$$

$$24a + 20 \times \frac{7}{32} = 5$$

$$\Rightarrow \quad 24a = 5 - \frac{140}{32}$$

$$= \frac{160 - 140}{32} = \frac{20}{32}$$

$$\Rightarrow \quad a = \frac{20}{32 \times 24} = \frac{5}{192}$$

$$\frac{1}{x + y} = \frac{5}{192}$$

$$\Rightarrow \quad 5x + 5y = 192 \qquad] \times 7$$

$$\frac{1}{x - y} = \frac{7}{32}$$

$$\Rightarrow \quad 7x - 7y = 32 \qquad] \times 5$$
$$35x + 35y = 1344$$
$$35x - 35y = 160$$
$$70x = 1504$$

$$x = \frac{1504}{70} = 21 \text{ km/hr}$$

II speed of boat = 16 km/hr
∴ Quantity I > Quantity II
Hence, option (B) is correct.

68. $$\frac{x^2}{5} + x + \frac{4}{5} = 0$$

$$\Rightarrow \quad x^2 + 5x + 4 = 0$$
$$\Rightarrow \quad x^2 + 4x + x + 4 = 0$$
$$\Rightarrow \quad x(x + 4) + 1(x + 4) = 0$$
$$\Rightarrow \quad (x + 4)(x + 1) = 0$$
$$\text{either } x = -4 \text{ or } x = -1$$
$$3y^2 + 4y + 1 = 0$$
$$\Rightarrow \quad 3y^2 + 3y + y + 1 = 0$$
$$\Rightarrow \quad 3y(y + 1) + 1(y + 1) = 0$$
$$\Rightarrow \quad (3y + 1)(y + 1) = 0$$

$$\text{either } y = -1 \text{ or } y = -\frac{1}{3}$$

Quantity I ≤ Quantity II
Hence, option (E) is correct.

69. Quantity I ≥ Quantity II
Hence, option (D) is correct.

81.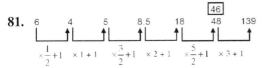

Hence, wrong number is 48.

82.

Hence, wrong number is 3.

83.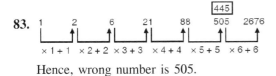

Hence, wrong number is 505.

84.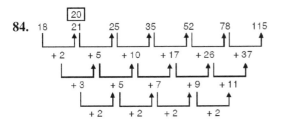

Hence, wrong number is 21.

85.

120	137	178	222	290	375	477

+ 17   + 34   + 51   + 68   + 85   + 102

17 × 1   17 × 2   17 × 3   17 × 4   17 × 5   17 × 6

Hence, wrong number is 178.

86. ∵ Area of rectangle = 150 m²

$$\Rightarrow \qquad\qquad xy = 150$$

$$\Rightarrow \qquad\qquad x = \frac{150}{y} \qquad ...(i)$$

Now, $(x - 5)(y + 2) = 120$

$$\Rightarrow \quad xy + 2x - 5y - 10 = 120$$

$$\Rightarrow \quad 150 + 2x - 5y - 10 = 120$$

$$\Rightarrow \qquad\qquad 2x - 5y = -20$$

$$\Rightarrow \qquad 2\left(\frac{150}{y}\right) - 5y = -20$$

$$\Rightarrow \qquad\qquad 300 - 5y^2 = -20y$$

$$\Rightarrow \qquad 5y^2 - 20y - 300 = 0$$

$$\Rightarrow \qquad\qquad y^2 - 4y - 60 = 0$$

$$\Rightarrow \qquad (y - 10)(y + 6) = 0$$

$$\Rightarrow \qquad\qquad y = 10 \text{ or } y = -6$$

which is not possible

∴ Breadth of rectangle = 10 m

Length of rectangle = 15 m

Side of square = 15 m

[∵ Length of rectangle = side of square given]

∴ Perimeter of square = 15 × 4 = 60 m.

87. Amount invested by A

= 4200 × 4 + 5200 × 6 = 48000

Amount invested by B

= 3600 × 6 + (3600 + x) × 4

= 21600 + 14400 + 4x

= 4x + 36000

Amount invested by C

= 2400 × 6 + (2400 + 2x)4

= 14400 + 9600 + 8x

= 24000 + 8x

A : B : C = 48000 : 4x + 36000 : 8x + 24000

$$\text{A's share} = \left(\frac{48000}{48000 + 12x + 60000}\right) \times 2820$$

$$\Rightarrow \quad 1200 = \left(\frac{48000}{12x + 108000}\right) \times 2820$$

$$\Rightarrow \quad 12x + 108000 = 282 \times 400 = 112800$$

$$\Rightarrow \quad 12x = 112800 - 10800 = 4800$$

$$x = \frac{4800}{12} = 400$$

Hence, B invested additional amount = ₹ 400.

88.

Milk	Water
100	20

Let amount of milk = 100 l

and amount of water = 20 l

24 l mix taken out

Amount of milk in 24 l mix

$$= \frac{5}{6} \times 24 = 20 l$$

Amount of water in 24 l mix

$$= \frac{1}{6} \times 24 = 4\,l$$

Now Amount of milk
$$= 100\,l = 80\,l + 24\,l \text{ (added)}$$
$$= 104\,l$$

Amount of water
$$= 20 - 4 = 16\,l$$

Again 15 l of mix taken out

Amount of milk in 15 l mix

$$= \frac{13}{15} \times 15 = 13\,l$$

Amount of water

$$= \frac{2}{15} \times 15 = 2\,l$$

Hence, the resultant quantity of milk in the mixture $= 104 - 13 = 91$ litres.

89. Let number of ball faced by D = 3x

then, number of ball faced by F = 4x

Total run scored by D = 72 × 3x

Total run scored by F = 66 × 4x

Per cent difference of run scored by F more than D

$$= \left(\frac{66 \times 4x - 72 \times 3x}{72 \times 3x} \right) \times 100$$

$$= \frac{4800}{216} = \frac{200}{9} = 22\frac{2}{9}\%.$$

90. Total run scored by E = 55 × 28 = 1540

Total run scored by E in first 25 matches
$$= 25 \times (55 - 9) = 1150$$

Total run scored by E in last 3 matches
$$= 1540 - 1150 = 390$$

Minimum run scored by E in 28th match
$$n \geq 390 - 127 - 126$$
$$n \geq 137$$
$$\therefore \quad n = 137.$$

91. Total run scored by A = 8x

Total ball faced = 8x − 74

Strike rate of A $= \left(\dfrac{8x}{8x - 74} \right) \times 100$

$\Rightarrow \qquad 129.6 = \dfrac{8x \times 100}{8x - 74}$

$\Rightarrow$ 129.6 × 8x − 8x × 100 = 129.6 × 74

$\Rightarrow$ 8x(129.6 − 100) = 129.6 × 74

$\Rightarrow \qquad x = \dfrac{129.6 \times 74}{8 \times 29.6} = \dfrac{81}{2}$

$\Rightarrow \qquad x = 40\dfrac{1}{2}$

$\therefore$ Average runs scored by A = 40.5.

93. Let no. of matches played by C = x

Total runs scored = 38 x

$$\text{Strike rate} = \left(\frac{38x}{400} \right) \times 100$$

$\Rightarrow \qquad 114 = \dfrac{38x}{4}$

$\therefore \qquad x = \dfrac{114 \times 4}{38} = 12$

Hence, total number of matches played by batsman C = 12

94. 1 man 1 day work $= \dfrac{1}{10 \times 12} = \dfrac{1}{120}$

1 child 1 day work $= \dfrac{1}{12 \times 16} = \dfrac{1}{192}$

1 women 1 day work $= \dfrac{1}{8 \times 20} = \dfrac{1}{160}$

(5 men + 12 children) 4 days work

$$= \left(\frac{5}{120} + \frac{12}{192} \right) \times 4$$

$$= \left(\frac{1}{24} + \frac{1}{16} \right) \times 4$$

$$= \left(\frac{2+3}{48} \right) \times 4 = \frac{5}{12}$$

Remaining work $= 1 - \dfrac{5}{12} = \dfrac{7}{12}$

(5 men + 4 women + 4 children) 1 day work

$$= \left(\frac{1}{24} + \frac{4}{160} + \frac{4}{192} \right) 1 \text{ day work}$$

$$= \left(\frac{1}{24} + \frac{1}{40} + \frac{1}{48}\right)$$

$$= \left(\frac{10 + 6 + 5}{240}\right) = \frac{21}{240} = \frac{7}{80}$$

$\because \dfrac{7}{80}$ part can do in 1 day

$\therefore \dfrac{7}{12}$ part can do in $\dfrac{80}{7} \times \dfrac{7}{12} = \dfrac{20}{3} = 6\dfrac{2}{3}$ days.

95. 60% of $x = 600$

$$x = \frac{600 \times 100}{60} = 1000$$

$(60 - 40)\% = 600$

20% of $x = 600$

$$x = \frac{600 \times 100}{20} = 3000.$$

96. Let present ages of son and daughter are x and y years.

According to the question,

$Z = x + y + 8$

Where Z = Present age of mother

$$\frac{y + 5}{x + 5} = \frac{7}{6}$$

$\Rightarrow 7x + 35 = 6y + 30$

$\Rightarrow 7x - 6y = -5$

$\Rightarrow 7x + 5 = 6y$

$$y = \frac{7x + 5}{6}$$

$$Z = x + y + 8 = x + \frac{7x + 5}{6} + 8$$

$\Rightarrow \qquad Z = \dfrac{6x + 7x + 5 + 48}{6} = \dfrac{13x + 53}{6}$

...(i)

Now, Father's age is equal to three times son's age $Z + 7 = 3x$

$\Rightarrow \qquad Z = 3x - 7$ \qquad ...(ii)

From (i) and (ii)

$$\frac{13x + 53}{6} = 3x - 7$$

$\Rightarrow \qquad 13x + 53 = 18x - 42$

$\Rightarrow \qquad 5x = 95$

$\Rightarrow \qquad x = 19$

$$y = \frac{7 \times 19 + 5}{6} = \frac{138}{6} = 23$$

Hence, present age of the daughter = 23 years.

97. X———————Y———————Z
$\qquad$ 20 km $\qquad$ 40 km

Let speed of the current = m km/hr

Speed of boat B in still water = 10 km/hr

Speed of B in upstream

$\qquad = (10 - m)$ km/hr

Speed of boat A in still water

$\qquad = (10 - m)$ km/hr

According to the question,

$$\frac{20}{10 - m + m} = \frac{40}{10 - m} - 3$$

$\Rightarrow \qquad 2 = \dfrac{40}{10 - m} - 3$

$\Rightarrow \qquad \dfrac{40}{10 - m} = 5$

$\Rightarrow \qquad 10 - m = 8$

$\qquad m = 2$

$\therefore$ Speed of the current = 2 km/hr

Hence, the speed of boat A

$= (10 - m)$ km/hr = (0-2) km/hr = 8 km/hr.

Previous Paper (Solved)

Institute of Banking Personnel Selection (IBPS) Specialist (HR/Personnel) Officer Scale-I Online Main Exam 2017*

PROFESSIONAL KNOWLEDGE

1. Match List 'A' with List 'B' and choose the right answer by using the codes given:

List–A	List–B
(a) Staffing	1. Motivation
(b) Planning	2. Training
(c) Directing	3. Forecasting
(d) Controlling	4. Comparison of Performance

   Codes:

	(a)	(b)	(c)	(d)
A.	1	2	3	4
B.	2	3	1	4
C.	3	2	4	1
D.	4	2	3	1

2. Which of the following pair is correctly matched?
   A. F.W. Taylor – Human Relations Approach
   B. Henry Fayol – Universality of Management
   C. Elton Mayo – Psychological Approach
   D. M. Parker Follet – Scientific Management

3. Arrange the following steps in disciplinary procedure in their right order:
   (a) Framing and issue of charge sheet
   (b) Domestic enquiry
   (c) Preliminary enquiry
   (d) Reporting of misconduct to disciplinary authority

   (e) Notice of enquiry
   (f) Findings of enquiry officer
   (g) Examination of evidences
   (h) Closure
   A. (d), (e), (a), (c), (b), (g), (h), (f)
   B. (d), (c), (a), (e), (b), (g), (h), (f)
   C. (d), (e), (a), (c), (b), (g), (f), (h)
   D. (d), (a), (c), (e), (b), (g), (f), (h)

4. Who among the following is associated with the types of personnel department such as independent, integrated; staff-coordinated and split function categories?
   A. Dale Yoder
   B. Dale S. Beach
   C. Richard P. Calhoon
   D. Dalton E. McFarland

5. Which of the following methods of training is also known as 'socio-drama' or 'psycho-drama'?
   A. Strategic planner   B. Mirroring
   C. Apprenticeship   D. Role-playing

6. The first of May in 1927 was for the first time celebrated as 'Labour Day' at
   A. Calcutta   B. Bombay
   C. Madras   D. Ahmedabad

7. Who started the publication of the Bengali Weekly, titled 'Janawani' in Calcutta?
   A. Shapurji Bengalee
   B. M.N. Roy
   C. Muzaffar Ahmad
   D. Diwan Chamanlal

---

* Based on Memory.

8. According to the Second National Commission on Labour, 'check-off system' must be made compulsory for members of all registered trade unions in establishments employing:
   A. 150 workers
   B. 200 workers
   C. 250 workers
   D. 300 workers

9. The Ahmedabad Textile Labour Association is an example of
   A. Craft Union
   B. Staff Union
   C. Industrial Union
   D. General Union

10. Which of the following is a non-statutory adhoc body?
    A. Central Implementation and Evaluation Committee
    B. Central Committee on Labour Research
    C. Committee on Conventions
    D. Wage Board

11. Which of the following statements relating to the First National Commission on Labour is correct?
    A. The Commission submitted its report in 1968.
    B. The Commission recommended that it would not be desirable to make union recognition compulsory under a Central Law.
    C. The Commission recommended that it would be desirable to make union recognition compulsory under a Central Law.
    D. The Commission recommended that a trade union seeking recognition should have at least 20 per cent membership of the workers of an establishment.

12. Which of the following is the prescribed qualification for appointment of a judge of an Employees' Insurance Court under the Employees' State Insurance Act, 1948?
    A. A judge of the High Court.
    B. Any presiding officer of a labour court with five years of experience.
    C. Any presiding officer of an Industrial Tribunal with three years of experience.
    D. Any person who is or has been a judicial officer or is a legal practitioner of five years standing.

13. Social security provided by a 'means test' is called
    A. Need based assistance
    B. Social assistance
    C. Social assurance
    D. Mutual assistance

14. Match the provisions provided under Column–A with the respective legislations under which they are covered under Column–B:

Column–A	Column–B
(a) Compulsory Insurance	1. The Payment of Gratuity Act, 1972
(b) Scheduled Employment	2. The Industrial Disputes Act, 1947
(c) Protected Workman	3. The Maternity Benefit Act, 1961
(d) Medical Bonus	4. The Minimum Wages Act, 1948

    Codes:

	(a)	(b)	(c)	(d)
A.	1	2	3	4
B.	4	3	2	1
C.	2	1	4	3
D.	1	4	2	3

15. Which of the following are ad-hoc bodies under the Industrial Disputes Act, 1947?
    (a) National Tribunal
    (b) Labour Court
    (c) Industrial Tribunal
    (d) Court of Inquiry
    (e) Grievance Redressal Committee
    A. (a), (c) and (d)
    B. (a), (d) and (e)
    C. (d) and (e)
    D. (a) and (d)

16. The provisions relating to Voluntary Arbitration was included in the Industrial Disputes Act, 1947 through an amendment in the year:
    A. 1948
    B. 1956
    C. 1962
    D. 1971

17. Who among the following is the first Indian to become the President of the International Labour Conference?

A. Shri Jagjivan Ram
B. Sir Atul Chatterjee
C. Dr. Nagendra Singh
D. Shri Ravindra Verma

18. As per the provisions of the Industrial Employment (Standing Orders) Act, 1946, for which of the following organisations the Central Government is not the appropriate Government?
A. Railways   B. Major Ports
C. Banks   D. Mine and Oilfields

19. The Second Industrial Truce Resolution was passed in the year _____.
A. 1948   B. 1956
C. 1962   D. 1991

20. Each labour legislation, which has been enacted, is based on certain underlying principles. Match the legislations with underlying principle:

List–I (Name of the Legislation)	List–II (Underlying Principle)
(a) Factories Act, 1948	1. Principle of Regulation
(b) Equal Remuneration Act, 1976	2. Principle of Social Security
(c) Industrial Employment (Standing Orders) Act, 1946	3. Principle of Protection
(d) Employees Compensation Act, 1923	4. Principle of Social Justice

Codes:

	(a)	(b)	(c)	(d)
A.	3	4	1	2
B.	1	2	3	4
C.	4	3	2	1
D.	1	3	2	4

21. The first craft union was organized by shoemakers in Philadelphia, USA in the year:
A. 1786   B. 1788
C. 1792   D. 1806

22. Which of the following theories of motivation classifies persons as 'Intrinsically motivated' and 'extrinsically motivated'?
A. Reinforcement Theory
B. Alderfer's ERG Theory
C. Adam's Equity Theory
D. Cognitive Evaluation Theory

23. Which of the following is not true relating to prohibition of strikes in public utility services under the Industrial Disputes Act, 1947?
A. Without giving to the employer notice of strike within six weeks before striking.
B. Before the expiry of the date specified in the notice of strike.
C. Within fourteen days of giving a notice of strike.
D. During the pendency of any conciliation proceedings and ten days after conclusion of such proceedings.

24. The method by which internal wage differentials are determined is called
A. Wage survey   B. Wage bargaining
C. Job evaluation   D. Wage regulation

25. The nature of employment relations in general in India is
A. Deregulated Competitive
B. Constrained Competitive
C. Regulated Protective
D. Protective Competitive

26. The Fish-Bone analysis is associated with which of the following?
A. Quality circles
B. Conflict Management
C. Performance Appraisal
D. Incentive Plan

27. Under the provisions of the Factories Act, 1948 the total number of hours of overtime in a quarter of a year shall not exceed:
A. Fifty hours   B. Fifty-six hours
C. Sixty hours   D. Forty-eight hours

28. Who suggested for setting up of Joint Workers' Councils?
A. Bombay Committee, 1920
B. Bengal Committee, 1920
C. Royal Commission on Labour, 1931
D. Government of India Act, 1935

29. Which of the following is not an element of planning?

A. Establishing leadership qualities

B. Finalising objectives

C. Evaluating alternatives

D. Establishing sequence of action

30. Which of the following statements is/are correct?

(a) Job enrichment does not need a motive to perform.

(b) Job enlargement is the expansion of number of different tasks performed by an employee in a single job.

(c) Moving employee from one job to other adds variety and reduces boredom.

(d) Participation cannot affect the enrichment process.

Code :

A. Both (a) and (c)

B. Both (b) and (c)

C. Only (c)

D. All (a), (b), (c) and (d)

31. Five phases constitute the strategic HRM process, they are :

(a) Identify Sources of Competitive Advantage

(b) Implementing HR Strategies

(c) Environmental Scanning

(d) Monitoring and Evaluating HR Strategies

(e) HR strategy formulation

Identify the correct sequence :

A. (c), (a), (d), (b), (e)

B. (a), (c), (d), (b), (e)

C. (c), (a), (e), (b), (d)

D. (c), (b), (d), (e), (a)

32. Which of the following is not an HR Demand Forecasting Technique?

A. Managerial Judgement

B. Ratio-Trend Analysis

C. Merrick Differential Plan

D. Work Study Technique

33. Which of the following describes "Command Groups"?

A. A group established to solve a particular problem.

B. A unit established by the organisation to accomplish specific tasks.

C. Group characterised by intimate, face-to-face association and cooperation.

D. Formal groups that consist of managers and their direct subordinates.

34. Match the Leadership Theories and their proponents given in Lists-I and II below :

List-I Leadership Theories	List-II Proponents
(a) Managerial Grid Theory	(i) Hollandder and Julian (1969)
(b) Iowa Leadership Studies	(ii) Albert Bandura (1977)
(c) Group and Exchange Theories of Leadership	(iii) Lippitt and White (1939)
(d) Social Learning Theories	(iv) Blake and Mouton (1978)

Code :

	(a)	(b)	(c)	(d)
A.	(ii)	(iii)	(iv)	(i)
B.	(i)	(ii)	(iv)	(iii)
C.	(iii)	(ii)	(i)	(iv)
D.	(iv)	(iii)	(i)	(ii)

35. The deliberate process through which someone becomes aware of personal skills, interests, knowledge, motivations and other characteristics, and establishes action plans to attain career specific goals is called :

A. Career Management

B. Career Development

C. Career Counselling

D. Career Planning

36. What is the correct sequence of following stages in manpower acquisition process?

(a) HR need forecast

(b) Assessing existing manpower

(c) Net manpower needed

(d) Organisational objectives and policies

(e) Recruitment process

Code :

A. (b), (a), (d), (c), (e)   B. (d), (a), (b), (c), (e)

C. (d), (a), (c), (b), (e)   D. (a), (b), (e), (d), (c)

37. Which of the following statements relating to labour-management cooperation is not correct?

A. It does not include information-sharing.

B. It includes problem sharing.

C. It includes joint consultation.

D. It includes workers' participation in management.

38. Match the following :

Philosophy	*Theory of Labour Welfare*
(*a*) Laws are made to prescribe minimum welfare for workers, implementation of which is periodically supervised and punishment for defaulting employers is levied.	(*i*) Religious Theory
(*b*) Labour welfare work is taken up in a spirit of atonement.	(*ii*) Placating Theory
(*c*) Labour welfare is extended in order to satisfy and appease the increasing demands of employees.	(*iii*) Public Relations theory
(*d*) Labour welfare is extended to build and improve 'employer branding'.	(*iv*) Policing Theory

Code :

	(*a*)	(*b*)	(*c*)	(*d*)
A.	(*ii*)	(*iii*)	(*i*)	(*iv*)
B.	(*iv*)	(*ii*)	(*iii*)	(*i*)
C.	(*iv*)	(*iii*)	(*i*)	(*ii*)
D.	(*iv*)	(*i*)	(*ii*)	(*iii*)

39. Which of the following concepts explains that welfare implies the welfare of man, his family, and his community?

A. The total concept of welfare

B. The social concept of welfare

C. The positive concept of welfare

D. The relative concept of welfare

40. Who said "Jobs, rather than men, should wait"?

A. Karl Marx

B. Higgins

C. Sir William Beveridge

D. D.R. Gadgil

41. According to classical theorists, the four pillars of organising are :

A. Division of labour, scalar and functional processes, structures and span of control.

B. Division of labour, identity, structures and cooperation.

C. Identity, structures, scalar chain and span of control.

D. Structures, scalar chain, span of control and specialisation.

42. Which of the following is not a publication of I.L.O.?

A. International Labour Review

B. Shram Ki Duniya

C. International Labour Statistics

D. Indian Labour Journal

43. Which of the following studies/approaches does not come under the In-plant Theories of industrial relations?

A. The 'systems' approach developed by John T. Dunlop.

B. The Human Relations approach of Elton Mayo.

C. The behaviouristic approach of Rensis Likert.

D. The Group Dynamics approach of Kurt Lewin, Chris Argyris and others.

44. The Leadership Theories based on the assumption that 'the leader's ability to lead is contingent upon various situational factors such as the leader's preferred style, the capabilities and behaviours of the followers etc.' is known as :

A. Situational Leadership Theory

B. Behavioural Theories

C. Contingency Theories

D. Trait Theories

45. What is a 'wild-cat strike'?

A. Strike perpetrated by workers with the support of the relevant union without giving notice to the employer.

B. Strike called by a group of workers on the spur of the moment without any formal notice to the employer or any consent from the relevant union.

C. Strike called by the union after resorting to a strike ballot.

D. Strike called by a union with a formal notice to the employer just a few minutes before the commencement of the strike.

46. Match the following :

List-I	List-II
(a) Hot-stove Rule	(i) Grievance handling
(b) Common Law	(ii) Disciplinary action
(c) Step-ladder system	(iii) Union security measure
(d) Protected workman	(iv) Principles of natural justice

Code :

	(a)	(b)	(c)	(d)
A.	(i)	(iii)	(ii)	(iv)
B.	(ii)	(iv)	(i)	(iii)
C.	(iii)	(ii)	(iv)	(i)
D.	(iv)	(iii)	(ii)	(i)

47. Which one of the following Articles of the Indian Constitution has been made effective with the enactment of the Equal Remuneration Act, 1976?
A. Article 41   B. Article 43
C. Article 39   D. Article 42

48. Knowledge Management refers to :
A. Providing the best skills to employees through planned training programmes.
B. Capturing, developing, sharing and using organisational knowledge.
C. Creating data bank of information about employees and customers.
D. Gathering information from employees for bringing planned change.

49. Quality of work life as a socio-technical concept was advanced by :
A. Fred Luthans   B. Eric Trist
C. A.K. Rice   D. Peter F. Drucker

50. What is the full form of AFL-CIO?
A. Asian Federation of Labour-Committee of Industrial Organizations.
B. African Federation of Labour-Confederation of Industrial Organizations.
C. American Federation of Labour-Congress of Industrial Organizations.
D. American Federation of Labour-Confederation of Industrial Organizations.

51. Institutions of workers participation in management is/are provided under which of the following legislations in India?
(a) Industrial Disputes Act, 1947
(b) Industrial Employment (standing orders) Act, 1946
(c) Factories Act, 1948
(d) Plantation Labour Act, 1951
Codes :
A. (a), (b) and (d) only
B. (a), (b) and (c) only
C. (b) and (d) only
D. (a) and (c) only

52. 'Glass ceiling' is a phenomena related to :
A. Solar energy conservation system
B. Inter-personal openness
C. Gender bias in career progression
D. Transparency in information sharing

53. Which one of the following types of strike is without the consent of official of union?
A. Jurisdictional strike
B. Wild cat strike
C. Sympathy strike
D. Slow down strike

54. Which one of the following describes the metamorphosis stage of employee socialisation?
A. Employee joins organisation with his values, attitudes and expectations.
B. Employee studies the organisation culture.
C. Employee evaluates the dichotomy between expectations and reality.
D. Employee becomes comfortable with organisation and internalises its norms.

55. When employees work longer days in exchange for longer weekends or other days off, it is called:
A. Flexy time
B. Job sharing
C. Compressed work week
D. Extended timing

56. In which of the following, the payment of bonus is linked to performance of specific employees or group of employees?

(*a*) Profit sharing

(*b*) Gain sharing plans

(*c*) Social system plans

Code:

A. (*a*) only

B. (*b*) only

C. Both (*a*) and (*b*)

D. (*a*), (*b*) and (*c*)

57. When an employee is willing to go above and beyond what is typically expected in his or her role, it is known as:

A. Employee Empowerment

B. Employee Engagement

C. Employee Enhancement

D. Employee Encouragement

58. Match the following and select the correct code of matching:

List–I	*List–II*
(*a*) F.W. Taylor	(*i*) Fair day's pay for fair day's work
(*b*) Henry L. Gantt	(*ii*) Motion study
(*c*) Frank and Lillian Gilbreth	(*iii*) Graphic scheduling for planning and controlling of work
(*d*) Max Weber	(*iv*) Bureaucratic organisation

Code :

	(*a*)	(*b*)	(*c*)	(*d*)
A.	(*i*)	(*ii*)	(*iii*)	(*iv*)
B.	(*i*)	(*iii*)	(*ii*)	(*iv*)
C.	(*iv*)	(*iii*)	(*ii*)	(*i*)
D.	(*iv*)	(*i*)	(*ii*)	(*iii*)

59. The achievement of goals with the least amount of resources is :

A. Effectiveness

B. Efficiency

C. Productivity

D. Both (A) and (B)

60. In which one of the following methods of performance appraisal, predetermined percentages of rates are placed in various performance categories?

A. Alternation Ranking Method

B. Forced Distribution Method

C. Paired Comparison Method

D. Check-list Method

ANSWERS

1	2	3	4	5	6	7	8	9	10
B	B	B	D	D	B	C	D	C	D

11	12	13	14	15	16	17	18	19	20
C	D	B	D	D	B	B	C	C	A

21	22	23	24	25	26	27	28	29	30
C	D	D	C	C	A	C	B	A	B

31	32	33	34	35	36	37	38	39	40
C	C	D	D	D	B	A	D	B	C

41	42	43	44	45	46	47	48	49	50
A	D	A	C	B	B	C	B	B	C

51	52	53	54	55	56	57	58	59	60
D	C	B	D	C	B	B	B	B	B

PROFESSIONAL KNOWLEDGE

HR/Personnel Management

1

Personal Management

The term 'human resource management' and human resources are largely replaced by 'personnel management' as describing the process of managing people in an organization. In many organizations, there may be person who is responsible for managing the welfare and performance of everyone within the organization. The task like overseeing programmes and setting policies that affect everyone associated with the organization can be referred to as personnel management as well human resource management.

The function of personnel manager usually begins with the staffing process. Determining the organization's policies and procedures as they relate to personnel is another important aspect of personnel management. HR function for any organization includes drafting vacation, sick leave and other policies that apply to all employees. The personnel management team might be responsible for administrating the benefits and other health insurance plans that are provided to employees.

Personnel managers and HR staff members often must draft and review the organization's handbook for employees, stating the policies and procedures, requirements for employment, recommendation, and disciplinary procedures and even things such as dress codes must be compared with legal guidelines before a handbook is issued among the employees.

Many personnel managers understand that happy and well-adapted employees are the asset to the organization. Depending on the size of the organization, it might be possible for one person to handle all of the personnel management functions. As an organization grows, however, it might be necessary to expand from a single personnel manager to a personnel management team. Although this adds to the cost, many organizations have found that overseeing the welfare of their personnel ultimately benefits the organization financially.

HRM is regarded by some personnel managers as just a set of initials or old wine in new bottles. It could indeed be no more and no less than another name for personnel management, but as usually perceived, at least it has the virtue of emphasizing the virtue of treating people as a key resource, to the management that is the direct concern of top management as part of the strategic planning processes of the enterprise. Although there is nothing new in the idea, insufficient attention has been paid to it in many organizations.

The difference between personnel management and human resource management appear to be substantial but they can be seen as a matter of emphasis and approach rather than one of substance.

FUNCTIONS, STRUCTURE OF PERSONNEL DEPARTMENT

Definition

Personnel management is defined like, 'Personnel management is concerned with obtaining,

3

organizing and motivating the human resources required by the enterprise.' *(Armstrong, 1977)*

Personnel management can be defined as obtaining, using and maintaining a satisfied workforce. It is a significant part of management concerned with employees at work and with their relationship within the organization.

According to Flippo, "Personnel management is the planning, organizing, compensation, integration and maintenance of people for the purpose of contributing to organizational, individual and societal goals."

According to Brech, "Personnel Management is that part which is primarily concerned with human resource of organization."

Nature of Personnel Management

Personnel management includes the functions of employment, development and compensation. These functions are performed primarily by the personnel management in consultation with other departments.

1. Personnel management is an extension to general management. It is concerned with promoting and stimulating competent work force to make their fullest contribution to the concern.

2. Personnel management exists to advice and assists the line managers in personnel matters. Therefore, personnel department is a staff department of an organization.

3. Personnel management lays emphasise on action rather than making lengthy schedules, plans, and work methods.

4. The problems and grievances of people at work can be solved more effectively through rationale personnel policies.

5. It is based on human orientation. It tries to help the workers to develop their potential fully to the concern.

6. It also motivates the employees through its effective incentive plans so that the employees provide fullest cooperation.

7. Personnel management deals with human resources of a concern. In context to human resources, it manages both individual as well as blue-collar workers.

Role of Personnel Manager

Personnel manager is the head of personnel department. He performs both managerial and operative functions of management. His role can be summarized as:

1. Personnel manager **provides assistance** to top management. The top management are the people who decide and frame the primary policies of the concern. All kinds of policies related to personnel or workforce can be framed out effectively by the personnel manager.

2. He **advices the line manager** as a staff specialist - Personnel manager acts like a staff advisor and assists the line managers in dealing with various personnel matters.

3. As a **counselor** - As a counselor, personnel manager attends problems and grievances of employees and guides them. He tries to solve them in best of his capacity.

4. Personnel manager acts as a **mediator** - He is a linking pin between management and workers.

5. He acts as a **spokesman** - Since he is in direct contact with the employees, he is required to act as representative of organization in committees appointed by government. He represents company in training programmes.

Functions of Personnel Management

Following are the four functions of Personnel Management:

1. Manpower planning
2. Recruitment
3. Selection
4. Training and Development

Following are the elements of Personnel Management:

1. **Organization:** Organization is said to be the framework of many activities taking place in view of goals available in a concern. An organization can be called as a physical framework of various interrelated activities.

Right from manpower planning to employees' maintenance, all activities take place within this framework. The nature of the organization is dependent upon its goal and the concern goal is being profit-making. Clubs, hospitals, schools, etc. are the goal being service. The objective of consultancy being providing sound advice. Therefore, it is organizational structure on which the achievement of goals of an enterprise depends upon. In personnel management, a manager has therefore to understand the importance of organizational structure.

2. **Job:** The second element, i.e., jobs tells us the activities to be performed in the organization. It is said that the goals of an enterprise can be achieved only through the functional department in it. Therefore, seeing the size of organization today, the nature of activities is changing. In addition to the three primary departments, personnel and research department are new additions. Various types of jobs available are :
   - Physical jobs
   - Creative jobs
   - Proficiency jobs
   - Intellectual jobs
   - Consultancy jobs
   - Technical jobs

3. **People:** The last and leading element in personnel management is people. In an organizational structure, where the main aim is to achieve the goals, the presence of manpower becomes vital to achieve the task. Therefore, in order to achieve departmental goals, different kinds of people with different skills are appointed. People shape the most important element because :
   - The organizational structure is meaningless without it.
   - It helps to achieve the goals of the enterprise.
   - It helps in resourcing both managerial and the functional areas.

- It helps in achieving the functional departmental goals.
- They give life to a physical organization.

The different types of people which are generally required in a concern are:
- Physically fit people
- Creative people
- Intellectuals
- Technical people
- Proficient and skilled people

In personnel management, a personnel manager has to understand the relationship of the three elements and their importance in organization. He has to understand basically three relationships:

1. Relationship between organization and job
2. Relationship between job and people
3. Relationship between people and organization.

Relationship between organization and job helps making a job effective and significant. Relationship between job and people makes the job itself important. Relationship between people and organization gives due importance to organizational structure and the role of people in it.

LINE AND STAFF

Line organization is the oldest and simplest method of administrative organization. According to this type of organization, the authority flows from top to bottom in a concern. The line of command is carried out from top to bottom. This is the reason for calling this organization as scalar organization which means scalar chain of command is a part and parcel of this type of administrative organization. In this type of organization, the line of command flows on an even basis without any gaps in communication and co-ordination taking place.

Features of Line Organization
1. It is the simplest form of organization.
2. Line of authority flows from top to bottom.
3. Specialized and supportive services do not take place in these organizations.

4. Unified control by the line officers can be maintained since they can independently take decisions in their area and spheres.

5. This kind of organization always helps in bringing efficiency in communication and bringing stability to a concern.

Merits of Line Organization

1. **Simplest:** It is the most simple and oldest method of administration.

2. **Unity of Command:** In these organizations, superior-subordinate relationship is maintained and scalar chain of command flows from top to bottom.

3. **Better discipline:** The control is unified and concentrates on one person and therefore, he can independently make decisions of his own. Unified control ensures better discipline.

4. **Fixed responsibility:** In this type of organization, every line executive has got fixed authority, power and fixed responsibility attached to every authority.

5. **Flexibility:** There is a coordination between the top most authority and bottom line authority. Since the authority relationships are clear, line officials are independent and can flexibly take the decision. This flexibility gives satisfaction of line executives.

6. **Prompt decision:** Due to the factors of fixed responsibility and unity of command, the officials can take prompt decision.

Demerits of Line Organization

1. **Over reliance:** The line executive's decisions are implemented to the bottom. This results in over-relying on the line officials.

2. **Lack of specialization:** A line organization flows in a scalar chain from top to bottom and there is no scope for specialized functions. It is so, expert advices whatever decisions are taken by line managers are implemented in the same way.

3. **Inadequate communication:** The policies and strategies which are framed by the top authority are carried out in the same way. This leaves no scope for communication from the other end. The complaints and suggestions of lower authority are not communicated back to the top authority. So there is one way communication.

4. **Lack of Co-ordination:** Whatever decisions are taken by the line officials, in certain situations may be wrong decisions, are carried down and implemented in the same way. Therefore, the degree of effective co-ordination is less.

5. **Authority leadership:** The line officials have tendency to misuse their authority positions. This leads to autocratic leadership and monopoly in the concern.

Line and staff organization is a modification of line organization and it is more complex than line organization. According to this administrative organization, specialized and supportive activities are attached to the line of command by appointing staff supervisors and staff specialists who are attached to the line authority. The power of command always remains with the line executives and staff supervisors guide, advice and direct the line executives. Personal Secretary to the Managing Director is a staff official.

Features of Line and Staff Organization

1. There are two types of staff:
   (a) Staff Assistants- P.A. to Managing Director, Secretary to Marketing Manager.
   (b) Staff Supervisor- Operation Control Manager, Quality Controller, PRO
2. Line and Staff Organization is a compromise of line organization. It is more complex than line concern.
3. Division of work and specialization takes place in line and staff organization.
4. The whole organization is divided into different functional areas to which staff specialists are attached.
5. Efficiency can be achieved through the features of specialization.
6. There are two lines of authority which flow at one time in a concern :
   (a) Line Authority (b) Staff Authority
7. Power of command remains with the line executive and staff serves only as counselors.

Merits of Line and Staff Organization

1. **Relief to line of executives:** In a line and staff organization, the advice and counseling which is provided to the line executives divides the work between the two. The line executive can concentrate on the execution of plans and they get relieved of dividing their attention to many areas.
2. **Expert advice:** The line and staff organization facilitates expert advice to the line executive at the time of need. The planning and investigation which is related to different matters can be done by the staff specialist and line officers can concentrate on execution of plans.
3. **Benefit of Specialization:** Line and staff through division of whole concern into two types of authority divides the enterprise into parts and functional areas. This way every officer or official can concentrate in its own area.
4. **Better co-ordination:** Line and staff organization through specialization is able to provide better decision making and concentration. This feature helps in bringing co-ordination in work as every official is concentrating in their own area.

5. **Benefits of Research and Development:** Through the advice of specialized staff, and the line executives get time to execute plans by taking productive decisions which are helpful for the concern. This gives a wide scope to the line executive to bring innovations and go for research work in those areas. This is possible due to the presence of staff specialists.
6. **Training:** Due to the presence of staff specialists and their expert advice serves as ground for training to line officials. Line executives can give due concentration to their decision making. This in itself is a training ground for them.
7. **Balanced decisions:** The factor of specialization which is achieved by line staff helps in bringing co-ordination. This relationship automatically ends up the line official to take better and balanced decision.
8. **Unity of action:** Unity of action is a result of unified control. Control and its action effectively take place when coordination is present in the concern. In the line and staff authority all the officials have got independence to make decisions. This serves as effective control in the whole enterprise.

Demerits of Line and Staff Organization

1. **Lack of understanding:** In a line and staff organization, there are two authorities flowing at one time. This results in the confusion between the two. As a result, the workers are not able to understand as to who is their commanding authority.
2. Difficulty in effective running.
3. **Lack of sound advice:** The line official get used to the expertise advice of the staff. At times the staff specialist also provides wrong decisions which the line executive has to consider. This can affect the efficient running of the enterprise.
4. **Line and staff conflicts:** Line and staff are two authorities which are flowing at the same time. The factors of designations, status influence sentiments which are related to their relation, can pose a distress on the minds of

the employees. This leads to minimizing of coordination which hampers a concern's working.

5. **Costly:** In line and staff concern, the concerns have to maintain the high remuneration of staff specialist. This proves to be costly for a concern with limited finance.

6. **Assumption of authority:** The power of concern is with the line official but the staff dislikes it as they are the one more in mental work.

7. **Staff steals the show:** In a line and staff concern, the higher returns are considered to be a product of staff advice and counseling. The line officials feel dissatisfied and a feeling of distress enters a concern. The satisfaction of line officials is very important for effective results.

Functional Organization

Functional organization has been divided to put the specialists in the top position throughout the enterprise. This is an organization in which we can define as a system in which functional department are created to deal with the problems of business at various levels. Functional authority remains limited to functional guidance to different departments. This helps in maintaining quality and uniformity of performance of different functions throughout the enterprise.

The concept of functional organization was suggested by F.W. Taylor who recommended the appointment of specialists at important positions. For example, the functional head and Marketing Director directs the subordinates throughout the organization in his particular area. This means that subordinates receives orders from several specialists, managers working above them.

Features of Functional Organization

1. The entire organizational activities are divided into specific functions such as operations, finance, marketing and personal relations.

2. Complex form of administrative organization compared to the other two.

3. Three authorities that exist are— Line, staff and function.

4. Each functional area is put under the charge of functional specialists and he has got the authority to give all decisions regarding the function whenever the function is performed throughout the enterprise.

5. Principle of unity of command does not apply to such organization as it is present in line organization.

Merits of Functional Organization

1. **Specialization:** Better division of labour takes place which results in specialization of function and its consequent benefit.

2. **Effective Control:** Management control is simplified as the mental functions are separated from manual functions. Checks and balances keep the authority within certain limits. Specialists may be asked to judge the performance of various sections.

3. **Efficiency:** Greater efficiency is achieved because of every function performing a limited number of functions.

4. **Economy:** Specialization compiled with standardization facilitates maximum production and economical costs.

5. **Expansion:** Expert knowledge of functional manager facilitates better control and supervision.

Demerits of Functional Organization

1. **Confusion:** The functional system is quite complicated to put into operation, especially when it is carried out at low levels. Therefore, co-ordination becomes difficult.

2. **Lack of Co-ordination:** Disciplinary control becomes weak as a worker is commanded not by one person but a large number of people. Thus, there is no unity of command.

3. **Difficulty in fixing responsibility:** Because of multiple authorities, it is difficult to fix responsibility.

4. **Conflicts:** There may be conflicts among the supervisory staff of equal ranks. They may not agree on certain issues.

5. **Costly:** Maintenance of specialist's staff of the highest order is expensive for a concern.

Delegation of Authority

Differences between Authority and Responsibility

Authority	*Responsibility*
It is the legal right of a person or a superior to command his subordinates.	It is the obligation of subordinate to perform the work assigned to him.
Authority is attached to the position of a superior in concern.	Responsibility arises out of superior subordinate relationship in which subordinate agrees to carry out duty given to him.
Authority can be delegated by a superior to a subordinate.	Responsibility cannot be shifted and is absolute
It flows from top to bottom.	It flows from bottom to top.

DELEGATION AND DECENTRALIZATION

Basis	*Delegation*	*Decentralization*
Meaning	Managers delegate some of their function and authority to their subordinates.	Right to take decisions is shared by top management and other level of management.
Scope	Scope of delegation is limited as superior delegates the powers to the subordinates on individual bases.	Scope is wide as the decision making is shared by the subordinates also.
Responsibility	Responsibility remains of the managers and cannot be delegated	Responsibility is also delegated to subordinates.
Freedom of Work	Freedom is not given to the sub-ordinates as they have to work as per the instructions of their superiors.	Freedom to work can be maintained by subordinates as they are free to take decision and to implement it.
Nature	It is a routine function	It is an important decision of an enterprise.
Need on purpose	Delegation is important in all concerns whether big or small. No enterprises can work without delegation.	Decentralization becomes more important in large concerns and it depends upon the decision made by the enterprise, it is not compulsory.
Grant of Authority	The authority is granted by one individual to another.	It is a systematic act which takes place at all levels and at all functions in a concern.
Grant of Responsibility	Responsibility cannot be delegated.	Authority with responsibility is delegated to subordinates.
Degree	Degree of delegation varies from concern to concern and department to department.	Decentralization is total by nature. It spread throughout the organization i.e. at all levels and all functions.
Process	Delegation is a process which explains superior subordinates relationship.	It is an outcome which explains relationship between top management and all other departments.

Basis	Delegation	Decentralization
Essentiality	Delegation is essential of all kinds of concerns.	Decentralization is a decision function by nature.
Significance	Delegation is essential for creating the organization.	Decentralization is an optional policy at the discretion of top management.
Withdrawal	Delegated authority can be . taken back	It is considered as a general policy of top management and is applicable to all departments.
Freedom of Action	Very little freedom to the subordinates.	Considerable freedom.

JOB ANALYSIS

Job analysis is primary tool in personnel management. In this method, a personnel manager tries to gather, synthesize and implement the information available regarding the workforce in the concern. A personnel manager has to undertake job analysis so as to put right man on right job.

Job Analysis is a systematic exploration, study and recording the responsibilities, duties, skills, accountabilities, work environment and ability requirements of a specific job. It also involves determining the relative importance of the duties, responsibilities and physical and emotional skills for a given job. All these factors identify what a job demands and what an employee must possess to perform a job productively.

There are two outcomes of job analysis:

1. Job description
2. Job specification

The information collected under job analysis is:

1. Nature of jobs required in a concern.
2. Nature / size of organizational structure.
3. Type of people required to fit that structure.
4. The relationship of the job with other jobs in the concern.
5. Kind of qualifications and academic background required for jobs.
6. Provision of physical condition to support the activities of the concern. For example, separate cabins for managers, special cabins for the supervisors, healthy condition for workers, and adequate store room for store keeper.

Advantages of Job Analysis

1. Job analysis helps the personnel manager at the time of recruitment and selection of right man on right job.
2. It helps him to understand extent and scope of training required in that field.
3. It helps in evaluating the job in which the worth of the job has to be evaluated.
4. In those instances where smooth work force is required in concern.
5. When he has to avoid overlapping of authority and responsibility relationship so that distortion in chain of command doesn't exist.
6. It also helps to chalk out the compensation plans for the employees.
7. It also helps the personnel manager to undertake performance appraisal effectively in a concern.

A personnel manager carries analysis in two ways:

a. Job description
b. Job specification

1. **JOB DESCRIPTION** is an organized factual statement of job contents in the form of duties and responsibilities of a specific job. The preparation of job description is very important before a vacancy is advertised. It tells in brief the nature and type of job. This

type of document is descriptive in nature and it constitutes all those facts which are related to a job such as :

a. Title/ Designation of job and location in the concern.
b. The nature of duties and operations to be performed in that job.
c. The nature of authority and responsibility relationships.
d. Necessary qualifications that is required for job.
e. Relationship of that job with other jobs in a concern.
f. The provision of physical and working condition or the work environment required in performance of that job.

Advantages of Job Description

a. It helps the supervisors in assigning work to the subordinates so that he can guide and monitor their performances.
b. It helps in recruitment and selection procedures.
c. It assists in man power planning.
d. It is also helpful in performance appraisal.
e. It is helpful in job evaluation in order to decide about rate of remuneration for a specific job.
f. It also helps in chalking out training and development programmes.

2. **JOB SPECIFICATION** is a statement which tells us minimum acceptable human qualities which helps to perform a job. Job specification translates the job description into human qualifications so that a job can be performed in a better manner. Job specification helps in hiring an appropriate person for an appropriate position. The contents are :

a. Job title and designation
b. Educational qualifications for that title
c. Physical and other related attributes
d. Physique and mental health
e. Special attributes and abilities
f. Maturity and dependability

g. Relationship of that job with other jobs in a concern.

Advantages of Job Specification

a. It is helpful in preliminary screening in the selection procedure.
b. It helps in giving due justification to each job.
c. It also helps in designing training and development programmes.
d. It helps the supervisors for counseling and monitoring performance of employees.
e. It helps in job evaluation.
f. It helps the management to take decisions regarding promotion, transfers and giving extra benefits to the employees.

From the above advantages, we can justify the importance of job analysis and its related products. Both job description as well as job specification is important for personnel manager in personnel management function. Therefore, **job analysis is considered to be the primary tool of personnel management.**

MAN POWER PLANNING— NEW CHALLENGES

Manpower Planning which is also called as Human Resource Planning consists of putting right number of people, right kind of people at the right place, right time, doing the right things for which they are suited for the achievement of goals of the organization. Human Resource Planning has got an important place in the arena of industrialization. Human Resource Planning has to be a systems approach and is carried out in a set procedure. The procedure is as follows:

1. Analyzing the current manpower inventory
2. Making future manpower forecasts
3. Developing employment programmes
4. Design training programmes

Steps in Manpower Planning

1. **Analyzing the current manpower inventory:** Before a manager makes forecast of future manpower, the current manpower status has

to be analyzed. For this the following things have to be noted:

- Type of organization
- Number of departments
- Number and quantity of such departments
- Employees in these work units

Once these factors are registered by a manager, he goes for the future forecasting.

2. **Making future manpower forecasts:** Once the factors affecting the future manpower forecasts are known, planning can be done for the future manpower requirements in several work units. The Manpower forecasting techniques commonly employed by the organizations are as follows:

- **Expert Forecasts:** This includes informal decisions, formal expert surveys and Delphi technique.
- **Trend Analysis:** Manpower needs can be projected through extrapolation (projecting past trends), indexation (using base year as basis), and statistical analysis (central tendency measure).
- **Work Load Analysis:** It is dependent upon the nature of work load in a department, in a branch or in a division.
- **Work Force Analysis:** Whenever production and time period has to be analyzed, due allowances have to be made for getting net manpower requirements.
- **Other Methods:** Several Mathematical models, with the aid of computers are used to forecast manpower needs, like budget and planning analysis, regression, new venture analysis.

3. **Developing employment programmes:** Once the current inventory is compared with future forecasts, the employment programmes can be framed and developed accordingly, which will include recruitment, selection procedures and placement plans.

4. **Design training programmes:** These will be based upon extent of diversification, expansion plans, development programmes, etc. Training

programmes depend upon the extent of improvement in technology and advancement to take place. It is also done to improve upon the skills, capabilities, knowledge of the workers.

Importance of Manpower Planning

1. **Key to managerial functions:** The four managerial functions, i.e., planning, organizing, directing and controlling are based upon the manpower. Human resources help in the implementation of all these managerial activities. Therefore, staffing becomes a key to all managerial functions.

2. **Efficient utilization:** Efficient management of personnel's becomes an important function in the industrialization world of today. Setting of large scale enterprises requires management of large scale manpower. It can be effectively done through staffing function.

3. **Motivation:** Staffing function not only includes putting right men on right job, but it also comprises of motivational programmes, i.e., incentive plans to be framed for further participation and employment of employees in a concern. Therefore, all types of incentive plans become an integral part of staffing function.

4. **Better human relations:** A concern can stabilize itself if human relations develop and are strong. Human relations become strong through effective control, clear communication, effective supervision and leadership in a concern. Staffing function also looks after training and development of the work force which leads to co-operation and better human relations.

5. **Higher productivity:** Productivity level increases when resources are utilized in best possible manner. Higher productivity is a result of minimum wastage of time, money, efforts and energies. This is possible through the staffing and its related activities (Performance appraisal, training and development, remuneration)

Need of Manpower Planning

Manpower Planning is a two-phased process because manpower planning not only analyses the current human resources but also makes manpower forecasts and thereby draw employment programmes. Manpower Planning is advantageous to firm in following manner:

1. Shortages and surpluses can be identified so that quick action can be taken wherever required.
2. All the recruitment and selection programmes are based on manpower planning.
3. It also helps to reduce the labour cost as excess staff can be identified and thereby overstaffing can be avoided.
4. It also helps to identify the available talents in a concern and accordingly training programmes can be chalked out to develop those talents.
5. It helps in growth and diversification of business. Through manpower planning, human resources can be readily available and they can be utilized in best manner.
6. It helps the organization to realize the importance of manpower management which ultimately helps in the stability of a concern.

Following are the main obstacles that organizations face in the process of manpower planning:

1. **Under Utilization of Manpower:** The biggest obstacle in case of manpower planning is the fact that the industries in general are not making optimum use of their manpower and once manpower planning begins, it encounters heavy odds in stepping up the utilization.
2. **Degree of Absenteeism:** Absenteeism is quite high and has been increasing since last few years.
3. **Lack of Education and Skilled Labour:** The extent of illiteracy and the slow pace of development of the skilled categories account for low productivity in employees. Low productivity has implications for manpower planning.

4. **Manpower Control and Review:**
   - Any increase in manpower is considered at the top level of management.
   - On the basis of manpower plans, personnel budgets are prepared. These act as control mechanisms to keep the manpower under certain broadly defined limits.
   - The productivity of any organization is usually calculated using the formula:
     Productivity = Output / Input
   - But a rough index of employee productivity is calculated as follows:

Employee Productivity = Total Production / Total no. of employees

   Exit Interviews: The rate of turnover and rate of absenteeism are source of vital information on the satisfaction level of manpower. For conservation of Human Resources and better utilization of men studying these conditions, manpower control would have to take into account the data to make meaningful analysis.

   Extent of Overtime: The amount of overtime paid may be due to real shortage of men, ineffective management or improper utilization of manpower. Manpower control would require a careful study of overtime statistics.

   Lack of HRIS: Few Organizations do not have sufficient records and information on manpower. Several of those who have them do not have a proper retrieval system. There are complications in resolving the issues in design, definition and creation of computerized personnel information system for effective manpower planning and utilization. Even the existing technologies in this respect are not optimally used. This is a strategic disadvantage.

RECRUITMENT AND SELECTION

Recruitment is of two types:

1. **Internal Recruitment:** In this, recruitment which takes place within the concern or organization. Internal sources of recruitment are readily available to an organization.

Internal sources are primarily three; they are transfers, promotions and re-employment of ex-employees. Re-employment of ex-employees is one of the internal sources of recruitment in which employees can be invited and appointed to fill vacancies in the concern. There are situations when ex-employees provide unsolicited applications also.

Internal recruitment may lead to increase in employee's productivity as their motivation level increases. It also saves time, money and efforts. But a drawback of internal recruitment is that it refines the organization from new blood. Also, not all the manpower requirements can be met through internal recruitment. Hiring from outside has to be done.

Internal sources are primarily three:

a. Transfers

b. Promotions (through Internal Job Postings) and

c. Re-employment of ex-employees: Re-employment of ex-employees is one of the internal sources of recruitment in which employees can be invited and appointed to fill vacancies in the concern. There are situations when ex-employees provide unsolicited applications also.

2. **External Recruitment:** External sources of recruitment have to be solicited from outside the organization. External sources are external to a concern. But it involves lot of time and money. The external sources of recruitment include, Employment at factory gate, advertisements, employment exchanges, employment agencies, educational institutes, labour contractors, recommendations etc.

   a. Employment at Factory Level: This is a source of external recruitment in which the applications for vacancies are presented on bulletin boards outside the Factory or at the Gate. This kind of recruitment is applicable generally where factory workers are to be appointed. There are people who keep on soliciting jobs from one place to another. These applicants are called as unsolicited applicants. These types of workers apply on their own for their job. For this kind of recruitment workers have a tendency to shift from one factory to another and therefore they are called as "badli" workers.

   b. Advertisement: It is an external source which has got an important place in recruitment procedure. The biggest advantage of advertisement is that it covers a wide area of market and scattered applicants can get information from advertisements. Medium used is Newspapers and Television.

   c. Employment Exchanges: There are certain Employment exchanges which are run by government. Most of the government undertakings and concerns employ people through such exchanges. Now-a-days recruitment in government agencies has become compulsory through employment exchange.

   d. Employment Agencies: There are certain professional organizations which look towards recruitment and employment of people, *i.e.* these private agencies run by private individuals supply required manpower to needy concerns.

   e. Educational Institutions: There are certain professional Institutions which serve as an external source for recruiting fresh graduates from these institutes. This kind of recruitment done through such educational institutions is called as Campus Recruitment. They have a special recruitment cell which helps in providing jobs to fresh candidates.

   f. Recommendations: There are certain people who have experience in a particular area. They enjoy goodwill and a stand in the company. There are certain vacancies which are filled by recommendations of such people. The biggest drawback of this source is that the company has to rely totally on such people which can later on prove to be inefficient.

g. **Labour Contractors:** These are the specialist people who supply manpower to the Factory or Manufacturing plants. Through these contractors, workers are appointed on contract basis, *i.e.* for a particular time period. Under conditions when these contractors leave the organization, such people who are appointed have to also leave the concern.

Employee Selection Process

Employee Selection is the process of putting right men on right job. It is a procedure of matching organizational requirements with the skills and qualifications of people. Effective selection can be done only when there is effective matching. By selecting best candidate for the required job, the organization will get quality performance of employees. Moreover, organization will face less of absenteeism and employee turnover problems. By selecting right candidate for the required job, organization will also save time and money. Proper screening of candidates takes place during selection procedure. All the potential candidates who apply for the given job are tested.

But selection must be differentiated from recruitment, though these are two phases of employment process. Recruitment is considered to be a positive process as it motivates more of candidates to apply for the job. It creates a pool of applicants. It is just sourcing of data. While selection is a negative process as the inappropriate candidates are rejected here. Recruitment precedes selection in staffing process. Selection involves choosing the best candidate with best abilities, skills and knowledge for the required job.

The **Employee Selection Process** takes place in following order:

1. **Preliminary Interviews:** It is used to eliminate those candidates who do not meet the minimum eligibility criteria laid down by the organization. The skills, academic and family background, competencies and interests of the candidate are examined during preliminary interview. Preliminary interviews are less formalized and planned than the final interviews. The candidates are given a brief up about the company and the job profile; and it is also examined how much the candidate knows about the company. Preliminary interviews are also called screening interviews.

2. **Application blanks:** The candidates who clear the preliminary interview are required to fill application blank. It contains data record of the candidates such as details about age, qualifications, reason for leaving previous job, experience, etc.

3. **Written tests:** Various written tests conducted during selection procedure are aptitude test, intelligence test, reasoning test, personality test, etc. These tests are used to objectively assess the potential candidate. They should not be biased.

4. **Employment interviews:** It is a one to one interaction between the interviewer and the potential candidate. It is used to find whether the candidate is best suited for the required job or not. But such interviews consume time and money both.

   Moreover the competencies of the candidate cannot be judged. Such interviews may be biased at times. Such interviews should be conducted properly. No distractions should be there in room. There should be an honest communication between candidate and interviewer.

5. **Medical examination:** Medical tests are conducted to ensure physical fitness of the potential employee. It will decrease chances of employee absenteeism.

6. **Appointment letter:** A reference check is made about the candidate selected and then finally he is appointed by giving a formal appointment letter.

Basis	Recruitment	Selection
Meaning	It is an activity of establishing contact between employers and applicants.	It is a process of picking up more competent and suitable employees.
Objective	It encourages large number of Candidates for a job.	It attempts at rejecting unsuitable candidates.
Process	It is a simple process.	It is a complicated process.
Hurdles	The candidates have not to cross over many hurdles.	Many hurdles have to be crossed.
Approach	It is a positive approach.	It is a negative approach.
Sequence	It precedes selection.	It follows recruitment.
Economy	It is an economical method.	It is an expensive method.
Time Consuming	Less time is required.	More time is required.

PLACEMENT AND INDUCTION

Orientation and Placement Programme

Once the candidates are selected for the required job, they have to be fitted as per the qualifications. Placement is said to be the process of fitting the selected person at the right job or place, *i.e.* fitting square pegs in square holes and round pegs in round holes. Once he is fitted into the job, he is given the activities he has to perform and also told about his duties. The freshly appointed candidates are then given orientation in order to familiarize and introduce the company to him. Generally the information given during the orientation programme includes:

- Employee's layout
- Type of organizational structure
- Departmental goals

- Organizational layout
- General rules and regulations
- Standing orders
- Grievance system or procedure

In short, during Orientation employees are made aware about the mission and vision of the organization, the nature of operation of the organization, policies and programmes of the organization.

The main aim of conducting Orientation is to build up confidence, morale and trust of the employee in the new organization, so that he becomes a productive and an efficient employee of the organization and contributes to the organizational success.

The nature of Orientation program varies with the organizational size, where smaller the organization the more informal is the Orientation and larger the organization more formalized is the Orientation programme.

Proper Placement of employees will lower the chances of employee's absenteeism. The employees will be more satisfied and contended with their work.

Training of Employees

Training is given on four basic grounds:

1. **New joins:** New candidates who join an organization are given training. This training familiarizes them with the organizational mission, vision, rules and regulations and the working conditions.
2. **Refreshment programme:** The existing employees are trained to refresh and enhance their knowledge.
3. **Change in technology:** If any update and amendments take place in technology, training is given to cope up with those changes. For instance, purchasing new equipment, changes in technique of production, computer implantment. The employees are trained about use of new equipments and work methods.
4. **New work environment:** When promotion and career growth becomes important, Training is given so that employees are

prepared to share the responsibilities of the higher level job.

The benefits of training can be summed up as:

1. **Improves morale of employees:** Training helps the employee to get job security and job satisfaction. The more satisfied the employee is and the greater is his morale, the more he will contribute to organizational success and the lesser will be employee absenteeism and turnover.

2. **Less supervision:** A well trained employee will be well acquainted with the job and will need less of supervision. Thus, there will be less wastage of time and efforts.

3. **Fewer accidents:** Errors are likely to occur if the employees lack knowledge and skills required for doing a particular job. The more trained an employee is, the less are the chances of committing accidents in job and the more proficient the employee becomes.

4. **Chances of promotion:** Employees acquire skills and efficiency during training. They become more eligible for promotion. They become an asset for the organization.

5. **Increased productivity:** Training improves efficiency and productivity of employees. Well trained employees show both quantity and quality performance. There is less wastage of time, money and resources if employees are properly trained.

Methods of Training

Training is generally imparted in two ways:

1. **On the job training:** On the job training methods are those which are given to the employees within the everyday working of a concern. It is a simple and cost-effective training method. The in-proficient as well as semi-proficient employees can be well trained by using such training method. The employees are trained in actual working scenario. The motto of such training is "learning by doing." Instances of such on-job training methods are job-rotation, coaching, temporary promotions, etc.

2. **Off the job training:** Off the job training methods are those in which training is provided away from the actual working condition. It is generally used in case of new employees. Instances of off the job training methods are workshops, seminars, conferences, etc. Such method is costly and is effective if and only if large number of employees have to be trained within a short time period. Off the job training is also called as vestibule training, here the employees are trained in a separate area (may be a hall, entrance, reception area, etc. known as a vestibule) where the actual working conditions are duplicated.

Employee Remuneration

Employee Remuneration refers to the reward or compensation given to the employees for their work performances. Remuneration provides basic attraction to an employee to perform job efficiently and effectively. Remuneration leads to employee motivation. Salaries constitute an important source of income for employees and determine their standard of living. Salaries affect the employee's productivity and work performance. Thus the amount and method of remuneration are very important for both management and employees.

There are mainly two types of Employee Remuneration:

1. **Time Rate Method**
2. **Piece Rate Method**

These methods of employee remuneration are explained below in detail.

Methods of Employee Remuneration

1. **Time Rate Method:** Under time rate system, remuneration is directly linked with the time spent or devoted by an employee on the job. The employees are paid a fixed pre-decided amount hourly, daily, weekly or monthly irrespective of their output. It is a very simple method of remuneration. It leads to minimum wastage of resources and lesser chances of accidents. Time Rate method leads to quality output and this method is very beneficial to new employees as they can learn their work

without any reduction in their salaries. This method encourages employee's unity as employees of a particular group/cadre get equal salaries.

There are some drawbacks of Time Rate Method, such as, it leads to tight supervision, indefinite employee cost, lesser efficiency of employees as there is no distinction made between efficient and inefficient employees, and lesser morale of employees.

Time rate system is more suitable where the work is non-repetitive in nature and emphasis is more on quality output rather than quantity output.

2. **Piece Rate Method:** It is a method of compensation in which remuneration is paid on the basis of units or pieces produced by an employee. In this system emphasis is more on quantity output rather than quality output. Under this system the determination of employee cost per unit is not difficult because salaries differ with output. There is less supervision required under this method and hence the per unit cost of production is low. This system improves the morale of the employees as the salaries are directly related with their work efforts. There is greater work-efficiency in this method.

There are some drawbacks of this method, such as; it is not easily computable, leads to deterioration in work quality, wastage of resources, lesser unity of employees, higher cost of production and insecurity among the employees.

Piece rate system is more suitable where the nature of work is repetitive and quantity is emphasized more than quality.

WAGES AND SALARY ADMINISTRATION

Wages and salary administration has been extremely important issue for both the employer and employee. This is because money is a crucial incentive and directly or indirectly related to the fulfillment of all human needs. Employees sell their hands and brains in order to fulfill their primary needs and employers hire them to achieve their organizational objectives. Wages and salaries are often one of the largest components of cost of production in most of the business enterprises. Labour cost can be reduced through technological changes resulting in increasing the productivity of workers. The major responsibility for wage and salary administration normally rest with the top management (*i.e.* Board of Directors in case of a company) or the chief executive officers, who is required to develop policies and procedures to achieve the company's objectives. Here the personnel managers play the vital role in developing the wage policies and procedures. However, no organization will come forward to pay higher wages because cost of production goes up and profits decrease to that extent. A number of factors, thus, influence the remuneration payable to the employees. These factors can be categorized into (i) External Factors and (ii) Internal Factors.

1. **External factors influencing Wage and Salary Administration**

   ● **Demand and supply:** The labour market conditions or demand and supply forces operate at the national and local levels and determine organizational wage structure. When the demand of a particular type of labour is more and supply is less than the wages will be more. On the other hand, if supply of labour is more demand on the other hand, is less then persons will be available at lower wage rates also. In the words of Mescon the supply and demand compensation criterion is very closely related to the prevailing pay, comparable wage and ongoing wage concepts since, in essence all of these remuneration standards are determined by immediate market forces and factors.

   ● **Cost of living:** The wage rates are directly influenced by cost of living of a place. The workers will accept a wage which may ensure them a minimum standard of living. Wages will also be adjusted according to price index number.

The increase in price index will erode the purchasing power of workers and they will demand higher wages. When the prices are stable then frequent wage increases may not be undertaken.

- **Trade unions bargaining power:** The wage rates are also influenced by the bargaining power of trade unions. Stronger the trade union higher well is the wage rates. The strength of a trade union is judged by its membership, financial position and type of leadership. Union's last weapon is strike which may also be used for getting wage increases. If the workers are disorganized and disunited then employers will be successful in offering low wages.

- **Government legislation:** To improve the working conditions of workers, government may pass legislation for fixing minimum wages of workers. This may ensure them a minimum level of living. In under developed countries bargaining power of labour is weak and employers try to exploit workers by paying them low wages. In India, Minimum Wages Act, 1948 was passed to empower government to fix minimum wages of workers.

- **Psychological and social factors:** Psychological the level of compensation is perceived as a measure of success in life. Management should take into considera-tion the psychological needs of the employees while fixing the wage rates so that the employees take pride in their work. Sociologically and ethically, the employees want that the wage system should be equitable, just and fair. These factors should also be taken into consideration while devising a wage programme.

- **Economy:** Economy also has its impact on wage and salary fixation. While it may be possible for some organizations to thrive in a recession, there is no doubt that economy affects remuneration

decisions. A depressed economy will probably increase the labour supply. This, in turn, should lower the going wage rate.

- **Technological development:** With the rapid growth of industries, there is a shortage of skilled resources. The technological developments have been affecting skills levels at faster rates. Thus, the wage rates of skilled employees constantly change and an organization has to keep its level up-to the mark to suit the market needs.

- **Prevailing market rates:** No enterprise can ignore prevailing or comparative wage rates. The wage rates paid in the industry or other concerns at the same place will form a base for fixing wage rates. If a concern pays low rates then workers leave their jobs whenever they get a job somewhere else. It will not be possible to retain good workers for long.

2. **Internal factors influencing Wage and Salary Administration**

- **Ability to pay:** The ability to pay of an enterprise will influence wage rates to be paid. If the concern is running into losses then it may not be able to pay higher wage rate. A profitable concern may pay more to attract good workers. During the period of prosperity, workers are paid higher wages because management wants to share the profits with labour.

- **Job requirements:** Basic wages depend largely on the difficulty level, and physical and mental effort required in a particular job. The relative worth of a job can be estimated through job evaluation. Simple, routine tasks that can be done by many people with minimum skills receive relatively low pay. On the other hand, complex, challenging tasks that can be done by few people with high skill levels generally receive high pay.

- **Management strategy:** The overall strategy which a company pursues should determine to remuneration to its employees. Where the strategy of the organization is to achieve rapid growth, remuneration should be higher than what competitors pay. Where the strategy is to maintain and protect current earnings, because of the declining fortunes of the company, remuneration level needs to be average or even below average.

● **Employee:** Several employees related factors interact to determine his remuneration.

1. Performance or productivity is always rewarded with a pay increase. Rewarding performance motivates the employees to do better in future.

2. *Seniority:* Unions view seniority as the most objective criteria for pay increases whereas management prefers performance to affect pay increases.

3. *Experience:* Makes an employee gain valuable insights and is generally rewarded.

4. *Potential:* Organizations do pay some employees based on their potential. Young managers are paid more because of their potential to perform even if they are short of experience.

Concept of Wages

Wage and Salary Administration refers to the establishment and implementation of sound policies and practices of employee compensation. The basic purpose of wage and salary administration is to establish and maintain an equitable wage and salary structure. Wages and salaries are often one of the largest components of cost of production and such have serious implications for growth and profitability of the company. On the other hand, they are the only source of workers' income. After the independence and particularly after 1948, some new terms relating to wages began to be used. These are:

1. Statutory Minimum Wages
2. Basic Minimum Wages
3. Minimum Wages
4. Fair Wages

5. Living Wages
6. Need Based Wages

1. **Statutory Minimum Wages:** By it we mean the minimum amount of wages which should essentially be given to the workers as per provisions of the Minimum Wages Act, 1948.

2. **Basic Minimum Wages:** This minimum wage is fixed through judicial pronouncement, awards, industrial tribunals and labour. The employers are essentially to give this minimum wage to the workers.

3. **Minimum Wages:** The concept of minimum wages has developed due to different standards in different countries. In Indian context, minimum wage means the minimum amount which an employer thinks necessary for the sustenance of life and preservation of the efficiency of the worker. According to Fair Wage Committee, the minimum wages must also provide for some measures of education- medical requirements and amenities.

4. **Fair Wages:** In order to bring about improved relations between labour and management an effort has been made in modern times that the labour gets a fair deal at the hands of owners and managers of industries. Various proposals were undertaken at the Industries Conference in 1947 and a resolution known as the Industrial Truce Resolution was passed. It is provided for the payment of fair wages to labour. The government of India appointed a Fair Wages Committee in 1948 to determine the principles on which fair wages should be based and to suggest the lines on which those principles should be applied. According to the report on this Committee, Fair Wages is that wages which the labourer gets for his work just near to minimum wages and living wages. Generally, the current rate of wages being paid in the enterprise is known as fair wages.

5. **Living Wages:** According to Fair Wage Committee Report, "The living wage should enable the male earner to provide for himself

and his family not merely the bare essentials of food, clothing and shelter, but also a measure of frugal comfort including education for children, protection against ill health, requirements of essential social needs and a measure of insurance against the more important misfortunes including old age." According to the Committee on Fair Wages, the living wages represent the highest level of the wages and include all amenities which a citizen living in a modern civilized society is to expect when the economy of the country is sufficiently advanced and the employer is able to meet the expanding aspirations of his workers. The Living Wage should be fixed keeping in view the National income and the capacity of the industry to pay.

6. **Need Based Wages:** The Indian Labour Conference at its 15th session held at New Delhi in July, 1957 suggested that minimum wage fixation should be need based. Following are the important points of the Resolution of the Conference.

   (*a*) The standard working class family should include three consumption units for the one earner.

   (*b*) Calculation of minimum food requirements should be made on the basis of the recommendation of Dr. Aykoroyed *i.e.* 27000 calories for an average Indian adult.

   (*c*) Calculation of cloth should be made @ 18 yards annually for one member. As such, a family consisting of four members will require 72 yards of cloth.

   (*d*) The workers should get minimum rent as per guidelines fixed by the government in the industrial housing policy.

   (*e*) Expenses for fuel, light and so on should be equal to 20% of the entire minimum wages.

Wage Determining Process

Wage determination is a complex process. However, wage determination process consists of the following steps:

1. **Job Analysis:** Job analysis describes the duties, responsibilities, working conditions and inter-relationships between the job as it is and the other jobs with which it is associated. It attempts to record and analyze details concerning the training, skills, required efforts, qualifications, abilities, experience, and responsibilities expected of an employee. After determining the job specifications, the actual process of grading, rating or evaluating the job occurs. A job is rated in order to determine its value relative to all the other jobs in the organization which are subject to evaluation. The next step is that of providing the job with a price. This involves converting the relative job values into specific monetary values or translating the job classes into rate ranges.

2. **Wage Survey:** In determining the wages for a specific job it is very necessary to work as to what wages are being given for the same job in other enterprises. If, on the basis of utility, the wages for a specific job are determined below the wages for the same job on other enterprises, following will be its disadvantages:

1. If such people are at all obtained for employment, they will shift to another enterprise after some time. It is, therefore, necessary to keep in mind the following in wage-survey:

   (*i*) Term of survey, (weekly or monthly)

   (*ii*) The whole wage-payment-knowledge of daily working hours or monthly payment.

   (*iii*) Definition of jobs.

   (*iv*) Appropriate questionnaire for collecting information.

   (*v*) Scientific technique of collecting the data.

2. **Group Similar Jobs into Pay Grades:** After the results of job analysis and salary surveys have been received, the committee can turn to the task of assigning pay rates to each job, but it will usually want to first group jobs into pay grades. A pay grade is comprises the jobs of approximately equal difficulty or

importance as determined by job evaluation. Pay grading is essential for pay purposes because instead of having to deal with hundreds of pay rates, the committee might only have to focus on a few.

3. **Price Each Pay Grade:** The next step is to assign pay rates to pay grades. Assigning pay rates to each pay grade is usually accomplished with a wage curve. The wage curve depicts graphically the pay rates currently being paid for jobs in each pay grade, relative to the points or ranking assigned to each job or grade by the job evaluation. The purpose of wage curve is to show the relationship between (*i*) the value of the job as determined by one of the job evaluation methods and (*ii*) the current average pay rates for the grades.

4. **Fine-Tune Pay Rates:** Fine tuning involves correcting out of line rates and developing rate ranges.

   (*i*) **Correcting out of Line Rates:** The average current pay for a job may be too high or too low, relative to other jobs in the firm. If a rate falls well below the line, a pay rise for that job may be required. If the rate falls well above the wage line, pay cuts or a pay freeze may be required.

   (*ii*) **Developing Rate Ranges:** Most employers do not pay just one rate for all jobs in a particular pay grade. Instead, they develop rate ranges for each grade so that there might be different levels and corresponding pay rates within each pay grade. The rate is usually built around the wage line or curve. One alternative is to arbitrarily decide on a maximum and minimum rate for each grade. As an alternative, some employers allow the rate for each grade to become wider for the higher pay ranges reflecting the greater demands and performance variability inherent in these more complex jobs.

5. **Wage Administration Rules:** The development of rules of wage administration has to be done in the next step. It is considered advisable in the interests of the concern and the employees that the information about average salaries and ranges in the salaries of group should be made known to the employees concerned; for secrecy in this matter may create dissatisfaction and it may also vitiate the potential motivating effects of disclosure. Finally, the employee is appraised and the wage is fixed for the grade he is found fit.

6. **Good persons and persons of merit will not be available.**

Methods of wage payment linking with productivity

Variable Pay or Pay for Performance Systems: Here the pay is linked to individual, group or organizational performance. Employees have to compete and deliver results. Three types of variable pay are commonly used:

- *Individual incentives: they link individual effort to pay*
- *Group incentives: they link pay to the overall performance of the entire group*
- *Organization: wide incentives: here employees are rewarded on the basis of the success of the organization over a specified time period.*

Essentials of a sound incentive plan are:

- Compensation administration
- Guaranteed minimum wages
- Simple equitable
- Economical flexible
- Supported by workers and unions
- Motivating prompt payment.

Methods of Wage Payment

Time wage system: A worker is paid on the basis of time spent on the work, irrespective of the amount of work done.

Plus points = Simple and easy to operate, Guaranteed wages to workers, Favoured by trade unions good for precision jobs.

Minus points = Makes no distinction between efficient and inefficient workers, offers very little to efficient workers, requires close supervision so that workers do not waste their time. No relationship exists between wages and productivity.

Piece rate system: A worker is paid at a stipulated rate per piece or unit of output. This method is suitable where quality of work is not important, work is repetitive in nature, there is sufficient demand for output to guarantee continuous work and the job is a standardized one. Plus points = Encourages efficient workers to produce more, Workers adopt better ways of getting things done, to earn more Idle time is reduced to the minimum, Workers take every precaution to avoid machine breakdowns. Cost of supervision is less in this method of Wage Payment.

Taylor's differential piece rate system: A worker is paid more if he finishes the assigned task before the stipulated time.

Merrick's differential piece rate system: This method uses three rates; up to 83% of the standard output workers are paid at the ordinary piece rate; between 83% to 100% at 110% of the ordinary piece rate and above 100% at 120% of the ordinary piece rate. Minus points are Delays beyond one's control could affect workers earnings adversely. Beginners and slow learners are left behind in the race. The focus on quantity would affect quality. Workers may stretch themselves to unhealthy levels to earn more Encourages rivalry between workers.

Individual Incentive Plans

Halsey plan: Here the worker gets a guaranteed wages based on the time, irrespective of whether the assigned work is completed or not. If the worker is able to finish the task in less than the standard time, he or she is entitled to get fifty (in some cases one third) per cent of time saved at time rate in addition to normal time wages.

Rowan plan: It assures minimum time wages. Bonus is paid on the basis of time saved. But unlike a fixed percentage, it is calculated thus Bonus = Time saved/Standard time multiply by Time taken multiply by hourly rate.

Gantt task and bonus plan: Here time wages are guaranteed. Standard time for each task is fixed. Workers, who fail to finish the job within the time limits, get time wages. A worker who reaches the standard is paid time wages plus bonus at a fixed percentage (20 percentages) of normal time wages.

If a worker exceeds the standards, he is paid a high piece rate.

Bedeaux plan: In this plan every operation is expressed in terms of standard minutes called as "B's" representing one minute. A worker gets time wages for 100% performance; *i.e.*, finishing the job exactly as per standards set. If actual performance exceeds the standard performance in terms of B's then 75% of the wages of time saved is paid to worker as bonus and 25% is given to the foreman.

Haynes manit plan: It is more or less like the Bedeaux plan. Here the bonus is only 50 per cent as against 75 per cent, being paid to the efficient worker. Of the remaining 50 per cent, 10% goes to the foreman and the rest to management.

Emerson's efficiency plan: If the worker achieves 67% efficiency, he gets bonus at a given rate. The rate of bonus increases gradually from 67% to 100%. Above 100% bonus will be at 20% of the basic rate plus 1% for each increase in efficiency.

Accelerate premium bonus plan: Here the premium is paid at varying rates for increasing efficiency. It is an incentive payment granted to a worker at the end of a particular year, in addition to one's normal standard wage.

The Payment of Bonus Act, 1965: The Act defines an employee who is covered by it as one earning ₹ 2,500 p.m. (w.e.f. 1.4.93) basic plus dearness allowance and specifies the formula for calculating the allocable surplus from which bonus is to be distributed. The minimum bonus to be paid has been raised from 4 per cent to 8.33 per cent (w.e.f. 25.9.75) and is sought to be linked to increased productivity in recent times. Through collective bargaining, the workers, through their representative union, can negotiate for more than what the Act provides and get the same ratified by the government, if necessary. In the absence of such a process, the Act makes it mandatory to pay bonus to employees (who have worked in the unit for not less than 30 working days in a year) following a prescribed formula for calculating the available surplus. The available surplus is normally the gross profits for that year after deducting depreciation, development rebate/investment allowance/ development allowance, direct tax and other sums referred to in Sec. 6. The Act applies to every factory or establishment in which 20 or more persons are employed in an accounting year. Currently the position is such that even if there is a loss, a minimum bonus needs to be paid treating the same as deficit to be carried forward and set off against profits in subsequent years (Sec. 15). The Act is proposed to be changed since the amount of bonus, the formula for calculating surplus, and the set off provisions have all been under serious attack from various quarters.

Merit Pay: Any salary increase awarded to an employee based on his or her performance is called merit pay. It is like rewarding the best performers with the largest increases in pay as an appreciative gesture from the employer. When high achievers are rewarded, they set the benchmarks for others to follow. But the whole process of recognizing merit, measuring performance, picking up the winners need to be followed objectively.

Commissions: For Sales People Compensation plans for sales personnel generally consist of a straight salary plan, a straight commission plan, or a combination of both.

Evaluation of Incentive Plans

Incentives based on performance would definitely motivate people to give their best to the organization. They can improve their standard of living. Other benefits include; better use of facilities, reduced supervision; reduced lost time, absenteeism and turnover. There is, of course, the dark side of the moon and the research evidence in this regard is somewhat mixed.

Reasons for the failure of **Pay for Performance** (PFP) systems

- Poor perceived connection between performance and pay
- Tendency of workers to speed up everything, leading to accidents, wastage of resources
- Workers may ignore basic safety precautions in order to produce more
- Workers have inflated ideas about performance

levels and when they fail to receive expected rewards, they blame management

- Jealousies may arise among workers because some are able to earn more than others.
- Unions, not surprisingly, are opposed to PFP systems because these would go against the spirit of "all for one and one for all". Often, setting acceptable, attainable, objective standards is not easy. All said and done, money is simply a hygiene factor and has only limited potential to spur people to superior performance.

Guidelines for PFP systems: Develop and implement PFP systems in an atmosphere of mutual trust and confidence make them easy to understand and implement. Establish the relationship between effort and reward directly and clearly, Recognize individual differences and set the targets keeping the expectations of people in mind. Show clearly what is there in the plan for an efficient worker, apart from the guaranteed wages.

Group or Team Based Incentive Plans: Here all team members receive an incentive bonus payment when production or service standards are met or exceeded. Methods in this category include: Preistman's production bonus, Rucker plan, Scanlon plan, Towne plan and Co-partnership. Under co-partnership, the worker gets his usual wages, a share in the profits of the company and a share in the management of the company as well. Compensation practices in India Companies like Mastek, Godrej and Boyce have tried to link their rewards to team based performance in recent times quite successfully.

Team based rewards: Best practices set quantifiable targets when evaluating team performance for rewards. Ensure that top performers in each team earn the highest level of rewards. Link team performance closely to the company's profits and overall financial health. Avoid subjectivity when assessing both the team and its member's performance.

Offer uniform non-team based incentives to employees within each grade. Other companies like Pfizer, Siemens have been linking rewards to shop floor workers based on the worker ability to meet productivity as well as performance targets. In any case, the emerging picture is quite clear especially in the post liberalization era in India. The start that need entrepreneurial action from its employees will have to offer large doses of cash, goal linked incentive pay and possibly stock options to link compensation to profits. Mature companies, whose focus is on managing their earnings per share and protecting market shares, will have to seek out managerial talent and reward it with flexible tax-friendly compensation packages with benefits designed to improve the quality of working life.

Organization Wide Incentive Plans: These plans reward employees on the basis of the success of the organization over a specified time period. Profit sharing: Here the organization agrees to pay a particular portion of net profits (given in cash or in the form of shares) to eligible employees.

Gain sharing: It is based on a mathematical formula that compares a baseline of performance with actual productivity during a given period. When productivity exceeds the base line an agreed upon savings is shared with employees. Unlike profit sharing plans which have deferred payments, gain sharing plans are current distribution plans. These are based on individual performance and are distributed on a monthly or quarterly basis. Employee stock ownership plan: It provides a mechanism through which certain eligible employees (based on length of service, contribution to the department etc) may purchase the stock of the company at a reduced rate.

Scanlon plan: Similar to gain sharing, but the distribution of gains is tilted toward the employees and is spread across the organization.

Profit sharing plans: Provide an organization wide incentive in the form of an annual bonus to all employees based on corporate profits.

Plus points: Empower the employee to participate in the growth of a company as part owner and get a fair share of the cake. Helps the company to retain talented employees and make them committed to the job and the company. Better industrial relations, reduced employee turnover, lesser supervision, are other benefits Organization Wide Incentive Plans.

Incentive Schemes for Indirect Workers: Since indirect workers also play a key role in manufacturing operations, their contributions need to be recognized and rewarded appropriately. The list of beneficiaries here would include repairs and maintenance staff, store staff, material handling staff, office staff etc. Such schemes, however, must be based on some agreed criteria aimed at improving the overall efficiency of the organization over a period of time.

Fringe Benefits: Fringe benefits include such benefits which are provided to the employees either having long-term impact like provident fund, gratuity, pension; or occurrence of certain events like medical benefits, accident relief, health and life insurance; or facilitation in performance of job like uniforms, canteens, recreation, etc.

JOB EVALUATION

Job evaluation is a process of determining the relative worth of a job. It is a process which is helpful even for framing compensation plans by the personnel manager. Job evaluation as a process is advantageous to a company in many ways:

1. **Reduction in inequalities in salary structure:** It is found that people and their motivation are dependent upon how well they are being paid. Therefore the main objective of job evaluation is to have external and internal consistency in salary structure so that inequalities in salaries are reduced.

2. **Specialization:** Because of division of labour and thereby specialization, a large number of enterprises have got hundred jobs and many employees to perform them. Therefore, an attempt should be made to define a job and thereby fix salaries for it. This is possible only through job evaluation.

3. **Helps in selection of employees:** The job evaluation information can be helpful at the time of selection of candidates. The factors that are determined for job evaluation can be taken into account while selecting the employees.

4. **Harmonious relationship between employees and manager:** Through job evaluation, harmonious and congenial relations can be maintained between employees and management, so that all kinds of salaries controversies can be minimized.

5. **Standardization:** The process of determining the salary differentials for different jobs become standardized through job evaluation. This helps in bringing uniformity into salary structure.

6. **Relevance of new jobs:** Through job evaluation, one can understand the relative value of new jobs in a concern.

According to *Kimball* and *Kimball*, "Job evaluation represents an effort to determine the relative value of every job in a plant and to determine what the fair basic wage for such a job should be."

Thus, job evaluation is different from performance appraisal. In job evaluation, worth of a job is calculated while in performance appraisal, the worth of employee is rated.

GRIEVANCE HANDLING AND DISCIPLINARY ACTION

Discipline means systematically conducting the business by the organizational members who strictly adhere to the essential rules and regulations. These employees/organizational members work together as a team so as to achieve organizational mission as well as vision and they truly understand that the individual and group aims and desires must be matched so as to ensure organizational success.

A disciplined employee will be organized and an organized employee will be disciplined always. Employee behaviour is the base of discipline in an organization. Discipline implies confirming with the code of conduct established by the organization. Discipline in an organization ensures productivity and efficiency. It encourages harmony and co-operation among employees as well as acts as a morale booster for the employees. In absence of discipline, there will be chaos, confusion, corruption and disobedience in an organization.

In short, discipline implies obedience, orderliness and maintenance of proper subordination among employees. Work recognition, fair and equitable treatment of employees, appropriate salary structure, effective grievance handling and job-security all contribute to organizational discipline.

Discipline is viewed from two angles/dimensions:

1. **Positive Discipline:** Positive discipline implies discipline without punishment. The main aim is to ensure and encourage self-discipline among the employees. The employees in this case identify the group objectives as their own objectives and strive hard to achieve them. The employees follow and adhere to the rules and regulations not due to the fear of punishment but due to the inherent desire to harmonize in achieving organizational goals. Employees exercise self-control to meet these goals.

2. **Negative Discipline:** Employees adhere to rules and regulations in fear of punishment which may be in form of fines, penalties, demotions or transfers. In this case, the employees do not perceive organizational goals as their own goals. The action taken by the management to ensure desired standard of behaviour/code of conduct from the employees in an organization is called negative discipline. The fear of punishment prevents the employees from going off-track.

Characteristics of a Sound Disciplinary System (Red Hot Stove Rule)

Discipline should be imposed without generating resentment. Mc George propounded the "red hot stove rule" which says that a sound and effective disciplinary system in an organization should have the following characteristics:

1. **Immediate:** Just as when you touch a red hot stove, the burn is immediate, similarly the penalty for violation should be immediate/immediate disciplinary action must be taken for violation of rules.

2. **Consistent:** Just as a red hot stove burns everyone in same manner; likewise, there

should be high consistency in a sound disciplinary system.

3. **Impersonal:** Just as a person is burned because he touches the red hot stove and not because of any personal feelings, likewise, impersonality should be maintained by refraining from personal or subjective feelings.

4. **Prior warning and notice:** Just as an individual has a warning when he moves closer to the stove that he would be burned on touching it, likewise, a sound disciplinary system should give advance warning to the employees as to the implications of not conforming to the standards of behaviour/ code of conduct in an organization.

In short, a sound disciplinary system presupposes:

1. **Acquaintance/Knowledge of rules:** The employees should be well aware of the desired code of conduct/ standards of behaviour in the organization. This code of discipline should be published in employee handbook.

2. **Timely action:** Timely enquiry should be conducted for breaking the code of conduct in an organization. The more later the enquiry is made, the more forgetful one becomes and the more he feels that punishment is not deserved.

3. **Fair and just action:** There should be same punishment for same offence/ misconduct. There should be no favouritism. Discipline should be uniformly enforced always.

4. **Positive approach:** The disciplinary system should be preventive and not punitive. Concentrate on preventing misconduct and not on imposing penalties. The employees should not only be explained the reason for actions taken against them but also how such fines and penalties can be avoided in future.

Types of Penalties for Misconduct/Indiscipline

For not following the standards of behaviour/ code of conduct in an organization, there are two kinds of penalties categorized as:

a. **Major penalties:** This includes demotion, dismissal, transfer, discharge, withholding increments, etc.

b. **Minor penalties:** This includes oral warning, written warning, fines, loss of privileges, etc.

Grievance may be any genuine or imaginary feeling of dissatisfaction or injustice which an employee experiences about his job and its nature, about the management policies and procedures. It must be expressed by the employee and brought to the notice of the management and the organization. Grievances take the form of collective disputes when they are not resolved. Also they will then lower the morale and efficiency of the employees. Unattended grievances result in frustration, dissatisfaction, low productivity, lack of interest in work, absenteeism, etc. In short, grievance arises when employees' expectations are not fulfilled from the organization as a result of which a feeling of discontentment and dissatisfaction arises. This dissatisfaction must crop up from employment issues and not from personal issues.

Grievance may result from the following factors:

a. Improper working conditions such as strict production standards, unsafe workplace, bad relation with managers, etc.

b. Irrational management policies such as overtime, transfers, demotions, inappropriate salary structure, etc.

Violation of organizational rules and practices.

The manager should immediately identify all grievances and must take appropriate steps to eliminate the causes of such grievances so that the employees remain loyal and committed to their work. Effective grievance management is an essential part of personnel management. The managers should adopt the following approach to manage grievance effectively:

1. **Quick action:** As soon as the grievance arises, it should be identified and resolved. Training must be given to the managers to effectively and timely manage a grievance. This will lower the detrimental effects of grievance on the employees and their performance.

2. **Acknowledging grievance:** The manager must acknowledge the grievance put forward by the employee as manifestation of true and

real feelings of the employees. Acknowledgement by the manager implies that the manager is eager to look into the complaint impartially and without any bias. This will create a conducive work environment with instances of grievance reduced.

3. **Gathering facts:** The managers should gather appropriate and sufficient facts explaining the grievance's nature. A record of such facts must be maintained so that these can be used in later stage of grievance redressal.

4. **Examining the causes of grievance:** The actual cause of grievance should be identified. Accordingly remedial actions should be taken to prevent repetition of the grievance.

5. **Decisioning:** After identifying the causes of grievance, alternative course of actions should be thought of to manage the grievance. The effect of each course of action on the existing and future management policies and procedure should be analyzed and accordingly decision should be taken by the manager.

6. **Execution and review:** The manager should execute the decision quickly, ignoring the fact, that it may or may not hurt the employees concerned. After implementing the decision, a follow-up must be there to ensure that the grievance has been resolved completely and adequately.

An effective grievance procedure ensures an amiable work environment because it redresses the grievance to mutual satisfaction of both the employees and the managers. It also helps the management to frame policies and procedures acceptable to the employees. It becomes an effective medium for the employees to express the feelings, discontent and dissatisfaction openly and formally.

MULTIPLE CHOICE QUESTIONS

1. Training an employee completes from his/her computer workstation. The training is accessible via the Internet (web) or CDs is termed as
   A. Systematic training
   B. Computer based training (CBT)
   C. Online training
   D. None of the above

2. Executive search firms is all about:
   A. External recruiting method
   B. Firms seek out candidates, or usually for executive
   C. Managerial or professional positions
   D. All the above

3. The interview in which an employee is informed of the fact that he or she has been dismissed is
   A. Termination Interview
   B. Insubordination
   C. Wrongful Discharge
   D. All the above

4. A spontaneous incentive awarded to individuals for accomplishments not readily measured by a standard is
   A. Spot bonus
   B. Hawthorne experiment
   C. Both A and B
   D. None of the above

5. Any plan that ties pay to productivity or profitability, usually as one-time lump Payments is
   A. Variable pay   B. Invariable pay
   C. Both A and B   D. None of the above

6. A system of pay based on the number of items processed by each individual worker in a unit of time, such as items per hour or items per day is
   A. Time based pay   B. Invariable pay
   C. Piecework   D. None of the above

7. Under this pay system each worker receives a set payment for each piece produced or processed in a factory or shop is
   A. Variable pay
   B. Pay system
   C. Straight piecework
   D. None of the above

8. The minimum hourly wage plus an incentive for each piece produced above a set number of pieces per hour is
   A. Guaranteed piecework plan
   B. Straight piecework plan
   C. Piecework plan
   D. None of the above

9. A plan by which a worker is paid a basic hourly rate, but is paid an extra percentage of his or her base rate for production exceeding the standard per hour or per day. Similar to piecework payment, but based on a percent premium is
   A. Guaranteed piecework plan
   B. Straight piecework plan
   C. Piecework plan
   D. Standard Hour plan

10. A plan in which a production standard is set for a specific work group, and its members are paid incentives if the group exceed the production standard is
    A. Guaranteed piecework plan
    B. Straight piecework plan
    C. Piecework plan
    D. Team or group incentive

11. Which of the following statements about the determinants of personality is true?
    A. Personality appears to be a result of external factors
    B. Personality appears to be a result of mainly hereditary factors
    C. Personality appears to be a result of mainly environmental factors
    D. Personality appears to be a result of both hereditary and environmental factors

12. Which of the following is NOT an important issue relating to goal-setting theory?
    A. Goal specificity
    B. Equity among co-workers
    C. Feedback
    D. Defining the goal

13. Shiva is the head of a group at an advertising agency working with artists and designers to come up with effective branding of new products. Why is it particularly important for him to keep his team happy?

   A. People are more conscientious when they are in a good mood
   B. People are more efficient when they are in a good mood
   C. People are more productive when they are in a good mood
   D. People are more creative when they are in a good mood

14. Which of the following is true of people of the Type A personality?
    A. They are generally content with their place in the world
    B. They generally feel little need to discuss their achievements
    C. They are easy going and relaxed that's why take no tension of work
    D. They have an intense desire to achieve and are extremely competitive

15. What is/are the key element(s) of motivation?
    A. Intensity
    B. Direction
    C. Persistence
    D. All of the given options

16. Which of the following theory is proposed by Clayton Alderfer?
    A. Theory X and Theory Y
    B. Hierarchy of Needs
    C. ERG Theory
    D. Theory Z

17. When your superior offers you a raise, you will perform additional work beyond the requirements of your job, he/she is exercising which of the following power?
    A. Legitimate   B. Coercive
    C. Reward   D. Personal

18. According to attribution theory, which of the following is an example of externally caused behaviour?
    A. An employee is late because of a flat tire
    B. An employee was promoted because of his abilities
    C. An employee was fired because he slept on the job
    D. An employee was promoted because he was hard working

19. For task conflict to be productive, it should be
    A. Kept high to low
    B. Kept at low to high
    C. Kept at moderate levels
    D. Kept at low-to-moderate levels

20. _____ of Hofstede's dimensions is the degree to which people in a country prefer structured to unstructured situations.
    A. Collectivism
    B. Power distance
    C. Long-term orientation
    D. Uncertainty avoidance

21. Which of the following answer choices is the best definition of attitude?
    A. Attitudes are the one that measures one's actions
    B. Attitudes are the emotional part of an evaluation of some person, object or event
    C. Attitudes are evaluative statements of what one believes about something or someone
    D. Attitudes are a measure of how the worth of an object, person or event is evaluated

22. Values are important to organizational behaviour because they
    A. Are considered as an integral part of culture
    B. Help to understand the attitudes and motivation
    C. Form the supporting foundation for the study of ethics
    D. Allow the study of alignment of organizational policies

23. When a bank robber points a gun at a bank employee, his base of power is
    A. Coercive   B. Punitive
    C. Positional   D. Authoritative

24. The highest level of trust is exhibited from the following type of trust is
    A. Reward-based
    B. Deterrence-based
    C. Knowledge-based
    D. Identification-based

25. Riti is an office worker who processes health insurance forms. She has worked at her present job for three years. Initially she was criticized by her supervisor for careless work, but in the months after that improved considerably. Now she consistently processes her forms without errors and above quota. However she has found her supervisor has not responded to the extra effort she puts in, giving her no praise and no financial reward. Riti, will most likely perceive that there is a problem in which of the following relationships?
    A. Rewards-personal goals
    B. Performance-reward
    C. Effort-performance
    D. Rewards-effort

26. The more consistent a behaviour, the more the observer is inclined to _____.
    A. Attribute it to interpretation
    B. Attribute it to internal causes
    C. Attribute it to consensus
    D. Attribute it to external causes

27. According to the goal-setting theory of motivation, highest performance is reached when goals are set to
    A. Impossible but inspirational
    B. Difficult but attainable
    C. Only marginally challenging
    D. Easy and attainable

28. Deepshi has composed a list of concerns along with her suggestions for improving conditions. Deepshi is dealing with her dissatisfaction through _____.
    A. Exit   B. Voice
    C. Loyalty   D. Neglect

29. Values like working hard, being creative and honest are the means which lead towards achieving organizational goals. Which of the following term best describes these values?
    A. Terminal values
    B. Instrumental values
    C. Theoretical values
    D. Social values

30. Rater Errors comprises all the following EXCEPT
    A. Central Tendency B. Leniency
    C. Miss-perception   D. Harshness

31. Your physician has advised you to take a series of medications. You comply because of his _____power.
    A. Referent   B. Formal
    C. Expert   D. Personal

32. Mrs. Hillary Clinton gained political capital by her marriage to the President Clinton is an example of which of the following power?
    A. Referent power   B. Legitimate power
    C. Reward power   D. Expert power

33. Maslow's Need theory was widely recognized by practicing managers during
    A. 1950s and 1960s   B. 1960s and 1970s
    C. 1970s and 1980s   D. 1980s and 1990s

34. Sanjay comes to you with a request for funds for a project. He reminds you that company policy supports his position. He is using the tactic of
    A. Coalitions   B. Consultation
    C. Legitimacy   D. Pressure

35. Which of the following is NOT consistent with rational decision-making?
    A. Consistency   B. Value-maximizing
    C. Restraints   D. Ranking of criteria

36. Which of the following fields has most helped us understand differences in fundamental values, attitudes, and behaviour among people in different countries?
    A. Anthropology
    B. Psychology
    C. Political science
    D. Operations research

37. Organizational members who intentionally violate established norms that result in negative consequences for the organization, its members, or both, shows
    A. Deviant Workplace Behaviour
    B. Emotional Labour
    C. Interpersonal Skills
    D. Social Skills

38. Explaining, measuring and changing behaviour of humans or animals are concerned with
    A. Operational analysts
    B. Scientists
    C. Psychologists
    D. Sociologists

39. Features of Maslow's need hierarchy theory are:
    A. Theory of human motives
    B. ERG theory
    C. Classifies basic human needs in a hierarchy
    D. Theory of human motivation

40. Cultural diversity brings with it concerns like
    A. Intra organizational conflicts
    B. Communication difficulties
    C. Intra organizational Turnovers
    D. All the above

41. In managing cultural diversity, organization must have a relatively non-bureaucratic structure.
    A. True   B. False
    C. Partially true   D. None of the above

42. Who has given the following definition of Organizational Behaviour, "understanding, predicting and controlling human behaviour at work"?
    A. Clyton   B. Robert Katz
    c. Mc Gregor   D. Fred Luthans

43. T.P.M stands for Total_____Management.
    A. Production   B. Performance
    C. People   D. Price

44. Repetitive tasks give rise to the same degree of boredom in all persons.
    A. True   B. False
    C. Partially true   D. None of the above

45. The esteem needs manifest itself in which of the following forms.
    A. Need for Status
    B. Need for Power
    C. Need of Recognition
    D. All of above

46. The leader who fails to guide, motivate and develop his subordinates is said to be practicing _____ leadership style.
    A. Free Rein   B. Autocratic
    C. Democratic   D. None of the above

47. _____ Communication is useful for flatter organizational structure.
A. Lateral   B. Vertical
C. Cross   D. None of the above

48. Cultural elements and their relationships create a pattern that is identical in all organizations.
A. True   B. False
C. Partially true   D. None of the above

49. The storming stage relating to development of a team is characterized by which of the following aspects?
A. Emergence of conflicts
B. Seeking task related guidance from the leader
C. Deciding the responsibilities of each team member
D. None of the above

50. A theory of motivation, what is the comment of Maslow on needs?
A. Needs can be structured in a hierarchy
B. Needs cannot be structured in a hierarchy
C. No requirement of Hierarchy
D. None of the above

51. The different types of fatigue are
A. Mental   B. Physical
C. Psychological   D. All the above

52. Organization with a strong culture has
A. Practices that include employee participation
B. Practices that only include top, middle levels
C. Dominating management
D. None of the above

53. Communication provides a means to release _____ and for fulfillment of social needs.
A. Emotional expression
B. Values
C. Perception
D. All the above

54. According to Frend, the human mind is composed of
A. Preconscious mind
B. Conscious mind
C. Unconscious mind
D. All the above

55. According to Herzberg, there are two sets of factors at the work life, viz. the motivators and the _____ factors.
A. Hygiene   B. Personal
C. Biological   D. All the above

56. _____ are the rules of pattern and behaviour that are expected from all team members.
A. Norms   B. Standards
C. Rules   D. Policy

57. Select the needs which are discussed by the need hierarch theory is
A. Physiological needs
B. Security needs
C. Self realization needs
D. All the above

58. Select the relevant parts of the communication process.
A. Encoding / Receiver
B. Decoding
C. Feedback
D. All the above

59. A person of lower than normal intelligence is less bored by _____ work.
A. Repetitive   B. Continuous
C. Batch   D. None of the above

60. Whatever an individual does, there is always some sort and some amount of stress on him.
A. True   B. False
C. Partially true   D. None of the above

61. The more successful, the organization is, the less effective is its internal communication.
A. True   B. False
C. Partially true   D. None of the above

62. In order to understand the Rogers' theory an individual to understand which of the following?
A. The self concept
B. The organism
C. The development of self
D. All the above

63. A change in the organization requires a corresponding change in the employee's individual personality.
A. True   B. False
C. Partially true   D. None of the above

64. The leadership process is a function which relates only to the leader and other situational variables.

    A. False   B. True

    C. Partially true   D. None of the above

65. The group _____ are more important to the group members than any financial incentive.

    A. Norms   B. Standards

    C. Rules   D. Procedures

66. _____ are the elements of the process of bringing about change in people as suggested by Lewin.

    A. Unfreezing   B. Refreezing

    C. Moving   D. All the above

67. On the managerial grid, a manager falling in the _____ category will have maximum concern for both people and production.

    A. 9.9   B. 9.1

    C. 1.9   D. 1.1

68. Which step concerned with the management of change involves the identification of the root cause?

    A. Diagnose the problem

    B. Terminate the problem

    C. Review the problem

    D. All the above

69. The communication process can be improved by _____.

    A. Reducing status barriers

    B. Increasing richness

    C. Clear goal setting

    D. All the above

70. Conceptual skill is the distinguishing feature of job performance at the operating level.

    A. False   B. True

    C. Partially true   D. None of the above

71. A subset of the labour force population that is available for selection using a particular recruiting approach is

    A. Interview

    B. Program

    C. Application population

    D. Public

72. A list of a job's duties, responsibilities, reporting relationships, working conditions, and supervisory responsibilities is

    A. Job analysis   B. Job description

    C. Job specification   D. Job enrichment

73. The procedure for determining the duties and skill requirements of a job and the kind of person who should be hired for it is

    A. Job analysis   B. Job description

    C. Job specification   D. Job enrichment

74. A list of a job's "human requirements," that is, the requisite education, skills, personality, and so on is

    A. Job analysis   B. Job description

    C. Job specification   D. Job enrichment

75. Daily listings made by workers of every activity in which they engage along with the time of each activity takes is made at

    A. Diary/log

    B. Record

    C. Entry Register

    D. Balance score card

76. Any abnormal condition or disorder, other than one resulting from an occupational injury, caused by exposure to factors associated with employment is

    A. Industry sickness

    B. Recruitment

    C. Placement

    D. Occupational illness/disease

77. A questionnaire used to collect quantifiable data concerning the duties and responsibilities of various jobs to analyses is

    A. Position analysis   B. Research

    C. Clarification   D. Cross check

78. A method for classifying jobs similar to the Department of Labour job analysis but additionally taking into account the extent to which instructions, reasoning, judgment, and verbal facility are necessary for performing the job tasks is

    A. Recruitment

    B. Placement

    C. Occupational illness/disease

    D. Functional job analysis

79. Used to classify specific occupations into a specific category, such as professionals, technical/hi-tech, administrative/clerical, Sales, service, retail, etc is
A. Position analysis
B. Research
C. Clarification
D. Occupational groups

80. _____ forecasting technique for determining future staff needs by using ratios between sales volume and number of employees needed.
A. Ratio analysis   B. Position analysis
C. Research   D. Clarification

81. An injury sustained during the course of employment, which results in the employee requiring medical treatment other then minor first aid and which results in the employee being absent from work as a result of such injury for one or more work days or results in work restrictions referred as
A. Selection
B. Occupational injury
C. Accident
D. Fringe benefits

82. Makes the hiring decision done by the official should immediately follow the final decision to hire a candidate, also known as
A. Orientation   B. Placement
C. Offer letter   D. Employer relation

83. To enhance learning and performance in organizations by practice of creating, acquiring, capturing, sharing and using knowledge, is
A. Enrichment
B. Knowledge management
C. Management function
D. HRIS

84. The processes that ensure that people are valued and rewarded for what they do and achieve and for the levels of skill and competence they reach, are called:
A. Goal achievement
B. Performance management
C. Reward management
D. Organizational behaviour

85. Used to define the periods of time during which an employee is totally and completely relieved of any and all job duties and is free to attend to his or her own personal activities is
A. Off duty hours
B. On duty hours
C. Absenteeism
D. Deputation period

86. A written qualified or non-qualified benefit plan, funded by employer and employee contributions, that provides retirement income benefits for employees is
A. Provident fund   B. Fixed amount
C. Reward plan   D. Retirement plan

87. Additional compensation awarded to employees who are required to remain on call during off-duty hours, are
A. Off-shore pay   B. On-call pay
C. Reward   D. Basic pay

88. Used to define periods of time when an employee is off duty but is required to remain on or close to the company premises or to respond to a call or page within a specified period of time, resulting in the employee being unable to effectively use such time to attend to his or her own personal activities, then the term is
A. On-call time   B. Notice period
C. Deputation   D. Temporary

89. Training that is provided for a certain job to enable an employee to acquire the necessary skills to work with new processes, procedures or equipment is
A. Training   B. Retraining
C. Retaining   D. Learning

90. Study of a firm's past employment needs over a period of years to predict future needs a
A. Trend analysis   B. Research
C. Planning   D. Presumption

91. Calculation showing the value of expenditures for HR activities is
A. Tax calculation
B. HR expenses
C. Return on investment (ROI)
D. HR accounting

92. A graphical method used to help identify the relationship between two variables is
A. Graph sheet
B. Pie diagram
C. Scatter plot
D. None of the above

93. A condition that may exist when a person is denied an opportunity because of preferences given to protected-class individuals who may be less qualified is
A. Reverse discrimination
B. Under employment
C. Employment opportunity
D. None of the above

94. Manual or computerized systematic records, listing employees' education, career and development interests, languages, special skills, and so on, is to be used in forecasting inside candidates for promotion means
A. Education
B. Register
C. Qualification inventories
D. Personnel management

95. The determination of future staff needs by projecting a firm's sales, volume of production, and personnel required to maintain this volume of output, using computers and software packages are
A. Computerized forecast
B. Planning
C. Computer package
D. Data collection

96. Company records showing present performance and promotability of inside candidates for the most important positions is
A. Position replacement
B. Position change
C. Personnel replacement
D. None of the above

97. A card prepared for each position in a company to show possible replacement candidates and their qualifications is
A. Position replacement
B. Promotion
C. Personnel replacement
D. None of the above

98. A formal or informal program used to recognize individual employee achievements, such as accomplishment of goals or projects or submission of creative ideas is
A. Reward system
B. Recording
C. Direction
D. Achievement of goal

99. Posting notices of job openings on company bulletin boards is an effective recruiting method refers as
A. Recruitment
B. Placement
C. Job posting
D. Job specification

100. The form that provides information on education, prior work record, and skills is
A. Application form
B. Registered
C. Diary
D. Log book

101. A standardized testing instrument used to measure how much an individual has learned or what skills he or she has attained as a result of education, training or past experience is
A. Performance appraisal
B. Job evaluation
C. Interview
D. Achievement test

102. Specific guidelines that regulate and restrict the behaviour of individuals is
A. Statement
B. Policy
C. Rule
D. Pamphlets

103. A learner-driven, continuous learning process where learning revolves around the need to find solutions to real problems is
A. Learning process
B. Action learning
C. Training methods
D. Problem solving

104. An outsourcing method that is based on transferring jobs away from higher cost urban areas to lower cost rural areas is
A. Rural sourcing
B. Outsourcing
C. Recruitment policy
D. All the above

105. The accuracy with which a test, interview, and so on measures what it purports to measure or fulfils the function it was designed to fill is
A. Test validity
B. Measurement
C. Sample
D. Data collection

106. An unstructured conversational-style interview, the interviewer pursues points of interest as they come up in response to questions is
    A. Formal interview
    B. Panel interview
    C. Non directive interview
    D. All the above

107. An interview following a set sequence of questions at interview process is
    A. Directive interview
    B. Non directive interview
    C. Informal interview
    D. All the above

108. An interview in which the applicant is made uncomfortable by a series of often rude questions. This technique helps identify hypersensitive applicants and those with low or high stress tolerance is
    A. Physiological style
    B. Stress interview
    C. Group discussion
    D. Selection procedure

109. A discussion following a performance appraisal in which supervisor and employee discuss the employee's rating and possible remedial actions is
    A. Appraisal interview
    B. Performance management
    C. Group discussion
    D. Stress interview

110. A series of job-related questions which focuses on how the candidate would behave in a given situation is
    A. Job description
    B. Unstructured interview
    C. Psychological assessment
    D. Situational interview

111. A series of job-related questions which focuses on relevant past job-related behaviours is
    A. Job related interview
    B. Job description
    C. Unstructured interview
    D. Psychological assessment

112. An interview in which the applicant is interviewed sequentially by interviewer is
    A. Structured sequential interview
    B. Job description
    C. Unstructured interview
    D. Psychological assessment

113. Several supervisors and each rates the applicant on a standard form is
    A. Communication
    B. Behaviourial aspect
    C. Training
    D. Interview

114. Applicant for employment is someone who
    A. submits expression of interest through the proper on-line application process
    B. is considered for employment in a particular position
    C. has submitted an expression of interest that indicates the basic qualifications for the position and does not remove him/herself from consideration prior to job offer.
    D. All the above

115. All persons who are actually evaluated for selection is termed as:
    A. Applicant
    B. Candidate
    C. Client
    D. Applicant pool

116. Any paper or computerized system that tracks the organization's data such as resumes/applications and internal job posting information is
    A. Application tracking
    B. Applying for a job
    C. Application pool
    D. None of the above

117. A system of indenture or other agreement, written or implied, to train a person in a recognized trade or craft in accordance with specified standards is
    A. Opportunity
    B. Employability
    C. Apprenticeship
    D. Job rotation

118. Tests that measure general ability to learn or acquire a skill is
    A. Testing
    B. Aptitude tests
    C. Interview
    D. Panel interview

119. When the interviewer asks each applicant questions from the same knowledge, skill, or ability area, then the questions, however, are not necessarily the same, also called a patterned interview is
A. Targeted interview
B. Panel interview
C. Group discussion
D. None of the above

120. Compensation plan used to protect expatriates from negative tax consequences is
A. Tax deduction
B. Tax benefited
C. Tax equalization plan
D. All the above

121. Organizational feedback and communication mechanism that asks employees to provide opinions on given topics, feelings and beliefs about their jobs or the organization, also known as climate survey is otherwise
A. Attitude survey
B. Observation survey
C. Questionnaire pattern
D. None of the above

122. A written or verbal notice given to employees who are being terminated or laid-off is
A. Letter   B. Notice
C. Communication   D. Pink slip

123. Fitting a person to the right job is
A. Placement   B. Placement goal
C. Positioning   D. All the above

124. Serve as objectives or targets in an affirmative action plan when the percentage of protected class workers is less than is reasonably expected given availability is
A. Placement   B. Placement goal
C. Positioning   D. All the above

125. A substantially different rate of selection in hiring, promotion or other employment decision that works to the disadvantage of a race, sex or ethnic group is
A. Adverse selection
B. Adverse committee
C. Adverse impact
D. All the above

126. Situation in which only higher-risk employees select and use certain benefits are
A. Adverse selection
B. Situation analysis
C. Both A and B
D. None of the above

127. An external recruiting method, that provide support and assistance to displaced employees, including career counseling, resume preparation, interview-tips, job referral assistance, and retraining is
A. Out placement firms
B. Consultant
C. Assessment centre
D. None of the above

128. A type of flexible staffing option, an independent company with expertise in operating a specific function contracts with a company to assume full operational responsibility for the function is meant as
A. Outplacement   B. Out sourcing
C. Consultant   D. Training period

129. A method of keeping employees informed of company programs and services available to them by utilizing such things as postings, newsletters, memos or meetings is
A. Outreach programs
B. Scheduled programs
C. Informal programmes
D. None of the above

130. Term used to define work that is performed in excess of 40 hours per week is
A. Overtime pay   B. Extra earning
C. Benefits   D. None of the above

131. The delivery of formal and informal training and educational materials, processes and programs via the use of electronic media is
A. Distance learning B. Online program
C. E-learning   D. None of the above

132. Plan that combines all time-off benefits into a total number of hours or days that employees can take off with pay is
A. Earned time plan   B. Over time pay
C. Extra income   D. None of the above

133. The planned introduction of new employees to their jobs, coworkers, and the organization is termed as
A. Fair well   B. Orientation
C. Induction   D. Placement

134. An advantage of recruitment from outside the company is
A. that it is cheaper than internal recruitment
B. that there is no need to advertise the vacancy
C. that it brings in new experience and skills to the firm
D. that it avoids jealousy within the firm

135. Ineffective planning of workforce would be highlighted by
A. Recruitment and selection problems
B. The need to outsource some of the production
C. A need to offer retraining to current employees
D. An opportunity to increase the use of mechanization

136. Which of the following will influence the method of recruitment and selection used by a company?
A. The state of the economy
B. The size of the organization
C. The type of training programmes used by the company
D. The possible expansion of UK business in Europe

137. An interview conducted by the responsible person at the time of an employee leaving the organization is
A. Lay-off
B. Retaining employee
C. Exit interview
D. Flexi hours

138. An interviewing style whereby the interviewer subjects a candidate to pressure or stress to ascertain how the candidate reacts under such conditions is
A. Stress
B. Stress management
C. Stress interview
D. Depression

139. This refers to a job ranking method in which evaluator compares each job with every other job being evaluated is
A. Point grading
B. Classification method
C. Paired-comparison method
D. Factor analysis

140. Group or team interview of a job candidate OR interview in which several interviewers interview the candidate at the same time is
A. Panel interview
B. Group discussion
C. Panel discussion
D. Debating

141. The design and implementation of workplace programs and services intended to combat employee stress and improve overall employee morale, effectiveness and productivity is
A. Stress
B. Stress management
C. Stress interview
D. Depression

142. Training that occurs internally through interactions and feedback among employees are
A. Formal training   B. Informal training
C. Assessment   D. None of the above

143. Employees are allocated a fund of money to spend on benefits from a menu. This is sometimes described as the "cafeteria approach".
A. Flex fund
B. Flex existing entitlement
C. Flex individual benefits
D. Flexible fund

144. Which Occupational Scheme is not provided?
A. Benefit on VRS
B. Benefit on Retirement
C. Benefit on death
D. Benefit on leaving on employer

145. Reward procedures deal with grading jobs, fixing rates of pay and handling appeals.
A. True   B. False
C. Myth   D. None of the above

146. Reward goals can be expressed in guiding principles or the objectives, defined for reward initiatives.
A. True   B. False
C. Myth   D. None of the above

147. The role of reward processes is "HR and reward specialists develop and implement reward strategies, policies and processes, administer and audit existing systems, and provide advice and guidance to line managers."
A. True   B. False
C. Myth   D. None of the above

148. Reward specialist do not need the skill to expertise design and manage complex system that meet the needs of users but they only require the expertise.
A. True   B. False
C. Myth   D. None of the above

149. Job analysis describes,
A. Duties   B. Responsibilities
C. Working conditions D. All the above

150. Group incentive plans may not become successful due to
A. Unevenness of performance of different members of groups
B. Ill-feeling among group members
C. No recognition for individual performance
D. All the above

151. For designing profit sharing plan, the company has to first
A. Analyze the need based
B. Determine organization's profit for year
C. Individuals Salary statement
D. None of the above

152. Job Analysis is the _____ process of collecting and making judgments about all the important information related to a job.
A. Managerial   B. Calculative
C. Systematic   D. None of the above

153. Techniques of Data Collection for job analysis
A. Questionnaires and Written narratives
B. Observation and Interviews
C. Log records
D. All the above

154. The jobs are fitted into different grades by comparing on the whole within the organization is
A. Job description   B. Job analysis
C. Job classification   D. None of the above

155. The methods of break down the jobs into compensable factors which are assigned some numerical values is
A. Qualitative methods
B. Quantitative methods
C. Both A and B
D. None of the above

156. Personnel management is not possible when
A. Large-sized concern
B. Small concern
C. Too small size concern
D. None of the above

157. The practice of placing a candidate at the right job is
A. Selection   B. Placement
C. Interview   D. None of the above

158. Recruitment is made
A. By centralized office
B. Through different department
C. Employment office
D. None of the above

159. An interview in which a group of interviewers questions the applicant is
A. Group interview
B. Group discussion
C. Panel interview
D. Appraisal interview

160. An error of judgment on the part of the interviewer due to interviewing one or more very good or very bad candidates just before the interview in question is
A. Candidate order error
B. Low performer
C. Average performer
D. Error on system

161. The practice of assessing the employer's current workforce to determine whether or not current employees possess the required skills or qualifications to fill specific vacancies either through promotion or transfer is

A. Internal recruitment
B. External recruitment
C. Human Resource Planning
D. None of the above

162. _____ describes a method of teaching intended to help people who have basic skills deficiencies, such reading or writing.
A. Remedial training
B. Refresher training
C. Role of ambiguity
D. None of the above

163. Often prepared by candidates (or by a professional hired by the candidate) to highlight candidates' work experience, strengths, skills, educational background, accomplishments and other related information is
A. Management Information system
B. Resumes
C. Registers
D. None of the above

164. An index number giving the relationship between a predictor and a criterion variable is
A. Correlation
B. Coefficient
C. Correlation coefficient
D. None of the above

165. Listing of all employees from highest to lowest in performance is
A. Sequential   B. Ranking
C. Point method   D. All the above

166. A rating method where the performance of a group, process or product is arranged in a particular order, such as highest to lowest is
A. Sequential   B. Rank order
C. Point method   D. All the above

167. Error that occurs when a rater's values or prejudices distort the rating is
A. Rater bias   B. Partiality
C. Both A and B   D. None of the above

168. According to Maslow's Need Hierarchy Theory, the lowest level needs are:
A. Physiological   B. Security
C. Self-esteem   D. All the above

169. 'Theory X' states that:
A. Workers prefer to be directed
B. Workers exercise self-direction and self-control
C. Workers have inherent disliking for work and will avoid it if they can
D. All the above

170. In the Herzberg's Hygiene theory of motivation, the hygiene factor causes:
A. Satisfaction of employees
B. Dissatisfaction of employees
C. Motivation of employees
D. No effect on satisfaction

171. If the General Manager asks the sales manager to recruit executives on his behalf, it is an instance of:
A. Centralization of authority
B. Delegation of authority
C. Delegation of responsibility
D. None of the above

172. Which is not Hershey Blanchard leadership model?
A. Telling / Directing
B. Participating / Supporting
C. Selling / Coaching
D. Performing / Doing

173. Theory X and Theory Y was propagated by
A. Frederick Herzberg   B. Mc Gregor
C. Victor Vroom   D. Adam

174. Motivation-hygiene theory was propagated by
A. Adam
B. Frederick Herzberg
C. Mc Gregor
D. Frank Gilbert

175. Contingency approach is also called
A. Error approach
B. Difficulty approach
C. Situational approach
D. Hindrance approach

176. GE matrix two dimensions are
A. Market attractiveness, Business Unit Strength
B. Market share, Profit
C. Profit, Loss
D. Market Growth, Market Share

177. Which of the following is one of Herzberg's 'motivational factors'?
A. People are primarily motivated by money
B. Opportunities to achieve some personal advancement within the organization
C. The application of respected supervision of employees by those responsible for this role within the organization
D. None of the above

178. _____ is commitment to systematic assessment of the company's main activities that have a social impact reporting to the society on relevant issues.
A. Social Audit
B. Social responsiveness
C. Corporate responsibility
D. None of the above

179. A Plan under which an employer pays to eligible employees, as an addition to their normal remuneration, special sums related to the profit of the business.
A. Stock sharing   B. Profit sharing
C. Gain sharing   D. Bonus sharing

180. There are _____ basic traditional systems of job evaluation.
A. 4 [four]   B. 5 [five]
C. 6 [six]   D. 8 [eight]

181. An insured person who is entitled to any of _____ benefits shall not be entitled to receive any other similar benefits under any other law.
A. Bonus benefits
B. Medical allowances
C. Maternity benefits
D. All the above

182. Towns are getting converted into cities and cities into Metro.
A. True   B. False
C. Cannot say   D. None of the above

183. A marketing strategy which aims to focus on small gaps or niches in the market, and then introduces suitable products at competitive prices to capture those small markets is
A. Strategy
B. Market niche strategy

C. Introduction stage
D. Product life cycle

184. Mathematical techniques for modeling, analysis and solution of management problems is
A. Operational research
B. Management science
C. Both A and B
D. None of the above

185. A formal, usually computerized, structure for providing management with complete and up-to-date information is
A. Information
B. Management Information System
C. Result
D. None of the above

186. A systematic, comprehensive examination of the quality of management in an organization in order to bring about improvement is
A. Management audit
B. Quality control
C. Product development
D. None of the above

187. A mathematical model used to determine the optimum allocation of limited resource to attain a goal is
A. Operations
B. Fundamentals of management
C. Linear programming model
D. None of the above

188. Communication between department of an organization that generally follows the work flow, thus providing a direct channel for coordination and problem solving is
A. Strategy formulation
B. Lateral communication
C. Both A and B
D. None of the above

189. Activities intended to ease an individual's entrance into an organization through introducing the individual to the organization and providing information on it is
A. Induction   B. Orientation
C. Both A and B   D. None of the above

190. An unofficial group created by members of an organization without the express encouragement of managers is
A. Informal group   B. Formal group
C. Get-together   D. None of the above

191. The monitoring within an organization of the validity, accuracy and completeness of its financial statement and records is
A. External audit   B. Internal audit
C. Both A and B   D. None of the above

192. The analysis and appraisal of an organization's current human resource is
A. Performance appraisal
B. Human resource audit
C. Both A and B
D. None of the above

193. The possibility that workers who receive special attention will perform better simply because they receive that attention; one interpretation of Elton Mayo and his subordinate studies is
A. Managerial grid   B. Hawthorne effect
C. SWOT analysis   D. All the above

194. Probability of loss or failure in a business venture or related to a particular decision or course of action is
A. Profit and loss account
B. Risk
C. Entrepreneurship
D. All the above

195. The degree of solidarity and positive feeling held by individuals toward their group is
A. Group cohesiveness
B. Introvert

C. Extrovert
D. All the above

196. The method of analyzing and predicting the rational behaviour of people in competitive and conflict situations is
A. Strategy planning
B. Strategy formulation
C. Strategy implementation
D. Game theory

197. Any conflict that has positive, constructive and non-divisive results is
A. Managerial conflict
B. Functional conflict
C. Labour welfare
D. All the above

198. The organizing of physical production arrangement to foster a specific purpose such as storage or sales is
A. Functional layout
B. Functional conflict
C. Managerial layout
D. Managerial conflict

199. The attitude that accepts both similarities and differences among countries and takes a balanced view towards the management of operations in every nation is
A. Geocentric   B. Ethnocentric
C. Egocentric   D. All the above

200. An educational or training activity in which a trainee is required to take decisions as if in real-life management problem and is then presented with the results of each decision is
A. Management game B. Business game
C. Both A and B   D. None of the above

ANSWERS

1	2	3	4	5	6	7	8	9	10
B	D	A	A	A	C	C	A	D	D
11	**12**	**13**	**14**	**15**	**16**	**17**	**18**	**19**	**20**
D	B	C	D	D	C	C	A	D	D
21	**22**	**23**	**24**	**25**	**26**	**27**	**28**	**29**	**30**
C	A	A	D	B	A	B	B	B	C
31	**32**	**33**	**34**	**35**	**36**	**37**	**38**	**39**	**40**
C	B	B	C	C	A	A	C	D	A

41	42	43	44	45	46	47	48	49	50
B	D	A	B	D	A	A	B	A	A

51	52	53	54	55	56	57	58	59	60
D	A	A	D	A	A	D	D	A	A

61	62	63	64	65	66	67	68	69	70
B	D	A	A	A	D	A	A	D	A

71	72	73	74	75	76	77	78	79	80
C	B	A	C	A	D	A	D	D	A

81	82	83	84	85	86	87	88	89	90
B	C	B	C	A	D	B	A	B	A

91	92	93	94	95	96	97	98	99	100
C	C	A	C	A	C	A	A	C	A

101	102	103	104	105	106	107	108	109	110
D	C	B	A	A	C	A	B	A	D

111	112	113	114	115	116	117	118	119	120
A	A	D	D	D	A	C	B	A	C

121	122	123	124	125	126	127	128	129	130
A	D	A	B	C	A	A	B	A	A

131	132	133	134	135	136	137	138	139	140
C	A	B	C	A	B	C	C	C	A

141	142	143	144	145	146	147	148	149	150
B	B	C	D	A	A	A	B	D	D

151	152	153	154	155	156	157	158	159	160
B	C	D	C	B	A	A	B	C	A

161	162	163	164	165	166	167	168	169	170
A	A	B	C	B	B	A	A	C	B

171	172	173	174	175	176	177	178	179	180
C	D	B	B	C	A	B	A	B	A

181	182	183	184	185	186	187	188	189	190
C	A	B	C	B	A	C	B	C	A

191	192	193	194	195	196	197	198	199	200
B	B	B	B	A	D	B	A	A	C

❖—❖—❖

2

Human Resource Development (HRD)

HRD: CONCEPT, IMPORTANCE, EVOLUTION, FUNCTION

The field of HRD or Human Resource Development encompasses several aspects of enabling and empowering human resources in organization. Whereas earlier HRD was denoted as managing people in organizations with emphasis on payroll, training and other functions that were designed to keep employees happy, the current line of management thought focuses on empowering and enabling them to become employees capable of fulfilling their aspirations and actualizing their potential. This shift in the way, human resources are treated has come about the sources of competitive advantage and not merely employees fulfilling their job responsibilities. The point here is that the current paradigm in HRD treats employees as value creators and assets based on the **RBV or the Resource Based View** of the firm that has emerged in the SHRM (Strategic Human Resource Management) field.

Further, the field of HRD now has taken on a role that goes beyond employee satisfaction and instead, the focus now is on ensuring that employees are delighted with the working conditions and perform their jobs according to their latent potential which is brought to the forefront. This has resulted that the HRD manager and the employees of the HRD department becoming partners in the organization's progress instead of just yet another line function. Further, the HR managers now routinely interact with the functional managers and the people managers to ensure high levels of job satisfaction and fulfillment. The category of people managers is a role that has been created in many multinational companies like Fidelity and IBM to specifically look into the personality related aspects of employees and to ensure that they bring the best to the table.

Finally, HRD is no longer just about payroll or timekeeping and leave tracking, directors of HRD in companies like Infosys are much sought after their inputs into the whole range of activities spanning the function and they are expected to add value rather than just consume resources.

Theories of HRD

When the field of management science and organizational behaviour was in its infancy, the HRD function was engaged as a department whose sole role was to look after payroll and wage negotiation. This was in the era of the assembly line and manufacturing where the HRD function's purpose was to check the attendance of the employees, process their pay and benefits and act as a mediator in disputes between the management and the workers.

Simultaneous with the rise of the services sector and the proliferation of technology and financial services companies, the role of the HRD function changed correspondingly.

The shift in the way the human resources were viewed as yet another factor of production to being viewed as sources of competitive advantage and the chief determinant of profits was mainly due to the changing perceptions of the workforce being central to the organization's strategy. For instance, many software and tech companies as well as other companies in the service sector routinely identify their employees as the chief assets and something that can give them competitive advantage over their rivals. Hence, the HRD function in these sectors has evolved from basic duties and is now looked upon as a critical support function.

With the advent of globalization and the opening up of the economies of several nations, there was again a shift in the way the HRD function was conceptualized. In line with the view of the resources as being international and ethnically diverse, the HRD function was thought of to be the bridge between the different employees in multiple locations and the management. Further, the present conceptualization also means that employees have to be not only motivated but also empowered and enabled to help them actualize their potential. The point here is that no longer were employees being treated like any other asset. On the contrary, they were the center of attraction and attention in the changed paradigm. This called for the HRD function to be envisaged as fulfilling a role that was aimed at enabling and empowering employees instead of being just mediators and negotiators.

Finally, the theory of HRD also morphed with the times and in recent years, there has been a perceptible shift in the way the HRD function that has come to encompass the extent of activities ranging from routine tasks like hiring and training and payroll to actually being the function that plays a critical and crucial role in the employee development. The theory has also transformed the function from being bystanders to the organizational processes to one where the HRD function is the layer between the management and employees to ensure that the decisions made at the top are communicated to the employees and the feedback from the employees is likewise communicated to the top.

Purpose of HRD

HRD is about adult human beings functioning in productive systems. The purpose of HRD is to focus on the resource that humans bring to the success equation in both personal success and organizational success.

The two core threads of HRD are:

(1) Individual and organizational learning and

(2) Individual and organizational performance (Ruona, 2000; Watkins & Marsick, 1996; Swanson, 1996a). Some view learning and performance as alternatives or rivals, while most see them as partners in a formula for success. Thus, assessment of HRD successes or results can be categorized into the domains of learning and performance. In all cases the intent is improvement.

Definition

HRD is a process for developing and unleashing human expertise through organization development and personnel training and development for the purpose of improving performance.

"Human Resource Development is any process or activity that, either initially or over the long term, has the potential to develop adults' work-based knowledge, expertise, productivity, and satisfaction, whether for personal or group/team gain, or for the benefit of an organization, community, nation, or, ultimately, the whole of humanity" (McLean & McLean, 2000).

Evolution

Evolution of Personnel management started in 19th century at that time there was a booming industrialization which leads to increase in franchising and influence of trade unions and harshness of industrial condition called for the better of industrial condition.

Human resource management emerged from personnel management and personnel management emerged from manpower planning. The consideration of changes taking place in managing human resource led to adaptation of strategic HRM the consideration of strategy and HRM system jointly led to the emergence of strategic human resource management SHRM which is crucial for achieving a corporation's long term goal. The historical evolution of HRM and changing roles of HR professional from time to time in order to considered employees as important assets which help in attaining goals of the organization. The fact that SHRM is not only PM or HRM but people are to be considered for modern industrialization that is to be used for creating and sustaining competitive advantage for the firm.

Origins of HRD

It is easy to logically connect the origins of HRD to the history of humankind and the training required to survive or advance. While HRD is a relatively new term, training the largest component of HRD can be tracked back through evolution of the human race. The field's history provides the long-range view of the profession. For now, it is important to recognize the massive development effort that took place in the United States during World War II as the origin of contemporary HRD.

Under the name of the "Training within Industry" project (Dooley, 1945), this massive development effort gave birth to systematic, (1) performance-based training, (2) improvement of work processes, and (3) the improvement of human relations in the workplace as contemporary HRD.

The brief interpretation of what motivates and frames the HRD profession is:

1. *Organizations are human-made entities that rely on human expertise to establish and achieve their goals.* This belief acknowledges that organizations are changeable and vulnerable. Organizations have been created by humankind and can soar or crumble, and HRD is intricately connected to the fate of any organization.

2. *Human expertise is developed and maximized through HRD processes and should be done for the mutual long- and/or short-term benefits of the sponsoring organization and the individuals involved.* HRD professionals have powerful tools available to get others to think, accept, and act. The ethical concern is

that these tools not been used for exploitation but rather for the benefit of all.

3. *HRD professionals are advocates of individual/ group, work process, and organizational integrity.* HRD professionals typically have a very privileged position of accessing information that transcends the boundaries and levels of individuals, groups, work processes, and the organization. Getting rich information and seeing things that others may not have a chance to see also carries a responsibility. At times harmony is required, and at other times the blunt truth is required.

Gilley and Maycunich (2000, pp. 79-89) have set forth a set of principles that guide the HRD. They contend that effective HRD practice

- integrates eclectic theoretical disciplines;
- is based on satisfying stakeholders' needs and expectations;
- is responsive but responsible;
- uses evaluation as a continuous improvement process;
- is designed to improve organization effectiveness;
- relies on relationship mapping to enhance operational efficiency;
- is linked to the organization's strategic business goals and objectives;
- is based on partnerships;
- is results oriented;
- assumes credibility as essential;
- utilizes strategic planning to help the organization integrate vision, mission, strategy, and practice;
- relies on the analysis process to identify priorities;
- is based on purposeful and meaningful measurement; and
- promotes diversity and equity in the workplace.

Most sets of principles are based on core beliefs that may or may not be made explicit. The pressures for stating principles of practice are greater than for stating over-arching core beliefs. Both have a place and deserve serious attention by the profession.

Function of HRD

The main functions of HRD are:

1. **Training and development:** Training and development is aimed at improving or changing the knowledge skills and attitudes of the employees. While training involves providing the knowledge and skills required for doing a particular job to the employees, developmental activities focus on preparing the employees for future job responsibilities by increasing the capabilities of an employee which also helps him perform his present job in a better way. These activities start when an employee joins an organization in the form of orientation and skills training. After the employee becomes proficient, the HR activities focus on the development of the employee through methods like coaching and counseling.

2. **Organization developments:** OD is the process of increasing the effectiveness of an organization along with the well being of its members with the help of planned interventions that use the concepts of behavioural science. Both micro and macro changes are implemented to achieve organization development. While the macro changes are intended to improve the overall effectiveness of the organization the micro changes are aimed at individuals of small groups. Employee involvement programmes requiring fundamental changes in work expectation, reporting, procedures and reward systems are aimed at improving the effectiveness of the organization. The human resource development professional involved in the organization development intervention acts as an agent of change. He often consults and advising the line manager in strategies that can be adopted to implement the required changes and sometimes becomes directly involve in implementing these strategies.

3. **Career development:** It is a continuous process in which an individual progresses through different stages of career each having a relatively unique set of issues and tasks. Career development comprises of two distinct processes—Career Planning and Career Management. Whereas career planning involves activities to be performed by the employee, often with the help of counselor and others, to assess his capabilities and skills in order to frame realistic career plan. Career management involves the necessary steps that need to be taken to achieve that plan. Career management generally focuses more on the steps that an organization that can take to foster the career development of the employees.

HRD as a Disipline and a Professional Field of Practice

The HRD profession is large and widely recognized. As with any applied field that exists in a large number and variety of organizations, HRD can take on a variety of names and roles. This can be confusing to those outside the profession and even sometimes confusing to those in the profession. We take the position that this variation is not always bad, and HRD, embracing the thinking underlying

- Training,
- Training and development,
- Employee development,
- Technical training,
- Management development,
- Executive and leadership development,
- Human performance technology,
- Organization development, and
- Organizational learning.

Thus, practitioners who work in HRD may have varying titles such as manager of management development, organization development specialist and director of technical training.

In addition, HRD roles can span the organization such as the chief learning officer, director of organizational effectiveness, or director of executive development. They can also fit within a subunit such as manager of sales, training, HRD coordinator (at a particular company location), or bank teller training specialist. Furthermore, a very large contingent in organizations is doing HRD work as part of their non-HRD jobs. For these people, HRD work is part of their larger job. It is almost impossible to calculate the total organizational commitment to HRD. Reports of chief executive officers leading executive development programs and shipping clerks doing on-the-job training of new employees are commonplace.

Estimates in the United States have led enormous financial numbers spent annually to conceptual comparisons. For example, it is estimated that the money spent on HRD in the workplace each year exceeds all the money spent on public education— kindergarten through universities, in the same time period. By any assessment, HRD is a huge profession with a huge annual expenditure.

We also see HRD as overlapping with the theory and practice underlying other closely linked domains, including the following:

● Career development
● Organizational and process effectiveness
● Performance improvement
● Strategic organizational planning
● Human resource management (HRM)
● Human resources (HR)

Probably the most apparent connection is with human resources (HR). HR can be conceived of as having two major components: HRD and HRM. As an umbrella term, HR is often confused with HRM. Thus, many HR departments are actually limited to HRM goals and activities such as hiring, compensation, and personnel compliance issues. Even when HRD and HRM are managed under the HR title, their relative foci tend to be fairly discrete.

HRD versus Personnel Function

The traditional personnel function is a service oriented activity, responding to the needs of the organization as and when they arise. On the other hand, HRD has productive functions which do not merely respond to organizational requirements but anticipates them and prepares the people and the organizations to face future challenges with confidence. HRD is wider in scope as it tries to develop the whole organization instead of focusing attention on people alone. Instead of concentrating on maintenance factors (wages, incentives, day to

day plans, operating procedures etc.) it tries to focus on motivating factors (job enrichment, developing potentialities of people, creating autonomous work groups, fostering innovation and creativity, developing trust etc). Personnel function, traditionally is viewed as the primary job of personnel department HRD, however, is the responsibility of all managers in the organization. The personnel function views higher morale and improved job satisfaction as the causes of improved performance. HRD on the other hand regards job challenges, creativity and opportunities for development as the main motivating forces.

Points of difference HRD and Personnel

Personnel Function

(1) Maintenance oriented
(2) An independent function with independent sub functions
(3) Reactive functions responding to events as and when they take place
(4) Exclusive responsibility of personnel department
(5) Emphases is put on monetary rewards
(6) Improved performances is the result of improved satisfaction and morale
(7) Tries to improve the efficiency of people and administration.

HRD (Human Resource Development)

(1) Development oriented
(2) Consists of inter-dependent parts.
(3) Proactive function, trying to anticipate and get ready with appropriate responses.
(4) Responsibility of all managers in the organization.
(5) Emphasis is on higher order needs such as — how to design jobs with stretch pull and challenge how to improve creativity and problem solving skills, how to empower people in all respects etc.
(6) Better use of human resources leads to improved satisfaction and morale.
(7) It tries to develop the organization and its culture as a whole.

ORGANIZATION OF HRD FUNCTION

In an organizational context, group think and group behaviour are important concepts as they determine the cohesiveness and coherence of the organizational culture and organizational communication. For instance, unless the HRD function communicates the policies clearly and cogently, the employees would not participate and comply with them wholeheartedly. Hence, molding group behaviour is important for organizations. However, this cannot be construed to mean that all employees must think and act alike. On the contrary, innovation cannot happen when group behaviour is the same across all levels. The point here is that while organizations must strive for cohesiveness and coherence, they must not sacrifice the principles of individual creativity and brilliance that are at the heart of organizational change and innovation. In these turbulent times, there is a need for individuals to take a stand and be firm on the direction that the organization seeks to take.

Of course, **group behaviour needs to be inculcated in organizations for the simple reason that employees must conform to the rules and regulations that govern organizations**. Hence, there is a need for uniformity and consistency in the way organizational group behaviour has to be molded. Towards this end, group think and group behavior must be encouraged by the HRD function as a means to ensure cohesiveness in the organization.

In the technology sector, we often find employees straight out of campuses behaving as though they are still in education institution. While some of this freethinking and freewheeling spirit is good for innovation, the HRD function must guard against the tendency to be offhand with the organizational rules and procedures. Further, competitiveness can be encouraged but it should not come at the expense of collaboration and cooperation that are at the heart of organizational success.

On the flip side, group behaviour can be detrimental to the organizational health as well. This happens when the decisions of the top management are not challenged or are followed blindly leading to the leadership thinking that whatever they do is right. It does not mean to say that there must be fractious fights in the organization. On the other hand, there must be a space for free expression of ideas and thoughts and true democratic decision-making ought to take place.

Finally, group think can be a powerful motivator as well as inhibitor. The motivating aspect happens, because of group think; employees feel bonding with their peers and colleagues and hence ensure that they give their best to the job. The inhibitor works when employees feel that their individual creativity and brilliance are being sacrificed at the altar of conformity. Hence, the leadership as well as the HRD function has their task cut out to ensure that group behaviour does more good than harm. There is a need for a sensibility to, awareness of and balanced approach towards group behaviour to leverage the individual creativity and at the same time not sacrifice organizational cohesiveness and coherence.

Motivation is one of the most important concepts in HRD. In most organizations, it is common to hear the refrain that a particular employee is not motivated and hence his or her performance has taken a backseat. This is the reason companies spend humungous amounts of money in arranging for training sessions and recreational events to motivate the employees. Motivation can be understood as the desire or drive that an individual has to get the work done. For instance, when faced with a task, it is the motivation to accomplish it that determines whether a particular individual would complete the task according to the requirements or not. Further, the absence of motivation leads to underperformance and loss of competitiveness resulting in loss of productive resources for the organization. It is for this reason that the HR managers stress on the employees having high levels of motivation to get the job done.

There are many theories of motivation and the ones being discussed here are:

Herzberg's hygiene theory states that for employees to be motivated, certain conditions need to exist and the absence of these conditions or the hygiene factors demotivate the employees. The point that is being made in this theory is that the presence of hygiene factors is a precondition for performance and is not a determinant of performance. On the other hand, the absence of these factors actually demotivates the employee. Hence, the bottom line is that companies should have the basic conditions under which employees work fulfilled so that there is no drag on the performance.

Maslow's need hierarchy theory postulates that individuals are motivated according to a hierarchy of needs which start from satisfaction of basic needs and then go on to need for recognition and finally, the need to actualize one's vision and reach the highest stage of personality. The point that is being made in the theory is that individual's progress from one stage to the other depending on how well the needs at each stage are met. So, organizations have to ensure that employees' needs are taken care of at each level so that by the time the employee reaches the top of the ladder, he or she is in a position to actualize them.

Finally, **McGregor's theory of motivation** alludes to the carrot and stick approach that is favoured by many managers. This theory states that employees can be motivated by a dual pronged strategy of rewarding them for good work and punishing them for bad work. The opposites of these reactions mean that employees have a strong incentive to do well as opposed to doing badly.

Motivation of employees is indeed important for the health of the companies. Only when employees are motivated sufficiently can they give their best. Typically, companies focus on compensation and perks and benefits as a strategy to motivate employees. However, as we have seen in this article, employees are motivated by factors other than pay and hence, the HRD function must take cognizance of this fact and proceed accordingly. This means that the need for job satisfaction and fulfillment have to be taken care of as well for the employees to reach their potential.

It is the practice in many organizations to conduct training programs periodically for their employees. Often, these training programs are conducted to enhance on the job skills and to

enable the employees to pick up valuable soft skills. Further, the training programs can be technical/job oriented or human resource skills oriented. For instance, it is common in technology companies and especially the big companies to provide a mandatory portion of training measured in hours per quarter for each employee. What these points add up to is the fact that organizational training is taken seriously in many companies. However, an aspect that is often sidelined is the effectiveness of the training programs and their linkage to organizational goals. This aspect makes the training programs lose their purpose and drains precious resources as well as waste of employee time that could have been used productively.

Organizations need to link training programs to Specific, Measurable, and Achievable, Realistic and Time Bound goals or the so-called SMART goals that is a proven method for ensuring that organizational goals are met. To explain, training programs have to be aimed at specific goals like training on a particular skill (technical or soft skill).

Conducting trainings on collection topics like leadership without focus on specific goals would render them useless. Next, the outputs from the training programs have to be measurable meaning that an exit test must be held at the end of the training program to assess the impact of the training program on employees. Further, the training programs have to have realistic goals like quantum jumps in skills and not aim for drastic improvements to the skill levels of the employee. The point here is that this focused approach to training pays off better than conducting trainings where the employees think more about what to do when they head back to their desks or are distracted by too many concepts being thrown at them.

Finally, training programs are time bound as mentioned earlier. This means that employees have to be trained periodically so that they retain their competitiveness and their edge and not become obtuse or blunted in their job. The reason for alluding to the SMART goals is that this tool has been proved to be effective in ensuring that organizational goals are linked to training programs and that the training programs are not vague or unconnected to the big picture. In some companies, it is common for employees to be trained offsite on experiential and exercise based training which involves physical activity. However, one should not miss the forest for the trees (literally as many of these experiential trainings happen in resorts in wooded and outskirts) and lose track of the larger goals for which the employees are being trained. The point here is that the SMART goals must be applied here as well with emphasis on focused approach to organizational goals to be derived from the training.

- In conclusion, trainings that are done without purpose or focus end up wasting the employees' time as well as drain of organizational resources. Hence, the aim that the HRD must strive for is to maximize the effectiveness of the training programs and increase the gains from such training.

- The practice of HRD is dominated by positive intentions for improving the expertise and performance of individuals, work groups, work process, and the overall organization. Most observers suggest that HRD evokes common sense thinking and actions. This perspective has good and bad consequences. One good consequence is the ease with which people are willing to contribute and participate in HRD processes. One bad consequence is that many of the people working in the field have little more than common sense to rely on.

- The underlying thinking and supporting evidence that allow HRD professionals to accept and apply sound theories and tools confidently. Such a foundation has the potential of ridding the profession of frivolous and invalid armchair theories and faddish practices.

PERFORMANCE APPRAISAL

Performance Appraisal is the systematic evaluation of the performance of employees and to understand the abilities of a person for further growth and development. Performance appraisal is generally done in systematic ways which are as follows:

1. The supervisors measure the pay of employees and compare it with targets and plans.

2. The supervisor analyses the factors behind work performances of employees.

3. The employers are in position to guide the employees for a better performance.

Objectives of Performance Appraisal

Performance Appraisal can be done with following objectives in mind:

1. To maintain records in order to determine compensation packages, wage structure, salaries raises, etc.

2. To identify the strengths and weaknesses of employees to place right men on right job.

3. To maintain and assess the potential present in a person for further growth and development.

4. To provide a feedback to employees regarding their performance and related status.

5. It serves as a basis for influencing working habits of the employees.

6. To review and retain the promotional and other training programmes.

Advantages of Performance Appraisal

It is said that performance appraisal is an investment for the company which can be justified by following advantages:

1. **Promotion:** Performance Appraisal helps the supervisors to sketch out the promotion programmes for efficient employees. In this regards, inefficient workers can be dismissed or demoted in case.

2. **Compensation:** Performance Appraisal helps in chalking out compensation packages for employees. Merit rating is possible through performance appraisal. Performance Appraisal tries to give worth to a performance. Compensation packages which include bonus, high salary rates, extra benefits, allowances and pre-requisites are dependent on performance appraisal. The criteria should be merit rather than seniority.

3. **Employees Development:** The systematic procedure of performance appraisal helps the supervisors to frame training policies and programmes. It helps to analyze strengths and

weaknesses of employees so that new jobs can be designed for efficient employees. It also helps in framing future development programmes.

4. **Selection Validation:** Performance Appraisal helps the supervisors to understand the validity and importance of the selection procedure. The supervisors come to know the validity and thereby the strengths and weaknesses of selection procedure. Future changes in selection methods can be made in this regard.

5. **Communication:** For an organization, effective communication between employees and employers is very important. Through performance appraisal, communication can be sought for in the following ways:

   a. Through performance appraisal, the employers can understand and accept skills of subordinates.

   b. The subordinates can also understand and create a trust and confidence in superiors.

   c. It also helps in maintaining cordial and congenial labour management relationship.

   d. It develops the spirit of work and boosts the morale of employees.

   All the above factors ensure effective communication.

6. **Motivation:** Performance appraisal serves as a motivation tool. Through evaluating performance of employees, a person's efficiency can be determined if the targets are achieved. This very well motivates a person for better job and helps him to improve his performance in the future.

Performance Appraisal Tools and Techniques

Following are the tools used by the organizations for Performance Appraisals of their employees.

1. Ranking
2. Paired Comparison
3. Forced Distribution
4. Confidential Report
5. Essay Evaluation
6. Critical Incident
7. Checklists
8. Graphic Rating Scale
9. BARS
10. Forced Choice Method
11. MBO
12. Field Review Technique

Performance Test

We will be discussing the important **performance appraisal tools and techniques** in detail.

Ranking Method

The ranking system requires the rater to rank his subordinates on overall performance. This consists in simply putting a man in a rank order. Under this method, the ranking of an employee in a work group is done against that of another employee. The relative position of each employee is tested in terms of his numerical rank. It may also be done by ranking a person on his job performance against another member of the competitive group.

Advantages of Ranking Method

   a. Employees are ranked according to their performance levels.

   b. It is easier to rank the best and the worst employee.

Limitations of Ranking Method

   a. The "whole man" is compared with another "whole man" in this method. In practice, it is very difficult to compare individuals possessing various individual traits.

   b. This method speaks only of the position where an employee stands in his group. It does not test anything about how much better or how much worse an employee is when compared to another employee.

   c. When a large number of employees are working, ranking of individuals become a difficult issue.

   d. There is no systematic procedure for ranking individuals in the organization. The ranking system does not eliminate the possibility of snap judgements.

Forced Distribution Method

This is a ranking technique where raters are required to allocate a certain percentage of rates to certain categories (e.g.: superior, above average, average) or percentiles (e.g.: top 10 percent, bottom 20 percent etc). Both the number of categories and percentage of employees to be allotted to each category are a function of performance appraisal design and format. The workers of outstanding merit may be placed at top 10 percent of the scale; the rest may be placed as 20 % good, 40 % outstanding, 20 % fair and 10 % fair.

Advantages of Forced Distribution
a. This method tends to eliminate raters bias
b. By forcing the distribution according to pre-determined percentages, the problem of making use of different raters with different scales is avoided.

Limitations of Forced Distribution
- The limitation of using this method in salary administration, however, is that it may lead low morale, low productivity and high absenteeism.

Employees who feel that they are productive, but find themselves in lower grade (than expected) feel frustrated and exhibit over a period of time reluctance to work.

Critical Incident Techniques
Under this method, the manager prepares lists of statements of very effective and ineffective behaviour of an employee. These critical incidents or events represent the outstanding or poor behaviour of employees or the job. The manager maintains logs of each employee, whereby he periodically records critical incidents of the workers behaviour. At the end of the rating period, these recorded critical incidents are used in the evaluation of the worker's performance. Example of a good critical incident of a Customer Relations Officer is: March 12, The Officer patiently attended to a customer's complaint. He was very polite and prompts in attending the customer's problem.

Advantages of Critical Incident techniques
a. This method provides an objective basis for conducting a thorough discussion of an employee's performance.
b. This method avoids recency bias (most recent incidents are too much emphasized).

Limitations of Critical Incident techniques
- Negative incidents may be more noticeable than positive incidents.
- The supervisors have a tendency to unload a series of complaints about the incidents during an annual performance review sessions.
- It results in very close supervision which may not be liked by an employee.
- The recording of incidents may be a chore for the manager concerned, who may be too busy or may forget to do it.

Checklists and Weighted Checklists
In this system, a large number of statements that describe a specific job are given. Each statement has a weight or scale value attached to it. While rating an employee the supervisor checks all those statements that most closely describe the behaviour of the individual under assessment. The rating sheet is then scored by averaging the weights of all the statements checked by the rater. A checklist is constructed for each job by having persons who are quite familiar with the jobs. These statements are then categorized by the judges and weights are assigned to the statements in accordance with the value attached by the judges.

Advantages of Checklists and Weighted Checklists
a. Most frequently used method in evaluation of the employee's performance.

Limitations of Checklists and Weighted Checklists
- This method is very expensive and time consuming.
- Rater may be biased in distinguishing the positive and negative questions.
- It becomes difficult for the manager to assemble, analyze and weigh a number of statements about the employee's characteristics, contributions and behaviours.
- Performance appraisals biasis.

Managers commit mistakes while evaluating employees and their performance. Biases and judgement errors of various kinds may spoil the performance appraisal process. Bias here refers to inaccurate distortion of a measurement. These are:

1. **First Impression (primacy effect):** Raters form an overall impression about the rate on

the basis of some particular characteristics of the rate identified by them. The identified qualities and features may not provide adequate base for appraisal.

2. **Halo Effect:** The individual's performance is completely appraised on the basis of a perceived positive quality, feature or trait. In other words this is the tendency to rate a man uniformly high or low in other traits if he is extra-ordinarily high or low in one particular trait. If a worker has few absences, his supervisor might give him a high rating in all other areas of work.

3. **Horn Effect:** The individual's performance is completely appraised on the basis of a negative quality or feature perceived. This results in an overall lower rating than may be warranted. "He is not formally dressed up in the office. He may be casual at work too!".

4. **Excessive Stiffness or Lenience:** Depending upon the raters own standards, values and physical and mental makeup at the time of appraisal, rate may be rated very strictly or leniently. Some of the managers are likely to take the line of least resistance and rate people high, whereas others, by nature, believe in the tyranny of exact assessment, considering more particularly the drawbacks of the individual and thus making the assessment excessively severe. The leniency error can render a system ineffective. If everyone is to be rated high, the system has not done anything to differentiate among the employees.

5. **Central Tendency:** Appraisers rate all employees as average performers. That is, it is an attitude to rate people as neither high nor low and follow the middle path. For example, a professor, with a view to play it safe, might give a class grade near the equal to B, regardless of the differences in individual performances.

6. **Personal Biases:** The way a supervisor feels about each of the individuals working under him — whether he likes or dislikes them as a tremendous effect on the rating of their performances. Personal Bias can stem from various sources as a result of information obtained from colleagues, considerations of faith and thinking, social and family background and so on.

7. **Spillover Effect:** The present performance is evaluated much on the basis of past performance. "The person who was a good performer in distant past is assured to be okay at present also".

8. **Recency Effect:** Rating is influenced by the most recent behaviour ignoring the commonly demonstrated behaviours during the entire appraisal period.

Therefore while appraising performances; all the above biases should be avoided.

360 degree feedback: 360 degree feedback is also known as multi-rater feedback or multi-dimensional feedback or multi-source feedback. It is a very good means of improving an individual's effectiveness (as a leader and as a manager). It is a system by which an individual gets a comprehensive/collective feedback from his superiors, subordinates, peers/co-workers, customers and various other members with whom he interacts. The feedback form is in a questionnaire format, which contains questions that are significant to both individual as well as organization from performance aspect. It is filled by anonymous people. The number of people from whom feedback is taken can range from 6-20. The individual's own feedback is also taken, *i.e.*, he self-rates himself and then his rating is compared with other individuals ratings. Self ratings compel the individual to sit down and think about his own strengths and weaknesses.

The primary aim of a 360 degree feedback is to assist an individual to identify his strengths and build upon them, to recognize priority fields of improvement, to encourage communication and people's participation at all levels in an organization, to examine the acceptance of any change by the employees in an organization and to promote self-development in an individual. It must be noted that the assessment of individual by other people is subjective. A 360-degree feedback is challenging, promoting and analytical. It should not be regarded as ultimate and concluding. It is a beginning point. Self-assessment is an ongoing process.

360 degree feedback provides a comprehensive view of the skills and competencies of the individual as a manager or as a leader. The individual gets a feedback on how other people perceive and assess him as an employee. 360 degree feedback is beneficial to both an individual as well as organization. It leads to pooling of information between individual and other organizational members. It encourages teamwork as there is full involvement of all the top managers and other individuals in the organization. It stresses upon internal customer satisfaction. It develops an environment of continuous learning in an organization. Based on a 360 degree feedback, the individual goals and the group goals can be correlated to the organizational strategy, *i.e.*, the individual and the group can synchronize their goals with the organizational goals.

The feedback must be confidential so as to ensure its reliability and legitimacy. The feedback must be accepted with positivity and an open-mind. The effectiveness of the feedback must be evaluated and analyzed on a regular basis.

Advantages of 360 Degree Feedback

- It is an effective medium for improving customer service and the inputs quality to the internal customers.
- It encourages participation of all and thus makes HR decisions more qualitative.
- It pinpoints the favouritism and biases of the supervisors present in conventional appraisal systems.
- The employees find 360 degree feedback more acceptable than the traditional feedback approaches.
- 360 degree feedback is more impartial and objective than a one-to-one assessment of employee traits.
- It concentrates and stresses upon internal customer satisfaction.
- It broadens the scope for employees to get various says for enhancing their job role, performance, and views.

- It can act as a supplement and not replacement to the conventional appraisal system.
- It can be motivating for the employees who undervalue themselves.
- It encourages teamwork.
- It is more credible as various people give almost same feedback from various sources.
- It brings into limelight the areas of employee development as it confirms the employee strengths and identifies his weaknesses on which he can work upon.
- It creates an environment of trust and loyalty in an organization.

Basics and Pre-requisites of 360 Degree Approach

It is essential that an organization should be prepared for 360 Degree feedback. Not only the organization, but also the candidate (the employee) should be prepared for accepting it.

Following are the essentials of an organization's preparedness for the 360 degree approach:

- The top level management must be keen to spend their time and efforts in giving feedback to their subordinates.
- Status and ego issues shouldn't overwhelm in the organization.
- The subordinates and the peer both should assess and analyze the top-level managers and the top-level management should be open to accept their feedback.
- Everyone in the organization should take the feedback considerately and constructively and utilize it for their development.
- Ethics and moral values should be predominant in the organization.
- The organization should encourage teamwork.
- There should be self-learning in the organization, especially for the managers.
- The personnel department of the organization should be highly credible.
- There should be no politics in the organization.
- Everyone in the organization should take the feedback seriously and should make an attempt to benefit from the same.

● It must be ensured that the feedback is confidential.

Following are the essentials of analyzing the candidate's (employee's) preparedness for the 360 degree approach:

● The employee should have an intention to be better.

● The employee should be open to accept the feedback and should respect the views of others.

● The employee should have a competitive feeling.

● The employee should be keen in knowing the viewpoints of others towards him.

● The employee should always learn on the job.

TRAINING AND DEVELOPMENT

Whenever training programs have to be conducted, there needs to be an assessment of the training needs which needs to preclude everything else. Assessment of the training needs should be done in an elaborate and methodical manner and should be comprehensive. Before we discuss how training needs are to be assessed, we need to understand what training needs are. To start with, employees in any organization often have to upgrade their skills or learn new skills to remain competitive on the job. This means that they need to be trained on the latest technologies or whatever skill is needed for them to get the job done. Further, employees moving up the ladder might need to be trained on managerial skills and leadership skills. All this means that each employee has a real need to get trained on either technical skills or soft skills. These form the basis for the training needs which need to be identified and acted upon.

● **Once training needs are identified, then the HRD function must prepare a checklist of employees and a matrix of each employee and his or her training needs.** This would give them a scientific method to assess how many employees need to be trained on what skill and whether they have the quorum necessary to conduct the trainings.

● Further, this matrix would help them in planning for the trainings in a structured and well thought out manner. There is another aspect here and that relates to the identification of training needs done by employees and their managers. The point here is that the specific needs that are identified by the managers might be different from those articulated by the employees. Hence, a gap analysis needs to be done which tallies both these and adds to the matrix discussed above.

● The third aspect is when the training needs are finalized and the process of preparing for the actual trainings starts, the HRD function must use the matrix of needs to identify those that are compatible with the organizational goals and prepare a final list of training needs that can be circulated to the managers for their approval. There are many back and forth discussions involved in this process because of the perceptual gaps that are common to organizational culture and organizational behaviour. After this, the training programs must be selected which would address these training needs and would be the catalysts for actualizing the training needs and satiating them.

● Finally, training needs vary from organization to organization and from employee to employee. There is no point in making all employees undergo specialized trainings and at the same time, there is the need to train all employees on the skills that they need to do their job well. So, the HRD function must be astute to recognize this asymmetry and hence their capability and understanding of the situation makes the difference between successful training programs and those that meander and ramble their way through.

● In conclusion, training is a basic aspect of any job and hence, the HRD functions in organizations must pay enough attention and thought to the process. Only where there is a comprehensive plan in place to train employees according to their needs and the alignment of these needs with organizational goals would ensure true progress for the organizations.

- Training methods pertain to the types of training that can be provided to employees to sharpen their existing skills and learn new skills. The skills that they learn can be technical or soft skills and for all categories of skills, some training methods are suggested here. The training methods can range from onsite classroom based ones, training at the office during which employees might or might not check their work.

- Experiential training methods which are conducted in resorts and other places where there is room for experiential learning.

- Training methods include many types of training tools and techniques and the commonly employed tools and techniques. For instance, it is common for trainers to use a variety of tools like visual and audio aids, study material, props and other enactment of scene based material and finally, the experiential tools that include sports and exercise equipment.

- If we take the first aspect of the different training methods that are location based, we would infer from the explanation that these training methods include the specific location based ones and would range from classroom training done at the trainers' location to the ones done on the office premises.

- Further, the experiential training methods can include use of resorts and other nature based locations so that employees can get the experience of learning through practice or the act itself rather than through study material. It needs to be remembered that the trainings conducted in the office premises often involve employees taking breaks to check their work and hence might not be ideal from the point of view of the organizations. However, provision can be done to locate the training rooms away from the main buildings so that employees can be trained in a relaxed manner. For instance, Infosys has training centers that are exclusively built for training and these centers give the employees enough scope and time for learning new skills.

- The next aspect of the training methods includes the use of visual and audio aids, study material, props and equipment. Depending on the kind of training that is being imparted, there can be a mechanism to use the appropriate tools and techniques based on the needs of the trainers and the trainees. The use of the training material often indicates the thoroughness of the training program and the amount of work that the trainers have put in to make the training successful. Of course, if the training material is good, it also means that the employees would benefit from the scope and depth of the material though they need to invest time and energy as well.

- Finally, the bottom line for any training to be successful is the synergy between the trainers and the trainees and this is where the HRD function can act as a facilitator for effective trainings and ensure that the trainers and trainees bond together and benefit in a mutual process of understanding and learning. In conclusion, there are various ways to approach trainings and some of the methods discussed above would be good starting points for follow up action and partnership between the training agencies and the organizations.

Many organizations have extensive training programs that cover all aspects of technical and soft skills. These trainings are conducted in such a way that employees get a mandatory number of hours of training every quarter or year. This is done to ensure that employees are enabled to perform their job duties to their potential. However, an aspect that needs elaboration is that more often than not, the training programs need to be implemented according to a rational consideration of training needs and moreover these training programs need to be evaluated for assessing their effectiveness. The point here is that training programs are conducted often without a clear articulation of training needs as well as not being implemented according to a set pattern. So, there are two aspects to training programs and they are to do with clear plan for implementation as well as potential evaluation of their effectiveness. To take the first aspect, training programs need to be implemented according to a careful consideration of training needs and the right training partners and the vendors have to be selected. This means that training programs are to be based according to the needs of the organization and not simply because there is a need for training to fill the mandatory number of hours.

- Apart from this, training programs need to be implemented based on a calendar that is drawn up taking into account the availability of participants. It is often the case that training programs are implemented without securing approvals from all the departments and divisions which mean that many potential participants would be unable to attend because they are busy with their work.

- The second aspect that needs to be considered is the evaluation of the effectiveness of the training programs that needs to be done based on how well the participants absorb the lessons and improve their skills. This can be done by conducting exit tests and other forms of assessment like presentation of case studies. These would help the trainers as well as the HRD department understand how well the training program succeeded in imparting knowledge and enhancing the skills of the participants. This is one way of ensuring that training is done that is pointed and focused and something which the participants would take seriously as well. There are many instances of training programs where the participants idle away their time and this has to be avoided and curbed as far as possible.

- Finally, training programs need to be conducted in organizations with a clear focus on linking them to organizational goals, selecting the right vendors, choosing a time that is convenient to all participants or at least a majority of them, publishing the training calendar in advance and most importantly, evaluating the effectiveness of the training programs by conducting exit tests and presentations to ensure that the lessons have been well received.

- In conclusion, it is not enough for HRD personnel to announce training programs and leave the rest to the trainers and participants. Instead, they need to play a proactive role in ensuring the success of the training programs by following these points that have been discussed here.

Training Programmes for Workers

Training and development is vital part of the human resource development. It is assuming ever important role in wake of the advancement of technology which has resulted in ever increasing competition, rise in customer's expectation of quality and service and a subsequent need to lower costs. It is also become more important globally in order to prepare workers for new jobs. In the current write up, we will focus more on the emerging need of training and development, its implications upon individuals and the employers.

Noted management author Peter Drucker said that the fastest growing industry would be training and development as a result of replacement of industrial workers with knowledge workers. In United States, for example, according to one estimate technology is de-skilling 75% of the population. This is true for the developing nations and for those who are on the threshold of development. In Japan for example, with increasing number of women joining traditionally male jobs, training is required not only to impart necessary job skills but also for preparing them for the physically demanding jobs. They are trained in everything from sexual harassment policies to the necessary job skills.

The Need for Training and Development

Before we say that technology is responsible for increased need of training inputs to employees, it is important to understand that there are other factors too that contribute to the latter. Training is also necessary for the individual development and progress of the employee, which motivates him to work for a certain organization apart from just money. We also require training update employees of the market trends, the change in the employment policies and other things.

The following are the two biggest factors that contribute to the increased need to training and development in organizations:

1. **Change:** The word change encapsulates almost everything. It is one of the biggest factors that contribute to the need of training and development. There is in fact a direct relationship between the two. Change leads to the need for training and development and training and development leads to individual and organizational change, and the cycle goes on and on. More specifically it is the technology that is driving the need; changing the way how businesses function, compete and deliver.

2. **Development:** It is again one the strong reasons for training and development becoming all the more important. Money is not the sole motivator at work and this is especially very true for the 21st century. People who work with organizations seek more than just employment out of their work; they look at holistic development of self. Spirituality and self awareness for example are gaining momentum world over. People seek happiness at jobs which may not be possible unless an individual is aware of the self. At Ford, for example, an individual can enroll himself / herself in a course on 'self awareness', which apparently seems inconsequential to ones performance at work but contributes to the spiritual well being of an individual which is all the more important.

The critical question however remains the implications and the contribution of training and development to the bottom line of organizations performance. To assume a leadership position in the market space, an organization will need to emphasize on the kind of programs they use to improvise performance and productivity and not just how much they simply spend on learning.

Training and development is one of the key HR functions. Most organizations look at training and development as an integral part of the human resource development activity. The turn of the century has seen increased focus on the same in organizations globally. Many organizations have mandated training hours per year for employees keeping in consideration the fact that technology is deskilling the employees at a very fast rate.

So what is training and development then? Is it really that important to organizational survival or they can survive without the former? Are training and development one and the same thing or are they different? Training may be described as an endeavour aimed to improve or develop additional competency or skills in an employee on the job one currently holds in order to increase the performance or productivity.

Technically training involves change in attitude, skills or knowledge of a person with the resultant improvement in the behaviour. For training to be effective it has to be a planned activity conducted after a thorough need analysis and target at certain competencies, most important it is to be conducted in a learning atmosphere.

While designing the training program it has to be kept in mind that both the individual goals and organizational goals are kept in mind. Although it may not be entirely possible to ensure a sync, but competencies are chosen in a way that a win-win is created for the employee and the organization.

Typically organizations prepare their training calendars at the beginning of the financial year where training needs are identified for the employees. This need identification called as 'training need analysis' is a part of the performance appraisal process. After need analysis the number of training hours, along with the training intervention are decided and the same is spread strategically over the next year.

Development

Lots of time training is confused with development, both is different in certain respects yet components of the same system. Development implies opportunities created to help employees grow. It is more of long term or futuristic in nature as opposed to training, which focus on the current job. It also is not limited to the job avenues in the current organization but may focus on other development aspects also.

For example, employees are expected to mandatorily attend training program on presentation skills however they are also free to choose a course on 'perspectives in leadership through literature'. Whereas the presentation skills program helps them on job, the literature based program may or may not help them directly.

Similarly many organizations choose certain employees preferentially for programs to develop them for future positions. This is done on the basis of existing attitude, skills and abilities, knowledge and performance of the employee. Most of the leadership programs tend to be of this nature with a vision of creating and nurturing leaders for tomorrow.

The major difference between training and development therefore is that while training focuses often on the current employee needs or competency gaps, development concerns itself with preparing people for future assignments and responsibilities.

With technology creating more unskilled workers and with industrial workers being replaced by knowledge workers, training and development is at the forefront of HRD. The onus is now on the human development department to take a proactive leadership role in responding to training and business needs.

Training is an expensive process not only in terms of the money spent on it but also the time and the other resources spent on the same. The most important question therefore is determining whether or not a need for training actually exists and whether the intervention will contribute to the achievement of organizational goal directly or indirectly? The answer to the above mentioned question lies in 'training needs analysis' which is the first step in the entire process of training and development.

Training needs analysis is a systematic process of understanding training requirements. It is conducted at three stages, at the level of organization, individual and the job, each of which

is called as the organizational, individual and job analysis. Once these analyses are over, the results are collated to arrive upon the objectives of the training program.

Another view of the training need is that, it is the discrepancy between 'what is' and 'what should be'. Taking cues from this the world bank conducted a needs analysis and arrived upon the conclusion that many of its units in eastern regions of Europe required transformation from state owned business to self sustaining organizations. A number of universities were then contacted to develop the necessary modules and conduct the training upon the same.

Although each step in the entire training process is unique in its own, needs analysis is special in that it lays the foundation for the kind of training required. The assessment gives insight into what kind of intervention is required, knowledge or skill or both. In certain cases where both of these are present and the performance is still missing then the problem may be motivational in nature. It thus highlights the need and the appropriate intervention which is essential to make the training effective.

QUALITY OF WORK LIFE

Meaning

There has been much concern today about decent wages, convenient working hours, conducive working conditions etc. Their term "Quality of work life" has appeared in research journals and the press in USA only in 1970s. There is no generally acceptable definition about this term. However, some attempts were made to describe the term quality of work life (QWL). It refers to the favourableness or unfavourableness of a job environment for people. QWL means different things to different people.

J. Richard and J. Loy define QWL as "the degree to which members of a work organization are able to satisfy important personnel needs through their experience in the organization."

Quality of work life improvements are defined as any activity which takes place at every level of an organization, which seeks greater organizational effectiveness through the enhancement of human dignity and growth ... a process through which the stockholders in the organization management, unions and employees learn how to work together better to determine for themselves what actions, changes and improvements are desirable and workable in order to achieve the twin and simultaneous goals of an improved quality of life at work for all members of the organization and greater effectiveness for both the company and the unions.

Richard E. Walton explains quality of work life in terms of eight broad conditions of employment that constitute desirable quality of work life. He proposed the same criteria for measuring QWL. Those criteria include:

(i) **Adequate and Fair Compensation:** There are different opinions about adequate compensation. The committee on Fair Wages defined fair wage as "... the wage which is above the minimum wage, but below the living wage."

(ii) **Safe and Healthy Working Conditions:** Most of the organizations provide safe and healthy working conditions due to humanitarian requirements and/or legal requirements. In fact, these conditions are a matter or enlightened self interest.

(iii) **Opportunity to Use and Develop Human Capacities:** Contrary to the traditional assumptions, QWL is improved... "to the extent that the worker can exercise more control over his or her work, and the degree to which the job embraces and entire meaningful task" ... but not a part of it. Further, QWL provides for opportunities like autonomy in work and participation in planning in order to use human capabilities.

(iv) **Opportunity for Career Growth:** Opportunities for promotions are limited in case of all categories of employees either due to educational barriers or due to limited openings at the higher level. QWL provides future opportunity for continued growth and security by expanding one's capabilities, knowledge and qualifications.

(v) **Social Integration in the Work Force:** Social integration in the work force can be established by creating freedom from prejudice, supporting primary work groups, a sense of community and inter-personnel openness, legalitarianism and upward mobility.

(vi) **Constitutionalism in the Work Organization:** QWL provides constitutional protection to the employees only to the level of desirability as it hampers workers. It happens because the management's action is challenged in every action and bureaucratic procedures need to be followed at that level. Constitutional protection is provided to employees on such matters as privacy, free speech, equity and due process.

(vii) **Work and Quality of Life:** QWL provides for the balanced relationship among work, non-work and family aspects of life. In other words family life and social life should not be strained by working hours including overtime work, work during inconvenient hours, business travel, transfers, vacations etc.

(viii) **Social Relevance of Work:** QWL is concerned about the establishment of social relevance to work in a socially beneficial manner. The workers' self esteem would be high if his work is useful to the society and the vice versa is also true.

CAREER MANAGEMENT AND CAREER PLANNING

Effective HRM encompasses career planning, career development and succession planning. An organization without career planning and career development initiatives is likely to encounter the highest rate of attrition, causing much harm to their plans and programmes. Similarly without succession planning managing of vacancies, particularly at higher levels, become difficult. There are examples of many organizations that had to suffer for not being able to find a right successor for their key positions. With the increase scope for job mobility and corporate race for global headhunting of good performers, it is now a well established fact that normal employment span for key performers remains awfully short.

The term career planning and career developments are used interchangeably in most of the organizations. It is also correct that but for their subtle difference in the definitional context, their process remains the same.

Definition

Career is a sequence of attitudes and behaviours associated with the series of job and work related activities over a person's lifetime. Yet in another way, it may be defined as a succession of related jobs, arranged in hierarchical order, through which a person moves in an organization. As the literal definition of career focuses on an individually perceived sequence, to be more accurate, career may be either individual-centred or organizational-centred. Therefore, career is often defined separately as external career and internal career.

External career refers to the objective categories used by society and organizations to describe the progression of steps through a given occupation, while **internal career** refers to the set of steps or stages which make up the individual's own concept of career progression within an occupation. For such two different approaches, in organizational context, career can be identified as an integrated pace of vertical lateral movement in an occupation of an individual over his employment span.

Elements of Career

Analyzing definitional context, it is clear that career has following important elements:

1. It is a proper sequence of job-related activities. Such job related activities vis-a-vis experience include role experiences at different hierarchical levels of an individual, which lead to an increasing level of responsibilities, status, power, achievements and rewards.
2. It may be individual-centered or organizational-centered, individual-centered career is an individually perceived sequence of career progression within an occupation.
3. It is better defined as an integrated pace of internal movement in an occupation of an individual over his employment span.

Overview

Career planning generally involves getting to know who you are, what you want, and how to get there. Keep in mind that career planning is a continuous process that allows you to move from one stage to another stage as your life changes. You may even find yourself going back to look at who you are again after exploring how to get there. Learning to negotiate the career planning process now is essential, considering most people will change careers several times in a lifetime.

If a career plan is to be effective, it must begin with an objective. When asked about career objectives, most managers will probably answer by saying that they want to be successful. What is success? Definition of success depends on personal aspirations, values, self-image, age, background and other different factors. Success is personally defined concept. In order to plan your career, you need to have an idea of what constitutes career success.

Do you want to be president of the company?

Do you want to be the senior executive in your field of expertise?

Would you be happier as a middle manager in your area?

Whatever the choice it must be yours.

Career management is a process by which individuals can guide, direct and influence the course of their careers.

General Periods in Careers

In the course of our career we move from one stage to another setting and implementing appropriate goals at each stage. Our goals differ from getting established on job at early career stage to career

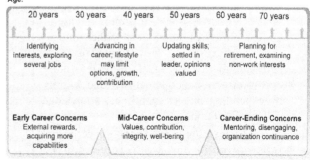

reappraisal, moving away from technical areas and becoming more of a generalist. Movement from one career stage to another will require individuals to update self and to appropriate change goals. When required danger exist that individuals may too long stay in a job they don't like or miss career opportunity.

A sensible early step in career planning is to diagnose. You might answer questions:

- What types of positions and career experiences do I need to achieve my goals?
- What personal traits characteristics and behaviours require change in order for me to improve my professional effectiveness?

Career Planning in Organization

Career planning is the process by which one selects career goals and the path to these goals. The major focus of career planning is on assisting the employees achieve a better match between personal goals and the opportunities that are realistically available in the organization. Career programmers should not concentrate only on career growth opportunities. Practically speaking, there may not be enough high level positions to make upward mobility a reality for a large number of employees. Hence, career-planning efforts need to pin-point and highlight those areas that offer psychological success instead of vertical growth.

Career planning is not an event or end in itself, but a continuous process of developing human resources for achieving optimum results. It must, however, be noted that individual and organizational careers are not separate and distinct. A person who is not able to translate his career plan into action within the organization may probably quit the job, if he has a choice. Organizations, therefore, should help employees in career planning so that both can satisfy each other's needs.

Career Planning vs Human Resource Planning

Human Resource planning is the process of analyzing and estimating the need for and availability of employees. Through Human Resource planning, the Personnel Department is able to prepare a summary of skills and potentials available within the organization. Career planning assists in finding those employees who could be groomed for higher level positions, on the strength of their performance.

Human Resource planning gives valuable information about the availability of human resources for expansion, growth, etc. (expansion of facilities, construction of a new plant, opening a new branch, launching a new product, etc.). On the other hand, career planning only gives us a picture of who could succeed in case any major developments leading to retirement, death, resignation of existing employees.

Human Resource planning is tied to the overall strategic planning efforts of the organization. There cannot be an effective manpower planning, if career planning is not carried out properly.

Need for the Career Planning

Every employee has a desire to grow and scale new heights in his workplace continuously. If there are enough opportunities, he can pursue his career goals and exploit his potential fully. He feels highly motivated when the organization shows him a clear path as to how he can meet his personal ambitions while trying to realize corporate goals.

Unfortunately, as pointed out by John Leach, organizations do not pay adequate attention to this aspect in actual practice for a variety of reasons. The demands of employees are not matched with organizational needs; no effort is made to show how the employees can grow within certain limits, what happens to an employee five years down the line if he does well, whether the organization is trying to offer mere jobs or long-lasting careers, etc. When recognition does not come in time for meritorious performance and a certain amount of confusion prevails in the minds of employees whether they are 'in' with a chance to grow or not, they look for greener pastures outside. Key executives leave in frustration and the organization suffers badly when turnover figures rise. Any recruitment effort made in panic to fill the vacancies is not going to be effective. So, the absence of a career plan is going to make a big difference to both the employees and the organization. Employees do not get right breaks at a right time; their morale will be low and they are always on their toes trying to find escape routes.

Organizations are not going to benefit from high employee turnover. New employees mean additional selection and training costs. Bridging the gaps through short-term replacements is not going to pay in terms of productivity. Organizations, therefore, try to put their career plans in place and educate employees about the opportunities that exist internally for talented people. Without such a progressive outlook, organizations cannot prosper.

Objectives

Career planning seeks to meet the following objectives:

   i. Attract and retain talent by offering careers, not jobs.
   ii. Use human resources effectively and achieve greater productivity.
   iii. Reduce employee turnover.
   iv. Improve employee morale and motivation.
   v. Meet the immediate and future human resource needs of the organization on a timely basis.

Career Planning Process

The career planning process involves the following steps:

   (i) **Identifying individual needs and aspirations:** Most individuals do not have a clear cut idea about their career aspirations, anchors and goals. The human resource professionals must, therefore, help an employee by providing as much information as possible showing what kind of work would suit the employee most, taking his skills, experience, and aptitude into account. Such assistance is extended through workshops/seminars while the employees are subjected to psychological testing, simulation exercises, etc. The basic purpose of such an exercise is to help an employee form a clear view about what he should do to build his career within the company. Workshops and seminars increase employee interest by showing the value of career planning. They help employees set career goals, identify career paths and uncover specific career development activities (discussed later). These individual efforts may be supplemented by printed or taped information. To assist employees in a better way, organizations construct a data bank consisting of information on the career histories, skill evaluations and career preferences of its employees (known as skill or talent inventory).

   (ii) **Analyzing career opportunities:** Once career needs and aspirations of employees are known, the organization has to provide career paths for each position. Career paths show career progression possibilities clearly. They indicate the various positions that one could hold over a period of time, if one is able to perform well. Career paths change over time, of course, in tune with employee's needs and organizational requirements. While outlining career paths, the claims of experienced persons lacking professional degrees and that of young recruits with excellent degrees but without experience need to be balanced properly.

   (iii) **Aligning needs and opportunities:** After employees have identified their needs and have realized the existence of career opportunities the remaining problem is one of alignment. This process consists of two steps: first, identify the potential of employees and then undertake career development programmers (discussed later on elaborately) with a view to align employee needs and organizational opportunities. Through performance appraisal, the potential of employees can be assessed to some extent. Such an appraisal would help reveal employees who need further training, employees who can take up added responsibilities, etc. After identifying the potential of employees certain developmental techniques such as special assignments, planned position rotation, supervisory coaching, job enrichment, understudy programs can be undertaken to update employee knowledge and skills.

(iv) **Action plans and periodic review:** The matching process would uncover gaps. These need to be bridged through individual career development efforts and organization supported efforts from time to time. After initiating these steps, it is necessary to review the whole thing every now and then. This will help the employee know in which direction he is moving, what changes are likely to take place, what kind of skills are needed to face new and emerging organizational challenges. From an organizational standpoint also, it is necessary to find out how employees are doing, what are their goals and aspirations, whether the career paths are in tune with individual needs and serve the overall corporate objectives, etc.

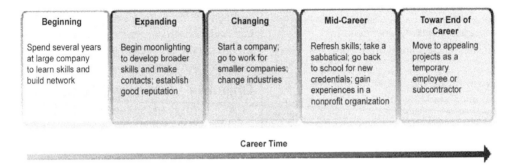

Beginning	Expanding	Changing	Mid-Career	Towar End of Career
Spend several years at large company to learn skills and build network	Begin moonlighting to develop broader skills and make contacts; establish good reputation	Start a company; go to work for smaller companies; change industries	Refresh skills; take a sabbatical; go back to school for new credentials; gain experiences in a nonprofit organization	Move to appealing projects as a temporary employee or subcontractor

Career Time →

The New "Portable" Career Path

CAREER PLANNING MODELS

There are many models one may use while career planning. The two main models are

Waterloo University Model

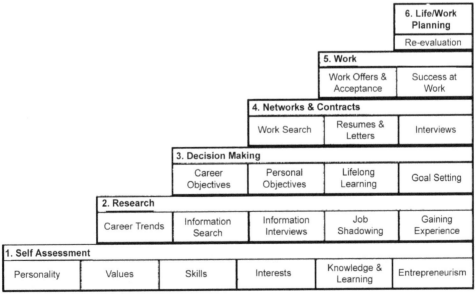

Waterloo University Model

The SODI Career Planning Model

Given the complexity of career development and the fluidity of the world of work, we need to be able to navigate our career paths with purpose and clarity.

Law and Watts (1977) devised a simple model of career education which has stood the test of time. This model has been changed slightly to become a career planning, rather than a career education model and named the SODI model where the last element is 'implementation' rather than 'transition learning', and 'decision learning' becomes 'decision-making and planning'.

The model encapsulates four concepts which are:

Self-awareness: Individual having knowledge about and understanding of their own personal development. Self-awareness in a careers context involves an understanding of kind of personal resources (both actual and potential) they bring to world.

Opportunity awareness: An understanding of the general structures of the world of work, including career possibilities and alternative pathways.

Decision-making and planning: An understanding of how to make career decisions, and being aware of pressures, influences, styles, consequences and goal setting.

Implementing plans: Having the appropriate skill level in a range of areas to be able to translate job and career planning into reality.

QUALITY CIRCLES

In Japanese culture, the group plays a dominate role. The Japanese end to do things in groups, to place to high value on group membership, and to strive to be as cohesive as possible. It was natural for this group orientation to be expressed in Quality-Control (Q-C) circles in Japanese industry. When American companies began to look to the Japanese for ways to compete in work markets, the most visible and transferable technique seemed to be Q-C groups. Several thousand, U.S. companies now make use of them.

A quality circle has been defined as a "self-governing group of workers with or without their supervisors who voluntarily meet regularly to identify, analyses and solve problems of their work field".

A group participation proves, quality circle typically are small groups of volunteers from the same work areas who meet regularly to identify, analyze, and solve quality and related problems in their area of responsibility. Members of a group choose a particular problem to study, gather data, and control charts to frame a recommendation that can be presented to management. Now groups are trained in communication and problem solving skills and quality/ measurement strategies and techniques.

Objective of Quality Circles

- To develop enhance and utilize human resources effectively.
- To improve quality of products/ services, productivity and reduce cost of production per unit of output.
- To satisfy the workers psychological needs for self-urge participation, recognition etc. with a view to motivate them.
- To improve various supervisory skills like leadership, problem solving inter-personal and conflict resolution.
- To utilize individual imaginative, creative and innovative skills through participation, creating and developing work interest, include problem solving techniques etc.

Techniques used for Discussion in Quality Circles

Brain-storming process

Under this technique complete free environment is created with a view to stimulate creativity and the employees can come out with as many ideas as possible. Later these ideas will be screened and best ideas will be chosen.

Cause and effect

Under this technique members are asked to find out the causes for the identified problem. They identify the causes and their effects.

Sampling and charting methods

Under this technique, members of the quality circle observe the events and their consequences in the form of positive or negative results.

They chart out all their observation either in sequence or in some other relationship which gives clear ideal of the problem.

These techniques will work effectively in attaining the objectives only when the organizational structure of Q-C is sound and systematic.

Quality Circle Process

Size of the each Q-C selects the problem from the operational problems suggested by management or by the members of the Q-C. After selecting the problem the members analyze it by using the various problem solving techniques. Then the members develop alternative solution, their effect and consequences on organization and members, cost benefit analysis and merits and demerits of each solution. The next stage is that members select the best solution from among the alternative solutions. Management reviews the solutions and may or may not accept the solution offered by the Q-C members. If the solution is accepted it is implemented.

Making Q-C Process Effective

The following factors should be recognized and practiced to make Q-C process of effective:

- All members should accept that there is more than one way to solve a problem successfully.
- All members to be encouraged to clarify and build on each other's ideas.
- Periodic summarizing of the activities by the leader or member to ensure common understanding.
- Avoidance of heated arguments in favour of one particular position.
- Avoidance of technique such as majority vote to obtain group agreement.

It has been stated in many forms that a major part of the responsibility for quality circles lies with the management than workers. Mr. Ishikawa, during a visit to India in 1987 had remarked that Q-Cs can contribute only about 30 percent to quality improvement and the rest has to be in the form of management efforts. The famous American expert Mr. Deming, after who, most of the quality awards are given, unhesitatingly says that a major part of the effort towards quality improvement has to come from management.

The secret of the success of the Japanese effort has been the continuous modification of their designs to overcome the quality problems faced by the customers and rectify them. This calls for a lot of upstream management and proper tools of analysis to be applied for successful efforts.

It is only in a climate of cohesion, mutual trust and understanding that there can be meaningful progress. For this, both managements and trade unions have to work jointly for the common organizational goal. It is not enough if only the management takes upon itself the task of achieving the desired results. It calls for the willing involvement of every section of employees, including those at the grassroots, leading to company wise true participation and open management. Finally, development of the most important of all resources, human resource has to find a place.

To achieve the prerequisites for excellence, many organizations are adopting various kinds of management tools in the fond hope of finding a place for all their problems in order to bring in greater involvement of employees in day-to-day affairs. Sweden and Yugoslavia (and some companies in India, too) had experimented with "work place democracy" and "work autonomy" but not with much success.

The task before India is to recreate the culture in which a sense of belonging to the organization is generated among all employees. If this is to happen, managements have to change their age-old attitudes.

Management, by itself, without actively involving task performers would not be able to achieve the organizational goals. This would be possible only through a holistic approach towards employees and humanization of work. Enrichment of the "quality of working life" and catering to the self-esteem and recognition needs of employees only would help develop in them a sense of involvement, participation and pride in the organizational progress.

The one road to achieve this goal is the effective implementation of small group activities such as "Employees Participation Circle" (EPC); "Small Group Activities" (SGA) and "Training at Work Teams" (TAWT). In India in the West they are called "Quality Circles". In Japan and many Southeast Asian countries, the small groups are known as "Quality Control Circles" because they got evolved in the sixties as a result of massive quality control training imparted to the employees.

The "Quality Circle" concept comes nearest to satisfying the pre-requisites for developing the capability to face the current and emerging challenges. Its unique features such as voluntariness, bottom up group synergy are now proved to being about tangible and intangible benefits to any organization, if practiced with sincerity of purpose as adapted to the Indian milieu. The number of organizations implementing quality circles in India has been steadily rising covering both the public and private sectors and government agencies.

This scheme will no doubt contribute to the organizational effectiveness and to enhance job satisfaction and sound human relations in all organizations.

Organizational Analysis

The organizational analysis is aimed at short listing the focus areas for training within the organization and the factors that may affect the same. Organizational mission, vision, goals, people inventories, processes, performance data are all studied. The study gives cues about the kind of learning environment required for the training. Motorola and IBM for example, conduct surveys every year keeping in view the short term and long term goals of the organization.

Job Analysis

The job analysis of the needs assessment survey aims at understanding the 'what' of the training

development stage. The kind of intervention needed is what is decided upon in the job analysis. It is an objective assessment of the job wherein both the worker oriented approach as well as the task oriented approach is taken into consideration. The worker approach identifies key behaviours and ASK for a certain job and the task oriented approach identifies the activities to be performed in a certain job. The former is useful in deciding the intervention and the latter in content development and program evaluation.

Individual Analysis

As evident from them name itself, the individual analysis is concerned with who in the organization needs the training and in which particular area. Here performance is taken out from the performance appraisal data and the same is compared with the expected level or standard of performance. The individual analysis is also conducted through questionnaires, 360 feedback, personal interviews etc. Likewise, many organization use competency ratings to rate their managers; these ratings may come from their subordinates, customers, peers, bosses etc. Apart from the above mentioned organizations also make use of attitude surveys, critical Incidents and Assessment surveys to understand training needs which will be discussed in detail in other articles.

The process of needs assessment happens at three stages or levels, the organizational, the job and the person or the individual. This is the basis for any needs assessment survey and remains the same more or less in all organizations around the globe. There are however many techniques for collecting the data for training need analysis. This article discusses some of the methods used for the same.

The needs assessment conducted at various stages tries to answer a different set of questions. Organizational analysis, for example, aims at the 'where in the organization' of the training. Person analysis similarly attempts to decipher the question of 'Whom in the organization'. There are therefore various instruments or techniques that are used to collect data for the analysis at each stage.

Techniques for Collecting Data at Organizational Level

As discussed already, in organizational analysis we try to ascertain the areas in the organization that require training interventions. For example, among the various kinds of interventions that organizations chose it was found out managerial training is picking up fast among corporations and also that managerial competencies amount for 98% of success in the jobs.

Personnel and skill inventories, organizational climate and efficiency indices, Management requests, Exit interviews, Management By Objectives (MBO) are the various kinds of techniques that are used at the level of organizational analysis for collecting data for training needs analysis.

Essentially all these tools collect data that is inferential in nature, but does not give a clear picture of the training needs. For example, the above mentioned tools may lead an organization to deduce that 'there is a need for aligning the work processes with the organizational goals / objectives', which is not very rich diagnostically. It may require further analysis, which is done with the help of tools at the level of job or the task.

The techniques for data collection at the level of the job include job description, performance standards, work sampling, job specifications, job literature analysis, and analysis of operational problems among others. These techniques are aimed at extracting data for understanding the target of training *i.e.* what exactly should be taught in training. Time management may be one critical intervention in project handling / management.

These techniques at the level of job are useful but yet not sufficient in helping understand who requires training and when. Taking the above example further, time management may be a critical intervention for Projects people, but there may already be some who are very efficient in time management and may require the intervention at other level, which is only possible to ascertain with the help of techniques used at the level of the individual or the person.

Training may prove worthless if it is conducted without studying individual data. Every member in a team is unique and works as well as performs at a certain level (n). There may be others who are at ($n + 1$) or ($n - 1$) or more. Thus, the same intervention may halt the progress of a certain individual and finally the organization. There are therefore certain tools that help in deciding interventions at the individual level. Performance appraisal data, questionnaires, attitude surveys, 360 degree feedback, assessment centres, critical incidents are some techniques that are employed to a good benefit. All these techniques are integral to the success of any training program. Although each one of these may be used independently but the combined use offers a holistic view of training within an organization.

Development of a training program is the next step after the training need analysis has been conducted and there is a clear consensus on the need of training within the organization. The next vital question to answer is whether the training should be conducted by an in house expert or from a consultant outside.

Many of the fortune 500 organizations around the world have their in house learning centers and many have even gone ahead to have their own training universities where they train people onboard and those who aspire to join in the future. Companies like Xerox, Good Year Tyres, Kodak, Mahindra and Mahindra, Birla etc. have such setups for generating prospective employees with the requisite skills and also for training the existing employees.

There are other organizations too that have tie ups with the best academic institutions for employee exchange programmes.

Nevertheless the prerequisites for development of a training program remain the same. We start with the development of a conducive learning environment, followed by a choice of the training methods and techniques.

Designing the Environment: Every individual is unique. One style of learning may not be applicable to each of the participants in a training program. Therefore 'how do various individuals learn' is what should be kept in mind while designing the training program. There are certain who learn the experiential way by doing and yet there are many who like the lecture based learning method. There are however pros and cons of both and the appropriate learning style is generally the discretion of the trainer / facilitator.

Establishing the Variables: Trainability is one factor that must be taken into consideration before developing any training program. It is the duty of the trainer to ensure that the employees are actually willing to sit and learn something in the training program. This is especially very true of sensitivity training that is not viewed positively by many. Trainability also implies that the employee is sufficiently motivated to learn apart from just the ability to do so. Before any training program sets off, it is the responsibility of the trainer to build excitement about the event and such that it attracts all types of employees from target audience within the organization.

There are both formal and informal ways of doing the same. Formal ways would be by sending mails to the employees who are supposed to attend the program. Informal ways would be just creating conditions for discussion in the cafeteria or the lounge where employees sit together, discuss and hear things on the grapevine.

Finally, once the training program has been delivered the evaluation of the same provides inputs for improving the process of training. These are called as the 'post learning inputs'. This evaluation which is conducted at various levels may be utilized accordingly. Most of the organizations evaluate training on the basis of Kirk Patrick Model. The feedback at each level — learning, reaction, behaviour and results can be used for effective design of training in future.

Cost Benefit Analysis for Training

Organizations use different methods to assess the benefits of training in terms of numbers *i.e.* the profits. Some of the frequently used methods are ROI and Utility analysis. There are many costs that are associated with the training apart from the direct

and apparent costs. These costs can be described under two headings:

1. There are costs incurred towards the training needs analysis, compensation of the training program designers, procurement of training material and various media like the computers, handouts, props, gifts and prizes, audio visuals etc.

2. Then there is another category is costs incidental to the training session itself such as trainer's fee / salary, facility costs / rental etc.

Finally there are costs involved is losing a man day of work (for those who are sent for training), travelling, boarding and lodging and training material that cannot be reused in some other training program. The various models that are used to estimate the benefits of the training program are as under.

The Return on Investment Model (ROI)

Organizations spend huge amount of money on employee development, it is therefore very important to ascertain the benefits of training. Different studies were conducted to evaluate the effectiveness of training programs. In one of the studies it was found out that sales and technical trainings gave better ROI compared to managerial training programs. Ford, for example, evaluates all the training programs against the profitability in a given product line. The basic formula for calculating the ROI for training is as:

ROI (in percent)
= Program benefits/Costs × 100

Utility Analysis

This is another way of reflecting upon the usefulness of a training program. Utility itself is a function of the duration up to which the training leaves an impact upon the trainee, the relative importance of the training program, the importance of the position or profile that received training and the cost of conducting the training. For example, leadership programs conducted for top and middle management tend to be high on value where as sales training programs for the front line sales staff tends to be low on value scale.

Utility analysis basically derives the effectiveness from analyzing the change in the behaviour of the trainee and the positive financial implications of the same. This model is not very famous because the deductions made are essentially subjective in nature.

Training Evaluation

Evaluation involves the assessment of the effectiveness of the training programs. This assessment is done by collecting data on whether the participants were satisfied with the deliverables of the training program, whether they learned something from the training and are able to apply those skills at their workplace. There are different tools for assessment of a training program depending upon the kind of training conducted.

Since organizations spend a large amount of money, it is therefore important for them to understand the usefulness of the same. For example, if a certain technical training was conducted, the organization would be interested in knowing whether the new skills are being put to use at the workplace or in other words whether the effectiveness of the worker is enhanced. Similarly in case of behavioural training, the same would be evaluated on whether there is change in the behaviour, attitude and learning ability of the participants.

Benefits of Training Evaluation

Evaluation acts as a check to ensure that the training is able to fill the competency gaps within the organization in a cost effective way. This is especially very important in wake of the fact the organizations are trying to cut costs and increase globally. Some of the benefits of the training evaluation are as under:

- **Evaluation ensures accountability:** Training evaluation ensures that training programs comply with the competency gaps and that the deliverables are not compromised upon.

- **Check the Cost:** Evaluation ensures that the training programs are effective in improving the work quality, employee behaviour, attitude and development of new skills within the employee within a certain budget. Since globally companies are trying to cut their costs without compromising upon the quality, evaluation just aims at achieving the same with training.

- **Feedback to the Trainer / Training:** Evaluation also acts as a feedback to the trainer or the facilitator and the entire training process. Since evaluation accesses individuals at the level of their work, it gets easier to understand the loopholes of the training and the changes required in the training methodology.

Not many organizations believe in the process of evaluation or at least do not have an evaluation system in place. Many organizations conduct training programs year after year only as a matter of faith and not many have a firm evaluation mechanism in place. Organizations like IBM, Motorala only, it was found out, have a firm evaluation mechanism in place.

MULTIPLE CHOICE QUESTIONS

1. Research method in which data is gathered first and for the specific project being conducted is
   A. Primary research   B. Data collection
   C. Data analysis   D. None of the above

2. Privacy refers to information about an employee which he or she regards as personal or private (*i.e.,* medical information, financial data, etc.) and that is the right of that individual not to have such information shared with others.
   A. Fact   B. Not factual
   C. Partially fact   D. None of the above

3. Error in which the rater gives greater weight to recent events when appraising an individual's performance is
   A. Recency effect   B. Mistake
   C. Median   D. None of the above

4. Self-employed is an individual who has earned income for the current or preceding year from self-employment, or an individual who would have had such income out of any business.
   A. Fact
   B. Not factual
   C. Partially fact
   D. None of the above

5. A contract, restricting an employee from obtaining employment with a competitor within a specified industry, distance and/or time frame referred as
   A. New contract
   B. Banned
   C. Non compete agreement
   D. None of the above

6. Semi-skilled workers have to be able to read, write and communicate but are usually not required to have educational or apprenticeship credentials to qualify for jobs.
   A. Fact   B. Not factual
   C. Partially fact D. None of the above

7. Length of employment as defined by the employer or applicable collective bargaining agreement is based on
   A. Seniority   B. Merit
   C. Both A and B   D. None of the above

8. A form of individual counseling geared toward increasing self-awareness and sensitivity to others. It aims to assist key employees in developing their leadership skills surrounding issues of diversity and harassment prevention. The process is
   A. Emotional training
   B. Development program
   C. Sensitivity training
   D. Role play

9. An appraisal method where the subordinate and the manager are evaluated by each other based on agreed-upon performance criteria is
   A. Understanding method
   B. Agreement based method
   C. Factor review
   D. Reciprocal review

10. An acknowledgement of an employee's exceptional performance or achievements expressed in the form of praise, commendation or gratitude is
    A. Appraisal   B. Performer
    C. Recognition   D. All the above

11. A method of analyzing how employee skill deficits can be addressed through current or future training and professional development programs, as well as determining the types of training/development programs required and how to prioritize training/development is
    A. Performance analysis
    B. Skill analysis
    C. Need analysis
    D. Personality analysis

12. A statistical measure used to discover relationships between variables such as performance ratings and promotions is
    A. Statistical analysis
    B. Time-series analysis
    C. Regression analysis
    D. Correlation analysis

13. A scale that allows the rater to mark an employee's performance on a continuum is
    A. Time series
    B. Regression analysis
    C. Graphic rating scale
    D. None of the above

14. A target level of performance expressed as a tangible, measurable objective against which actual performance can be compared, including a goal expressed as a quantitative standard, value, or rate is
    A. Performance management
    B. Performance appraisal
    C. Performance goal
    D. None of the above

15. Processes used to identify, encourage, measure, evaluate, improve, and reward employee performance is
    A. Performance management system
    B. Performance appraisal system
    C. Performance goal setting
    D. None of the above

16. The practice of monitoring employees while they perform their jobs through the use of surveillance cameras, telephone or computer monitoring is
A. Performance management
B. Performance appraisal
C. Performance goal
D. Performance monitoring

17. The amount of clear information received about how well or how poorly one has performed is
A. Appraisal   B. Feedback
C. Data feeding   D. None of the above

18. Several practice sessions spaced over a period of hours or days are
A. Spaced practice B. Orientation
C. Both A and B   D. None of the above

19. Questions that can usually be answered with yes or no is
A. Multiple choice question
B. Closed question
C. Descriptive question
D. None of the above

20. Daily training and feedback given to employees by immediate supervisors is
A. Training   B. Workshop
C. Coaching   D. All the above

21. A form of training that enforces organizational rules are
A. Need identify   B. Discipline
C. Behaviour   D. None of the above

22. Differences among people is
A. Diversity   B. Level
C. Society   D. None of the above

23. An amount advanced from and repaid to future commissions earned by the employee is
A. Draw   B. Commission
C. Loan   D. None of the above

24. A score derived from the mean performance of a group on a test, as well as the comparative performance of all the individuals who took the test as
A. Marks   B. Points
C. Standard score   D. None of the above

25. A prescribed written procedure outlining how recurring tasks, duties and functions are to be performed organization wide is
A. Standard operating procedures
B. Standard managing procedures
C. Standard performance procedures
D. None of the above

26. Making a decision regarding the appropriateness of a test or other assessment instrument based on appearance rather than objective criteria is
A. Test validity   B. Sample work test
C. Face validity   D. Assessment centre

27. A policy or practice designed to help families spend more time together and/or enjoy a better quality of life is
A. Quality circle   B. Balance work life
C. Social   D. Family-friendly

28. A term used to describe employees who have exhibited strong potential for promotion and are being primed for higher level professional or technical positions within the organization is
A. Merit based   B. Seniority based
C. Fast-trackers   D. None of the above

29. Alternative dispute resolution method in which a panel of employees hears appeals from disciplined employees and make recommendations or decisions are
A. 360 degree appraisal
B. Peer review panel
C. Stereotyping
D. Central tendency

30. The process of evaluating how well employees perform their jobs when compared to a set of standards, and then communicating that information are
A. Training evaluation
B. Performance appraisal
C. Performance management
D. None of the above

31. One-time payment made to an employee; often called a lump-sum increase is
A. Performance bonus
B. Performance appraisal
C. Performance management
D. None of the above

32. A situation where an individual's performance is the basis for either the amount or timing of pay increases _____
    A. Performance-based pay
    B. Merit pay
    C. Both A and B
    D. None of the above

33. A plan that gives an individual the right to buy stock in a company, usually at a fixed price for a period of time is
    A. Stock option   B. Stock verification
    C. Stock maintenance D. None of the above

34. A pay system in which wages are determined by multiplying the number of units produced by the piece rate for one unit is
    A. Pay-for performance
    B. Straight piece-rate system
    C. Time based
    D. None of the above

35. The process of taking a long-term approach to Human Resource Management through the development and implementation of HR programs that address and solve business problems and directly contribute to major long-term business objectives are
    A. Strategy human resource
    B. Strategic HR
    C. HR planning
    D. None of the above

36. A training method whereby participants are divided into small groups, given a specific problem to handle within a short period of time (typically less than 10 minutes) and then report their findings back to the larger collective group is
    A. Group performance B. Case study
    C. Huddle group   D. None of the above

37. Functions such as caring for oneself, performing manual tasks, walking, seeing, hearing, speaking, breathing, learning, and working is
    A. Career succession plan
    B. Life activities
    C. Life and career plan
    D. None of the above

38. Activities that help people identify their life and career objectives is
    A. Career succession plan
    B. Life activities
    C. Life and career planning activities
    D. None of the above

39. A document outlining and representing the core priorities in the organization's culture is
    A. Report   B. Book
    C. Value statement   D. All the above

40. A form of training conducted outside of the workplace to acclimate newly hired employees with procedures and equipment or tools to be used in their jobs is
    A. Orientation
    B. Variance identification
    C. Vestibule training
    D. None of the above

41. A person with responsibility of performing a variety of HR activities is
    A. HR specialist   B. HR generalist
    C. Both A and B   D. None of the above

42. The analysis of data from HR records to determine the effectiveness of past and present HR practices is
    A. Research study
    B. HR research
    C. Research methodology
    D. None of the above

43. A person with in-depth knowledge and expertise in a limited area of HR is
    A. Research study
    B. HR research
    C. Research methodology
    D. HR Specialist

44. The means used to aid the organization in anticipating and managing the supply and demand for human resources is
    A. Corporate governance
    B. Environmental analysis
    C. HR strategies
    D. None of the above

45. A process whereby people acquire capabilities to aid in the achievement of organizational goals is
    A. Learning   B. Training
    C. Development   D. All the above

46. Any form of audio or visual materials used for training purposes is
A. Training aids
B. Instruments
C. Tools
D. None of the above

47. A process dealing primarily with transferring or obtaining knowledge, attitudes and skills needed to carry out a specific activity or task is
A. Recruitment and selection
B. Performance management
C. Training and development
D. All the above

48. A method used to determine what people need to learn and which training programs may be beneficial, the result of the analysis is training needs report identifying training needs and the interventions needed to reduce key performance gaps are referred as
A. Human Resource Planning
B. Training needs analysis (TNA)
C. Performance oriented
D. None of the above

49. Moving an employee from one position, shift or department to another within the organization is
A. Job assessment
B. Transfer
C. Transfer and promotion
D. None of the above

50. Physical or emotional exhaustion, lack of motivation or decreased morale resulting from an individual being exposed to excessive or prolonged stress and frustration caused by personal problems, work pressures, financial difficulties, etc. are termed as
A. Exhausted
B. Burnout
C. Mental abnormality
D. None of the above

51. Rights of an employee to displace another employee due to a layoff or other employment action as defined in a collective bargaining agreement or other binding agreement is
A. Contract employee
B. Employability right
C. Individual rights
D. Bumping rights

52. Any salary increase awarded to an employee based on his or her individual performance is
A. Merit pay
B. Merit raise
C. Both A & B
D. None of the above

53. A training program designed to assist a group of people to work together as a team while they are learning is
A. Team building
B. Team manager
C. Both A and B
D. None of the above

54. The practice of individuals working together in order to bring a variety of talents and experiences to achieve a common goal is
A. Team work
B. Individual performance
C. Group
D. All the above

55. Managers who are responsible for translating the general goals and plans developed by strategic managers into more specific objectives and activities is by
A. Line manager
B. Supervisor
C. Technical manager
D. All the above

56. Working from a remote location (often one's home workstation) using computers, telephones, facsimile machines and other remote capabilities, rather than commuting via automobile or other mode of transportation to and from an employer's work site to perform equivalent work is termed as
A. Telecommuting
B. Communication
C. Tele-Conference
D. None of the above

57. The term used to describe increasingly mobile organizations that are performing their operations in foreign countries is
A. Globalization
B. Liberalization
C. Privatization
D. All the above

58. Pay practices relating to employees who are working on assignments in international locations as service premium and additional incentives are often included in the compensation package to offset differences in taxes and cost of living is termed as
A. Compensation management
B. Global compensation system
C. Salary & wages
D. None of the above

59. An organization that has corporate units in a number of countries that are integrated to operate as one organization worldwide are defined as
A. Global organization
B. International organization
C. Global assignment
D. Trade

60. The process of transferring an individual's residence from their home country to a foreign country for the purpose of completing an international job assignment is
A. Global relocation   B. Global restricting
C. Global change   D. None of the above

61. An individual who works on either short or long term assignments with an employer without being treated as a permanent employee and lacking the benefits of permanent employees and is normally utilized by employer to meet seasonal or other demands that they do not have the internal resources to meet is
A. Expatriate
B. Impatriate
C. Temporary employee
D. Permanent employee

62. Restraining and/or protective orders are examples of orders issued by a court restraining the conduct of an individual and protecting a victim from the activities of an abusive person is
A. Temporary restraining order
B. Permanent restraining order
C. Restraining order
D. None of the above

63. A teaching tool used to help employees become more safety-conscious in all aspects of safety is
A. Safety training
B. Environment analysis
C. Individual behaviour
D. Group levels

64. The concept that people learn best if reinforcement is given as soon as possible after training is
A. Learning skill
B. Teaching skill
C. Immediate confirmation
D. Behaviourial theory

65. Functions such as caring for oneself, performing manual tasks, walking, seeing, hearing, speaking, breathing, learning, and working is
A. Career succession plan
B. Life activities
C. Life and career plan
D. None of the above

66. A permanent reassignment to a position with a lower pay grade, skill requirement or level of responsibility than the employee's current position is
A. Demotion   B. Promotion
C. Transfer   D. None of the above

67. A performance appraisal strategy whereby an employee is reviewed by his or her peers who have sufficient opportunity to examine the individual's job performance is
A. 360 degree appraisal
B. Peer appraisal
C. Stereotyping
D. Central tendency

68. A statement outlining the long-term results, accomplishments or objectives, is that an organization seeks to attain
A. Goal
B. Human resource metrics
C. HR audit
D. HR accounting

69. The process of setting and assigning a set of specific and attainable goals to be met by an individual, group or organization is
A. Human resource metrics
B. HR audit
C. HR accounting
D. Goal setting

70. A computer database used to gather, store, maintain and retrieve relevant employee and HR-related information that is helpful in HR decision making is
A. Human resource metrics

B. HR audit

C. Human resource information system (HRIS)

D. HR accounting

71. The design of formal systems in an organization to ensure the effective and efficient use of human talent to accomplish the organizational goals is
A. Human resource metrics
B. HR audit
C. HR accounting
D. Human resource management

72. A software application combining various human resource functions, such as benefits, payroll, recruiting, training, etc., into one package is
A. Human resource metrics
B. HR audit
C. HR accounting
D. Human resource management system (HRMS)

73. Measurements used to determine the value and effectiveness of HR strategies. Typically includes such items as cost per hire, turnover rates/costs, training and human capital ROI, labour /productivity rates and costs, benefit costs per employee, etc. is
A. Human resource metrics
B. HR audit
C. HR accounting
D. All the above

74. The process of analyzing and identifying the need for and availability of human resources so that the organization can meet its objectives is
A. Recruitment
B. Selection
C. Human resource planning (HRP)
D. Job analysis

75. An organization whose structure is comprised of both vertical and horizontal models are
A. Acquisition
B. Merging
C. Hybrid organization
D. Cross functional management

76. Characteristics of the workplace, such as company policies, working conditions, pay, and supervision that make a job more satisfying is
A. Two factor theory
B. Hygiene theory
C. Satisfied and not satisfied factor
D. Hygiene factor

77. Studies conducted by Frederick Herzberg used to better understand employee attitudes and motivation and what factors cause job satisfaction and dissatisfaction, also referred to as the Motivation-Hygiene theories are
A. Two factor theory
B. Hygiene theory
C. Satisfied and not satisfied factor
D. All the above

78. The dimension of culture that refers to the extent to which people in a country prefer to act as individuals instead of members of groups is
A. Team   B. Group
C. Department   D. Individualism

79. Programs designed to introduce and acclimate newly hired employees into the organization is
A. Orientation program
B. Induction program
C. Placement activity
D. None of the above

80. Efforts to improve employees' ability to handle a variety of assignments are
A. Human development
B. Organization effectiveness
C. Market growth
D. None of the above

81. A person who has the job of criticizing ideas to ensure that different viewpoints are fully explored is
A. Devil's advocate   B. Bargaining
C. Negotiation   D. None of the above

82. A facilitator-directed meeting consisting of groups of individuals gathered to study a specific subject matter is
A. Work shop   B. Conference
C. Seminar   D. All the above

83. A type of employee counseling used to correct performance or behaviour-related issues is
    A. Performance management
    B. Remedial counseling
    C. Employee counseling
    D. All the above

84. False defamation expressed as spoken words, signs or gestures, which cause damage to the character or reputation of the individual being defamed are referred as
    A. Slander
    B. Body language
    C. Individual behaviour
    D. All the above

85. The process of improving employee performance and productivity by providing the employee with feedback regarding areas where he or she is doing well and areas that may require improvement is
    A. Remedial counseling
    B. Mentor
    C. Performance counseling
    D. All the above

86. A plan implemented by a manager or supervisor that is designed to provide employees with constructive feedback, facilitate discussions between an employee and his or her supervisor regarding performance-related issues, and outline specific areas of performance requiring improvement is
    A. Performance improvement plan
    B. Performance appraisal plan
    C. Feedback plan
    D. None of the above

87. A development technique that requires participants to analyze a situation and decide the best course of action based on the data given is
    A. Simulation   B. Training
    C. Observation   D. All the above

88. The sequence of work-related position for a person occupies throughout life is
    A. Job   B. Career
    C. Job design   D. Career enrichment

89. Type of formula used to determine benefits under a defined benefit pension plan, based on a percentage of pay for each year the employee is in the plan or a percentage of career-average pay times years of service is
    A. Career-average formula
    B. Labour turnover
    C. Maximizing formula
    D. None of the above

90. An office set up within an organization to be used for the purpose of providing outplacement counseling and job placement services to displaced workers is
    A. Office   B. HR department
    C. Career centre   D. Assessment centre

91. Guiding individuals through the career planning and career decision-making process by helping them to make informed decisions regarding educational and occupational choices, as well as providing resources needed to further developing job search and placement skills is
    A. Mentor
    B. Career assessment centre
    C. Career counseling
    D. All the above

92. The process by which individuals establish their current and future career objectives and assess their existing skills, knowledge or experience levels and implement an appropriate course of action to attain their desired career objectives is
    A. Career development
    B. Job enrichment
    C. Job enlargement
    D. All the above

93. The progression of jobs in an organization's specific occupational fields ranked from highest to lowest based on level of responsibility and pay is
    A. Career growth
    B. Career development
    C. Career ladder
    D. None of the above

94. The propensity to make several career changes during an individual's lifetime instead of committing to a long-term career within a specific occupational field is
A. Career development
B. Demand and supply of labour
C. Career advertisement
D. Career mobility

95. The progression of jobs in an organization's specific occupational fields ranked from lowest to highest in the hierarchical structure is
A. Career path   B. Career growth
C. Career developmentD. None of the above

96. The process of establishing career objectives and determining appropriate educational and developmental programs to further develop the skills required to achieve short or long-term career objectives is
A. Career analysis
B. Research based on career
C. Career planning
D. None of the above

97. Occurs when an employee has reached the highest position level he or she can possibly obtain within an organization and has no future prospect of being promoted due to a lack of skills, corporate restructuring or other factors is
A. Career opportunity
B. Career advertisement
C. Career plateau
D. All the above

98. A multi-rater assessment strategy that allows for a performance evaluation of a person, team, project or organization from various sources such as peers, team members, clients, employees, or managers. When individuals and groups receive feedback from various co-workers then it is
A. Performance management
B. Human resource process
C. Implementation
D. 360 degree performance evaluation

99. A career development method whereby less experienced employees are matched with more experienced colleagues for guidance either through formal or informal programs is
A. Guide
B. Well wisher
C. Mentoring
D. Parents

100. Career planning that focuses on individuals' careers rather than on organizational needs is
A. Career planning
B. Group-centered career planning
C. Individual-centered career planning
D. All the above

101. A scale that lists a number of traits and a range of performance for each. The employee is then rated by identifying the score that best describes his or her performance for each trait is
A. Graphic rating scale
B. Alternative ranking method
C. Paired comparison method
D. Forced distribution method

102. Ranking employees from best to worst on a particular trait is
A. Graphic rating scale
B. Alternative ranking method
C. Paired comparison method
D. Forced distribution method

103. Ranking employees by making a chart of all possible pairs of the employees for each trait and indicating which the better employee of the pair is
A. Graphic rating scale
B. Alternative ranking method
C. Paired comparison method
D. Forced distribution method

104. Similar to grading on a curve, predetermined percentages of rates are placed in various categories is
A. Graphic rating scale
B. Alternative ranking method
C. Paired comparison method
D. Forced distribution method

105. Keeping a record of uncommonly good or undesirable examples of an employee's work-related behaviour and reviewing it with the employee at predetermined times is
A. Critical incident method
B. Alternative ranking method
C. Paired comparison method
D. Forced distribution method

106. An appraisal method that aims at combining the benefits of narrative and quantified ratings by anchoring a quantified scale with specific narrative examples of good and poor performance. This is termed as
A. Management by objectives
B. Halo effect
C. Behavioural Anchored Rating Scale (BARS)
D. None of the above

107. _____ setting specific measurable goals with each employee and then periodically reviewing the progress made.
A. Management by objectives
B. Halo effect
C. Behavioural Anchored Rating Scale
D. None of the above

108. An appraisal scale that is too open to interpretation, instead, it includes descriptive phrases that define each trait and what is meant by standards like "good" or "unsatisfactory". This is referred as
A. Management by objectives
B. Halo effect
C. Behavioural Anchored Rating Scale
D. Unclear performance standards

109. The informational role manager's play when they share information with people outside their departments or companies is
A. Spokesperson role
B. Managerial role
C. Leader role
D. All the above

110. In performance appraisal, the problem that occurs when a supervisor's rating of a subordinate on one trait biases the rating of that person on other traits is termed as

A. Management by objectives
B. Halo effect
C. Behaviourial Anchored Rating Scale
D. None of the above

111. A tendency to rate all employees the same way, avoiding the high and the low ratings is
A. Central tendency
B. Halo effect
C. Behaviourial Anchored Rating Scale
D. All the above

112. The problem that occurs when a supervisor has a tendency to rate all subordinates either high or low is
A. Strictness bias   B. Leniency bias
C. Both A & B   D. None of the above

113. The tendency to allow individual differences such as age, race, and sex to affect the appraisal rates these employees receive is
A. Strictness bias
B. Leniency bias
C. Bias
D. None of the above

114. An interview in which the supervisor and subordinate review the appraisal and make plans to remedy deficiencies and reinforce strengths is
A. Performance appraisal
B. Appraisal Interviews
C. Both A and B
D. None of the above

115. The deliberate process through which a person becomes aware of personal career-related attributes and the lifelong series of stages that contributes to his or her career fulfillment is
A. Human resource planning
B. Career planning and development
C. Personality development programme
D. None of the above

116. Results of a period that may occur at the initial career entry when the new employee's high job expectations confront the reality of a boring, unchallenging job is
A. Reality shock   B. Initial stage
C. Both A and B   D. None of the above

117. A training method in which each participant purposely acts out or assumes a particular character or role is
A. Drama
B. Role play
C. Performance management
D. None of the above

118. The process of acquiring control of another corporation by purchase or stock exchange is
A. Acquisition   B. Merging
C. Risk management D. None of the above

119. The performance of job-related tasks and duties by trainees during training is
A. Active practice
B. Performance management
C. Training period
D. All the above

120. A training method where employees are rotated among a variety of different jobs, departments or company functions for a certain period of time is
A. Job schedule   B. Rotational training
C. Direction   D. Planning

121. The process of learning new knowledge, skills and behaviours through taking specific actions or performing specific tasks is
A. Knowledge management
B. Task oriented
C. Goal oriented
D. Active learning

122. Act that determined that older workers may not be discriminated against by performance-based pay systems is
A. Performance appraisal
B. ADEA (Age Discrimination in Employment Act)
C. Wage Act
D. Labour welfare

123. Investigations conducted by local management, local Personnel Representatives and/or Employee Relations in response to complaints or concerns that generally are non-criminal in nature is
A. Administrative process
B. Administrative function

C. Administrative nature
D. Administrative investigation

124. A classical management approach that attempted to identify major principles and functions that managers could use to achieve superior organizational performance is
A. Scientific management
B. Policy and procedures
C. Administrative management
D. Hierarchy function

125. Individual who are beyond post secondary education age, are employed on a full or part-time basis and are enrolled in a formal or informal educational program is
A. Systematic education
B. Adult learner
C. Part time work
D. Full time education

126. Any act by an employer that result in an individual or group of individuals being deprived of equal employment opportunities is
A. Adverse Action   B. Employment policy
C. Job analysis   D. All the above

127. Broadly defined as the implementation of integrated strategies or systems designed to increase workplace productivity by developing improved processes for attracting, developing, retaining and utilizing people with the required skills and aptitude to meet current and future business needs.
A. Implement process
B. Strategic management
C. Talent management
D. Skill management

128. A system that addresses competency gaps, particularly in mission-critical occupations, by implementing and maintaining programs to attract, acquire, develop, promote, and retain quality talent is
A. Implement process
B. Strategic management
C. Talent management system
D. Skill management

129. A type of validity based on showing that scores on the test (predictors) are related to job performance is
A. Score card
B. Criterion validity
C. Stratification
D. Measurement

130. _____ is one in which the test contains a fair sample of the tasks and skills actually needed for the job in question.
A. Test validity
B. Content validity
C. HR accounting
D. HR audit

131. Training provided to employees by managers and supervisors, conducted at the actual worksite utilizing demonstration and actual performance of job tasks to be accomplished.
A. On-the job training
B. Off-the job training
C. Job rotation
D. Abroad training

132. The characteristic which refers to the consistency of scores obtained by the same person when retested with the identical or equivalent tests is
A. Value
B. Reliability
C. Factor analysis
D. All the above

133. A graph showing the relationship between test scores and job performance for a large group of people is
A. Performance feed back
B. 360 degree feedback
C. Expectancy chart
D. Balance score card

134. Typically begin with what, where, why, when, or how is
A. Open question
B. Close question
C. Neither A nor B
D. Either A or B

135. Encourages employees to meet with an immediate supervisor or manager to discuss workplace problems is
A. Direct control
B. Indirect reporting
C. Quality circle
D. Open-door policy

136. Actual job tasks used in testing applicants' performance is
A. Work samples
B. Job analysis
C. Observation
D. Sample work

137. A detailed projection of all projected income and expenses during a specified future period is
A. Tax counting
B. Operating budget
C. HR investment
D. Operating cost

138. A written document issued by government agencies used to provide a ruling on a particular issue.
A. Opinion letter
B. Suggestion box
C. Notice
D. Pamphlets

139. A testing method based on measuring performance on actual job tasks is
A. Performance based
B. Sampling techniques
C. Job description
D. Work sample techniques

140. A situation in which management candidates are asked to make decisions in hypothetical situations and are scored on their performance is
A. Management assessment centre
B. Situation analysis
C. Performance management
D. Performance appraisal

141. A tool used to solicit and assess employee opinions, feelings, perceptions and expectations regarding a variety of managerial and organizational issues is
A. Opinion survey
B. Survey
C. Historical survey
D. Internal survey

142. A verbal warning given to an employee by a manager or supervisor as a means of correcting inappropriate behaviour or conduct is
A. Oral reprimand
B. Communication system
C. Conversation
D. All the above

143. What is meant by the term 'Management By Objectives'?
A. A system of giving the authority to carry out certain jobs by those lower down the management hierarchy.
B. The system of management that is based on bringing together experts into a team.

C. The setting of objectives to bring about the achievement of the corporate goals.

D. The control of the organization by those in the 'head office'.

144. 'Management by objectives' is to think about how targets can be used to monitor performance and objectives need to be reviewed and updated regularly, or else they will become out of date.

A. True

B. False

C. Neither true nor false

D. None of the above

145. Economic value added (EVA) is a firm's net operating profit after the cost of capital is deducted.

A. True   B. False

C. Either true or false D. None of the above

146. An active leader who creates a positive work environment in which the organization and its employees have the opportunity and the incentive to achieve high performance.

A. Effective manager   B. HR manager

C. Line manager   D. None of the above

147. The extent to which goals have been met.

A. Efficient   B. Effectiveness

C. Measuring tool   D. None of the above

148. The degree to which operations are done in an economical manner OR the ratio of outputs to inputs.

A. Efficiency   B. Effectiveness

C. Measuring tool   D. None of the above

149. Employee assistance program (EAP) is a program that provides counseling and help to employees having emotional, physical, or personal problems.

A. True   B. False

C. Either true or false D. None of the above

150. Listen and respond to employees and find the right balance between demands on employees and resources available to employees is termed as

A. Worker's participation

B. Trade union

C. Employee's right

D. Employee champion

ANSWERS

1	2	3	4	5	6	7	8	9	10
A	A	A	A	C	A	A	C	D	C
11	**12**	**13**	**14**	**15**	**16**	**17**	**18**	**19**	**20**
C	C	C	C	A	D	B	C	B	C
21	**22**	**23**	**24**	**25**	**26**	**27**	**28**	**29**	**30**
B	A	A	C	A	C	D	C	B	B
31	**32**	**33**	**34**	**35**	**36**	**37**	**38**	**39**	**40**
A	C	A	B	B	C	B	C	C	C
41	**42**	**43**	**44**	**45**	**46**	**47**	**48**	**49**	**50**
B	B	C	C	B	A	C	B	B	B
51	**52**	**53**	**54**	**55**	**56**	**57**	**58**	**59**	**60**
D	C	A	D	C	A	A	B	A	A
61	**62**	**63**	**64**	**65**	**66**	**67**	**68**	**69**	**70**
C	A	A	C	B	A	B	A	D	C
71	**72**	**73**	**74**	**75**	**76**	**77**	**78**	**79**	**80**
D	D	A	C	C	D	D	D	B	A
81	**82**	**83**	**84**	**85**	**86**	**87**	**88**	**89**	**90**
A	C	B	A	C	A	A	B	A	C

91	92	93	94	95	96	97	98	99	100
C	A	C	D	A	C	C	D	C	C
101	**102**	**103**	**104**	**105**	**106**	**107**	**108**	**109**	**110**
A	B	C	D	A	C	A	D	A	B
111	**112**	**113**	**114**	**115**	**116**	**117**	**118**	**119**	**120**
A	C	C	B	B	C	B	A	A	B
121	**122**	**123**	**124**	**125**	**126**	**127**	**128**	**129**	**130**
D	B	D	C	B	A	C	C	B	B
131	**132**	**133**	**134**	**135**	**136**	**137**	**138**	**139**	**140**
A	B	C	A	D	A	B	A	D	A
141	**142**	**143**	**144**	**145**	**146**	**147**	**148**	**149**	**150**
A	A	C	A	A	A	B	A	A	D

3

Organizational Behaviour

Organizational behaviour is a study of individuals and it is a study of groups. It studies the aspects of motivation, leader behaviour, power, interpersonal relations and communication, group structure and problems, learning, attitudes, perception, change process, conflict, job design and work stress etc. The history of organizational behaviour dates back from 1920' with "Hawthorne studies" of Elton Mayo and R.J. Roethlisberger. Later McGeorge threw light on understanding behaviour to motivate people through his work known as "Theory X and Theory Y". The study of organizational behaviour is an interdisciplinary approach consisting of Psychology, Sociology, Anthropology, Economics, and Political science. The study involves interaction among the formal structure, the tasks to be undertaken, the technology employed and the method of carrying out work, the behaviour of people, the process of management and the external environment in which an organization is functioning.

Organizational Behaviour is the key aspect to maintain and enhance interaction levels amongst employees in the company. Other attributes like leadership, openness to discuss problems, challenge-initiative is all tied in to this base concept of Organizational Behaviour to help the business achieve its strategic and in some cases business objectives. The proper definition of organizational behaviour with its understanding and management has resulted in development of few key offshoots to the concept of Organizational Behaviour.

Organizational behaviour is the study of the behaviour of people within an organization setting. It involves the understanding, prediction and control of human behaviour and the factors which influence the performance of people in all types of organization.

Definitions

According to Keith Davis, organizational behaviour is the study and application of knowledge about how people act within organizations. It relates to other system elements such as structure, technology and the external social environment. In the words of Stephen P. Robbins, organizational behaviour is the study of the impact that individuals, groups and structure, technology and the external social environment.

The concepts and the definition of Organization Behaviour

- **Organization Design:** This is the simple structure of creating roles and formal reporting relationships for employees in an organization. An effective organization design is reflected in the joining letter which is handed over to a new employee. The joining letter would talk about his role, his direct line manager and the processes which he would need to adhere to.

● **Organization Development:** Every organization has a mission statement and the time when the organization formalizes the mission statement it may not have the resources or the expertise to execute the mission effectively. Organization Development involves the combined, planned effort of all the resources of the company to ensure that the company carries its mission forward. As defined by Richard Beckhard, organization development would involve a site-wide, planned effort from all the employees, with the top management overriding in the organization purposes.

● **Organizational empowerment:** This is one of the buzzwords of organizational behaviour principles in most of the companies which are evolving today. Organizational empowerment means the level of responsibility that an organization places on its employees at all levels so that decisions can be taken without any manager interference. The key is here though many organizations advocate this approach; most of them have a certain element of mentoring and guidance to their employees at all times.

● **Organizational engineering:** This is a distinctive advancement of Organization development with the only difference that it takes a completely mathematical approach to organization development. The mathematical equations of the company's business model is studied and different people are inserted into the model based on formulas, and better still the outcomes are predicted from the people's roles. This is done to ensure that company's efficiency is increased and it gets more effective with its communication.

● It is most important to understand that any definition of organization behaviour would be incomplete without studying the change management curve of the employees. If you are a company planning to introduce some organizational behaviour initiatives, would need to ensure that the organizational behaviour initiatives are transitioned out smoothly to the employees. This needs to be done very carefully because this may lead to a lot of discontented employees if enough care is not taken to transitioning the processes. If one had to define organizational behaviour, it will be a set of principles followed by employees at all levels to ensure that the company meets its strategic objectives.

Evolution of Organizational Behaviour

● **Traditional Organizational Theory:** Management theory was a philosophy born of 19th century industrialization. Mass production factories were packed with individuals with unique personalities and motivations. These employees had to form teams and work through their differences for the good of the organization. The first management theories focused mostly on how to help supervisors through bureaucracy and authority. Traditional organizational concerns included company hierarchy, labour divisions and company rule. Later organizational theory came to include scientific study of behaviour and group dynamics, which leads to the motivations-based management that we often see in today's top businesses.

● **Behavioural Management:** Organizational Behaviour Management (OBM) applies group dynamics and organizational behaviour theory to performance management. In this system, a manager analyzes how each individual (and each individual group) contributes to the entire system. The individual's actions are broken down into the antecedent (cause of the action), the behaviour and the outcome. Undesirable outcomes are traced back to dysfunctional antecedents. Managers adjust the outcome to higher performance by changing the predecessor. Managers also use this system to change the direction of the whole organization.

● **Organizational Behaviour:** Organizational behaviour considers individual motivations and applies those drives to the organization. Motivations are unique to individuals; some people are motivated more by money, while others seek appreciation or more free time with their family and friends. Individual motivations create roles for people that are further defined by other group members and the entire organization. Organizational leaders offer motive-based incentives to encourage productivity and group cooperation. Many companies use a wide variety of incentives to meet employees' various motives.

• **Group Dynamics:** Group dynamics describes the behaviour of the group, different types of groups and the attitudes of various individuals involved in the group. According to the Social Exchange Theory, groups are formed because individuals need beneficial interactions that are driven by obligation and backed by trust. The formation of a group provides obligation and implies trust. Stages of group progress include formation, storming, normalizing, performing and adjourning. Not all groups go through every stage; for example, perpetual groups may never adjourn.

The basic approaches of organizational behaviour:

1. Interdisciplinary approach
2. Human resource approach
3. Contingency approach
4. Productivity approach
5. System approach

Managing a group in organization is more difficult than managing individuals. When individual are in groups, they act differently rather than they do when they are alone. The fact is that the group exhibit patterns of behaviour that are different from the behaviours of members in their individual capacity. Many factors influence human behaviour in the workplace. Complex interactions come with a diversity of consequences and outcomes. To achieve maximum efficiency and successful teamwork at the office, it is important for managers and their employees to understand group dynamics.

Organizations of today are increasingly complex and must respond to rapid changes to sustain their effectiveness. Due to these developments, expertise is required to deal with the issues and challenges arising from the person and the environment. The field of organizational behaviour is an area of study offering insights that can improve or restore proper functioning. According to several sources, the aim of organizational behaviour is to "explain, predict, and control" in order to enhance the performance of organizations. Groups serve an increasingly important function in the operation of organizations.

The discipline Organizational Behaviour, works in teams, streamline processes, enhance employee participation, and improve quality. John Schermerhorn, author of Management and Organizational Behaviour wrote that groups can "increase resources for problem-solving, foster creativity and innovation, improve quality of decision-making, enhance members' commitments to tasks, raise motivation through collective action, help control and discipline members, and help satisfy individual needs as organizations grow in size."

Stephen R. Robbins defined group as two or more individuals interacting and interdependent, who have come together to achieve particular objectives. Group in general is a social phenomenon in which two or more person decide to, (*i*) Interact with in another, (*ii*) Share common ideology and (*iii*) Perceive themselves as a group. The field of anthropology, psychology and sociology has contributed to the development of the concept of a group.

Characteristics of Group

(*i*) Strong desire of association
(*ii*) Development of leadership
(*iii*) Awareness among members
(*iv*) Properties of individuals
(*v*) Cohesiveness
(*vi*) Perceive themselves as a group.

The major function of Group is to socialization of new employees, getting the job done and decision-making. *Organizational Behaviour* and *Human Decision Processes*, Kevin Tasa and Glen Whyte examined vigilant problem-solving in the context of group decision-making. According to them, it entails

- Identify the objectives to be achieved by the decision and specifying the major requirements of a successful choice,
- Generating a comprehensive list of well-developed alternatives,
- Searching widely for relevant information with which to determine the quality of the alternatives,
- Engaging in the unbiased and accurate processing of information relevant to the assessment of the alternatives,
- Reconsidering and re-examining all the pros and cons of the alternatives,
- Recognizing, evaluating, and adjusting to more desirable levels the costs, benefits, and risks of the preferred choice, and
- Developing plans to implement the decision, monitor the results, and react in the event that known risks become a reality.

If nothing else, the above serves as a bench-mark against which to judge and compare work processes of organizational teams. Due to myriad circumstances however, it sounds more like an ideal than a reality. Like most mission statements, criteria are easy to state but hard to live up to. Many teams fall short for a number of reasons. Groups provide a means for communication and mechanisms for the performance of necessary activities of a complex nature.

ORIGINS OF GROUP DYNAMICS

Humans cannot escape from their fate as social creatures. The individual's well-being is inextricably tied in with group harmony, they must vigilantly respond to the sometimes unpredictable whims of their society in order to safeguard their own security. This is where the use of the study of group psychology comes in.

Kurt Lewin, widely regarded as one of the founding fathers of social psychology, was one of the pioneers in the fruitful field of group dynamics. Lewin believed that in order to explain behaviour, the person's entire environment has to be taken into consideration. This means the dynamics of different environmental and individual factors and their interrelations have to be given due consideration. This is the principle of "field theory".

The field represents the complete picture of the individual and the environment and behaviour results from interactions between the person's self-perceptions and the environmental influences. Group dynamics grew out of the Lewin's work in field theory and his work inspired many psychologists to further investigate and advance our understanding of group dynamics and its impact on society.

Many schools of thought arose from this seminal breakthrough and when theories formed, new terms were coined to describe various group phenomena that have influenced decisions undertaken which turned major events in human history. In order to understand group dynamics, we need to know about the various group-level phenomena that have been observed throughout the span of time where its manifestations have sparked debate or caught the eye of scholars and researchers.

Conformity

One of the most commonly known effects of groups is conformity. This phenomenon had been thoroughly examined in great depth by many talented scholars but none more than the legendary social psychologist Solomon Asch. In truly daring fashion, his experimental design elegantly demonstrated on empirical grounds the distortion of fact by judgments formed in the face of group pressure. Not since Asch has anyone come as close to epitomizing the art of elegance in the field of experimentation at least in the domain of the social sciences.

Security

Unity is strength "By joining a group, we can reduce the insecurity of standing alone", we feel stronger, and we have fewer self-doubts and are more resistant to threats. The appeal of unions—if management creates an environment in which employees feel insecure, they are likely to turn to unionization to reduce their feelings of insecurity.

Risky Shift

Another phenomenon associated with groups is known as risky shift. This effect is more aptly described as the tendency for groups to express riskier or more extreme opinions when composed as a group instead of individuals. Riskier choices are explained in part by diffusion of responsibility when individuals coalesce into a group. Sergei Moscovici and Marisa Zavaloni conducted an experiment to examine this phenomenon and concluded that group members' commitment to consensus made as a group may be a factor contributing to this occurrence.

Groupthink

One of the most prominent theories put forward to describe a group-level phenomenon is known as Groupthink, famously associated with psychologist Irving Janis. This is a state where members of a group care too much for group harmony and cohesiveness which gives rise in part to a sense of invulnerability. Symptoms associated with this phenomenon include group members that override a complete and thorough evaluation of the situation and fail to adequately consider alternative courses of action, are biased towards their own point of view, or are afraid of voicing opposition for fear of ostracizing themselves.

Affiliation

People join group for their affiliation to be obtained from the group members as well an opportunity for social interaction while off the job. Their instinct of affiliation is satisfied by such interaction on the job, by the status, esteem, power, rewards, goals achieved etc.

Social Loafing

Apart from excessive group pressure which impedes objectivity in assessing team-based decisions, members of work teams also need to watch out for another commonly known drawback associated with group work, a phenomenon called social loafing. This is when responsibility becomes diffused throughout the team and one or a few members of work teams take unfair advantage and do not pull their weight in completing their assignments. This gives rise to disproportionate distribution of effort amongst team members or incomplete work.

Gender Dynamics

The decisional outcomes of workgroups are also impacted by the gender of its members. Stereotypes about gender roles do exist and are abound in the literature. Traditional feminine roles are conceptualized as expressive and masculine roles instrumental. However, individuals differ greatly as to how they approximate to these traits among one another. Therefore whether these traits cast an overriding influence across all people in all situations remains to be seen. Men are frequently assigned stereotypical roles of being task-oriented and logical while women are looked upon as nurturing, intuitive thinkers who go to extra length to hold relationships together.

Women supposedly lead more in an interpersonally-oriented style and men in a more task-oriented style. No sweeping statement can justifiably summarize the superiority or inferiority of one gender or style over the other. One thing we can be sure of however is that the characteristic each individual brings into a group scenario has strengths and merits of their own and we should not fall into the trap of stereotyping.

Group Formation Process

An analysis of group dynamics will not be complete without touching on the group formation process in organizations. According to Schermerhon, corroboration of studies has revealed they can be subdivided into five stages:

- **Forming:** Forming refers to the initial get-to-know stages, where individuals feel for the boundaries and get acquainted.
- **Storming:** Storming is a highly emotional stage whereby individuals identify common interest, try to impose certain standards on others, or even establish status differentials.
- **Norming:** Norming is the stage whereby rules or codes of conduct become built up consciously or unconsciously.
- **Performing:** Performing is the beginning of productivity, as group members become a coordinated work unit.

- **Adjourning:** Finally, adjourning is the stage whereby groups disband after accomplishing their goals.

Benefits of Successful Teamwork

In spite of the many shortcomings, many experts agree that teamwork is of great use because of the "synergy" effect. Synergy occurs when individuals compose into a group to work towards a common purpose and emergent advantages accumulate to give the company with better teamwork the edge. This is also known as the "whole is greater than the sum of its parts" argument.

When broken down into its components, teams can be said to derive their strength from numerous areas which include a greater sum total of knowledge and information from different members, a wider range of approaches to solving problems, lower chance of running out of ideas, greater acceptance due to consensus being obtained among more numbers, and better understanding due to partaking in the road taken to reach the decision.

MOTIVATION

Motivation is the word derived from the word 'motive' which means needs, desires, wants or drives within the individuals. It is the process of stimulating people to actions to accomplish the goals. In the work goal context the psychological factors stimulating the people's behaviour can be:

- desire for money
- success
- recognition
- job-satisfaction
- team work, etc.

One of the most important functions of management is to create willingness amongst the employees to perform in the best of their abilities. Therefore the role of leader is to arouse interest in performance of employees in their jobs. The process of motivation consists of three stages:

1. A felt need or drive
2. A stimulus in which needs have to be aroused
3. When needs are satisfied, the satisfaction or accomplishment of goals.

Therefore, we can say that motivation is a psychological phenomenon which means needs and wants of the individuals have to be tackled by framing an incentive plan.

- Motivation
  - The set of forces that cause people to behave in certain ways.
  - The goal of managers is to maximize desired behaviours and minimize undesirable behaviours.

The Importance of Motivation in the Workplace

- Determinants of individual performance
- Motivation, the desire to do the job.
- Ability, the capability to do the job.
- Work environment, the resources needed to do the job.

The Motivation Framework

Motivational Challenges

Motivation seems to be a simple function of management, but in practice it is more challenging. **The reasons for motivation being challenging job are as follows:**

One of the main reasons of motivation being a challenging job is due to the changing workforce. The employees become a part of their organization with various needs and expectations. Different employees have different beliefs, attitudes, values, backgrounds and thinking. But all the organizations are not aware of the diversity in their workforce and thus are not aware and clear about different ways of motivating their diverse workforce.

Motivation of employees becomes challenging especially when the organizations have considerably changed the job role of the employees, or have lessened the hierarchy levels of hierarchy, or have chucked out a significant number of employees in the name of down-sizing or right-sizing. Certain firms have chosen to hire and fire and paying for performance strategies nearly giving up motivational efforts. These strategies are unsuccessful in making an individual overreach himself.

Good Motivation System

- Motivation is a state of mind. High motivation leads to high morale and greater production. A motivated employee gives his best to the organization. He stays loyal and committed to the organization. A sound motivation system in an organization should have the following features:
- Superior performance should be reasonably rewarded and should be duly acknowledged.
- If the performance is not consistently up to the mark, then the system must make provisions for penalties.
- The employees must be dealt in a fair and just manner. The grievances and obstacles faced by them must be dealt instantly and fairly.
- Carrot and stick approach should be implemented to motivate both efficient and inefficient employees. The employees should treat negative consequences (such as fear of punishment) as stick, an outside push and move away from it. They should take positive consequences (such as reward) as carrot, an inner pull and move towards it.
- Performance appraisal system should be very effective.
- Ensure flexibility in working arrangements.
- A sound motivation system must be correlated to organizational goals. Thus, the individual/employee goals must be harmonized with the organizational goals.
- The motivational system must be modified to the situation and to the organization.
- A sound motivation system requires modifying the nature of individual's jobs. The jobs should be redesigned or restructured according to the requirement of situation. Any

of the alternatives to job specialization, job rotation, job enlargement, job enrichment, etc. could be used.

- The management approach should be participative. All the subordinates and employees should be involved in decision-making process.
- The motivation system should involve monetary as well as non-monetary rewards. The monetary rewards should be correlated to performance. Performance should be based on the employees' action towards the goals, and not on the fame of employees.
- "Motivate yourself to motivate your employees" should be the managerial approach.
- The managers must understand and identify the motivators for each employee.

Sound motivation system should encourage supportive supervision whereby the supervisors share their views and experiences with their subordinates, listen to the subordinates views, and assist the subordinates in performing the designated job. The motivation concepts were mainly developed around 1950's. Three main theories were made during this period. These three classical theories are:

Content Perspectives of Motivation

- Maslow's Hierarchy of Needs
- Herzberg's Two-Factor Theory
- Theory X and Theory Y
- McClelland's, Achievement, Power, and Affiliation Needs

Process Perspectives of Motivation

- Expectancy Theory
- Porter-Lawler Extension of Expectancy Theory
- Equity Theory
- Goal-Setting Theory

Maslow's Hierarchy of Needs Theory

Abraham Maslow is well renowned for proposing the Hierarchy of Needs Theory in 1943. This theory is a classical depiction of human motivation. This theory is based on the assumption that there is a hierarchy of five needs within each individual. The urgency of these needs varies. These five needs are as follows:

Maslow's Need Hierarchy Model

1. **Physiological needs:** These are the basic needs of air, water, food, clothing and shelter. In other words, physiological needs are the needs for basic amenities of life.
2. **Safety needs:** Safety needs include physical, environmental and emotional safety and protection. For instance: Job security, financial security, protection from animals, family security, health security, etc.
3. **Social needs:** Social needs include the need for love, affection, care, belongingness, and friendship.
4. **Esteem needs:** Esteem needs are of two types: internal esteem needs (self-respect, confidence, competence, achievement and freedom) and external esteem needs (recognition, power, status, attention and admiration).
5. **Self-actualization need:** This include the urge to become what you are capable of becoming/ what you have the potential to become. It includes the need for growth and self-contentment. It also includes desire for gaining more knowledge, social-service, creativity and being aesthetic. The self-actualization needs are never fully satiable. As an individual grows psychologically, opportunities keep cropping up to continue growing.

According to Maslow, individuals are motivated by unsatisfied needs. As each of these needs is significantly satisfied, it drives and forces the next need to emerge. Maslow grouped the five needs into two categories—**Higher-order needs** and **Lower-order needs**. The physiological and the safety needs constituted the lower-order needs. These lower-order needs are mainly satisfied externally. The social, esteem, and self-actualization needs constituted the higher-order needs. These higher-order needs are generally satisfied internally, *i.e.*, within an individual. Thus, we can conclude that during boom period, the employees lower-order needs are significantly met.

Implications of Maslow's Hierarchy of Needs Theory for Managers

- As far as the physiological needs are concerned, the managers should give employees appropriate salaries to purchase the basic necessities of life. Breaks and eating opportunities should be given to employees.
- As far as the safety needs are concerned, the managers should provide the employees job security, safe and hygienic work environment, and retirement benefits so as to retain them.
- As far as social needs are concerned, the management should encourage teamwork and organize social events.
- As far as esteem needs are concerned, the managers can appreciate and reward employees on accomplishing and exceeding their targets. The management can give the deserved employee higher job rank / position in the organization.
- As far as self-actualization needs are concerned, the managers can give the employees challenging jobs in which the employees' skills and competencies are fully utilized. Moreover, growth opportunities can be given to them so that they can reach the peak.
- The managers must identify the need level at which the employee is existing and then those needs can be utilized as push for motivation.

Limitations of Maslow's Theory

- It is essential to note that not all employees

are governed by same set of needs. Different individuals may be driven by different needs at same point of time. It is always the **most powerful unsatisfied need that motivates an individual.**

- The theory is not empirically supported.
- The theory is not applicable in case of starving artist as even if the artist's basic needs are not satisfied, he will still strive for recognition and achievement.

Herzberg's Two-Factor Theory of Motivation

In 1959, Frederick Herzberg, a behavioural scientist proposed a two-factor theory or the motivator-hygiene theory. According to Herzberg, there are some job factors that result in satisfaction while there are other job factors that prevent dissatisfaction. According to Herzberg, the opposite of "Satisfaction" is "No Satisfaction" and the opposite of "Dissatisfaction" is "No Dissatisfaction".

Herzberg's view of satisfaction and dissatisfaction

Herzberg classified these job factors into two categories:

(a) **Hygiene factors:** Hygiene factors are those job factors which are essential for existence of motivation at workplace. These do not lead to positive satisfaction for long-term. But if these factors are absent / if these factors are non-existent at workplace, then they lead to dissatisfaction. In other words, hygiene factors are those factors which when adequate/reasonable in a job, pacify the employees and do not make them dissatisfied. These factors are extrinsic to work. Hygiene factors are also called as **dissatisfiers or maintenance factors** as they are required to avoid dissatisfaction. These factors describe the job environment/scenario. The hygiene factors symbolized the physiological needs which the individuals wanted and expected to be fulfilled.

(b) **Motivational factors:** According to Herzberg, the hygiene factors cannot be regarded as motivators. The motivational factors yield positive satisfaction. These factors are inherent to work. These factors motivate the employees for a superior performance. These

factors are called satisfiers. These are factors involved in performing the job. Employees find these factors intrinsically rewarding. The motivators symbolized the psychological needs that were perceived as an additional benefit. Motivational factors include:

- Recognition: The employees should be praised and recognized for their accomplishments by the managers.
- Sense of achievement: The employees must have a sense of achievement. This depends on the job. There must be a fruit of some sort in the job.
- Growth and promotional opportunities: There must be growth and advancement opportunities in an organization to motivate the employees to perform well.
- Responsibility: The employees must hold themselves responsible for the work. The managers should give them ownership of the work. They should minimize control but retain accountability.
- Meaningfulness of the work: The work itself should be meaningful, interesting and challenging for the employee to perform and to get motivated.

➤ Pay: The pay or salary structure should be appropriate and reasonable. It must be equal and competitive to those in the same industry in the same domain.

➤ Company policies and administrative policies: The company policies should not be too rigid.

➤ They should be fair and clear: It should include flexible working hours, dress code, breaks, vacation, etc.

➤ Fringe benefits: The employees should be offered health care plans (medi-claim), benefits for the family members, employee help programmes, etc.

➤ Physical working conditions: The working conditions should be safe, clean and hygienic. The work equipments should be updated and well-maintained.

➤ Status: The employees' status within the organization should be familiar and retained.

➤ Interpersonal relations: The relationship of the employees with his peers, superiors and subordinates should be appropriate and acceptable. There should be no conflict or humiliation element present.

➤ Job security: The organization must provide job security to the employees.

Limitations of Two-Factor Theory

The two factor theory is not free from limitations:

1. The two-factor theory overlooks situational variables.

2. Herzberg assumed a correlation between satisfaction and productivity. But the research conducted by Herzberg stressed upon satisfaction and ignored productivity.

3. The theory's reliability is uncertain. Analysis has to be made by the raters. The raters may spoil the findings by analyzing same response in different manner.

4. No comprehensive measure of satisfaction was used. An employee may find his job acceptable despite the fact that he may hate/object part of his job.

5. The two factor theory is not free from bias as it is based on the natural reaction of

employees when they are enquired the sources of satisfaction and dissatisfaction at work. They will blame dissatisfaction on the external factors such as salary structure, company policies and peer relationship. Also, the employees will give credit to themselves for the satisfaction factor at work.

6. The theory ignores blue-collar workers. Despite these limitations, Herzberg's Two-Factor theory is acceptable broadly.

Implications of Two-Factor Theory

The Two-Factor theory implies that the managers must stress upon guaranteeing the adequacy of the hygiene factors to avoid employee dissatisfaction. Also, the managers must make sure that the work is stimulating and rewarding so that the employees are motivated to work and perform harder and better. This theory emphasize upon job-enrichment so as to motivate the employees. The job must utilize the employee's skills and competencies to the maximum. Focusing on the motivational factors can improve work-quality.

Theory X and Theory Y

Douglas McGregor, an American social psychologist, proposed his famous X-Y theory in his 1960 book 'The Human Side of Enterprise'. Theory X and theory Y are still referred to commonly in the field of management and motivation, and whilst more recent studies have questioned the rigidity of the model, McGregor's X-Y Theory remains a valid basic principle from which to develop positive management style and techniques. McGregor's XY Theory remains central to organizational development, and to improving organizational culture.

McGregor's X-Y theory is a salutary and simple reminder of the natural rules for managing people, which under the pressure of day-to-day business are all too easily forgotten.

McGregor's ideas suggest that there are two fundamental approaches to managing people. Many managers tend towards theory X, and generally get poor results. Enlightened managers use theory Y, which produces better performance and results, and allows people to grow and develop.

McGregor's ideas significantly relate to modern understanding of the psychological, which provides many ways to appreciate the unhelpful nature of X-Theory leadership, and the useful constructive beneficial nature of Y-Theory leadership.

Assumption of Theory X and Theory Y

- Employees can perceive their job as relaxing and normal. They exercise their physical and mental efforts in an inherent manner in their jobs.
- Employees may not require only threat, external control and coercion to work, but they can use self-direction and self-control if they are dedicated and sincere to achieve the organizational objectives.
- If the job is rewarding and satisfying, then it will result in employees' loyalty and commitment to organization.
- An average employee can learn to admit and recognize the responsibility. In fact, he can even learn to obtain responsibility.
- The employees have skills and capabilities. Their logical capabilities should be fully utilized. In other words, the creativity, resourcefulness and innovative potentiality of the employees can be utilized to solve organizational problems.

Thus, we can say that Theory X presents a pessimistic view of employees' nature and behaviour at work, while Theory Y presents an optimistic view of the employees' nature and behaviour at work. If correlate it with Maslow's theory, we can say that Theory X is based on the assumption that the employees emphasize on the physiological needs and the safety needs; while Theory X is based on the assumption that the social needs, esteem needs and the self-actualization needs dominate the employees.

McGregor views Theory Y to be more valid and reasonable than Theory X. Thus, he encouraged cordial team relations, responsible and stimulating jobs, and participation of all in decision-making process.

Implications of Theory X and Theory Y

- Quite a few organizations use Theory X today. Theory X encourages use of tight control and supervision. It implies that employees are reluctant to organizational changes. Thus, it does not encourage innovation.
- Many organizations are using Theory Y techniques. Theory Y implies that the managers should create and encourage a work environment which provides opportunities to employees to take initiative and self-direction. Employees should be given opportunities to contribute to organizational well-being. Theory Y encourages decentralization of authority, teamwork and participative decision-making in an organization. Theory Y searches and discovers the ways in which an employee can make significant contributions in an organization. It harmonizes and matches employees' needs and aspirations with organizational needs and aspirations.

McClelland Theory of Motivation

David McClelland and his associates proposed McClelland's theory of Needs / Achievement Motivation Theory. This theory states that human behaviour is affected by three needs: Need for Power, Achievement and Affiliation. Need for **achievement** is the urge to excel, to accomplish in relation to a set of standards, to struggle to achieve success. Need for **power** is the desire to influence other individual's behaviour as per your wish. In other words, it is the desire to have control over others and to be influential. Need for **affiliation** is a need for open and sociable interpersonal relationships. In other words, it is a desire for relationship based on co-operation and mutual understanding.

The individuals with high achievement needs are highly motivated by competing and challenging work. They look for promotional opportunities in job. They have a strong urge for feedback on their achievement. Such individuals try to get satisfaction in performing things better.

High achievement is directly related to high performance. Individuals who are better and above average performers are highly motivated. They assume responsibility for solving the problems at work. McClelland called such individuals as gamblers as they set challenging targets for themselves and they take deliberate risk to achieve those set targets. Such individuals look for innovative ways of performing job. They perceive achievement of goals as a reward, and value it more than a financial reward.

The individuals who are motivated by power have a strong urge to be influential and controlling. They want that their views and ideas should dominate and thus, they want to lead. Such individuals are motivated by the need for reputation and self-esteem. Individuals with greater power and authority will perform better than those possessing less power. Generally, managers with high need for power turn out to be more efficient and successful managers.

They are more determined and loyal to the organization they work for. Need for power should not always be taken negatively. It can be viewed as the need to have a positive effect on the organization and to support the organization in achieving its goals.

The individuals who are motivated by affiliation have an urge for a friendly and supportive environment. Such individuals are effective performers in a team. These people want to be liked by others. The manager's ability to make decisions is hampered if they have a high affiliation need as they prefer to be accepted and liked by others, and this weakens their objectivity. Individuals having high affiliation needs prefer working in an environment providing greater personal interaction. Such people have a need to be on the good books of all. They generally cannot be good leaders.

Modern Theories of Motivation

As far as contemporary theories of motivation are concerned all were supported with evidence whereas, the classical theories of motivation are not empirically supported. Some of the contemporary / modern theories of motivation are explained below:

- ERG theory
- Goal setting theory
- Reinforcement theory
- Equity theory of motivation
- Expectancy theory of motivation

ERG Theory of Motivation

To bring Maslow's need hierarchy theory of motivation in synchronization with empirical research, Clayton Alderfer redefined it in his own terms. His rework is called as ERG theory of motivation. He recategorized Maslow's hierarchy of needs into three simpler and broader classes of needs:

- **Existence needs:** These include need for basic material necessities. In short, it includes an individual's physiological and physical safety needs.
- **Relatedness needs:** These include the aspiration individual's have for maintaining significant interpersonal relationships (be it with family, peers or superiors), getting public fame and recognition. Maslow's social needs and external component of esteem needs fall under this class of need.
- **Growth needs:** These include need for self-development and personal growth and advancement. Maslow's self-actualization needs and intrinsic component of esteem needs fall under this category of need.

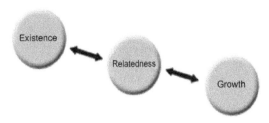

The significance of the three classes of needs may vary for each individual.

Difference between Maslow Need Hierarchy Theory and Alderfer's ERG Theory

- *ERG Theory states that at a given point of time, more than one need may be operational.*
- *ERG Theory also shows that if the fulfillment of a higher-level need is subdued, there is an increase in desire for satisfying a lower-level need.*
- *According to Maslow, an individual remains at a particular need level until that need is satisfied. While according to ERG theory, if a higher-level need aggravates, an individual may revert to increase the satisfaction of a lower-level need. This is called frustration-regression aspect of ERG theory. For instance- when growth need aggravates, then an individual might be motivated to accomplish the relatedness need and if there are issues in accomplishing relatedness needs, then he might be motivated by the existence needs. Thus, frustration/aggravation can result in regression to a lower-level need.*
- *While Maslow's need hierarchy theory is rigid as it assumes that the needs follow a specific and orderly hierarchy and unless a lower-level need is satisfied, an individual cannot proceed to the higher-level need; ERG Theory of motivation is very flexible as he perceived the needs as a range/variety rather than perceiving them as a hierarchy.*
- *According to Alderfer, an individual can work on growth needs even if his existence or relatedness needs remain unsatisfied. Thus, he gives explanation to the issue of "starving artist" who can struggle for growth even if he is hungry.*

Implications of the ERG Theory

Managers must understand that an employee has various needs that must be satisfied at the same time. According to the ERG theory, if the manager concentrates solely on one need at a time, this will not effectively motivate the employee. Also, the frustration-regression aspect of ERG Theory has an added effect on workplace motivation.

For instance: if an employee is not provided with growth and advancement opportunities in an organization, he might revert to the relatedness need such as socializing needs and to meet those socializing needs, if the environment or circumstances do not permit, he might revert to the need for money to fulfill those socializing needs. The sooner the manager realizes and discovers this, the more immediate steps they will take to fulfill those needs which are frustrated until such time that the employee can again pursue growth.

Goal-Setting Theory

- Assumptions
  - Behaviour is a result of conscious goals and intentions.
  - Setting goals influences the behaviour of people in organizations.
- Characteristics of Goals
  - Goal difficulty
    - Extent to which a goal is challenging and requires effort.
    - People work harder to achieve more difficult goals.
    - Goals should be difficult but attainable.
- Characteristics of Goals (cont'd)
  - Goal specificity
    - Clarity and precision of the goal.
    - Goals vary in their ability to be stated specifically.
  - Acceptance
    - The extent to which persons accept a goal as their own.
  - Commitment

The extent to which an individual is personally interested in reaching a goal

The Expanded Goal-Setting Theory of Motivation

Reinforcement Perspectives on Motivation
- Reinforcement Theory
  - The role of rewards as they cause behaviour to change or remain the same over time.
  - Assumes that:
- Behaviour that results in rewarding consequences is likely to be repeated, whereas behaviour that results in punishing consequences is less likely to be repeated.

Kinds of Reinforcement in Organizations
- Positive reinforcement
  - Strengthens behaviour with rewards or positive outcomes after a desired behaviour is performed.
- Avoidance
  - Strengthens behaviour by avoiding unpleasant consequences that would result if the behaviour is not performed.
- Punishment
  - Weakens undesired behaviour by using negative outcomes or unpleasant consequences when the behaviour is performed.
- Extinction
  - Weakens undesired behaviour by simply ignoring or not reinforcing that behaviour.
- Reinforcement schedules
  - Fixed interval schedule: reinforcement applied at fixed time intervals, regardless of behaviour.
  - Variable interval: reinforcement applied at variable time intervals.

- Fixed ratio: reinforcement applied after a fixed number of behaviours, regardless of time.

Variable Ratio: reinforcement applied after a variable number of behaviours, regardless of time.

- Behaviour modification (OB Mod)
  - A method for applying the basic elements of reinforcement theory in an organizational setting.
  - Specific behaviours are tied to specific forms of reinforcement.

Equity Theory
- People are motivated to seek social equity in the rewards they receive for performance.
- Equity is an individual's belief that the treatment he or she receives is fair relative to the treatment received by others.
- Individuals view the value of rewards (outcomes) and inputs of effort as ratios and make subjective comparisons of themselves to other people:

$$\frac{\text{Outcomes (self)}}{\text{Inputs (self)}} = \frac{\text{Outcomes (other)}}{\text{Inputs (other)}}$$

- Conditions of and reactions to equity comparisons:
  - Feeling equitably rewarded.
    - ⋆ Maintain performance and accept comparison as fair estimate.

– Feeling under-rewarded-try to reduce inequity.
– Feeling over-rewarded.
  * Increase or decrease inputs.
  * Distort ratios by rationalizing.
  * Help the object person gain more outcomes.

Expectancy Theory

- Motivation depends on how much we want something and how likely we are to get it.
- Assumes that:
  – Behaviour is determined by a combination of personal and environmental forces.
  – People make decisions about their own behaviour in organizations.
  – Different people have different types of needs, desires, and goals.

People choose among alternatives of behaviours in selecting one that leads to a desired outcome

- Model of Motivation
  Suggests that motivation leads to effort, when combined with ability and environmental factors, that results in performance which, in turn, leads to various outcomes that have value (valence) to employees.

The Expectancy Model of Motivation

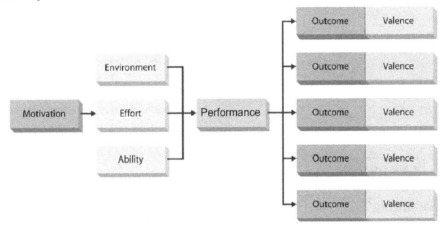

Elements of Expectancy Theory

- Effort-to-Performance Expectancy
  – The individual's perception of the probability that effort will lead to a high level of performance.
- Performance-to-Outcome Expectancy
  – The individual's perception of the probability that performance will lead to a specific outcome, or consequence or reward in an organizational setting.
  – Outcomes (Consequences) and Valences.
  – Valence is an index of how much an individual values a particular outcome. It is also the attractiveness of the outcome to the individual.

– Attractive outcomes have positive valences and unattractive outcomes have negative valences.
– Outcomes to which an individual is indifferent have zero valences.

- For individual motivated behaviour (effort) to occur:
  – Effort-to-performance expectancy (the belief that effort will lead to high performance) must be greater than zero.
  – Performance-to-outcome expectancy (performance will result in certain outcomes) must be greater than zero.
  – The sum of the valences must be greater than zero—the outcome/reward must have value to the individual.

Porter-Lawler Extension of Expectancy Theory

- Assumptions:
  - If performance in an organization results in equitable and fair rewards, people will be more satisfied.
- High performance can lead to rewards and high satisfaction.
- Types of rewards:
  - Extrinsic rewards—outcomes set and awarded by external parties (e.g., pay and promotions).
  - Intrinsic rewards—outcomes that are internal to the individual (e.g., self-esteem and feelings of accomplishment.

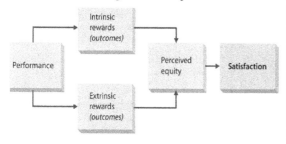

LEADERSHIP

What is Leadership?

Leadership is a process by which an executive can direct, guide and influence the behaviour and work of others towards accomplishment of specific goals in a given situation. Leadership is the ability of a manager to induce the subordinates to work with confidence and passion.

Leadership is the potential to influence behaviour of others. It is also defined as the ability to influence a group towards the realization of a goal. Leaders are required to develop future visions, and to motivate the organizational members to want to achieve the visions.

According to Keith Davis, "Leadership is the ability to persuade others to seek defined objectives enthusiastically. It is the human factor which binds a group together and motivates it towards goals."

George R Terry, "Leadership is the activity if influencing people to strive willingly for group activities".

Robert Tannenbaum, defines, "leadership as interpersonal influence exercised in a situation and directed through the communication process towards the attainment of a specified goal or goals".

Effective management of human resources requires understanding the capabilities of subordinates, assigning them appropriate tasks, helping them to acquire new capabilities in which the staff enjoys doing the tasks assigned to them.

Characteristics of Leadership

1. It is a inter-personal process in which a manager is into influencing and guiding workers towards attainment of goals.
2. It denotes a few qualities to be present in a person who includes intelligence, maturity and personality.
3. It is a group process. It involves two or more people interacting with each other.
4. A leader is involved in shaping and moulding the behaviour of the group towards accomplishment of organizational goals.
5. Leadership is situation bound. There is no best style of leadership. It all depends upon tackling with the situations.
6. A leader can influence the people either by compliance, identification and internalization.

Leadership is an important function of management which helps to maximize efficiency and to achieve organizational goals. The following points justify the importance of leadership in a concern.

1. **Initiates action:** Leader is a person who starts the work by communicating the policies and plans to the subordinates from where the work actually starts.
2. **Motivation:** A leader proves to be playing an incentive role in the concern's working. He motivates the employees with economic and non-economic rewards and thereby gets the work from the subordinates.
3. **Providing guidance:** A leader has to not only supervise but also play a guiding role for the

subordinates. Guidance here means instructing the subordinates the way they have to perform their work effectively and efficiently.

4. **Creating confidence:** Confidence is an important factor which can be achieved through expressing the work efforts to the subordinates, explaining them clearly their role and giving them guidelines to achieve the goals effectively. It is also important to hear the employees with regards to their complaints and problems.

5. **Building morale:** Morale denotes willing co-operation of the employees towards their work and getting them into confidence and winning their trust. A leader can be a morale booster by achieving full co-operation so that they perform with best of their abilities as they work to achieve goals.

6. **Builds work environment:** Management is getting things done from people. An efficient work environment helps in sound and stable growth. Therefore, human relations should be kept into mind by a leader. He should have personal contacts with employees and should listen to their problems and solve them. He should treat employees on humanitarian terms.

7. **Co-ordination:** Co-ordination can be achieved through reconciling personal interests with organizational goals. This synchronization can be achieved through proper and effective co-ordination which should be primary motive of a leader.

Following are the main roles of a leader in an organization:

1. **Required at all levels:** Leadership is a function which is important at all levels of management. In the top level, it is important for getting co-operation in formulation of plans and policies. In the middle and lower level, it is required for interpretation and execution of plans and programmes framed by the top management. Leadership can be exercised through guidance and counseling of the subordinates at the time of execution of plans.

2. **Representative of the organization:** A leader, *i.e.*, a manager is said to be the representative of the enterprise. He has to represent the concern at seminars, conferences, general meetings, etc. His role is to communicate the rationale of the enterprise to outside public. He is also representative of the own department which he leads.

3. **Integrates and reconciles the personal goals with organizational goals:** A leader through leadership traits helps in reconciling/ integrating the personal goals of the employees with the organizational goals. He is trying to co-ordinate the efforts of people towards a common purpose and thereby achieves objectives. This can be done only if he can influence and get willing co-operation and urge to accomplish the objectives.

4. **He solicits support:** A leader is a manager and besides that he is a person who entertains and invites support and co-operation of sub-ordinates. This he can do by his personality, intelligence, maturity and experience which can provide him positive result. In this re-gard, a leader has to invite suggestions and if possible implement them into plans and programmes of enterprise. This way, he can solicit full support of employees which re-sults in willingness to work and thereby ef-fectiveness in running of a concern.

5. **As a friend, philosopher and guide:** A leader must possess the three dimensional traits in him. He can be a friend by sharing the feelings, opinions and desires with the employees. He can be a philosopher by utilizing his intelligence and experience and thereby guiding the employees as and when time requires. He can be a guide by supervising and communicating the employees the plans and policies of top management and secure their co-operation to achieve the goals of a concern. At times he can also play the role of a counselor by counseling and a problem-solving approach. He can listen to the problems of the employees and try to solve them.

Qualities of leader

A leader has got multidimensional traits in him whom makes him appealing and effective in behaviour. The following are the requisites to be present in a good leader:

1. **Physical appearance:** A leader must have a pleasing appearance. Physique and health are very important for a good leader.

2. **Vision and foresight:** A leader cannot maintain influence unless he exhibits that he is forward looking. He has to visualize situations and thereby has to frame logical programmes.

3. **Intelligence:** A leader should be intelligent enough to examine problems and difficult situations. He should be analytical who weighs pros and cons and then summarizes the situation. Therefore, a positive bent of mind and mature outlook is very important.

4. **Communicative skills:** A leader must be able to communicate the policies and procedures clearly, precisely and effectively. This can be helpful in persuasion and stimulation.

5. **Objective:** A leader has to be having a fair outlook which is free from bias and which does not reflects his willingness towards a particular individual. He should develop his own opinion and should base his judgement on facts and logic.

6. **Knowledge of work:** A leader should be very precisely knowing the nature of work of his subordinates because it is then he can win the trust and confidence of his subordinates.

7. **Sense of responsibility:** Responsibility and accountability towards an individual's work is very important to bring a sense of influence. A leader must have a sense of responsibility towards organizational goals because only then he can get maximum of capabilities exploited in a real sense. For this, he has to motivate himself and arouse and urge to give best of his abilities. Only then he can motivate the subordinates to the best.

8. **Self-confidence and will-power:** Confidence in him is important to earn the confidence of the subordinates. He should be trustworthy and should handle the situations with full will power.

9. **Humanist:** This trait to be present in a leader is essential because he deals with human beings and is in personal contact with them. He has to handle the personal problems of his subordinates with great care and attention. Therefore, treating the human beings on humanitarian grounds is essential for building a congenial environment.

10. **Empathy:** It is an old adage "Stepping into the shoes of others". This is very important because fair judgement and objectivity comes only then. A leader should understand the problems and complaints of employees and should also have a complete view of the needs and aspirations of the employees. This helps in improving human relations and personal contacts with the employees.

From the above qualities present in a leader, one can understand the scope of leadership and its importance for scope of business. A leader cannot have all traits at one time. But a few of them helps in achieving effective results.

1. While management includes focus on planning, organizing, staffing, directing and controlling; leadership is mainly a part of directing function of management. Leaders focus on listening, building relationships, teamwork, inspiring, motivating and persuading the followers.

2. While a leader gets his authority from his followers, a manager gets his authority by virtue of his position in the organization.

3. While managers follow the organization's policies and procedure, the leaders follow their own instinct.

4. Management is more of science as the managers are exact, planned, standard, logical and more of mind. Leadership, on the other hand, is an art. In an organization, if the managers are required, then leaders are a must/essential.

5. While management deals with the technical dimension in an organization or the job

content; leadership deals with the people aspect in an organization.

6. While management measures/evaluates people by their name, past records, present performance; leadership sees and evaluates individuals as having potential for things that can't be measured, *i.e.*, it deals with future and the performance of people if their potential is fully extracted.

7. If management is reactive, leadership is proactive.

8. Management is based more on written communication, while leadership is based more on verbal communication.

9. While managers lay down the structure and delegates authority and responsibility, leaders provides direction by developing the organizational vision and communicating it to the employees and inspiring them to achieve it.

The organizations which are over managed and under-led do not perform up to the benchmark. **Leadership accompanied by management sets a new direction and makes efficient use of resources to achieve it.** Both leadership and management are essential for individual as well as organizational success.

LEADERSHIP STYLES

All leaders do not possess same attitude or same perspective. As discussed earlier, few leaders adopt the carrot approach and a few adopt the stick approach. Thus, all of the leaders do not get the things done in the same manner. Their style varies. The leadership style varies with the kind of people the leader interacts and deals with. A perfect/ standard leadership style is one which assists a leader in getting the best out of the people who follow him.

Autocratic leadership style: In this style of leadership, a leader has complete command and hold over their employees/team. The team cannot put forward their views even if they are best for the teams or organizational interests. They cannot criticize or question the leader's way of getting

things done. The leader himself gets the things done. The advantage of this style is that it leads to speedy decision-making and greater productivity under leader's supervision. Drawbacks of this leadership style are that it leads to greater employee absenteeism and turnover. This leadership style works only when the leader is the best in performing or when the job is monotonous, unskilled and routine in nature or where the project is short-term and risky. This leader determines policies for the group without consulting the subordinates.

Decorative/Participative leadership

This type is also consultative or ideographic style of leadership. The leader invites and encourages the team members to play an important role in decision-making process through ultimate decision-making power rests with the leader. The leaders guide the employees on what is to be performed and how to perform, while the employees communicate to the leader their experience and suggestions if any. It is considered as a highly motivating technique of leadership as employees feel elevated when they become a part of the process of decision-making, leaders to the efficiency of the employees. It provides organizational stability by raising morale of the employees. It leads to better understanding and co-operation between the management and the employees and reduces the number of complaints and grievances.

Laissez-Faire Style/Free-rein style: Means giving complete freedom to subordinates. In this style, the leader once determines policy, programmes and limitations for action and the entire process is left to subordinates. The leader totally trusts their employees/ team to perform the jobs themselves. He just concentrates on the intellectual/rational aspect of his work and does not focus on the management aspects of his work. The team/ employees are welcomed to share their views and provide suggestions which are best for organizational interests. This style works only when the employees are skilled, loyal, experienced and intellectual.

The paternalistic style: Under this technique, leader assumes paternal of fatherly role. He is to guide, protect and keep his followers happy, who work together as members of a family. He makes provisions for good working conditions and other necessary services. It is expected that under such leadership workers will work hard out of gratitude. But in the present conditions, this type of attitude may not result out of gratitude. But in the present conditions, this type of attitude may not result in maximum motivation. Instead, it may generate resentment in the subordinates.

Bureaucratic Leadership: Here the leaders strictly adhere to the organizational rules and policies. Also, they make sure that the employees/team also strictly follows the rules and procedures. Promotions take place on the basis of employees' ability to adhere to organizational rules. This leadership style gradually develops over time. This leadership style is more suitable when safe work conditions and quality are required. But this leadership style discourages creativity and does not make employees self-contented.

Theories of leadership

There are three main theories with regard to the nature of leadership:

1. Trait theory
2. Situation theory
3. Behavioural theory
4. **Trait Theory:** The trait theory says that there are certain identifiable qualities or characteristics that are unique to leaders and that good leader possess such qualities. The Trait theorist have identified a list of qualities that are as follows:

   (*i*) **Intelligence:** A leader should be intelligent enough of understanding the context and contents of his position and function. He should be able to grasp the dynamics of environmental variables, both internal as well as external, which affect the activities of the enterprise. He should also have technical competence and sound general knowledge.

   (*ii*) **Personality:** The term personality here means not only the physical appearance but also inner-personality qualities. Such qualities include emotional stability and

maturity, self-confidence, decisiveness, strong drive, extrovert, achievement, orientation, purposefulness, discipline, skill in getting along with others, integrity in character and a tendency to be co-operative.

(*iii*) In addition a good business leader should possess qualities such as open mindedness, scientific sprit, social sensitivity, ability to communicate, objectivity and a sense of realism.

Leaders are essentially those who know their goals and have the power to influence the thoughts and actions of others to support and cooperation to achieve these goals. The trait theory of leadership is criticized on the account of those inadequacies as follows:

1. Skill are sometimes mistaken as traits.
2. It is not based on any research or systematic development of concepts and principles.
3. Researchers have shown that leadership should be looked beyond personal qualifications and traits of the individuals.
4. The theory do not have a scale of measurement to measure traits of individuals.
5. Leaders must display different leadership characteristics at different times and under different situations.

SITUATIONAL LEADERSHIP— MEANING AND CONCEPT

The situation approach does not reject the importance of individuals' traits in leadership but further extent and asserts that leadership pattern is the product of a situation in a particular group and that leadership will be different in different situation.

Bavelas and Barrett, that no individual emerges as leader when all the participants have equal access to the information and that the individuals commanding maximum information will sooner or later emerge as a leader. Thus it is obvious that a leader can so structure the organization that a favourable situation is created for the subordinates to emerge as a leader.

Fred E. Fiedler has developed a contingency model of leadership effectiveness. This approach was the result of the most extensive programme of research about leadership styles and effective group performance carried out by him.

The model encourages the leaders to analyze a particular situation in depth and then lead in the most appropriate manner, suitable for that situation. The three aspects that need could be considered in a situation are:

- Employees' competences
- Maturity of the employees
- Complexity of the task
- Leadership style

In the situational leadership model, the leadership style has been divided into 4 types:

- **S1-Telling:** Telling style is associated with leaders who minutely supervise their followers, constantly instructing them about why, how and when of the tasks that need to be performed.

- **S2-Selling:** Selling style is when a leader provide controlled direction and is a little more open and allows two way communication between him/herself and the followers thus ensuring that the followers buy in the process and work towards the desired goals.

- **S3-Participating:** This style is characterized when the leaders seeks opinion and participation of the followers to establish how a task should be performed. The leader in this case tries creating relationship with the followers:

- **S4-Delegating:** In this case, the leader plays a role in decisions that are taken but passes on or delegates the responsibilities of carrying out tasks to his followers. The leader however monitors and reviews the process.

It is also represented by a diagram most often which is below:

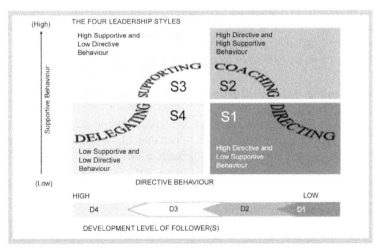

The developmental level of follower is an important indication for a leader to decide the most appropriate leadership style for them:

- **D4-High Competence, High Commitment:** The followers who are identified in this category are the ones who have high competence and high commitment towards tasks to be performed. It might happen so that they turn out better than their leaders in performing these tasks. (For *e.g.* cricketing legend Sachin Tendulkar playing in the

Indian cricket team under the captainship of Mahendra Singh Dhoni)

- **D3-High Competence, Variable Commitment:** This category consists of followers who have the competence to do the job but their commitment level is inconsistent. They also tend to lack the confidence to go out and perform task alone. (*e.g.* President Barack Obama)

- **D2-Some Competence, Low Commitment:** In this case, the followers have a certain level of competence which might be sufficient to do the job but they are low on commitment towards the tasks. Despite of having relevant skills to perform the task they seek external help when faced with new situations. (A team member made the trainer for new joiners)

● **D1-Low Competence, High Commitment:** This category of followers may not have the specific skill required but they display a high level of commitment towards the task they have to perform, with confidence and motivation, they figure out ways to complete the tasks. (*e.g.* Mohandas Karamchand Gandhi, a lawyer by profession who spearheaded the Indian Freedom Struggle)

The above information regarding the style of leadership and the type of followers sure has a correlation to each other which forms the basis of situational leadership. So, a situational leader would try to accommodate his leadership style as per the situation and the level of competence and commitment of his followers. This information is also an important aspect to consider when senior leaders act as coaches for their subordinates in the organizations.

Impact of situational leadership and performance and motivation

Situational Leadership has all the more relevance when teams work together especially across functions or locations. In these cases the team members might be physically separated from the leaders and the work situations might rapidly change, in such cases, maintaining the involvement and motivation level of team members becomes important. To create a high performance team that works effectively, the style that the leader would have to choose may be unique for each team.

Apart from this, a leader has to provide a vision to the people; it is the visions which help them direct and redirect their efforts towards it. In the recent times where changes are rapid in the organizations, the leaders have to be fully sensitized to what style would work the best, sometimes they might have to use a combination of styles to address issues effectively. For e.g. for a new change that is being introduced, the initial approach has to be

Selling, where people are educated about the change, the next step becomes Telling, where the people have to be instructed as to how the change would be carried out. When the change starts settling in and people adopt it, they style can become Participating, where the people get an opportunity to partner in the change and take it ahead. The last change would then become delegating when the change can now be carried on by the others. The ultimate aim of any leader is to smoothly arrive at a stage where he/she can easily delegate tasks without worrying about its completion or effectiveness.

The leadership style also has a bearing when leaders are to act as mentors and coaches for their subordinates. The learning style of the subordinates can be interpreted in the terms of Telling, Selling, Participating and Delegating. Some subordinates learn when they know exactly what is to be done, some learn when they know the importance of the task, some learn when they understand the how of what is to be done, and ultimately some learn when they are actually allowed to perform the task. When a leader acts as a coach he/she has to keep in mind what works best for the coachee and the fact that what works for one might not work for the other.

It is the leadership style practiced by the manager which to quite an extent is responsible for such a situation to arise. Every team has people who have different level of competence and commitment towards the work they do, some are proactive and others need to be pushed. In either case, the role of the manager as a leader becomes all the more important where he/she needs to be flexible with the kind of leadership style they can practice with each subordinate.

Let's try to understand the relationship between leadership styles and subordinate development in a little detail. Recall the four situational leadership styles identified by Hersey and Blanchard. They were:

● Telling
● Selling
● Participating
● Delegating

Now, have a look at the following diagram which depicts the development level of the followers based on their competence and commitment towards their work.

So, which leadership style would be appropriate with each of these levels? A manager as a leader has to partner in the developmental journey of his/her subordinate. For a subordinate who is at a level D1, where he has low competence but high motivation, the leadership style could be Participative where the leader involves the subordinate and further motivates him to build on his competence to increase his/her effectiveness at tasks.

For a subordinate, who stands at a level D2 where he has some competence but lacks or shows inconsistent commitment, the leader can resort to the Telling style. In this case, the subordinate cannot be relied upon to complete the task without instructions and guidance. For the subordinates who fall into the category of D3 or high competence but variable commitment, the leadership style could be Selling as the leader would have to create a buy in from these subordinates to secure their commitment towards the task. Since they have the necessary competence to do the task, instructions are not required but such subordinates wish to see the value of the work they are doing to get committed to it.

And lastly, if the subordinate fall into the category of D4 where they have both high commitment and high motivation, the leadership style best suited could be Delegating, where the leaders need to understand, acknowledge and appreciate the competence and commitment of the subordinates and entrust them with responsibilities. Leaders have to be aware of their surroundings and sensitized to the abilities and motivations of their followers/subordinates in order to be able to take effective decisions.

BEHAVIOURAL THEORIES

Behavioural theory takes a different approach, focusing more on patterns of leadership behaviour than on the individual leader. It suggests that certain behavioural patterns may be identified as leadership styles. Applications of behavioural theory promote the value of leadership styles with an emphasis on concern for people and participative decision-making, encouraging collaboration and team development by supporting individual needs and aligning individual and group objectives. In practice, trait and behavioural theories may be used to develop our own ideas about successful leadership, and it may be useful to consider which leadership traits would be beneficial in particular situations. It may also be instructive to consider how our behavioural style as a manager affects our relationship with the team and promotes their commitment and contribution to the organizational goals.

MANAGERIAL GRID

Robert Blake & Jane Mouton (1964) developed a theory known as the "Managerial Grid". It is based on two variables: focus on task and focus on relationships. The grid includes five possible leadership styles based on concern for task or concern for people. Using a specially designed testing instrument, people can be assigned a numerical score depicting their concern for each variable. Numerical indications, such as 9, 1 or 9, 9 or 1, 9 or 1, 1 or 5, 5 can then be plotted on the grid using horizontal and vertical axes. Although their work is also often classified as a Leadership Theory, it is typical of the specially designed analysis and instruments of the systems theorists.

Details: The treatment of task orientation and people orientation as two independent dimensions was a major step in leadership studies. Many of the leadership studies conducted in the 1950s at the University of Michigan and the Ohio State University focused on these two dimensions. Building on the work of the researchers at these Universities, Robert Blake and Jane Mouton (1960s) proposed a graphic portrayal of leadership styles through a *managerial grid* (sometimes called *leadership grid*). The grid depicted two dimensions of leader behaviour, *concern for people* (accommodating people's needs and giving them priority) on *y*-axis and *concern for production* (keeping tight schedules) on *x*-axis, with each dimension ranging from low (1) to high (9), thus creating 81 different positions in which the leader's style may fall. (See figure).

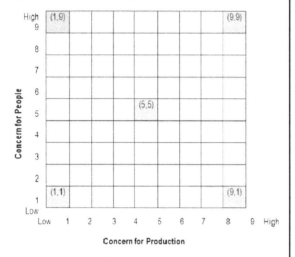

Managerial Grid

The five resulting leadership styles are as follows:

1. **Impoverished Management (1, 1):** Managers with this approach are low on both the dimensions and exercise minimum effort to get the work done from subordinates. The leader has low concern for employee satisfaction and work deadlines and as a result disharmony and disorganization prevail within the organization. The leaders are termed ineffective wherein their action is merely aimed at preserving job and seniority.

2. **Task management (9, 1):** Also called dictatorial or perish style. Here leaders are more concerned about production and have less concern for people. The style is based on theory X of McGregor. The employees' needs are not taken care of and they are simply a means to an end. The leader believes that efficiency can result only through proper organization of work systems and through elimination of people wherever possible. Such a style can definitely increase the output of organization in short run but due to the strict policies and procedures, high labour turnover is inevitable.

3. **Middle-of-the-Road (5, 5):** This is basically a compromising style wherein the leader tries to maintain a balance between goals of company and the needs of people. The leader does not push the boundaries of achievement resulting in average performance for organization. Here neither employee nor production needs are fully met.

4. **Country Club (1, 9):** This is a collegial style characterized by low task and high people orientation where the leader gives thoughtful attention to the needs of people thus providing them with a friendly and comfortable environment. The leader feels that such a treatment with employees will lead to self-motivation and will find people working hard on their own. However, a low focus on tasks can hamper production and lead to questionable results.

5. **Team Management (9, 9):** Characterized by high people and task focus, the style is based on the theory Y of McGregor and has been termed as most effective style according to Blake and Mouton. The leader feels that empowerment, commitment, trust, and respect are the key elements in creating a team atmosphere which will automatically result in high employee satisfaction and production.

Advantages of Blake and Mouton's Managerial Grid

The Managerial or Leadership Grid is used to help managers analyze their own leadership styles through a technique known as grid training. This is done by administering a questionnaire that helps managers identify how they stand with respect to their concern for production and people. The training is aimed at basically helping leaders reach to the ideal state of 9, 9.

Limitations of Blake and Mouton's Managerial Grid

The model ignores the importance of internal and external limits, matter and scenario. Also, there are some more aspects of leadership that can be covered but are not.

CONTINGENCY THEORIES OF LEADERSHIP

Tannenbaum and Schmidt's leadership model

A criticism of early work on leadership styles is that they show leadership in strictly black and white terms. The autocratic and democratic styles or task-oriented and relationship-oriented styles which they described are extremes, whereas in practice the behaviour of most leaders will be somewhere between the two. Contingency theorists, Robert Tannenbaum and Warren Schmidt (1958, 1973), proposed that leadership behaviour varies along a continuum and that as leaders move away from the autocratic extreme the amount of follower participation and involvement in decision taking increases.

They identified three forces that led to the leader's action: the forces in the **situation**, the forces in the **follower** and also forces in the leader. This recognizes that the leader's style is highly variable, and even such distant events as a family argument can lead to the displacement activity of a more aggressive stance in an argument than usual.

They proposed a more detailed approach to defining leadership styles. Their model shows the spectrum of possible styles along a continuum linking autocratic leaders, who tell their staff what to do at one extreme, with those who delegate authority for decision-making to subordinates, at the other. The two extremes represent the ideas characterised by Theory X and Theory Y managers. Managers may move along this continuum as external factors alter and situations change. This is shown in figure below.

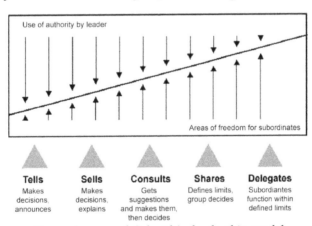

Tannenbaum and Schmidt's leadership model

It may seem as if the ideal is a position somewhere between the two extremes, but the truth is that the nature of decision-making an effective leader displays can swing constantly between them.

FIEDLERS' CONTINGENCY THEORY

Fred E. Fiedlers' contingency theory of leadership effectiveness was based on studies of a wide range of group effectiveness, and concentrated on the relationship between leadership and organizational performance. This is one of the earliest situation-contingent leadership theories given by Fiedler. According to him, if an organization attempts to achieve group effectiveness through leadership, then there is a need to assess the leader according to an underlying trait, assess the situation faced by the leader, and construct a proper match between the two.

Leader's trait

In order to assess the attitudes of the leader, Fiedler developed the 'least preferred co-worker' (LPC) scale in which the leaders are asked about the person with whom they least like to work. The scale is a questionnaire consisting of 16 items used to reflect a leader's underlying disposition toward others. The items in the LPC scale are pleasant / unpleasant, friendly / unfriendly, rejecting / accepting, unenthusiastic / enthusiastic, tense / relaxed, cold / warm, helpful / frustrating, cooperative / uncooperative, supportive / hostile, quarrelsome / harmonious, efficient / inefficient, gloomy / cheerful, distant / close, boring / interesting, self-assured / hesitant, open / guarded. Each item in the scale is given a single ranking of between one and eight points, with eight points indicating the most favourable rating.

Friendly _____ Unfriendly
　　8　7　6　5　4　3　2　1

Fiedler states that leaders with high LPC scores are relationship-oriented and the ones with low scores are task-oriented. The high LPC score leaders derived most satisfaction from interpersonal relationships and therefore evaluate their least preferred co-workers in fairly favourable terms. These leaders think about the task accomplishment only after the relationship need is well satisfied. On the other hand, the low LPC score leaders derived satisfaction from perfor-mance of the task and attainment of objectives and only after tasks have been accomplished, these leaders work on establishing good social and interpersonal relationships.

Situational factor

According to Fiedler, a leader's behaviour is dependent upon the favourability of the leadership situation. Three factors work together to determine how favourable a situation is to a leader.

These are:

- **Leader-member relations:** The degree to which the leaders is trusted and liked by the group members, and the willingness of the group members to follow the leader's guidance.
- **Task structure:** The degree to which the group's task has been described as structured or unstructured, has been clearly defined and the extent to which it can be carried out by detailed instructions.
- **Position power:** The power of the leader by virtue of the organizational position and the degree to which the leader can exercise authority on group members in order to comply with and accept his direction and leadership.

With the help of these three variables, eight combinations of group-task situations were constructed by Fiedler. These combinations were used to identify the style of the leader.

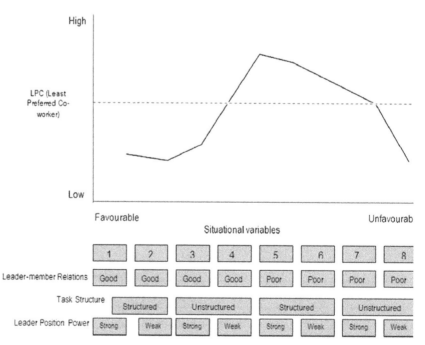

Leadership Effectiveness

The leader's effectiveness is determined by the interaction of the leader's style of behaviour and the favourableness of the situational characteristics. The most favourable situation is when leader-member relations are good, the task is highly structured, and the leader has a strong position power.

Research on the contingency model has shown that task-oriented leaders are more effective in highly favourable (1, 2, 3) and highly unfavourable situation (7, 8), whereas relationship-oriented leaders are more effective in situations of intermediate favourableness (4, 5, 6). Fiedler also suggested that leaders may act differently in different situations. Relationship-oriented leaders generally display task-oriented behaviours under highly favourable situations and display relationship-oriented behaviours under unfavourable intermediate favourable situations. Similarly, task-oriented leaders frequently display task-oriented in unfavourable or intermediate favourable situations but display relationship-oriented behaviours in favourable situations.

LIKERT'S SYSTEM-4 MANAGEMENT

Rinsis Likert (1967) suggests that manager operates under four systems. In system-1 the manager operates in very authoritarian manner and exploits the subordinates. In system-2 the manager is benevolent autocrat, behaves in a paternalistic manager and still tries to be autocratic. In system-3 manager adopts a consultative approach. He consults subordinates but takes the final decision. In system-4 manager uses a democratic style. Manager presents the problem and makes the decision by consent. The typical characteristics of the four systems are indicated as follows:

Leadership characteristics	System 1 Exploitative Autocratic	System 2 Benevolent Autocratic	System 3 Participative	System 4 Democratic
Leadership process	No confidence and trust in subordinates	Condescending confidence and trust in subordinates	Substantial but not complete confidence and trust in subordinates	Complete confidence and trust in subordinates
Motivational forces	Physical security, economic needs and some use for desire for status	Economic needs and moderate use of ego motives	Economic needs and considerable use of ego and other major motives	Full use of economic, ego and other major motives arising from group goals
Communication	Very little	Little	Quite	Much between individual and group
Interaction	Little interaction and always with fear and distrust	Little interaction and usually with some condescension by superiors, fear and caution by subordinates	Moderate interaction, often with fair amount of confidence amount	Extensive friendly interaction with high degree of confidence and trust
Decision-making	Bulk of decision at top of organization	Policy at top, many decisions with prescribed framework made at lower levels but usually checked with top before decision is taken	Broad policy decision at top, more specific decision at lower levels	Decision-making widely done throughout organization, well integrated through linking process provided by overlapping groups
Goal setting	Orders issued	Orders issued but opportunity to comment may exist	Goals are set or orders are issued after discussion with subordinates of problems and planned action	Except in emergencies, goals are usually established by group participation

Job satisfaction

- **Organization's view.** Organizations hire people to perform specific tasks that help them to achieve their business goals. They want to hire the talent necessary to achieve organizational goals that are consistent with their mission and profitability. The process of selecting employees is dependent on accurate job descriptions and job specification, reasonable expectations and realistic, self-aware applicants. When an organization successfully finds people who "fit" the job requirements, who enjoy and are skilled in the tasks assigned to meet the organization's goals, and appreciate the organization's salary/benefit strategy, a win-win situation is created for the employer and employee.

- Traditionally, the focus of organizations has been to establish a generally acceptable organizational culture. Organization-provided satisfiers are offered to employees in exchange for outcomes the organization considers valuable, such as high levels of performance and loyalty. Organizations benchmark their compensation and benefit strategies to remain competitive in hiring and retaining talent. They also face increasing expenses in benefits such as healthcare, retirement investments and tuition reimbursement.

- Employers that understand another critical aspect of job satisfaction will gain an advantage in recruiting, retaining and developing talent. This second aspect is referred to as job-related satisfiers, the satisfiers and enjoyment that an individual employee experiences from performing the actual work or tasks of his or her job.

- **Employee's view.** Starting with the end in mind, reflect for a moment on what people might be looking for when they take a job. Maybe their health benefits are most important, or a good retirement plan? Some people may be interested in reimbursement, opportunities for advancement, or to learn new skills. All of these types of critical rewards that are determined by the organization based

on their strategy to be profitable and competitive in recruiting and retaining people. This is the heart of how employees and organizations negotiate the value of the labour exchange.

- Job-related satisfiers have to do with the employee's desire to use his/her abilities to make a contribution, to do meaningful work, and to be valued. These satisfiers are more directly related to how much we enjoy our day-to-day tasks and our role in the organization. How we perform on daily tasks is related to our productivity, and we expect to discuss the assignment and performance of our work with an immediate supervisor or manager.

- The annual performance review is typically the main conversation to explore productivity and satisfaction. Since these conversations focus more on evaluation of performance, goal attainment and salary adjustments, they seldom get to meaningful conversations about satisfaction with tasks or the "fit" of the current or future work itself. Also, managers juggle multiple demands to achieve organizational goals, so they can easily under-appreciate the powerful influence that job-related satisfiers have on employees' overall satisfaction. By taking the initiative to communicate with their managers, employees can help ensure that managers are better able to provide the necessary guidance or coaching support.

- In summary, it is challenging for an organization and manager to identify and promote employee satisfaction at an individual level. This is surprising because these job-related satisfiers are highly motivating when met, (de-motivating when not met), and are at the heart of productivity and performance.

Job Satisfaction Model

- Employees are in a better position for achieving success and satisfying work once they understand and can communicate how their own unique work profiles (aptitudes/

abilities, interests, personality style & values) can meet an organization's work-related requirements and opportunities.

- A simple job satisfaction model shown of the following page demonstrates the organizing relationship of these different concepts. The model is divided so the concepts on the left side identify what the employer wants and what it offers as rewards and benefits of the organization-provided satisfiers. The right side of the model shows what the employee contributes to accomplish specific tasks (circle 2) and ultimately the organization's goals. The more self-aware an individual is about their aptitudes, personal style, and values, the greater is the potential to identify and select jobs that fit. The more accurate the job description, the better the odds of attracting the right pool of applicants (circle 3). When there is a clear fit between the person and the job, there is a greater chance of successfully accomplishing goals (circle 4). This in turn leads to an increase in personal satisfaction (circles 6 and 7). In today's complex work environment, job descriptions are developing as we take on special projects or are assigned to teams. This expanded complexity increases the need to be proactive in determining fit.

- **Performance & fit the core of satisfaction:** Job performance and fit are at the center of the diagram because they comprise the core of a win-win relationship between employer and employee, (circles 3 & 4). When we are relatively satisfied with our salary, vacation time and other organization-related rewards and we find a fit and enjoy our work, feel appreciated and understand that our contributions are needed (our job-related satisfiers), we develop a personal, higher level of commitment to the achievement of goals and thereby the success of the organization. Collectively, when individuals achieve higher levels of job satisfaction and performance, an organization is better positioned to meet its goals with improved productivity and profitability.

- **What happens when the job no longer fits?:** We might select a position that is an excellent fit at any point in our working years. We perform well and enjoy the work, the benefits and rewards are in the right range but over time the things begin to change. This can be the result of new and different goals that no longer use our full range of aptitudes/abilities, the introduction of technology that alters the work, the need for new knowledge or skills to accomplish the tasks, or perhaps the lack of anything new. These types of changes and others impact our level of satisfaction. The key is to take a step back, conduct an evaluation of what has changed and identify what specifically is impacting our current level of satisfaction.

- First, it is important to determine whether any of the actual work requirements and expectations, or organization-provided satisfiers has changed. We may discover that the job is still satisfying, but the organization may be facing increased competition or costs that have impacted their profitability and capability to maintain its current salary and/or benefit strategy. This change may impact our satisfaction with the way the organization rewards us. In today's changing economy, a situational analysis should include industry trends to determine if the changes are specific to your organization or are industry-wide.

- Second, since there are many aspects of job satisfaction, it may be time to re-evaluate what is most important for you. Our needs change over time. We may have experienced changes in our personal life or entered a new stage of life.

- Finally, if the job itself has become unsatisfactory, determining what has changed is critical to planning effective next steps in your career decision-making process. Unfortunately, without an analysis of what is contributing to our personal level of satisfaction, many of us make uninformed choices that don't actually improve our circumstances or satisfaction.

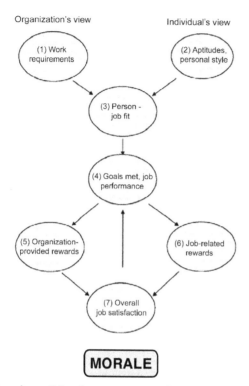

Organization's view   Individual's view

(1) Work requirements

(2) Aptitudes, personal style

(3) Person - job fit

(4) Goals met, job performance

(5) Organization-provided rewards

(6) Job-related rewards

(7) Overall job satisfaction

MORALE

Meaning: Morale represents the attitudes of individuals and groups in an organization towards their work environment. Morale is an indicator of the attitude of employees towards their jobs, superiors and their organizational environment. It is a collection of the employees' attitude, feelings and sentiments.

Some researchers take job satisfaction as individual and morale as group phenomenon. Morale is an important factor for organizational success as it reflects the attitudes and sentiments of individuals or group towards the organizational objectives. People with high morale are enthusiastic in their work environment. Morale is linked with job satisfaction. A person with a high morale has confidence in himself and in people with whom he works.

Definition

According to William Spriegel, **"morale is the co-operative attitude or mental health of a number of people who are related to each other on some basis".**

According to Leighton, **"morale is the capacity of a group of people to pull together persistently and consistently in pursuit of a common purpose".**

Characteristics of Morale

1. Morale is basically a psychological concept.
2. Morale is intangible therefore it is very difficult to measure the degree of morale accurately.
3. Morale is contagious in the sense that people learn from each other.
4. Morale in dynamic in nature. It cannot be developed overnight. Managers have to make continuous efforts to build and maintain high morale. It is a long-term concept.
5. Morale is a group phenomenon consisting of a pattern of attitudes. It is the sum total of employees' attitudes, feelings and sentiments.
6. High morale is sound behavioural climate in the organization.

Significance of Morale

● Morale is the vital ingredient of organizational success because attitudes and sentiments of employees greatly influence productivity and satisfaction of employees.

● Morale describes a state of complex attitudes and feelings about work situation whereas motivation deals with the propensity of particular behaviour pattern.

● Morale may be high or low; when the morale of the employees is high, they co-operate fully with the management towards the achievement of organizational objectives.

● High morale leads to good discipline, high degree of interest in the job, loyalty to the organization and high performance.

Consequences of Low Morale

Low morale indicates the presence of mental unrest. This mental tension or unrest not only hampers production and productivity but also leads to ill-health of the working people. The other consequences of low morale are the following:

1. Low morale results in inefficiency
2. High rate of labour turnover

3. High rate of absenteeism
4. Excessive complaints and grievances
5. Resistance to change
6. Lack of discipline
7. Antagonism towards the organization and its management
8. Low quantity and quality of output

Low morale can be fatal to the organization. In order to avoid the evil consequences of low morale, every manager should attempt to build high morale amongst his subordinates.

Steps to build High Morale

Every manager should attempt to build high morale of his subordinates. Both individual and collective efforts are required to develop and maintain high morale. The following measures are taken to improve the morale of employees in the organization:

1. A fair system of wage and salary payments should be evolved.
2. A sense of security of job should be ensured.
3. The promotion policy should be sound and should be followed promptly.
4. Competent supervisors should be appointed.
5. The channel of communication should be effective.
6. The employees should be made to feel proud of being employed in the organization.
7. Employees' welfare schemes like housing, medical benefits, education facilities for children, canteen, credit facilities, and safety measures should be provided as they are very helpful in developing positive attitude among the employees.
8. Workers should be given proper training so that they may perform their jobs without frustration and get job satisfaction.

Morale can be measured by assessing attitudes and job satisfaction. There are several techniques to measure employee attitudes, inference, prediction from behavioural data, interviews and questionnaires and scales. Interview has been frequently used to measure attitudes. Questionnaires and scales have been used either in combination with interview and independently to get increased reliability and objectivity. There are three basic methods for selecting and scaling items to be incorporated in a scale:

(i) The Thurston method of equal appearing intervals.
(ii) Likert method of summarized rating.
(iii) Guttman method of scale analysis.

Factors Determining Morale

The degree of morale in any organization is determined by several factors. Some of them are merely psychological and difficult to identify, however, researchers have succeeding in figuring out the following factors:

- **Confidence in leadership:** If the leader of the organization is able to win the confidence of the employees, morale will be high. For employees, the leader being mentioned is the immediate supervisor/superior. If the leader is systematic, fair, honest, helpful and friendly, he may win over the confidence of his subordinates and boost their morale.

- **Job Satisfaction:** The morale of the employee would be high if he is satisfied with his job. Hence right men should be placed in the right job to boost up their morale in their jobs.

- **Confidence in co-workers:** Mani is a social being and he finds himself more enthusiastic in the company of others. If he finds that his companions or fellow workers are co-operating with him, his morale would be high.

- **Sound and efficient organization:** Sound and effective organization is an important factor affecting the employee's morale. At the same time, the chance of communication should be effective and the personal problems of the employee should be heard and redressed as quickly as possible.

- **Fair remuneration:** Fair and reasonable remuneration is essential to secure enthusiasm and willingness of the workers to do the job. The wages should be comparable with those paid in similar concerns. Besides, monetary incentives should be provided to them as and when necessary and possible.

- **Security of job:** If the employee feels secured, they will be willing and co-operative to do the job allotted to them.
- **Opportunity to rise:** The employees should also be made to realize that if they work properly, they will be promoted and adequately rewarded. This feeling of recognition will definitely boost their morale.
- **Working conditions:** The conditions of work at which the employees are required to work also affect their morale. Providing safety measures, hygienic facilities, clean workplace etc. give them satisfaction and boost their morale.
- **Physical & mental health:** An employee with weak health cannot be co-operative and willing to work. Similarly his mental strain shall also reduce his motivation of morale. Both physical and mental illness are detrimental to an individual's work and thereby the organizational output.

Fatigue, monotony: Routine repetitiveness of the job without any change for longer periods causes monotony and fatigue. Fatigue is the "reduction in ability to do work". Fatigue may be physical and mental also. Length of work period, speed of work and the extent of physical work may cause fatigue. Fatigue and monotony can be reduced by enrichment and enlargement of the job.

Morale can be improved by several other measures such as employee's contest to improve morale, special recognition and award to long service employees, providing coffee during the rest pauses, more informal get together may enhance the morale. There is no limit for the devices, but the organization has to continuously measure the effectiveness of these measures and make the necessary changes whenever necessary.

Organizational change and development

The organizational development (OD) tradition is a practitioner-driven intervention-oriented approach to effecting organizational change via individual change, with view to increasing effectiveness. It is implemented within a problem-solving model, places a heavy accent on survey-based problem diagnosis and subordinates people to a vision of the future. Commitment-based strategies of effecting change assume that the impetus for change must come from the bottom up, whilst compliance-based strategies involve the creation of behavioural imperatives for change.

Various 'employee involvement' strategies are reviewed, but there is little evidence for their effectiveness either as a means of securing commitment or enhanced performance, or as a means of leverage for change. Culture is assumed to be the primary vehicle for change within the OD tradition, although the relationship between culture and the change process is ill understood. Finally, the assumptions underpinning team development, and its implementation, are critically examined.

The organizational culture literature itself is fraught with epistemological debate. Practitioners are interested in management by measurement and manipulation of culture. Theoreticians of culture, however, aim to understand the depth and complexity of culture. Unresolved issues remain regarding how to define culture, the difference between culture and climate, measurement/levels of analysis, and the relationship between organizational culture and performance.

Interest in corporate identity is relatively recent, and is mainly driven by marketing and strategic management considerations. More psychological approaches to the analysis of corporate identity include an interest in how corporate identity is reflected in the identity and self-esteem of employees, and the implications of this for managing organizational change.

The classic OD approach to organizations and organizational change has been somewhat 'side tracked' today in favour of 'knowledge management', where knowledge and its creation is seen as critical to organizational sustainability and competitive advantage in today's constantly changing global economy. Knowledge management raises issues about the potentially highly complex relationship between structure, technology and people. The dangers of a too tightly coupled understanding of the relationship between organizational structure and technology are highlighted.

OD has become a vital component in the management of change for many organizations, and has resulted in the increased employment of external (and, increasingly, internal) 'change agents', responsible for planning, implementing and evaluating organizational changes.

The following model is an *example* of how many cultural change programmes are pursued using a variety of methods. The model assumes that:

- the change agent has zero knowledge of the company prior to commencement of the project;
- the cultural change to be effected is company-wide;
- the change agent has been requested to assist in effecting the change by senior management;
- the budget for the programme is large and the timescale relaxed;
- replacing managerial staff is outside the remit of the change agent.

Clearly, these assumptions may, in some cases, not be accurate for all change management projects.

The basic model is as follows:

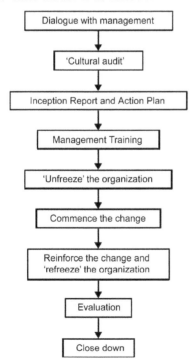

The portion of the above model which directly addresses the process of culture change is based on Lewin's (1951) 'unfreezing-change-refreezing' model of change, the detail of which forms part of the following discussion. Each of the above stages contains a variety of sub stages, some of which are effected directly by the change agent and others of which are achieved through the training and empowering of management to communicate the prescribed changes to the organization. Each of the above stages will be discussed in detail below, including, where appropriate, consideration of particular issues which must be attended to at each stage.

Stage 1: Dialogue with senior management/decision-makers

This stage of the process is primarily concerned with establishing a functional relationship with the management staff proposing the cultural change programme. Ideally, this should include the following:

- Establishing a contractual agreement (legal and psychological) that management must take ownership of the change process, and that any input by the change agent will be purely in facilitating and informing that process.
- Establishing single points of contact within the Human Resources department, any other departments of relevance and within senior management for the reporting of progress and requesting of information.
- Establishing the nature and perceptions of the problem through asking questions:
  - ➢ What do they perceive as the problem(s)?
  - ➢ What do they expect to gain from cultural change?
  - ➢ What measures/steps have already been taken to improve the situation?
  - ➢ Where is the company now?
  - ➢ Where should the company be?
  - ➢ What do they expect from the change agent?
  - ➢ What alternative solutions to the problem have been discussed/rejected?

- Provision of basic company information required for the subsequent cultural audit.
- Agreement of information to be gathered through the cultural audit and agreement that the process of data collection will be promoted by management whenever possible.
- Identification of any specific problems which may present themselves during the cultural audit/any later stage of the project.

It should be noted that, throughout the project, dialogue with management should be continuous, through appointed contacts within the organization, to ensure that the project remains focused and that additional information can be transmitted from change agent to management and *vice versa* as easily as possible.

Stage 2: 'Cultural audit'

Assuming the full agreement and support of senior management, a cultural audit is conducted, which should attempt to access and analyze the following data sources:

- Staff attitudes and perceptions of the existing culture (via questionnaires and structured interviews). Anonymity of respondents should be guaranteed to facilitate candid responses. Dimensions of interest may be selected depending on initial discussions with management, but should include: psychological climate; level of teamwork/conflict; supervision/management; role/goal ambiguity/clarity; information flow; nature/depth of support, and so on. These data should provide a means of bypassing 'managerial rhetoric' likely to have been obtained during Stage 1, in order to tap into the 'true' culture of the organization.
- Staff views on how things should/could be changed (via questionnaires and structured interviews). This will promote a sense of 'involvement' for staff at an early stage in the change process.
- Company information, including:
  - ➢ financial data;
  - ➢ external market situation;

- ➢ human resources data, for example, performance appraisals, absenteeism/turnover figures, and so on;
- ➢ company procedures;
- ➢ other factors identified in initial dialogue with management as being 'problematic'
- Organizational structure, including:
  - ➢ 'Type' of management structure;
  - ➢ Communication processes/lines;
  - ➢ Position of company within overall corporate structure.

It should be noted that prior to this stage, management may be required to provide some introductory information to staff in order to facilitate the data collection process. Without this, activities of the change agent may be treated with suspicion and may result in obstruction of the audit, or in biased (and therefore useless) self-report responses to questionnaires/interviews, if staffs are suspicious/nervous about the anonymity of responses. This may be especially evident in an existing culture based on 'fear' and on directive, authoritarian management.

Stage 3: Inception report

On the basis of analysis/interpretation of data from Stage 2 and of discussions conducted in Stage 1, an inception report should be produced and discussed with management, to ensure that details and focus are accurate and appropriate. The report should:

- Identify the principle characteristics of the company (as detailed above);
- Identify the major driving forces and restraining forces prevalent in the company (Umstat, 1988);
- Identify any practical resistance to change;
- Identify the principle affective components of the workforce, that is, attitudes, beliefs, and so on.

Stage 4: Action plan

On the basis of the inception report and on the initial discussions with management, an action plan is developed in order to crystallize the proposed cultural change in terms of goals and objectives. Should the 'fit' between management's identified problems, aims and objectives and the results from the inception report be poor, it may be necessary to suggest alternative solutions to those proposed by management, and point out results from the cultural audit of which management were unaware. For example, Snyder (1988), in an example from a cultural change which took place in Lockheed during the early 1980s, points out that technical barriers were presenting the most significant barriers to performance within a particular factory, and that reduction of these barriers was likely to be far more important to increasing production than the prevailing culture of the organization. Ultimately, the change agent and management must agree on definition of the problem and on the objectives for cultural change. This agreement should take the following form:

- Recommendations to management on the basis of agreed information obtained during stages 1-3;
- Actions for key staff members' unanimous support is crucial here.

Emphasis is on the role of management in achieving cultural change management must take ownership.

Stage 5: Management training

Assuming that support for the action plan has been secured, a series of briefing sessions/seminars/ training sessions are conducted with key management staff, that is, those people who are crucial to the successful adoption and acceptance of the proposed changes. These training sessions typically comprise:

- explanation of process of cultural change (as illustrated in the flow chart above);
- emphasis on the importance of empathy, communication and participation with workers;
- explanation of key aspects of process for management, including:
  - ➢ clear articulation of desired visions and associated practices;
  - ➢ translation of vision into memorable reality, for example, 'attack the problem, not the person' (Snyder, 1988);

- ➢ endorsement of top management and 'modelling' by management, resulting in, for example, 'vicarious learning' (Bandura, 1969) through meeting workers, 'spreading the word', and so on;
- ➢ Building a new team, if necessary, to reinforce the new values/approach;
- ➢ engaging in symbolic acts, for example, team/company presentations, changing uniforms to symbolize team spirit, and so on;
- explanation of proposed goals and aims to be achieved through change and how these will impact on the organization and, ultimately, on organizational performance, that is, translation of a 'soft' process into 'hard' financial results;
- training management in 'transformational' leadership skills, and in the understanding of group processes and group dynamics.

Stage 6: 'Unfreeze' the organization

By Stage 6, this process, as envisaged by Lewin (1951), should be well underway. Management, with the assistance of the change agent, now take responsibility for the following, in order to prepare the organization for change:

- application of the principles learned during Stage 5 in order to make the organization aware of the need for change;
- ensuring that a climate of openness is developed between management and staff, regarding aims and consequences of proposed changes, by;
  - ➢ presenting the change programme to workers (and ensuring that this is pitched correctly);
  - ➢ adopting an open door policy;
  - ➢ increasing the visibility of management in the workplace;
  - ➢ encouraging participation of workers through seminars, workshops, and so on.

Note: Facilitating an atmosphere of openness may be difficult to achieve, especially if the previous climate has been one of distance and conflict between management and staff.

- highlighting threats to the organization if change does not take place, while encouraging workers to believe that change is possible and desirable (Schein, 1987);
- ensuring a climate of participation is developed by involving staff, especially influential supervisory staff, and so on, by involving them early in the change process;
- promoting *worker* ownership of the change by encouraging participation (to allow internalization by workers of new values).

Stage 7: Commence the Change

Management, with the assistance of the change agent, will typically begin the change process, by:

- communicating aims:
  - ➢ explaining goals and objectives to the workforce;
  - ➢ retaining openness and willingness for discussion;
  - ➢ building expectations for success;
- utilizing methods such as:
  - ➢ presentations/seminars;
  - ➢ workshops for team and skill building;
  - ➢ training/retraining programmes, following job analysis, especially if the change involves technical considerations;
  - ➢ continuous modeling of the change by senior/middle management.

Stage 8: Reinforce the change and 'refreeze' the organization

In order to effect a transition of values, norms and working practices, management is expected to:

- systematically reward adoption of new working practices;
- systematically punish adherence to old directions (while retaining useful aspects of the old system);
- promote adoption of required behaviours through:
  - ➢ incentive programmes (remuneration);
  - ➢ staff presentations concerning progress and feedback with the change programme;

- ➢ provision of personal counseling to workers who require it;
- Implement new rituals and artifacts, for example, new uniforms, and so on.

Stage 9: Evaluation

The initial post-change evaluation is usually conducted by the change agent, in consultation with management. The evaluation sets initial agreed aims and objectives against the current, post-change situation, and typically comprises criteria such as:

- behaviours (observational/absenteeism or turnover figures);
- performance ratings (peer/supervisory);
- financial/production (turnover/profit/production/sales/market share);
- Worker attitudes and satisfaction.

Results from this evaluation should be presented to management, summarizing:

- areas where change has been successful;
- recommendations for areas for improvement and suggestions as to how improvements could be achieved using in-house resources;
- unsuccessful elements of the programme compared against original objectives;
- areas requiring monitoring;
- suggested rolling evaluation programme.

Stage 10: Close down

At this final stage, the change agent should explain the following to management:

- Cultural change is an ongoing process which is evaluated and monitored on a continuous basis. Not undertaking this may result in a slow slide back into the 'old methods'.
- This involves:
  - ➢ presentations to staff on feedback and progress, both with change and with market success;
  - ➢ provision of personal counseling;
  - ➢ climate of openness and trust;
  - ➢ 'Management by objectives' and 'management by walking about', if possible.

The above model describes a staged process for effecting a cultural change within an occupational setting. Clearly, different industries will require emphasis to be placed on different aspects of the culture, which would need to be built into the programme. It is also clear that in the case of many organizations, internal politics may present the greatest barrier to cultural change; the above model assumes that agendas of management and staff are stated openly, and that subversive or sabotaging behaviours are minimized. In practice, such factors may require drastic measures such as replacement of staff or disciplinary procedures. However, through preparing adequately for cultural change, entering into a continuous dialogue with management, ensuring management support for proposals and objectives and by providing the necessary human resources support during the change process, a change agent can prove a valuable facilitator to the organizational development of companies requiring significant cultural, and other, change.

Diagnosing Organizational Development Needs:

The process that we advocate is based upon over eight years of field research:

1. Plan-to-plan
2. Decide on the need
3. Agree goals & brief
4. Gather senior mgt data
5. Gather staff data
6. Collate
7. Feedback set priorities
8. Action plan
9. Implement & review

This is the process which surrounds the Business Improvement Review (BIR) when implemented fully.

ORGANIZATIONAL EFFECTIVENESS

Organizational behaviour helps the manager to effectively handle individuals, groups and organizational resources. The knowledge of behaviour helps to achieve the goals of the organization. Organizational effectiveness is a term that is more comprehensive by mere performance and productivity of members. This is all about how effectively the organization can discharge its obligations with respect to all its constituencies including employees, shareholders, say other stakeholders. The growth, development, motivation, morale and satisfaction of the employees in the system combine with the good image projection of the organization to the society. Thus, organizational effectiveness is reflected in how well the organization is equipped to,

1. Handle its survival function through successful coping and
2. Its growth in future creative adaption strategies.

Rinsis Likerts identifies three variables as factors affecting the organizational effectiveness are as, casual, intervening, and end-result.

Casual variables are those factors that influence the course of developments within an organization, and the results or accomplishments. These independent variables can be altered by the management and its organization. They are not beyond the control of the organization like general business conditions, leadership strategies, skills and behaviour, management's decisions and the policies and structure of the organization are examples of casual variables.

Intervening variables are leadership strategies, skills and behaviour and other casual variables affect the human resource in an organization. According to Likert, intervening variables represent the current conditions of the internal state of the organization. They are reflected in the commitment to objectives, motivation and morale of members and their skills in leadership, communications, conflict resolution, decision-making and problem solving.

Output or end results are the variables that are dependent variables that reflect the achievements of the organizations. In evaluating effectiveness, perhaps more than 90 percent of managers in organization look for these measures of output alone. Based on all this aspect N.S. Gupta (1988) identified the parameters which may be helpful in

understanding the concept of effectiveness are:
1. General characteristics of effectiveness
2. Environmental setting
3. Achievement of short-term and long-term goals
4. Efficiency attainable within the organization.

Components of organizational effectiveness are:
1. Personal effectiveness
2. Managerial effectiveness
3. Organizational characteristics
4. Environmental characteristics
5. Employee characteristics
6. Managerial policies and practices.

Effectiveness is a continuous process in an organization and is brought out by the managers in the context of ever changing organization goals by restructuring available resources, altering technologies, modifying climate, and developing goal-oriented strategy of performance by objectives. Contingency has been the genesis of effectiveness. Change whether in goal or technology or resources composition or employee behaviour was needed because contingency arises due to the environmental factors. Organization can follow either of approaches for it effectiveness say the goal attainment approach or by the systems approach, or by both the approach applied in the appropriate areas.

MULTIPLE CHOICE QUESTIONS

1. An organizational restructuring strategy meant to reduce the organization's existing levels of managers or supervisors is
   A. De-layering   B. Cost cutting
   C. Retrenchment   D. None of the above

2. A small group of employees (normally six to twelve) invited to actively participate in a structured discussion with a facilitator is
   A. Small group   B. Large team
   C. Focus group   D. None of the above

3. An organizational network that operates over the Internet is
   A. Internet   B. Intranet
   C. Communication   D. None of the above

4. The act of creating new products and processes with an organization refers to
   A. Corporate entrepreneur
   B. Intrapreneurship
   C. Both A and B
   D. None of the above

5. An organizational team composed of individuals who are assigned a cluster of tasks, duties, and responsibilities to be accomplished is typically assumed as
   A. Autocratic team
   B. Self-directed team
   C. Task oriented team
   D. None of the above

6. A consensus planning tool used to identify the strengths of an organization, department or division, whereby participants are brought together to discuss important issues, problems and solutions is
   A. Team work
   B. Group discussion
   C. Analyzing tools
   D. Nominal group technique

7. An individual who works independently to assist and advise client organizations with various organizational functions and responsibilities on a fee-for-service basis is
   A. Employee   B. Consultant
   C. Citizen   D. Workers

8. A written statement that reflects the employer's standards and objectives relating to various employee activities and related matters is
   A. Oral communication
   B. Rules
   C. Standards
   D. Policy

9. General guidelines that focus organizational actions are
   A. Oral communication
   B. Rules
   C. Standards
   D. Policies

10. An organizational team composed of a core of members, resource experts who join the team as appropriate, and part-time/temporary members as needed is
   A. Shamrock team   B. Department team
   C. Sham team   D. Peer team

11. Rethinking and redesigning work to improve cost, service, and speed is
   A. Reengineering   B. Restructuring
   C. Both A and B   D. None of the above

12. The systematic approach and application of knowledge, tools and resources to deal with new corporate strategies, structures, procedures and technologies to deal with changes in external conditions and the business environment are
   A. Updating
   B. Change management
   C. Restructuring
   D. None of the above

13. Organizational feedback and communication mechanism that asks employees to provide opinions on given topics, feelings and beliefs about their jobs or the organization is
   A. Attitude Survey   B. Climate survey
   C. Both A and B   D. None of the above

14. An organizational team that is formed to address specific problems and may continue to work together to improve work processes or the quality of products and services is
   A. Work schedule
   B. Special-purpose team
   C. Committee members
   D. All the above

15. The assignment of different tasks to different people or groups are
   A. Management task
   B. Line authority
   C. Division of labour
   D. None of the above

16. Reducing the size of an organizational workforce is
   A. Cost cutting   B. Downsizing
   C. Both A and B   D. None of the above

17. Groups and individuals who affect and are affected by the achievements of the organization's mission, goals, and strategies is
   A. Stockholders
   B. Stakeholders
   C. Owners
   D. None of the above

18. Retirement benefits established and funded by employers and employees is
   A. Pay structure   B. Pension plans
   C. Lump sum amount   D. None of the above

19. The concept that people be trained best, if reinforcement is given as soon as possible after training is
   A. Learning skill
   B. Teaching skill
   C. Immediate confirmation
   D. Behavioural theory

20. _____ are the parts of an organization's intangible assets that relate specifically to knowledge, expertise, information, ideas, best practices, intellectual property and other capabilities.
   A. Knowledge assets
   B. Power of individuals
   C. Mindset
   D. None of the above

21. A salary differentiation system that bases compensation on an individual's education, experience, knowledge, skills or specialized training is
   A. Knowledge-based pay
   B. Skill-based pay
   C. Both A and B
   D. None of the above

22. The individual who facilitates the creation, sharing and use of knowledge in an organization by linking individuals with providers are termed as
   A. Knowledge-based pay
   B. Skill-based pay
   C. Knowledge broker
   D. None of the above

23. _____ is broadly defined as the assimilation, extraction, transformation and loading of information from disparate systems into a single more unified, consistent and accurate data store used for evaluating, manipulating and reporting information.
    A. Knowledge-based pay
    B. Skill-based pay
    C. Knowledge integration
    D. None of the above

24. The collective knowledge, skills and abilities of an organization's employees is
    A. Knowledge management
    B. Organizational behaviour
    C. Personality development
    D. Human capital

25. A group of employees responsible for a given end product is
    A. Product based
    B. Work team
    C. Organization members
    D. None of the above

26. Dimension of culture that values people, emphasize for the future, as opposed to short-term values focusing on the present and the past event is
    A. Long-term orientation
    B. Specified period training
    C. Development programs
    D. None of the above

27. A document outlining and representing the core priorities in the organization's culture is
    A. Report   B. Book
    C. Value statement   D. All the above

28. Organizational behaviour is not:
    A. A field of study
    B. An applied field
    C. Studying what people do in an organization
    D. An intuitive analysis of human behaviour

29. The four management functions do not include one of the following:
    A. Controlling   B. Planning
    C. Staffing   D. Organizing

30. A management theory stating that different situations call for different leadership styles and that essentially there is no one best way to lead is
    A. Charisma leader
    B. Autocratic leader
    C. Situational leader
    D. None of the above

31. _____ is a disciplined, data-driven methodology used to eliminate defects and improve processes and cut costs from manufacturing to transactional and from product to service.
    A. Research   B. Deduction
    C. Quality   D. Six sigma

32. Specific abilities resulting from knowledge, information, practice, and aptitude are
    A. Talent   B. Skill
    C. Both A and B   D. None of the above

33. Both parties enter into discussion with fair and open minds and a sincere desire to arrive at an agreement is, Generally means that
    A. Good-faith bargaining
    B. Bad-faith bargaining
    C. Negotiating
    D. All the above

34. The effort and action an organization puts forth to correct goals and specific problem areas is
    A. Good-faith bargaining
    B. Bad-faith bargaining
    C. Good-faith effort
    D. None of the above

35. A change in a company's strategy, mission and vision is
    A. New strategy
    B. Strategy restricting
    C. Change management
    D. Strategic change

36. A change in a company's shared values and aims, is about
    A. Structural change
    B. Behavioural change
    C. Cultural change
    D. Change management

37. The reorganizing-redesigning of an organization's departmentalization, coordination, span of control, reporting relationships, or centralization of decision making is
    A. Structural change
    B. Behavioural change
    C. Cultural change
    D. Change management

38. Modifications to the work methods an organization uses to accomplish its tasks is
    A. Structural change
    B. Behavioural change
    C. Cultural change
    D. Technological change

39. HR-based techniques aimed at changing employees' attitudes, values and behaviour is
    A. Organizational development interventions
    B. Organizational development
    C. Organizational behaviour
    D. Organizational climate

40. A method aimed at changing attitudes, values, and beliefs of employees so that employees can improve the organizations is
    A. Organizational development interventions
    B. Organizational development
    C. Organizational behaviour
    D. Organizational climate

41. A work team that uses consensus decision making to choose its own team members, to solve job-related problems, design its own jobs, and schedule its own break time is
    A. Individual performance
    B. Group formation
    C. Self-directed team
    D. None of the above

42. The redesign of business processes to achieve improvements in such measures of performance as cost, quality, service, and speed is
    A. Construction
    B. Destruction
    C. Business process reengineering
    D. None of the above

43. According to the text, the best approach for obtaining knowledge about human behaviour is

A. The common sense approach
B. An observational approach
C. A systematic approach
D. A theoretical approach

44. A conference established between two or more people or groups of people who are in different locations, made possible by the use of such telecommunications equipment as closed-circuit television is
   A. Telecommuting   B. Communication
   C. Teleconferencing   D. None of the above

45. _____ means that organizations are becoming more heterogeneous in terms of gender, race, and ethnicity.
   A. Globalization
   B. Workforce diversity
   C. Affirmative action
   D. Organizational culture

46. _____ has helped us understand differences in fundamental values, attitudes, and behaviour between people in different countries.
   A. Anthropology
   B. Psychology
   C. Social psychology
   D. Political science

47. _____ is the behavioural science discipline has made the most significant contributions to understanding individual behaviour.
   A. Sociology   B. Social psychology
   C. Psychology   D. Anthropology

48. Which of the following is the BEST description of OB's current state?
   A. It is based on universal truths.
   B. It is based on contingencies.
   C. There is little disagreement among OB researchers and scholars.
   D. Cause-effect principles have been isolated which tend to apply to all situations.

49. At individual level independent variables include
   A. Technology
   B. Organizational culture
   C. Perception
   D. Human resource policy

50. Organizational behaviour is a field of study that investigates the impact that individuals, groups, and structure have on behaviour within organizations, for the purpose of applying such knowledge toward improving an organization's effectiveness.
    A. True   B. False
    C. Not fact   D. None of the above

51. Managers get things done through other people.
    A. Fact   B. Non factual
    C. Myths   D. None of the above

52. Robert Katz has identified three management skills: technical, human, and conceptual.
    A. True   B. False
    C. Partially true   D. None of the above

53. Behaviour is generally predictable, and the systematic study of behaviour is a means to making reasonably accurate predictions.
    A. True   B. False
    C. Partially true   D. None of the above

54. Workforce diversity means that organizations are becoming more homogeneous in terms of gender, race, and ethnicity.
    A. True   B. False
    C. Partially true   D. None of the above

55. Learning, perception, and personality have been OB topics whose contributions have generally come from sociology.
    A. True   B. False
    C. Partially true   D. None of the above

56. Social psychology is an area within psychology, blending concepts from both psychology and political science.
    A. True   B. False
    C. Partially true   D. None of the above

57. In tight labour markets, those managers who don't understand human behaviour risk having no one to manage.
    A. True   B. False
    C. Partially true   D. None of the above

58. Today's managers must learn to cope with ongoing stability.
    A. True   B. False
    C. Partially true   D. None of the above

59. There are three levels of analysis in OB, and as we move from the individual level to the group level, to the organization systems level, we add systematically to our understanding of behaviour in organizations.
    A. True
    B. False
    C. Partially true
    D. None of the above

60. _____ is the process of managing the way people leave an organization.
    A. Organizational entry
    B. Organizational exit
    C. Either A or B
    D. None of the above

61. The systematic presentation of data to groups with the intent of stimulating discussion of problem areas, generating potential solutions, and stimulating motivation for change is
    A. Organizational feedback
    B. Performance appraisal
    C. Meeting
    D. None of the above

62. A formal research effort that evaluates the current state of HR management in an organization is
    A. HR accounting
    B. HR information system
    C. HR audit
    D. None of the above

63. The process of transforming an organization's goals, objectives, philosophy and mission into practices and policies is
    A. Strategic management
    B. Corporate governance
    C. Management function
    D. Organization planning

64. Information that provides a graphical presentation of the organizational units, including their interrelationships is
    A. Department
    B. Organizational profile
    C. Key resource area
    D. None of the above

65. The design of an organization that identifies the organization's hierarchal reporting and authority relationships is
A. Organizational structure
B. Hierarchy
C. Organization planning
D. Organization objective

66. The process of evaluating and analyzing an organization's structure and other major components to determine whether they are suitably meeting the organization's current and future needs is
A. Research survey
B. Social survey
C. Organizational survey
D. None of the above

67. Any discrete component at which there is a level of supervision responsible and accountable for the selection, compensation, etc., of employees within the unit is
A. Departments
B. Organizational area
C. Organizational unit
D. None of the above

68. A set of planned activities intended to provide the organization with the skills it requires to meet current and future business demands is
A. Human resource management
B. Personnel management
C. Human resource department
D. Line authority

69. Career planning that focuses on jobs and on constructing career paths that provide for the logical progression of people between jobs in an organization is
A. Individual growth
B. Organization-centered career planning
C. Human resource department
D. None of the above

70. The function dealing with the management of people employed within the organization is
A. Management function
B. Planning
C. Department function
D. Human resource function

71. Which of the following types of teams would most likely empower its team members to make work-related decisions?
A. Technical   B. Self-managed
C. Problem-solving   D. Management

72. _____ focuses on the study of people in relation to their social environment.
A. Psychology   B. Sociology
C. Corporate strategy D. Political science

73. _____ of the following techniques most restricts discussion or interpersonal communication during the decision-making process.
A. Nominal group   B. Brainstorm
C. Electronic meeting D. Formal process

74. _____ creates problem for employees when their job requires to display emotions incompatible with their actual feelings
A. Depression   B. Emotional Labour
C. Stress   D. Anxiety

75. Self-managed teams are typically comprised of how many members?
A. 2-5   B. 5-10
C. 10-15   D. Over 100

76. In attribution theory, what is distinctiveness?
A. Whether an individual displays consistent behaviours in different situations
B. Whether an individual displays different behaviours in different situations
C. Whether an individual displays consistent behaviours in similar situations
D. Whether an individual displays different behaviours in similar situations

77. Ravi has a low absenteeism rate. He takes responsibility for his health and has good health habits. He is likely to have a(an):
A. Internal locus of control
B. External locus of control
C. Core locus of control
D. High emotional stability level

78. When we rank an individual's values in order of their _____, we obtain the person's value system.
A. Intensity   B. Content
C. Context   D. Social needs

79. An individual most likely to engage in political behaviour would have all of the following except a
   A. High need for power
   B. High need of achievement
   C. High ability to self monitor
   D. High charisma rating

80. The advertisers believe that the celebrities have which of the following power?
   A. Personal   B. Referent
   C. Expert   D. Legitimate

81. Which of the following is the term used to refer to establishing effective relationships with key people inside and/or outside an organization?
   A. Networking   B. Politicking
   C. Interest group   D. Lobbying

82. Decrease in tenure can increase,
   A. Innovation   B. Productivity
   C. Creativity   D. Absenteeism

83. What is the term used for a general impression about an individual based on a single characteristic such as intelligence, sociability, or appearance?
   A. The contrast effect B. Personal bias
   C. The halo effect   D. Projection

84. Which of the following is NOT true of charismatic leaders?
   A. They have behaviour that is unconventional
   B. They are willing to take high personal risk
   C. They have a vision and the ability to articulate the vision
   D. They show consistency with their followers' behaviours

85. Rahul is undergoing a great deal of stress at his job. Rahul performs several duties during the course of a day and finds that the accomplishment of one duty directly competes or interferes with the successful accomplishment of another duty. It can be said that Rahul is most probably experiencing:
   A. Role conflict
   B. Personal conflict
   C. Relationship conflict
   D. Role ambiguity

86. If you support the idea that conflict should be eliminated, you are supporting which of the following views of conflict?
   A. The traditional view
   B. The human relations view
   C. The interactionist view
   D. The positivistic view

87. _____ can be defined as a loss in performance due to low leader expectations?
   A. Golem effect   B. Galatea effect
   C. Halo effect   D. Marshal effect

88. A motivational theory suggesting that an individual will behave in a manner that helps him or her avoids potential negative outcomes and achieve agreeable outcomes is
   A. Organizational behaviour modification theory
   B. Organizational development theory
   C. Organizational transformation theory
   D. Change management theory

89. The process of establishing and arranging the elements of an organization's structure is,
   A. Organization structure
   B. Organization design
   C. Organization components
   D. Organization flow chart

90. Workforce planning involves all of the following except
   A. examining production plans in a factory
   B. forecasting the individual output
   C. maintain individuals output
   D. organizing the training plan.

91. A pattern of shared values and beliefs giving members of an organization meaning and providing them with rules for behaviour is
   A. Organization structure
   B. Organization culture
   C. Organization components
   D. Organization flow chart

92. Which of the following theories is a process theory of motivation?
   A. Maslow's Need Hierarchy
   B. Vroom's valence expectancy
   C. Motivation–hygienic
   D. Equity theory

93. A leader exercising very little control or influence over the subordinates is called:
   A. Autocratic leader
   B. Participative leader
   C. Democratic leader
   D. Laissez-faire leader

94. In which type of leadership is the entire group involved and accepts responsibility for Goal setting and achievement?
   A. Authoritarian leadership
   B. Democratic leadership
   C. Laissez-faire leadership
   D. None of the above

95. Who formulated the contingency model of leadership?
   A. Chris Agrys
   B. R. Likert
   C. Ohio State University
   D. F.E. Fiedler

96. 'Theory X and 'Theory Y' were given by:
   A. Maslow   B. Herzberg
   C. McGregor   D. Taylor

97. According to Tuckman's theory of group formation, Group process starts with
   A. Creating   B. Norming
   C. Performing   D. Forming

98. Changing an organizational structure in order to make it more efficient and cost effective is,
   A. Restructuring
   B. Change management
   C. Procrastination
   D. None of the above

99. An organization-wide change, such as restructuring operations, introducing new technologies, processes, services or products, implementing new programs, re-engineering, etc. is known as
   A. Organizational behaviour
   B. Organizational development
   C. Organizational transformation
   D. Change management

100. A planned organization-wide effort to improve and increase the organization's effectiveness, productivity, return on investment, and overall employee job satisfaction through planned interventions in the organization's processes is referred as
   A. Organizational behaviour
   B. Organizational development
   C. Organizational transformation
   D. Change management

101. Maslow Need Hierarchy starts with
   A. Social
   B. Physiological needs
   C. Esteem
   D. Self Actualisation

102. In TOWS matrix, S stands for
   A. Situation   B. Society
   C. Strength   D. Skill

103. Which is not a part of Porters Five force Model?
   A. Threat of Suppliers
   B. Threat of New Entrants
   C. Threat of Substitutes
   D. Threat of Environment

104. _____ capacity of a firm to adapt to its changing societal conditions.
   A. Social Responsiveness
   B. Social Obligation
   C. Social Responsibility
   D. None of the above

105. In developmental phase, the dotcom companies concentrate on,
   A. Balancing phase   B. Building brand
   C. Both A and B   D. None of the above

106. The expenditure on medical treatment and stay abroad will be exempt only to the extent permitted by
   A. National bank
   B. Government of India
   C. Private banks
   D. Reserve Bank of India

107. At germination stage, to attract and retain talent, dotcom companies offer
   A. Stock option
   B. Flexi time
   C. Flexi-Working system
   D. None of the above

108. The motivation framework - arrange in order
   (*i*) Need or deficiency
   (*ii*) Search for ways to satisfy need
   (*iii*) Choice of behaviour evaluation of need satisfaction
   (*iv*) Determination of future needs and search/choice for satisfaction
   A.   (*i*)   (*ii*)   (*ii*)   (*iv*)
   B.   (*ii*)   (*iii*)   (*iv*)   (*i*)
   C.   (*iii*)   (*iv*)   (*i*)   (*ii*)
   D.   (*iv*)   (*i*)   (*ii*)   (*iii*)

109. In motivational theory, Focus on needs and deficiencies of individuals, is termed as
   A. Content perspectives of motivation
   B. Process perspectives of motivation
   C. Both A and B
   D. None of the above

110. In motivational theory, the Focus on why people choose certain behavioural options to satisfy their needs and how they evaluate their satisfaction after they have attained their goals is termed as
   A. Content perspectives of motivation
   B. Process perspectives of motivation
   C. Both A and B
   D. None of the above

111. Which of the following is not Content Perspectives of Motivation?
   A. Maslow's Hierarchy of Needs
   B. Herzberg's Two-Factor Theory
   C. McClelland's - Achievement
   D. Goal-Setting Theory

112. Which of the following is not, Process Perspectives of Motivation?
   A. Power, and Affiliation Needs
   B. Expectancy Theory
   C. Porter-Lawler Extension of Expectancy Theory
   D. Equity Theory

113. The People's satisfaction and dissatisfaction are influenced by independent sets of factors—motivation factors and hygiene factors is related to the theory of
   A. The Two-Factor Theory (Herzberg)
   B. Goal setting theory

   C. Maslow's theory
   D. None of the above

114. The outcomes set and awarded by external parties (*e.g.*, pay and promotions) is
   A. Extrinsic rewards   B. Intrinsic rewards
   C. Bothe A and B   D. None of the above

115. The outcomes that is internal to the individual (*e.g.*, self-esteem and feelings of accomplishment).
   A. Extrinsic rewards   B. Intrinsic rewards
   C. Both A and B   D. None of the above

116. In Designing Effective Reward Systems
   A. Reward system must meet an individual's needs and must recognize different needs.
   B. Rewards should compare favourably with other organizations.
   C. Distribution of rewards must be perceived to be equitable.
   D. All the above

117. The Types of rewards are
   A. Extrinsic rewards   B. Intrinsic rewards
   C. Both A and B   D. None of the above

118. It is an individual's belief that the treatment of he or she receives is fair relative to the treatment received by others.
   A. Equity theory   B. Fair treatment
   C. Policy   D. None of the above

119. Those incentives like Days off, additional paid vacation time are termed as
   A. Non-monetary   B. Monetary
   C. Increment   D. Allowances

120. Match the Reinforcement schedules
   (*a*) Fixed interval schedule — (*i*) Reinforcement applied at fixed time intervals, regardless of behaviour.
   (*b*) Variable interval — (*ii*) Reinforcement applied at variable time intervals.
   (*c*) Fixed ratio — (*iii*) Reinforcement applied after a fixed number of behaviours, regardless of time.
   (*d*) Variable Ratio — (*iv*) Reinforcement applied after a variable number of behaviours, regardless of time.

	(a)	(b)	(c)	(d)
A.	(i)	(ii)	(ii)	(iv)
B.	(ii)	(iii)	(iv)	(i)
C.	(iii)	(iv)	(i)	(ii)
D.	(iv)	(i)	(ii)	(iii)

121. The term LOC in the study of personality stands for:
A. Locus of control
B. Line of control
C. Levels of communication
D. Loss of compensation

122. Social self is the way an individual appears to self.
A. False
B. True
C. Myths
D. None of the above

123. Group formed because of some common entertaining interest is
A. Formal Group
B. Informal Group
C. Interest Group
D. Friendship Group

124. The ability and willingness of group members to set goals and work towards their accomplishment is known as _____.
A. Group Maturity
B. Group Cohesiveness
C. Group Dynamics
D. None of the above

125. Organizational objectives can be achieved by
A. Group work
B. Division of labour
C. Hierarchy of authority
D. All of above

126. Valence refers to the degree of favourableness or unfavourableness towards object.
A. True
B. False
C. Cannot say
D. None of the above

127. The senior executive of XYZ Ltd., Mr. Roy, had given complete freedom to his subordinates. He essentially provided no leadership. What category suitably defines the leadership style being practiced by Mr. Roy?
A. Laissez-faire
B. Autocratic
C. Democratic
D. Reinforcement

128. From the following which is classified as a hygiene factor according to Herzberg's theory of motivation?
A. Salary
B. Recognition
C. Achievement
D. Basic needs

129. A group of 6 employees has been formed within an organization; the initial discussions in the group were based on the environmental factors of the concerned issue. As the group started to work on the measures to rectify the core factors responsible for the concerned issue, the discussions always ended up in conflicts within the group members. This conflict was hampering the group's effectiveness. What is the level of conflict that is being highlighted in this case?
A. Intra-group
B. Inter-group
C. Inter personnel
D. Intra personnel

130. Any organizational change faces employee resistance because it is perceived as loss of something of value as a result of the change.
A. True
B. False
C. May be
D. None of the above

131. At _____ stage of team building, cooperation and a sense of shared responsibility is developed amongst the team members.
A. Norming
B. Storming
C. Performing
D. None of the above

132. What are the sources of attitudes for an individual?
A. Personal experiences/ Institutional factors
B. Peer groups and society
C. Friend's experiences
D. All the above

133. Alderfer's ERG needs model is very rigid in nature.
A. False
B. True
C. May be
D. None of the above

134. Rest provides the opportunity to recover from fatigue.
A. True
B. False
C. May be
D. None of the above

135. Traditional win-lose situations can be solved using _____ negotiations.
A. Distributive
B. Inter-organizational
C. Negative
D. Positive

136. Mismatch between personality and organization may lead to
A. Confusion and chaos
B. Loss of interest by members in organization
C. Low morale and job satisfaction
D. All the above

137. There is one leadership style which gives good results when the leader is required to deal with the unskilled workers doing repetitive tasks, this leadership style is
A. Autocratic   B. Participative
C. Free Rein   D. Democratic

138. In Supportive organization model, employee orientation is
A. Job performance   B. Security
C. Both A and B   D. None of the above

139. The relationship in which one person influences others to work together willingly on related tasks is known as _____.
A. Leadership   B. Subordinateship
C. Colleagues   D. Team

140. Congruent change in attitude means movement is in
A. The same direction B. Different direction
C. No way   D. None of the above

141. In the case of intra-organizational negotiations, groups often negotiate as representatives.
A. True   B. False
C. Cannot say   D. None of the above

142. Cultural elements and their relationships create a pattern that is identical in all organizations.
A. False   B. True
C. Cannot say   D. None of the above

143. Research activity emphasizes least collaboration and team work among workers.
A. False   B. True
C. Cannot say   D. None of the above

144. The discipline of Organizational _____ tries to synchronize internal organizational environment with external social environment.
A. Behaviour   B. Development
C. Change   D. None of the above

145. The _____ job loading is also known as job enlargement.
A. Horizontal   B. Vertical
C. Cross   D. Functional

146. The primary concern of ego is to determine whether the action proposed by superego is right or wrong.
A. False   B. True
C. Cannot say   D. None of the above

147. The stress which refers to a state of happiness is known as _____.
A. Eu-stress   B. Distress
C. Hyper stress   D. Hypo stress

148. Whatever an individual does, there is always some sort and some amount of stress on him.
A. True   B. False
C. Myths   D. None of the above

149. Noise is regarded as a distracter, because it interferes with/affects
A. Personal Life   B. Performance
C. Work efficiency   D. None of the above

150. What is the other name for vertical job loading?
A. Job enlargement   B. Job enrichment
C. Job rotation   D. All the above

ANSWERS

1	2	3	4	5	6	7	8	9	10
A	C	B	C	B	D	B	D	D	A

11	12	13	14	15	16	17	18	19	20
C	B	C	B	C	B	B	B	C	A

21	22	23	24	25	26	27	28	29	30
C	C	C	D	B	A	C	B	C	C

31	32	33	34	35	36	37	38	39	40
D	C	A	C	D	C	A	D	A	B

41	42	43	44	45	46	47	48	49	50
C	C	C	C	B	A	C	D	C	A

51	52	53	54	55	56	57	58	59	60
A	A	A	A	B	B	A	B	A	B

61	62	63	64	65	66	67	68	69	70
A	C	D	B	A	C	C	C	B	D

71	72	73	74	75	76	77	78	79	80
B	B	A	B	C	B	A	A	D	B

81	82	83	84	85	86	87	88	89	90
D	D	C	D	D	A	A	A	B	A

91	92	93	94	95	96	97	98	99	100
B	D	D	C	D	C	D	A	C	B

101	102	103	104	105	106	107	108	109	110
B	C	D	A	C	C	A	A	A	B

111	112	113	114	115	116	117	118	119	120
D	A	A	A	B	D	C	A	A	A

121	122	123	124	125	126	127	128	129	130
A	B	C	A	D	A	A	A	A	A

131	132	133	134	135	136	137	138	139	140
A	D	A	A	A	D	A	A	A	A

141	142	143	144	145	146	147	148	149	150
A	A	A	A	A	A	A	A	C	B

4

Industrial Relations

Industrial relations comprise one of the most delicate and complex problems of the modern industrial society. This event of a new complex industrial set-up is directly attributable to the surfacing of "Industrial Revolution". The pre-industrial revolution period was characterized by a simple process of manufacture, small scale investment, local markets and small number of persons employed. All this led to close proximity between the managers and to be managed. Due to personal and direct relationship between the employer and the employee it was easier to secure cooperation for managing. Any grievance or misunderstanding on the part of either party could be promptly removed with necessary proceedings. Also, there was no interference by the State in the economic activities of the people. Under such a set-up industrial relations were simple, direct and personal. This situation underwent a marked change with the introduction of industrial revolution – size of the business increased needing investment of enormous financial and human resources, there emerged a new class of professional managers causing separation between ownership and management, and relations between the employer and the employer became absorbed and gradually aggressive. This new set-up rendered the old philosophy of industrial relation irrelevant and gave rise to complex, indirect, and impersonal industrial relations.

Then the origin of the industrial relation lies in the employer-employees relationships. The workers are wage earners and depend upon wages for their livelihood. In the beginning the relationship between an employer and employees was informal, personnel and intimate since the business and industrial establishment were small. Formal institution have grown up to regulate the relationships depending on those factors like the intervention of the State, the growth of the trade unions and their federations, employer's associations, the growth of sciences of personnel management, industrial psychology and industrial sociology have all tended to influence the spirit and the course of relationship between employers and employees. Industrial relations are a by-product of industrial revolution and it owes origin from excessive exploitation of workers by the owners of industries.

Industry today is neither viewed as a venture of employers alone nor profit if considered as its sole objective. It is considered to be a venture based on purposeful cooperation between management and labour in the process of production and maximum social good is regarded as its ultimate end and both management and employees contribute in their own way towards its success. Similarly, labour today is no more an unorganized mass of ignorant works ready to obey without resentment or protest the arbitrary and discretionary dictates of management. The management has to deal with employees today into as individuals but also as members of organized social groups who are very much conscious about their rights and have substantial bargaining strength. Hence, the objective of evolving and maintaining sound industrial relations is not only to find our ways and means to solve conflicts to resolve differences but also to secure the cooperation among the employees in the conduct of industry.

But maintaining smooth industrial relation is not an easy task. Almost all the industrialized countries of the world fact the problem of establishing and maintaining good management worker relationships in their industries. Each country has sought to find our solution, depending upon its economic, social and political environment. However, industrial conflict still arises and therefore establishment and maintenance of satisfactory industrial relations forms an important platform in the personnel policies of modern organization.

Meaning

In the broad sense, industrial relations cover all such relationships that a business enterprise maintains with various sections of the society such as workers, state, customers and public who come into its contact.

The labour dictionary defines "industrial relation", "as the relation between employers and employees in industry".

In the narrow sense, it refers to all types of relationships between employer and employees, trade union and management, works and union and between workers and workers. It also includes all sorts of relationships at both formal and informal levels in the organization.

The term 'industrial relations' has been variously defined. J.T. Dunlop defines industrial relations as "the complex interrelations among managers, workers and agencies of the governments". According to Dale Yoder "industrial relations is the process of management dealing with one or more unions with a view to negotiate and subsequently administer collective bargaining agreement or labour contract".

In industrial relations, therefore, one seeks to study how people get on together at their work place, what difficulties arise between them, how their relations including wages and working conditions etc., are regulated. Industrial relations, thus, include both 'industrial relations' and 'collective relations' as well as the role of the state in regulating these relations. Such a relationship is therefore complex and multidimensional resting on economic, social, psychological, ethical, occupational, political and legal levels.

There are mainly two set of factors that determine the state of industrial relations, whether good or poor in any country. The first set of factors, described as 'institutional factors' include type of labour legislation, policy of state relating to labour and industry, extent and stage of development of trade unions and employers' organizations and the type of social institutions. The other set of factors, described as 'economic factors' include the nature of economic organization capitalist, socialist technology, the sources of demand and supply in the labour market, the nature and composition of labour force etc.

INDUSTRIAL RELATION: CONCEPT, SCOPE

What are Industrial Relations?

The concept of industrial relations has been defined using various terminologies, but in the strictest sense, it is essentially the relationship between management and labour. The full concept of industrial relations is the organization and practice of multi-pronged relationships between labour and management, unions and labour, unions and management in an industry. Dale Yoder defines it as a "whole field of relationships that exists because of the necessary collaboration of men and women in the employment process of an industry".

Evolution of Industrial Relations

The evolution of industrial relations in India began a long time ago. The caste system greatly influenced the ancient industries and their development. Due to successive foreign invasions in India, the living conditions of slave and artesian couldn't be differentiated. Furthermore, under the autocratic regime of Muslim rulers, the conditions of employees worsened. Wages were not guaranteed, the living conditions of workers were harsh, and there was no proper management. The coming of the British didn't improve the working conditions. After some time, however, most Indian industries were modeled after the British system of business, and this led to growth in various sectors.

Industrial Relations Under British Rule

During British rule, India was expected to be a colonial market for British goods up until a cotton mill was established in Mumbai in 1853 and a jute mill was established in Kolkata in 1955. The working conditions of workers, however, were still very harsh with low pay, and this gave rise to various disputes involving the management and employees. On the other hand, Tata Iron and Steel industry was also established in Jamshedpur in 1911. While there was great demand of iron and steel before and during the First World War, the working conditions of workers hadn't improved. Hence, the Factories Act of 1881 was established, and it granted workers certain rights.

Industrial Relations in First World War

The First World War was an opportunity in disguise for local factories in India. Prices of virtually all products went up and profits soared, however, wages of lower employees were still the same. There were various strikes and disputes between management and employees. During this time, the Workmen's Compensation Act (1923), the Trade Union Act (1926), and the Trade Disputes Act (1917) were established. While the wages of employees remained the same, they were given a certain share of profits made by their hiring industry. Strikes, however, were sometimes prohibited under the Emergency Rules. The years following World War II involved the most workers' turmoil, and saw the establishment of Industrial Employment Act (1946) and Industrial Disputes Act (1947).

Post-Independence Industrial Relations

The post-independence era saw a developing relation between industry and labour. A conference called the Industrial Truce Resolution took place in 1947, and foresaw the establishment of the Minimum Wages Act, Factories Act, and Employees State Insurance Act in 1948. This ensured peace between labour and industry. While industrial relations in India have evolved a long way, some features of the early system still exist today. Modern industrial relations are dynamic, and may integrate industrial policies of American and British businesses.

Role of Industrial Relations

Industrial relations are associated with labour, management, labour unions, and the state. The scene of industrial relations has grown tremendously, and cannot be represented merely by relations between management and labour. It has become a comprehensive and total concept embracing the sum total of relationship that exists at various levels of the organizational structure. Additionally, it connotes relationships between workers themselves within the labour class, and relations among the management within the managerial class. In an open sense, industrial relations denote all types of relations within a group and outside a group, both formal and informal relations. Many other events happened which accelerated the pace of industrial relations during the period. They are,

- The success of Russian Revolution 1917.
- ILO was established in 1919 and it influenced through its conventions and recommendations.
- AITUC was established in 1920.
- The happening of Carnatic and Birmingham milks in which Mr.B.P.Wadie was arrested 1923.
- In 1924 left wing emerged on the Indian political horizon.
- In 1924 labour party government was formed in U.K.
- British industrialists of Bancashere and Birmingham put pressure on government.
- The Trade Dispute Act 1926 was promulgated and passed in the year of 1929.
- Royal Commission on Labour (1929-31) was formed which made a comprehensive study

of Indian Labour problems regarding health, safety and welfare of workers and made recommendations of far reaching consequences.

Scope

The scope of industrial relations includes all aspects of relationships such as bringing cordial and healthy labour management relations, creating industrial peace and developing industrial democracy.

The cordial and healthy labour management relations could be brought in:

- by safeguarding the interest of the workers;
- by fixing reasonable wages;
- by providing good working conditions;
- by providing other social security measures;
- by maintaining healthy trade unions;
- by collective bargaining.

The industrial peace could be attained:

- by setting industrial disputes through mutual understanding and agreement;
- by evolving various legal measure and setting up various machineries such as Works Committee, Boards of Conciliation, Labour Courts etc.

The industrial democracy could be achieved:

- by allowing workers to take part in management; and
- by recognition of human rights.

Objectives of Industrial Relations

1. To bring better understanding and cooperation between employers and workers.
2. To establish a proper channel of communication between workers and management.
3. To ensure constructive contribution of trade unions.
4. To avoid industrial conflicts and to maintain harmonious relations.
5. To safeguard the interest of workers and the management.
6. To work in the direction of establishing and maintaining industrial democracy.
7. To ensure workers' participation in decision-making.

8. To increase the morale and discipline of workers.
9. To ensure better working conditions, living conditions and reasonable wages.
10. To develop employees to adapt themselves for technological, social and economic changes.
11. To make positive contributions for the economic development of the country.
12. To protect management and labour interests by securing mutual relations between the two groups.
13. Avoid disputes between management and labour, and create a harmonizing relationship between the groups so productivity can be increased.
14. Ensure full employment and reduce absenteeism, hence, increasing productivity and profits.
15. Emphasize labour employer partnership to establish and maintain industrial democracy. This is done to ensure the sharing of profit gains, and personal developmental of all employees.
16. Provide better wages and living conditions to labour, so misunderstandings between management and labour are reduced to a minimum.
17. To bring about government control over plants where losses are running high, or where products are produced in the public interest.
18. To bridge a gap between various public factions and reshape the complex social relationships emerging out of technological advances by controlling and disciplining members, and adjusting their conflicts of interests.

Significance of Industrial Relations

Maintenance of harmonious industrials relations is on vital importance for the survival and growth of the industrials enterprise. Good industrial relations result in increased efficiency and hence prosperity, reduced turnover and other tangible benefits to the organization. The significance of industrial relations can be summarized as below:

1. *It establishes industrial democracy:* Industrial relations means settling employee's problems through collective bargaining, mutual cooperation and mutual agreement amongst the parties *i.e.*, management and employees' unions. This helps in establishing industrial democracy in the organization which motivates them to contribute their best to the growth and prosperity of the organization.

2. *It contributes to economic growth and development:* Good industrial relations lead to increased efficiency and hence higher productivity and income. This will result in economic development of the economy.

3. *It improves morale of the work force:* Good industrial relations, built-in mutual cooperation and common agreed approach motivate one to contribute one's best, result in higher productivity and hence income, give more job satisfaction and help improve the morale of the workers.

4. *It ensures optimum use of scare resources:* Good and harmonious industrial relations create a sense of belongingness and group-cohesiveness among workers, and also a congenial environment resulting in less industrial unrest, grievances and disputes. This will ensure optimum use of resources, both human and materials, eliminating all types of wastage.

5. *It discourages unfair practices on the part of both management and unions:* Industrial relations involve setting up machinery to solve problems confronted by management and employees through mutual agreement to which both these parties are bound. This results in banning of the unfair practices being used by employers or trade unions.

6. *It prompts enactment of sound labour legislation:* Industrial relations necessitate passing of certain labour laws to protect and promote the welfare of labour and safeguard interests of all the parties against unfair means or practices.

7. *It facilitates change:* Good industrial relations help in improvement of cooperation, team work, performance and productivity and hence in taking full advantages of modern inventions, innovations and other scientific and technological advances. It helps the work force to adjust themselves to change easily and quickly.

Causes of Poor Industrial Relations

Perhaps the main cause or source of poor industrial relations resulting in inefficiency and labour unrest is mental laziness on the part of both management and labour. Management is not sufficiently concerned to ascertain the causes of inefficiency and unrest following the laissez-faire policy, until it is faced with strikes and more serious unrest. Even with regard to methods of work, management does not bother to devise the best method but leaves it mainly to the subordinates to work it out for themselves. Contempt on the part of the employers towards the workers is another major cause. However, the following are briefly the causes of poor industrial relations:

1. Mental inertia on the part of management and labour;

2. An intolerant attitude of contempt of contempt towards the workers on the part of management;

3. Inadequate fixation of wage or wage structure;

4. Unhealthy working conditions;

5. Indiscipline;

6. Lack of human relations skill on the part of supervisors and other managers;

7. Desire on the part of the workers for higher bonus or DA and the corresponding desire of the employers to give as little as possible;

8. Inappropriate introduction of automation without providing the right climate;

9. Unduly heavy workloads;

10. Inadequate welfare facilities;

11. Dispute on sharing the gains of productivity;

12. Unfair labour practices, like victimization and undue dismissal;

13. Retrenchment, dismissals and lockouts on the part of management and strikes on the part of the workers;

14. Inter-union rivalries; and

15. General economic and political environment, such as rising prices, strikes by others, and general indiscipline having their effect on the employees' attitudes.

INDUSTRIAL RELATION APPROACH

Approaches to Industrial Relations

Industrial conflicts are the results of several socio-economic, psychological and political factors. Various lines of thoughts have been expressed and approaches used to explain his complex phenomenon. One observer has stated, "An economist tries to interpret industrial conflict in terms of impersonal markets forces and laws of supply demand.

To a politician, industrial conflict is a war of different ideologies – perhaps a class-war. To a psychologist, industrial conflict means the conflicting interests, aspirations, goals, motives and perceptions of different groups of individuals, operating within and reacting to a given socio-economic and political environment".

Psychological Approach

According to psychologists, problems of industrial relations have their origin in the perceptions of the management, unions and rank and file workers. These perceptions may be the perceptions of persons, of situations or of issues involved in the conflict. The perceptions of situations and issues differ because the same position may appear entirely different to different parties. The perceptions of unions and of the management of the same issues may be widely different and, hence, clashes and may arise between the two parties. Other factors also influence perception and may bring about clashes.

The organizational behaviour of inter-groups of management and workers is of crucial importance in the pattern of industrial relations.

The group-dynamics between the two conflicting groups in industrial relations tend to shape the behavioural pattern.

Sociological Approach

Industry is a social world in miniature. The management goals, workers' attitudes, perception of change in industry, are all, in turn, decided by broad social factors like the culture of the institutions, customs, structural changes, status-symbols, rationality, acceptance or resistance to change, tolerance etc. Industry is, thus inseparable from the society in which it functions. Through the main function of an industry is economic, its social consequences are also important such as urbanization, social mobility, housing and transport problem in industrial areas, disintegration of family structure, stress and strain, etc. As industries develop, a new industrial-cum-social pattern emerges, which provides general new relationships, institutions and behavioural pattern and new techniques of handling human resources. These do influence the development of industrial relations.

Human Relations Approach

Human resources are made up of living human beings. They want freedom of speech, of thought of expression, of movement, etc. When employers treat them as inanimate objects, encroach on their expectations, throat-cuts, conflicts and tensions arise. In fact major problems in industrial relations arise out of a tension which is created because of the employer's pressures and workers' reactions, protests and resistance to these pressures through protective mechanisms in the form of workers' organization, associations and trade unions.

Dunlop's Systems Theory: Dunlop has developed a systems approach to industrial relations as the systems model of industrial relations consisting of workers, organizations, managers, governmental agencies and so on. The interaction of those components creates a set of rules in the form of agreements, orders regulations, policies etc. which facilitates the smooth functioning of the organization. This approach emphasis on direct relationship between the industrial relations subsystems and objectives of the company. According to this approach, human resource plays a key role in opening up new opportunities for increasing productivity and promoting both the industrial and organizational growth. Workers, managers and their organizations, government, agencies confront an environment comprising of factors such as technology, market constrains power relation and ideas, beliefs held by them to help fund or integrate the industrial relations systems. The rules are framed to govern the actors at work place by collective bargaining agreements, awards, law customs etc. The model focuses on institutiona-lization of conflict and establishment of orderly industrial relations. The approach is quite helpful in studying the industrial relations in the sense that it focuses on participants in the process environment forces and the output and studies and inter-relationship studies and inter-relationship among different factors of industrial relations systems.

Participative approach: This approach in industrial relations emphasis on face-to-face relationships, better understanding between workers and management so that cordial industrial relations may be developed and a great willingness any help in carrying through decisions once made this approach involves the need for flow of ideas in the organization and is helpful in developing individuals for higher responsibilities.

Pluralist theory of Flanders: According to Flanders conflict is inherent in an industrial system since the organization is composed of individuals who make up distinct sectional groups, each with its own interests objectives and leadership. This give rise to competing interest groups. The conflicts between management and employees are rational and inevitable. Collective bargaining is required as formal system to settle conflicts. Collective bargaining is central to the industrial relations system. The rule of the system are viewed as being determined through the rule making process of collective bargaining, which is regarded as a political institution involving a power relationship between employers and employees.

Gandhian Approach: This is based on the fundamental principles of truth, non-violence and non-possession. He advocated peaceful coexistence of capital and labour and if the employers follow the principles of trusteeship than there is no scope for conflict of interest between them and labour trusteeship implied cooperation between capital and labour. He advocated rules to resolve industrial conflicts workers can resort to Satyagraha to have their grievance redressed. Gandhiji accepted the workers to go on strike but strikes should be avoided and only resorted to as last measure. The workers should avoid strikes as far as possible in industries of essential services, and if they have to organize a strike, trade union should exercise this right in a peaceful and non-violent manner. Workers should seek redressal of demands through collective bargaining and take resource to voluntary arbitration where direct settlement fails.

Through tension is more direct in work place; gradually it extends to the whole industry and sometimes affects the entire economy of the country. Therefore, the management must realize that efforts are made to set right the situation. Services of specialists in Behavioural Sciences (namely, psychologists, industrial engineers, and human relations expert and personnel managers) are used to deal with such related problems. Assistance is also taken from economists, anthropologists, psychiatrists, pedagogists, and technology. In resolving conflicts, understanding of human behaviour – both individual and groups – is a pre-requisite for the employers, the union leaders and the government – more so for the management. Conflicts cannot be resolved unless the management must learn and know what the basic what the basic needs of men are and how they can be motivated to work effectively.

It has now been increasingly recognized that much can be gained by the managers and the worker, if they understand and apply the techniques of human relations approaches to industrial relations. The workers are likely to attain greater job satisfaction, develop greater involvement in their work and achieve a measure of identification of their objectives with the objectives of the organization; the manager, on their part, would develop greater insight and effectiveness in their work.

Principle of Good Industrial Relations

- The willingness and ability of management and trade unions to deal with the problems freely, independently and with responsibility.
- Recognition of collective bargaining.
- Desirability of associations of workers and managements with the Government while formulating and implementing policies relating to general economic and social measures affecting industrial relations.
- Fair redressal of employee grievances by the management.
- Providing satisfactory working conditions and payment of fair wage.
- Introducing a suitable system of employee's education and training.
- Developing proper communication system between management and employees.
- To ensure better working conditions, living conditions and reasonable wages.
- To develop employees to adapt themselves for technological, social and economic changes.
- To make positive contributions for the economic development of the country.

Role of State in Industrial Relations

In recent years the State has played an important role in regulating industrial relations but the extent of its involvement in the process is determined by the level of social and economic development while the mode of intervention gets patterned in conformity with the political system obtaining in the country and the social and cultural traditions of its people. The degree of State intervention is also determined by the stage of economic develop. For example, in a developing economy like ours, work-stoppages to settle claims have more serious consequences than in a developed economy and similarly, a free market economy may leave the parties free to settle their relations through strikes and lockouts but in other systems varying degrees of State participation is required for building up sound industrial relations.

In India, the role played by the State is an important feature in the field of industrial relations and State intervention in this area has assumed a more direct form. The State has enacted procedural as well as substantive laws to regulate industrial relations in the country.

Role of Management in Industrial Relations

The management has a significant role to play in maintaining smooth industrial relations. For a positive improvement in their relations with employees and maintaining sound human relations in the organization, the management must treat employees with dignity and respect. Employees should be given 'say' in the affairs of the organization generally and wherever possible, in the decision-making process as well. A participative and permissive altitude on the part of management tends to give an employee a feeling that he is an important member of the organization, a feeling that encourages a spirit of cooperativeness and dedication to work.

- Management must make genuine efforts to provide congenial work environment.
- They must make the employees feel that they are genuinely interested in their personal development. To this end, adequate opportunities for appropriate programmes of 18-training and development should be provided.
- Managements must delegate authority to their employees commensurate with responsibility.
- They must evolve well conceived and scientific wage and salary plan so that the employees may receive just compensation for their efforts. They must devise, develop and implement a proper incentive plan for personnel at all levels in the organization.
- There must be a well-planned communication system in the organization to pass on information and to get feedback from the employees.
- Managements must pay personal attention to the problems of their employees irrespective

of the fact whether they arise out of job environment or they are of personal nature.

● They must evolve, establish and utilize appropriate machineries for speedy redressal of employee's grievances.

● Managements must provide an enlightened leadership to the people in the organization.

An environment of mutual respect, confidence, goodwill and understanding on the part of both management and employees in the exercise of their rights and performance of their duties should prevail for maintaining good industrial relations.

Role of Trade Unions in Maintaining Industrial Relations

The trade unions have a crucial role to play in maintaining smooth industrial relations. It is true that the unions have to protect and safeguard the interests of the workers through collective bargaining. But at the same time they have equal responsibility to see that the organization does not suffer on account of their direct actions such as strikes, even for trivial reasons. They must be able to understand and appreciate the problems of managements and must adopt a policy of 'give and take' while bargaining with the managements. Trade unions must understand that both management and workers depend on each other and any sort of problem on either side will do harm to both sides. Besides public are also affected, particularly when the institutions involved are public utility organizations.

The Labour Management Synergy

Planning for healthy Industrial Relations is one of the most delicate and complex problems of present day industrial society, representing diverse 'points of flexion' and 'bases of industrial edifice'. How people get on together at their work, what difficulties arise between them, how their relations, including wages and working conditions, are regulated and what organizations are set up for the protection of different interests. These are some of the major issues of industrial relations system.

The Triangle of Industrial Relations System represents multi-pronged relationship between management, trade unions and workers.

Industrial Relations System's responsibility implies: (a) Inter-vertex Relationship (amongst management, trade unions and workers) and, (b) Inter-societal obligations.

Management relationship vis-a-vis trade unions is based on increasing realization that trade unionism has to come to stay as a necessary concomitant of the contemporary capitalist them; and, that trade unions movement is the expression of the workers' collective determination to recover emotional security lost through Industrial revolution.

Management relationship vis-a-vis workers revolves round the themes like attitude towards work; industrial democracy; urge for greater degree of control over work situation; search for an environment, where worker can take roots and where he belongs to; and, identification of the functions, where he sees the purpose of his work and feels important in achieving it.

Management approach towards itself presupposes management as a social task. Since life is based on conflict, the management task in the long-run is directed towards harmonizing this conflict inside and outside the enterprise. The art and science of management is highly sophisticated with theories, concepts and models of management.

Trade union relationship vis-a-vis management is conditioned by accepting the fact that management presents an indissoluble partnership amongst interest, power and responsibility in the societal context.

Trade Union relationship vis-a-vis workers implied that it should appreciate workers' aspirations and expectations that trade union is essentially a protective, friendly society, meant primarily to manage and handle their economic, social and cultural problems. Often aspirations of workers are at variance with those of leaders in the trade union movement. Trade union approach towards itself is based on the premise that trade unionism is a management system. Trade Unions as organizations generally viewed themselves as an 'end' rather than as a 'means' centering on 'cause' and not on 'man', which, in turn, creates an attitude of convalescence and the cause of unconsciousness. There is often a tendency in trade unionism to promote 'mass movement' instead of an 'organization', and its membership is often based on 'calamity features' rather than on 'positive factors'. In a changing situation like India, ideological postures are of limited relevance in the realm of trade unionism, which has to undertake responsi-bilities in a dynamic situation, influenced by external and internal environment and focusing on:

- The primary purpose
- Organization
- Adjustment and adaptation
- Attitudes
- Representation
- Economic responsibility
- Discipline

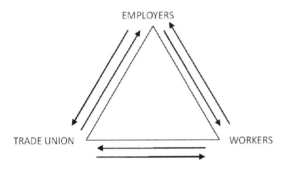

There is an imperative need of strengthening the democracy and freedom within the trade unions, encourage workers' participation in the process of decision-making and developing new perspectives in the personnel problems of the trade unionism.

Management and trade unions both have to be aware of the changing value system, the needs of a 'new breed' of employee, the ever-increasing generational gap in attitudes towards money, emphasis on quality of life, public's lower frustration tolerance, changing attitudes towards work and leisure, education's impact on peoples' self-image, rejection of authoritarianism and dogmatism, greater stress on pluralism and individualism, and search of identity, self-esteem and self-realization. The

ideology based on rationality; moral absolutes leading to situational ethics; and, economic efficiency resulting in social justice; are the new bases and postulates for shaping the future industrial relations system in the Indian context.

INDUSTRIAL RELATION SYSTEM

In future organization systems, employees would consider themselves to be partners in management and expect their talents to be utilized to the fullest. With increased self-esteem and self-image, young graduates will resist authority and would challenge prevailing management prerogatives. Tomorrow's management control centers, advanced OR models will aid future managers in the use of resources, they would need to balance humanistic values with the flow of advancing science and technology.

According to Victor Fuchs, "In future, the large corporation is likely to be over-shadowed by the hospital, university, research institutes, government offices and professional organizations that are the hallmarks of a service economy". Following the concept of 'corporate citizenship', the 'responsible corporation' has to develop as a social institution, where people share success and failure, create ideas, interact and work for development and realization of the individual's potential as human being.

Since Industrial Relations is a function of three variables – management, trade unions and workers, a workable approach towards planning for healthy labour-management relations can be developed by:

- Defining the acceptable boundaries of employer/ employee action;
- Granting the freedom to act within these boundaries; and
- Monitoring the resulting developments.

For achieving the objectives of improved management, trade union the following line of action is suggested:

- A realistic attitude of managers towards employees and *vice versa* for humanizing industrial relations.
- Proper organization climate and extension of area of Industrial Relations.

- Institutionalism of industrial relations and effective forms for interaction between management and trade unions at plant, industry and national levels.
- A comprehensive system of rules and discipline.
- The maintenance of an efficient system of communication.
- An objective follow-up pattern for industrial relations system.
- Respect for public opinion and democratic values.
- An integrated industrial relations policy incorporating rational wage policy; trade union and democratic rights, sanctity of ballot, collective bargaining and tripartite negotiations.

Whatever, labour laws may lay down, it is the approach of the management and union which matters and unless both are enlightened, industrial harmony is not possible. In fact both managements and workers need a change in their philosophy and attitudes towards each other. In all fairness, both management and workers should not look upon themselves as two separate and distinct segments of an organization, but on the contrary, realize that both are partners in an enterprise working for the success of the organization for their mutual benefit and interest. It is becoming increasingly obvious that industrial peace amongst all participants in the industrial relations systems requires truth as foundation, justice as its rule, love as its driving force, and liberty as its atmosphere.

INDUSTRIAL DISPUTE: CAUSES, EFFECTS, TRENDS METHODS

Meaning

According to Section 2(K) of the Industrial Disputes Act, 1947, and 'industrial dispute' means any dispute or difference between employers and employees or between employers and workmen or between workmen and workmen, which is connected with the employment or non-employment or the terms of employment or with the conditions of labour of any person.

Thus form the legal point of view, industrial dispute does not merely refer to difference between labour and capital as is generally thought, but it refers to differences that affect groups of workmen and employers engaged in an industry. Essentially, therefore, the differences of opinions between employers and workmen in regard to employment, non-employment, terms of employment or the conditions of labour where the contesting parties are directly and substantially interested in maintaining their respective contentious constitute the subject-matter of an industrial dispute.

Causes of Industrial Disputes

The causes of industrial conflict or disputes have been much varied. These may be described partly a psychological or social and partly political, but predominantly economic. Some important factors responsible for industrial conflict and poor industrial relations many are briefly stated as follows:

- Management's general apathetic towards workers or employees because of their contention that they want more and more economic or monetary rewards and want to do less work.
- Mental inertia on the part of both management and labour.
- Lack of proper fixation of wages inconformity with cost of living and a reasonable wage structure generally.
- Bad working conditions.
- Attempts by management to introduce changes (such a rationalization, modernization or automation) without creating a favourable to appropriate climate or environment for the same.
- Lack of competence or training on the part of first-line supervision as well management at upper levels in the practice of human relations.
- Assignment of unduly heavy work-loads to worker, unfair labour practices (such as victimization or undue dismissal).
- Lack of strong and healthy trade unionism, lack of a proper policy of union recognition and inter-union rivalries.

● A spirit of non-cooperation and a general tendency among employees to criticize or oppose managerial policies or decisions even when they may be in the right directions.

● A fall in the standard of discipline among employees largely due to wrong or improper leadership, often resulting in insubordination or disobedience on the part of employees.

● Difference in regard to sharing the gains of increased productivity.

● Inadequate collective bargaining agreements.

● Legal complexities in the industrial relations machinery or settlement of industrial disputes.

● Lack of necessary changes in the working of government in accordance with changing needs and circumstances.

● Combination of too much law and too little respect for law even at high levels.

● Growing factional and personal difference among rank-and-file employees who are union members or union leaders and a tendency on the part of the management in some cases to prefer having with outside leaders and not give due respect to worker-leaders.

● Political environment of the country; and

● Agitation and wrong propaganda by selfish labour leaders to further their own interests of their own party.

Forms of Disputes

Strikes, lockouts and gheraos are the most common forms of disputes.

Strike

"Strike" means a cessation of work by a body of persons employed in any industry acting in combination; or a concerted refusal or a refusal under a common understanding or an number of persons who are or have been so employed to continue to work or to accept employment.

The following points may be noted regarding the definition of strike:

● Strike can take place only when there is a cessation of work or refusal to work by the workmen acting in combination or in a concerted manner.

● A concerted refusal or a refusal under a common understanding of any number of persons to continue to work or to accept employment will amount to a strike. A general strike is one when there is a concert of combination of workers stopping or refusing to resume work. Going on mass casual leave under a common understanding amounts to a strike.

● If on the sudden death of a fellow-worker, the workmen acting in concert refuse to resume work, it amounts to a strike (National Textile Workers' Union Vs. Shree Meenakshi Mills (1951) II L.L.J. 516).

● The striking workman must be employed in an 'industry' which has not been closed down.

● Even when workmen cease to work, the relationship of employers and employees is deemed to continue albeit in a state of belligerent suspension.

Types of Strike

● *Go-slow:* Go-slow does not amount to strike, but it is a serious case of is conduct.

● *Sympathetic strike:* Cessation of work in the support of the demands of workmen belonging to other employer is called a sympathetic strike. The management can take disciplinary action for the absence of workmen. However, in Ramalingam Vs. Indian Metallurgical Corporation, Madras, 1964-I L.L.J.81, it was held that such cessation of work will not amount to a strike since there is no intention to use the strike against the management.

● *Hunger strike:* Some workers may resort to fast on or near the place of work or residence of the employers. If it is peaceful and does not result in cessation of work, it will not constitute a strike. But if due to such an fact, even those present for work, could not be given work, it will amount to strike (Pepariach Sugar Mills Ltd. Vs. Their Workmen).

● *Stay-in, sit-down, pen-down strike:* In all such cases, the workmen after taking their seats refuse to do work. All such acts on the part of the workmen acting in combination, amount to a strike.

- *Lightning or wildcat strike:* A wildcat strike is an unofficial strike *i.e.* a strike not sanctioned by the union. Such strikes occasionally occur in violation of the no-strike pledge in collective bargaining agreements. In such a situation union is obliged to use its best efforts to end the strike. Such strikes are prohibited in public utility services under Section 22 of the Industrial Disputes Act, 1947. Further, the standing order of a company generally required for notice.
- *Work-to-rule*: Since there is a no cessation of work, it does not constitute a strike.

Lockout

Section 2(1) of the Industrial Disputes Act, 1947 defines "lockout" to mean the temporary closing of a place of employment or the suspension of work, or the refusal by an employers to continue to employ any number of persons employed by him, lockout, thus, is the counterpart of strike, the corresponding weapon the hands of employer to resist the collective demands of workmen or to enforce his terms. It has been held by the courts that the suspension of work as a disciplinary measure does not amount to lockout. Similarly, temporary suspension of work called lay-off is not lock-out.

Gherao

Gherao means encirclement of the managers to criminally intimidate him to accept the demands of the workers. It amounts to criminal conspiracy under Section 120-A of the I.P.C. and is not saved by Sec. 17 of the Trade Unions Act on the grounds of its being a concerted activity.

Regulation of Strikes and Lockouts

Employees do not have an unfettered right to go on strike nor do employers have such right to impost lockout. The Industrial Disputes Act lays down several restrictions on the rights of both the parties. A strike or lockout commenced or continued in contravention of those restrictions is termed illegal and there is serve punishment provided for the same.

Illegal strikes and lockout are of two types:

- Those which are illegal form the time of their commencement; and
- Those which are not illegal at the time of commencement but become illegal subsequently.

Section 22 and 23 of the IDA provide for certain restrictions which if not followed make strikes and lockouts illegal from their very commencement.

According to this section, no person employed shall go on strike in breach of contract;

- Without giving notice of strike to the employer, as here matter provided, within six week before striking; or
- Within fourteen days of giving such notice; or
- Before the expiry of the date of strike specified in any such notice as aforesaid; or
- During the pendency of any conciliation proceedings before a Conciliation Officer and seven days after the conclusion of such proceedings.

Consequences of Illegal Strikes and Lockouts

- *Penalty for illegal strikes [Sec.26(1)]:* Any workman who commences, continues or otherwise acts in furtherance of a strike which is illegal, shall be punishable with imprisonment for a term which may extend to 1 month, or with fine which may extend to ₹ 50, or with both.
- *Penalty for illegal lockout [Sec.26(2)]:* Any employer who commences, continues or otherwise acts in furtherance of a lockout which is illegal, shall be punishable with imprisonment for a term which may extend to 1 month, or with fine which may extend to ₹ 1,000 or with both.
- *Penalty for instigation, etc. [Sec. 27]:* Any person who instigates or incites others to take part in, or otherwise acts in furtherance of, a strike or lockout which is illegal, shall be punishable with imprisonment for a term which may extend to 6 months, or with fine which may extend to ₹ 1,000 or with both.

- *Penalty for giving financial aid for illegal strikes and lockouts [Sec. 28]* : Any person who knowingly expends or applies any money in direct furtherance or support of any illegal strike or lockout shall be punishable with an imprisonment for a term which may extend to 6 months, or with fine which may extend to ₹ 1,000 or with both.

MACHINERY FOR THE SETTLEMENT OF INDUSTRIAL DISPUTES

Machinery for Prevention and Settlement of Industrial Relations

The machinery for prevention and settlement of the disputes has been given in the following figure:

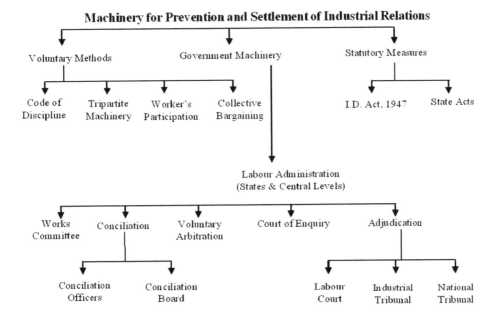

Machinery for Prevention and Settlement of Industrial Relations

Voluntary Methods

Code of Discipline

Formally announced in 1958, the Code of Discipline provides guidelines for the workers, unions and employers. The code which was approved by major national trade unions and principal organization of employers enjoyed on them to create an environment of mutual trust and cooperation and to settle the disputes by mutual negotiation, conciliation and voluntary arbitration. It required the employers and workers to utilize the existing machinery for the settlement of disputes.

Code of Discipline

The Fifteenth Indian Labour Conference discussed the question of discipline in industry and lain down the following general principles:

- There should be no lockout or strike without notice.
- No unilateral action should be taken in connection with any industrial matter.
- There should be no recourse to go-slow tactics.
- No deliberate damage should be caused to plant or property.
- Acts of violence, intimidation, coercion or instigation should not be resorted to.
- The existing machinery for settlement of disputes should be utilized.
- Awards and agreements should be speedily implemented.
- Any agreement which disturbs cordial industrial relations should be avoided.

The Code embodies four parts. Part I contains

the duties and responsibilities of employees, workers and the government in maintaining discipline in industry. Part II enlists the common obligations of management and unions. Part III deals with the obligations of management only, while Part IV relates to those of the unions only. In additions, Annexure-A to the Code embodies the national level agreement on the criteria for the recognition of unions. A supplementary document contains the rights of recognized unions and a model grievance procedure. Thus, the Code is highly comprehensive and ethical in its approach to the industrial relations system. It has been reproduced below.

Part –I: To maintain discipline in industry (both in public and private sectors) :

There has to be: (i) a just recognition by employers and workers of the rights and responsibilities of either party, as defined by the laws and agreements (including bipartite and tripartite agreements arrived at all levels from time to time); and ii) a proper and willing discharge by either party of its obligation consequent on such recognition.

Part – II: To ensure better discipline in industry, management and union(s) agree:

- that no unilateral actions should be taken in connection with any industrial matter and that disputes should be settled at appropriate level;
- that the existing machinery for settlement of disputes should be utilized with the utmost expedition;
- that there should be no strike or lockout without notice;
- that affirming their faith in democratic principles, they bind themselves to settle all future differences, disputes and grievances by mutual negotiation, conciliation and voluntary arbitration;
- that neither will have recourse to (a) coercion, (b) intimidation, (c) victimization, and (d) go-show;
- that they will avoid (a) litigation, (b) sit-down and stay-in-strikes, and (c) lockouts;
- that they will promote constructive cooperation between their representatives at all levels and

as between workers themselves and abide by the spirit of agreements mutually entered into;

- that they will establish upon a mutually agreed basis a Grievance Procedure which will ensure a speedy and full investigation leading to settlement;
- that they will abide by various stages in the Grievance Procedure and take no arbitrary action which would by-pass this procedure; and
- that they will educate the management personnel and workers regarding their obligations to each other.

Part–III: Management agrees

- not to increase work-loads unless agreed upon or settled otherwise;
- not to support or encourage any unfair labour practice such as: (a) interference with the right of employees to enroll or continue as union members; (b) discriminations, restraint or coercion against any employee because of recognized activity of trade unions; and (c) victimization of any employee and abuse of authority in any form;
- to take prompt actions for (a) settlement of grievance, and (b) implementation of settlements, awards, decisions and orders;
- to display in conspicuous places in the undertaking the provision of this Code in local language(s);
- to distinguish between actions justifying immediate discharge and those where discharge must be preceded by a warning, reprimand, suspension or some other form of disciplinary action and to arrange that all such disciplinary action should be subject to an appeal through normal Grievance Procedure;
- to take appropriate disciplinary action against its officers and members in cases where enquiries reveal that they were responsible for precipitate action by workers leading to indiscipline; and
- to recognize the unions in accordance with

the criteria (Annexure A given below) evolved at the 16th session of the Indian Labour Conference held in May, 1958.

Part–IV: Union(s) agrees

- not to encourage any form of physical duress;
- not to permit demonstrations which are not peaceful and not to permit rowdyism in demonstration;
- that their members will not engage or cause other employees to engage in any union activity during working hours, unless as provided for by law, agreement or practice;
- to discourage unfair labour practices such as: (a) negligence of duty, (b) careless operation, (c) damage to property, (d) interference with or disturbance to normal work, and (e) insubordination;
- to take prompt actions to implement awards, agreements, settlements and decisions;
- to display in conspicuous places in the union offices, the provision of this Code in the local language(s); and
- to express disapproval and to take appropriate action against office bearers and members for indulging in action against the spirit of this Code.

The Code does not have any legal section but the following moral sanctions are behind it:

1. The Central Employers' and Workers' Organizations shall take the following steps against their constituent units guilty of breaches of Code:
   - to ask the unit to explain the infringement of the Code;
   - to give notice to the unit to set right the infringement within a specific period;
   - to warn, and in case persistent violation of the Code; and
   - not to give countenance, in any manner, to non-members who did not observe the Code; and
   - not to give countenance, in any manner, to non-members who did not observe the Code.

2. Grave, willful and persistent breaches of the Code by any party should be widely publicized.
3. Failure to observe the Code would entail derecognition normally for a period of one year. This period may be increased or decreased by the implementing Committee concerned.
4. A dispute may not ordinarily be referred for adjudication if there is a strike or lockout without proper notice or in breach of the code as determined by an Implementation.

The Code of Discipline worked well at the beginning of its introduction and had a considerable impact on the industrial relations scene. But, however, the impact of the Code was not sustained over a long period of time due to several problems in its application and implementation. The spirit of the Code has not been imbibed by the central organizations which were signatories to it.

According to the National Commission on Labour, the Code has had only limited success and was obviously not the answer to the industrial relations problems. The Code began to rust and the parties were more eager to take it off; they developed an attitude of indifference. As regards the future of the Code, the Commission was in favour of giving a legal form to its important provisions regarding recognition of unions, grievance procedure, unfair labour practices, and the like. With the removal of these provisions from the Code to give them a statutory shape, the Code will have no useful function to perform.

Discipline is a two-way traffic and a breach of discipline on the part of either party in industry will cause unrest. The approach to managing discipline depends to a great extent upon managerial philosophy, culture and attitude towards the employees. A negative approach to discipline relies heavily on punitive measures and in the line with the traditional managerial attitude of "hire and fire" and obedience to orders. On the other hand, a constructive approach stress on modifying forbidden behaviour by taking positive steps like educating, counseling etc. The concept of positive discipline promotion aims at the generation of a sense of self-discipline and disciplined behaviour in all the human beings in a dynamic organizational setting, instead of discipline imposed by force or punishment. In brief, the approach to the disciplinary action in most cases should be corrective rather than punitive.

A few important provisions of code of discipline are:

- Strikes and lockout cannot be declared without proper notice.
- The parties should not take any action without consulting each other.
- There should be no go slow statistics or any resort to deliberate damage to plant or property or resort to acts of violence, intimidation, coercion etc.

The code has moral sanction only and it does not entail any legal liability or punishment.

Tripartite Machinery

Tripartite machinery consists of various bodies like Indian Labour Conference, the Standing Labour Committee, the International Committees, the Central Implementation and Evaluation Committee and the Committee on conventions. Generally, these committees include representatives from centre and the states, and the same number of workers' and employers' organizations. These various committees are basically of advisory nature, yet they carry considerable weight among the government, workers and employers.

Workers' Participation in Management

Workers participation in management is in essential ingredient of industrial democracy. The concept of workers participation in management is based in "Human Relations" approach to management which brought about new set of values to labour and management.

Traditionally, the concept of Workers' Participation in Management (WPM) refers to participation of non-managerial employees in the decision-making process of the organisation. Workers' participation in management meets the psychological needs of the workers to a greater extent. That way it may also be treated as the process of delegation of authority in the general areas of managerial functions.

According to one view, workers participation is based on the fundamental concept that the ordinary worker invest his labour in, and ties his fate to, his place of work and, therefore, he has a legitimate right to have a share in influencing the various aspects of company policy.

To quote the version of British Institute of Management, "Workers' participation in management is the practice in which employees take part in management decisions and it is based on the assumption of commonality of interest between employer and employee in furthering the long term prospects of the enterprise and those working in it".

According to G.S. Walpole, participation in management gives the workers a sense of importance, price and accomplishment; it given him the freedom and the opportunity for self-expression; a feeling of belonging to his place of work and a sense of workmanship and creativity. It provides for the integration of his interest with those of the management and makes him a joint partner in the enterprise.

Dr. Alexander considers a management to be participative, "if it gives scope to the workers to influence its decision-making process on any level or sphere or if it shares with them some if its managerial prerogatives".

Clegg says, "It implies a situation where workers' representatives are, to some extent, involved in the process of management decision-making, but where the ultimate power is in the hands of the management".

According to Dr. Davis, "it is a mental and emotional involvement of a person in a group situation which encourages him to contribute to goals and share responsibilities in them".

According to Dr. Davis, "it is a mental and emotional involvement of a person in a group situation which encourages him to contribute to goals and share responsibilities in them".

In should be borne in mid that when individuals are provided with opportunities for expression and share in decision-making, they show much initiative and accept responsibility substantially. The rationale of workers' participation in management lies in that it helps in creation amongst the workers a sense of involvement in their organization, a better understanding of their role in the smooth functioning of industry and provides them a means of self-realization, thereby, promoting efficiency and increased productivity.

Thus the concept workers' participation in management encompasses the following:

- It provides scope for employees in the decision-making of the organization.
- The participation may be at the shop level, departmental level or at the top level.
- The participation includes the willingness to share the responsibility by works as they have a commitment to execute their decisions.
- The participation is conducted through the mechanism of forums which provide for association of workers representatives.
- The basic idea is to develop self-control and self-discipline among workers, so that the management becomes "Auto Management".

Objectives

The scheme has economic, psychological, ethical and political objectives.

- Its psychological objective of the scheme is to secure full recognition of the workers. Association of worker with management provides him with a sense of importance, involvement and a feeling of belongingness. He considers himself to be an indispensable constituent of the organization.
- Socially, the need for participation arises because modern industry is a social institution with the interest of employer, the share-holders, the community and the workers equally invested in it.
- The ethical objective of participation is to develop workers free personality and to recognize human dignity.
- The political objective of participation is to develop workers conscious of their democratic rights on their work place and thus bring about industrial democracy.

Levels of Participation

Workers' participation is possible at all levels of management; the only difference is that of degree and nature of application. For instance, it may be vigorous at lower level and faint at top level. Broadly speaking there is following five levels of participation:

1. *Information participation:* It ensures that employees are able to receive information and express their views pertaining to the matters of general economic importance.

2. *Consultative participation:* Here works are consulted on the matters of employee welfare such as work, safety and health. However, final decision always rests at the option of management and employees' views are only of advisory nature.

3. *Associative participation:* It is extension of consultative participation as management here is under moral obligation to accept and implement the unanimous decisions of employees.

4. *Administrative participation:* It ensures greater share of works in discharge of managerial functions. Here, decision already taken by the management come to employees, preferably with alternatives for administration and employees have to select the best from those for implementation.

5. *Decisive participation:* Highest level of participation where decisions are jointly taken on the matters relation to production, welfare etc. is called decisive participation.

Forms of Workers' Participation in Management

The forms of workers participation in management vary from industry to industry and country to country depending upon the political system, pattern of management relations and subject or area of participation. The forms of workers participation may be as follows:

1. *Joint consultation model:* In joint consultation model the management consults with the workers before taking decisions. The

workers represent their view through 'Joint Consultative Committees'. This form is followed in U.K., Sweden and Poland.

2. *Joint decision model:* In this form both the workers and management jointly decide and execute the decisions. This form of participation is followed in U.S.A. and West Germany.

3. *Self management or Auto management:* In this model, the entire control is in the hands of workers. Yugoslavia is an example to this model. Where the state industrial units are run by the workers under a scheme called 'Self Management or Auto Management Scheme'.

4. *Workers' representation on board:* Under this method, the workers elect their representative and send them to the Board to participate in the decision-making process.

The participation of workers may be formal or informal. In the formal participation, it takes the forms of formal structures such as Works Committee, Shop Councils, Production Committee, Safety Committee, Joint Management Councils, Canteen Committee etc. The informal participation may be such as the supervisor consulting the workers for granting leave, overtime, and allotment of worked or transfer of workers from one department to another.

Workers' Participation in Management in India

Workers participation in management in India was given importance only after independence. Industrial Disputes Act of 1947 was the first step in this direction, which recommended for the setting up of Works Committees. The Joint Management Councils were established in 1950 which increased the participation of labour in management. The management scheme, 1970 gave birth to 'Board of Management'. Since July 1975, the two-tire participation model called 'Shop Council' at the shop level and 'Joint Councils' at the enterprise level were introduced.

Based on the review and performance of previous schemes a new scheme was formulated in 1983. The new scheme of workers' participation was applicable to all central public sector enterprises, except those specifically exempted. The scheme with equal number of representatives will operate both at shop as well as plant level. The various functions of participative forum laid down in the scheme could be modified with the consent of parties. The scheme could not make such head way due to lack of union leaders consensus of the mode of representation and workers' tendency to discuss ultra-virus issues *e.g.* pay scales, wages etc.

Prior to WPM Bill, 1990 all the schemes of participation were non-statutory and concentrated on particular levels. For effective and meaningful participation at all levels, a bill was introduced in Parliament on 25th May, 1990. The bill provide for effective participation at all level by formulating schemes of participation. For electing representatives for participation it also provides for secret ballot. The appropriate government may also appoint inspectors to review participation schemes and the bill also has provision of punishment for those who contravene any of the provision of the Act.

Thus the workers' participation schemes in India provide wide scope for application and up liftmen of workers. But in practice, these schemes have not met with success though they are successful in some private sector units. The factors responsible for the failure are:

- Attitude of the management towards the scheme is not encouraging. The preventatives of workers are not given due recognition by the management.
- The attitude of trade unions towards the schemes is negative as they consider these schemes are reducing the power of Trade Unions. Some Trade Unions boycott Joint Management Council meetings.

  The success these schemes require certain conditions.

- Management should appreciate the scheme and accept them in full faith.
- Trade unions have to cooperate with the schemes.
- Workers have to be educated.

Thus workers' participation in management in India has yet to succeed. It can be done by educating the workers, creating an environment in the organization for coordination of workers and management.

Workers' participation in management is an essential ingredient of Industrial democracy. The concept of workers' participation in management is based on Human Relations approach to Management which brought about a new set of values to labour and management. Traditionally the concept of Workers' Participation in Management (WPM) refers to participation of non-managerial employees in the decision-making process of the organization. Workers' participation is also known as 'labour participation' or 'employee participation' in management. In Germany it is known as co-determination while in Yugoslavia it is known as self-management. The International Labour Organization has been encouraging member nations to promote the scheme of Workers' Participation in Management.

Workers' participation in management implies mental and emotional involvement of workers in the management of Enterprise. It is considered as a mechanism where workers have a say in the decision.

The philosophy underlying workers' participation stresses:

1. democratic participation in decision-making;
2. maximum employer-employee collaboration;
3. minimum state intervention;
4. realization of a greater measure of social justice;
5. greater industrial efficiency; and
6. Higher level of organizational health and effectiveness.

It has been varyingly understood and practiced as a system of joint consultation in industry; as a form of labour management cooperation; as recognition of the principle of co-partnership, and as an instrument of industrial democracy. Consequently, participation has assumed different forms, varying from mere voluntary sharing of information by management with the workers to formal participation by the latter in actual decision-making process of management.

Collective Bargaining

Collective bargaining is a source of solving the problems of employees in the work situation collectively. It provides a good climate for discussing the problems of workers with their employers. The employees put their demands before the employers and the employers also give certain concession to them. Thus it ensures that the management cannot take unilateral decisions concerning the work ignoring the workers. It also helps the works to achieve reasonable wages, working conditions, working hours, fringe benefits etc. It provides them a collective strength to bargain with the employer. It also provides the employer some control over the employees.

The process of collective bargaining is bipartite in nature *i.e.*, the negotiations are between the employers without a thirds party's intervention. Thus collective bargaining serves to bridge the emotional and physiological between the workers and employers through direct discussions.

Definitions

Collective bargaining has different meanings for different individuals or groups. Trade Unions, management and public interpret the term in their own ways. Let us now discuss some leading definitions:

According to the Encyclopedia of social sciences, "Collective bargaining is a process of discussion and negotiation between two parties, one or both of whom is a group of persons acting in concert. The resulting bargain is an understanding as to the terms and conditions which a continuing service is to be performed. More specifically, collective bargaining is a procedure, by which employer and a group of employees agree upon the conditions of work".

Richardson says, "Collective bargaining takes place when a number of work people enter into negotiation as a bargaining unit with an employer or a group of employers with the object of reaching agreement on conditions of the employment of the work people".

The I.L.O. workers manual defines collective bargaining as, "negotiation about working conditions and terms of employment between an employer, a group of employers or one or more employer's organizations, on the one hand, and one or more representative workers' organization on the other with a view of reaching an agreement.

Salient Features

- It is a collective process in which representatives of employers and employees participate mutually.
- It is a flexible and dynamic process wherein no party adopts a rigid attitude.
- It is a bipartite process whereas the representatives of workers and management get an opportunity for clear and face to face negotiation.
- It is a continuous process which can establish regular and stable relationship between worker's organization and management.
- It is a practical way to establish an industrial democracy.
- It is a good method of promoting industrial jurisprudence.
- It is good form of interdisciplinary system (*i.e.* a function embodying economic psychological, administrative, ethical and other aspects.)
- It is a process that includes efforts from preliminary preparations to the presentation of conflicting view points, collection of necessary facts, understanding of view points, taking correct decisions etc.

Importance

Whatever labour laws may lay down, it is the approach of employers and trade unions which matters and unless both are enlightened, industrial harmony is not possible. Therefore, the solution to common problems can be found directly through negotiation between both parties and in this context the scope of collective bargaining is very great.

Collective bargaining is really beneficial forms the stand part of employees and their unions as well as management. If it works well, it develops a sense of self-responsibility and self-respect among the employees concerned and thus significantly paves the way for improved employee morale and productivity.

Collective bargaining restricts management's freedom for arbitrary action and thereby management learns a new code of behaviour by conceiving of the union as a method of dealing with employees. The management also comes to know the grievances of workers in advance and it gives an opportunity to take precautionary measure. Moreover, collective bargaining opens the channel of communication between top and bottom levels of an organization.

From the point of view of the society, collective bargaining; if property conducted, result in the establishment of a harmonious industrial climate which helps for the socio-economic development of the nation. It builds up a system of industrial jurisprudence by introducing civil rights in industry and ensures that management is conduct by rules rather than by a arbitrary decisions. It extends the democratic principles from the political to industrial field.

Functions

Prof. Butler has viewed the functions as:

- a process of social change
- a peace treaty between two parties
- a system of industrial jurisprudence

Collective Bargaining as a Process of Social Change

Collective bargaining enhances the status of the working class in the society. Wage earners have enhanced their social and economic position in relation to other groups.

Employers have also retained high power and dignity through collective bargaining.

Collective Bargaining as a Peace Treaty

Collective bargaining serves as a peace treaty between the employers and employees. However, the settlement between the two parties is a compromise.

Collective Bargaining as an Industrial Jurisprudence

Collective bargaining creates a system of "Industrial Jurisprudence". It is a method of introducing civil rights into industry. It establishes rules which define and restrict the traditional authority exercised by employers over their employees placing part of the authority under joint control of union and management.

In addition to the above, its functions include:

- Increasing the economic strength to employers and employees.
- Improving working conditions and fair wages.
- Maintaining peace in industry
- Prompt and fair redressel of grievances.
- Promoting stability and prosperity of the industry.

Principles of Collective Bargaining

The success of collective bargaining is based on certain principles. These principles are to be followed by the employers and unions. Prof. Arnold. F. Campo has laid down certain principles for union and management, for management and for union.

For both Union and Management

1. Collective bargaining process should give due consideration to hear the problems on both sides. This will develop mutual understanding of a problem which is more important for arriving at the solutions.
2. Both the management and union should analyze the alternatives to arrive at the best solution.
3. There must be mutual respect on both the parties. The management should respect the unions and the unions should recognize the importance of management.
4. Both the union and management must have good faith and confidence in discussion and arriving at a solution.
5. Collective bargaining required effective leadership on both sides, on the union side and management side to moderate discussions and create confidence.

6. In collective bargaining both the union and management should observe the laws and regulations in practice in arriving at a solution.
7. In all negotiations, the labour should be given due consideration – in wage fixation, in working conditions, bonus etc.

For Management

1. Management should think of realistic principles and policies for labour regulations.
2. The recognitions of a trade union to represent the problems are more essential. If there are more than one union, the management can recognize on which is having the support of majority of workers.
3. Management should follow a policy of goodwill, and cooperation in collective bargaining rather than an indifferent attitude towards the union.
4. Managements need not wait for trade union to represent their grievances for settlement. Management can voluntarily take measures to settle the grievances.
5. Managements should give due consideration to social and economic conditions of workers in collective bargaining.

For Unions

1. Unions should avoid unconstitutional practices.
2. Unions have to recognize their duties to the management also before emphasizing their demands.
3. Unions have to consider the benefits to all workers rather than a section of workers.
4. Strike lockouts should be resorted to, only as a last measure. As far as possible they have to be avoided by compromise and discussion.

Forms of Collective Bargaining

The forms of collective bargaining differ from country to country and time to time in India. Collective bargaining takes the following forms:

1. *Settlements under industrial disputes act*: According to this, negotiations are carried

out by officers according to the Industrial Disputes Act.

2. *Settlements by parties*: In this case settlements are arrived at by parties themselves without the interference of a third party.

3. *Consent awards*: Here the agreements are negotiated by the parties on a voluntary basis when disputes are subjudiced. Later these are submitted to the labour courts.

4. *Direct negotiation*: In this agreements are arrived at by both the parties after direct negation. The enforcement of these agreements depends upon the goodwill and cooperation of the parties.

On the basis of the level (in which collective bargaining takes place) it can be classified as:

1. Plant level bargaining
2. Industry level bargaining
3. National level bargaining

Plant Level Bargaining

It is the micro level bargaining. It takes place in the particular unit between the management and the trade unions of that unit.

Industry Level Bargaining

Several unions of the same industry form and association and negotiate with the employers.

National Level Bargaining

In this, the representatives of trade unions and employers at the national level will negotiate.

The Contents of Collective Bargaining Agreements

The scope of collective bargaining has increased during the recent years. Prof. Randle observes that the increase in the scope of collective bargaining is due to the growth of trade unions, increased response by the managements, increased response by the managements, increased prices and the legislations.

Problems relating to security of trade unions, wages, promotions, transfers, hours and conditions or work, holidays and leave with wages, safety and health etc. are included in the collective bargaining.

The Institute of Personal Management includes the following in a collective agreement.

● Nature, scope, definition and purpose of agreement.

● Rights and responsibilities of management and trade unions.

● Wages, bonus, production norms, leave, retirement's benefits and other benefits and terms and conditions of service.

● Grievance redressal procedure.

● Methods and machinery for the settlements of possible future, disputes, and

● A termination clause.

Thus collective bargaining includes not only the negotiation of wages, but also working condition, labour welfare and organizational matters.

Process of Collective Bargaining

The process of collective bargaining consists of two stages, (i) the negotiation stage, and (ii) the contract administration.

Negotiation Stage

At the negotiation stage certain proposals are put forward for mutual agreement after careful consideration. The negotiation stage consists of three steps.

● Preparation for negotiation
● Negotiation procedure
● Follow up action

Preparation for Negotiation

First the union will submit their fresh contract to the management before the expiry of existing contract (usually 30 to 60 days before the expiry). Both the management and unions will take considerable time to the preparation and negotiation.

They collect the required data relating to large number of issues such as wage, salary, seniority, overtime allowance, the cost of living, the policies of trade unions and management, nature of agreement in other companies etc.

The company will collect such information its internal sources such as balance sheet, contract agreements, market research reports, Govt. reports etc. The trade union also collects such data from their own central organization, research staff from various Department etc.

The personal department prepares a personal, which includes:

- Specific proposals of the company including the objectives of negotiation.
- Estimating the cost of implementing the proposals.
- Classifying the demands as demands acceptable before negotiation, demands acceptable after negotiation, demands which cannot be accepted. Such proposals are based on company's commitment to shareholders, consumers, workers and public.

Negotiation Technique or Procedure

In this step, a negotiation committee is to be formed by both the parties. From the management side the representative include the chief executives. The unions are represented by the leaders and centrals leaders. The committee consists of three to six members.

The demands are classified as demands which need bargaining and demands which may be rejected. During negotiations, normally the easier demands are taken up first. Both parties should have a "bargaining cushion", and make counter proposals. For example, a demand for wage increase by the union may be accompanied by a counter proposal for increase in production by the management. Such negotiations go on till the "point of no return" is being reached. A rigid or irrevocable stance should always be avoided.

Follow-up Action

At this stage, the agreement is printed and circulated among all the employees. The supervisors will be enlightened about the agreements for their effective implementation.

Contract Administration

Agreement will be useful if they are executed properly. As observed by Profs. Illiamson and Harries, "if anything is more important to industrial relations than the contract itself, it is the administration of the contract".

Prof. Campo has laid down the following general principles for administering the contact effectively;

- Cooperation between both the parties is essential. Both the parties should have a tolerant attitude towards each other and have a spirit of accommodation and goodwill.
- Proper procedure should be adopted for the redressal of grievances by providing opportunity to exchange views.
- When a conference over the redressal of grievance reaches an impasse, the grievance should be referred to arbitration.
- Both the parties should honour the commitment.

Pre-requisite for Successful Collective Bargaining

Collective bargaining will be more effective under the following conditions:

Negotiating Team

Negotiating team should represent all groups including production, finance and industrial relations experts. The team should be headed by an appropriate person with adequate authority to take decisions.

Recognition of Unions

The management should recognize the trade union and analyze the facts in their representation of grievances. Mutual understanding encourages mutual agreement.

Open Mind

Both the management and union should have open minds to listen and appreciate each other's point of view with flexibility and adjustment.

'Home Work' on Demands

The union and management have to collect relevant data relating wages, conditions of work, welfare schemes, cost of benefits.

Routine Problems

The management and unions have to identify the grievances on routine basis and take appropriate action then and there.

Internal Union Democracy

Trade unions should encourage internal union democracy by consulting the rank and file members.

Importance to Output

Trade unions should also give importance to output, quality of the products, company's image etc., in addition to their wages, bonus, working conditions etc.

Strikes/Lockouts

Strikes and lockouts should be resorted to as last measure. Before taking any decision, both the union and management should conduct periodic discussions to avoid strikes and lockouts.

Collective bargaining has gradually been taking roots in Indian soil. Most of the collective bargaining agreements were concluded at plant level. Some industry level agreements were also concluded in textile industries in Bombay and Ahemadabad.

The scope is widening. It includes matters relating to productivity, bonus, modernization, standing orders, voluntary arbitration, incentive schemes and job evaluation etc. The number of agreement has been increasing. Most of the agreements were relating to wages. In a study conducted by E.F.I. shows that out of 109 agreements 96 were relating to wages.

Thus collective bargaining is an important method of solving problems, through mutual understanding. If used properly it can solve the problems of the parties, management and union through mutual confidence.

Collective bargaining is also used as a tool for bringing coordination between workers and managements. It also serves as tool of communication of views by both management and works. In the long-run it will serve as an instrument for labour participation in management and pave way for the cordial industrial relations in India.

Collective Bargaining in Central Public Sector Undertakings

Collective bargaining in central public sector undertakings is done according to the guidelines issued by the Departments of Public Enterprises (earlier known as the Bureau of Public Enterprises). This department gives the content and limits of financial commitments which a public enterpriser can make with the union during the course of bargaining. However, in many instances these limits are circumvented by the management by making gentleman's promises with the unions on several issues outside the written agreement and implementing these promises over a period through administrative orders.

In core industries like steel, ports and docks and banks, collective bargaining is done at the national level for the industry as a whole. Thus, in steel industry, one main collective agreement is entered into by the National Joint Consultative Forum on behalf of all private and public sector steel units with other unions. This is followed by several supplementary agreements being entered into at the plant level to cover aspects not resulted in creating uniform wage structures and fringe benefit patterns in all public sector units irrespective of the nature of industry (labour or capital intensive) and the paying capacity of a unit as determined by its financial performance. This is in sharp contrast to a private sector unit where its wages and fringe benefits are more geared to its specific requirements and circumstances.

Government Machinery

The Ministry of Labour and Employment at the centre is the key agency for the policy formulation and administration in all the matters pertaining to labour. The State governments with the cooperation of their labour departments are responsible for the enforcement thereof. The Directorate General of Employment and Training (DGET), Office of Chief Labour Commissioner (CLC) (Central), the Director General of Mines Safety (DGMS), the Director General of Factory Advice and Labour Institutes, and Industrial Tribunals are some of the agencies through which the Central Government discharges its functions related to framing of labour laws and settlement of industrial disputes. The Labour Secretary is the overall in charge of policy formulation and administration, and commissioners of labour in the States are the operative arms for the effective implementation of Labour Laws.

Statutory Measures – Industrial Disputes Act, 1947

The States are free to frame their own labour laws as the labour falls in the concurrent list, some States like Maharashtra, M.P., U.P. and Rajasthan have their own Acts. In the rest of the States, Industrial Disputes Act, 1947 applies. However, in the States having their own Acts, the IDA, 1947 will be applicable to the industries not covered by the State Legislation. Formally announced in 1947, the Industrial Disputes Act has been amended several times since then. Under the Act the following authorities have been proposed for the investigation and settlement of industrial disputes.

Works Committees

The IDA, 1947 provides for setting up works committees in every organization having 100 or more employees. Having representatives of employees and employees, these are consultative bodies and are set up for maintaining harmonious relations at the work place and sort out the difference if any. Though the act does not define the jurisdiction of these committees, yet their functions mainly include providing proper working conditions and amenities for the welfare of employees at the work place or away from the work. A work committee aims at promoting measures for securing the preserving amity and good relations between employees and workers.

Conciliation

When the services of a neural party are availed for the amicable solution of a dispute between the disputing parties, this practice is known as conciliation. The IDA, 1947 provides for conciliation and it can be utilized either by appointing Conciliation Officer or by setting up Board or Conciliation.

The Conciliation Officers are appointed by the Government by notifying in the Official Gazette. Usually at the State level, Commissioners of Labour, Additional and Deputy Commissioners of Labour act as Conciliation Officer for disputes arising in any undertaking employing less than twenty workers. In the conciliation process the officer ties to bring the disputing parties together towards a settlement of the dispute and hence works as a mediator. The intervention of conciliation officer may be mandatory or discretionary. But in the disputes related to public utilities in respect of which proper notice is served to him, his intervention becomes mandatory.

The Board of Conciliation is a higher forum and is constituted for a specific dispute. It consists of equal number of representatives of employers and employees under the chairmanship of an independent person, appointed by the government. The Board has to submit its report to the government regarding the dispute within two months from the date dispute was referred to it. However, depending on the case, the period can be extended.

Voluntary Arbitration

Industrial Disputes (Amendment) Bill, 1956 incorporated Section 10A favouring voluntary arbitration. In case of existed or apprehended dispute, the disputing parties can enter into an arbitration agreement in writing. The success of voluntary arbitration depends on "a sufficient degree of mutual confidence in decision by agreement on subjects which may be submitted for arbitration".

Court of Enquiry

The IDA, 1947 empowers the appropriate government to constitute a Court of Enquiry. This body basically is a fact-finding agency, constituted just to reveal the causes of the disputes and does not care much for the settlement thereof. The Court of Enquiry is required to submit its report to the government ordinarily within six months from the commencement of enquiry. The report of the court shall be published by the government within 30 days of its receipt.

Adjudication

If the dispute is not settled by any other method, the government may refer it for adjudication. Hence it is a compulsory method which provides for three-tier system for adjudication of industrial disputes.

This machinery consists of Labour Court, Industrial Tribunals and National Tribunal. The first two bodies can be set up either by State or Central Government but the National Tribunal can be constituted by Central Government only, when it thinks that the solution of dispute is of national significance. A Labour Court consists of one person only, called Presiding Officer, who is or has been a judge of a High Court. The jurisdiction of Industrial Tribunal is comparatively wider than Labour Courts, and further the Presiding Officer of Tribunal can have two assessors may be appointed by the Central Government to help its Presiding Officer.

Labour Courts and Tribunals are now required to submit award to the appropriate government within three months in case of individual disputes. The submitted award shall be published by government within 30 days from the date of its receipt. It shall come into force on the expiry of 30 days from the date if its publication and shall be operative for a period of one year, unless declared otherwise by the appropriate government.

INTERNATIONAL LABOUR ORGANIZATION (ILO)

The International Labour Organization (ILO) was set up in 1919 by the Versailles Peace Conference as an autonomous body associated with the League of Nations. The ILO was the only international organization that survived the Second World War even after the dissolution of its parent body. It became the first specialized agency of the United Nations in 1946 in accordance with an agreement entered into between the two organizations. India has been a member of the ILO since its inception. A unique feature of the ILO, as distinct from other international institutions, is its tripartite character.

The aims and objectives of ILO are set out in the preamble to its Constitution and in the Declaration of Philadelphia (1944) which was formally annexed to the Constitution in 1946. The preamble affirms that universal and lasting peace can be established only if it is based upon social justice, draws attention to the existence of conditions of labour involving injustice, hardship and privation

of a large number of people, and declares that improvement of these conditions is urgently required through such means as the regulation of hours of work, prevention of unemployment, provision of an adequate living wage, protection of workers against sickness, disease, and injury arising out of employment, protection of children, young persons and women, protection of the interests of migrant workers, recognition of the principle of freedom of association, and organization of vocational and technical education. The Preamble also states that the failure of any nation to adopt human conditions of labour is an obstacle in the way of other nations desiring to improve labour conditions in their own countries.

The three main functions of the ILO are:

● to establish international labour standards;
● to collect and disseminate information on labour and industrial conditions; and
● to provide technical assistance for carrying out programmes of social and economic development.

From the very beginning, the ILO has been confronted with the tremendous task of promoting social justice by improving the work and conditions of life in all parts of the world.

The ILO consists of three principal organs, namely, the International Labour Conference, the Governing Body and the International Labour Office. The work of the Conference and the Governing Body is supplemented by that of Regional Conferences, Regional Advisory Committees, Industrial Committees, etc. The meeting of the General Conference, held normally every year, are attended by four delegates from each member State, of whom two are government delegates and one each representing respectively the employers and the work people of the State. The International Labour Conference is the supreme organ of the ILO and acts as the legislative wing of the Organization. The General Conference elect the Governing Body, adopt the Organization's biennial programme and budget, adopt international labour standards in the form of conventions and Recommendations and provide a forum for discussion of social and labour issues. The

Governing Body is the executive wing of the Organization. It appoints the Director-General, draws up the agenda of each session of the Conference and examines the implementation by member countries of its Conventions and Recommendations. The International Labour Office, whose headquarters are located at Geneva, provides the secretariat for all conferences and other meetings and is responsible for the day-to-day implementation of the administrative and other decisions of the Conference, the Governing Body, etc. The Director-General is the chief executive of the International Labour Office. An important aspect of its work relates to the provision of assistance to member States. It also serves as a clearing house of information on all labour matters.

In order to achieve its objective, the ILO has relied on its standard-setting function. The international labour standards take the form of Conventions and Recommendations. A Convention is a treaty which, when ratified, creates binding international obligations on the country concerned. On the other hand, a Recommendation creates no such obligations but is essentially a guide to national actions. The ILO adopted a series of Conventions and Recommendations covering hours of work, employment of women, children and your persons, weekly rest, holidays leave with wages, night work, industrial safety, health, hygiene, labour inspection, social security, labour-management, relations, freedom of association, wages and wage fixation, productivity, employment, etc. One of the fundamental obligations imposed on governments by the Constitutions of the ILO is that they must submit the instruments before the competent national or State or provincial authorities within a maximum period of 18 months of their adoption by the Conference for such actions as might be considered practicable. These dynamic instruments continue to be the principal means at the disposal of the ILO to strive for establishing a just, democratic and changing social order necessary for lasting peace. In fact, these instruments have been included in the category of "international labour legislation". These Conventions and Recommendations taken together are known as the "International Labour Code". Wilfred Jenks describes the International Labour Code as the corpus juries of social justice.

Grievances Handling

A grievance is a sign of the employees' discontent with job and its nature. It is caused due to the difference between employee expectation and management practice.

Beach defines a grievance as, 'any dissatisfaction or feeling of injustice in connection with one's employment situation that is brought to the notice of the management.

Jucius defines a grievance as 'any discontent or dissatisfaction, whether exposed or not, whether valid or not, arising out of anything connected with the company which an employee thinks, believes or even feels to be unfair, unjust and inequitable'.

A grievance is a problem submitted by an employee or by a few employees of different types. It may be concerning a situation or may likely to affect the terms and conditions of employment of one worker or a few workers.

In the Indian context, 'grievance' may be said to "the representation by a worker, a group of workers or the unions to the management relation to the terms and conditions of employment, breach of the freedom of association or the provisions of standing orders or non-implementation of the Government orders, conciliation agreements or adjudicators' awards". It may also include representation against non-compliance with provision of a collective agreement in an establishment where it has been signed.

Grievances usually result in definite and considerable loses to employee morale, efficiency and productivity. The accumulation of grievance leads to strikes, lockouts and other forms of conflicts. Therefore, proper disposal of grievances deserves special and adequate consideration in any programme of harmonizing industrial relations.

Areas of Grievances

Grievances resulting from working conditions
  - Poor physical conditions of work place.
  - Lack of proper tools, machines and equipments.

● Frequent changes in schedules or procedures.
● Rigid production standards.
● Improper matching of the worker with the job.
● Poor relationship with the supervisor.

Grievances resulting from management policy and practices

● Poor payment
● Lack of job security
● Inadequate benefits such as medical benefits, leave, travel concession etc.
● Leave facilities
● Seniority
● Transfer
● Promotion
● Lack of career planning and development
● Hostility towards labour union
● Defective leadership style
● Communication gap

Grievances resulting from alleged violations of

● Violation collective bargaining agreement
● Violation of Central/State laws
● Violation of common rules

Grievances resulting from personal maladjustment

● Over ambition
● Excessive self-esteem

Methods of Identifying Grievances

The following methods can help the employer to identify the grievances:

1. *Directive observation*: Knowledge of human behaviour is requisite quality of every good manager. From the changed behaviour of employees, he should be able to snuff the causes of grievances. This he can do without its knowledge to the employee. This method will give general pattern of grievances. In addition to normal routine, periodic interviews with the employees, group meetings and collective bargaining are the specific occasions where direct observation can help in unfolding the grievances.

2. *Grip boxes*: The boxes (like suggestion boxes) are placed at easily accessible spots to most employees in the organization. The employees can file anonymous complaints about their dissatisfaction in these boxes. Due to anonymity, the fear of managerial action is avoided. Moreover management's interest is also limited to the free and fair views of employees.

3. *Open door policy*: Most democratic by nature, the policy is preached most but practiced very rarely in Indian organizations. But this method will be more useful in absence of an effective grievance procedure; otherwise the organization will do well to have a grievance procedure. Open door policy demands that the employees, even at the lowest rank, should have easy access to the chief executive to get his grievances redressed.

4. *Exit interview*: Higher employee turnover is a problem of every organization. Employees leave the organization either due to dissatisfaction or for better prospects. Exit interviews may be conducted to know the reasons for leaving the job. Properly conducted exit interviews can provide significant information about the strengths and weaknesses of the organization and can pave way for further improving the management policies for its labour force.

Principles or Guidelines for Grievance Handling

1. In handling grievances, a considerable amount of time must be spent in talking to employees; gathering data from them and passing on various types of information. Such talks to be most effective, should confirm to definite patterns and adhere to well tested rules.

2. The manager must seek to develop an attitude towards employees that should be helpful in gaining their confidence. The management should also display a sincere interest in the problems of employees and their constructive willingness to be to help to them with a view to gain not only their confidence but also

their utmost loyal by and genuine cooperation.

3. The procedure adopt by the management in handling the grievances must be apparent.

4. Grievances should be handled in terms of their total effect on the organization and not solely their immediate or individual effect.

Steps in Handling Grievances

It is important that grievance must be handled in a systematic manner. The following steps should be taken in handling grievances:

1. Defining, describing or expressing the nature of the grievances as clearly and fully as possible;

2. Gathering all facts that serve to explain when, how, where, to whom and why the grievance occurred;

3. Establishing tentative solutions or answers to the grievances;

4. Gathering additional information to check the validity of the solutions and thus ascertain the best possible solution;

5. Applying the solution, and

6. Following up the case to see that it has been handled satisfactorily and the trouble has been eliminated.

Grievance Handling Procedures

Grievance procedure is the most significant channel through which dissatisfaction of employees can be communicated to management. A grievance procedure is an ordered multistep process that the employer and employee jointly use to redress grievances and resolve disputes that arise. Thus a formal procedure which attempts to resolve the differences of parties involved, in an orderly, peaceful and expeditious manner, may be defined as grievance procedure or grievance redressal machinery. The steps in this machinery vary from organization to organization.

For handling grievances, as a first step, the management is required to designate the persons for each of the various departments to be approached by the works and the department heads for handling grievances as the second step. A Grievance Committee may also be constituted with representatives of workers and management.

The model grievance producer gives the various steps through which a grievance should be processed.

First, the grievance is taken to the departmental representative of the management who has to give an answer within 48 hours. Failing this, the aggrieved worker/employee can beat the departmental head along with the departmental representative of the management and this step is allotted three days. Above this, the grievance is taken up by the Grievance Committee which should make its recommendations to the manager within seven days. The final decision of the management has to be communicated to the workers or employee concerned within three days of the Grievance Committee's recommendations. If the employee is not satisfied, he can make an appeal for revision and the management has to communicate its decision within a week. In the case of non-settlement, the grievance may be referred to voluntary arbitration. The formal conciliation machinery will not be invoked till the final decision of the top management has been found unacceptable by the aggrieved employee.

In the case of any grievance arising out of discharge or dismissal, the workman or employee has the right to appeal either to the dismissing authority or to a senior authority specific by the management within a week from the date of dismissal or discharge.

Although the grievance procedure gives the employees opportunity to raise their grievances to the highest possible level of management, yet they should be resolved as close as possible to their source. The main object of grievance procedure is to resolve the grievance at earliest possible stage. The management must convince itself that justice is not only done, but seen to be done and the presence of a trade union representative with the aggrieved party helps to ensure fair play not only for the employee concerned, but also for his management.

Wage Administration and Industrial Relation

Wage is remuneration to labour for the work done or the service rendered by it to the employees. Wage payment if the most vital and important problem that an industrial workers is confronted with it is also one of the most difficult areas in our present industrial relations system. The wages constitute the earning for the workmen, which, in turn, determine his standard of living and that of his family. They also determine the standard of his efficiency and consequently, the level of productivity. Wage administration is also important to the employer as it constitutes one of the principal items that enter into the cost of production of his product. The government and the community at large are also vitally concerned with the problem because of a large number of industrial disputes center round the questions of wages and allowances. Therefore, evolution of a suitable wage structure and wage fixing machinery is important for the prosperity of industry, for the well-being of labour, and for the economic development of the country. However the problem of wage fixation in a modern democratic society is by far the most difficult of all employer-employee relationship. The concerned parties, namely, the employers, the works and the consumers have seemingly conflicting interests. A delicate balance has to be struck between wages paid to the workers, the profits passed on to the shareholders, and the services rendered to the community. It cannot also be considered in isolation from the larger economic and social background prevailing in the country.

Wage Policy

The term 'wage policy' refers to legislation or government action undertaken to regulate the level or structure of wages, or both for the purpose of achieving specific objectives of social and economic policy. The social objectives of wage policy may aim at eliminating the exceptionally low wages, the establishing of fair standards, the protection of wage earners from the impact of inflationary tendencies; and at increasing the economic welfare of the community as a whole.

"The social and economic aspects of wage policy are normally inter-related; measures inspired by social considerations inevitably have economic effects and action designed to achieve specific economic results has social implications. When the social and economic implication of measures of wage-policy conflict, a choice has to be made."

A wage policy may be viewed from three different angles. At the macroeconomic level, the problem is that of resolving the conflict between the objectives of an immediate rise in the standard of living of workers, additional employment and capital formation. At the semi-aggregative level, the problem is that of evolving a wage structure which is conducive to economic development. At the plant level, the problem is that of a system which provides incentives to increasing productivity and improving the quality of workers.

Objectives of a Wage Policy

The ILO publication has enumerated the following objectives of a wage policy in developing countries:

- To abolish malpractices and abuses in wage payment.
- To set minimum wages for workers whose bargaining position is weak because they are unorganized or inefficiently organized, accompanied by separate measures to promote the growth of trade unions and collective bargaining.
- To obtain for the workers a just share in the fruits of economic development, supplemented by appropriate measures to keep workers' expenditure on consumption goods in step with available supplies so as to minimize inflationary pressure; and
- To bring about a more efficient allocation and utilization of manpower through wage differentials and where appropriate, systems of payment by results.

In India, the objectives of a national wage policy may be stated thus:

- To provide minimum wages to workers employed in sweated industries
- To fix wage ceilings
- To improve the existing wage-structure

- To control inflationary tendencies
- To accelerate export promotion and
- Other objectives.

Provision of Minimum Wages in Sweated Industries

In a country like India, where labourers are exploited in the sweated industries, the basic need is to provide for "safety net" wages to prevent its exploitation. According to Turner, "The protection of workers against exploitation or unduly low wages remains wager policy's major pre-occupation for the under-developed areas". The fixing of minimum wage is also necessary to boost up industrial employment, partly to smooth the flow of labour from the farm to expanding modern industries; and partly to cover the differentials in wage rates so that wages paid to employees doing identical work are rationalized. Thus, the wage policy should aim at a minimum wage in sweated occupation as well as a floor for entry to industrial employment.

Fixation of Wage Ceilings

Ceilings on wages need be fixed to save employees from the pinch of inflationary tendency that follow from uncontrolled price movement. The workers should get a just share in the fruits of economic development and increased productivity. Productivity and efficiency can be boosted by giving incentives to them and by improving the investment capacity of industries by plaguing back a part of the profit in the industry.

Improvement in Existing Wage Structure

Desirable or rational wage structure facilitates the acquisition of productive skills, serves as an incentive to higher productivity and wage income, and encourages the allocation of labour to the expanding sectors of economy in which labour is in great demand. Justice and fairness demand that a sound relationship should exist between rates of wage for different groups in similar occupations.

The jobs which demand a higher degree of skill, training, experience, responsibility, mental and physical effort and hazards should be paid more than those having lower requirement. According to

Clark Kerr, "improving worker efficiency and performance, encouraging the acquisition of skills and providing and incentive of labour mobility should be the real purpose of a wage policy in a developing economy".

Control over Inflationary Tendencies

Controlling inflationary pressures should be an essential element of wage policy, for increasing prices erode workers' real income and lower down their standard of living and ultimately cause industrial unrest. The wage policy should, therefore, aim at stabilizing prices by tying wage increases to productivity.

Acceleration of Export Promotion

To get imports of essential capital goods, technical knowhow, trained manpower and raw materials, foreign exchange need be earned by promoting exports through increased productivity of exportable goods and price stability or price reduction wherever possible. A wage policy should help to accelerate a nations' development process.

Other objectives

- To bring social justice to workers and equal opportunities of personal development through the development of socialistic pattern of society; as provided by the Directive Principles of the State Policy in the Constitution.
- To maintain industrial peace, which cannot be achieved only through statutory measures and ban on strikes and lockouts and compulsory arbitration.
- To provide guidance to various authorities charged with the task of wage fixation and revision.
- To develop the skill of newly recruited industrial labour and other manpower resources.

Dr. Giri has said, "A national wage policy must aim at establishing wages at the highest possible level, which the economic conditions of the country as a whole resulting from economic development".

Thus, it may be said that "the protection of workers against exploitation or unduly low wages, improving workers' efficiency and performance, encouraging acquisition of strikes, providing an incentive to labour mobility, stabilizing prices and acceleration of the nation's development process should be the real purpose and the need for a national wage policy."

It may be observed that no serious attempt has so far been made at the level, for formulating a national wage policy; and there does not appear to be a formally proclaimed wage policy in India.

Wage Regulation Machinery

In unorganized industries, wages are fixed and revised under the Minimum Wages Act, 1948. But for other industrial workers, they are fixed by several well-established procedures or practices available for wage-fixation and wage revision. These are settlements in conciliation of wage disputes, collective bargaining at the plant level, bipartite wage revision committees in several industries, adjudication, and arbitration. Lately, Wage Boards have also been created.

Wage Board

Wage Board is a tripartite body, having representation of the employers and labour besides, independent members. The representatives of the former two interests are nominated by their central organizations; others are nominated by the Government. It is an important machinery of State regulation of wages.

Growth and Development

After independence, the Industrial Disputes Act was enacted under which disputed regarding wages could be settled through adjudication. But the parties were not satisfied with this system. The idea of setting up of tripartite Wage Boards was, therefore, mooted and endorsed in the First Plan. But no action was taken during that Plan period.

However, the Second Plan emphasized the need to determine wages through industrial wage boards. It observed, "The existing machinery for settlement of wage disputes has not given full satisfaction to the parties concerned. More acceptable machinery for settling wage disputes will be one which gives the parties themselves a more responsible role in reaching decisions. An authority like a tripartite

Wage Board, consisting of equal representative of employers and workers and an independent chairman will probably ensure more acceptable decisions. Such wage boards should be instituted for individual industries in different areas".

This recommendation was subsequently reiterated by the 15th Indian Labour Conference in 1957 and various Industrial Committees. The Government decision to set up the first wage board in cotton textile and sugar industries in 1957 was also influence by the Report of the ILO's expert.

Composition and Functions of Wage Board

The composition of wage boards is, as a rule, tripartite representing the interests of labour, management and the public. Labour and management representatives are maintained in equal numbers by the government, with consultation and consent of the major central organizations. Generally, the labour and management representatives are selected from the particular industry being investigated. These boards are chaired by government-nominated members representing the public.

They function industry-wise with broad terms for reference, which include recommending the minimum wage, differential cost of living compensation, regional wage differentials, gratuity, hours of work, etc.

The Wage Boards are required to:

● determine which categories of employees (manual, clerical, supervisory etc.) are to be brought within the scope of the wage fixation;

● to work out a wage structure based on principles of fair wages as formulated by the Committee on Fair Wages;

● the system of payment by results;

● to work out the principles that should govern of bonus to workers in respective industries.

In addition to these common items, some wage boards may also be asked to deal with the question of "bonus" (like that of the wage boards for cement, sugar and jute industries); gratuity (like that of the wage boards for the iron ore mining, limestone and dolomite mining industries and the second wage board on cotton textile industry; demands in respect of payments other than wages (wage boards of jute and iron and steel industry); hours of work (rubber plantation industry), interim relief (like that of the wage boards for jute industry and port and dock workers).

Some wage boards (like that of the wage boards for sugar, jute, iron ore, rubber, tea and coffee plantation, limestone and dolomite mining industries) have been required to take into account the 'special features of the industry'.

Thus, wage boards have to deal with a large range of subjects of which the fixation of wage-scales on an industry-wise basis constitutes the biggest of all the issues before them.

Evaluation of Wage Boards

The Committee set up by the National Commission on Labour identified three major problems from which the wage boards suffer:

- Majority of the recommendations of wage boards are not unanimous;
- The time taken by the wage boards to complete their task has been rather unduly long; and
- Implementation of the recommendations of the wage boards has been difficult. The Committee made some important recommendations as below:
- The Chairman of the wage board should be selected by common consent of the organization of employees and employees in the industry concerned.
- In future the wages board should function essentially as machinery for collective bargaining and should strive for unity.
- Wage boards should be assisted by technical assessors and experts.
- Terms of reference of wage boards should be decided by Government in consultation with the organization of employers and the workers concerned.
- A central wage board should be set up in the Union Ministry of Labour on a permanent basis to serve all wage boards through the supply of statistical and other material and lending of the necessary staff.

- Unanimous recommendations of wage boards should be accepted and in case of non-unanimous recommendations, government should hold consultations with the organization of employers and employees before taking a final decision.
- Wage boards should not be set up under any statues, but their recommendations as finally accepted by the Government should be made statutorily binding in the parties.
- For Industries covered by wage boards, a permanent machinery should be created for follow-up action; and
- Wage-boards should complete their work in one year's time and the operation of the recommendation of a wage board should be between two or three years, after which need for a subsequent wage boards should be considered on merit.

By these recommendations are accepted, the working of wage boards may be made more effective.

The institution of wage boards has come to be widely accepted in India as a viable wage determination mechanism. Both unions and employers' organizations have supported it from its very inception, and have been willing to accept changes to make it more efficient and productive. It has succeeded in promoting industry-wise negotiations, as contrasted to enterprise-level decisions under adjudications, more acceptable agreements on wages and other conditions of employment of industrial peace. Furthermore, in addition to encouraging greater participation by the parties and freedom in decision-making, the boards have functioned with responsibility and restraint and their recommendations have not undermined the efficiency of the industry.

However, delays involved in actual working of the boards and imperfect implementation of the reconditions has been often the cause of anxiety, but these can be reduce considerably if collection and tabulation of basic information and relevant data on wage fixation is done on a running and continuing basis in respect of all major industries/employments.

MULTIPLE CHOICE QUESTIONS

1. Collective bargaining issues that are not mandatory but relate to certain jobs is
   A. Mandatory issues   B. Permissive issues
   C. Employees' issues   D. None of the above

2. Contract or agreement, either oral or in writing, that force employees to agree not to join a union or participate in any union activity as a condition of employment is
   A. Yellow-dog contracts
   B. Illegal contracts
   C. Misbehaviours
   D. None of the above

3. A labour relations term used to define periodic suspensions of negotiations in order to provide both sides with an opportunity to consider their relevant positions is
   A. Mediator   B. Caucus
   C. Observation   D. None of the above

4. A formal written complaint or allegation by an employee or group of employees made to unfair treatment or violation of a union contract is
   A. Quarrel   B. Grievance
   C. Illegal   D. All the above

5. The relationship between a Professional Employer Organization (PEO) or employee leasing firm and an employer, based on a contractual sharing of liability and responsibility for employees is
   A. Industrial relation
   B. Employment relations
   C. Co-employment relations
   D. None of the above

6. The process of utilizing an impartial third party, not employed by the organization, to examine all pertinent facts surrounding a complaint is
   A. Third opinion   B. Fact finding
   C. Grievance handling D. None of the above

7. An informal meeting directed by the EEOC to settle discrimination complaints between an employer and the plaintiff is

A. Meeting
B. Adjudication
C. Fact-finding conference
D. Organization committee

8. The measurement of how employees spend their time and the number of work units being produced by employees over a specific period of time is
   A. Work observation B. Supervision
   C. Work sampling   D. None of the above

9. Tests that require an applicant to perform a simulated job task is
   A. Work observation B. Supervision
   C. Work sampling   D. Work sample tests

10. People's belief that they can influence events, even they have no control over what will happen is
    A. Illusion of control
    B. Span of control
    C. Work plan
    D. None of the above

11. Intervention in which a neutral third party tries to assist the principals in reaching agreement is
    A. Mediation   B. Arbitration
    C. Middle man   D. All the above

12. The most definitive type of third-party intervention, in which the arbitrator usually has the power to determine and dictate the settlement terms is
    A. Mediation   B. Arbitration
    C. Middle man   D. All the above

13. A strike that results from a failure to agree on the terms of a contract that involve wages, benefits, and other conditions of employment is termed as
    A. Strike   B. Economic strike
    C. Environment strike D. None of the above

14. Unfair Labour Practice Strike is a strike aimed at protesting illegal conduct by the employer.
    A. True   B. False
    C. Partially true   D. None of the above

15. An unauthorized strike occurring during the term of a contract is
A. Strike
B. Wildcat strike
C. Bear strike
D. Economic strike

16. A strike that takes place when one union strikes in support of another is
A. Sympathy strike
B. Wildcat strike
C. Bear strike
D. Economic strike

17. An organized effort by the union that exerts pressure on the corporation by pressuring the company's other unions, shareholders, directors, customers, creditors, and government agencies, often directly is
A. Stake holders
B. Corporate campaign
C. Corporate governance
D. None of the above

18. The combined refusal by employees and other interested parties to buy or use the employer's products is
A. Strike
B. Lockout
C. Boycott
D. Slow down

19. A refusal by the employer to provide opportunities to work is
A. Strike
B. Lockout
C. Boycott
D. Slow down

20. Any factor involving wages, hours, or conditions of employment that is used as a complaint against the employer.
A. Grievance
B. Lockout
C. Boycott
D. Slow down

21. An employee is defined as a salaried employee who is among the highest-paid 10% of all workers employed by the employer within a 75-mile radius OR he/she is defined as a plan participant who is a highly compensated officer or company owner remains as
A. Group of employees
B. Leader
C. Manager
D. Key employee

22. Collective bargaining issues that would require either party to take illegal action referred as
A. Legal action
B. Illegal action
C. Legal issue
D. Illegal issues

23. Those collective bargaining items that is unlawful by statue is
A. Legal action
B. Illegal subjects
C. Legal issue
D. Illegal issues

24. Individuals who report real or perceived wrongs committed by their employers is
A. Brainstorming
B. Training
C. Whistle-blowers
D. Orientation

25. Process by which a third party assists negotiators in their discussions and also suggests settlement proposals is
A. Arbitration
B. Adjudication
C. Mediation
D. None of the above

26. Work stoppages involving the primary employer-employee relationship that are neither sanctioned nor stimulated by the union is
A. Strikes
B. Lay-off
C. Wildcat strikes
D. None of the above

27. Studying the workflow, activities, context, & output of a job is
A. Schedules
B. Work analysis
C. Job description
D. Job specification

28. Process that uses a neutral third party to make a decision is
A. Arbitration
B. Adjudication
C. Middle person
D. None of the above

29. A collection of instruments and exercises designed to diagnose a person's development needs is
A. Training centre
B. Assessment center
C. Rehabilitation center
D. Psychological test

30. An employer's written standards regarding the requirement for employees to be on time and present at work during regularly scheduled work periods is
A. Register
B. Observation
C. Attendance policy
D. None of the above

31. _____ refers to signs or labels attached to equipment to warn others not to activate it.
A. Access
B. Tag out
C. Reference
D. None of the above

32. _____ refers to time lost when employees report to work late.
A. Lateness
B. Delay
C. Tardiness
D. All the above

33. A professional individual who is authorized to practice law and can be legally appointed by either a plaintiff or a defendant to provide legal advice or act as a legal agent on their behalf during legal proceedings is termed as
A. Attorney
B. Personnel representative
C. Legal proceedings
D. None of the above

34. A term used to describe voluntary and involuntary terminations, deaths and employee retirements that result in a reduction to the employer's physical workforce.
A. Attrition
B. Exploitation
C. Orientation
D. None of the above

35. An analysis that identifies the number of protected class members (minorities and women) available to work in the appropriate labour markets in given jobs.
A. Labour demand
B. Availability analysis
C. Demand and supply
D. None of the above

36. A group of services provided to displace employees to give them support and assistance such as job counseling, training and job finding assistance that is appropriate to his or her talents and needs is
A. Assessment centre
B. Out placement
C. Training
D. Work shop

37. A standard used in sexual harassment suits, referring to conduct or behaviour so offensive in nature that any reasonable person, regardless of sex, would agree the conduct or behaviour should be illegal is termed as
A. Ragging
B. Punishment
C. Reasonable person standard
D. None of the above

38. An interim or Final Order pertaining to Industrial Dispute passed by Industrial Tribunal / Labour Court is called
A. Judgment
B. Order
C. Award
D. None of the above

39. The temporary closing of a place of employment or the suspension of work, or refusal by an employer is called
A. Lay off
B. Lockout
C. Retrenchment
D. None of the above

40. The rate of Subsistence allowance paid to an employee under suspension for first 90 days is?
A. 75%
B. 60%
C. 50%
D. None of the above

41. Contract Labour (Regulation & Abolition), Act was enacted in _____.
A. 1948
B. 1946
C. 1970
D. 1965

42. Chapter V-A of ID Act, 1947 Envisages about _____.
A. Closure
B. Grievance redressal
C. Lay-off retrenchment
D. None of the above

43. An oral or written reproach given to an employee as part of disciplinary action is
A. Caution notice
B. Reprimand
C. Pleaser
D. None of the above

44. Behaviour modeling is a copying someone else's behaviour.
A. The statement is right
B. The statement is not right
C. The statement is partially right
D. None of the above

45. Type of interview in which the interviewer focuses on how the applicant previously handled real work situations is
A. Behaviour-based interview
B. Group interview
C. Standard interview
D. Repetitive interview

46. Assesses an employee's behaviours instead of other characteristics is
   A. Sensitive training
   B. Emotional intelligence
   C. Behaviourial rating approach
   D. None of the above

47. Training methods that deal less with physical skills than with attitudes, perceptions, and interpersonal issues is
   A. Sensitive training
   B. Emotional intelligence
   C. Behaviourial experience training
   D. None of the above

48. Bell-shaped curve is representing the normal distribution of a rating or test score.
   A. The statement is right
   B. The statement is not right

   C. The statement is partially right
   D. None of the above

49. The systematic process of comparing an organization's products, services and practices against those of competitor organizations or other industry leaders to determine what it is they do that allows them to achieve high levels of performance is
   A. Strategic management
   B. Environmental analysis
   C. Benchmarking
   D. None of the above

50. Jobs used as reference point when setting up a job classification system is
   A. Career   B. Job
   C. Benchmark job   D. Job satisfaction

ANSWERS

1	2	3	4	5	6	7	8	9	10
B	A	B	B	C	B	C	C	D	A

11	12	13	14	15	16	17	18	19	20
A	B	A	A	B	A	B	C	B	A

21	22	23	24	25	26	27	28	29	30
D	D	B	C	C	C	B	A	B	C

31	32	33	34	35	36	37	38	39	40
B	D	A	A	B	B	C	C	B	C

41	42	43	44	45	46	47	48	49	50
C	C	B	A	A	C	C	A	C	C

5

Trade Unions

Trade Unionism

Trade unionism is a worldwide movement and the highly strategic position occupied by the unions in modern industrial society which has been widely recognized. In most cases, employees' associations or trade unions seem to have emerged as 'protest movements' reaching against the working relationships and conditions created by industrialization. When industrialization begins, organization members have to be generally recruited from the ranks of former agricultural labour and artisans who have to adapt themselves to the changed conditions of industrial employment. They have to be provided with new types of economic security – wages/salaries, benefits and services etc. Often they may have to learn to live together in newly developing industrial townships and cities and also to adopt themselves to new working conditions and new pattern of work-rules imposing discipline and setting pace of work to which they are unfamiliar. Their old habits and traditions do not suffice to guide them in their daily work-behaviour and in consequence they may be disorganized and frustrated. Thus the growth of modern industrial organizations involving the employment of a large number of workers/employees in new type of working conditions and environment makes them helpless in bargaining individually for their terms of employment. As observed by Frank Tannenbaum, "The emergence of trade unionism lies in the Industrial Revolution which disrupted the older way of life and created a new society forged by the shop, the factory, the mine and the industry.

Meaning of Trade Union, Organized Labour and Labour Movement

- The term 'Trade Union' has been defined in various ways because of wide differences in the use of this term in different countries. Of all the definitions of a trade union, the classic definition of the Webbs has been most popular. According to them a trade union is "a continuous association of wage-earners for the purpose of maintaining or improving the condition of their working lives". Since this definition does not cover all the extensions of trade union activities in modern times, a trade union with some modification may be redefined as "a continuous association of wage-earners or salaried employees for maintaining the conditions of their working lives and ensuring them a better and healthier status in industry as well as in the society".

- The term 'Organized Labour' is used to distinguish workers/employees who are members of trade unions or employee association from those who are unorganized, i.e. who are not members of any union.

• The term 'Labour Movement' is generally applied to all the various types of long-term association of workers/employees that the formed in industrialized or industrializing economies. According to Encyclopedia of Social Sciences, labour movement is conceived as "all of the organized activity of wage-earners to better their own conditions either immediately or in the more or less distant future". According to G.D.H. code, "Labour movement implies, in some degree, a community of outlook. Thus the labour movement in a country emerges from a common need to serve a common interest. It seeks to develop amongst employees a spirit of combination, class-consciousness and solidarity of interest and generates a consciousness for self-respect and creates organizations for their self protection, safeguarding of their common interest and betterment of their economic and social conditions. A trade union is thus an essential basis of labour movement. The labour movement without trade unions cannot exist. Trade unions are the principal institutions in which the employees learn the lesson of self-reliance and solidarity.

Objectives of Trade Unions

The following are the broad objectives of trade unions:

1. **Ensure Security of Workers:** This involves continued employment of workers, preventing retrenchment, layoffs or lockouts; restricting the application of "fir" or "dismissal or discharge", etc.

2. **Obtain Better Economic Returns:** This involves wage hike at periodic intervals, bonus at higher rates, other admissible allowances, subsidized canteen and transport facilities, etc.

3. **Improve working Environment and Welfare Measures:** This involves better workplace. Ventilation, lighting, safety, healthcare, sanitation, less pollution, welfare measures for working ladies, maternity facilities, children' education, housing insurance, social-security schemes, old-age covers etc.

4. **Secure Power to Influence Management:** This involves the worker's participation in management, decision-making, the role of unions in policy decision affecting workers, etc.

5. **Secure Power to Influence the Government:** This involves influence on the government to pass labour legislation that improves working conditions; safety, welfare, security and retirement benefits of the workers and their dependents; curbing the power of punishment by employers; seeking redress of grievances, etc.

Functions of Trade Unions

(*i*) **Militant functions:** Rise in wages, rise in the status of workers, protection against injustice.

(*ii*) **Fraternal functions:** Measures to boost up the workers' morale, Foster self confidence, Develop sincerity and discipline, Protection to women workers against discrimination.

• Functions relating to members
• Functions relating to organization
• Functions relating to the union; and
• Functions relating to the society.

Functions relating to trade union members

1. To safeguard workers against all sorts of exploitation by the employers, by union leaders and by political parties.

2. To protect workers from the atrocities and unfair practices of the management.

3. To ensure healthy, safe and conducive working conditions, and adequate conditions of work.

4. To exert pressure for enhancement of rewards associated with the work only after making a realistic assessment of its practical implications.

5. To ensure a desirable standard to living by providing various types of social service – health, housing, educational, recreational, cooperative, etc. and by widening and consolidating the social security measures.

6. To guarantee a fair and square deal and social security measures.

7. To remove the dissatisfaction and redress the grievances and complaints of workers.

8. To encourage worker's participation in the management of industrial organization and trade union, and to foster labour-management cooperation.

9. To make the workers conscious of their rights and duties.

10. To impress upon works the need to exercise restraint in the use of rights and to enforce them after realistically ascertaining their practical implications.

11. To stress the significance of settling disputes through negotiation, joint consultation and voluntary arbitration.

12. The raise the status of trade union members in the industrial organization and in the society at large.

Functions relating to industrial organization

1. To highlight industrial organization as a joint enterprise between workers and management and to promote identity of interests.

2. To increase production quantitatively and qualitatively, by laying down the norms or production and ensuring their adequate observance.

3. To help in the maintenance of discipline.

4. To create opportunities for worker's participation in management and to strengthen labour-management cooperation.

5. To help in the removal of dissatisfaction and redressal of grievances and complaints.

6. To promote cordial and amicable relations between the workers and management by settling disputes through negotiation, joint consultation and voluntary arbitration, and by avoiding litigation.

7. To create favourable opinion of the management towards trade unions and improve their status in industrial organization.

8. To exert pressure on the employer to enforce legislative provision beneficial to the workers, to share the profits equitably, and to keep away from various types of unfair labour practices.

9. To facilitate communication with the management.

10. To impress upon the management the need to adopt reformative and not punitive, approach towards workers' faults.

Functions relating to trade unions organization

1. To formulate policies and plans consistent with those of the industrial organization and society at large.

2. To improve financial position by fixing higher subscription, by realizing the union dues and by organizing special fund-raising campaigns.

3. To preserve and strengthen trade union democracy.

4. To train members to assume leadership position.

5. To improve the network of communication between trade union and its members.

6. To curb inter-union rivalry and thereby help in the creating of unified trade union movement.

7. To resolve the problem of factionalism and promote unity and solidarity within the union.

8. To eradicate casteism, regionalism and linguism within the trade union movement.

9. To keep away from unfair labour practices.

10. To save the union organization from the exploitation by vested interests of personal and political.

11. To continuously review the relevance of union objectives in the context of social change, and to change them accordingly.

12. To prepare and maintain the necessary records.

13. To manage the trade union organization on scientific lines.

14. To publicize the trade union objectives and functions, to know people's reaction towards them, and to make necessary modifications.

Functions relating to society

1. To render all sorts of constructive cooperation in the formulation and implementation of plans and policies relating to national development.

2. To actively participate in the development of programmes of national development, e.g., family planning, afford station, national integration, etc.

3. To launch special campaigns against the social evils of corporation, nepotism, communalism, casteism, regionalism, linguism, price rise, hoarding, black marketing, smuggling, sex, inequality, dowry, untouchability, illiteracy, dirt and disease.

4. To create public opinion favourable to government's policies and plans, and to mobilize people's participation for their effective implementation.

5. To create public opinion favourable to trade unions and thereby to raise their status.

6. To exert pressure, after realistically ascertaining its practical implications, on the government to enact legislation conducive to the development of trade unions and their members.

Need for Trade Union

- One of the main reasons of workers joining a trade union been their belief to get wages increased and maintained at a reasonable standard through collective action and their realization that individual bargaining was utterly useless for this purpose.

- Since the employee, as an individual, feels especially weak, he prefers to join an organization that may afford him an opportunity to join others for the achievement of those objectives that he considers as socially desirable.

- The employees may join the unions to ensure a just and fair dealing by management.

- Through collective strength, they restrain the management from taking any such action which may be irrational, illogical, discriminatory or contrary to their general interests.

- Another reason of employees joining some union may be the broader realization on their part that unions fulfil the important need for adequate machinery for proper maintenance of labour-management relations.

- Employees may join the unions because of their belief that it is an effective way to secure adequate protection from various types of hazards and income insecurity such as accident injury, illness, unemployment etc.

- The employees may join the unions because of their feeling that this would enable them to communicate their views, ideas, feelings and frustrations to the management effectively.

- Individuals may join the unions in the hope of finding a job through their influence in the company management.

Difference between Labour Movement and Trade Union Movement

- There is lot of confusion on the use of the terms 'labour movement' and 'trade union movement'. Often the two are used interchangeably. However, there is a slight distinction between the two. The 'labour movement' is 'for the worker'; whereas the 'trade union movement' is 'by the workers'. This distinction needs to be noticed all the more because till the workers organized themselves into trade unions, efforts were made mainly by the social reformers to improve the working and living conditions of labour. These efforts should be taken as forming a part of the labour movement and not that of the trade union movement. The labour movement thus conveys a higher degree of consciousness amongst workers than conveyed by mere trade union movement.

THEORIES AND STRUCTURE OF TRADE UNIONS

There is no one theory of Trade Unionism, but many contributors to these theories are revolutionaries like Marx and Engels, Civil servants like Sydney Webb, academics like Common and Hoxie and labour leader like Mitchall. Important theories of trade unionism are as follows:

1. **Political Revolutionary Theory of Labour Movement of Marx and Engels:** This theory is based on Adam Smith's theory of labour value. Its short run purpose is to eliminate competition among labour, and the ultimate purpose is to overthrow capitalist business-man. Trade union is a pure, simple class struggle, and proletarians have nothing to lose but their chains and have a world to win.

2. **Webbs' Theory of Industrial Democracy:** Webb's book 'Industrial democracy' is the Bible of trade unionism. According to Webb, trade unionism is an extension of democracy from political sphere to industrial sphere. Webb agreed with Marx that trade unionism is a class struggle and modern capitalist state is a transitional phase which will lead to democratic socialism. He considered collective bargaining as the process which strengthens labour.

3. **Cole's Theory of Union Control of Industry:** Cole's views are given in his book "World of Labour" 1913. His views are somewhere in between Webb and Marx. He agrees that unionism is class struggle and the ultimate is the control of industry by labour and not revolution as predicted by Marx.

4. **Common's Environment Theory:** He was skeptical of generalizations and believed only that which could be proved by evidence. He agreed that collective bargaining was an instrument of class struggle, but he summarized that ultimately there will be partnership between employers and employees.

5. **Mitchell's Economic Protection Theory of Trade Unionism:** Mitchell, a labour leader, completely rejected individual bargaining. According to him unions afford economic protection to.

6. **Simons Theory of Monopolistic, anti-Democratic Trade Unionism:** He denounced trade unionism as monopoly founded on violence. And he claimed monopoly power has no use save abuse.

7. **Perlman's Theory of the "Scarcity Consciousness" of Manual Workers:** He rejected the idea of class consciousness as an explanation for the origin of the trade union movement but substituted it with what he called job consciousness. According to him, 'working people in reality felt an urge towards collective control of their employment opportunities, but hardly towards similar control of industry'. Perlman observed that three dominant factors emerged from the rich historical data:

   (*i*) The capacity or incapacity of the capitalist system to survive as a ruling group in the face of revolutionary attacks (e.g., failure in Russia).

   (*ii*) The source of the anti-capitalist influences being primarily from among the intellectuals in any society.

   (*iii*) The most vital factor in the labour situation was the trade union movement. Trade unionism, which is essentially pragmatic, struggles constantly not only against the employers for an enlarged opportunity measure in income, security and liberty in the shop and industry, but struggles also, whether consciously or unconsciously, actively or passively, against the intellectual who would frame its programmes and shape its policies.

But Perlman also felt that a theory of the labour movement should include a theory of the psychology of the labouring man. For instance, there was a historical continuity between the guilds and trade unions, through their common fundamental psychology; the psychology of seeking a livelihood in the face of limited economic opportunity. It was when manual workers became aware of a scarcity of opportunity, that they banded together into unions for the purpose of protecting their jobs and distributing employment opportunities among themselves equitably, and to subordinate the interests of the individual to the whole labour organism. Unionism was ruled thus by this fundamental scarcity consciousness (Perlman, 1970).

8. **Hoxies Functional Classification of Unionism:** He classified Unionism on the basis of their functions. His classification were Business Unionism for protecting the interest of various craftsmen, "Uplift unionism" for the purpose of contributing better life such as association of sales engineers etc. "Revolutionary Unionism" which is eager to replace existing social order, "Predatory Unionism" which rests on these support of others. Robert Hoxie's Social Psychological Theory was propounded in 1920. He classified unionism on the basis of its functions and structure. According to him to understand the nature of trade unionism one has to take into accounts not only environmental conditions but also temperamental characteristics of the workers concerned. Thus the differences in group psychology cause different types of unions to appear. Business Unionism for protecting the interest of various craftsman and lays emphasis on immediate goals the enhancement in wages, reduction in hours of work, improvement in working conditions and so on.

9. **Tannenbaum's Theory of Man vs. Machine:** According to him Union is formed in reaction to alienation and loss of community in an individualistic and unfeeling society. In his words, the union returns to the workers his society, which he left behind him when he migrated from a rural background to the anonymity of an urban industrial location. The union gives the worker a fellowship and a value system that he shares with others like him. Institutionally, the trade union movement is an unconscious effort to harness the drift of our time and reorganize it around the cohesive identity that men working together always achieve.

10. **Protest/General Theory**: Kerr, Dunlop and Myre observed that worker protest in inherent in industrialization. The type of labour organization that develops in a country is related to the type of industrializing elite. This stress and strain of industrialization compel the workers to form labour organization and the nature and role of such labour organization is dependent on a number of factors like particular culture and environment of the country, the industrialization process etc, the workers does not get the compensation commensurate with their contribution and protest in an organized way like absenteeism, sabotage strikes, etc.

11. **Sarvodaya Theory:** Mahatma Gandhi's approach is known as Sarvodaya Theory/ approach because it is based upon the Sarvodaya principles of Truth, Non-violence and Trusteeship. According to him, trade unions were reformist organization, not anti-capitalistic, less political and their main function is to raise the moral and intellectual supplementary during strike may be reducing to the minimum. Unions work conscientiously and do not take from the employer no more what is rightly due to the labourers.

TRADE UNION STRUCTURE

The structure of trade unions refers to the basis on which unions are organized and to the pattern whereby the plant unions are linked to regional level or national level federations of unions. Trade unions are classified into following three categories.

1. **Craft Union:** A craft union is formed by workers belonging to same occupation or specialization irrespective of industry. The carpenters working in different industries may form a union of carpenters. The Indian pilots guild and International Wood Carvers are the examples of craft union. This union exists among non-manual workers like administrative staff professional, technicians etc.

2. **Industrial Union:** Industrial unions is formed on the basis of industry rather than on a craft, *i.e.,* the workers of a cotton textile factory may from a union consisting of workers of different crafts to avoid separate bargaining by each employee union *i.e.,* cotton textile

factory Rashtriya Mill Mazdoor Sangh Mumbai.

3. **General Union:** General unions embraces all workers whatever industry of craft in a place. Its membership covers workers employed in different industries and crafts, *i.e.,* Jamshedpur labour unions. In our country most of the trade unions have been organized by industry-wise.

The other way of structuring trade union is by the relationship between national level, regional level, local level and plant level:

1. **Plant Level:** These unions' functions at lowest level or at the plant level and does not have more influence independently. But the generally unite is a particular craft or industry for strength.

2. **Local Level Federation:** The plant level unions at the local level in a particular craft or industry are held together by the local level federations.

3. **Regional Level Federation:** This is due to variation in style of living language, customs, and traditions; working conditions from region to region workers are organized at regional or state level. Regional level federations are organizations of all the constituent unions in a particular state or region. Regional federations may be independent or may get affiliated to some national federation.

4. **National Federation:** The apex bodies at the top of the structure and act as coordinating bodies. The plant level unions, local level unions, or regional level unions may get affiliated to national level bodies. The national federations may have their own regional or state level coordinating bodies which the plant level unions may get affiliated.

TRADE UNION MOVEMENT IN INDIA

The trade union movement's origin in a sense can be traced back to very early date to the time when villages had panchayats and guilds for settling disputes between the masters and their members. The panchayats prescribed the code of conduct which was rigidly observed by its members. Its non-observance resulted in expulsion from the community. Trade unions, as understood today, however originated in the first quarter of the present century, although the groundwork was laid during the last quarter of the 19th century. In Mumbai, as early as in 1875, a movement was started by reformers under the leadership of Sorabji Shapurji. They protested against the appealing conditions of the factory workers and appealed for introduction of adequate legislation to prevent them. The credit of laying the foundation of the organized labour movement in India is at time accorded to Mr. N.M. Lokhande, a factory worker himself. An agitation was organized by him 1884 in Mumbai. This resulted in certain amenities being extended to the mill workers which led to the organization of the Mumbai Milhands Association.

Actually a real organized labour movement in India started at the end of the First World War. Rising prices, without a corresponding increase in wages, despite the employers making huge profits, led to a new awakening. Many trade unions were formed throughout India. There were a number of strikes during 1919 to 1922. To this was added the influence of the Russian Revolution, the establishment of the ILO (International Labour Organization) and the All-India Trade Union Congress. They speeded up the pace of the trade union movement. Following the Second World War, there was a spiralling of prices. The workers once again became restive. This further indirectly strengthened the movement in India.

The labour world in India is dominated mainly by four central organization of labour. These unions are, in fact, federations of affiliated union – units which function on regional, local and craft bases. These are:

1. *All-India Trade Union Congress (AITUC):* An important event in the history of trade union movement in India was the organization of the All-India Trade Union Congress in 1920. Mr. Nehru took a prominent part in the organization of this Congress. It followed the

pattern of the trade unions in the United Kingdom. The effort toward unified action in the matter of labour was, however, short-lived and soon it came under the domination of the Communists and Radicals. This lineated any prominent people who did not subscribe to the views and ideology of the communists. At present, it is the second largest union of workers and is still controlled by Communists and fellow-travellers.

2. *Indian National Trade Union Congress (INTUC)*: In May, 1947 the Indian National Trade Union Congress was organized by the Congress party on its labour front. This was formed with the help of the Hindustan Mazdoor Sewak Sangh which consisted of those who believed in Gandhian methods and had left the AITUC under of leadership of Mr. M.N. Roy. The INTUC received the blessings of the top congress leaders at the Centre like Mr. Nehru and Sardar Patel. The prominent leaders of ATLA and HMSS were elected office-bearers of INTUC. One of the important points of the constitution of Indian National Trade Union Congress is that every affiliated union has to agree to submit to arbitration every individual dispute in which settlement is not reached thorough negotiations. There must be no strikes till other means of settlement are exhausted. In 1948, the Government of India declared that INTUC, and not AITUC, was the most representative organization of labour in the country entitled to represent Indian labour in I.L.O.

3. *Hind Mazdoor Sangha (HMS)*: The socialists in the Congress disapproved not only the Communist run AITUC but also the Congress-sponsored INTUC, particularly because it advocated compulsory arbitration as a method of resolving industrial disputes. For some time the activities of socialist leaders were coordinated by the Hind Mazdoor Panchayat. Subsequently when they left the Congress, they met in Kolkatta in December, 1948 and a new federation by the Hind Mazdoor

domination by employers, Government and political parties.

4. *United Trade Union Congress (UTUC)*: The dissidents from the Socialist Leaders' Conference held at Kolkatta in December, 1948 proceeded to establish yet another federation of trade unions in April-May 1949 under the name of United Trade Union Congress. The UTUS is more radical than HMS but less revolutionary in its objectives and policies than AITUC.

Problems of Trade Union

The following are some of the most important problems of the trade unions in India:

1. Multiplicity of Trade Unions and Inter-union Rivalry
2. Small Size of Unions
3. Financial Weakness
4. Leadership Issues
5. Politicization of the Unions
6. Problems of Recognition of Trade Unions

Multiplicity of Trade Unions

Multiple rival unionisms are one of the great weaknesses of the Indian trade union movement. "Multiple unions are mainly the result of political outsiders wanting to establish unions of their own, with a view to increasing their political influence". The existence of different conflicting or rival organizations, with divergent political views, is greatly responsible for inadequate and unhealthy growth of the movement. Within a single organization one comes across a number of groups comprising or 'insiders and outsiders', 'new-comers', and 'old-timers', moderates' and radicals', and 'high' and low caste' people. This develops small unions. Inter-union and intra-union rivalry undermines the strength and solidarity of the workers in many ways.

Multiplicity of unions lead to inter-union rivalries, which ultimately cuts at the very root of unionism, weakens the power of collective bargaining, and reduces the effectiveness of workers in securing their legitimate rights. Therefore, there should be "One union in one Industry".

Small Size of Unions

The small size of unions is due to various factors, namely:

- The fact that by seven workers may form a union under the Trade Union Act of 1926, and get it registered and a large number of small unions have grown.
- The structure of the trade union organization in the country which is in most cases the factory or the unit of employment; so whenever employees in a particular factory or mine are organized, a new union is formed.
- Unionism in India started with the big employers and gradually spread to smaller employers. This process is still continuing and has pulled down the average membership. Though the number of unions and union membership are increasing; average membership is declining.
- Rivalry among the leaders and the Central Organization has resulted in multiplicity of unions.

The small size of unions creates problems such as:

- Lack of funds to help its members.
- Lack of ability among the leaders and members.
- Low bargaining power.
- Rivalry between the unions
- Lack of unity among workers.

LEADERSHIP, FINANCE, UNION POLITICS, INTER AND INTRA-UNION RIVALRY

Leadership issues

Another disquieting feature of the trade unions is the 'outside' leadership, *i.e.* leadership of trade unions by persons who are professional politicians and lawyers and who have no history of physical work in the industry. There are several reasons for this phenomenon, namely:

- The rank and the file are largely illiterate as such they cannot effectively communicate with the management;

- The union's lack of formal power tends to put a premium on the charismatic type of the leader, usually a politician, who can play the role of the defender of the workers against the management;
- For ensuring a measure of 'equation of power' in collective bargaining where the workers are generally uneducated and have a low status;
- For avoiding victimisation of worker-office-bearers of the trade unions; and
- For lack of financial resources to appoint whole time office-bearers.

These political leaders are inevitably concerned with "maximizing their individual standing as political leaders rather than with, maximizing the welfare of their members". Further, in bigger unions, direct contact with the rank and file membership and the top leaders is missing because of their hold on a number of trade unions in varied fields; they fail to pay adequate attention to any one union. Again, often these union leaders are not adequately aware of the actual needs and pressing problems of the members. They therefore cannot put forth the case of the union effectively.

Outside leadership of the unions leads to political unionism (each union having an allegiance to a different political party), which in turn, leads to multiplicity of unions, leading to intra-union rivalry, which cause low membership leading to unsound finances and in turn, lack of welfare and other constructive activities which may infuse strength into unions and to conduct collective bargaining effectively the unions depend on outside leadership, and the vicious circle thus goes on and on.

Over and again it has been realized that "a reorientation of policy is desirable by a switchover to working class leadership". The National Commmission on Labour gave a good deal of thought to the issue whether outside leadership should be retained. It felt that, "there should be no ban on non-employees holding positions in the executive body of the unions as that would be a very drastic step". The Commission also refers to the ILO convention (No. 87) concerning "freedom of association" and protection of the right to organize, and the workers' organization shall have the right to elect their representative in full freedom.

The commission's own estimate was that outsiders in the union's executive bodies would be about 10%, much less than the number legally permitted. It makes the following recommendations to deal with the problem of outside leadership:

- Ex-employees of an industrial enterprise should not be treated as outsiders;
- Intensification of worker's education;
- Penalties for victimization and similar unfair labour practices such as would discourage the growth of internal leadership;
- Intensification of efforts by trade union organizers to train workers in union organization.
- Limiting the proportion of outsiders in the union execute;
- Establishing a convention that no union office-bearer will concurrently hold an office in a political party.

Hence, leadership should be promoted from within the rank and file and given a more responsible role. Initiative should come from the workers themselves through the launching of a vigorous programme for Workers' Education. This will enable them to participate in the decision-making and managing the union affairs effectively.

Politicization of the unions

One of the biggest problems of the country's trade union movement faces is the influence of the political parties, *i.e.,* the most distressing feature is its political character. Harold Crouch has observed, "Even to the most casual observer of the Indian trade union scene, it must be clear that much of the behaviour of Indian unions, whether it be militant or passive behaviour can be explained in political terms.

Dr. Raman's observations are: "Trade union multiplicity in India is directly traceable to the domination and control of the trade union movement by rival political parties…. The clay of unionism is possibly an effervescent industrial

labourers, but the sculptors chiselling it into shape have certainly been members of political parties.

In a recent study, Dr. Pandey had reached the conclusion: "The unions are closely aligned with political parties, and political leaders continue to dominate the unions even now... The supreme consequence of political involvement of unions in India in general, formed to safeguard and promote the social and economic interests of workers, have tended to become tools of party politics".

It should be noted that decisions in the trade union fields are taken by the respective political parties to which the unions are attached and, therefore, with the changing political situation, the decisions also change. With the split in the political ideology, there develops factional split in the same trade union professing the same political ideology. The divisions and sub-divisions, thus made, have affected adversely the trade union movement. It has become fragmented and disjointed. Each section pulls itself in different directions; with the result that "instead of becoming a unity and mighty torrential river, the movement is sub-divided into numerous rivulets".

Dr. Raman has very aptly concluded that: "The use of political methods by trade unions may be to their advantage, but the union cause is endangered when unions allow themselves to become pawns in political fights. Political unionism has prevented the development of a movement or organization that could be termed the workers' own and turned the soil upside down to such a degree that it has become impossible for a genuine labour-inspired, labour-oriented, worker-led trade union movement to take root".

Financial weakness

The financial weakness of the union may be attributed to the small size of union and poor ability of its members to contribute. The other reasons are low subscriptions and irregular payments of subscriptions by the members.

Problems of recognition of trade unions

This is one of the basic issues in our industrial relation system because employers are under no obligation to give recognition to any union. In the initial stages, the attitudes of the employers towards the trade unions have been very hostile. The employers many a times have refused recognition to trade unions either on the basis that unions consist of only a minority of employees; or that two or more unions existed.

Recommendations of National Commission on Labour for Strengthening Trade Unions

The National Commission on Labour has made a large number of recommendations on different aspects of trade unions, as given below:

Enlargement of functions

The N.C.L. has stated that the "unions must pay greater attention to the basic needs of its members which are:

- to secure for workers fair wages;
- to safeguard security of tenure and improved conditions of service;
- to enlarge opportunities for promotion and training;
- to improve working and living conditions;
- to provide for educational, cultural and recreational facilities;
- to cooperate in and facilitate technological advance by broadening the understanding of workers on its underlying issues;
- to promote identity of interests of the workers with their industry;
- to offer responsible cooperation in improving levels of production and productivity, discipline, and high standard of quality; and generally;
- to promote individual and collective welfare".

In addition, "unions should also undertake social responsibilities such as;

- promotion of national integration,
- influencing the socio-economic policies of the community through active participation in the formulations of these policies, and
- instilling in their members a sense of responsibility towards industry and community".

The main objective should be to draw unions as closely as possible into the entire development process.

Leadership

Regarding leadership the N.C.L. has recommended that "(*i*) There should be not ban on non-employees holding the position in the executive of the unions; (*ii*) steps should be taken to promote international leadership and give it more responsible role (*iii*) internal leadership should be kept outside the pale of victimization; (*iv*) permissible limit of outsiders in the executive of the unions should be reduced to 25%; and (*v*) ex-employees should not be treated as outsiders".

Registration

The Commission has recommended that registration should be cancelled if: (*a*) its membership fell below the minimum prescribed for registration; (*b*) the union failed to submit its annual report; (*c*) it submitted defective returns and defects were not rectified within the prescribed time; and (*d*) an application for re-registration should not be entertained within six months of the date of cancellation of registration.

Improvement of financial condition

To improve the financial conditions of the unions, the Commission recommended for the increase of membership fees.

Verification of membership

The Industrial Relations Commission should decide the representative character of a union, either by examination of membership records or if it consider necessary by holding an election by secret ballot open to all employees.

Recognition of the unions

The N.C.L. has been of the opinion that, "it would be desirable to make recognition compulsory under a Central Law in all undertakings employing 100 or more workers or where the capital invested in above a stipulated size. A trade union seeking recognition as a bargaining agent from an individual employer should have a membership of at least 30 per cent of workers in that establishment. The minimum membership should be 25 per cent, if recognition is sought for an industry in a local area".

Trade Unionism in the International Context

To be understood in the international context, trade unionism must be examined as part of a wider concept—the labour movement as a whole. That movement consists of several more or less intimately relative related organization such as labour parties, workers' mutual insurance organizations, producers' or consumers' cooperatives, and workers' education and sports association. All have the common objective of improving the material, cultural, and social status of their members.

What distinguish one organization from another is the particular aspects of that broad objective it is endeavouring to pursue, and the particular method it employs. The relationship among the various parts of the labour movement varies from country to country and from period to period. Not all countries have produced the entire gamut of organization referred to above; in some countries the term "labour movement" is virtually synonymous with "trade unionism".

Origins and background of the trade union movement

Early forms of labour organizations

Union oriented, mainly in Great Britain and the U.S.A in the late 18th and early 19th centuries, as, associations of workers using the same skill. There is no connection between trade unions and medieval craft guilds, for the latter were composed of master craftsmen who owned capital and often employed several workers. The early unions were formed a partly as social clubs but soon became increasingly concerned with improving wages and working conditions, primarily by the device of collective bargaining. Progressing from trade to trade within the same city or area, the clubs formed local associations which, because they carried on their main activities on a purely local level, were almost self-sufficient. With industrial development, however, local associations sooner or later followed

the expansion of production beyond the local market and developed into national unions of the same trade. These in turn formed national union federations.

Factors favouring unionism

The unions of the early 19th century were almost exclusively based upon a particular craft. But as mass production industries – which required large numbers of rapidly trained, semiskilled workers – developed, a trend toward large-scale union organization grew, and toward the end of the 19th century Great Britain was including unskilled workers. Unions that recruited members from such groups – whose ranks were expanding rapidly as a result of new technologies – emerged either as industrial unions or as general unions. Industrial unions attempted to organize all works employed in producing a given product or service, sometimes including even the general office or white-collar workers. General unions included skilled workers and labourers of all grades from different industries, even though they usually started from a base in one particular industry. But changing technologies, union mergers, and ideological factors led to the development of various kinds of unions that would not fit easily into any of the above categories.

Obstacles to union organization

In most Western countries, labour movements arose out of the protest of workers and intellectuals against social and political systems based upon discrimination according to ancestry, social status, income and property. Such a system offered few avenues for individual or collective advancement. Discrimination in political franchise (restriction on or outright denials of the vote) and a lack of educational opportunities, anti-union legislation, and the whole spirit of a society founded upon acknowledged class distinction were the main sources of the social protest at the root of modern labour movements.

International Trade Union Organization

The large trade union movements of various countries for many years have maintained loose alliances by joining international organizations of labour; federations of unions, rather than individual unions, usually hold membership. In 1901, the International Federation of Trade Unions was established, chiefly under the guidance of German unions. It proved to be ineffective and disappeared during World War I. In 1919 it was revived at Amsterdam, but immediately came into collision with the Red International of Labour Unions, established by the new government of the Soviet Union. The Communist organization had a brief period of expansion but soon dwindled away and had disappeared before 1939.

World Federation of Trade Unions (WFTU)

Origin

The WFTU was founded in 1945 on a worldwide basis, representing trade union organizations in more than 50 Communist and Non-Communist countries. From the outset, the American Federation of Labour declined to participate. In January 1949, with the WFTU under Communist control, British, USA and Netherlands trade union organizations withdrew and went on to found the ICFTU; by June 1951 all Non-Communist trade unions and the Yogoslav Federation had withdrawn.

By the 1990s, after the collapse of the European Communist regimes, membership became uncertain; unions broke their links with the Communist parties and most were later accepted into the ICFTU. Most of the national trade union centers in Africa and Latin America moved to the ICFTU after 1989, and the French Confederation Generale du Travail have proposed withdrawal to its members.

At the Nov. 1994 Congress in Damascus, most WFTU delegates come from the developing countries (Cuba, India, South Korea, Vietnam).

In a move towards decentralization, regional offices have been set up in New Delhi (India), Havana (Cuba), Dakar (Senegal), Damascus (Syria) and Moscow (Russia).

World Confederation of Labour (WCL)

Founded in 1920 as the International Federation of Christian Trade Unions, it went out of existence in 1940 as a large proportion of its 3.4 million members were in Italy and Germany, where affiliated unions were suppressed by the Fascist and Nazi regimes. Reconstituted in 1945 and declining to merge with the WFTU or ICFTU, its policy was based on the papal encyclicals Return novarum (1891) and Quadragesimo anno (1931), and in 1968 it became the WCL and dropped its openly confessional approach.

Today, it has Protestant, Buddhist and Muslim member confederations, as well as a mainly Roman Catholic membership. In its concern to defend trade union freedoms and assist trade union development, the WCL differs little in policy from the ICFTU above. A membership of 11 million in about 90 countries is claimed. The biggest group is the Confederation of Christian Trade Unions (CSC) of Belgium (1.2 million).

Organization

The WCL is organized on a federative basis which leaves wide discretion to its autonomous constituent unions. Its governing body is the Congress, which meets every 4 years. The Congress appoints (or re-appoints) the Secretary-General at each 4-yearly meeting. The General Council which meets at least once a year, is composed of the members of the Confederal Board (at least 22 members, elected by the Congress) and representatives of national confederations, international trade federations, and trade union organizations where there is not confederation affiliated to the WCL. The Confederal Board is responsible for the general leadership of the WCL, in accordance with the decisions and directive of the Council and Congress. Its headquarters is at Belgium. There are regional organization in Latin America (Caracas), Africa (Banjul, Gambia) and Asia (Manila) and a liaison centre in Montreal.

A much smaller international organization, the International Federation of Christian Trade Unions (IFCTU), now called the WCL (World Confederation of Labour), is made up largely of Catholic labour unions in France, Italy and Latin America. The ICFT, at its founding congress in 1949, invited the affiliates of the IFCTU to join, but the invitation was rejected. On the international scene, the WCL has been a comparatively ineffective organization. Its influence limited to a few countries in Europe and Latin America.

International Confederation of Free Trade Unions (ICFTU)

Origin

The founding congress of the ICFTU was held in London in December 1949 following the withdrawal of some Western trade unions from the World Federation of Trade Unions (WFTU), which had come under Communist Control. The constitution, as amended, provides for cooperation with the UN and the ILO, and for regional organization to promote free trade unionism, especially in developing countries. The ICFTU represents some 124m. Workers across 196 affiliated organizations in 136 countries.

Aims

The ICFTU aims to promote the interests of the working people and to secure recognition of worker's organization as free bargaining agents; to reduce the gap between rich and poor; and to defend fundamental human and trade union rights. In 1996, it campaigned for the adoption by the WTO of a social clause, with legally binding minimum labour standards.

Organization

The Congress meets every 4 years. It elects the executive Board of 50 members nominated on an area basis for a 4-years period; 5 seats are reserved for women nominated by the Women's Committee; and the Board meets at least once a year, Various Committees cover economic and social policy, violation of trade union and other human rights, trade union cooperation projects and also the administration of the International Solidarity Fund. There are joint ICFTU-International Trade Secretariat Committees for coordinating activities.

The ICFTU has its headquarters at Belgium; branch offices in Geneva and New York, and regional organizations in America (Caracas), Asia (Singapore) and Africa (Nairobi).

Purposes of ICFTU

Striving for world peace, the spreading of democratic institutions, increasing the standard of living for workers everywhere, a worldwide strengthening of free trade unions, and support to colonial people in their struggle for freedom. The ICFTU consistently opposed Fascist as well as Communist dictatorships, and implemented that policy by giving such aid as was possible to free labour in Spain and certain Latin American countries. It also furnished direct financial assistance to workers in Hungary and Tibet and campaigned against racialist policies in South Africa.

Failures and successes of the ICFTU

Lack of homogeneity among affiliates hindered the activity of the ICFTU in many fields, chiefly because of difference among its affiliates in the approach to unions in Communist-controlled countries. It found its work to be most effective in the area of international education. By 1960 it has created an international Solidarity Fund of $2,000,000 to aid workers who became victims of oppression and to promote democratic trade unionism in economically under-developed countries. Problems of union organization were discussed at ICFTU seminars in various parts of the world, with experienced labour leaders and labour spokesmen from the less industrialized countries participating.

To facilitate the functioning of its widespread activities, the ICFTU established headquarters in Brussels, Belgium, with regional or sub-regional offices in many other countries. Form one or more of those centers it conducted numerous educational conferences, maintained a residential trade union training college in Calcutta, India and assisted in founding an African Labour College in Kampala, Uganda. It provided assistance to inexperienced works in areas in the first stages of industrialization and sent organizers to Lebanon, Okinawa, Cyprus, Cameroon, India, Indonesia, Nigeria and elsewhere.

It has been the consistent policy of the ICFTU to cooperate with the United Nations Educational, Scientific, and Cultural Organization and with the International Labour Office in Geneva. It is wholly financed by contributions from its affiliates.

Union rivalries

In regard to union rivalries, the Commission was of the opinion that its recommendation regarding recognition of unions, building up of internal leadership, shift to collective bargaining and institution of an independent authority for union recognition would reduce them. Intra-union rivalries should be left to the central organization concerned to settle and if it is unable to resolve the dispute the Labour Court should be set up at the request of either group or on a motion by the government.

Inter-union rivalry

Another vexing problem is that of intra-union rivalry. Trade rivalry is acute and pervades the entire industrial scene in India. Practically in every important industry, there exists parallel and competing unions, e.g., on the Indian Railways, there are two parallel Federations, the Indian Railway Men's Federation and Indian National Federation of Railway-men.

The multiplicity of unions emerging from political affiliations and led by external political leaders brought to fore the politics of many and the dynamics associated with it. Unions became competitive, and the survival of the fittest led to inter-union conflicts and mutual accusations being traded freely. This became advantageous for the management, which followed the policy of "divide and rule". The predominance of the inter-union rivalry has entered pushed them to the periphery in the current global economic environment.

Intra-union rivalry

Indian trade unionism has also demonstrated the intra-union rivalry coming to the forefront and hampering production and industrial relations. The National Commission on Labour remarked that while healthy rivalry and opposition are necessary within the democratic structure of any trade union, it can have pernicious effects when motivated by personal considerations. The NCL recommended that intra-union rivalries should best be left to the central workers' organizations concerned to settle disputes, and that labour courts should step in central organization was unable to resolve the dispute.

MULTIPLE CHOICE QUESTIONS

1. Contract stipulation that the union agrees not to strike during the duration of the contract is
   A. Arbitration
   B. Adjudication
   C. No-strike clause
   D. All the above

2. Removes the authority of the bargaining representative to enter into and enforce a union security clause is
   A. Authorized
   B. De-authorization
   C. Both A and B
   D. None of the above

3. A voting process whereby a union is removed as the representative of a group of employees is
   A. Election
   B. Decertification
   C. Certification
   D. None of the above

4. A common-law tort; defined as injuring someone's reputation either through verbal (slander) or written (libel) statements are
   A. Offensive
   B. Defamation
   C. Both A and B
   D. None of the above

5. All employees eligible to select a single union to represent and bargain collectively for them is
   A. Trade union
   B. Bargaining unit
   C. Craft union
   D. Guild

6. The term means that a union's conduct may not be arbitrary, discriminatory, or in bad faith is
   A. Standard justice
   B. Union leader
   C. Fair representation
   D. None of the above

7. An unfair labour practice occurring when a union requires an employer to pay an employee for services he or she did not perform OR When unions try to require the employment of more workers than is necessary is
   A. Featherbedding
   B. Unionism
   C. Disciplinary action
   D. None of the above

8. A group of autonomous national and international unions are
   A. ILO
   B. Federation
   C. International associations
   D. None of the above

9. Agreement that union members were not required handling goods made by non-union labour or a struck plant; illegal except for provisions in the construction and clothing industries is
   A. Strike
   B. Work stoppage
   C. Hot cargo clauses
   D. All the above

10. A work stoppage occurs when employees cease to perform their jobs as a means of showing their support for a specific cause or as a way of voicing a grievance is meant as
    A. Strike   B. Work stoppage
    C. Hot cargo clauses D. All the above

11. _____ is a disciplinary action, is intended to provide the employee with an opportunity to correct conduct or performance issues before any action is made to change the employee's job duties or pay.
    A. Letter   B. Notice
    C. Greetings   D. Written warning

12. A full-time union official employed by the union to operate the union office and assist union members is
    A. Business agent B. Broker
    C. Middle men   D. All the above

13. A form of union security in which the company can hire only union members. This was outlawed in 1947 but still exists in some industries (such as printing) is
    A. Closed shop   B. Open shop
    C. Union shop   D. None of the above

14. A form of union security in which the company can fire nonunion people, but they must join the union after a prescribed period of time and pay dues is termed as
    A. Closed shop   B. Open shop
    C. Union shop   D. None of the above

15. A form of union security in which employees that do not belong to the union must still pay union dues on the assumption that union efforts benefit all workers is
    A. Closed shop
    B. Open shop
    C. Union shop
    D. Agency shop

16. Perhaps the least attractive type of union security from the union's point of view, the workers decide whether or not to join the union; and those who join must pay dues is
    A. Closed shop
    B. Open shop
    C. Union shop
    D. None of the above

17. _____ to union organizing tactics by which workers who are in fact employed full-time by a union as undercover organizers are hired by unwitting employers.
    A. Union meeting
    B. Union coordination
    C. Union salting
    D. None of the above

18. In order to petition for a union election, the union must show that at least 30% of employees may be interested in being unionized is by
    A. Unauthorized cards
    B. Authorization cards
    C. Unionized
    D. None of the above

19. The union will be authorized to represent the group of employees by
    A. Bargaining unit
    B. Negotiating
    C. Collective bargaining
    D. None of the above

20. The process through which representatives of management and the union meet to negotiate a labour agreement is by
    A. Negotiating
    B. Collective bargaining
    C. Management function
    D. None of the above

21. A term that means both parties are communicating and negotiating and those proposals are being matched with counterproposals with both parties making every reasonable effort to arrive at agreements. It does not mean that either party is compelled to agree to a proposal. The process is
A. Negotiating
B. Collective bargaining
C. Good faith bargaining
D. None of the above

22. Items in collective bargaining over which bargaining is neither illegal nor mandatory, neither party can be compelled against its wishes to negotiate over those items is
A. Negotiating
B. Collective bargaining
C. Voluntary bargaining items
D. None of the above

23. Items in collective bargaining that are forbidden by law, for example, the clause agreeing to hire "union members exclusively" would be illegal in a right-to-work state refer
A. Negotiating
B. Collective bargaining
C. Illegal bargaining items
D. None of the above

24. Items in collective bargaining that a party must bargain over if they are introduced by the other party refers
A. Mandatory bargaining
B. Negotiating
C. Collective bargaining
D. None of the above

25. The involvement and empowerment of employees in decision-making within the organization by such methods as joint labour management committees, work teams, quality circles, employee task forces are termed as
A. Industrial Psychology
B. Individual Psychology
C. Industrial democracy
D. Nation democracy

26. Applied psychology concerned with the study of human behaviour in the workplace and how efficiently to manage an industrial labour force and problems encountered by employees is termed as
A. Physiology
B. Psychology
C. Industrial Psychology
D. Individual Psychology

27. Programs designed to get employees who have been injured on the job back into the workforce and off workers' compensation is
A. Rehabilitation centre
B. Industrial union
C. Industrial rehabilitation
D. Labour community

28. A union that includes many persons working in the same industry or company, regardless of jobs held is
A. Industrial relation
B. Industrial union
C. Trade union
D. International labour organization

29. A common-law tort implying that a contract need not be in writing to be enforceable, an express oral contract can be created when an employer and an employee exchange promises related to employment is
A. Document
B. Report
C. Record contact
D. Express oral contact

30. Organizationally controlled incentives, such as pay, benefits, incentives, achievement awards, etc., used to reinforce motivation and increase performance is
A. Intrinsic motivator
B. Extrinsic motivator
C. Peer group motivator
D. All the above

31. Work-related rewards that have a measurable monetary value, unlike intrinsic rewards, such as praise or satisfaction in a job well done referred as
A. Extrinsic reward   B. Intrinsic reward
C. Neither A nor B   D. All the above

32. Entrepreneurship: The act of forming a new business.
A. Owner   B. Proprietor
C. Entrepreneurship   D. All the above

33. The process of studying the environment of the organization to pinpoint opportunities and threats refers
A. Environment scanning
B. SWOT analysis
C. Strategic approach
D. All the above

34. A policy statement that equal consideration for a job is applicable to all individuals and that the employer does not discriminate based on race, colour, religion, age, marital status, national origin, disability or sex. The concept that individuals should have equal treatment in all employment related actions is termed as
A. Demographic data
B. Employability opportunity
C. Equal employment opportunity (EEO)
D. All the above

35. The degree to which an interview, test, or other selection device measures the knowledge, skills, abilities, or other qualifications that are part of the job is
A. Behavioural aspect B. Learning aspect
C. Contingent factor   D. Content validity

36. _____ refers to an individual employed in a job that does not have an explicit contract for long-term employment (i.e., independent contractor or temporary employee).
A. Permanent worker B. Contingent worker
C. Contractual worker D. All the above

37. Rights based on a specific contractual agreement between employer and employee is
A. Contractual right   B. Individual right
C. Legal measures   D. All the above

38. Tendency to rate people relative to other people rather than to performance standards are
A. Mistake   B. Poor performance
C. Good performance D. Contrast error

39. Pension plan in which the money for pension benefits is paid by both employees and employers are
A. Long term plan
B. Short term plan
C. Contributory plan
D. None of the above

40. Employee's payment of a portion of the cost of both insurance premiums and medical care is
A. Co-payment   B. Fringes
C. Benefits   D. None of the above

41. The skills, knowledge and abilities which employees must possess in order to successfully perform job functions that are essential to business operations are
A. Ability   B. Skill
C. Core competencies D. None of the above

42. The tasks or functions within an organization considered essential to the organization's business operations are
A. Co-workers activity
B. Core workers activity
C. Employees activity
D. Employer objective

43. Employees who are considered to be vital to the organization's successful business operations is
A. Co-workers   B. Core workers
C. Employees   D. Employer

44. The beliefs, values and practices adopted by an organization that directly influence employee conduct and behaviour are
A. Corporate governance
B. Corporate values
C. Corporate image
D. Corporate culture

45. The way in which an organization is viewed by clients, employees, vendors or the general public is
A. Corporate governance
B. Corporate values
C. Corporate image
D. All the above

46. The prescribed standards, behaviours, principles or concepts that an organization regards as highly important are
    A. Corporate governance
    B. Corporate values
    C. Corporate image
    D. All the above

47. An index number giving the relationship between a predictor and a criterion variable is
    A. Correlation
    B. Coefficient
    C. Correlation coefficient
    D. None of the above

48. Process by which union members vote to accept the terms of a negotiated labour agreement is
    A. Recruiting process
    B. Reasonable accommodation
    C. Ratification
    D. None of the above

49. A modification or adjustment to a job or work environment that enables a qualified individual with a disability to have equal employment opportunity is
    A. Recruiting process
    B. Reasonable accommodation
    C. Job specialization
    D. None of the above

50. CITU full form is
    A. Centre for Indian Trade Union
    B. Centre for Indo Tibet Union
    C. Central Indian Trade Union
    D. None of the above

51. INTUC is
    A. Indian National Trade Union Congress
    B. Indian National Trade Union Centre
    C. Indian National Trade Union Committee
    D. None of the above

52. AITUC is
    A. All India Trade Union Committee
    B. All India Trade Union Congress
    C. All Indian Trade Union Company
    D. None of the above

53. Human Relation Approach to Industrial Relation is based on

A. Freedom of speech, expression
B. Freedom of capital
C. Existence of labour
D. None of the above

54. A formal association of workers that promotes the interests of its members through collective action is
    A. Grid   B. Society
    C. Union   D. Craft person

55. Card signed by an employee to designate a union as his or her collective bargaining agent is
    A. Employment Identity card
    B. Union authorization card
    C. Union card
    D. Red card

56. Contract provisions to aid the union in obtaining and retaining members is
    A. Labour welfare
    B. Welfare opportunities
    C. Union security provisions
    D. None of the above

57. A form of union security that requires employees to join the union, usually 30 to 60 days after being hired or after a compulsory unionism contract is executed, and to maintain their membership as a condition of employment is
    A. Union office   B. Union procedures
    C. Union shop   D. None of the above

58. An employee of a firm or organization who is elected to serve as the first-line representative of unionized worker is
    A. Union leader   B. Union member
    C. Union steward   D. None of the above

59. The total labour cost per unit of output, which is the average cost of workers divided by their average level of output is
    A. Unit labour cost   B. Capital cost
    C. Labour investment   D. None of the above

60. A structure in which each worker reports to one boss, who in turn reports to one boss is
    A. Unit of command   B. Span of control
    C. Both A and B   D. None of the above

61. The practice of hiring retired former employees whose skills or qualifications are in need is
A. Earlier employability
B. Unretirement
C. Employee referrals
D. None of the above

62. Incidents that result from unsafe behaviour on the part of the employee, such as operating equipment at high speeds is
A. Accident zone   B. Unsafe acts
C. Misbehaviour   D. None of the above

63. Mechanical or physical hazards that may lead to injury, such as defective equipment or improper lighting is
A. Unsafe conditions   B. Accident zone
C. Caution   D. None of the above

64. An indication of employee dissatisfaction that has not been submitted in writing is
A. Report writing
B. First incident reporting
C. Complaint
D. All the above

65. Disagreement between individuals or groups within the organization stemming from the needs to share scare resources or engaged in interdependent work activities, or from differing statuses, goals, or cultures are termed as
A. Functional conflict
B. Individual conflict
C. Role conflict
D. Organizational conflicts

66. Any conflict that results in decreased efficiency and greater factionalism within an organization is
A. Functional conflict
B. Individual conflict
C. Role conflict
D. Dysfunctional conflict

67. The pertaining relations between the management and the workers or between the representatives of employees and the representatives of employees is said as
A. Industrial relations
B. Labour relation

C. Functional organization
D. All the above

68. The assumption that an organization is composed of a group of people under a single/unified loyalty structure, it is therefore, the prerogative of the management to make decisions regarding how an enterprise is to be run and how the employees are to be dealt with is
A. Unitary perspective
B. Pluralistic perspective
C. Both A and B
D. None of the above

69. The assumption that is based on the organization composed of individuals who coalesce into a variety of distinct sectional groups, each with its own interests objectives, and leadership is
A. Unitary perspective
B. Pluralistic perspective
C. Both A and B
D. None of the above

70. The notion that the production system is privately owned and is motivated by profit, where control over production is exercised by managers who are agents of the owners is
A. Radical perspective
B. Marxian perspective
C. Both A and B
D. None of the above

71. Match the following:
(a) Sarvodaya Theory: (i) Mahatma Gandhi's approach
(b) Protest/General Theory: (ii) Kerr, Dunlop and Myre
(c) Theory of Man vs. Machine: (iii) Tannenbaum's
(d) Functional Classification of Unionism: (iv) Robert Hoxies

	(a)	(b)	(c)	(d)
A.	(i)	(ii)	(iv)	(iii)
B.	(iii)	(ii)	(i)	(iv)
C.	(i)	(ii)	(iii)	(iv)
D.	(ii)	(iii)	(iv)	(i)

72. Sequence the labour organization in order when it got organized year wise.
    (a) All-India Trade Union Congress (AITUC): 1920
    (b) Indian National Trade Union Congress (INTUC):1937
    (c) Hind Mazdoor Sangha (HMS) : 1948
    (d) United Trade Union Congress (UTUC): 1949
    A. (a), (b), (c), (d)   B. (d), (c), (b), (a)
    C. (c), (b), (a), (d)   D. (b), (a), (c), (d)

73. Multiplicity of unions lead to
    A. Intra-union rivalries
    B. Inter-union rivalries
    C. Both A and B
    D. None of the above

74. The small size of unions creates problems such as
    A. Lack of funds to help its members.
    B. Lack of ability among the leaders and members.
    C. Low bargaining power.
    D. All the above

75. In some countries the term "labour movement" is virtually synonymous with "trade unionism".
    A. True   B. False
    C. Myth   D. None of the above

ANSWERS

1	2	3	4	5	6	7	8	9	10
C	B	B	C	B	C	A	B	C	B

11	12	13	14	15	16	17	18	19	20
D	A	A	C	D	B	C	B	A	B

21	22	23	24	25	26	27	28	29	30
C	C	C	A	C	C	C	B	D	B

31	32	33	34	35	36	37	38	39	40
A	D	D	C	D	B	A	D	C	A

41	42	43	44	45	46	47	48	49	50
C	B	B	D	C	B	C	C	B	A

51	52	53	54	55	56	57	58	59	60
A	B	A	C	B	C	C	C	A	C

61	62	63	64	65	66	67	68	69	70
B	B	A	C	D	D	A	B	B	C

71	72	73	74	75
C	A	B	D	A

 ❖—❖—❖

6

Labour Legislation and Administration

LABOUR LEGISLATION: OBJECTIVES, PRINCIPLES, CLASSIFICATION

Labour is one of the basic resources for any country and the industries located there over. Labour has an important bearing on the performance and goals of the organization.

This phenomenon of a new complex industrial set-up is directly attributable to the emergence of "Industrial Revolution". The pre-industrial revolution period was characterized by a simple process of manufacture, small scale investment, local markets and small number of persons employed.

It is considered to be a venture based on purposeful cooperation between management and labour in the process of production and maximum social good is regarded as its ultimate end and both management and employees contribute in their own way towards its success. There are mainly two set of factors that determine the state of industrial relations – whether good or poor in any country. The first set of factors, described as 'institutional factors' include type of labour legislation, policy of state relating to labour and industry, extent and stage of development of trade unions and employers' organizations and the type of social institutions. The other set of factors, described as 'economic factors' include the nature of economic organization capitalist, socialist technology, the sources of demand and supply in the labour market, the nature and composition of labour force etc.

Distinction between Human Relations and Industrial Relations

The term 'human relations' lays stress upon the processes of inter-personal relationships among individuals as well as the behaviour of individuals as members of groups. The term 'industrial relations' is used widely in industrial organizations and refers to the relations between the employers and workers in an organization, at any specified time.

Thus, while problem of human relations are personal in character and are related to the behaviour of individuals where moral and social element predominate, the term 'industrial relations' is comprehensive covering human relations and the relations between the employers and workers in an organization as well as matters regulated by law or by specific collective agreement arrived at between trade unions and the management.

However, the concept of 'industrial relations' has undergone a considerable change since the objective of evolving sound and healthy industrial relations today is not only to find out ways and means to solve conflicts or resolve difference but also to secure unreserved cooperation and goodwill to divert their interest and energies toward constructive channel. The problems of industrial relations are therefore, essentially problems that may be solved effectively only by developing in conflicting social groups of an industrial undertaking, a sense of mutual confidence, dependence and respect and at the same time

(1799) Prof. Know. (HRM)–25

encouraging them to come closer to each other for removing misunderstanding if any, in a peaceful atmosphere and fostering industrial pursuits for mutual benefits.

Significance of Industrial Relations

Maintenance of harmonious industrial relations is on vital importance for the survival and growth of the industrials enterprise. Good industrial relations result in increased efficiency and hence prosperity, reduced turnover and other tangible benefits to the organization. The significance of industrial relations can be summarized as below:

1. *It establishes industrial democracy:* Industrial relations means settling employee's problems through collective bargaining, mutual cooperation and mutual agreement amongst the parties *i.e.,* management and employees' unions. This helps in establishing industrial democracy in the organization which motivates them to contribute their best to the growth and prosperity of the organization.

2. *It contributes to economic growth and development:* Good industrial relations lead to increased efficiency and hence higher productivity and income. This will result in economic development of the economy.

3. *It improves morale in work force:* Good industrial relations, built-in mutual cooperation and common agreed approach motivate one to contribute one's best, result in higher productivity and hence income, give more job satisfaction and help improve the morale of the workers.

4. *It ensures optimum use of scare resources:* Good and harmonious industrial relations create a sense of belongingness and group-cohesiveness among workers, and also a congenial environment resulting in less industrial unrest, grievances and disputes. This will ensure optimum use of resources, both human and materials, eliminating all types of wastage.

5. *It discourages unfair practices on the part of both management and unions:* Industrial relations involve setting up machinery to solve problems confronted by management and employees through mutual agreement to which both these parties are bound. This results in banning of the unfair practices being used by employers or trade unions.

6. *It prompts enactment of sound labour legislation:* Industrial relations necessitate passing of certain labour laws to protect and promote the welfare of labour and safeguard interests of all the parties against unfair means or practices.

7. *It facilitates change:* Good industrial relations help in improvement of cooperation, team work, performance and productivity and hence in taking full advantages of modern inventions, innovations and other scientific and technological advances. It helps the work force to adjust themselves to change easily and quickly.

Causes of Poor Industrial Relations

Perhaps the main cause or source of poor industrial relations resulting in inefficiency and labour unrest is mental laziness on the part of both management and labour. Management is not sufficiently concerned to ascertain the causes of inefficiency and unrest following the laissez-faire policy, until it is faced with strikes and more serious unrest. Even with regard to methods of work, management does not bother to devise the best method but leaves it mainly to the subordinates to work it out for themselves. Contempt on the part of the employers towards the workers is another major cause. However, the following are briefly the causes of poor industrial relations:

1. Mental inertia on the part of management and labour;

2. An intolerant attitude of contempt of contempt towards the workers on the part of management;

3. Inadequate fixation of wage or wage structure;

4. Unhealthy working conditions;

5. Indiscipline;

6. Lack of human relations skill on the part of supervisors and other managers;

7. Desire on the part of the workers for higher bonus or DA and the corresponding desire of the employers to give as little as possible;

8. Inappropriate introduction of automation without providing the right climate;

9. Unduly heavy workloads;

10. Inadequate welfare facilities;

11. Dispute on sharing the gains of productivity;

12. Unfair labour practices, like victimization and undue dismissal;

13. Retrenchment, dismissals and lockouts on the part of management and strikes on the part of the workers;

14. Inter-union rivalries; and

15. General economic and political environment, such as rising prices, strikes by others, and general indiscipline having their effect on the employees' attitudes.

Objectives of Industrial Relations

1. To bring better understanding and cooperation between employers and workers.

2. To establish a proper channel of communication between workers and management.

3. To ensure constructive contribution of trade unions.

4. To avoid industrial conflicts and to maintain harmonious relations.

5. To safeguard the interest of workers and the management.

6. To work in the direction of establishing and maintaining industrial democracy.

7. To ensure workers' participation in decision-making.

8. To increase the morale and discipline of workers.

9. To ensure better working conditions, living conditions and reasonable wages.

10. To develop employees to adapt themselves for technological, social and economic changes.

11. To make positive contributions for the economic development of the country.

Scope

The scope of industrial relations includes all aspects of relationships such as bringing cordial and healthy labour management relations, creating industrial peace and developing industrial democracy.

The cordial and healthy labour management relations could be brought in:

● by safeguarding the interest of the workers;
● by fixing reasonable wages;
● by providing good working conditions;
● by providing other social security measures;
● by maintaining healthy trade unions;
● by collective bargaining

The industrial peace could be attained:

● by setting industrial disputes through mutual understanding and agreement;
● by evolving various legal measure and setting up various machineries such as Works Committee, Boards of Conciliation, Labour Courts etc.

The industrial democracy could be achieved:

● by allowing workers to take part in management; and
● by recognition of human.

In India, we have an excess of Laws which deals with issues concerning Labour administration, labour welfare, regulation of industrial relations between the management and the workers. For the effective and efficient management of labour in an industry or an organization it is necessary to have a complete knowledge of the Laws, bye laws, regulations and ordinances applicable to the industry in general and to the company or organization specifically.

The salient features of the Central Labour Acts in force in India are given here under: The Indian Factories Act of 1948 provides for the health, safety and welfare of the workers. The Shops and Commercial Establishment Act regulates the conditions of work and terms of employment of workers engaged in shops, commercial establishments, theatres, restaurants, etc. The Maternity Benefit Act provides for the grant of cash benefits to women workers for specified periods before and after confinements. The Employment of Children Act, 1938, prohibits the employment of young children below the age of 15 years in certain risky and unhealthy occupations. The payment of wages Act, 1936, regulates the timely payment of wages without any unauthorized deductions by the employers. The Minimum Wages Act, 1948, ensures the fixation and revision of minimum rates of wages in respect of certain scheduled industries involving hard labour. The Industrial Disputes Act, 1947, provides for the investigation, and settlement of industrial disputes by mediation, conciliation, adjudication and arbitration, there is scope for payment of compensation in cases of lay-off and retrenchment. The Industrial Employment (Standing Orders) Act, 1946, requires employers in Industrial establishments to define precisely the conditions of employment under them and make them known to their workmen.

These rules, once certified, are binging on the parties for a minimum period of six months. The Workmen's Compensation Act, 1923, provides for compensation to injured workmen of certain categories and in the case of fatal accidents to their dependants if the accidents arose out of and in the course of their employment. It also provides for payment of compensation in the case of certain occupational diseases. The Indian Trade Unions Act, 1926, recognizes the right of workers to organize into trade unions, and when registered, they have certain rights and obligations and function as autonomous bodies. The Employees' State Insurance Act, 1948, provides for sickness benefit, maternity benefit, disablement benefit and medical benefit. The Employees' Provident Fund Act, 1952, seeks to make a provision for the future of industrial worker after he retires or in case he is retrenched, or for his dependents in case of his early death.

The labour welfare work, thus, covers a wide range of activities and in its present form is widely recognized and is regarded as an integral part of the industrial system and management.

What is Labour Law?

Wikipedia, the internet encyclopedia defines labour law as "Labour Law is the body of laws, administrative rulings, and precedents which address the relationship between and among employers, employees, and labour organizations, often dealing with issues of public law". The terms Labour Laws and Employment Laws, are often interchanged in the usage. This has led to a big confusion as to their meanings. Labour Laws are different from employment laws which deal only with employment contracts and issues regarding employment and workplace discrimination and other private law issues.

Employment Laws cover broader area than labour laws in the sense that employment laws cover all the areas of employer/employee relationship except the negotiation process covered by labour law and collective bargaining.

Labour Laws harmonize many angles of the relationship between trade unions, employers and employees. In some countries (like Canada), employment laws related to unionized workplaces are different from those relating to particular individuals. In most countries however, no such distinction is made.

The final goal of labour law is to bring both the employer and the employee on the same level, thereby mitigating the differences between the two ever-warring groups.

Origins of Labour Laws

Labour laws emerged when the employers tried to restrict the powers of workers' organizations and keep labour costs low. The workers began demanding better conditions and the right to organize so as to improve their standard of living. Employer's costs increased due to workers demand to win higher wages or better working conditions. This led to a chaotic situation which required the intervention of Government. In order to put an end to the disputes between the ever-warring employer and employee, the Government enacted many labour laws.

In India the labour laws are so numerous, complex and ambiguous that they promote litigation rather than the resolution of problems relating to industrial relations. The labour movement has contributed a lot for the enactment of laws protecting labour rights in the 19th and 20th centuries. The history of labour legislation in India can be traced back to the history of British colonialism. The influences of British political economy were naturally dominant in sketching some of these early laws. In the beginning it was difficult to get enough regular Indian workers to run British establishments and hence laws for chartering workers became necessary. This was obviously labour legislation in order to protect the interests of British employers.

The British enacted the Factories Act with a really self-centered motive. It is well known that Indian textile goods offered serious competition to British textiles in the export market. In order to make India labour costlier, the Factories Act was first introduced in 1883 because of the pressure brought on the British parliament by the textile moguls of Manchester and Lancashire. Thus we received the first stipulation of eight hours of work, the abolition of child labour, and the restriction of women in night employment, and the introduction of overtime wages for work beyond eight hours. While the impact of this measure was clearly for the welfare of the labour force the real motivation was undoubtedly the protection their vested interests.

India provides for core labour standards of ILO for welfare of workers and to protect their interests. India has a number of labour laws addressing various issues such as resolution of industrial disputes, working conditions, labour compensation, insurance, child labour, equal remuneration etc. Labour is a subject in the concurrent list of the Indian Constitution and is therefore in the jurisdiction of both Central and State governments. Both Central and State governments have enacted laws on labour issues. Central laws grant powers to officers under Central government in some cases and to the officers of the State governments in some cases.

Classification of Various Labour Laws

There are over 45 legislations on labour from the Central Government and the number of legislations enacted by the State Governments is close to four times that of the Central Acts.

Labour Laws can be classified into the following eight categories:

(*i*) Laws related to Industrial Relations

(*ii*) Laws related to Wages

(*iii*) Laws related to Specific Industries

(*iv*) Laws related to Equality and Empowerment of Women

(*v*) Laws related to Deprived and Disadvantaged Sections of the Society

(*vi*) Laws related to Social Security

(*vii*) Laws related to Employment & Training

(*viii*) Others.

Laws Related to Industrial Relations

1. The Trade Unions Act, 1926
2. The Industrial Employment (Standing Orders) Act, 1946
   The Industrial Employment (Standing Orders) Rules, 1946
3. The Industrial Disputes Act, 1947.

Laws Related to Wages

1. The Payment of Wages Act, 1936
   The Payment of Wages Rules, 1937
2. The Minimum Wages Act, 1948
   The Minimum Wages (Central) Rules, 1950
3. The Working Journalist (Fixation of Rates of Wages) Act, 1958
   Working Journalist (Conditions of service) and Miscellaneous Provisions Rules, 1957
4. The Payment of Bonus Act, 1965
5. The Payment of Bonus Rules, 1975.

Laws Related to Specific Industries

1. The Factories Act, 1948
2. The Dock Workers (Regulation of Employment) Act, 1948
3. The Plantation Labour Act, 1951
4. The Mines Act, 1952
5. The Working Journalists and other Newspaper Employees' (Conditions of Service and Misc. Provisions) Act, 1955
   The Working Journalists and other Newspaper Employees' (Conditions of Service and Misc. Provisions) Rules, 1957

6. The Merchant Shipping Act, 1958
7. The Motor Transport Workers Act, 1961
8. The Beedi & Cigar Workers (Conditions of Employment) Act, 1966
9. The Contract Labour (Regulation & Abolition) Act, 1970
10. The Sales Promotion Employees (Conditions of Service) Act, 1976

    The Sales Promotion Employees (Conditions of Service) Rules, 1976
11. The Inter-State Migrant Workmen (Regulation of Employment and Conditions of Service) Act, 1979
12. The Shops and Establishments Act
13. The Cinema Workers and Cinema Theatre Workers (Regulation of Employment) Act, 1981

    The Cinema Workers and Cinema Theatre Workers (Regulation of Employment) Rules, 1984

    The Cine Workers' Welfare Fund Act, 1981.
14. The Dock Workers (Safety, Health & Welfare) Act, 1986
15. The Building & Other Construction Workers (Regulation of Employment & Conditions of Service) Act, 1996
16. The Dock Workers (Regulation of Employment) (inapplicability to Major Ports) Act, 1997
17. The Mica Mines Labour Welfare Fund Act, 1946
18. The Limestone & Dolomite Mines Labour Welfare Fund Act, 1972
19. The Beedi Workers Welfare Fund Act, 1976
20. The Beedi Workers Welfare Cess Act, 1976
21. The Iron Ore Mines, Manganese Ore Mines & Chrome Ore Mines Labour Welfare Fund Act, 1976
22. The Iron Ore Mines, Manganese Ore Mines & Chrome Ore Mines Labour Welfare Cess Act, 1976
23. The Cine Workers Welfare Fund Act, 1981
24. The Cine Workers Welfare Cess Act, 1981
25. The Employment of Manual Scavengers and Construction of Dry latrines Prohibition Act, 1993
26. The Coal Mines (Conservation and Development) Act, 1974.

Laws Related to Equality and Empowerment of Women

1. The Maternity Benefit Act, 1961
2. The Equal Remuneration Act, 1976

Laws Related to Deprived and Disadvantaged Sections of the Society

1. The Bonded Labour System (Abolition) Act, 1976
2. The Child Labour (Prohibition & Regulation) Act, 1986.

Laws Related to Social Security

1. The Workmen's Compensation Act, 1923
2. The Employees' State Insurance Act, 1948
3. The Employees' Provident Fund & Miscellaneous Provisions Act, 1952
4. The Payment of Gratuity Act, 1972.

Laws Related to Employment & Training

1. The Employment Exchanges (Compulsory Notification of Vacancies) Act, 1959

   The Employment Exchanges (Compulsory Notification of Vacancies) Rules, 1959
2. The Apprentices Act, 1961.

Others

1. The Fatal Accidents Act, 1855
2. The War Injuries Ordinance Act, 1943
3. The Weekly Holiday Act, 1942
4. The National and Festival Holidays Act
5. The War Injuries (Compensation Insurance) Act, 1943
6. The Personal Injuries (Emergency) Provisions Act, 1962
7. The Personal Injuries (Compensation Insurance) Act, 1963
8. The Labour Laws (Exemption from Furnishing Returns and Maintaining Register by Certain Establishments) Act, 1988
9. The Public Liability Insurance Act, 1991.

EVOLUTION OF LABOUR LEGISLATION IN INDIA

Labour Policy of India

Labour policy in India has been evolving in response to specific needs of the situation to suit requirements of planned economic development and social justice and has two-fold objectives, viz., maintaining industrial peace and promoting the welfare of labour.

Labour Policy Highlights

- Creative measures to attract public and private investment.
- Creating new jobs.
- New Social security schemes for workers in the unorganized sector.
- Social security cards for workers.
- Unified and beneficial management of funds of Welfare Boards.
- Reprioritization of allocation of funds to benefit vulnerable workers.
- Model employee-employer relationships.
- Long term settlements based on productivity.
- Vital industries and establishments declared as 'public utilities'.
- Special conciliation mechanism for projects with investments of ₹150 crores or more.
- Industrial Relations committees in more sectors.
- Labour Law reforms in tune with the times. Empowered body of experts to suggest required changes.
- Statutory amendments for expediting and streamlining the mechanism of Labour Judiciary.
- Amendments to Industrial Disputes Act in tune with the times.
- Efficient functioning of Labour Department.
- More labour sectors under Minimum Wages Act.
- Child labour act to be aggressively enforced.
- Modern medical facilities for workers.
- Rehabilitation packages for displaced workers.

- Restructuring in functioning of employment exchanges. Computerization and updating of data base.
- Revamping of curriculum and course content in industrial training.
- Joint cell of labour department and industries department to study changes in laws and rules.

IMPACT OF ILO

International Labour Organization (ILO)

The International Labour Organization (ILO) was set up in 1919 by the Versailles Peace Conference as an autonomous body associated with the League of Nations. The ILO was the only international organization that survived the Second World War even after the dissolution of its parent body. It became the first specialized agency of the United Nations in 1946 in accordance with an agreement entered into between the two organizations. India has been a member of the ILO since its inception. A unique feature of the ILO, as distinct from other international institutions, is its tripartite character.

The aims and objectives of ILO are set out in the preamble to its Constitution and in the Declaration of Philadelphia (1944) which was formally annexed to the Constitution in 1946. The preamble affirms that universal and lasting peace can be established only if it is based upon social justice, draws attention to the existence of conditions of labour involving injustice, hardship and privation of a large number of people, and declares that improvement of these conditions is urgently required through such means as the regulation of hours of work, prevention of unemployment, provision of an adequate living wage, protection of workers against sickness, disease, and injury arising out of employment, protection of children, young persons and women, protection of the interests of migrant workers, recognition of the principle of freedom of association, and organization of vocational and technical education. The Preamble also states that the failure of any nation to adopt human conditions of labour is an obstacle in the way of other nations desiring to improve labour conditions in their own countries.

The three main functions of the ILO are;

- to establish international labour standards;
- to collect and disseminate information on labour and industrial conditions; and
- to provide technical assistance for carrying out programmes of social and economic development.

From the very beginning, the ILO has been confronted with the tremendous task of promoting social justice by improving the work and conditions of life in all parts of the world.

The ILO consists of three principal organs, namely, the International Labour Conference, the Governing Body and the International Labour Office. The work of the Conference and the Governing Body is supplemented by that of Regional Conferences, Regional Advisory Committees, Industrial Committees, etc. The meeting of the General Conference, held normally every year, are attended by four delegates from each member State, of whom two are government delegates and one each representing respectively the employers and the work people of the State. The International Labour Conference is the supreme organ of the ILO and acts as the legislative wing of the Organization. The General Conference elect the Governing Body, adopt the Organization's biennial programme and budget, adopt international labour standards in the form of conventions and Recommendations and provide a forum for discussion of social and labour issues. The Governing Body is the executive wing of the Organization. It appoints the Director-General, draws up the agenda of each session of the Conference and examines the implementation by member countries of its Conventions and Recommendations. The International Labour Office, whose headquarters are located at Geneva, provides the secretariat for all conferences and other meetings and is responsible for the day-to-day implementation of the administrative and other decisions of the Conference, the Governing Body, etc. The Director-General is the chief executive of the International

Labour Office. An important aspect of its work relates to the provision of assistance to member States. It also serves as a clearing house of information on all labour matters.

In order to achieve its objective, the ILO has relied on its standard-setting function. The international labour standards take the form of Conventions and Recommendations. A Convention is a treaty which, when ratified, creates binding international obligations on the country concerned. On the other hand, a Recommendation creates no such obligations but is essentially a guide to national actions. The ILO adopted a series of Conventions and Recommendations covering hours of work, employment of women, children and your persons, weekly rest, holidays leave with wages, night work, industrial safety, health, hygiene, labour inspection, social security, labour-management, relations, freedom of association, wages and wage fixation, productivity, employment, etc. One of the fundamental obligations imposed on governments by the Constitutions of the ILO is that they must submit the instruments before the competent national or State or provincial authorities within a maximum period of 18 months of their adoption by the Conference for such actions as might be considered practicable. These dynamic instruments continue to be the principal means at the disposal of the ILO to strive for establishing a just, democratic and changing social order necessary for lasting peace. In fact, these instruments have been included in the category of "international labour legislation". These Conventions and Recommendations taken together are known as the "International Labour Code". Wilfred Jenks describes the International Labour Code as the corpus juris of social justice.

LABOUR LEGISLATION AND INDIAN CONSTITUTION

Labour and the Constitution

Constitutional Framework

The Constitution of India has guaranteed some Fundamental Rights to the citizens and has also laid down certain Directive Principles of State Policy for the achievement of a social order based on Justice, Liberty, Equality and Fraternity, The Constitution amply provides for the upliftment of labour by guaranteeing certain fundamental rights to all. Article 14 lays down that the State shall not deny to any person equality before the law or the equal protection of laws. There shall be equality of opportunity to all citizens in matters relating to employment or appointment or appointment to any office under the State. People have the right to form associations or unions. Traffic in human beings and forced labour and the employment of children in factories or mines or other hazardous work is prohibited. The Directive Principles, though not enforceable by any court, are nevertheless fundamental in the governance of the country, and it shall be the duty of the State to apply those principles in making laws from time to time.

Labour is in the Concurrent List on which both the Centre as well as the States have the power to make laws, Article 254 has been enacted to clarify the position. Normally, as laid down in clause(I), in case of any repugnancy between the Union and the State legislation, the legislation of the Union shall prevail. To this, there is one exception embodied under clause(II) of Art. 354, where, a law enacted by a State with respect to the matter enumerated in the Concurrent List, reserved for the consideration enumerated in the Concurrent List, reserved for the consideration of the President, has received his assent, such law shall prevail in the State, and provisions of that law repugnant to the provision of an earlier law made by the Parliament or any existing law with respect to that matter have priority over the Central legislation.

Articles 39, 41, 42 and 43 have a special relevance in the field of industrial legislation and adjudication. In fact, they are the sub-stratum of industrial jurisprudence.

Article 39 accentuates the basic philosophy of idealistic socialism which is enshrined in the Preamble of the Constitution and provides a motivation force to the Directive Principles by laying down that the State shall direct its policy towards equal pay for both men and women.

Article 41 lays down that the State shall, within the limits of its economic capacity and development, make effective provision for securing the right to work, to education and to public assistance in cases of unemployment, old age, sickness and disablement, and in other cases of undeserved want.

Social security is guaranteed in our Constitution under Arts. 39, 41 and 43. The Employees' State Insurance Act, 1948, is a pioneering piece of legislation in the field of social insurance. The benefits provided to the employees under the scheme are: (1) sickness benefit and extended sickness benefit; (2) maternity benefit; (3) disablement benefit; (4) dependants' benefit; (5) funeral benefit; and (6) medical benefit. All the benefits are provided in cash except the medical which is in kind.

The administration of the scheme is entrusted to an autonomous corporation called the Employees' State Insurance Corporation. The Employees' Provident Funds and Miscellaneous Provisions Act, 1952 and the Maternity Benefit Act, 1961, are also social security measures to help fulfill the objectives of Directive Principles of our Constitution.

- The Provident Fund Scheme aimed at providing substantial security and timely monetary assistance to industrial employees and their families. This scheme has provided protection to employees and their dependants in case of old age, disablement, early death of the bread-winner and in some other contingencies.

- A scheme of Family Pension-cum-Life Assurance was introduced with a view to providing long-term recurring financial benefit to the families in the event of the members' premature death while in service. The Employees' Provident Fund Organization is in charge of three important schemes, viz., the Employees' Provident Funds Scheme, the Employees' Family Pension Scheme and the Employees' Deposit-linked Insurance Scheme.

- The Maternity Benefit Scheme is primarily designed to provide full wages and security of employment. They enable a female employee to get maternity leave with full wages at least for 6 weeks before and 6 weeks after confinement.

- The object of the Payment of Gratuity Act, 1972 is to provide a scheme for the payment of gratuity to employees employed in factories, mines, oil fields, plantations, ports, railways, shops and establishments. All employees who have rendered a minimum number of years' continuous service in the above mentioned establishments are entitled to gratuity at the time of superannuation, retirement, resignation, death or if they leave their job due to accident, disablement. Under the Act, employers are required to pay gratuity at the rate of 15 days' wages for every completed year of service subject to a maximum of 20 months' wages.

Article 42 enjoins the State government to make provision for securing just and humane conditions of work and for maternity relief.

Substantial steps have been taken to fulfil the object of Article 42 of the Constitution. The Factories Acticle, 1948, provides for health, safety, welfare, employment of young persons and women, hours of work for adults and children, holidays, leave with wages etc. Labour welfare funds have been set up to provide welfare facilities to the workers employed in different mines such a coal, mica, iron ore and limestone. The Contract Labour (Regulation and Abolition) Act of 1970, a piece of social legislation, provides for the abolition of contract labour wherever possible and to regulate the conditions of contract labour in establishments or employments where the abolition of contract labour system is not considered feasible for the time being. The Act provides for licensing of contractors and registration of establishments by the employers employing contract labour.

Article 43 makes it obligatory for the State to secure by suitable legislation or economic organization or in any other manner to all workers, agricultural, industrial, or otherwise, work, a living wage, condition of work ensuring a decent standard of life and full enjoyment of leisure and social and cultural opportunities.

To ensure this, the Minimum Wages Act, 1948, was enacted. It provides for the fixation of minimum rates of wages by the Central or State governments within a specified period for workers employed in certain scheduled employments. These rates vary from State to State, area to area and from employment to employment. The minimum wage in any event must be paid irrespective of the capacity of the industry to pay. Living wage is the higher level of wage and of the industry to pay and naturally, it would include all amenities which a citizen living in a modern civilized society is entitled to. Fair wage is something above the minimum wage which may roughly be said to approximate to the need-based minimum wage. It is a mean between the living wage and the minimum wage.

Article 43A makes it obligatory on the State to take steps by suitable legislation or otherwise to secure the participation of workers in the management of undertakings and industrial establishments. As observed by the National Commission on Labour in its report, "in accepting the Directive Principles, the country is committed morally and ethically to see that the governance of the country is carried on with a view to implementing these Directive Principles in course of time".

Social Justice

In industrial adjudication, the concept of social justice has been given wide acceptance. Different views have been expressed by different authorities about the exact meaning and scope of this concept. According to the Supreme Court, it was a vague and indeterminate expression and that no definition could be laid down which would cover all situations. According to Justice Holmes, social justice is "an inarticulate major premise which is personal and individual to every court and every judge".

In a democratic society, administration of justice is based on the Rule of Law, which, as conceived by modern jurists, is dynamic and includes within its important social justice. It has been given a place of pride in our Constitution. The philosophy of social justice has now become an integral part of industrial jurisprudence. The philosophy of social justice has now become an integral part of industrial jurisprudence. The concept of social justice is a very important variable in the function of industrial relations. In a welfare State it is necessary to apply the general principles of social and economic justice to remove the imbalances in the political, economic and social life of the people.

Judicial System in India

The judicial system in India is quite well-established and independent. The Supreme Court of India in New Delhi is the highest Court of Appeal. Each State has a High Court along with subsidiary District Courts, which enforce the rule of law and ensure fundamental rights of citizens, guaranteed by the Constitution of India.

India has a three-tier court system with a typical Indian litigation starting from a District Court and reaching its logical conclusion in the Supreme Court of India. The High Courts along with the various State level forums, situated mostly in the State capitals, constitute the middle rung of this three-tier system. District level courts are the courts of first instance in dispute resolution except in cases where they are prevented from being so by virtue of lack of pecuniary jurisdiction. Cases involving violation of fundamental rights are filed in respective High Court or Supreme Court. A number of special courts and tribunals have been constituted in India to deal with specific disputes:

1. Tax Tribunals
2. Consumer Dispute Redressal Forums
3. Insurance Regulatory Authority of India
4. Industrial Tribunals
5. Debts Recovery Tribunals
6. Company Law Board
7. Motor Accidents Claims Tribunals
8. Labour Courts

Where to file?

Most of the labour disputes are referred to the Labour Courts/Industrial Tribunals through the Department of Labour under the respective State Government. The process for labour dispute starts with filing of a petition before Labour Conciliation Officer and in case no compromise is possible, the said officer sends a failure report to the Government. After consideration of the said report, the Government may send a reference to the Labour Court/Industrial Tribunal. In certain matters, the labour dispute can be directly filed in the court concerned.

Labour Courts

These courts are found in every district and they form the courts of original jurisdiction under which various labour laws and rules are enforced.

Appellate Labour Courts

These courts hear only the Appeals and revisions originating from the judgements and orders of the subordinate original labour courts and officers, under the provisions of various labour and related laws.

(a) When an industrial dispute has been referred to a Labour Court for adjudication, it is the duty of the Labour Court to
   (i) Hold proceedings expeditiously, and
   (ii) To submit its award to the appropriate Government soon after the conclusion of the proceedings.

(b) However, no deadline has been laid down with respect to the time within which the completion of proceedings has to be done. Nonetheless, it is expected that these Courts hold their proceedings without getting into the technicalities of a Civil Court.

(c) It has been held that the provisions of Article 137 of the Limitation Act do not apply to reference of disputes to the Labour Courts. These Courts can change the relief granted by refusing payment of back wages or directing payment of past wages too.

Court Fee

No Court fee is payable on the petitions filed before Labour Courts and Industrial Tribunals.

What matters fall within the jurisdiction of Industrial Tribunals?

1. Wages, including the period and mode of payment
2. Compensatory and other allowances

3. Hours of work and rest intervals
4. Leave with wages and holidays
5. Bonus, profit sharing, provident fund and gratuity
6. Shift working otherwise than in accordance with standing orders
7. Classification by grades
8. Rules of discipline
9. Retrenchment of workmen and closure of establishment.

What matters fall within the Jurisdiction of Labour Courts?

1. The propriety or legality of an order passed by an employer under the standing orders
2. The application and interpretation of standing order
3. Discharge or dismissal of workmen including reinstatement of, or grant of relief to, workmen wrongfully dismissed.
4. Withdrawal of any customary concession or privilege
5. Illegality or otherwise of a strike or lockout; and
6. All matters other than those being referred to Industrial Tribunals.

Stages of adjudication in labour or industrial disputes

The first is receiving a reference from the appropriate Government or filing of the labour dispute in the Labour Court. The next step is sending notice to the Management and after filing of the response by them, the matter is fixed for adjudication. The fourth step is recording the evidence of the parties and hearing the arguments. It is appropriate to mention here that advocates cannot appear in Labour Courts/Industrial Tribunals, unless permitted.

The final conclusion of the dispute

After hearing the parties, the Labour Court/Industrial Tribunal decides the dispute and the said final decision is called an Award. A copy of the award is to be published by the Labour Department as per rules. Copies of the same are also sent to the parties concerned.

Execution of Awards

In case the management does not comply with the terms of the award, the workman may pray for its execution by moving an application before the concerned Conciliation Officer.

Mediation in Labour Disputes

Mediation is an exercise of resolving a dispute by settlement with the help of a Mediator who is a neutral third party. The mediator may be:

(*a*) A judicial officer (retired or sitting judge)
(*b*) An Advocate
(*c*) An otherwise trained professional.

When a sitting judicial officer acts as a mediator in a case, his services are available free of cost and without any other charges on any of the parties.

Role of the Mediator

A mediator helps the parties in arriving at an amicable solution through negotiation. He facilitates the parties in reaching a mutually acceptable agreement. The parties need not agree to the terms of settlement, if they are not satisfied. Judges and arbitrators make decisions that are imposed on parties but a mediator helps the parties to evaluate the probable outcome of a dispute and then leads them to an acceptable settlement.

Process of Mediation

A mediator meets both the parties in a joint mediation session. The initial meeting provides for:

(*a*) An introduction to the participants and the mediation process.
(*b*) An opportunity to discuss issues affecting settlement that are important for the mediator to know.
(*c*) An opportunity to determine what information would be helpful for the mediator to have at or in advance of the mediation.

The joint session provides an opportunity for each participant, either directly or through counsel, to express their view of the case to the other participants and how they would like to approach settlement. The opening statements are intended to begin the settlement process, not to be adversarial or a restatement of positions.

Mediation Procedure

Formal procedures as in a Court or arbitration are completely absent in mediation proceedings. Both parties and their advocates participate freely without any set procedures or any rules of evidence. The absence of formality provides for an open discussion of the issues and allows a free interchange of ideas making it easier for the parties to determine their interest and fashion a solution accordingly. A mediator may, if necessary, meet the disputing parties individually and in private. Such meetings are completely confidential and are intended to understand the needs of each participant and what prevents him or her from reaching a settlement. In these private meetings, the mediator often assists parties to prioritize their interest and options for settlement and to assess the relative strengths and weaknesses of their positions. Once a settlement is reached, the mediator records it with the signatures of the parties.

Some important points in the Mediation Process

(a) All mediation proceedings are *confidential*. Documents generated for the mediation are also confidential and may not be introduced during a subsequent trial should the case not settle.

(b) Counsel and parties with *settlement authority* must attend mediation sessions. Certain exceptions may be granted for institutional parties or if a party is a unit of government.

(c) Unless the presiding judge indicates otherwise, referral of a case to mediation *does not stay* other proceedings in the case or alter applicable litigation deadlines. A judicial officer may, while referring a case to mediation, fix a time limit for completing the mediation process.

Advantages of Mediation Method for Dispute Resolution

(i) Procedures more satisfying results

(a) Helps settle all or part of the dispute much sooner than regular trial.

(b) Permits a mutually acceptable solution that a court would not have the power to order.

(c) Saves time and money.

(d) Preserve ongoing business or personal relationships.

(e) Increases satisfaction and thus results in a greater likelihood of a lasting resolution.

(ii) Allows more flexibility, control and participation

(a) Tailors the procedures used to seek a resolution.

(b) Broadens the interests taken into consideration.

(c) Fashions a business-driven or other creative solution that may not be available from the court.

(d) Protects confidentiality.

(e) Eliminates the risks of litigation.

(iii) Enables a better understanding of the case

(a) Provides an opportunity for clients to communicate their views directly and informally.

(b) Helps parties get to the core of the case and identify the disputed issues.

(c) Helps parties agree to exchange key information directly.

(iv) Improves case management

Narrows the issues in dispute and identifies areas of agreement and disagreement.

(v) Reduces hostility

(a) Improves the quality and tone of communication between parties.

(b) Decreases hostility between clients and lawyers.

(c) Reduces the risk that parties will give up on settlement efforts.

How to Initiate Mediation?

Where both the parties agree in a pending case to try to get their dispute settled through Mediation, the Court will record the same and send the file to Mediation Centre.

FACTORIES ACT 1948

Objectives

The main object of the Factories Act 1948 is **to ensure adequate safety measures and to promote the health and welfare of the workers** employed in factories. The Act also makes provisions regarding employment of women and young persons (including children and adolescents), annual leave with wages etc.

Applicability of the Act

1. Applicable to the whole of India including Jammu & Kashmir.
2. Covers all manufacturing processes and establishments falling within the definition of 'factory'.
3. Applicable to all factories using power and employing 10 or more workers, and if not using power, employing 20 or more workers on any day of the preceding 12 months.
4. Unless otherwise provided it is also applicable to factories belonging to Central/State Governments.

Scheme of the Act

1. The Act consists of 120 Sections and 3 Schedules.
2. Schedule 1 contains list of industries involving hazardous processes.
3. Schedule 2 is about permissible level of certain chemical substances in work environment.
4. Schedule 3 consists of list of notifiable diseases.

Important Definitions and Provisions of the Act

Adult: "Adult" means a person who has completed his eighteenth year of age. [Section 2(a)]

Adolescent: "Adolescent" means a person who has completed his fifteenth year of age but has not completed his eighteenth year. [Section 2(b)]

Calendar year: "Calendar Year" means the period of twelve months beginning with the first day of January in any year. [Section 2(bb)]

Child: "Child" means a person who has not completed his fifteenth year of age. [Section 2(c)]

Competent Person: "Competent Person" in relation to any provision of this Act, means a person or an institution recognized as such by the Chief Inspector for the purposes of carrying out tests, examinations and inspections required to be done in a factory under the provisions of this Act having regard to

(i) The qualifications and experience of the person and facilities available at his disposal; or

(ii) The qualifications and experience of the persons employed in such institution and facilities available therein.

With regard to the conduct of such tests, examinations and inspections and more than one person or institution can be recognized as a competent person in relation to a factory. [Section 2(ca)]

Hazardous Process: "Hazardous Process" means any process or activity in relation to an industry specified in the First Schedule where, unless special care is taken, raw material used therein or the intermediate or finished products, by-products, wastes or effluents thereof would

(i) Cause material impairment to the health of the persons engaged in or connected therewith, or

(ii) Result in the pollution of the general environment.

Provided that the State Government may, by notification in the official Gazette amend the First Schedule by way of addition, omission or variation of any industry specified in the said Schedule. [Section 2(cb)]

Young Person: "Young Person" means a person who is either a child or an adolescent. [Section 2(d)]

Day: "Day" means a period of twenty four hours beginning at mid-night. [Section 2(e)]

Week: "Week" means a period of seven days beginning at mid-night on Saturday night or such other night as may be approved in writing for a particular area by the Chief Inspector of Factories [Section 2(f)].

Power: "Power" means electrical energy or any other form of energy which is mechanically transmitted and is not generated by human or animal agency. [Section 2(g)]

Prime Mover: "Prime Mover" means any engine, motor or other appliance which generates or otherwise provides power. [Section 2(h)]

Transmission Machinery: "Transmission Machinery" means any shaft, wheel, drum, pulley, system of pulleys, coupling, clutch, driving belt or other appliance or device by which the motion of a prime-mover is transmitted to or received by any machinery or appliances. [Section 2(i)]

Machinery: The term machinery includes prime-movers, transmission machinery and all other appliances whereby power is generated, transformed, transmitted or applied. [Section 2(j)]

Factory: "Factory" includes any premises including the precincts thereof.

Essential elements of a factory:

(*i*) There must be premises.

(*ii*) There must be a manufacturing process which is being carried on or is so ordinarily carried on in any part of such a premises.

(*iii*) There must be ten or more workers who are/ were working in such a premises on any day of the last 12 months where the said manufacturing process is carried on with the aid of power. But where the manufacturing process is carried on without the aid of power, the required number of workers should be twenty or more.

The following are not covered by the definition of factory:

(*i*) Railway running sheds, (*ii*) mines, (*iii*) mobile units of armed forces, (*iv*) hotels, eating places or restaurants, (*v*) electronic data processing unit or a computer unit if no manufacturing process is being carried on in such premises or part thereof.

The word "premises" means open land or land with building or building alone.

The term 'precincts' is usually understood as a space enclosed by walls.

Manufacturing Process: Means any process for:

(*i*) Making, altering, repairing, ornamenting, finishing, packing, oiling, washing, cleaning, breaking up, demolishing, or otherwise, treating or adopting any article or substance with a view to its use, sale transport, delivery or disposal; or

(*ii*) Pumping oil, water or sewage or any other substance; or

(*iii*) Generating, transforming, transmitting power; or

(*iv*) Composing types for printing, printing by letter-press, lithography, photogravure or other similar process, or book-binding; or

(*v*) Constructing, reconstructing, repairing, refitting, finishing or breaking up ships or vessels; or

(*vi*) Preserving or storing any article in cold storage. [Section 2(k)]

What is not a manufacturing process?

No definite test can be prescribed for determining the question whether a particular process is a manufacturing process. Each case must be judged on its own facts regard being had to the nature of the process employed, the eventual result achieved and the prevailing business and commercial notions of the people. In deciding whether a particular business is a manufacturing process or not, regard must be had to the circumstances of each particular case.

Following process is not manufacturing processes:

(*i*) Exhibition of films process in cinema halls,

(*ii*) Industrial school or institute imparting training, producing cloths not for sale,

(*iii*) Receiving of news from various sources on a reel in a tele-printer of a newspaper office is not a manufacturing process in as much as news is not the article or substance,

(*iv*) Any preliminary packing of raw materials for delivering it to the factory,

(*v*) Finished goods and packing thereof.

Worker: "Worker" means a person employed

directly or by or through any agency (including a contractor) with or without the knowledge of the principal employer, whether for remuneration or not, in any manufacturing process, or in cleaning any part of the machinery or premises used for a manufacturing process, or in any other kind of work incidental to, or connected with the manufacturing process, or the subject of the manufacturing process but does not include any member of the armed forces of the union.

Occupier: Section 2(n) of the Act defines the term "occupier" as a person who has ultimate control over the affairs of the factory.

Provided that:

1. In the case of a firm or other association of individuals that any one of the individual, partners or members thereof shall be deemed to be the occupier.

2. In the case of a company that any one of the directors shall be deemed to be the occupier.

3. In case of a factory owned or controlled by the Central Government or any State Government or any local authority – the person or persons appointed to manage the affairs of the factory by the Central Government, the State Government or the local authority, as the case may; be shall be deemed to the occupier.

The important test, "whether a person is an occupier or not" is the possession or vesting in of the ultimate control of the factory. The control should be an ultimate one, though it may be remote. There was a lot of controversy regarding 'Occupier in case of a company, as the Section 2 (n) (ii), provides that any one of the directors of the company shall be deemed to be occupier of the factory.

General Duties of the Occupier

Section 7A provides that:

1. Every occupier shall ensure, so far as is reasonably practicable, the health, safety and welfare of all workers while they are at work in the factory.

2. The matters to which such duty extends shall include:

(a) The provision and maintenance of plant and systems of work in the factory that are safe and without risks to health;

(b) The arrangement in the factory for ensuring safety and absence of risks to health in connection with the use, handling, storage and transport of articles and substances;

(c) The provisions of such information, instruction, training and supervision as are necessary to ensure the health and safety of all workers at work;

(d) The maintenance of all places of work in the factory in a condition that is safe and without risks to health and provisions and maintenance of such means of access to, and egress from, such places as are safe and without such risks;

(e) The provision, maintenance or monitoring of such working environment in the factory for the workers that is safe, without risks to health and adequate as regards facilities and arrangements for their welfare at work.

3. Except in such cases as may be prescribed, every occupier shall prepare, and as often as may be appropriate revise, a written statement of his general policy with respect to the health and safety of the workers at work and arrangements for the time being in force for carrying out that policy, and shall bring the statement and any revision thereof to the notice of all the workers in such manner as may be prescribed.

Exemption of occupier or manager from liability in certain cases

Section 101 provides exemptions from liability of occupier or manager. It permits an occupier or manager of a factory who is charged with an offence punishable under the Act to bring into the court any other person whom he charges as actual offender and also prove to the satisfaction of the Court that

(a) He has used due diligence to enforce the execution of this Act, and

(b) That the offence in question was committed without his knowledge, consent or connivance by the said other person.

The other person shall be convicted of the offence and shall be liable to the like punishment as if he were the occupier or manager of the factory.

In such a case occupier or manager of the factory is discharged from liability.

The section is an exception "to principle of strict liability but benefit of this would be available only when the requirements of this section are fully complied with and the court is fully satisfied about the proof of facts contemplated in (a) and (b) above.

Measures to be Taken by Factories for Health, Safety Welfare of Workers

Such measures are provided under Chapters III, IV and V of the Act which are as follows:

A. Health

Chapter III of the Act deals with the following aspects.

(*i*) **Cleanliness:** Section 11 ensures the cleanliness in the factory. It must be seen that a factory is kept clean and it is free from effluvia arising from any drain, privy or other nuisance. The Act has laid down following provisions in this respect:

1. All the accumulated dirt and refuse on floors, staircases and passages in the factory shall be removed daily by sweeping or by any other effective method. Suitable arrangements should also be made for the disposal of such dirt or refuse.

2. Once in every week, the floor should be thoroughly cleaned by washing with disinfectant or by some other effective method [Section 11 (1) (b)].

3. Effective method of drainage shall be made and maintained for removing water to the extent possible, which may collect on the floor due to some manufacturing process.

4. To ensure that interior walls and roofs, etc. are kept clean, it is laid down that:

   (*a*) White wash or colour wash should be carried at least once in every period of 14 months;

   (*b*) Where surface has been painted or varnishing, repair or revarnished should be carried out once in every five years, if washable then once in every period of six months;

   (*c*) Where they are painted or varnished or where they have smooth impervious surface, it should be cleaned once in every period of 14 months by such method as may be prescribed.

5. All doors, windows and other framework which are of wooden or metallic nature shall be kept painted or varnished at least once in every period of five years.

6. The dates on which such processes are carried out shall be entered in the prescribed register.

If the State Government finds that a particular factory cannot comply with the above requirements due to its nature of manufacturing process, it may exempt the factory from the compliance of these provisions and suggest some alternative method for keeping the factory clean [Section 11(2)].

(*ii*) **Disposal of waste and effluents:** Every occupier of a factory shall make effective arrangements for the treatment of wastes and effluents due to the manufacturing process carried on in the factory so as to render them innocuous and for their disposal. Such arrangements should be in accordance with the rules, if any, laid down by the State Government. If the State Government has not laid down any rules in this respect, arrangements made by the occupier should be approved by the prescribed authority if required by the State government (Section 12).

(*iii*) **Ventilation and temperature:** Section 13 provides that every factory should make suitable and effective provisions for securing and maintaining (1) adequate ventilation by the circulation of fresh air; and (2) such a temperature as will secure to the workers reasonable conditions of comfort and prevent injury to health. The State Government has been empowered to lay down the standard of adequate ventilation and reasonable temperature for any factory or class or description of factories or parts thereof. It may direct that proper measure instruments at such places and in such position as may be specified shall be provided and prescribed records shall be maintained.

(*iv*) **Dust and fume:** There are certain manufacturing processes like chemical, textile or jute, etc., which generates lot of dust, fume or other impurities. It is injurious to the health of workers employed in such manufacturing process.

Following measures should be adopted in this respect:

1. Effective measures should be taken to prevent the inhalation and accumulation of dust, fumes etc., in the work-rooms.
2. Wherever necessary, exhaust appliances should be fitted, as far as possible to the point of origin of dust fumes or other impurities. Such point shall also be enclosed as far as possible.
3. In stationery internal combustion engine and exhaust should be connected into the open air.
4. In cases of other internal combustion engine, effective measures should be taken to prevent the accumulation of fumes there from (Section 14).

(*v*) **Artificial humidification:** Humidity means the presence of moisture in the air. In certain industries like cotton, textile, cigarette, etc., higher degree of humidity is required for carrying out the manufacturing process. For this purpose, humidity of the air is artificially increased. This increase or decrease in humidity adversely affects the health of workers.

Section 15(1) empowers the State Government to make rules (*i*) prescribing the standards of humidification, (*ii*) regulating methods to be adopted for artificially increasing the humidity of the air, (*iii*) directing prescribed tests for determining the humidity of the air to be correctly carried out, and recorded, and (*iv*) prescribing methods to be adopted for securing adequate ventilation and cooling of the air in the work-room.

Section 15(2) lays down that water used for artificial humidification should be either purified before use or obtained from a public supply or other source of drinking water.

Where the water is not purified as stated above. Section 15(3) empowers the Inspector to order, in writing, the manager of the factory to carry out specified measures, before a specified date, for purification of the water.

(*vi*) **Overcrowding:** Overcrowding in the work-room not only affect the workers in their efficient discharge of duties but their health also.

Section 16 has been enacted with a view to provide sufficient air space to the workers,

1. Section 16(1) prohibits the overcrowding in the work-rooms to the extent it is injurious to the health of the workers.
2. Apart from this general prohibition Section 16(2) lays down minimum working space for each worker as 14.2 cubic metres of space per worker in every workroom.

(*vii*) **Lighting:** Section 17 of the Factories Act makes following provisions in this respect:

1. Every factory must provide and maintain sufficient and suitable lighting, natural, artificial or both, in every part of the factory where workers are working or passing;
2. All the glazed windows and sky lights should be kept clean on both sides;
3. Effective provisions should be made for the prevention of glare from a source of light or by reflection from a smooth or polished surface;
4. Formation of shadows to such an extent causing eye-strain or the risk of accident to any worker, should be prevented; and
5. The state government is empowered to lay down standard of sufficient and suitable lighting for factories for any class or description of factories or for any manufacturing process.

(*viii*) **Drinking water:** Section 18 makes following provisions with regard to drinking water.

1. Every factory should make effective arrangements for sufficient supply of drinking water for all workers in the factory;
2. Water should be wholesome, *i.e.,* free from impurities;

3. Water should be supplied at suitable points convenient for all workers;

4. No such points should be situated within six meters of any washing place, urinals, latrine, spittoon, open drain carrying sullage or effluent or any other source of contamination, unless otherwise approved in writing by the Chief Inspector;

5. All such points should be legibly marked Drinking Water in a language understood by majority of the workers;

6. In case where more than 250 workers are ordinarily employed, effective arrangements should be made for cooling drinking water during hot weather. In such cases, arrangements should also be made for the distribution of water to the workers; and

7. The State Government is empowered to make rules for the compliance of above stated provisions and for the examination, by prescribed authorities, of the supply and distribution of drinking water in factories.

(*ix*) **Latrines and urinals:** Every factory shall make suitable arrangement for the provision of latrines and urinals for the workers. These points as stated below are subject to the provisions of Section 19 and the rules laid down by the State Government in this behalf.

1. Every factory shall make provision for sufficient number of latrines and urinals of prescribed standard. These should be conveniently situated and accessible to all workers during working hours;

2. Separate arrangement shall be made for male and female workers;

3. All these places shall have suitable provisions for lighting and ventilation;

4. No latrine or urinal shall communicate with any work-room unless in between them there is provision of open space or ventilated passage;

5. All latrines and urinals shall be kept in a clean and sanitary conditions at all times;

6. A sweeper shall be employed whose exclusive job will be to keep clean all latrines and urinals;

7. Where more than 250 workers are ordinarily employed in a factory, following additional measures shall be taken under Section 19(2):

    (*i*) All latrines and urinals accommodation shall be of prescribed sanitary type;

    (*ii*) All internal walls upto ninety centimeters, and the floors and the sanitary blocks shall be laid in glazed tiles or otherwise furnished to provide a smooth polished impervious surface;

    (*iii*) The floors, walls, sanitary pan, etc., of latrines and urinals shall be washed and cleaned with suitable detergents and/or disinfectants, at least once in every seven days.

8. The State Government is empowered to make rules in respect of following:

    (*i*) Prescribing the number of latrines and urinals to be provided to proportion to the number of male and female workers ordinarily employed in the factory.

    (*ii*) Any additional matters in respect of sanitation in factories;

    (*iii*) Responsibility of the workers in these matters.

(*x*) **Spittoons:** Every factory should have sufficient number of spittoons situated at convenient places. These should be maintained in a clean and hygienic condition. (Section 20)

B. SAFETY

Chapter IV of the Act contains provisions relating to safety. These are discussed below:

(*i*) **Fencing of machinery:** Fencing of machinery in use or in motion is obligatory under Section 21. This section requires that following types of machinery or their parts, while in use or in motion, shall be securely fenced by safeguards of substantial construction and shall be constantly maintained and kept in position, while the parts of machinery they are fencing are in motion or in use. Such types of machinery or their parts are:

1. Every moving parts of a prime-mover and flywheel connected to a prime-mover. It is immaterial whether the prime-mover or fly-wheel is in the engine house or not;

2. Head-race and tail-race of water wheel and water turbine;

3. Any part of stock-bar which projects beyond the head stock of a lathe;

4. Every part of an electric generator, a motor or rotary converter or transmission machinery unless they are in the safe position;

5. Every dangerous part of any other machinery unless they are in safe position.

(*ii*) **Safety measures in case of work on or near machinery in motion:** Section 22 lays down the procedure for carrying out examination of any part while it is in motion or as a result of such examination to carry out the operations mentioned under clause (i) or (ii) of the proviso to Section 21(1). Such examination or operation shall be carried out only by specially trained adult male worker wearing tight fitting clothing (which shall be supplied by the occupier) whose name has been recorded in the register prescribed in this behalf and who has been furnished with a certificate of appointment and while he is so engaged. No woman or young person shall be allowed to clean, lubricate or adjust any part of a prime-mover or any transmission machinery while the prime-mover or transmission machinery is in motion or to clean, lubricate or adjust any part of any machine if the cleaning, lubrication and adjustment thereof would expose the woman or the young person to risk of injury from any moving part either of that machine or of any adjacent machinery [Section 22(2)].

(*iii*) **Employment of young person's on dangerous machines:** Section 23 provides that no young person shall be required or allowed to work at any machine to which this section applies unless he has been fully instructed as to dangers arising in connection with the machine and the precautions to be observed and (*a*) has received sufficient training in work at the machine, or (*b*) is under adequate supervision by a person who has a thorough knowledge and experience of the machine.

(*iv*) **Striking gear and devices for cutting off power:** Section 24 provides that in every factory suitable striking gears or other efficient mechanical appliances shall be provided and maintained and used to move driving belts to and from fast and loose pullyes which form part of the transmission machinery and such gear or appliances shall be so constructed, placed and maintained as to prevent the belt from creeping back on the fast pulley. Further, driving belts when not in use shall not be allowed to rest or ride upon shafting in motion. Suitable devices for cutting off power in emergencies from running machinery shall be provided and maintained in every work-room in every factory. It is also provided that when a device which can inadvertently shift from 'off' to 'on' position in a factory, cutoff power arrangements shall be provided for locking the devices on safe position to prevent accidental start of the transmission machinery or other machines to which the device is fitted.

(*v*) **Self-acting machines:** Section 25 provides further safeguard for workers from being injured by self-acting machines. It provides that no traverse part of self-acting machine in any factory and no material carried thereon shall, if the space over which it runs is a space over which any person is liable to pass whether in the course of his employment or otherwise, be allowed to run on its outward or inward traverse within a distance of forty five centimeters from any fixed structure which is not part of the machines. However, Chief Inspector may permit the continued use of a machine installed before the commencement of this Act, which does not comply with the requirement of this section, on such conditions for ensuring safety, as he may think fit to impose.

(*vi*) **Casing of new machinery:** Section 26 provides further safeguards for casing of new machinery of dangerous nature. In all machinery driven by power and installed in any factory (*a*) every set screw, bolt or key on any revolving shaft, spindle, wheel or pinion shall be so sunk, encased or otherwise effectively guarded as to prevent danger; (*b*) all spur, worm and other toothed or friction gearing which does not require frequent adjustment while in motion, shall be completely encased unless it is so situated as to be so safe as it would be if it were completely encased. The section places statutory obligation on all persons who sell or let on hire or as agent of seller or hire to comply with the section and in default shall be liable to punishment with imprisonment for a term which may extend to 3 months or with fine which may extend to ₹ 500 or with both.

(*vii*) **Prohibition of employment of woman and children near cotton openers:** According to Section 27, no child or woman shall be employed in any part of factory for pressing cotton in which a cotton opener is at work. However, if the feed-end of a cotton opener is in a room separated from the delivery end by a partition extending to the roof or to such height as the inspector may in any particular case specify in writing, women and children may be employed on the side of partition where the feed-end is situated.

(*viii*) **Hoists and lifts:** Section 28 provides that in every factory: (i) every hoist and lift shall be of good mechanical construction, sound material and adequate strength. It shall be properly maintained and thoroughly examined by a competent person at least once in every period of six months and a register shall be kept containing the prescribed particulars every such examination, (ii) every hoist way and lift way shall be sufficiently protected by an enclosure fitted with gates and the hoist or lift and every such enclosure shall be so constructed as to prevent any person or thing from being trapped between any part of the hoist or lift and any fixed structure or moving part, (iii) the maximum safe working load shall be marked on every hoist or lift and no load greater, than such load shall be marked on every hoist or lift and no load greater than such load shall be carried thereon, (iv) the cage of every hoist and lift shall be fitted with a gate on each side from which access is afforded to a landing (v) such gates of the hoist and lift shall be fitted with interlocking or other efficient device to secure that the gate cannot be opened except when the cage is at the landing and that the cage cannot be moved unless the gate is closed.

(*ix*) **Lifting machines, chains, ropes and lifting tackles:** In terms of Section 29, in any factory the following provisions shall be complied with respect of every lifting machine (other than a hoist and lift) and every chain, rope and lifting tackle for the purpose of raising or lowering persons, goods or materials:

(*a*) All parts including the working gear, whether fixed or movable, shall be (*i*) of good construction, sound material and adequate strength and free from defects; (*ii*) properly maintained; (*iii*) thoroughly examined by a competent person at least once in every period of 12 months or at such intervals as Chief Inspector may specify in writing and a register shall be kept containing the prescribed particulars of every such examination;

(*b*) no lifting machine or no chain, rope or lifting tackle, shall, except for the purpose of test, be loaded beyond the safe working load which shall be plainly marked thereon together with an identification mark and duly entered in the prescribed register and where it is not practicable, a table showing the safe working loads of every kind and size of lifting machine or chain, rope or lifting tackle in use shall be displayed in prominent positions on that premises;

(*c*) while any person is employed or working on or near the wheel track of a travelling crane in any place where he would be liable to be struck by the crane, effective measures shall be taken to ensure that the crane does not approach within 6 meters of that place.

(*x*) **Safety measures in case of use of revolving machinery:** Section 30 of the Act prescribes for permanently affixing or placing a notice in every factory in which process of grinding is carried on. Such notice shall indicate maximum safe working peripheral speed of every grindstone or abrasive wheel, the speed of the shaft or spindle upon such shaft or spindle necessary to secure such safe working peripheral-speed. Speed indicated in the notice shall not be exceeded and effective measures in this regard shall be taken.

(*xi*) **Pressure plant:** Section 31 provides for taking effective measures to ensure that safe working pressure of any plant and machinery, used in manufacturing process operated at pressure above atmospheric pressure, does not exceed the limits. The State Government may make rules to regulate such pressures or working and may also exempt any part of any plant or machinery from the compliance of this section.

(*xii*) **Floor, stairs and means of access:** Section 32 provides that in every factory (*a*) all floors, steps, stairs passages and gangways shall be of sound construction and properly maintained and shall be kept free from obstruction and substances likely to cause persons to slip and where it is necessary to ensure safety, steps, stairs passages and gangways shall be provided with substantial handrails, (*b*) there shall, be so far as is reasonably practicable, be provided, and maintained safe means of access of every place at which any person is at any time required to work; (*c*) when any person has to work at a height from where he is likely to fall, provision shall be made, so far as is reasonably, practicable, by fencing or otherwise, to ensure the safety of the person so working.

(*xiii*) **Pits, sumps, openings in floors etc.:** Section 33 requires that in every factory every fixed vessel, sump, tank, pit or opening in the ground or in a floor which, by reason of its depth, situation, construction, or contents is or may be source of danger shall be either securely covered or securely fenced. The State Government may exempt any factory from the compliance of the provisions of this Section subject to such conditions as it may prescribe.

(*xiv*) **Excessive weights:** Section 34 provides that no person shall be employed in any factory to lift, carry or make any load so heavy as to be likely to cause him injury. The State Government may make rules prescribing the maximum weights which may be lifted, carried or moved by adult men, adult women, adolescents and children employed in factories or in any class or description of factories or in carrying on any specified process.

(*xv*) **Protection of eyes:** Section 35 requires the State Government to make rules and require for providing the effective screens or suitable goggles for the protection of persons employed on or in immediate vicinity of any such manufacturing process carried on in any factory which involves (i) risk of injury to the eyes from particles or fragments thrown off in the course of the process or; (ii) risk to the eyes by reason of exposure: excessive light.

(*xvi*) **Precautions against dangerous fumes, gases etc.:** Section 36 provides (1) that no person shall be required or allowed to enter any camber, tank, vat, pit, pipe, flue or other confined space in any factory in which any; as, fume, vapour or dust is likely to be present to such an extent as to involve risk to persons being overcome thereby, unless it is provided with a manhole of adequate size or other effective means of egress, (2) No person shall be required or allowed to enter any confined space as is referred to in sub-section (1), until all practicable measures have been taken to remove any gas, fume, vapour or dust, which may be present so as to bring its level within the permissible limits and to prevent any ingress of such gas, fume, vapour and unless

(*a*) A certificate in writing has been given by a competent person, based on a test carried out by himself that the space is reasonably free from dangerous gas, fume, vapour or dust; or

(*b*) Such person is wearing suitable breathing apparatus and a belt securely attached to a rope, the free end of which is held by a person outside the confined space.

(*xvii*) **Precautions regarding the use of portable electric light:** Section 3GA of the Act provides that in any factory (1) no portable electric light or any other electric appliance of voltage exceeding 24 volts shall be permitted for use inside any chamber, tank, vat, pit, pipe, flue or other confined space unless adequate safety devices are provided; and (2) if any inflammable gas, fume or dust is likely to be present in such chamber, tank, vat, pit, pipe, flue or other confined space unless adequate safety devices are provided, no lamp or light other than that of flame proof construction shall be permitted to be used therein.

(*xviii*) **Explosive or inflammable dust gas, etc.:** Sub-section (1) of section 37 of the Act provides that in every factory where any manufacturing process produces dust, gas, fume or vapour of such character and to such extent to be likely to explode on ignition, all practicable measures shall be taken to prevent any such explosion by (*a*) effective enclosure of the plant or machinery used in the process (*b*) removal or prevention of the accumulation of such dust, gas fume or vapour, and (*c*) exclusion or effective enclosure of all possible sources of ignition.

(*xix*) **Precautions in case of fire:** Section 38 provides that in every factory all practicable measures shall be taken to outbreak of fire and its spread, both internally and externally and to provide and maintain (*a*) safe means of escape for all persons in the event of fire, and (*b*) the necessary equipment and facilities for extinguishing fire.

Effective measures shall be taken to ensure that in every factory all the worker are familiar with the means of escape in case of fire and have been adequately trained in the outline to be followed in such case.

(*xx*) **Power to require specification of defective parts or test to stability:** Section 39 states that when the inspector feels that the conditions in the factory are dangerous to human life or safety; he may serve on the occupier or manager or both notice in writing requiring him before the specified date to furnish such drawings, specifications and other particulars as may be necessary to determine whether such building, machinery or plant can be used with safety or to carry out such test in such a manner as may be specified in the order and to inform the inspector of the results thereof.

(*xxi*) **Safety of buildings or machinery:** Section 40 provides that the inspectors in case of dangerous conditions of building or any part of ways, machinery or plant requires the manager or occupier or both to take such measures which in his opinion should be adopted and require them to be carried out before a specified date. In case the danger to human life is immediate and imminent from such usage of building, ways of machinery he may order prohibiting the use of the same unless it is repaired or altered.

(*xxii*) **Maintenance of buildings:** Section 40-A provides that if it appears to the inspector that any building or part of it is in such a state of disrepair which may lead to conditions detrimental to the health and welfare of workers; he may serve on the manager or occupier or both, an order in writing specifying the measures to be carried out before a specified date.

(*xxiii*) **Safety officers:** Section 40-B provides that in every factory (i) where 1,000 or more workers are ordinarily employed or (ii) where the manufacturing process or operation involves risk of bodily injury, poisoning or disease or any other hazard to health of the persons employed therein, the occupier shall employ such number of safety officers as may be specified in the notification with such duties and qualifications and conditions of service as may be prescribed by State Government.

(*xxiv*) **Power to make rules to supplement this Chapter:** This is vested in the State Government under Section 41 for such devices and measures to secure the safety of the workers employed in the factory.

C. WELFARE

Following provisions under Chapter (v) of the Act, relate to the measures to be taken for the welfare of workers.

(*i*) **Washing facilities:** Section 42 provides that every factory should provide and maintain adequate and suitable washing facilities for its workers. For the use of male and female, such facilities should be separate and adequately screened. Such facilities should be conveniently accessible for all workers and be kept in a state of cleanliness. The State Government is empowered to make rules prescribing standards of adequate and suitable washing facilities.

(*ii*) **Facilities for storing and drying clothing:** Section 43 empowers the State Government in respect of any factory or class or description of factories to make rules requiring the provision, therein of (i) suitable places for keeping clothing not worn during working hours, and (ii) for drying of wet clothing.

(*iii*) **Facilities for sitting**: There are certain operations which can be performed by the workers only in a standing position. This not only affects the health of a worker but his efficiency also.

According to Section 44(1), every factory shall provide and maintain suitable facilities for sitting, for those who work in standing position so that they may make use of them as an when any opportunity comes in the course of their work. If, in the opinion of the Chief Inspector, any work can be efficiently performed in a sitting position, he may direct, in writing, the occupier of the factory, to provide before a specified date such seating arrangements as may be practicable, for all workers so engaged. The State Government, may by a notification in the Official Gazette, declares that above provisions shall not apply to any specified factory or any manufacturing process.

(*iv*) First aid appliances: As per Section 45, the following arrangements should be made in every factory in respect of first-aid facilities.

(*a*) Provision of at least one first-aid box or cup-board, subject to following conditions, for every 150 workers ordinarily employed at any one time factory.

(*b*) It should be equipped with prescribed contents and nothing else should be stored in it.

(*c*) It should be properly maintained and readily accessible during all working hours.

(*d*) A responsible person who holds a certificate in first-aid treatment, recognized by the State Government should be made the in-charge of such first-aid box or cup-board. Such a person should be readily available during working hours of the factory. Where there are different shifts in the factory, a separate person may be appointed for each shifts provided he is a responsible person and trained in first-aid treatment.

(*e*) Where more than 500 workers are ordinarily employed in a factory, an ambulance room should be provided and maintained by every such factory. Such room should be of prescribed size containing prescribed equipments and is in charge of such medical and nursing staff as may be prescribed.

(*v*) Canteen: (1) The State Government may make rules requiring that in any specified factory wherein more than 250 workers are ordinarily employed, a canteen shall be provided and maintained by the occupier for the use of workers. (2) Such rules may relate to any of the following matter:

(*i*) The date by which canteen shall be provided;

(*ii*) The standards in respect of construction, accommodation, furniture and other equipment of the canteen;

(*iii*) The foodstuffs to be served and the prices to be charged;

(*iv*) The items of expenditure in the running of the canteen which are not to be taken into account in fixing the cost of foodstuffs and which shall be borne by the employer;

(*v*) The constitution of a Managing Committee for the canteen and the representation of the workers in the management of the canteen; and

(*vi*) The delegation, to the chief inspector, subject to such conditions as may be prescribed, of the power to make rules under clause (iii). (Section 46). Where the statute casts an obligation to own a canteen in the factory, and the establishment runs a canteen through a contractor who brings the workers for the canteen would be part and parcel of the establishment and the canteen workers would be deemed to be regular employees of the establishment entitled to arrears of salary and other monetary benefits **(Tamil Manila Thozilalar Sangam v. Chairman TNEB, 1994 CLA 34 Mad. 63.)**

(*vi*) Shelters, rest rooms and lunch rooms: The provision of some sort of shelter is a must, where the workers can take their meals brought by them during rest interval. The following provisions under Section 47 of the Act have been made in this respect:

1. In every factory where more than 150 workers are ordinarily employed, the occupier should make adequate and suitable arrangements for shelters or rest rooms and lunch-room with provision of drinking water where the workers can take rest of or eat meals brought by them. However, any canteen which is maintained in accordance with provisions of Section 45 shall be regarded as part of the requirements of this sub-section. Where a lunch room exists no worker shall eat any food in the workroom.

2. Such places should be equipped with the facility of drinking water.

3. Such places should be sufficiently lighted, ventilated and kept in cool and clean conditions.

4. The construction and accommodation, furniture and equipment of such place should conform to the standards, if any, laid down by the State Government.

By a notification in the Official Gazette, the State Government may exempt any factory from the compliance of these provisions. Further, where any canteen is maintained under Section 45, then provision of such shelter room, etc., is not necessary.

(*vii*) **Crèches:** Following provisions have been made in respect of crèches in the factories:

1. In every factory wherein more than 30 women workers are ordinarily employed, the facility of suitable room or rooms should be provided and maintained for the use of children under the age of six years of such women.

2. There should be adequate accommodation in such rooms.

3. These places should be sufficiently lighted and ventilated and kept in clean and sanitary conditions.

4. Women trained in the case of children and infants should be made in charge of such rooms.

The State Government is empowered to make rules in respect of following matters:

1. Location and standards in respect of construction, accommodation, furniture and other equipment of such places.

2. Provisions of facilities for washing and changing clothing of children or any other additional facility for their care.

3. Provisions of free-milk or refreshment or both for children.

4. Facilities for the mothers of such children to feed them at suitable intervals in the factory (Section 48).

(*viii*) **Welfare officers:** According to Section 49(1), in every factory wherein 500 or more workers are ordinarily employed, the occupier should employ such number of welfare officers as may be prescribed.

The State Government is empowered to prescribe the duties, qualifications and conditions of service of such welfare officers. The provisions of Section 49 also apply to seasonal factories like sugar factories etc.

The State Government is empowered to lay down rules as to the conditions of service of welfare officers. The conditions of service may include matters in respect of pay grades, period of probation and confirmation, dismissal or termination or retirement etc.

(*ix*) **Powers to make rules to supplement this chapter:** The State Government is empowered to make rules exempting factory or class or description of factories from the compliance of provisions of this chapter, provided alternative arrangements for workers welfare have been made to the satisfaction of the authorities. Such rules may require that workers representatives shall be associated with the management of the welfare arrangements of the workers (Section 50).

Working Hours of Adults

Chapter VI contains provision for regulating working hours for the adult workers and the same are explained below:

(*i*) **Weekly hours:** An adult worker shall be allowed to work only for forty eight hours in any week (Section 51).

(*ii*) **Weekly holidays:** Section 52 provides that there shall be holiday for the whole day in every week and such weekly holiday shall be on the first day of the week. However, such holiday may be substituted for any one of the three days immediately before or after the first day of the week provided the manager of the factory has:

(*a*) Delivered a notice at the office of the Inspector; and

(*b*) Displayed a notice in the factory to this effect.

The effect of all this is that subject to above said conditions (*a*) and (*b*) there shall be a holiday during ten days. In other words no adult worker shall work for more than ten days consecutively without a holiday for the whole day. It is not possible for an employer to change the weekly off solely on the ground that there was no material available for work to be provided on a particular date, avoiding requirements to be fulfilled under Section 25(m) of Industrial Disputes Act regarding lay off (LAB 1C 1998 Bom. 1790).

Such notices of substitution may be cancelled by an appropriate notice but not later than the day of weekly holiday or the substituted holiday whichever is earlier.

(*iii*) **Compensatory holidays:** When a worker is deprived of any of the weekly holiday as result of passing of an order or making of a rule exempting a factory or worker from the provisions of Section 52, he is entitled to compensatory holidays of equal number of the holidays so lost. These holidays should be allowed either in the same month in which the holidays became due or within next two months immediately following that month (Section 53).

(*iv*) **Daily hours:** According to Section 54, an adult worker, whether male or female shall not be required or allowed to work in a factory for more than 9 hours in any day. Section 54 should be read with Section 59. In other words, the daily hours of work should be so adjusted that the total weekly hours does not exceed 48. The liability of the employer, under this Section cannot be absolved on the ground that the workers are willing work for longer hours without any extra payment.

The daily maximum hours of work specified in Section 54 can be exceeded provided:

(*a*) It is to facilitate the change of shift; and

(*b*) The previous approval of the Chief Inspector has been obtained.

(*v*) **Intervals for rest:** No adult worker shall work continuously for more than 5 hours unless a rest interval of at least half an hour is given to him [Section 55(1)].

(*vi*) **Spread over:** Section 56 provides that the daily working hours should be adjusted in such a manner, that inclusive of rest interval under Section 55, they are not spread over more than 10-1/2 hours on any day. Thus, we see this Section restricts the practice of forcing the stay of workers in the factory for unduly long periods without contravening the provision of Section 54 relating to daily hours of work.

Proviso to Section 56 provides that the limit may be extended upto 12 hours for reasons to be specified in writing to the Chief Inspector.

(*vii*) **Night shifts:** Where a worker in a factory works in nightshifts, i.e., shift extending beyond night:

(*a*) The weekly or compensatory holiday shall be a period of 24 consecutive hours beginning when his shift ends;

(*b*) The following day shall be deemed to the period of 24 hours beginning shift ends, and the hours he has worked after midnight shall be counted in the previous day (Section 57).

(*viii*) **Prohibition of overlapping shifts:** According to Section 58(1), where the work in any factory is carried on by means of multiple shifts, the period of shifts should be arranged in such a manner that not more than one relay of workers is engaged in work of the same kind at the same time.

In case of any factory or class or description of factories or any department or section of a factory or any category or description of workers, the State Government or subject to the control of the State Government, the Chief Inspector may, by written order and for specified reasons, grant exemption from the compliance of the provisions of Section 58(1) on such condition as may be deemed expedient [Section 58(2)].

(*ix*) **Extra wages for overtime:** The following provisions have been made in respect of overtime wages:

Where a worker works in a factory for more than 9 hours in any day or more than 48 hours in any week, he shall, in respect of overtime work, be entitled to wages at the rate of twice his ordinary rate of wages [Section 59(1)].

(*x*) **Restriction on double employment:** According to Section 60, no adult worker shall be required or allowed to work in any factory on any day if he has already been working in any other factory on that day. However, in certain exceptional circumstances as may be prescribed, the double employment may be permitted.

(*xi*) **Notice of period of work for adults:** As per Section 61(1), a notice of period of work, showing clearly for everyday the periods during which adult workers may be required to work, shall be displayed and correctly maintained in every factory. The display of notice should be in accordance with the provisions of [Section 108(2)].

(*xii*) **Register of adult workers:** The manager of every factory shall maintain a register of adult workers to be available to the inspector at all times during working hours containing the following particulars:

(*a*) The name of worker;

(*b*) The nature of his work;

(*c*) The group, if any, in which he is included;

(*d*) Where his group works on shifts, the relay to which he is allotted; and

(*e*) Other particulars as may be prescribed.

Where any factory is maintaining a muster roll or a register which contains the above mentioned particulars, the Inspector may, by order in writing, direct that such muster roll or register shall be maintained in place of and be treated as the register of adult workers in that factory (Section 62). Further, an adult worker shall not be required or allowed to work in the factory unless his particulars have been entered in this register [Section 62(IA)].

(*xiii*) **Hours of work to correspond with notice under Section 61 and register under Section 62:** No adult worker shall be required or allowed to work in any factory otherwise than in accordance with the notice of period of work for adults displayed in the factory and the entries made before had against his name in the register of adult workers of the factory (Section 63).

(*xiv*) **Power to make exempting rules:** (1) The State Government is empowered under Section 64, to make rules defining certain persons holding supervisory or managerial or confidential positions and granting exemptions to them from the provisions of this chapter except Section 66(1) (b) and proviso to Section 66(1) provided that such person shall be entitled for extra wages in respect of overtime under Section 59 if his ordinary rate of wages is not more than ₹ 750 per month.

Additional Provisions Regulating Employment of Women in Factory

We have discussed the provisions relating to working hours of adult workers both male and female. However, certain additional restrictions have been found necessary on the working hours of female workers. Section 66 makes following provisions in this respect.

1. No exemption may be granted to female worker, from the provisions of Section 54 relating to daily hours of work.

2. Women workers shall not be employed except between the hours of 6 a.m. and 7 p.m. However, the State Government may by a notification in the Official Gazette, vary these limits to the extent that no woman shall be employed between the hours of 10 p.m. and 5 a.m.

3. There shall be no change of shifts except after a weekly holiday or any other holiday.

Exemptions from the above restriction

The State Government has been empowered to make rules granting exemptions from above stated restriction in respect of women working in fish-curing or fish canning factories. This has been done with a view to prevent damage to or deterioration in any raw material. However, before granting any exemption, the State Government may lay down any condition as it thinks necessary. Such rules made by the State Government shall remain in force for not more than three years at a time [Section 66(3)].

Employment of Young Persons and Children

Most of the civilized nations restrict the employment of children in the factories. The Royal Commission on Labour observed that this is based on the principle that the supreme right of the State to the guardianship of children controls the natural rights of the parent when the welfare of society or of the children themselves conflicts with parental rights. Workers as young as five years of age may be found in some of these places working without adequate meal, intervals or weekly rest days at as low as 2 annas in the case of those tenderest years. Therefore, to curb these and other evil practices of employing children, following legislative measures have been adopted.

(*a*) **General prohibition as to employment of children:** According to Section 67, a child who has not completed his fourteenth year of age, shall not be employed in any factory.

(*b*) **Employment of children and Adolescents— Conditions:** According to Section 68, children completing their fourteenth year or an adolescent, shall not be required to work in any factory, unless following conditions are fulfilled:

(*i*) The manager of the factory has obtained a certificate of fitness granted to such young person under Section 69;

(*ii*) While at work, such child or adolescent carries a token giving reference to such certificate.

Working hours for children

Section 71, lays down further restrictions on the employment of children in the factories. These restrictions as stated below relate to working hours for children.

1. A child shall not be employed or permitted to work for more than 4-1/2 hours in any day [Section 71 (1) (a)].

2. He is not permitted to work during night, *i.e.,* during a period of at least 12 consecutive hours, including intervals, between 10 p.m. and 6 a.m.

3. The period of work shall be limited to two shifts only [Section 71(2)].

4. These shifts shall not overlap.

5. Shifts should not spread over more than 5 hours each.

6. Each child shall be employed in only one of the relays.

7. The relays should not be changed more frequently than once in a period of 30 days, otherwise previous permission of the Chief Inspector should be sought in writing.

8. The provision relating to weekly holiday under Section 52, also apply to child workers. But Section 7(3) does not permit any exemption in respect of these provisions.

9. No child shall be required or allowed to work in any factory on any **day** on which he has already been working in another factory [Section 71(4)].

10. No female child shall be required or allowed to work in any factory except between 8 a.m. and 7 p.m.

The Act not only prohibits the double employment of a child by the occupier or manager, but also prohibits under Section 99 his parent or guardian or person having custody of or control over him or obtaining any direct benefit from his wages, from allowing him to go for double employment. If they contravene this provision, they can be punished with a fine extending upto one thousand rupees unless the child works without the consent or connivance of his parent or guardian or such other person.

Annual Leave with Wages

Under Section 79, the following provisions have been made with regard to annual leave with wages.

Basis of leave

(*a*) According to Section 79(1), where a worker has worked for a minimum period of 240 days or more in a factory during any calendar year, *i.e.,* the year beginning from 1st January, he is entitled to leave with wages on the following basis:

(*i*) For adults - One day for every 20 days of work performed by them during the previous calendar year.

(*ii*) For children - One day for every fifteen days of work performed by him during the previous calendar year.

(*b*) If a worker does not commence his services from 1st January, he is entitled to these leaves at the above mentioned rates provided he has worked 2/3rd of the total number of days in the remaining part of the calendar year.

(*c*) These leaves are exclusive of all holidays whether occurring during or at either end of the period of leave.

(*d*) In calculating leave, fraction of leave of half a day or more shall be treated as one full day's leave and fraction of less than half a day shall be ignored.

(*e*) Computation of qualifying period of 240 days: For the purpose of calculating the minimum period, following periods are also included:

(*i*) Any days of lay-off as agreed or as permissible under the Standing Orders.

(*ii*) For female workers, period of maternity leave not exceeding 12 weeks

(*iii*) Leave earned in the year prior to that in which the leave is enjoyed.

Accumulation or carry forward of leaves

If any worker does not avail any earned leave entitled to him during the calendar year, it can be carried forward to the next calendar year subject to the maximum of 30 days for an adult worker and 40 days for a child worker.

Wages during leave period

According to Section 80(1), for the leave allowed to a worker under Section 78 or 79, he shall be entitled to wages at a rate equal to the daily average of his total full time earnings for the days on which he actually worked during the month immediately preceding his leave. Such full time earning will also include the dearness allowance and cash equivalent of the advantage accruing through the concessional sale to the workers of food grains and other articles. But will exclude any overtime wages and bonus.

Payment in advance in certain cases

Section 81 provides that where an adult worker has been allowed leave for not less than 4 days and a child worker for not less than 5 days, wages due for the leave period should be paid in advance, *i.e.,* before his leave begins.

Mode of recovery of unpaid wages

Any unpaid wages due to the workers under this Chapter can be recovered as delayed wages under the provisions of the Payment of Wages Act, 1936 (Section 82).

Penalties and Procedures

(1) **General penalties for offence**: If there is any contravention of any of the provisions of this Act or any rules or order made there under, the occupier and manager shall each be guilty of an offence and punishable with imprisonment for a term which may extend to two years or with fine which may extend to ₹ one lakh or with both and if the contravention is continued after conviction, with a further fine of ₹ one thousand for each, day till contravention continues.

The provisions of Section 92 further provides penalty for contravention of any of the provisions of Chapter IV or any rule made there under or under Section 87 which has resulted in an accident causing death or serious bodily injury, the fine shall not be less than ₹ 25,000 in the case of an accident causing death and ₹ 5,000 in case of serious bodily injury.

(2) **Liabilities of owner of premises in certain circumstances:** Section 93 provides that where in any premises separate building are being leased out by the owner to different occupiers for use as separate factories, the owner of the premises shall be responsible for the provision and maintenance of common

facilities and services such as approach roads, drainage, water-supply, lighting and sanitation [Section 93(1)].

Where in any premises, independent floors or flats are leased to different occupiers for use as separate factories, the owner shall be liable as if he were the manager or occupier of a factory for any contravention of the provisions of this Act in respect of (*i*) latrines, urinals, washing facilities and common supply of water for this purpose; (*ii*) fencing of machinery and plant belonging to the owner and not entrusted to the custody or use of an occupier; (*iii*) safe means of access to floors or flats and maintenance and cleanliness of staircase and common passages; (*iv*) precautions in case of fire; (*v*) maintenance of hoists and lifts; and (*vi*) maintenance of any other common facilities provided in the premises [Section 93(3)].

But the liability of the owner [under Section 93(3) arises only wherein any premises, independent rooms with common latrine, urinals and washing facilities are leased to different occupiers for use as separate factories so that the owner should also comply with the provisions of maintaining such facilities. (Section 93(5)].

For the purposes of sub-sections (5) and (7) computing the total number of workers employed, the whole of the premises shall be deemed to be single factory [Section 93(3)].

The Chief Inspector has been empowered to issue orders to the owners in respect of the carrying out of the provisions as mentioned above but subject to the control of the State Government.

(3) **Penalty for obstructing Inspector:** Section 95 lays down penalty of imprisonment for six months or fine of ₹ 10,000 or with both for willfully obstructing an inspector in the exercise of any power conferred on him by or under this Act or fails to produce any registers or other documents to him on demand or concealing or preventing any worker from appearing before or being examined by an Inspector.

(4) **Penalty for wrongfully disclosing of results of analysis under Section 91:** Section 96 provides imprisonment extending up to a term of six months and fine upto ₹ 10,000 or both for the wrongful disclosure of results of analysts of the analysis done under Section 91 of the Act.

(4A) **Penalty for contravention of Sections 41B, 41C and 41H:** Section 96A provides punishment of 7 years imprisonment or fine which may extend to ₹ 2 lakhs for the non-compliance with or contravention of any of the provisions of Sections 41B, 41C, or 41H or rules made there under by any person. In case the failure or contravention continues, with additional fine which may extend to five thousand rupees for every day during which such failure or contravention continues after the conviction for the first such failure or contravention. If such failure, contravention continues beyond a period of one year after the date of conviction, the offender be punishable with imprisonment for a term which may extend to ten years.

(5) **Offences by workers and penalties therefore:**

(*i*) Section 97 lays down that if any worker contravenes the provision of this Act or any rules or orders made there under imposing any duty or liability on workers he will be punishable with fine which may extend to ₹ 500.

(*ii*) Section 98 imposes penalty for using false certificate of fitness. Such punishment involves imprisonment for such a term which may not extend two months or with fine which may extend to ₹ 1,000 or with both.

(6) Penalty for permitting double employment of child by parents or guardians is stipulated under Section 99. Such an act is punishable with fine extending up to ₹ 1,000 unless it appears to the Court that the child so worked without consent and connivance of such parents, guardian or person.

(7) Onus of providing limits of what is practicable etc.: Onus of proving is on person who is alleged to have failed to comply with such duty etc. to prove that has taken all measures or it was not reasonable practicable (Section 104A).

Display on Notice Board: A notice containing abstract of the Factories Act and the rules made there under, in English and local language should be displayed. Name and address of Factories Inspector and the certifying surgeon should also be displayed on notice board [Section 108(1)].

Notice of Accidents, Diseases Etc.: Notice of any accident causing disablement of more than 48 hours, dangerous occurrences and any worker contacting occupational disease should be informed to Factories Inspector [Section 88]. Notice of dangerous occurrences and specified diseases should be given [Sections 88A and 89].

Obligation regarding Hazardous Processes/Substances: Information about hazardous substances/processes should be given. Workers and general public in vicinity should be informed about dangers and health hazards. Safety measures and emergency plan should be ready. Safety Committee should be appointed.

THE EMPLOYEES STATE INSURANCE ACT (ESI ACT), 1948

The ESI Act has been passed to provide for certain benefits to employees in case of sickness, maternity and employment injury and to make provisions for related matters. As the name suggests, it is basically an 'insurance' scheme *i.e.* employee gets benefits if he is sick or disabled. The Act has been amended by the Employees' State Insurance (Amendment) Act, 2010.

ESIC - Employees State Insurance Corporation (ESIC) has been formed to supervise the scheme under Section 3 of the Act. The Corporation supervises and controls the ESI scheme.

Employees' State Insurance Act, 1948 extends to the whole of India.

It shall apply, in the first instance, to all factories (including factories belonging to the Government) other than seasonal factories.

Nothing contained in the Act shall apply to a factory or establishment belonging to or under the control of the government whose employees are otherwise in receipt of benefits substantially similar or superior to the benefits provided under this Act.

The appropriate government may, in consultation with the ESI Corporation and where the appropriate government is a State Government, with the approval of the Central Government, after giving six months' notice of its intention of so doing by notification in the Official Gazette, extend the provisions of this Act, to any other establishment or class of establishments, industrial, commercial, agricultural or otherwise.

Under these enacting provisions, the Act has been extended by many State Governments to shops, hotels, restaurants, cinemas, including preview theaters, newspaper establishments, road transport undertaking etc., employing 20 or more persons.

A factory or an establishment to which this Act applies shall continue to be governed by this Act notwithstanding that the number of persons employed therein at any time falls below the limit specified by or under this Act or the manufacturing process therein ceases to be carried on with the aid of power.

The coverage under the Act is at present restricted to employees drawing wages not exceeding ₹ 15000 per month.

Definitions

Appropriate government means, in respect of establishment under the control of the Central Government or a railway administration or a major port or a mine or oilfield, the Central Government, and in all other cases, the State Government.

Contribution means the sum of money payable to the corporation by the principal employer in respect of an employee and includes any amount payable by or on behalf of the employee in accordance with the provisions of this Act.

Confinement means labour resulting in the issue of living child or labour after twenty-six weeks of pregnancy resulting in the issue of a child whether alive or dead.

Corporation means the Employees' State Insurance Corporation set up under this Act.

Dependent under Section 2 (6A) of the Act (as amended by the Employees' State Insurance (Amendment) Act, 2010) means any of the following relatives of a deceased insured person namely:

(*i*) A widow, a legitimate or adopted son who has not attained the age of twenty-five years, an unmarried legitimate or adopted daughter,

(*ia*) A widowed mother,

(*ii*) If wholly dependent on the earnings of the insured person at the time of his death, a legitimate or adopted son or daughter who has attained the age of 25 years and is infirm;

(*iii*) If wholly or in part dependent on the earnings of the insured person at the time of his death:

(*a*) A parent other than a widowed mother,

(*b*) A minor illegitimate son, an unmarried illegitimate daughter or a daughter legitimate or adopted or illegitimate if married and minor or if widowed and a minor,

(*c*) A minor brother or an unmarried sister or a widowed sister if a minor,

(*d*) A widowed daughter-in-law,

(*e*) A minor child of pre-deceased son,

(*f*) A minor child of a pre-deceased daughter where no parent of the child is alive or,

(*g*) A paternal grant parent if no parent of the insured person is alive.

Employment injury means a personal injury to an employee caused by accident or an occupational decease arising out of and in the course of his employment, being an insurable employment, whether the accident occurs or the occupational disease is contracted within or outside the territorial limit of India.

Employee means any person employed for wages in or in connection with the work of a factory or establishment to which this Act applies and—

(*i*) Who is directly employed by the principal employer or any work of, or incidental or preliminary to or connected with the work of, the factory or establishment whether such work is done by the employee in the factory or establishment or elsewhere; or

(*ii*) Who is employed by or through an immediate employer on the premises of the factory or establishment or under the supervision of the principal employer or his agent on work which is ordinarily part of the work of the factory or establishment or which is preliminary to the work carried on in or incidental to the purpose of the factory or establishment; or

(*iii*) Whose services are temporarily lent or let on hire to the principal employer by the person with whom the person whose services are so lent or let on hire has entered into a contract of service;

But does not include

(*a*) Any member of the Indian naval, military or air force; or

(*b*) Any person so employed whose wages (excluding remuneration for overtime work) exceed such wages as may be prescribed by the Central Government (> ₹ 15,000 per month).

Exempted employee means an employee who is not liable under this Act to pay the employee's contribution.

Insured person means a person who is or was an employee in respect of whom contributions are or were payable under this Act and who is, by reason thereof, entitled to any of the benefits provided by this Act.

Permanent partial disablement means such disablements of a permanent nature, as reduces the earning capacity of an employee in every employment which he was capable of undertaking at the time of the accident resulting in the disablement.

Permanent total disablement means such disablement of a permanent nature as incapacitates an employee for all work which he was capable of performing at the time of the accident resulting in such disablement.

Principal employer means the following:

(*a*) In a factory, owner or occupier of the factory and includes the managing agent of such owner or occupier, the legal representative of a deceased owner or occupier and where a person has been named as the manager of the factory under the Factories Act, 1948, the person so named.

(*b*) In any establishment under the control of any department of any Government in India, the authority appointed by such Government in this behalf or whose no authority is so appointed the head of the Department.

(*c*) In any other establishment, any person responsible for the supervision and control of the establishment [Section 2(17)].

Family means under Section 2(11) as amended by the Employees' State Insurance Amendment Act, 2010 means all or any of the following relatives of an insured person namely:

(*a*) A spouse.

(*b*) A minor legitimate or adopted child dependent upon the insured person.

(*c*) A child who is wholly dependent on the earnings of the insured person and who is:

  (*i*) Receiving education, till he or she attains the age of twenty-one years,

  (*ii*) An unmarried daughter;

(*d*) A child who is infirm by reason of any physical or mental abnormality or injury and is wholly dependent of the earnings of the insured person, so long as the infirmity continues.

(*e*) Dependent parents whose income from all sources does not exceed such income as may be prescribed by the Central Government.

(*f*) In case the insured person is unmarried and his or her parents are not alive, a minor brother or sister wholly dependent upon the earnings of the insured person.

Factory as per ESI Act: The 'Factory' means any premises including the precincts thereof whereon ten or more persons are employed or were employed on any day of the preceding twelve months, and in any part of which a manufacturing process is being carried on or is ordinarily so carried on, but does not including a mine subject to the operation of the Mines Act, 1952 or a railway running shed.

Seasonal factory means a factory which is exclusively engaged in or more of the following manufacturing processes namely, cotton ginning, cotton or jute pressing, decortications of groundnuts, the manufacture of coffee, indigo, lac, rubber, sugar (including gur) or tea or any manufacturing process which is incidental to or connected with any of the aforesaid processes and includes a factory which is engaged for a period not exceeding seven months in a year.

Sickness means a condition which requires medical treatment and attendance and necessitates abstention from work on medical grounds [Section 2 (20)].

Temporary disablement means a condition resulting from an employment injury which requires medical treatment and renders an employee as a result of such injury, temporarily incapable of doing the work which he was doing prior to or at the time of injury [Section 2 (21)].

Wages means all remuneration paid or payable in cash to an employee if the terms of the contract of employment, express or implied, were fulfilled and includes any payment to an employee in respect of any period of authorized leave, lockout, strike which is not illegal or lay-off and other additional remuneration if any, paid at intervals not exceeding two months but does not include:

(*a*) Any contribution paid by the employer to any pension fund or provident fund, or under this Act;

(*b*) Any travelling allowance or the value of any travelling concession;

(*c*) Any sum paid to the person employed to defray special expenses entailed on him by the nature of his employment; or

(*d*) Any gratuity payable on discharge [Section 2 (22)].

No Dismissal or Punishment During Period of Sickness: Section 73 of the Act provides that no employer shall dismiss, discharge or reduce or otherwise punish an employee during the period employee is in receipt of sickness benefit or maternity benefit. He also cannot dismiss, discharge or otherwise punish employee when he is in receipt of disablement benefit or is under medical treatment or is absent from work due to sickness.

This gives protection to employee when he is in receipt of sickness benefit or maternity benefit. Employer cannot take disciplinary action against employee in such cases. This provision is grossly misused by employees.

However, in Buckingham & Carnatic Co v. Venkatayya - AIR 1964 SC 1272 = 1963(7) FLR 343 = (1964) 4 SCR 265 = (1963) 2 LLJ 638 = 25 FJR 25 (SC), it was rightly held that this provision (of Section 73) is applicable only in case of punitive action for all kinds of misconduct during which employee has received sickness benefits. This protection is not applicable in case of abandonment of employment or when termination is automatic as per contract – followed in Rajveer Singh v. Judge 1996 LLR 61 (Raj HC), where it was hold that provisions of Section 73 are not applicable when termination of an employee is automatic.

Registration of Factories and Establishments Under This Act

Section 2A of the Act lays down that every factory or establishment to which this Act applies shall be registered within such time and in such manner as may be specified in the regulations made in this behalf.

Employees' State Insurance

Section 38 of the Act makes compulsory that subject to the provisions of the Act all the employees in factories or establishments to which this Act applies shall be insured in the manner provided by this Act. Such insured persons shall pay contributions towards Insurance Fund through their employers who will also pay their own contribution. Such insured persons are entitled to get certain benefits from that fund which shall be administered by the Corporation. Any dispute will be settled by the Employees' Insurance Court.

Regional Offices/Branch Offices Get Covered: Regional offices of a factory, which have their connection to the factory and where the Principal Employer has control over the regional offices, the regional offices will be covered under ESIC - Hyderabad Asbestos Cement Products v. ESIC - AIR 1978 SC 356 = (1978) 2 SCR 345 = (1978) 1 SCC 194. If head office is covered under ESIC, branch offices are also covered when branch and principal office are inter-dependent and there is unity of relationship - Transport Corporation of India v. ESIC 1999(7) SCALE 63 = 2000 LLR 113 = 83 FLR 970 = 1999 AIR SCW 4340 = AIR 2000 SC 238 (SC 3 member bench).

Outside agencies can be covered: In PM Patel v. UOI (1986) 1 SCC 32 = AR 1987 SC 447 = 1985 II CLR 322 (SC), workers were given work of making 'bidis' at home. Right of rejection of bidis was with employer. It was held that test of control and supervision lies in the right of rejection. It was held that employees working outside can be covered under ESIC, if there is master servant relationship.

Construction Workers Not Covered: Construction workers employed in construction activities are not covered under ESIC. – ESIC circular No. P-12(11)-11/27/99 Ins. IV dated 14-6-1999. However, if administrative office employs 20 or more eligible employees, that establishment and employees working in administrative office will be covered.

Administration of Employees' State Insurance Scheme

For the administration of the scheme of Employees' State Insurance in accordance with the provisions of this Act, the Employees' State Insurance Corporation Standing Committee and Medical Benefit Council have been constituted. Further, ESI Fund has been created which is held and administered by ESI Corporation through its executive committee called Standing Committee with the assistance, advice and expertise of Medical Council, etc. and Regional and Local Boards and Committees.

Employees' State Insurance Corporation

Section 3 of this Act provides for the establishment of Employees' State Insurance Corporation by the Central Government for administration of the Employees' State Insurance Scheme in accordance with the provisions of Act. Such Corporation shall be body corporate having perpetual succession and a common seal and shall sue and be sued by the said name.

Constitution

The Central Government appoints a chairman, a vice-chairman and other members representing interests of employers, employees, state government/union territories and medical profession. Three members of Parliament and the Director General of the Corporation are its ex-officio members [Section 4].

Powers and Duties if the Corporation

Section 19 empowers the Corporation, to promote (in addition to the scheme of benefits specified in the Act), measures for the improvement of the health and welfare of insured persons and for the rehabilitation and re-employment of insured persons who have been disabled or injured or in respect of such measures expenditure from the funds of the Corporation within such limits as may be prescribed by the Central Government.

Section 29 empowers the Corporation (*a*) to acquire and hold property both movable and immovable, sell or otherwise transfer the said property; (*b*) it can invest and reinvest any moneys which are not immediately required for expenses and or realize such investments; (*c*) it can raise loans and discharge such loans with the previous sanction of Central Government; (*d*) it may constitute for the benefit of its staff or any class of them such provident or other benefit fund as it may think fit. However, the powers under Section 29 can be exercised subject to such conditions as may be prescribed by the Central Government.

Appointment of Regional Boards etc

The Corporation may appoint Regional Boards, Local Committees and Regional and Local Medical Benefit Councils in such areas and in such manner, and delegate to them such powers and functions, as may be provided by the regulations (Section 25).

Wings of the Corporation

The Corporation to discharge its functions efficiently has been provided with two wings:

1. Standing Committee
2. Medical Benefit Council

1. **Standing Committee:** The Act provides for the constitution of a Standing Committee under Section 8 from amongst its members. The Standing Committee has to administer affairs of the Corporation and may exercise any of the powers and perform any of the functions of the Corporation subject to the general superintendence and control of the Corporation. The Standing Committee acts as an executive body for administration of Employees State Insurance Corporation.

2. **Medical Benefit Council:** Section 10 empowers the Central Government to constitute a Medical Benefit Council. Section 22 determines the duties of the Medical Benefit stating that the Council shall:

   (*a*) Advice the Corporation and the Standing Committee on matters relating to administration of medical benefit, the certification for purposes of the grant of benefit and other connected matters;

   (*b*) Have such powers and duties of investigation as may be prescribed in relation to complaints against medical practitioners in connection with medical treatment and attendance matters;

   (*c*) Perform such other duties in connection with medical treatment and attendance as may be specified in the regulations.

Contribution to ESIC Fund: Both employee and employer have to make contribution to ESIC. The employer has to deduct contribution from wages of employee and pay to ESIC both the employer's contribution as well as employees' contribution [Section 39(1)].

The contribution is payable for 'wage period' *i.e.* the period in respect of which wages are payable to employee [Section 39(2)]. Normally, 'wage period' is a month. The employee's contribution is 1.75% of wages. It should be rounded off to next 5 paise. Employees contribution is not payable when daily wages are below ₹ 15.

Employer's contribution is 4.75% of total wage bill of all employees in respect of every wage period. Thus, it is not necessary to calculate employer's contribution separately for each employee. 4.75% of gross wages should be calculated and rounded off to next 5 paise. Employees drawing wages lower than ₹ 25 per day do not have to pay employee's share. The contribution has to be paid within 21 days from close of the month. It is payable by a challan in authorized bank. If the contribution is not paid in time, interest @ 12% is payable. [Section 39(5) (a)].

In addition, ESIC authorities can impose 'damages' varying between 5% to 25% of arrears of contribution u/s 85B.

Employer cannot deduct employer's contribution from the salary of employee [Section 40(3)].

Liability of Principal Employer: In case of employees of contractor, liability is of Principal Employer. In Britannia Industries v. ESIC (2001) 98 FJR 520 (Mad HC), it was held that Principal Employer will be liable to penalty and damages also if contribution is not paid on due date. Same view in Padmini Products v. ESIC 2000(2) Kar LJ 369 (Karn HC).

Contribution Period and Benefit Period: Contribution period is (*a*) 1st September to 31st March (*b*) 1st April to 30th September. The corresponding benefit period is (*a*) following 1st July to 31st December (*b*) following 1st January to 30th June. Thus, 'benefit period' starts three months after the 'contribution period' are over. The relevance of this definition is that sickness benefit and maternity benefit is available only during 'benefit period'. Thus, an employee gets these benefits only after 9 months after joining employment and paying contribution. However, other benefits are available during contribution period also.

Benefits to employees covered under ESI Act: The insured persons, their dependants or the persons hereinafter mentioned, as the case may be, shall be entitled to the following benefits, namely,

(*a*) Periodical payments to any insured person in case of his sickness certified by a duly appointed medical practitioner or by any other person possessing such qualifications and experience as the Corporation may, by regulations, specify in this behalf (thereinafter referred to as sickness benefit);

(*b*) Periodical payments to an insured woman in case of confinement or miscarriage or sickness arising out of pregnancy, confinement, premature birth of child or miscarriage, such woman being certified to be eligible for such payments by an authority specified in this behalf by the regulations (hereinafter referred to as maternity benefit);

(*c*) Periodical payments to an insured person suffering from disablement as a result of an employment injury sustained as an employee under this Act and certified to be eligible for such payments by an authority specified in this behalf by the regulations (hereinafter referred to as disablement benefit);

(*d*) Periodical payments to such dependants of an insured person who dies as a result of an employment injury sustained as an employee under this Act, as are entitled to compensation under this Act (hereinafter referred to as dependants' benefit);

(*e*) Medical treatment for and attendance on insured persons (i.e. medical benefit); and

(*f*) Payment to the eldest surviving, member of the family of an insured person who has died, towards the expenditure on the funeral of the deceased insured person or, to the person who actually incurs the expenditure on the funeral of the deceased insured person (to be known as funeral expenses):

Provided that the amount of such payment shall not exceed such amount as may be prescribed by the C.G, and the claim for such payment shall be made within three months of the death of the insured person or within such extended period as the

Corporation or any officer or authority authorized by it in this behalf may allow.

An employee is entitled to get benefits which are medical benefits as well as cash benefits. He also can get disablement benefit.

The Employees State Insurance Corporation, ESIC, has on the 15th of June 06, taken a historic decision to take over the ESI scheme in the States subject to the willingness of the State Governments. The decision was taken at the 136th meeting of the ESI Corporation held under the chairmanship of the former Labour and Employment Minister, Shri Chandrasekhar Rao.

Benefits not to be combined

1. An, insured person shall not be entitled to receive for the same period:
   (a) Both sickness benefit and maternity benefit; or
   (b) Both sickness benefit and disablement benefit for temporary disablement; or
   (c) Both maternity benefit and disablement benefit for temporary disablement.
2. Where a person is entitled to more than one of the benefits mentioned in sub-section (1), he/she shall be entitled to choose which benefit he shall receive.

Difference between - Sickness Benefit and Medical Benefit

Sickness benefit: Sickness benefit is periodical payment to any insured person in case his sickness is certified by a duty appointed medical practitioner or by any person having such qualification and experience as the ESI Corporation may specify in this behalf.

The qualification of a person to claim sickness benefit, the conditions subject to which such benefit may be given, the rates and period thereof shall be such as may be prescribed by the Central Government.

Medical benefit: Medical benefit is given to an insured person or a member of his family (in case such medical benefit is extended to his family) whose condition requires medical treatment and attendance.

Such medical benefit may be given either in the form of out-patient treatment and attendance in a hospital or dispensary, clinic or other institution or by visits to the home of the insured person or treatment as in-patient in a hospital or other institution.

A person is entitled to medical benefit during any period for which he is qualified to claim sickness benefit or maternity benefit or disablement benefits.

An insured person is not entitled to receive benefit of sickness with benefit of maternity or disablement, etc.

Employees' Insurance Court (E.I. Court)

Constitution

Section 74 of the Act provides that the State Government shall by notification in the Official Gazette constitute an Employees' Insurance Court for such local area as may be specified in the notification. The Court shall consist of such number of judges as the State Government may think fit. Any person who is or has been judicial officer or is a legal practitioner of 5 years standing shall be qualified to be a judge of E.I. Court. The State Government may appoint the same Court for two or more local areas or two or more Courts for the same local area and may regulate the distribution of business between them.

Matters to be decided by E.I. Court

(i) **Adjudication of disputes:** The Employees' Insurance Court has jurisdiction to adjudicate disputes, namely, whether any person is an employee under the Act, rate of wages/contribution, as to who is or was the principal employer, right of a person to any benefit under the Act.

(ii) **Adjudication of claims:** The E.I. Court also has jurisdiction to decide claims for recovery of contribution from principal employer or immediate employer, action for failure or negligence to pay contribution, claim for recovery of any benefit admissible under the Act.

Proceedings in both the above cases can be initiated by filing application in the prescribed form by the employee or his dependent or employer or the corporation depending who has cause of action.

No Civil Court has power to decide the matters falling within the purview/ jurisdiction of E.I. Court.

Exemptions

The appropriate Government may exempt any factory/establishment from the purview of this Act, as well as any person or class of persons employed in any factory/establishment, provided the employees employed therein are in receipt of benefits superior to the benefits under the Act. Such exemption is initially given for one year and may be extended from time to time. The applicant has to submit application justifying exemption with full details and satisfy the concerned Government.

PAYMENT OF GRATUITY ACT, 1972

Gratuity is a lump sum payment to employee when he retires or leaves service. It is basically a retirement benefit to an employee so that he can live life comfortably after retirement. However, under Gratuity Act, gratuity is payable even to an employee who resigns after completing at least 5 years of service.

In DTC Retired Employees v. Delhi Transport Corporation 2001(4) SCALE 30 = 2001 AIR SCW 2005, it was observed that gratuity is essentially a retiring benefit which as per Statute has been made applicable on voluntary resignation as well. Gratuity is reward for good, efficient and faithful service rendered for a considerable period.

The payment of Gratuity Act has been amended from time to time to bring it in tune with the prevailing situation. Recently the Act has been amended twice to enhance the ceiling on amount of gratuity from ₹ 3.50 lakh to ₹ 10 lakh as well as to widen the scope of the definition of 'employee' under section 2 (e) of the Act. These amendments have been introduced by the Payment of Gratuity (Amendment) Act, 2010 with effect from May 24, 2010 and the Payment of Gratuity (Amendment) Act, 2009 with effect from April 3, 2007, 1997 respectively.

Application of the Act

Application of the Act to an employed person depends on two factors. Firstly, he should be employed in an establishment to which the Act applies. Secondly, he should be an 'employee' as defined in Section 2(e).

Establishments to Which the Act Applies

According to Section 1(3), the Act applies to:

(a) Every factory, mine, oilfield, plantation, port and Railway Company;

(b) Every shop or establishment within the meaning of any law for the time being in force in relation to shops and establishments in a State, in which ten or more persons are employed, or were employed, on any day of the preceding twelve months;

(c) Such other establishments or class of establishments in which ten or more employees are employed, or were employed, on any day of the preceding twelve months as the Central Government may, by notification specify in this behalf.

In exercise of the powers conferred by clause (c), the Central Government has specified Motor transport undertakings, Clubs, Chambers of Commerce and Industry, Inland Water Transport establishments, Solicitors offices, Local bodies, Educational institutions, Societies, Trusts and Circus industry, in which 10 or more persons are employed or were employed on any day of the preceding 12 months, as classes of establishments to which the Act shall apply.

A shop or establishment, to which the Act has become applicable once, continues to be governed by it, even if the number of persons employed therein at any time after it has become so applicable falls below ten (Section 3A).

Who is an Employee?

The definition of 'employee' under section 2 (e) of the Act has been amended by the Payment of Gratuity (Amendment) Act, 2009 to cover the teachers in educational institutions retrospectively with effect from 3rd April, 1997. The amendment to the definition of 'employee' has been introduced in pursuance to the judgment of Supreme Court in Ahmedabad Private Primary Teachers' Association vs. Administrative Officer, AIR 2004 SC 1426. The ceiling on the amount of gratuity from ₹ 3.50 lakh to ₹ 10 lakh has been enhanced by the Payment of Gratuity (Amendment) Act, 2010.

Employees eligible for gratuity: 'Employee' means any person (other than apprentice) employed on wages in any establishment, factory, mine, oilfield, plantation, port, railway company or shop, to do any skilled, semi-skilled or unskilled, manual, supervisory, technical or clerical work, whether terms of such employment are express or implied, and whether such person is employed in a managerial or administrative capacity. However, it does not include any Central/State Government employee [Section 2(e)]. Thus, the Act is applicable to all employees - workers as well as persons employed in administrative and managerial capacity.

Gratuity is payable to a person on (*a*) resignation (*b*) termination on account of death or disablement due to accident or disease (*c*) retirement (*d*) death. Normally, gratuity is payable only after an employee completes five years of continuous service. In case of death and disablement, the condition of minimum 5 years' service is not applicable [Section 4(1)].

The Act is applicable to all employees, irrespective of the salary.

Other Important Definitions

Appropriate Government

"Appropriate Government" means:

(*i*) In relation to an establishment

(*a*) Belonging to, or under the control of, the Central Government,

(*b*) Having branches in more than one State,

(*c*) Of a factory belonging to, or under the control of the Central Government.

(*d*) Of a major port, mine, oilfield or railway company, the Central Government.

(*ii*) In any other case, the State Government [Section 2(a)].

It may be noted that many large establishments have branches in more than one State. In such cases the 'appropriate Government' is the Central Government and any dispute connected with the payment or non-payment of gratuity falls within the jurisdiction of the 'Controlling Authority' and the 'Appellate Authority' appointed by the Central Government under Sections 3 and 7.

Continuous Service

According to Section 2A, for the purposes of this Act:

1. An employee (shall be said to be in 'continuous service' for a period if he has, for that period been in uninterrupted service, including service which may be interrupted on account of sickness, accident, leave, absence from duty without leave not being absence in respect of which an order treating the absence as break in service has been passed in accordance with the standing orders, rules or regulations governing the employees of the establishment), layoff, strike or a lockout or cessation of work not due to any fault of the employee, whether such uninterrupted or interrupted service was rendered before or after the commencement of this Act;

2. Where an employee (not being an employee employed in a seasonal establishment) is not in continuous service within the meaning of clause (1) for any period of one year or six months, he shall be deemed to be in continuous service under the employer:

(*a*) for the said period of one year, if the employee during the period of twelve calendar months preceding the date with reference to which calculation is to be made, has actually worked under the employer for not less than:

(*i*) one hundred and ninety days in the case of an employee employed below the ground in a mine or in an establishment which works for less than six days in a week; and

(*ii*) two hundred and forty days in any other case;

(*b*) for the said period of six months, if the employee during the period of six calendar months preceding the date with reference to which the calculation is to be made, has actually worked under the employer for not less than:

    (*i*) ninety five days, in the case of an employee employed below the ground in a mine or in an establishment which works for less than six days in a week; and

    (*ii*) one hundred and twenty one days in any other case.

Family

Family, in relation to an employee, shall be deemed to consist of:

  (*i*) In case of a male employee, himself, his wife, his children, whether married or unmarried, his dependent parents and the dependent parents of his wife and the widow and children of his predeceased son, if any,

  (*ii*) In the case of a female employee, herself, her husband, her children whether married or unmarried, her dependent parents and the dependent parents of her husband and the widow and children of her predeceased son, if any [Section 2(h)].

Retirement

'Retirement' means termination of the service of an employee otherwise than on superannuation. [Section 2(q)].

Superannuation

'Superannuation' in relation to an employee, means the attainment by the employee of such age as is fixed in the contract or conditions of service as the age of the retirement of which the employee shall vacate the employment [Section 2 (r)].

Wages

"Wages" means all emoluments which are earned by an employee while on duty or on leave in accordance with the terms and conditions of his employment and which are paid or are payable to him in cash and includes dearness allowance but does not include any bonus, commission, house rent allowance, overtime wages and any other allowance [Section 2(s)].

When is Gratuity Payable?

According to Section 4(1) of the Payment of Gratuity Act, 1972, gratuity shall be payable to an employee on the termination of his employment after he has rendered continuous service for not less than five years:

  (*a*) On his superannuation, or

  (*b*) On his retirement or resignation, or

  (*c*) On his death or disablement due to accident or disease.

Note: The completion of continuous service of five years is not necessary where termination of the employment of any employee is due to death or disablement.

To Whom is Gratuity Payable?

It is payable normally to the employee himself. However, in the case of death of the employee, it shall be paid to his nominee and if no nomination has been made, to his heirs and where any such nominees or heirs is a minor, the share of such minor, shall be deposited with the controlling authority who shall invest the same for the benefit of such minor in such bank or other financial institution, as may be prescribed, until such minor attains majority.

Amount of gratuity payable: Gratuity is payable @ 15 days wages for every year of completed service. In the last year of service, if the employee has completed more than 6 months, it will be treated as full year for purpose of gratuity. In case of seasonal establishment, gratuity is payable @ 7 days wages for each season [Section 4(2)].

Wages shall consist of basic plus D.A, as per last drawn salary. However, allowances like bonus, commission, HRA, overtime etc. are not to be considered for calculations [Section 2(s)].

In case of employees paid on monthly wages basis, per day wages should be calculated by dividing monthly salary by 26 days to arrive at daily wages e.g., if last drawn salary of a person (basic plus DA) is ₹ 2,600 per month, his salary per day will be ₹ 100 (2,600 divided by 100). Thus, the employee is entitled to get ₹ 1,500 [15 days multiplied by ₹ 100 daily salary] for every year of completed service. If he has completed 30 years of service, he is entitled to get gratuity of ₹ 45,000 (₹ 1,500 multiplied by 30). Maximum gratuity payable under the Act is ₹ 3.50 lakhs (the ceiling was ₹ 1,00,000 which was increased to 2.50 lakhs on 24.9.97 by an ordinance which was later increased to ₹ 3.50 lakhs while converting the ordinance into Act].

Nomination

An employee covered by the Act is required to make nomination in accordance with the Rules under the Act for the purpose of payment of gratuity in the event of his death. The rules also provide for change in nomination.

Forfeiture of Gratuity

The Act deals with this issue in two parts. Section 4(6) (a) provides that the gratuity of an employee whose services have been terminated for any act of willful omission or negligence causing any damage or loss to, or destruction of, property belonging to the employer, gratuity shall be forfeited to the extent of the damage loss or caused. The right of forfeiture is limited to the extent of damage. In absence of proof of the extent of damage, the right of forfeiture is not available (LLJ- 11-19:-515 MP).

Section 4(6) (b) deals with a case where the services of an employee have been terminated:

(a) For riotous and disorderly conduct or any other act of violence on his part,

(b) For any act which constitutes an offence involving moral turpitude provided that such offence is committed by him in the course of his employment.

Exemptions

The appropriate Government may exempt any factory or establishment covered by the Act or any employee or class of employees if the gratuity or pensionary benefits for the employees are not less favourable than conferred under the Act.

The Controlling Authority and the Appellate Authority

The controlling authority and the Appellate Authority are two important functionaries in the operation of the Act. Section 3 of the Act says that the appropriate Government may by notification appoint any officer to be a Controlling Authority who shall be responsible for the administration of the Act. Different controlling authorities lay be appointed for different areas.

Section 7(7) provides for an appeal being preferred against an order of the Controlling Authority to the appropriate Government or such other authority as may be specified by the appropriate Government in this behalf.

Rights and Obligations of Employees

Application for Payment of Gratuity

Section 7(1) lays down that a person who is eligible for payment of gratuity under the Act or any person authorized, in writing; to act on his behalf shall send a written application to the employer. Rule 7 of the Payment of Gratuity (Central) Rules, 1972, provides that the application shall be made ordinarily within 30 days from the date gratuity becomes payable. The rules also provide that where the date of superannuation or retirement of an employee is known, the employee may apply to the employer before 30 days of the date of superannuation or retirement.

A nominee of an employee who is eligible for payment of gratuity in the case of death of the employee shall apply to the employer ordinarily within 30 days from the date of the gratuity becomes payable to him [Rule 7(2)].

Although the forms in which the applications are to be made have been laid down, an application on plain paper with relevant particulars is also accepted.

The application may be presented to the employer either by personal service or be registered post with acknowledgement due. An application for payment of gratuity filed after the period of 30 days mentioned above shall also be entertained by the employer if the application adduces sufficient cause for the delay in preferring him claim. Any dispute in this regard shall be referred to the Controlling Authority for his decision.

Rights and Obligations of the Employer

Employers Duty to Determine and Pay Gratuity

Section 7(2) lays down that as soon as gratuity becomes payable the employer shall, whether the application has been made or not, determine the amount of gratuity and give notice in writing to the person to whom the gratuity is payable and also to the Controlling Authority, specifying the amount of gratuity so determined.

Section 7(3) of the Act says that the employer shall arrange to pay the amount of gratuity within thirty days from the date of its becoming payable to the person to whom it is payable

Section 7(3A): If the amount of gratuity payable under sub-section (3) is not paid by the employer within the period specified in sub-section (3), the employer shall pay from the date on which the gratuity becomes payable to the date on which it is paid, simple interest at the rate of 10 per cent per annum.

Provided that no such interest shall be payable if the delay in the payment is to the fault of the employee and the employer has obtained permission in writing from the controlling authority for the delayed payment on this ground.

Dispute as to the Amount of Gratuity or Admissibility of the Claim

If the claim for gratuity is not found admissible, the employer shall issue a notice in the prescribed form to the applicant employee, nominee or legal heir, as the case may be, specifying reasons why the claim for gratuity is not considered admissible. A copy of the notice shall be endorsed to the Controlling Authority.

If the disputes relates as to the amount of gratuity payable, the employer shall deposit with the Controlling Authority such amount as he admits to be payable by him. According to Section 7(4)

(e), the Controlling Authority shall pay the amount of deposit as soon as may be after a deposit is made:

  (*i*) To the applicant where he is the employee; or
  (*ii*) Where the applicant is not the employee, to the nominee or heir of the employee if the Controlling Authority is satisfied that there is no dispute as for the right of the applicant to receive the amount of gratuity.

Recovery of Gratuity

Section 8 provides that if the gratuity payable under the Act is not paid by the employer within the prescribed time, the Controlling Authority shall, on an application made to it in this behalf by the aggrieved person, issue a certificate for that amount to the Collector, who shall recover the same together with the compound interest thereon at such rate as the Central Government may, by notification, specify, from the date of expiry of the prescribed time, as arrears of land revenue and pay the same to the person entitled thereto.

Act provides for minimum gratuity only: The Gratuity Act provides only for minimum gratuity payable. If employee has right to receive higher gratuity under a contract or under an award, the employee is entitled to get higher gratuity [Section 4(5)].

Employers liable under the scheme: The Act applies to every factory, mine, plantation, port, and Railway Company. It also applies to every shop and establishment where 10 or more persons are employed or were employed on any day in preceding 12 months [Section 1(3)]. Since the Act is also applicable to all shops and establishments, it will apply to motor transport undertakings, clubs, chambers of commerce and associations, local bodies, solicitor's offices etc., if they are employing 10 or more persons.

Maximum gratuity payable: Maximum gratuity payable is ₹ 4 lakhs [Section 4(3)]. [Of course, employer can pay more. Employee has also right to get more if obtainable under an award or contract with employer, as made clear in Section 4(5)].

Income-tax exemption: Gratuity received up to ₹ 3.50 lakhs is exempt from Income Tax. Gratuity paid above that limit is taxable [Section 10(10) of Income Tax Act]. However, employee can claim relief u/s 89 in respect of the excess amount.

No Compulsory insurance of gratuity liability – Section 4A provides that every employer must obtain insurance of his gratuity liability with LIC or any other insurer. However, Government companies need not obtain such insurance. If an employee is already member of gratuity fund established by an employer, he has option to continue that arrangement. If an employer employing more than 500 persons establishes an approved gratuity fund, he need not obtain insurance for gratuity liability. However, this Section has not yet been brought into force. Hence, presently, such compulsory insurance is not necessary.

Gratuity cannot be attached - Gratuity payable cannot be attached in execution of any decree or order of any civil, revenue or criminal court, as per Section 13 of the Act.

WORKMEN'S COMPENSATION ACT 1923

The Workmen's Compensation Act, aims to provide workmen and/or their dependents some relief in case of accidents arising out of and in the course of employment and causing either death or disablement of workmen. It provides for payment by certain classes of employers to their workmen compensation for injury by accident.

Object and Scope

The Employees' Compensation Act is social security legislation. It imposes statutory liability upon an employer to discharge his moral obligation towards his employees when they suffer from physical disabilities and diseases during the course of employment in hazardous working conditions. The Act also seeks to help the dependents of the employee rendered destitute by the 'accidents' and from the hardship arising out from such accidents. The Act provides for cheaper and quicker mode of disposal of disputes relating to compensation through special proceedings than possible under the civil law. The Act extends to the whole of India.

Who is a Workman

Workman means any person (other than a person whose employment is of a casual nature and who is employed otherwise than for the purposes of the employer's trade or business) who is:

(*i*) a railway servant as defined in section 3 of the Indian Railways Act, 1890 not permanently employed in any administrative, district or sub-divisional office of a railway and not employed in any such capacity as is specified in Schedule II, or

(*ii*) employed in any such capacity as is specified in Schedule II whether the contract of employment was made before or after the passing of this Act and whether such contract is expressed or implied, oral or in writing.

The provisions of the Act have been extended to cooks employed in hotels, restaurants using power, liquefied petroleum gas or any other mechanical device in the process of cooking.

Employees Entitled to Compensation

Every employee (including those employed through a contractor but excluding casual employees), who is engaged for the purposes of employer's business and who suffers an injury in any accident arising out of and in the course of his employment, shall be entitled for compensation under the Act.

Employer's Liability for Compensation (Accidents)

The employer of any establishment covered under this Act, is required to compensate an employee:

(*a*) Who has suffered an accident arising out of and in the course of his employment, resulting into (*i*) death, (*ii*) permanent total disablement, (*iii*) permanent partial disablement, or (iv) temporary disablement whether total or partial, or

(*b*) Who has contracted an occupational disease?

However the Employer Shall not be Liable

(*a*) In respect of any injury which does not result in the total or partial disablement of the workmen for a period exceeding three days;

(*b*) In respect of any injury not resulting in death, caused by an accident which is directly attributable to:

(*i*) the workmen having been at the time thereof under the influence of drugs, or

(*ii*) The willful disobedience of the workman to an order expressly given, or to a rule expressly framed, for the purpose of securing the safety of workmen, or

(*iii*) The willful removal or disregard by the workmen of any safeguard or other device which he knew to have been provided for the purpose of securing the safety of workmen. The burden of proving intentional disobedience on the part of the employee shall lie upon the employer.

(*iv*) When the employee has contacted a disease which is not directly attributable to a specific injury caused by the accident or to the occupation; or

(*v*) When the employee has filed a suit for damages against the employer or any other person, in a Civil Court.

Contracting Out

Any contract or agreement which makes the workman give up or reduce his right to compensation from the employer is null and void insofar as it aims at reducing or removing the liability of the employer to pay compensation under the Act.

What is Disablement

Disablement is the loss of the earning capacity resulting from injury caused to a workman by an accident. Disablement's can be classified as (*a*) Total, and (*b*) Partial. It can further be classified into (*i*) Permanent, and (*ii*) Temporary, Disablement, whether permanent or temporary is said to be total when it incapacitates a worker for all work he was capable of doing at the time of the accident resulting in such disablement. Total disablement is considered to be permanent if a workman, as a result of an accident, suffers from the injury specified in Part I of Schedule I or suffers from such combination of injuries specified in Part II of Schedule I as would be the loss of earning capacity when totalled to one hundred per cent or more. Disablement is said to be permanent partial when it reduces for all times, the earning capacity of a workman in every employment, which he was capable of undertaking at the time of the accident. Every injury specified in Part II of Schedule I is deemed to result in permanent partial disablement. Temporary disablement reduces the earning capacity of a workman in the employment in which he was engaged at the time of the accident.

Accident Arising Out of and in the Course of Employment

An accident arising out of employment implies a casual connection between the injury and the accident and the work done in the course of employment. Employment should be the distinctive and the proximate cause of the injury. The three tests for determining whether an accident arose out of employment are:

1. At the time of injury workman must have been engaged in the business of the employer and must not be doing something for his personal benefit;

2. That accident occurred at the place where he was performing his duties; and

3. Injury must have resulted from some risk incidental to the duties of the service, or inherent in the nature condition of employment.

The general principles that are evolved are: There must be a casual connection between the injury and the accident and the work done in the course of employment.

The onus is upon the applicant to show that it was the work and the resulting strain which contributed to or aggravated the injury. It is not necessary that the workman must be actually working at the time of his death or that death must occur while he was working or had just ceased to work; and where the evidence is balanced, if the evidence shows a greater probability which satisfies a reasonable man that the work contributed to the causing of the personal injury it would be enough for the workman to succeed. But where the accident involved a risk common to all humanity and did not involve any peculiar or exceptional danger resulting from the nature of the employment or where the accident was the result of an added peril to which the workman by his own conduct exposed himself, which peril was not involved in the normal performance of the duties of his employment, then the employer will not be liable.

Compensation in Case of Occupational Diseases

Workers employed in certain types of occupations are exposed to the risk of contracting certain diseases, which are peculiar and inherent to those occupations. A worker contracting an occupational disease is deemed to have suffered an accident out of and in the course of employment and the employer is liable to pay compensation for the same. Occupational diseases have been categorized in Parts A, B and C of Schedule III. The employer is liable to pay compensation:

(*a*) When a workman contracts any disease specified in Part B, while in service for a continuous period of 6 months under one employer. (Period of service under any other employer in the same kind of employment shall not be included),

(*b*) When a workman contracts any disease specified in Part C, while he has been in continuous service for a specified period, whether under one or more employers. (Proportionate compensation is payable by all the employers, if the workman had been in service under more than one employer).

If an employee has after the cessation of that service contracted any disease specified in the said Part B or Part C, as an occupational disease peculiar to the employment and that such disease arose out of the employment, the contracting of the disease shall be deemed to be an injury by accident within the meaning of the Act.

Calculation of Compensation

The amount of compensation payable by the employer shall be calculated as follows:

(*a*) In case of death - 50% of the monthly wages X Relevant Factor or ₹ 50,000, whichever is more and ₹1000 for funeral expenses.

(*b*) In case of total permanent disablement Specified under Schedule I - 60% of the monthly wages X Relevant Factor or ₹ 60,000, whichever is more.

(*c*) In case of partial permanent disablement specified under Schedule I - Such percentage of the compensation payable in case (*b*) above as is the percentage of the loss in earning capacity (specified in Schedule I).

(*d*) In case of partial permanent disablement not specified under Schedule I - Such percentage of the compensation payable in case (*b*) above, as is proportionate to the loss of earning Capacity (as assessed by a qualified medical practitioner).

(*e*) In case of temporary disablement (whether total or partial). A half-monthly installment equal to 25% of the monthly wages, for the period of disablement or 5 years, whichever is shorter.

When Compensation to be Deposited with Commissioner?

The amount of compensation is not payable to the workman directly. It is generally deposited along with the prescribed statement, with the Commissioner who will then pay it to the workman. Any payment made to the workman or his dependents, directly, in the following cases will not be deemed to be a payment of compensation:

(*i*) in case of death of the employee;

(*ii*) in case of lump sum compensation payable to a woman or a minor or a person of unsound mind or whose entitlement to the compensation is in dispute or a person under a legal disability.

(*iii*) Besides, compensation of ₹ 10 or more may be deposited with the Commissioner on behalf of the person entitled thereto. The receipt of deposit with the Commissioner shall be a sufficient proof of discharge of the employer's liability.

Amounts Permissible to be Paid to the Workman/Dependents Directly

Following amounts may be paid directly to the workman or his dependents:

(a) In case of death of the workman, any advance on account of compensation up to [an amount equal to three months' wages of such workman] may be paid to any dependent.

(b) In case of lump sum compensation payable to an adult male worker not suffering from any legal disability. In case of half-monthly payments payable to any workman.

Registration of Agreements of Compensation

1. Where the amount payable as compensation has been settled by agreement a memorandum thereof shall be sent by the employer to the Commissioner, who shall, on being satisfied about its genuineness, record the memorandum in a registered manner.

2. However, where it appears to the Commissioner that the agreement ought not to be registered by reason of the inadequacy of the sum or amount, or by reason that the agreement has been obtained by fraud or undue influence or other improper means he may refuse to record the agreement and may make such order including an order as to any sum already paid under the agreement as he thinks just in the circumstances.

3. An agreement for payment of compensation which has been registered shall be enforceable under this act notwithstanding anything contained in the Indian Contract Act, or any other law for the time being in force.

Effect of Failure to Register Agreement

When a memorandum of any agreement is not sent to the Commissioner for registration, the employer shall be liable to pay the full amount of compensation, which he is liable to pay under the provisions of this Act.

Filing of Claims

A claim for the compensation shall be made before the Commissioner. No claim for compensation shall be entertained by the Commissioner unless the notice of accident has been given by the workman in the prescribed manner, except in the following circumstances:

(a) in case of death of workman resulting from an accident which occurred on the premises of the employer, or at any place where the workman at the time of the accident was working: died on such premises or such place or in the vicinity of such premises or place;

(b) in case the employer has knowledge of the accident from any other source, at or about the time of its occurrence;

(c) in case the failure to give notice or prefer the claim, was due to sufficient cause.

Limitation

Workman, to the Commissioner, may file the claim for accident compensation in the prescribed form, within 2 years from the occurrence of the accident or from the date of death. The claim must be preceded by,

(i) A notice of accident, and

(ii) The claimant-employee must present himself for medical examination if so required by the employer.

Duties of Employers/Employees

To pay compensation for an accident suffered by an employee, in accordance with the Act. To submit a statement to the Commissioner (within 30 days of receiving the notice) in the prescribed form, giving the circumstances attending the death of a workman as result of an accident and indicating whether he is liable to deposit any compensation for the same.

To submit accident report to the Commissioner in the prescribed form within 7 days of the accident, which results in death of a workman or a serious bodily injury to a workman? To maintain a notice book in the prescribed from at a place where it is readily accessible to the workman.

To submit an annual return of accidents specifying the number of injuries for which compensation has been paid during the year, the amount of such compensation and other prescribed particulars.

Duties of Employees

To send a notice of the accident in the prescribed form, to the Commissioner and the employer, within such time as soon as it is practicable for him. The notice is precondition for the admission of the claim for compensation. To present himself for medical examination, if required by the employer.

Appeal/Bar to Civil Remedy

An appeal against and order of the Commissioner lies to the High Court, within 60 days of the order. The employer is required to deposit the compensation before filing the appeal. No right to compensation in respect of any injury shall exist under this act if he has instituted in Civil Court a suit for damages in respect of the injury against the employer or any other person; and no suit for damages shall be maintainable by a workmen in any Court of law in respect of any injury:

(*a*) if he has instituted a claim to compensation respect of the injury before a Commissioner; or

(*b*) if an agreement has come to between the workman and his employer providing for the payment of compensation in respect of the injury in accordance with the provisions of the Act.

MATERNITY BENEFITS ACT 1961

Introduction

Prior to the enactment of the Maternity Benefits Act of 1961, there were in force several central and state maternity benefits Act in the country. However, there was no uniformity in their provisions for all women workers in the country. It is true that its object was achieved by the enactment of the Employees' State Insurance Act, 1948, which superseded the provision of several Maternity Benefits Acts. But the ESI did not cover all women workers in the country. The Maternity Benefit Act of 1961 was therefore, passed to provide uniform maternity benefit for women workers in certain industries not covered by the Employees' State Insurance Act, 1948. The Act is amended by the Act No. 29 of 1995. The Amendment Act has come into force with effect from 1 February 1996.

The object of maternity leave and benefit is to protect the dignity of motherhood by providing for the full and healthy maintenance of women and her child when she is not working. With the advent of modern age, as the number of women employees is growing, the maternity leave and other maternity benefits are becoming increasingly common. But there was no beneficial piece of legislation in the horizon which is intended to achieve the object of doing social justice to women workers employed in factories, mines and plantation.

With the object of providing maternity leave and benefit to women employee the Maternity Benefit Bill was passed by both the Houses of Parliament and subsequently it received the assent of President on 12th December, 1961 to become an Act under short title and numbers "THE MATERNITY BENEFIT ACT, 1961 (53 OF 1961)".

1. To provide for maternity benefit to women workers in certain establishment.

2. To regulate the employment of women workers in such establishment for a certain period before and after child birth.

It is enacted by Parliament in the Twelfth Year of the Republic of India as follows:-

1. Short title, extent and commencement:

(1) This Act may be called the Maternity Benefit Act, 1961.

(2) It extends to the whole of India.

(3) It shall come into force on such date2as may be notified in this behalf in the Official Gazette:

(*a*) In relation to mines and to any other establishment wherein persons are employed for the exhibition of equestrian, acrobatic and other performances, by the Central Government; and (*b*) In relation to other establishments in a State, by the State Government.

2. Application of Act.:

It applies, in the first instance:

(*a*) to every establishment being a factory, mine or plantation including any such establishment belonging to Government and to every establishment wherein persons are employed for the exhibition of equestrian, acrobatic and other performances;

(*b*) to every shop or establishment within the meaning of any law for the time being in force in relation to shops and establishments in a State, in which ten or more persons are employed, or were employed, on any day of the preceding twelve months.

Provided that the State Government may, with the approval of the Central Government, after giving not less than two months notice of its intention of so doing, by notification in the Official Gazette, declare that all or any of the provisions of this Act shall apply also to any other establishment or class of establishments, industrial, commercial, agricultural or otherwise.

Save as otherwise provided in [sections 5A and 5B] nothing contained in this Act shall apply to any factory or other establishment to which the provisions of the Employees, State Insurance Act, 1948 (34 of 1948), apply for the time being.

MULTIPLE CHOICE QUESTIONS

1. A health condition requiring inpatient, hospital, or residential medical care or continuing physician care is
   A. Treatment
   B. Serious health condition
   C. Medical reimbursement
   D. None of the above

2. Sex discrimination is discriminatory conduct or actions based on sex or pregnancy, as it relates to conditions of employment, benefits, pay and opportunities for advancement is
   A. Fact
   B. Not factual
   C. Partially fact
   D. None of the above

3. Sexual harassment is an action that are sexually directed, are unwanted, and subject the worker to adverse employment conditions or create a hostile work environment is
   A. Fact
   B. Not factual
   C. Partially fact
   D. None of the above

4. The focus of a person's amorous or erotic desires and feelings toward members of the opposite or the same gender is
   A. Sex discrimination
   B. Sexual harassment
   C. Sexual orientation
   D. All the above

5. The Prohibits regarding discrimination based on physical or mental disabilities is
   A. Rehabilitation Act
   B. Reinforcement
   C. Both A and B
   D. None of the above

6. The practice of providing positive feedback to an individual or groups of individuals after completion of a particular project or achievement of a particular goal is
   A. Rehabilitation Act
   B. Reinforcement
   C. Both A and B
   D. None of the above

7. Statutory rights are the rights based on laws.
   A. True
   B. False
   C. Partially true
   D. None of the above

8. A court order requiring a person to perform, or to refrain from performing, a designated act is
   A. Talent hunting
   B. Injunctive relief
   C. Suspension
   D. None of the above

9. A physical or mental condition resulting from injury or illness, which diminishes an individual's faculties such as ability to hear, see, walk, talk, etc, are
   A. Destruction
   B. Impairment
   C. Both A and B
   D. None of the above

10. A common-law tort existing when an agreement is implied from circumstances, even though there has been no express agreement between the employer and the employee is
A. Implied contact   B. overt contact
C. Both A and B   D. None of the above

11. _____ indicates the work-related injuries and illnesses and the number of lost workdays per 100 employees.
A. Error
B. Incidence rate statistics
C. Sampling
D. None of the above

12. A legal proceeding occurring in a federal or state court of law to determine and enforce legal rights is
A. Litigation   B. Industrial relation
C. Both A and B   D. None of the above

13. The agency created by the Wagner Act to investigate unfair labour practice charges and to provide for secret-ballot is
A. National Labour Relations Board (NLRB)
B. National Labour Relations Act
C. Wagner Act
D. None of the above

14. This law banned certain types of unfair labour practices and provided for secret-ballot elections and majority rule for determining whether or not a firm's employees want to unionize is by
A. National Labour Relations Act
B. Wagner Act
C. Both A and B
D. None of the above

15. This _____ prohibited union unfair labour practices and enumerated the rights of employees as union members.
A. National Labour Relations Act
B. Wagner Act
C. Taft-Hartley Act
D. None of the above

16. Strikes that might "imperil the national health and safety" is by
A. National emergency strikes
B. State emergency strike

C. Wild cat strike
D. None of the above

17. The law aimed at protecting union members from possible wrongdoing on the part of their unions is by
A. Landrum-Griffin Act
B. Griffin Act
C. Landrum Act
D. None of the above

18. This law marked the beginning of the era of strong encouragement of unions and guaranteed to each employee the right to bargain collectively "free from interference, restraint, or coercion" is
A. Norris-LaGuardia Act
B. LaGuardia Act
C. Both A and B
D. None of the above

19. Shutdown of company operations undertaken by management to prevent union members from working.
A. Strike   B. Lockout
C. Boycott   D. Slow down

20. The process that refers to the employment contract restrictions used as a means of protecting the organization's trade secrets or proprietary information is
A. Trade clause   B. Gag clause
C. Both A & B   D. None of the above

21. A court action in which a portion of an employee's wages is set aside to pay a debt owed to a creditor is
A. Garnishment
B. Labour contract
C. Compensation management
D. None of the above

22. An individual who possesses the capabilities to perform more than one diversified function, rather than specializing in or having responsibility for one specific function is
A. Generalist
B. Operative function
C. Managerial function
D. None of the above

23. As related to international labour relations, groups of workers and management representatives charged with examining how to improve company performance, working conditions, job security, etc. are
    A. Trade union   B. Grids
    C. Work councils   D. None of the above

24. Reflects management decisions regarding specific actions to be taken, or avoid in a given situation is
    A. Rules and regulations
    B. Work rule
    C. Punishment
    D. None of the above

25. An accommodation made for an employee, such as time off from work, so that he or she may observe a religious holiday or attend a religious ceremony, is termed as
    A. Rest room
    B. Reception
    C. Empty room
    D. Religious accommodation

26. A type of benefit offered to employees who accept work assignments in new locations, typically takes the form of assistance with moving costs, travel expenses, temporary lodging and home buying/ selling is
    A. Transfer
    B. Relocation assistance
    C. Movement
    D. Migrate

27. A procedure that corrects or punishes a subordinate because a rule of procedure has been violated, is termed as
    A. Obedient
    B. Discipline
    C. Industrial regulation
    D. Factory regulation

28. Involuntary termination of an employee's employment with the firm is
    A. Dismissal
    B. Discipline
    C. Industrial regulation
    D. Factory regulation

29. The idea, based in law, that the employment relationship can be terminated at will by either the employer or the employee for any reasons said as Termination at will is
    A. Possible   B. Not possible
    C. Partially   D. None of the above

30. Willful disregard or disobedience of the boss's authority or legitimate orders, criticizing the boss in public is
    A. Insubordination   B. Disobedience
    C. Both A and B   D. None of the above

31. An employee dismissal that does not comply with the law or does not comply with the contractual arrangement stated or implied by the firm via its employment application forms, employee manuals, or other promises is
    A. Termination
    B. Insubordination
    C. Wrongful Discharge
    D. All the above

32. The perceived fairness of the relation between what a person does (inputs) and what the person receives (outcomes) is termed as
    A. Equity   B. Content validity
    C. Balance approach D. None of the above

33. Who is an adult as per Factories Act, 1948?
    A. Who has completed 18 years of age
    B. Who is less than 18 years
    C. Who is more than 14 years
    D. Who is more than 15 years

34. Who is an Adolescent as per Factories Act, 1948?
    A. Who has completed 17 years of age
    B. Who is less than 18 years
    C. Who has completed 15 years but less than 18 years.
    D. None of the above

35. Canteen is to be provided if engaging employees more than _____ persons.
    A. 250   B. 230
    C. 300   D. 275

36. The Ambulance Room is to be provided if engaging employees more than _____
    A. 400   B. 350
    C. 500   D. 450

37. Which act provides for the Health, Safety and Welfare of Apprentices?
A. Apprenticeship Act
B. Factories Act, 1948
C. Workmen Compensation Act
D. None of the above

38. The employees drawing up to ₹ _____ as wages are only covered under ESI, Act, 1948?
A. 6500   B. 8500
C. 10000   D. None of the above

39. Which one of the following is not a welfare provision under Factories Act, 1948?
A. Canteen   B. Creches
C. First Aid   D. Drinking water.

40. When was the Minimum Wages Act enacted?
A. 1947   B. 1946
C. 1948   D. None of the above

41. Any imbalance in input-output relation in any incentive payment scheme can result in
A. Tension   B. Lower productivity
C. More absenteeism D. All the above

42. In the history of Indian IT industry, the year 2001-2002 will be remembered as _____.
A. The great success B. Year of lay-offs
C. Highest pay masters D. None of the above

43. Documents useful for the purpose of wage analysis are
A. Wage sheets
B. Payroll
C. Accounting registers
D. All the above

44. For a normal adult the net intake of calories should be
A. 2700   B. 2800
C. 2600   D. 2750

45. Basic compensation systems are
A. Time rate system B. Piece rate system
C. Both A and B   D. None of the above

46. Minimum wages are not to be fixed in an industry which employs less then how many employees in the entire state?
A. 1000   B. 1500
C. 2000   D. 2500

47. _____ is that portion of which Government declares to be paid for all purposes and for inflation in cost.
A. Increment   B. Dearness Pay
C. Incentives   D. All the above

48. Major components of compensation
A. Salary   B. Basic salary
C. Consolidated salary D. All the above

49. Components of wage & salary are
A. Basic wage
B. Overtime wage
C. Dearness allowance
D. All the above

50. Incentive schemes should be installed right from beginning of production.
A. True   B. False
C. No command   D. None of the above

51. The occupational diseases are listed under which schedule of factories Act
A. First schedule   B. Second schedule
C. Third schedule   D. None of the above

52. This is used to define occupations or specific fields where women typically comprise less than 25 per cent of the workforce is
A. Traditional employment
B. Non-Traditional employment
C. Employability rights
D. None of the above

53. Works Committee is to be constituted in an Industry which is employing _____ or more employees?
A. 75   B. 90
C. 100   D. 80

54. The process by which a Third Party Persuades disputants to come to an amicable adjustment of claims is called?
A. Arbitration
B. Collective Bargaining
D. Conciliation
D. None of the above

55. The Maximum Amount of Gratuity Payable under Payment of Gratuity Act is _____
A. ₹ 3,00,000   B. ₹ 3,50,000
C. ₹ 3,75,000   D. None of the above

56. The Gratuity is payable to person who has rendered service of _____ years?
    A. 5   B. 3
    C. 6   D. 4

57. The provision for cooling water during hot weather should be made by the organization if it employees _____ or more employees.
    A. 200   B. 250
    C. 300   D. 150

58. Safety Officers are to be appointed if Organization is engaging _____ or more employees.
    A. 1000   B. 2000
    C. 500   D. 750

59. What percentage is the employer's contribution under ESI Act, 1948?
    A. 4.75 %   B. 4%
    C. 5 %   D. 3.5%

60. What percentage is the employee's contribution under ESI Act, 1948?
    A. 2.75 %   B. 3%
    C. 1.75 %   D. 3.75%

61. An adult worker can up to ____ hrs in a day as per factories Act, 1948
    A. 8   B. 9
    C. 10   D. 12

62. Leave with wages is allowed for employees if they work for _____ days in a month.
    A. 15   B. 25
    C. 20   D. 28

63. What is the percentage of Maximum bonus Payable?
    A. 25%   B. 20%
    C. 22%   D. 26%

64. What is the percentage of Minimum bonus Payable ?
    A. 7.33%   B. 8.33%
    C. 9.33%   D. 6.33%

65. Employee's State Insurance Act, _____ is a pioneering measure in the field of social insurance of our country.
    A. 1948   B. 1947
    C. 1949   D. 1946

66. Who is an adult as per Factories Act, 1948?
    A. Who has completed 18 years of age
    B. Who is less than 18 years
    C. Who is more than 14 years
    D. Who is more than 15 years

67. The space for every worker employed in the Factory after the commencement of Factories Act, 1948 should be _____ Cubic Metres.
    A. 9.9   B. 10.2
    C. 14.2   D. 13.2

68. A survey of expert opinion that includes each expert's review of the other's ideas; the expert's identity is not disclosed to the others in order to ensure that the decision is not through consensus is
    A. Management Information System
    B. Delphi method
    C. Quality audit
    D. None of the above

69. It is the obligation to carry out responsibility and exercise authority in terms of performance standards established is
    A. Responsibility   B. Accountability
    C. Both A and B   D. None of the above

70. A corporate portfolio management approach that examines the rate of market growth and market share of each of a corporation's business units to help top management develop a balance between those business units that absorb cash and those that provide it is
    A. Management game B. Business game
    C. BCG matrix   D. Kaizen

71. The main functions of the ILO is
    A. to establish international labour standards
    B. to collect and disseminate information on labour and industrial conditions; and
    C. to provide technical assistance for carrying out programmes of social and economic development
    D. All the above

72. The ESI Act has been passed to provide for certain benefits to employees in case of
    A. Sickness   B. Maternity
    C. Employment injury D. All the above

73. Employees' State Insurance Act, 1948 extends to the whole for
   A. Few State in IndiaB. India
   C. State capital   D. None of the above

74. The coverage under the ESI Act is at present restricted to employees drawing wages not exceeding
   A. ₹ 18000 per month   B. ₹ 13000 per month
   C. ₹ 15000 per month   D. None of the above

75. Payment of Gratuity Act, was amended in
   A. 1972   B. 1975
   C. 1912   D. 1919

76. Gratuity is a lump sum payment to employee when he retires or leaves service.
   A. True   B. False
   C. As pension   D. None of the above

77. The first Factories Act was enacted in
   A. 1881   B. 1895
   C. 1897   D. 1885

78. A person who has ultimate control over the affairs of the factory under Factories Act, 1948 is called as _____.
   A. Occupier   B. Manager
   C. Chairman   D. Managing Director

79. Following are the main causes of industrial dispute
   A. Wages/ Allowance/ Bonus/ Work Load
   B. Leave/ Working hours/ Work conditions
   C. Retrenchment/ Layoffs/ Indiscipline/ Violence
   D. All the above

80. Match the following
   (*i*) Economic strike (*a*) for demands like wages and bonus
   (*ii*) Sympathetic strike (*b*) to support the strike in other units.
   (*iii*) General strike (*c*) Strike by all the unions in an industry or region.
   (*iv*) Sit down strike (*d*) Workers come to the work place but do not work
   (*v*) Slow down strike (*e*) Workers work but at a low efficiency

   (*vi*) Sick (*f*) A large number of members call in sick on the same day.
   (*vii*) Wild cat strikes (*g*) Carried out with the consent of unions

	(*i*)	(*ii*)	(*iii*)	(*iv*)	(*v*)	(*vi*)	(*vii*)
A.	(*a*)	(*c*)	(*d*)	(*e*)	(*b*)	(*g*)	(*h*)
B.	(*b*)	(*g*)	(*h*)	(*d*)	(*c*)	(*e*)	(*a*)
C.	(*c*)	(*h*)	(*d*)	(*a*)	(*e*)	(*g*)	(*b*)
D.	(*a*)	(*b*)	(*c*)	(*d*)	(*e*)	(*f*)	(*g*)

81. Which of the following is not rightly matched of some of the central trade unions in India below:
   (*i*) AITUC - All India Trade Union Congress
   (*ii*) BMS - Hind Mazdoor Sabha
   (*iii*) CITU - Centre of Indian Trade Unions
   (*iv*) HMKP - Hind Mazdoor Kisan Panchayat
   (*v*) HMS - Bhartiya Mazdoor Sangh
   (*vi*) IFFTU - Indian Federation of Free Trade Unions
   (*vii*) INTUC - Indian National Trade Union Congress
   (*viii*) NFITU - National Front of Indian Trade Unions
   (*ix*) NLO - National Labour Organization
   (*x*) TUCC - Trade Unions Co-ordination Centre
   (*xi*) UTUC - United Trade Union Congress
   (*xii*) UTUC - LS - United Trade Union Congress - Lenin Sarani
   A. (*ii*) and (*v*)   B. (*i*) and (*v*)
   C. (*ii*) and (*vi*)   D. None of the above

82. (*i*) Militant functions - Rise in wages, rise in the status of workers, protection against injustice
   (*ii*) Fraternal functions- Measures to boost up the workers' morale, Foster self confidence, Develop sincerity and discipline, Protection to women workers against discrimination.
   A. Statement (*i*) is right
   B. Statement (*ii*) is right
   C. Both Statement (*i*) and (*ii*) are right
   D. Both Statement (*i*) and (*ii*) are wrong

83. Indian labour market can be mainly classified into:
   A. Rural workers   B. Organized
   C. Unorganized   D. All the above

84. Match the following

(*a*) Distributive bargaining — (*i*) This kind of bargaining aims at achieving the consensus within the trade union and management group.

(*b*) Integrative bargaining — (*ii*) This type of bargaining mainly aims at developing a change in the attitude of the management and the employees. The purpose is to reduce the bitterness and develop a congenial atmosphere.

(*c*) Attitudinal restructuring — (*iii*) Also termed as co-operative bargaining, this form of bargaining is for overall improvement in the working of the organization. No party loses here, so, the level of co-operation is more.

(*d*) Intra-organizational bargaining — (*iv*) Also termed as conjunctive bargaining, this form of bargaining aims at re-distribution of benefits between the management and the group of workers. In this form of bargaining, one group gains while the other loses something

	(*a*)	(*b*)	(*c*)	(*d*)
A.	(*iv*)	(*ii*)	(*iii*)	(*i*)
B.	(*ii*)	(*iv*)	(*i*)	(*iii*)
C.	(*ii*)	(*i*)	(*iii*)	(*iv*)
D.	(*i*)	(*ii*)	(*iii*)	(*iv*)

85. Before the enactment of Employees' Compensation Act, 1923, workers suffering a personal injury in course of employment claimed damages under
A. Economic Law   B. Social Law
C. Common Law   D. None of the above

ANSWERS

1	2	3	4	5	6	7	8	9	10
B	A	A	C	A	A	A	B	C	A
11	**12**	**13**	**14**	**15**	**16**	**17**	**18**	**19**	**20**
B	A	A	C	C	A	A	A	B	B
21	**22**	**23**	**24**	**25**	**26**	**27**	**28**	**29**	**30**
A	A	C	B	D	B	B	A	A	C
31	**32**	**33**	**34**	**35**	**36**	**37**	**38**	**39**	**40**
C	A	A	C	A	C	B	A	D	C
41	**42**	**43**	**44**	**45**	**46**	**47**	**48**	**49**	**50**
D	B	D	A	C	A	B	D	D	B
51	**52**	**53**	**54**	**55**	**56**	**57**	**58**	**59**	**60**
C	B	C	C	B	A	B	A	A	C
61	**62**	**63**	**64**	**65**	**66**	**67**	**68**	**69**	**70**
B	C	B	B	A	A	C	B	B	C
71	**72**	**73**	**74**	**75**	**76**	**77**	**78**	**79**	**80**
D	D	B	C	A	A	A	A	D	D
81	**82**	**83**	**84**	**85**					
A	C	D	D	C					

❖—❖—❖

7

Settlements of Industrial Disputes and Wage Legislation

TRADE UNION ACT 1926

Trade Union is formed by the means of any combination whether temporary or permanent, but the primarily purpose is to:

1. Regulating the relations
   (a) Between workmen and employers, or
   (b) Between workmen and workmen, or
   (c) Between employers and employers, or
2. For imposing restrictive conditions on the conduct of any trade or business and includes any federation of two or more Trade Unions.

Provided that this Act shall not affect:

(a) Any agreement between partners as to their own business.
(b) Any agreement between an employer and those employed by him as to such employment; or
(c) Any agreement in consideration of the sale of the goodwill of a business or of instruction in any profession, trade or handicraft.

The definition of trade union not only recognizes the combination of workers but any combination of employers will also come within the scope of the term trade union. However, deciding factor will be the purpose for which this combination is formed. Thus a combination of employers in a jute industry, imposing restrictions on the members in respect of prices to be charged from customers is covered under the definition of trade union.

Registration of Trade Unions

Registration of trade union is not compulsory but is desirable since a registered trade union enjoys certain rights and privileges under the Act.

Procedure for Registration

Minimum seven members of an established (or seven employers) can form a trade union and apply to the Registrar for the registration. The application for registration should be in the prescribed form and accompanied by the prescribed fee, a copy of the rules of the union signed by at least 7 members and a statement containing:

(a) The name, address and occupation of the members making the application.
(b) The name of the trader union and the address of its head office.
(c) The titles, names, ages, addresses and occupations of its office bearers.

If the union has been existence for more than a year, then a statement of its assets and liabilities in the prescribed form should also be submitted along with the application.

The executive committee/office bearers of the union should be constituted in accordance with the provisions of the Act.

Registration

The Registrar shall register a Trade Union by entering in a register to be maintained in Form B the particulars relating to the Trade Union after being satisfied that the Trade Union has complied with all the requirements in regards to registration. If all the terms of Act are complied with, it is obligatory upon the Registrar to register a Union and he has no discretion in the matter.

Certificate of Registration

The Registration on registering a Trade Union under section 8 shall issue a certificate of Registration in Form C which shall be conclusive evidence that the Trade Union has been duly registered under the Act, the certifiable of Registration continues to be valid, until it is cancelled (1992 IILW 1987).

The Trade Unions Act 1926 has been an Act to provide registration of Trade Unions and in certain aspect define the law relating to register Trade unions does not cast any obligation on the employer to maintain any register, record/books etc, nor does it require filling of a return/ notice.

Power to call for further particulars

The Registrar may call for further information for satisfying himself that the application is complete and is in accordance with the provisions of section 5 and 6 and that the proposed name of the union does not resemble with the name of any existing trade union.

Rules of a union

The rules of a trade union should clearly mention its name and objects the purpose for which its funds can be used provision for maintenance of a list of members, procedure for admission of ordinary, honorary or temporary members rate of subscription procedure for amending or rescinding rules, manner of appointing executive committee and other office bearers, safe custody of funds, audit and inspection of account book, procedure for dissolution of the union and changing the union.

Legal status of a Registered Trade Union

(*i*) A registered trade union is a body corporate with perpetual succession and a common seal.

(*ii*) It can acquire, hold sell or transfer any movable or any immovable property and can be a party to contracts.

(*iii*) A registered trade union can sue and be sued in its own name.

(*iv*) No civil suit or other legal proceeding can be initiated against a registered trade union in respect of any act done in furtherance of trade dispute under certain conditions.

(*v*) No agreement between the members of a registered trade union shall be void or voidable merely on the ground that any of its objects is in restraint of trade.

Cancellation of Registration

The Registrar can withdraw or cancel registration of a trade union on an application being made for its cancellation or by giving at least 2 months notice under any of the following circumstances:

(*i*) If the registration has been obtained by fraud or mistake,

(*ii*) If the union has ceased to exist,

(*iii*) If it has willfully contravened any of the provisions of the Act, or

(*iv*) If any rule which is required under section 6 has been deleted.

The registrar should satisfy himself that the withdrawal or cancellation of registration has been approved of the majority of the members. For this he may call or examine any person or particulars.

Registered Office

All communications and notices to a registered Trade Union may be addressed to its registered office. Notice of any change in the address of the head office shall be given within fourteen days of such change to the registrar in writing and changed address shall be recorded in the register.

Membership of Trade Union

Any person can become a member of the trade union. The members of the union must be those who are actually engaged in the trade or industry with which the union is concerned. But there is nothing in the Act which debars trade unions from admitting outsiders as its members. A person does not have the absolute right to be admitted as members. A person does not have the absolute right to be admitted as a member of the trade union. He may however claim this right if there is an express provision in the constitution of the union that no one having the requisite qualification can be refused membership.

Certain Acts not apply to Registered Trade Unions

The following Acts shall not apply to a registered Trade Unions and the registration of any such trade union under such Act shall be void:

1. The societies registration Act 1860.
2. The cooperative societies Act 1912.
3. The companies Act 1956 (section 14).

Dissolution of Trade Union

A registered trade union can be dissolved in accordance with the rules of the union. A notice of dissolution designed by any seven members and the secretary of the Union should be sent to the Registrar within 14 days of the dissolution. On being satisfied, the registrar shall register the notice and the union shall stand dissolved from the date. The funds of the union shall be divided by the registrar amongst its members in the manner prescribed under the rules of the union or as laid down by the government.

Amalgamation of Trade Union

Any registered trade union may amalgamate with any other union(s) provided that at least 50% of the member of each such union record their votes and at least 60% of the votes so recorded are in favour of amalgamation. A notice of amalgamation signed by the secretary and at least seven members of each amalgamation union should be sent to the Registrar and the amalgamation shall be in operation after the Registrar registers the notice.

Rights of Registered Trade Union

A trade union has a right to demonstrate. A trade union has a right to appeal against an order of the Registrar either refusing or cancelling registration to the Civil court/ High court within the prescribed time.

Obligations of Registered Trade Unions

1. The general funds of a registered trade union should be spent only for the objects specified under section 15 such as:
   (a) Payment of salaries, allowances and expenses of its office bearers,
   (b) Its administrative and audit expenses,
   (c) Prosecution or defense of any legal proceedings for securing or protecting its rights,
   (d) Conduct of trade disputes,
   (e) Provisions of educational, social or religions benefits and allowances on account of death, old age, sickness accident or unemployment to its member,
   (f) Publication of labour journals.
2. The trade unions may set up separate political funds for furtherance of civic and political interests of members, contribution to this fund shall not be compulsory.
3. The account books and membership register of the trade union should be kept open for inspection by any of its members or office bearers.
4. A copy of every alteration made is the rules of the union should be sent to the Registrar within 15 days of making the alteration.
5. An annual statement of receipt are expenditures and assets and liabilities of the union for the year ending on 31st December, prepared in the prescribed forms and duly audited should be accompanied by a statement showing changes in office bearers during the year and a copy of the rules as amended up to date.

INDUSTRIAL EMPLOYMENT (STANDING ORDER) ACT 1946

The employer could hire or fire workman, without following any set of procedure of giving them any opportunities to define themselves. Such arbitrary dismissals and discharges created constantly observed and the experience has shown that standing orders defining the conditions of recruitment, discharge, disciplinary action, holidays leave etc, go along was towards minimizing friction between the management and workers in industrial undertakings.

Discussions on the subject in the tripartite labour conferences in 1943, 1944, and 1945 revealed consensus of opinion in favour of a separate central enactment making it obligatory, on the part of the employers in large industrial undertakings in the country to frame and enforce with the approval of the Government Standing orders defining precisely the conditions of employment under them. For improving industrial relations the Government considered it necessary to standardize conditions of employment in private industry including any disciplinary action. The Industrial Employment (standing orders) Act was thus passed in 1946.

Object of the Act

The Act requires the employers in industrial establishment to define with sufficient precision the conditions of employment for workers under them and make the said conditions known to workmen employed by them.

The objects of the Act are:

1. To enforce uniformity in the conditions of services under different employers in different industrial establishments.
2. The employer, once having made the conditions of employment known to his employed workmen cannot change them to their detriment or to the prejudice of their rights and interests.
3. With the express or written conditions of employment, it is open for the prospective worker to accept them and join the industrial establishment.
4. For maintaining industrial peace and continued productivity, the significance of the express written conditions of employment cannot be minimized or exaggerated.

The object of the Act is to have uniform standing orders in respect of matters enumerated in the Schedule to the Act, applicable to all workers irrespective of their time of appointment **[Baruni**

Refinery Pragati Sheel **Parshad v. Indian Oil Corporation Ltd. (1991)]**

Scope of the Act

The Act extends to the whole of India and applies to every industrial establishment wherein 100 or more workmen are employed on any day during the preceding twelve months.

Further the appropriate Government may, after giving not less than 2 months notice of its intention to do so by notification in the Official Gazette, extend the provisions of this Act to any industrial establishment employing such number of persons less than 100 as may be specified in the notification.

However, the Act does not apply to:

1. Any industry to which provisions of Chapter VII of the Bombay Industrial Relations Act, 1946, apply: or
2. Any industrial establishment to which provisions of Madhya Pradesh Industrial Employment (Standing Orders) Act, 1961 apply.

Notwithstanding anything contained in the said Act, the provisions of this Act shall apply to all industrial establishments under the control of Central Government.

Further, Section 14 provides that the appropriate Government may by notification in the Official Gazette **exempt** conditionally or unconditionally any industrial establishment or class of industrial establishments from all or any of the provisions of this Act.

DEFINITIONS

Appellate Authority

It means an authority appointed by the appropriate Government by notification in the Official Gazette, to exercise in such area as may be specified in the notification the functions of an Appellate authority under this Act [Section 2 (a)].

Appropriate Government

Appropriate Government means in respect of industrial establishments under the control of the Central Government or a Railway administration or a major port, mine or oilfield the Central Government and in all other cases the State Government.

Certifying Officer

Certifying Officer means a Labour Commissioner or a Regional Labour Commissioner, and includes any other appointed by the appropriate Government by NIOG, to perform all or any of the functions of a certifying Officer under this Act [Section 2(c)].

Employer

Employer means the owner of an industrial establishment to which this Act applies and also includes the following persons:

(*i*) A manager so named under Section 7(1)(f) of the Factories Act, 1948.

(*ii*) The head of the department or any authority appointed by the Government in any industrial establishment under its control.

(*iii*) Any person responsible to the owner for the supervision and control of any other industrial establishment which is not under the control of Government [Sec. 2(d)].

Industrial Establishment

It means:

(*i*) An industrial establishment defined by Sec. 2(*ii*) of the Payment of Wages Act, 1936 or

(*ii*) A factory as defined by section 2 (m) of the Factories Act, 1948.

(*iii*) A railway as defined by Section 2 (4) of the Indian Railways Act, 1890, or

(*iv*) The establishment of a person who, for the purpose of fulfilling a contract with the owner of any industrial establishment, employs workmen [Section 2 (e)].

Standing Orders

Standing Orders means rules relating to matters set out in the Schedule to the Act [Section 2(g)].

Wages and workmen

The terms "Wages" and "Workmen" have the meanings respectively assigned to them in clauses (r) and (s) of Section 2 of the **Industrial Disputes Act, 1947** [Section 2 (*i*)].

Certification of Draft Standing Orders

Section 3 provides that within **six months** from the date on which this Act becomes applicable to an industrial establishment, the employer of that establishment shall submit to the Certifying Officer five copies of the draft Standing Orders proposed by him for adoption in that establishment.

Such Draft Standing Orders shall be in conformity with the Model Standing Orders, if any, and shall contain every matter set out in the Schedule which may be applicable to the industrial establishments.

The draft Standing Orders shall be accompanied by a statement containing prescribed particulars of the workmen, employed in the industrial establishment including the name of the trade union, if any, to which they belong.

If the industrial establishments are of similar nature, a group of employers owning those industrial establishments may submit a joint draft of Standing Orders subject to such conditions as may be prescribed.

Conditions for certification of Standing Orders

According to Section 4 of the Act, Standing Orders shall be certifiable if –

(*a*) Provision is made therein for every matter stated in the Schedule to the Act which is applicable to industrial establishment; and

(*b*) The Standing Orders are otherwise in conformity with the provisions of the Act.

Fairness or Reasonableness of Standing Orders

The Act has imposed a duty on the Certifying Officer, to consider the reasonableness and fairness of the Standing Orders before certifying the same. The Certifying Officer is under a legal duty to consider that the Standing Orders are in conformity with the Act. If the Certifying Officer finds that some provisos, as proposed by the employer relate to matters which are not included in the Schedule, or if he finds some provisions are unreasonable, he must refuse to certify the same. Certification of any such Standing Order would be without jurisdiction.

The Certifying Officer has a mandatory duty to discharge and he acts in a quasi-judicial manner. Where a matter is not included in the Schedule and the concerned appropriate Government has not added any such item to the Schedule, neither the employer has a right to frame a Standing Order enabling him to transfer his employees nor does the Certifying Officer has jurisdiction to certify the same. The consent of the employees to such standing orders would not make any difference (**Air gases Mazdoor Sangh, Varanasi v. Indian Air Gases Ltd., 1977 Lab. I.C. 575**).

Certification of Standing Orders

Procedure to be followed by the Certifying Officer: On receipt of the draft Standing Order from the employer, the Certifying Officer shall forward a copy thereof to the trade union of the workmen or where there is no trade union, then to, the workmen in such manner as may be prescribed, together with a notice requiring objections, if any, which the workmen may desire to make in the draft Standing Orders.

These objections are required to be submitted to him within 15 days from the receipt of the notice.

On receipt of such objections he shall provide an opportunity of being heard to the workmen and the employer and will make amendments, if any, required to be made therein and this will render the draft Standing Orders certifiable under the Act and he will certify the same.

A copy of the certified Standing Orders will be sent by him to both the employer and the employees association within seven days of the certification.

Effect of certification: The Act is a special law in regard to matters enumerated in the Schedule and the regulations made by the employer with respect to any of those matters.

These are of no effect unless such regulations are notified by Government under Sec. 13B or certified by the Certifying Officer under Section 5 of the Act.

Register of Standing Orders: Section 8 empowers the Certifying Officer to file a copy of all the Standing Orders as certified by him in a register maintained for the purpose in the prescribed form.

He shall furnish a copy of the same to any person applying therefore on payment of the prescribed fee.

Appeals

The order of the Certifying Officer can be challenged by any employer, workman, trade union or any other prescribed representatives of the workmen, who can file an appeal before the appellate authority within 30 days from the date on which copies are sent to employer and the workers representatives.

The appellate authority, whose decision shall be final, has the power to confirm the Standing Orders as certified by the Certifying Officer or to amend them.

The appellate authority is required to send copies of the Standing Orders as confirmed or modified by it, to the employer, workers representatives **within 7 days** of its order.

The Appellate authority has no power to set aside the order of Certifying Officer; it can confirm or amend the Standing Orders (**Khadi Gram Udyog Sangh v. Jit Ram**).

The appellate authority cannot remand the matter for fresh consideration [**Kerala Agro Machinery Corporation (1998)**].

Date of Operation of Standing Orders

Standing Orders shall come into operation **on the expiry of 30 days** from the date on which the authenticated copies are sent to employer and workers' representatives OR where an appeal has been preferred, they will become effective **on the expiry of 7 days** from the date on which copies of the order of the appellate authority are sent to employer and workers' representatives. (Section 7)

Posting of Standing Orders

The text of the Standing Orders as finally certified under this Act shall be prominently posted by the employer in English and in the language understood by the majority of his workmen on special boards to be maintained for the purpose at or near the entrance through which the majority of the workmen enter the industrial establishment and in all departments thereof where the workmen are employed. (Section 9)

Duration and Modification of Standing Orders

Section 10 prohibits an employer to modify the Standing Orders once they are certified under this Act except on agreement between the employer and the workmen or a trade union or other representatives' body of the workmen.

Such modification will not be affected until the expiry of 6 months from the date on which the Standing Orders were last modified or certified as the case may be.

This section further empowers an employer or the workmen or a trade union or other representatives' body of the workmen to apply to the: Certifying Officer to have the Standing Orders modified by making an application to the certifying Officer.

Such application should be accompanied by 5 copies of the proposed modifications and where such modifications are proposed to be made by agreement between the employer and the workmen or a trade union or other representative body of the workmen, a certified copy of such agreement should be filed along with the application.

Workmen are entitled to apply for modification of the Standing Orders.

Sec. 10(2) does not contain any time limit for making modification application. It can be made at any time. **[Indian Express Employees Union vs. Indian Express (Madurai) Ltd. (Kerala)]**

Payment of Subsistence Allowance

Statutory provision for payment of subsistence allowance has been made under section 10A of the Act which was inserted by the amending Act of 1982. **Section 10A** provides as follows:

Where any workman is suspended by the employer pending investigation or inquiry into complaints or charges of misconduct against him. The employer shall pay to such a workman the subsistence allowance:

(a) At the rate of fifty per cent of the wages which the workman was entitled to immediately preceding the date of such suspension, for the first ninety days of suspension, and

(b) At the rate of seventy five per cent of such wages for the remaining period of suspension, if the delay in the completion of disciplinary proceedings against such workman is not directly attributable to the conduct of such workman.

Any dispute regarding subsistence allowance may be referred by the workman or the employer to the Labour Court constituted under the Industrial Disputes Act, 1947.

However, if the provisions relating to payment of subsistence allowance under any other law for the time being in force are more beneficial, then the provisions of such other law shall be applicable.

Interpretation of Standing Orders

Section 13A of the Act provides that question relating to application or interpretation of a Standing Order certified under this Act, can be referred to any Labour Court constituted under the Industrial Disputes Act, 1947 by any employer or workman or a trade union or other representatives body of the workmen. The labour Court to whom the question is so referred, shall decide it after giving the parties an opportunity of being heard. Such decision shall be final and binding on the parties.

Temporary Application of Model Standing Orders

Section 12A provides that for the period commencing on the date on which this Act becomes applicable to an industrial establishment and ending with the date on which the Standing Orders as finally certified under this Act come into operation in that establishment, the prescribed model Standing Orders shall be deemed to be adopted in that establishment and the provisions of Sections 9, 13(2), and 13A shall apply.

Where there are two categories of workers, daily rated and monthly rated but the certified Standing Orders are in respect of daily rated workmen only, and then model Standing Orders can be applied to monthly rated workmen. (Indian Iron and Steel Co. Ltd. Ninth Industrial Tribunal, 1977 Lab. I.C. 607).

In case where there are no certified Standing Orders applicable to an industrial establishment the prescribed Model Standing Orders shall be deemed to be adopted and applicable.

INDUSTRIAL DISPUTE ACT 1947

Object and Significance of the Act

The Industrial Disputes Act, 1947 makes provision for the investigation and settlement of industrial disputes and for certain other purposes. It ensures progress of industry by bringing about harmony and cordial relationship between the employers and employees. Definitions of the words 'industrial dispute, workmen and industry' carry specific meanings under the Act and provide the framework for the application of the Act.

This Act extends to whole of India. The Act was designed to provide a self-contained code to compel the parties to resort to industrial arbitration for the resolution of existing or apprehended disputes without prescribing statutory norms for varied and variegated industrial relating norms so that the forums created for resolution of disputes may remain unhampered by any statutory control and devise rational norms keeping pace with improved industrial relations reflecting and imbibing socio-economic justice. This being the object of the Act, the Court by interpretative process must strive to reduce the field of conflict and expand the area of agreement and show its preference for upholding agreements sanctified by mutuality and consensus in larger public interest, namely, to eschew industrial strife, confrontation and consequent wastage (*Workmen, Hindustan Lever Limited* v. *Hindustan Lever Limited,* (1984)1 SCC 728).

Important Definitions

Industry means any business, trade, undertaking, manufacture or calling of employers and includes any calling service, employment, handcraft, or industrial occupation or avocation of workmen [Section 2 (j)].

Industrial Disputes means any dispute or difference between employers and employers, or between employers and workmen, or between workmen and workmen, which is connected with the employment or the terms of employment or with the conditions or labour, of any person [Section 2 (k)].

Workman means any person (including an apprentice) employed in any industry to do any manual, unskilled, skilled, technical, operational, clerical or supervisory work for hire or reward, whether the terms of employment be expressed or implied and for the purposes of any proceeding under this Act in relation to an industrial dispute, includes:

(*a*) any such person who has been dismissed, discharged or retrenched in connection with, or as a consequence of that dispute, or

(*b*) any person whose dismissal, discharge or retrenchment has led to that dispute, but does not include any such person:

   (*i*) who is subject to the Army Act, 1950, or the Air Force Act, 1950 or the Navy Act, 1957; or

   (*ii*) who is employed in the police service or as an officer or other employee of a prison; or

   (*iii*) Who is employed mainly in a managerial or administrative capacity; or

   (*iv*) Who is employed in a supervisory capacity drawing more than ₹ 1,600 per month as wages; or

   (*v*) Who is exercising either by the nature of the duties attached to the office or by reason of the powers vested in him, functions mainly of a managerial nature [Section 2(s)].

Works Committee: Joint Committee with equal number of employers and employees' representatives for discussion of certain common problems. Sec. 3

Conciliation: It is an attempt by a third party in helping to settle the disputes. Sec. 4

Adjudication: Labour Court, Industrial Tribunal or National Tribunal to hear and decide the dispute. **Secs. 7, 7A & 7B**

Strike means a cessation of work by a body of persons employed in any industry acting in combination, or a concerted refusal, or a refusal under a common understanding of any number of persons who are or have been so employed to continue to work or to accept employment [Section 2(q)].

Lockout means the temporary closing of a place of employment, or the suspension of work, or the refusal by an employer to continue to employ any number of persons employed by him [Section 2(1)].

In lockout, the employer refuses to continue to employ the workman employed by him even though there is no intention to close down the unit. The essence of lockout is the refusal of the employer to continue to employ workman. Even if Suspension of work is ordered, it would constitute lockout. But mere suspension of work, unless it is accompanied by an intention on the part of employer as retaliation, will not amount to lockout.

Locking out workmen does not contemplate severance of the relationship of employer and the workmen. In the case Lord Krishna Sugar Mills Ltd. v. State of U.P., (1964) if LLJ 76 (Ail), a closure of a place of business for a short duration of 30 days in retaliation to certain acts of workmen (i.e. to teach them a lesson) was held to be a lockout. But closure is not a lockout.

Lay-off (with its grammatical variations and cognate expressions) means the failure, refusal or inability of an employer to give employment due to following reasons, to a workman whose name appears on the muster-rolls of his industrial establishment and who has not been retrenched:

(*a*) Shortage of coal, power or raw materials, or

(*b*) Accumulation of stocks, or

(*c*) Break-down of machinery, or

(*d*) Natural calamity, or

(*e*) For any other connected reason [Section 2(kkk)].

Award means an interim or a final determination of any industrial dispute or of any question relating thereto by any Labour Court, Industrial Tribunal or National Industrial Tribunal and includes award made under Section 10-A [Section 2 (b)].

Arbitrator means an umpire [Section 2 (aa)].

Average pay means the average of the wages payable to a workman:

(*i*) In the case of monthly paid workman, in the three complete calendar months;

(*ii*) In the case of weekly paid workman, in the four complete weeks;

(*iii*) In the case of daily paid workman, in the twelve full working days preceding the date on which the average pay becomes payable if the workman had worked for three complete calendar months or four complete weeks or twelve full working days as the case may be, and where such calculation cannot be made, the average pay shall be calculated as the average of the wages payable to a workman during the period he actually worked [Section 2(aaa)].

Closure means the permanent closing down of a place of employment or a part thereof [Section 2(cc)].

Controlled Industry means any industry the control of which by the Union has been declared by any Central Act to be expedient in the public interest [Section 2(ee)].

Employer means:

(*i*) In relation to an industry carried on by or under the authority department of the Central Government or a State Government, the authority prescribed in this behalf, or where no authority is prescribed, the head of the department;

(*ii*) In relation to an industry carried on by or on behalf of a local authority the chief executive officer of that authority [Section 2(g)].

Employer includes among others an agent of an employer, general manager, director, occupier of factory etc. Executive in relation to a Trade Union means the body, by whatever name called, to which the management of the affairs of the trade union is entrusted [Section 2(gg)].

Independent

A person shall be deemed to be 'independent' for the purpose of his appointment as the chairman or other member of a Board, Court or Tribunal if he is unconnected with the industrial dispute referred to such Board, Court or Tribunal, or with any industry directly affected by such dispute.

Provided that no person shall cease to be independent by reason only of the fact that he is a shareholder of an incorporated company which is connected with, or likely to be affected by, such industrial dispute; but in, such a case, he shall disclose to the appropriate Government, the nature and extent of the shares held by him in such company [Section 2(1)].

Office Bearer

In relation to a trade union, includes any member of the executive thereof, but does not include an auditor [Section 2(111)].

Public Utility Service means:

(*i*) Any railway service or any transport service for the carriage of passengers or goods by air;

(*ia*) Any service in, or in connection with the working of, any major port or dock;

(*ii*) Any section of an industrial establishment, on the working of which the safety of the establishment or the workman employed therein depends;

(*iii*) Any postal, telegraph or telephone service;

(*iv*) Any industry which supplies power, light or water to the public;

(*v*) Any system of public conservancy or sanitation;

(*vi*) Any industry specified in the First Schedule which the appropriate Government may, if satisfied that public emergency or public interest so requires, by notification in the Official Gazette, declare to be a public utility service for the purposes of this Act, for such period as may be specified in the notification:

Settlement means a settlement arrived at in the course of conciliation proceeding and includes a written agreement between the employer and workmen arrived at otherwise than in the course of conciliation proceeding where such agreement has been signed by the parties thereto in such manner as may be prescribed and a copy thereof has been sent to an officer authorized in this behalf by the appropriate Government and the conciliation officer [Section 2(p)].

Trade Union means a trade union registered under the Trade Unions Act, 1926 [Section 2(qq)].

Unfair labour practice means any of the practices specified in the Fifth Schedule [Section 2(ra)].

Wages means all remuneration capable of being expressed in terms of money, which would, if the terms of employment, expressed or implied, were fulfilled, be payable to workman in respect of his employment or of work done in such employment, and includes;

(*i*) Such allowance (including dearness allowance) as the workman is for the time being entitled to;

(*ii*) the value of any house accommodation, or of supply of light, water, medical attendance or other amenity or of any service or of any concessional supply of food grains or other articles;

(*iii*) Any travelling concession, but does not include:

(*a*) Any bonus;

(*b*) Any contribution paid or payable by the employer to any pension fund or provident fund or for the benefit of the workman under any law for the time being in force;

(*c*) Any gratuity payable on the termination of his service;

(*d*) Any commission payable on the promotion of sales or business or both [Section 2(rr)].

Power of Labour Court to give Appropriate Relief

Labour Court/Industrial Tribunal can modify the punishment of dismissal or discharge of workmen and give appropriate relief including reinstatement. Sec. 11A

Right of a Workman during Pendency of Proceedings in High Court

Employer to pay last drawn wages to reinstated workman when proceedings challenging the award of his reinstatement are pending in the higher Courts. **Sec. 17B**

Persons Bound by Settlement

- When in the course of conciliation proceedings etc., all persons working or joining subsequently.
- Otherwise than in course of settlement upon the parties to the settlement. **Sec. 18**

Period of Operation of Settlements and Awards

- A settlement for a period as agreed by the parties, or
- Period of six months on signing of settlement.
- An award for one year after its enforcement. **Sec. 19**

Notice of Change

21 days by an employer to workmen about changing the conditions of service as provided in Schedule (*iv*). **Sec. 9A**

Prior Permission for Lay off

When there are more than 100 workmen during proceeding 12 months. **Sec. 25-M**

Lay off Compensation

Payment of wages except for intervening weekly holiday compensation 50% of total or basic wages and DA for a period of lay off up to maximum 45 days in a year. **Sec. 25-C**

Prior Permission by the Government for Retrenchment

- When there are more than 100 (in UP 300 or more) workmen during preceding 12 months.
- Three months' notice or wages thereto.
- Form QA.
- Compensation @ 15 days' wages. **Sec. 25-N**

Prohibition of unfair labour practice either by employer or workman or a trade union as stipulated in fifth schedule

Both the employer and the Union can be punished. **Sec. 25-T**

Closure of an Undertaking

60 days' notice to the labour authorities for intended closure in Form QA. **Sec. 25FFA**

Prior permission at least 90 days before in Form-O by the Government when there are 100 or more workmen during preceding 12 months (in UP 300 or more workmen) **Sec. 25-O**

Prohibition of Strikes & Lockouts

- Without giving to the employer notice of strike, as hereinafter provided, within six weeks before striking.
- Within fourteen days of giving such notice.
- Before the expiry of the date of strike specified in any such notice as aforesaid.
- During the pendency of any conciliation proceedings before a conciliation officer and seven days after the conclusion of such proceedings.
- During the pendency of conciliation proceedings before a Board and seven days after the conclusion of such proceedings.
- During the pendency of proceedings before a Labour Court, Tribunal or National.
- Tribunal and two months, after the conclusion of such proceedings.
- During the pendency of arbitration proceedings before an arbitrator and two months after the conclusion of such proceedings, where a notification has been issued under Sub-Section(3A) of Section 10A.
- During any period in which a settlement or award is in operation, in respect of any of the matters covered by the settlement or award. **Secs. 22&23**

Conditions of service etc. to remain unchanged under certain circumstances during pendency of proceedings

- Not to alter to the prejudice of workmen concerned the condition of service.
- To seek Express permission of the concerned authority by paying one month's wages on dismissal, discharge or punish a protected workman connected with the dispute.
- To seek approval of the authority by paying one month's wages before altering condition of service, dismissing or discharging or punishing a workman. **Sec. 33**

Retrenchment of Workmen Compensation & Conditions

- Workman must have worked for 240 days.
- Retrenchment compensation @ 15 days' wages for every completed year to be calculated at last drawn wages.
- One month's notice or wages in lieu thereof.
- Reasons for retrenchment
- Complying with principle of 'last come first go'.
- Sending Form P to Labour Authorities.

Conditions of service etc. to remain unchanged under certain circumstances during pendency of proceedings

- Not to alter to the prejudice of workmen concerned the condition of service.
- To seek Express permission of the concerned authority by paying one month's wages on dismissal, discharge or punish a protected workman connected with the dispute.
- To seek approval of the authority by paying one month's wages before altering condition of service, dismissing or discharging or punishing a workman. **Sec. 33**

Penalties

1. **Penalty for illegal strikes:** Any workman, who commences, continues or otherwise acts in furtherance of a strike which is illegal under this Act, shall be punishable with imprisonment for a term which may extend to one month, or with fine which may extend to fifty rupees or with both [Section 26(1)].

   In the case of Vijay Kumar Oil Mills vs. Their Workmen, it was held that the act of a workman to participate in an illegal strike gives the employer certain rights against the workman, which are not the creation of the Statute but are based on policy, and the employer has every right to waive such rights. In a dispute before the Tribunal, waiver can be a valid defense by the workman. However, waiver by the employer cannot be a defense against prosecution under Section 26 and something which is illegal by Statute cannot be made legal by waiver (Punjab National Bank vs. Their Workmen).

2. **Penalty for illegal lockout:** Any employer, who commences, continues, or otherwise, acts in furtherance of a lockout which is illegal under this Act, shall be punishable with imprisonment for a term which may extend to one month, or with fine which may extend to one thousand rupees, or with both [Section 26(2)].

3. **Penalty for instigation etc.:** Any person who instigates or incites others to take part in, or otherwise acts in furtherance of, a strike or lockout which is illegal under this Act, shall be punishable with imprisonment for a term which may extend to six months, or with fine which may extend to one thousand rupees, or with both (Section 27).

4. **Penalty for giving financial aid to illegal strikes and lockouts:** Any person who knowingly expends or applies any money in direct furtherance or support of any illegal strike or lockout shall be punishable with imprisonment for a term which may extend to six months, or with fine which may extend to one thousand rupees, or with both (Section 28).

5. **Penalty for breach of settlement or award:** Any person who commits a breach of any term of any settlement or award which is binding on him under this Act, should be punishable with imprisonment for a term which may extend to six months, or with fine or with both, and where the breach is a continuing one with a further fine which may extend to two hundred rupees for everyday during which the breach continues after the conviction for the first, and the Court trying the offence, if it fines the offender, may direct that the whole or any part of the fine realized from him shall be paid, by way of compensation to any person who, in its opinion has been injured by such breach (Section 29).

6. **Penalty for disclosing confidential information:** Any person who willfully

discloses any such information as is referred to in Section 21 in contravention of the provisions of that section shall, on complaints made by or on behalf of the trade union or individual business affected, be punishable with imprisonment for a term which may extend to six months or with fine which may extend to one thousand rupees, or with both (Section 30).

7. **Penalty for closure without notice:** Any employer who closes down any undertaking without complying with the provisions of Section 25-FFA shall be punishable with imprisonment for a term which may extend to six months or with fine which may extend to five thousand rupees, or with both (Section 30-A).

8. **Penalty for other offences:** Any employer who contravenes the provisions of Section 33 shall be punishable with imprisonment for a term which may extend to six months, or with fine which may extend to one thousand rupees, or with both.

   Further, whoever contravenes any of the provisions of this Act or any rules made there under shall, if no other penalty is elsewhere provided by or under this Act for such contravention, be punishable with fine which may extend to one hundred rupees (Section 31).

9. **Offence by companies, etc:** Where a person committing an offence under this Act is a company, or other body corporate, or an association of persons (whether incorporated or not) every director, manager, secretary, agent or other officer or person concerned with management thereof shall, unless he proves that the offence was committed without his knowledge or consent, be deemed to be guilty of such offence (Section 32).

MINIMUM WAGES ACT 1948

The Minimum Wages Act, 1948, it came into force on 15th March 1948, and was enacted to safeguard the interests of workers, mostly in the unorganized sector by providing for the fixation of minimum wages in certain specified employments. It binds the employers to pay their workers the minimum wages fixed under the Act from time to time.

Under the Act, both the Central Government and the State Governments are the appropriate Governments to fix, revise, review and enforce the payment of minimum wages to workers in respect of 'scheduled employments' under their respective jurisdictions. There are 45 scheduled employments in the Central sphere and as many as 1530 in State sphere.

In the Central sphere, the Act is enforced through the Central Industrial Relations Machinery (CIRM). CIRM is an attached office of the Ministry of Labour and is also known as the Chief Labour Commissioner (Central) [CLC (c)] organization. The CIRM is headed by the Chief Labour Commissioner (Central). While, the State Industrial Relations Machinery ensures the enforcement of the Act at the State level.

The appropriate Government is required to appoint an Advisory Board for advising it, generally in the matter of fixing and revising minimum rates of wages. The Central Government appoints a Central Advisory Board for the purpose of advising the Central and State Governments in the matters of the fixation and revision of minimum rates of wages as well as for coordinating the work of Advisory Boards.

Minimum wage and an allowance linked to the cost of living index and are to be paid in cash, though payment of wages fully in kind or partly in kind may be allowed in certain cases. The minimum rate of wages consists of a basic wage and a special allowance, known as 'Variable Dearness Allowance (VDA)' linked to the Consumer Price Index Number. The allowance is revised twice a year, once in April and then in October.

Important Definitions

Appropriate Government [Section 2 (b)]

   Appropriate Government means:

   (*i*) In relation to any scheduled employment carried on by or under the authority of the Central or a railway administration, or in relation to a mine, oilfield or major port or any corporation established by a Central Act - the Central Government, and

(*ii*) In relation to any other scheduled employment - the State Government.

Employee [Section 2(i)]

'Employee' means any person who is employed for hire or reward to do any work, skilled or unskilled, manual or clerical in a scheduled employment in respect of which minimum rates of wages have been fixed, and includes an outworker to whom any articles or materials are given out by another person (*i.e.* employer) to be made up, cleaned, washed, altered, ornamented, finished, repaired, adapted or otherwise processed for sole purpose of the trade or business of that other person where the process is to be carried out either in the home of the out-worker or in some other premises, not being premises under the control and management of that person; and also includes an employee declared to be an employee by the appropriate government; but does not include any member of Armed Forces of the union.

Employer [Section 2 (e)]

'Employer' means any person who employs, whether directly or through another person, or whether on behalf of himself or any other person, one or more employees in any scheduled employment in respect of which minimum rates of wages have been fixed under this Act.

Scheduled employment [Section 2(g)]

'Scheduled employment' means an employment specified in the Schedule or any process or branch of work forming part of such employment.

Wages [Section 2 (h)]

'Wages' means all remunerations capable of being expressed in terms of money which would, if the terms of the contract of employment, express or implied, were fulfilled, be payable to a person employed in respect of his employment or of work done in such employment and includes house rent allowance but does not include:

(*i*) The value of:

(*a*) Any house accommodation, supply of light, water, medical;

(*b*) Any other amenity or any service excluded by general or special order of the appropriate Government,

(*ii*) Contribution by the employer to any Pension Fund or Provident Fund or under any scheme of deposit insurance.

(*iii*) Any travelling allowance or the value of any travelling concession;

(*iv*) Any sum paid to the person employed to defray special expenses entailed on him by the nature of his employment.

(*v*) Any gratuity payable on discharge.

Fixation of Minimum Rates of Wages [Section 3(l)(a)]

Section 3 lays down that the appropriate Government shall fix the minimum rates of wages, payable to employees in an employment specified in Part I and Part II of the Schedule, and in an employment added to either part by notification under Section 27.

In case of the employments specified in Part II of the Schedule the minimum rates of wages may not be fixed for the entire State. Parts of the State may be left out altogether. In case of an employment specified in Part I, minimum rates of wages must be fixed for the entire State, no pails of the State being omitted. The rates to be fixed need not be uniform. Different rates can be fixed for different zones or localities. [Basti Ram v. State of A.P.]

Revision of Minimum Wages

According to Section 3(l) (b), the appropriate Government may review at such intervals as it may think fit, such intervals not exceeding 5 years, and revise the minimum rate of wages, if necessary. This means that minimum wages can be revised earlier than 5 years also.

Manner of Fixation/Revision of Minimum wages

According to Section 3(2), the appropriate Government may fix minimum rate of wages for:

(*a*) Time work, known as a Minimum Time Rate;

(*b*) Piece work, known as a Minimum Piece Rate;

(*c*) A 'Guarantee Time Rate' for those employed in piece work for the purpose of securing to such employees a minimum rate of wages on a time work basis; (This is intended to meet a situation where operation of minimum piece rates fixed by the appropriate Government may result in a worker earning less than the minimum wage); and

(*d*) A 'Over Time Rate' *i.e.* minimum rate whether a time rate or a piece rate to apply in substitution for the minimum rate which would otherwise be applicable in respect of overtime work done by employee.

Section 3(3) provides that different minimum rates of wages may be fixed for:

(*i*) Different scheduled employments;

(*ii*) Different classes of work in the same scheduled employments;

(*iii*) Adults, adolescents, children and apprentices;

(*iv*) Different localities.

Under the Minimum Wage Act, there are two methods for fixation/revision of minimum wages, namely:

- **Committee method:** Under this method, committees and sub-committees are set up by the appropriate Governments to hold enquiries and make recommendations with regard to fixation and revision of minimum wages, as the case may be.

- **Notification method:** Under this method, Government proposals are published in the Official Gazette for information of the persons likely to be affected thereby and specify a date not less than two months from the date of the notification on which the proposals will be taken into consideration.

After considering the advice of the Committees/Sub-committees and all the representations received by the specified date in Notification method, the appropriate Government shall, by notification in the Official Gazette, fix/revise the minimum wage in respect of the concerned scheduled employment and it shall come into force on expiry of three months from the date of its issue. The Government may review the minimum rates of wages and revise the minimum rates at intervals not exceeding five years.

The fixation of minimum wages depends on a number of factors such as level of income and paying capacity, prices of essential commodities, productivity, local conditions, etc. Since these factors vary from State to State, the wages accordingly differ throughout the country. Hence, in the absence of a uniform national minimum wage, the Central Government introduced a 'national floor level minimum wage'. Initially, this minimum wage level was fixed at ₹ 35 per day and has been revised periodically.

Minimum Wages India 2013—Current Minimum Wage Rate in India

Legislative protection for workers to receive a minimum wage can be considered as the hallmark of any progressive nation. It is one of the fundamental premises of decent work. In India, the Minimum Wages Act, 1948 provides for fixation and enforcement of minimum wages in respect of scheduled employments.

The Act aims to prevent the exploitation of labour through the payment of low wages by ensuring a minimum subsistence wage for workers. The Act also requires the appropriate government [both central and state] to fix minimum rates of wages in respect of employments specified in the schedule and also review and revise the same at intervals not exceeding five years.

With effect from November 2009, the National Floor Level of Minimum Wage has been increased to ₹ 100 per day from ₹ 80 per day (which was in effect since 2007). Recently with effect from April 1, 2011 the National Floor Level of Minimum wage has been raised to ₹ 115 per day.

Since the respective state governments have been empowered to independently fix minimum wages, disparities between wages in neighboring states are common. In order to reduce this problem and bring comparability the Central government has set up five regional committee for harmonization of minimum wages.

All the States/UTs Governments are required to ensure that fixation/revision of minimum rates of wages in all the scheduled employments is not below this national minimum wage.

Also, in order to bring uniformity in the minimum wages of scheduled employments, the Union Government has requested the States to form regional Committees. Hence, five Regional Minimum Wages Advisory Committees have been formed in the country. These include:

Region	*States/UTs covered*
Eastern Region	West Bengal, Odisha, Bihar, Jharkhand and Andaman & Nicobar Islands.
North Eastern Region	Arunachal Pradesh, Assam, Manipur, Meghalaya, Mizoram, Sikkim, Nagaland and Tripura.
Southern Region	Andhra Pradesh, Karnataka, Kerala, Tamil Nadu, Pondicherry and Lakshadwadeep.
Northern Region	Punjab, Rajasthan, Himachal Pradesh, Jammu & Kashmir, Haryana, Uttar Pradesh, Uttarakhand, Delhi and Chandigarh.
Western Region	Maharashtra, Gujarat, Goa, Madhya Pradesh, Chhattisgarh, Dadra & Nagar Haveli and Daman & Diu.

Wages: According to section 2 (h)

Wages means all remuneration capable of being expressed in terms of money, which would, if the terms of the contract of employment, express or implied, were fulfilled, be payable to a person employed in respect of his employment or of work done in such employment and includes house rent allowances but does not include:

(*i*) The value of,

    (*a*) Any house accommodation, supply of light, water, medical attention, or

    (*b*) Any other amenity or any service excluded by general or social order of the appropriate Government.

(*ii*) Any contribution by the employer to any pension fund of provident fund or under any scheme of social insurance.

(*iii*) Any travelling allowance or the value of any travelling concession.

(*iv*) Any sum paid to the person employed to defray special expenses entailed on him.

(*v*) Any gratuity payable on discharge.

Offences and Penalties

Section 22 of the Act provides that any employer who (a) pays to any employee less than the minimum rates of wages fixed for that employee's class of work or less than the amount due to him under the provisions of this Act or contravenes any rule or order made under section 13, shall be punishable with imprisonment for a term which may extend to six months or with fine which may extend to five hundred rupees or with both.

While imposing any fine for an offence under this section the court shall take into consideration the amount of any compensation already awarded against the accused in any proceedings taken under section 20.

It is further stipulated under Section 22A of the Act that any employment, who contravenes any provision of this Act or of any rule or order made there under shall if no other penalty is provided for such contravention by this Act be punishable with fine which may extend to five hundred rupees.

PAYMENT OF WAGES ACT 1936

Objectives: To ensure regular and prompt payment of wages and to prevent the exploitation of a wage earner by prohibiting arbitrary fines and deductions from his wages.

Applicability of the Act

● Application for payment of wages to persons employed in any factory.

● Not applicable to wages which average ₹ 6,500 per month or more.

● Wages include all remuneration, bonus, or sums payable for termination of service, but do not include house rent reimbursement, light vehicle charges, medical expenses, TA, etc.

Important provisions of the Act

- Responsibility of the employer for payment of wages and fixing the wage period.
- Procedures and time period in wage payment.
- Payment of wages to discharged workers.
- Permissible deductions from wages.
- Nominations to be made by employees.
- Penalties for contravention of the Act.
- Equal remuneration for men and women.
- Obligations and rights of employers.
- Obligations and rights of employees.

The Act is to regulate payment of wages to certain class of employed persons. The main purpose of this Act is to ensure regular and timely payment of wages to the employed persons, to prevent unauthorized deductions being made from wages and arbitrary fines being imposed on the employed persons. The Act extends to the whole of India.

Application of the Act

The Act applies to payment of wages to persons employed in factory or railways. It also applies to any 'industrial or other establishment' specified in Section 2(*ii*). [Section 1(4)]. 'Factory' means factory as defined in Section 2(m) of Factories Act. — Industrial or other establishment specified in Section 2(*ii*) are:

* Tramway or motor transport services * Air transport services * Dock wharf or jetty * Inland vessels * Mines, quarry or oil-field * Plantation * Workshop in which articles are produces, adopted or manufactured. The Act can be extended to other establishment by State/Central Government.

Presently, the Act applies to employees drawing wages upto ₹ 6,500. [Section 1(6)]. Every employer is responsible for payment to persons employed by him on wages. [Section 3].

Meaning of Wages: Wages means all remuneration expressed in terms of money and include remuneration payable under any award or settlement, overtime wages, wages for holiday and any sum payable on termination of employment. However, it does not include bonus which does not form part of remuneration payable, value of house accommodation, contribution to PF, travelling allowance or gratuity. [Section 2(*vi*)]

How Wages Should be Paid: Wages can be paid on daily, weekly, fortnightly or monthly basis, but wage period cannot be more than a month. [Section 4]. Wages should be paid on a working day. Wages are payable on or before 7th day after the 'wage period'. In case of factories employing more than 1,000 workers, wages can be paid on or before 10th day after 'wage period' is over. [Section 5(1)]. [Normally, 'wage period' is a 'month'. Thus, normally, wages should be paid by 7th of following month and by 10th if the number of employees are 1,000 or more]. Wages should be paid in coins and currency notes. However, with authorisation from employee, it can be paid by cheque or by crediting in his bank account. [Section 6].

Deductions Permissible: Deduction on account of absence of duty, fines, house accommodation if provided, recovery of advance, loans given, income tax, provident fund, ESI contribution, LIC premium, amenities provided, deduction by order of Court etc. is permitted. Maximum deduction can be 50%. However, maximum deduction upto 75% is permissible if deduction is partly made for payment to cooperative society. [Section 7].

Fines: Specific notice specifying acts and omissions for which fine can be imposed should be exhibited on notice board etc. Such notice can be issued only after obtaining specific approval from State Government. Fine can be imposed only after giving employee a personal hearing. Fine can be maximum 3% of wages in a month. Fine cannot be recovered in instalments. [Section 8].

EQUAL REMUNERATION ACT 1976

The Equal Remuneration Act 1976 aims to provide for the payment of equal remuneration to men and women workers and for the prevention of discrimination, on the ground of sex, against women in the matter of employment and for matters connected therewith or incidental thereto. According to the Act, the term 'remuneration' means "the basic wage or salary and any additional emoluments whatsoever payable, either in cash or in kind, to a person employed in respect of employment or work done in such employment, if the terms of the contract of employment, express or implied, were fulfilled". Nothing in this Act shall apply: (*i*) to cases affecting the terms and conditions of a woman's employment in complying with the requirements of any law giving special treatment to women; or (*ii*) to any special treatment accorded to women in connection with the birth or expected birth of a child, or the terms and conditions relating to retirement, marriage or death or to any provision made in connection with the retirement, marriage or death.

The Central Industrial Relation Machinery (CIRM) in the Ministry of Labour is responsible for enforcing this Act. CIRM is an attached office of the Ministry and is also known as the Chief Labour Commissioner Central [CLC (c)] organization. The CIRM is headed by the Chief Labour Commissioner (Central).

The main provisions of the Act are:

- No employer shall pay to any worker, employed by him/ her in an establishment, a remuneration (whether payable in cash or in kind) at rates less favourable than those at which remuneration is paid by him/ her to the workers of the opposite sex in such establishment for performing the same work or work of a similar nature. Also, no employer shall, for the purpose of complying with the provisions of this Act, reduce the rate of remuneration of any worker.

- No employer shall, while making recruitment for the same work or work of a similar nature, or in any condition of service subsequent to recruitment such as promotions, training or transfer, make any discrimination against women except where the employment of women in such work is prohibited or restricted by or under any law for the time being in force.

- Every employer shall maintain such registers and other documents in relation to the workers employed by him/her in the prescribed manner.

- If any employer: (*i*) makes any recruitment in contravention of the provisions of this Act; or (*ii*) makes any payment of remuneration at unequal rates to men and women workers for the same work or work of a similar nature; or (*iii*) makes any discrimination between men and women workers in contravention of the provisions of this Act; or (*iv*) omits or fails to carry out any direction made by the appropriate Government, then he/she shall be punishable with fine or with imprisonment or with both.

- Where an offence under this Act has been committed by a company, every person who at the time the offence was committed, was in charge of, and was responsible to the company for the conduct of the business of the company, as well as the company, shall be deemed, to be guilty of the offence and shall be liable to be proceeded against and punished accordingly.

PAYMENT OF BONUS ACT 1965

The term "bonus" has not been defined in the Payment of Bonus Act, 1965. Webster's International Dictionary, defines bonus as "something given in addition to what is ordinarily received by or strictly due to the recipient". The Oxford Concise Dictionary defines it as "something to the good into the bargain (and as an example) gratuity to workmen beyond their wages". The purpose of payment of bonus is to bridge the gap between wages paid and ideal of a living wage.

Establishments to which the Act is applicable: The Act applies to— (*a*) every factory; and (*b*) every other establishment in which twenty or more persons are employed on any day during an accounting year [Section 1(3)].

An establishment to which this Act applies shall continue to be governed by this Act not with standing that the number of persons employed there in falls below twenty.

Act not to apply to certain classes of employees: Section 32 of the Act provides that the Act shall not apply to the following classes of employees:

- Employees employed by:
  - The Indian Red Cross Society or any other institution of a like nature including its branches;
  - Universities and other educational institutions;
  - Institutions (including hospitals, chambers of commerce and social welfare institutions) established not for the purpose of profit;
- Employees employed by the Reserve Bank of India;
- Employees employed by any insurer carrying on general insurance business and the employees employed by the Life Insurance Corporation of India;
- Employees employed by:
  - The Industrial Finance Corporation of India;
  - Any Financial Corporation established under Section 3, or any Joint Financial Corporation established under Section 3A of the State Financial Corporations Act, 1951;
  - The Deposit Insurance Corporation;
  - The National Bank for Agriculture and Rural Development;
  - The Unit Trust of India;
  - The Industrial Development Bank of India;
- The Small Industries Development Bank of India established under Section 3 of the Small Industries Development Bank of India Act, 1989;
- The National Housing Bank;
  - Any other financial institution (other than Banking Company) being an establishment in public sector, which the Central Government may by notification specify having regard to (*i*) its capital structure; (*ii*) its objectives and the nature of its activities; (*iii*) the nature and extent of financial assistance or any other concession given to it by the Government; and (*iv*) any other relevant factor.

- Employees registered or listed under any scheme made under the Dock Workers (Regulations of Employment) Act, 1948, and employed by registered or listed employers;
- Employees employed by an establishment engaged in any industry carried on by or under the authority of any department of Central Government or State Government or local authority;
- Employees employed through contractors on building operations; **(Contract labour in building operations is eligible for bonus now);**
- Seamen as defined in clause (42) of Section 3 of the Merchant Shipping Act, 1958;
- Employees employed by inland water transport establishments [IWTE] operating on routes passing through any other country.

Apart from the above, the appropriate Government has necessary powers under Section 36 to exempt any establishment or class of establishments from all or any of the provisions of the Act for a specified period having regard to its financial position and other relevant circumstances and it is of the opinion that it will not be in the public interest to apply all or any of the provisions of this Act thereto. It may also impose such conditions while according the exemptions as it may consider fit to impose.

An employee in the following cases is entitled to bonus:

(*i*) A temporary workman is entitled to bonus on the basis of total number of days worked by him.

(*ii*) An employee of a seasonal factory is entitled to proportionate bonus and not the minimum bonus as prescribed under section 10 of the Act.

(*iii*) A part time employee as a sweeper engaged on a regular basis is entitled to bonus. **[Automobile Karamchari Sangh vs. Industrial Tribunal]**

(*iv*) A retrenched employee is eligible to get bonus provided he has worked for minimum qualifying period. [East Asiatic Co. (P) Ltd, vs. Industrial Tribunal]

(v) A probationer is an employee and as such is entitled to bonus. [Bank of Madura Ltd. vs. Employee's Union]

(vi) If an employee is prevented from working and subsequently reinstated in service with back wages, employer's statutory liability for bonus cannot be said to have been lost. Nor can the employer refuse for bonus to such employee. Employee can claim bonus from employer. [ONGC vs. Sham Kumar Sehgal [1995]

(vii) A piece rated worker is entitled to bonus. [Mathuradas vs. L.A. Tribunal]

An employee in the following cases is NOT entitled to bonus:

1. An apprentice is not entitled to bonus. [Wheel & RIM Co. vs. Government of T.N.]

2. An employee who is dismissed from service on the ground of misconduct as mentioned in Section 9 is disqualified for any previous outstanding bonus, and not merely for bonus of the accounting year in which is dismissed. [Pandian Roadways Corporation Ltd. vs. Presiding Officer]

L.A.T Formula regarding payment of bonus

A dispute relating to payment of bonus by the Cotton Mills of Bombay was decided by the Industrial Court, Bombay. An appeal against the award of the Industrial Court was considered by the Full Bench of the then Labour Appellate Tribunal (Mill Owners' Association, Bombay vs. Rashtriya Mill Mazdur Sangh, Bombay, 1959 II LLJ 1247).

In its decision, the LAT laid down the principles involved in the grant of bonus to workers. These principles are known as the LAT Formula. According to the formula, the following prior charges were to be deducted from gross profits:

● Provision for depreciation;
● Reserve for rehabilitation;
● Return of 6 per cent on the paid up capital; and

● Return on the working capital at a lower rate than the return on paid-up capital.

● The balance, if any, was called "available surplus" and the workmen were to be awarded a reasonable share out of it by way of bonus for the year.

Bonus is really a reward for good work or share of profit of the unit where the employee is working. Often there were disputes between employer and employees about bonus to be paid. It was thought that legislation will solve the problem and hence Bonus Act was passed. Unfortunately, in the process, bonus has become almost as deferred wages due to provision of payment of minimum 8.33% and maximum 20% bonus. Bonus Act has not in any way reduced the disputes.

The Act is applicable to (a) any factory employing 10 or more persons where any processing is carried out with aid of power (b) Other establishments (established for purpose of profit) employing 20 or more persons. Minimum bonus payable is 8.33% and maximum is 20%. Bonus is payable annually within 8 months from close of accounting year. Bonus is payable to all employees whose salary or wages do not exceed ₹ 3,500 per month provided they have worked for at least 30 days in the accounting year. However, for calculation of bonus, maximum salary of ₹ 2,500 is considered.

Once the Act is applicable, it continues to apply even if number of employees fall below 20. The Act is applicable to Government companies and corporations owned by Government which produces goods or renders services in competition with private sector.

However, the Act is not applicable to Government employees, the employees of Municipal Corporation or Municipality, railway employees, university and employees of educational institutions, public sector insurance employees, employees of RBI and public sector financial institutions, charitable hospitals, social welfare organizations and defense employees. The Act does not apply to any institution established not for purposes of profit.

Important Definitions

Accounting Year

(*i*) "Accounting Year" means: In relation to a corporation, the year ending on the day on which the books and accounts of the corporation are to be closed and balances;

(*ii*) In relation to a company, the period in respect of which any profit and loss account of the company laid before it in annual general meeting is made up;

(*iii*) In any other case

- The year commencing on the 1st day of April; or
- If the accounts of an establishment maintained by the employer thereof are closed and balances on any day other than the 31st day of March, then, at the option of the employer, the year ending on the day on which its accounts are so closed and balanced.

Provided that an option once executed by the employer under paragraph (b) of this sub-clause shall not again be exercised except with the previous permission in writing of the prescribed authority and upon such conditions as that authority may think fit. [Section 2(1)]

Allocable Surplus

It means (*a*) in relation to an employer, being a company (other than a banking company) which has not made the arrangements prescribed under the Income-tax Act for the declaration and payment within India of the dividends payable out of its profits in accordance with the provisions of Section 194 of that Act, 67% of the available surplus in an accounting year.

(*b*) In any other case, 60% of such available surplus [Section 2(4)].

Available Surplus

It means the available surplus under Section 5. [Section 2(6)]

Award

"Award" means an interim or a final determination of any industrial dispute or of any question relating thereto by any Labour Court, Industrial Tribunal or National Tribunal constituted under the Industrial Disputes Act, 1947 or by any other authority constituted under any corresponding law relating to investigation and settlement of industrial disputes in force in a State and includes an arbitration award made under Section 10A of that Act or under that law [Section 2(7)].

Employee

"Employee" means any person (other than an apprentice) employed on a salary or wage of maximum ten thousand rupees per month in any industry to do any skilled or unskilled, manual, supervisory, managerial, administrative, technical or clerical work or hire or reward, whether the terms of employment be express or implied. [Section 2(13)]

Part time permanent employees working on fixed hours are employees.

Employer

"Employer" includes:

(*i*) In relation to an establishment which is a factory, the owner or occupier of the factory, including the agent of such owner or occupier, the legal representative of a deceased owner or occupier, and where a person has been named as a manager of the factory under clause (f) of Sub-section 7(1) of the Factories Act, 1948, the person so named; and

(*ii*) In relation to any other establishment, the person who, or the authority which, has the ultimate control over the affairs of the establishment and where the said affairs are entrusted to a manager, managing director or managing agent, such manager, managing director or managing agent. [Section 2(14)]

Establishment in Private Sector

It means any establishment other than an establishment in public sector. [Section 2(15)]

Salary or Wages

The "Salary or Wage" means all remuneration (other than remuneration in respect of over-time work) capable of being expressed in terms of money, which would, if the terms of employment, express or implied, were fulfilled, be payable to an employee in respect of his employment or of work done in such employment and includes dearness allowance (that is to say, all cash payments, by whatever name called, paid to an employee on account of a rise in the cost of living) but does not include:

(*i*) any other allowance which the employee is for the time being entitled to;

(*ii*) the value of any house accommodation or of supply of light, water, medical attendance or any other amenity or of any service or of any concessional supply of food grains or other articles;

(*iii*) any travelling concession;

(*iv*) any bonus (including incentive, production and attendance bonus);

(*v*) any contribution paid or payable by the employer to any pension fund or provident fund or for the benefit of the employee under any law for the time being in force;

(*vi*) any retrenchment compensation or any gratuity or other retirement benefit payable to the employee or any ex-gratia payment made to him;

(*vii*) any commission payable to the employee [Section 2(21)].

Explanation: Where an employee is given in lieu of the whole or part of the salary or wages payable to him, free food allowance or free food by his employer, such food allowance or the value of such food shall, for the purpose of this clause, be deemed to form part of the salary or wages of such employee.

Meaning of 'Establishment': The word 'establishment' is not defined in the Act. Normally, 'establishment' is a permanently fixed place for business. The term 'establishment' is much wider than 'factory'. It covers any office or fixed place where business is carried out.

Establishment in Public Sector Covered Only in Certain Cases: The Act applies to establishment in public sector only if the establishment in public sector sells the goods or renders services in competition with an establishment in private sector, and the income from such sale or services or both is not less than twenty per cent, of the gross income of the establishment in public sector for that year. [Section 20(1)]. In other cases, the provisions of this Act do not apply to the employees employed by any establishment in public sector. [Section 20(2)]. As per section 32(*v*)(c), the Act does not apply to any institution established not for purposes of profit.

Establishment in public sector means an establishment owned, controlled or managed by— (*a*) a Government company as defined in section 617 of the Companies Act, 1956 (1 of 1956) (*b*) a corporation in which not less than forty per cent of its capital is held (whether singly or taken together) by the Government; or the Reserve Bank of India; or a corporation owned by the Government or the Reserve Bank of India. [Section 2(16)]. Establishment which is not in public sector is 'establishment in private sector' [Section 2(15)].

"Corporation" means anybody corporate established by or under any Central Provincial or State Act but does not include a company or a co-operative society. [Section 2(11)].

Establishments to Include Departments, Undertakings and Branches: Where an establishment consists of different departments or undertakings or has branches, whether situated in the same place or in different places, all such departments or undertakings or branches shall be treated as parts of the same establishment for the purpose of computation of bonus under this Act. [Section 3]

Duties/Rights of Employer

Duties

- To calculate and pay the annual bonus as required under the Act.
- To submit an annual return of bonus paid to employees during the year, in Form D, to the Inspector, within 30 days of the expiry of the time limit specified for payment of bonus.
- To co-operate with the Inspector, produce before him the registers/records maintained, and such other information as may be required by them.

- To get his account audited as per the directions of a Labour Court/Tribunal or of any such other authority.

Rights

An employer has the following rights:

Right to forfeit bonus of an employee, who has been dismissed from service for fraud, riotous or violent behaviour, or theft, misappropriation or sabotage of any property of the establishment.

Right to make permissible deductions from the bonus payable to an employee, such as, festival/interim bonus paid and financial loss caused by misconduct of the employee.

Right to refer any disputes relating to application or interpretation of any provision of the Act, to the Labour Court or Labour Tribunal.

Eligibility for Bonus if Worked for Minimum 30 Days: Every employee shall be entitled to be paid be his employer in an accounting year, bonus, in accordance with the provisions of this Act, provided he has worked in the establishment for not less than thirty working days in that year. [Section 8]

Computation of amount available for distribution as bonus: The establishment has to prepare a balance sheet and profit and loss account of the year and calculate the 'gross profit', 'available surplus' and 'allocable surplus' as per method and formula given in Bonus Act.

The first step is to calculate 'Gross Profit'. As per section 4, the gross profit in respect of any accounting year is required to be calculated as per First Schedule to Act in case of banking company and as per second schedule in case of other establishments. After calculation of 'Gross Profit' as per section 4, next step is to calculate 'Available Surplus'. As per section 5, 'available surplus' is calculated by deducting sums as specified in section 6 from 'gross profit' arrived at as per section 6 and adding difference equal to income tax on the bonus paid in the preceding year.

Thus, Available Surplus is equal to Gross Profit [as per section 4] less prior charges allowable as deduction u/s 6 plus amount equal to income tax on bonus portion calculated as per proviso (b) to section 5.

Allocable surplus is equal to 60% of 'available surpluses calculated as per provisions of section 5. [In case of company which does not deduct tax at source as per provisions of section 194 of Income Tax Act, 'allocable surpluses will be 67% of 'available surpluses]. This 'allocable surplus' has to be distributed as bonus among employees in proportion to the salary or wages actually earned by each employee during the year. However, this is subject to minimum 8.33% and maximum 20% as explained below.

Calculation of Bonus Simplified

The method for calculation of annual bonus is as follow:

1. Calculate the gross profit in the manner specified in:

   First Schedule, in case of a banking company, or Second Schedule, in any other case.

2. Calculate the Available Surplus.

   Available Surplus = A + B, where A = Gross Profit – Depreciation admissible u/s 32 of the Income tax Act - Development allowance - Direct taxes payable for the accounting year (calculated as per Sec.7) – Sums specified in the Third Schedule.

   B = Direct Taxes (calculated as per Sec. 7) in respect of gross profits for the immediately preceding accounting year – Direct Taxes in respect of such gross profits as reduced by the amount of bonus, for the immediately preceding accounting year.

3. Calculate Allocable Surplus

   Allocable Surplus = 60% of Available Surplus, 67% in case of foreign companies.

   Make adjustment for 'Set-on' and 'Set-off'. For calculating the amount of bonus in respect of an accounting year, allocable surplus is computed after considering the amount of set on and set off from the previous years, as illustrated in Fourth Schedule. The allocable surplus so computed is distributed amongst the employees in proportion to salary or wages received by them during the relevant accounting year.

4. In case of an employee receiving salary or wages above ₹ 2,500 the bonus payable is to be calculated as if the salary or wages were ₹ 2,500 p.m. only.

Set off and set on provisions: It may happen that in some years, the allocable surplus is more than the amount paid to employees as bonus calculating it @ 20%. Such excess 'allocable surplus' is carried forward to next year for calculation purposes. This is called 'carry forward for being set on in succeeding years'. The ceiling on set on that is required to be carried forward is 20% of total salary and wages of employees employed in the establishment. In other words, even if actual excess is more than 20% of salary/wages, only 20% is required to be carried forward. The amount set on is carried forward only up to and inclusive of the fourth accounting year. If the amount carried forward is not utilized in that period, it lapses [section 15(1)].

Similarly, in a particular year, there may be lower 'allocable surplus' or no 'allocable surplus' even for payment of 8.33% bonus. Such shortfall is also carried to next year. This is called 'carry forward for being set off in succeeding years'. Thus, in every year, 'allocable surplus' is calculated. To this amount, set on from previous years is added. Similarly, set off, if any, from previous years is deducted. This gives amount which is available for distribution as bonus. The amount set off is carried forward only up to and inclusive of the fourth accounting year. If the amount carried forward is not set off in that period, it lapses. [Section 15(2)]

Minimum bonus: Every employer shall be bound to pay to every employee in respect of any accounting year, a minimum bonus which shall be 8.33 per cent of the salary or wage earned by the employee during the accounting year or one hundred rupees, whichever is higher, whether or not the employer has any allocable surplus in the accounting year. Where an employee has not completed fifteen years of age at the beginning of the accounting year, the minimum bonus payable is 8.33% or ₹ 100 whichever is higher. [Section 10].

While computing number of working days, an employee shall be deemed to have worked in an establishment even on the days on which (a) He was laid off (b) He was on leave with salary/wages (c) He was absent due to temporary disablement caused by accident arising out of and in course of employment and (d) Employee was on maternity leave with salary/wages [Section 14].

Payment of maximum bonus: Where in respect of any accounting year, the allocable surplus exceeds the amount of minimum bonus payable to the employees, the employer shall, in lieu of such minimum bonus, be bound to pay to every employee in respect of that accounting year bonus which shall be an amount in proportion to the salary or wage earned by the employee during the accounting year subject to a maximum of twenty per cent of such salary or wage [Section 11(1)].

In computing the allocable surplus under this section, the amount set on or the amount set off under the provisions of section 15 shall be taken into account in accordance with the provisions of that section [Section 11(2)].

Thus, maximum bonus payable to employee is 20% in any accounting year.

Special Provisions with respect to certain newly set up establishments: In the case of newly set up establishments following provisions have been made under Section 16 for the payment of bonus:

Where an establishment is newly set up whether before or after commencement of this Act, the employees of such establishment shall be entitled to be paid bonus under this Act in accordance with the provisions of sub-sections (1-A), (1-B) and (1-C).

(1-A): In the first five accounting years following the accounting year in which the employer sells the goods produced or manufactured by him or renders services as the case may be, from such establishment, bonus shall be payable only in respect of the accounting year in which the employer derives profit from such establishment and such bonus shall be calculated in accordance with the provisions of this Act in relation to that year, but without applying the provisions of Section 15.

(1-B): For the sixth and seventh accounting year in which the employer sells the goods produced or manufactured by him or renders services as the case may be, from such establishment, the provisions of Section 15 shall apply subject to the following modifications, namely:

For the sixth accounting year:

Set on set off, as the case may be, shall be made in the manner illustrated in the Fourth Schedule taking into account the excess or deficiency, if any as the case may be, of the allocable surplus set on or set off in respect of the fifth and sixth accounting year.

For the seventh accounting year:

Set on or set off, as the case may be, shall be made in the manner illustrated in the Fourth Schedule taking into account the excess or deficiency, if any, as the case may be of the allocable surplus set on or set off in respect of the fifth, sixth and seventh accounting years.

(1-C): From the eighth accounting year following the accounting year in which the employer sells the goods produced or manufactured by him or renders services, as the case may be from such establishment, the provisions of Section 15 shall apply in relation to such establishment as they apply in relation to any other establishment.

Explanation I: For the purpose of sub-section (1) an establishment shall not be deemed to be newly set up merely by reason of a change in its location, management or ownership.

Explanation II: For the purpose of sub-section (IA), an employer shall not be deemed to have derived profit in accounting year unless:

He has made provision for that year's depreciation to which he is entitled under the Income-tax Act or, as the case may be, under the Agriculture Income tax law, and

The arrears of such depreciation and losses incurred by him in respect of the establishment for the previous accounting years have been fully set off against his profits.

Explanation III: For the purposes of sub-section (1A), (1B) and (1C), sale of the goods produced or manufactured during the course of the trial running of any factory or of the prospecting stage of any mine or an oil field shall not be taken into consideration and where any question arises with regard to such production or manufacture, the decision of the appropriate Government, made after giving the parties a reasonable opportunity of representing the case, shall be final and shall not be called in question by any court or other authority.

(2) The provisions of sub-sections (1A), (1B) and (1C) shall, so far as may be, apply to new departments or undertakings or branches set up by existing establishments:

Provided that if an employer in relation to an existing establishment consisting of different departments or undertakings or branches (whether or not in the same industry) set up at different periods has, before the 29th May, 1965, been paying bonus to the employees of all such departments or undertakings or branches were set up, on the basis of the consolidated profits computed in respect of all such departments or undertakings or branches, then, such employer shall be liable to pay bonus in accordance with the provisions of this Act to the employee of all such departments or undertakings or branches (whether set up before or after that date) on the basis of the consolidated profits computed as aforesaid.

Within the meaning of Section 16(1-A) the word "profit" must obviously be construed according to its ordinary sense. A sense which is understood in trade and industry because the rationale behind Section 16(1-A) is that it is only when the employer starts making profits in the commercial sense that he should become liable to pay bonus under the Act.

Profit in the commercial sense can be ascertained only after deducting depreciation and since there are several methods of computing depreciation, the one adopted by the employer, in the absence of any statutory provision to the contrary, would govern the calculation. Explanation II to Section 16(1-A) says that the employer shall not be deemed to have derived profits unless he has made provision for that years' depreciation to which he is entitled to under the Income-tax Act. This explanation embodies a clear legislative mandate that in determining for the purpose of sub-section (1A) of Section 16 whether the employer has made profit from the establishment in accounting year, depreciation should be provided in accordance with the provisions of the Income-tax Act.

Clearly, therefore, if depreciation is as prescribed in the Income-tax Act. There is no profit for the year in question and there is no liability on the part of the employer to pay bonus under the Act (The Management of Central Coal Washery vs. Workmen, 1978-II Labour Law Journal 350).

Adjustment of customary or interim bonus

Where in any accounting year: (*a*) an employer has paid any Puja bonus or other customary bonus to an employee; or (*b*) an employer has paid a part of the bonus payable under this Act to an employee before the date on which such bonus becomes payable; then, the employer shall be entitled to deduct the amount of bonus so paid from the amount of bonus payable by him to the employee under this Act in respect of that accounting year and the employee shall be entitled to receive only the balance (Section 17).

Deductions of certain amounts from bonus

Where in any accounting year, an employee is found guilty of misconduct causing financial loss to the employer, then, it shall be lawful for the employer to deduct the amount of loss from the amount of bonus payable by him to the employee under this Act, in respect of that accounting year only and the employee shall be entitled to receive the balance, if any. (Section 18)

Time limit for payment of bonus

Where there is a dispute regarding payment of bonus pending before any authority under Section 22, all amounts payable to an employee by way of bonus under this Act shall be paid in cash by his employer, within a month from the date from which the award becomes enforceable or the settlement comes into operation, in respect of such dispute.

In any other case, the bonus should be paid within a period of eight months from the close of the accounting year. However, the appropriate Government or such authority as the appropriate Government may specify in this behalf may, upon an application made to it by the employer and for sufficient reasons, by order, extend by the said period of 8 months to such further period or periods as it thinks fit, so, however, that the total period so extended shall not in any case exceed two years (Section 19).

Reference of disputes under the Act

Where any dispute arises between an employer and his employee with respect to the bonus payable under this Act or with respect to the application of this Act to an establishment in public sector, then, such dispute shall be deemed to be an industrial dispute within the meaning of the Industrial Disputes Act, 1947, or any corresponding law relating to investigation and settlement of industrial disputes in force in a State and provisions of that Act or, as the case may be, such law, shall, save as otherwise expressly provided, apply accordingly. (Section 22)

Accuracy of Accounts

Where any industrial dispute arises with respect to bonus payable under the Act, the audited balance sheet and profit and loss account of a corporation or a company or a banking company shall be presumed to be correct. Similarly, in the case of employers not being corporation, company or banking company, audited accounts will be presumed to be correct for the purpose of payment of bonus.

Bonus linked with production or productivity

Section 31A enables the employees and employers to evolve and operate a scheme of bonus payment linked to production or productivity in lieu of bonus based on profits under the general formula enshrined in the Act. However, bonus payments under Section 31A are also subject to the minimum of 8.33% and maximum of 20%. In other words, a minimum of 8.33% is payable in any case and the maximum cannot exceed 20% (Section 31A).

Agreements inconsistent with the Act

Subject to the provisions of Section 31A, the provisions of this Act shall be in addition to and not in derogation of the Industrial Disputes Act, 1947, or any corresponding law relating to investigation and settlement of industrial disputes in force in a State.

Power of Exemption

If the appropriate Government, having regard to the financial position and other relevant circumstances of any establishment or class of establishments, is of opinion that it will not be in public interest to apply all or any of the provisions of this Act thereto, it may, by notification in the Official Gazette, exempt for such period as may be specified therein and subject to such conditions as it may think fit to impose, such establishment or class of establishments from all or any of the provisions of this Act. (Section 36)

Government should consider public interest, financial position and whether workers contributed to the loss, before grant of exemption (J.K Chemicals vs. Maharashtra, 1996 III CLA Bom 12).

Application of certain laws not barred

Save as otherwise expressly provided, the provisions of this Act shall be in addition to and not in derogation of the Industrial Disputes Act, 1947, or any corresponding law relating to investigation and settlement of industrial disputes in force in a State (Section 39).

Recovery of Bonus Due

Where any bonus is due to an employee by way of bonus, employee or any other person authorized by him can make an application to the appropriate government for recovery of the money due.

If the government is satisfied that money is due to an employee by way of bonus, it shall issue a certificate for that amount to the collector who then recovers the money.

Such application shall be made within one year from the date on which the money became due to the employee.

However the application may be entertained after a year if the applicant shows that there was sufficient cause for not making the application within time.

Offences and Penalties

Penalties

For contravention of the provisions of the Act or rules the penalty is imprisonment up to 6 months or fine up to ₹ 1000, or both.

For failure to comply with the directions or requisitions made the penalty is imprisonment up to 6 months or fine up to ₹ 1000, or both.

Offences

1. If the person committing an offence under this Act is a company, every person who. at the time the offence was committed was in charge of, and was responsible to, the company for the conduct of business of the company, as well as the company, shall be deemed to be guilty of the offence and shall be liable to be proceeded against and punished accordingly:

    provided that nothing contained in this sub-section shall render any such person liable to any punishment if he proves that the offence was committed without his knowledge or that he exercised all due diligence to prevent the commission of such offence.

2. Notwithstanding anything contained in sub-section (1), where an offence under this Act has been committed by a company and it is proved that the offence has been committed with the consent or connivance of, or is attributable to any neglect on the part of, any director, manager, secretary or other officer of the, company, such director, manager, secretary or other officer shall also be deemed to be guilty of that offence and shall be liable to be proceeded against and punished accordingly.

    Explanation: For the purposes of this section

    (a) "Company" means anybody corporate and includes a firm or other association of individuals; and

    (b) "Director" in relation to a firm means in a partner in the firm.

MULTIPLE CHOICE QUESTIONS

1. A benefit designed to provide temporary income replacement for worker absent due to illness or injury, but who is expected to return to work within a specified timeframe is,
   A. Short-term disability
   B. Long-term disability
   C. Absenteeism
   D. None of the above

2. A firm that requires individuals to join a union before they can be hired is,
   A. Opened shop   B. Closed shop
   C. Both A and B   D. None of the above

3. As related to international labour relations, groups of workers and management representatives charged with examining how to improve company performance, working conditions, job security, etc. are,
   A. Trade union   B. Grids
   C. Work councils   D. None

4. The progress that reflects management decisions regarding specific actions to be taken, or avoid in a given situation is,
   A. Rules and regulations
   B. Work rule
   C. Punishment
   D. None of the above

5. Provides lower rates for the employer or employee and includes all employees, including new employees, regardless of health or physical condition is,
   A. Life insurance
   B. Group life insurance
   C. Insurance
   D. None of the above

6. A prepaid health care system that generally provides routine round-the-clock medical services as well as preventative medicine in a clinic-type arrangement for employees, who pay a nominal fee in addition to the fixed annual fee the employer pays is,
   A. Health Maintenance Organization (HMO)
   B. Human Maintenance Organization
   C. Both A and B
   D. None of the above

7. Groups of health care providers that contract with employer's insurance companies, or third-party payers to provide medical care services at a reduced fee is,
   A. Preferred Provider Organization (PPO)
   B. Principle Provider Organization
   C. Both A and B
   D. None of the above

8. Amendment to title VII of the Civil Rights Act that prohibits sex discrimination based on "pregnancy, childbirth, or related medical conditions." It requires employers to provide benefits - including sick leave and disability benefits and health and medical insurance - the same as for any employee not able to work because of disability. The term relates to,
   A. Pregnancy Discrimination Act
   B. Pre mature Discrimination
   C. Hospital management
   D. None of the above

9. Provides three types of benefits: retirement income at age 62 and thereafter, survivors or death benefits payable to the employee's dependents regardless of age at time of death; and disability benefits payable to disabled employees and their dependents. These benefits are payable only if the employee is insured under the,
   A. Employee security B. Women security
   C. Social security   D. None of the above

10. Plans that provide a fixed sum when employees reach a predetermined retirement age or when they can no longer work due to disability is,
    A. Retirement plan   B. Pension plan
    C. Gratuity plan   D. None of the above

11. Defined Benefit Pension Plan is a plan that contains a formula for determining retirement benefits.
    A. True   B. False
    C. Not true or false D. None of the above

12. A plan in which the employer's contribution to employee's retirement or savings funds is specified as,

A. Defined contribution plan
B. Insurance plan
C. Benefits plan
D. None of the above

13. A plan in which a certain amount of profits is credited to each employee's account, payable at retirement, termination, or death is referred as,
A. Deferred profit sharing plan
B. Retirement plan
C. Termination plan
D. None of the above

14. Vesting Provision that money placed in a pension fund cannot be forfeited for any reason.
A. True   B. False
C. Maximum   D. Minimum

15. Signed into law by President Ford in 1974 to require that pension rights be vested, and protected by a government agency is by,
A. Deferred profit sharing plan
B. Retirement plan
C. Termination plan
D. Employee Retirement Income Security Act (ERISA)

16. Established under ERISA to ensure that pensions meet vesting obligations, also insures pensions is under _____.
A. Pension Benefits Guarantee Corporation (PBGC)
B. Retirement plan
C. Termination plan
D. None of the above

17. Offers to current employees aimed at encouraging them to retire early, perhaps even with the same pensions they would expect if they retired at, say, age 65 is,
A. Deferred profit sharing plan
B. Retirement plan
C. Termination plan
D. Golden offering

18. A type of golden offering by which employees are encouraged to retire early, the incentive being liberal pension benefits plus perhaps a cash payment is,
A. Golden offering
B. Early Retirement window
C. SWOT plan
D. None of the above

19. A formal employer program for providing employees with counseling and/or treatment programs for problems such as alcoholism, gambling, or stress is,
A. Employee Assistance Program
B. Retirement plan
C. Termination plan
D. None of the above

20. Individualized plans allowed by employers to accommodate employee preferences for benefits is,
A. Employee Assistance Program
B. Flexible Benefits Program
C. Both A and B
D. None of the above

21. Employees to whom employers are not required to pay overtime under the Fair Labour Standards Act is,
A. Exempt employee
B. Appraised employee
C. Outstanding employee
D. All the above

22. An interview in which those leaving the organization are asked to identify the reasons for their departure is,
A. Daily report   B. Exit interview
C. Both A and B   D. None of the above

23. Persons who live in one country and are employed by an organization based in another country, also called international assignees,
A. Expatriate   B. Repatriate
C. Impatriate   D. None of the above

24. Research to determine how factors respond when changes are made in one or more variables, or conditions is,
A. Experiment   B. Research
C. Survey   D. Sample

25. An employee assistance program (EAP) which is conducted by a trained professional counselor hired as an employee by the employer to handle all aspects of the company's EAP by,
A. In-company counseling
B. In-house counseling
C. Both A and B
D. None of the above

26. A self-employed individual who performs specific services on a contract basis is,
    A. Dependant contractors
    B. Independent contractors
    C. Both A and B
    D. None of the above

27. A law passed in 1931 that sets wage rates for labourers employed by contractors working for the federal government is under,
    A. Factory Act   B. Wage Act
    C. Humanity   D. Davis-Bacon Act

28. A law enacted in 1936 that requires minimum-wage and working conditions for employees working on any government contract amounting to more than $10,000 is under,
    A. Walsh-Healey Public Contract Act
    B. Minimum wage Act
    C. Fair labour standards Act
    D. None of the above

29. Congress passed this Act in 1936 to provide for minimum wages, maximum hours, overtime pay, and child labour protection. The law has been amended many times and covers most employees is under,
    A. Walsh-Healey Public Contract Act
    B. Minimum Wage Act
    C. Fair Labour Standards Act
    D. None of the above

30. Amendment to the Fair Labour Standards Act designed to require equal pay for women doing the same work as men is under,
    A. Equal Pay Act of 1963
    B. Walsh-Healey Public Contract Act
    C. Minimum Wage Act
    D. Fair Labour Standards Act

31. This law makes it illegal to discriminate in employment because of race, colour, religion, sex, or national origin is under,
    A. Equal Pay Act of 1963
    B. Walsh-Healey Public Contract Act
    C. Civil Right Act
    D. Fair Labour Standards Act

32. The law that provides government protection of pensions for all employees with company pension plans. It also regulates vesting rights (employees who leave before retirement may claim compensation from the pension plan) is under,
    A. Employee Retirement Income Security Act (ERISA)
    B. Equal Pay Act
    C. Wage Act
    D. Insurance Act

33. Casual workers come under _____ class of workers.
    A. Skilled   B. Unskilled
    C. Semi-skilled   D. None of the above

34. A person who has ultimate control over the affairs of the factory under Factories Act, 1948 is called as _____.
    A. Occupier   B. Manager
    C. Chairman   D. Managing Director

35. The provision for cooling water during hot weather should be made by the organization if it employees _____ or more employees.
    A. 200   B. 250
    C. 300   D. 150

36. Which the types of Compensation, for the employees are;
    A. Direct and indirect compensation
    B. Base compensation
    C. Allowances and Incentives
    D. Monetary rewards

37. The employer exchanges monetary rewards for work done is,
    A. Base compensation
    B. Allowances and Incentives
    C. Monetary rewards
    D. Direct compensation

38. Employer-provided benefits—like health insurance—that are provide employees for being a member of the organization is,
    A. Indirect compensation
    B. Base compensation
    C. Allowances and Incentives
    D. Monetary rewards

39. Match the following:
    (a) Pay for position (i) creating a grading structure.
    (b) Pay for person (ii) based on market-competitive pay for competence

(c) Pay for performance
(iii) Individuals variables and fluctuates of work done yearly.

(d) Motivation
(iv) The set of forces that cause to behave in certain ways

Codes:

	(a)	(b)	(c)	(d)
A.	(i)	(ii)	(iii)	(iv)
B.	(ii)	(iii)	(iv)	(i)
C.	(iii)	(iv)	(i)	(ii)
D.	(iv)	(i)	(ii)	(iii)

40. Pay is awarded to employees on the basis of the relative value of their contribution to the organization.
A. Merit reward system B. Compensation
C. Job performance D. Annual salary

41. The percentage of an employee's sales to customers that is paid to an employee as a reward for selling the firm's products or services is,
A. Base salary B. Performance reward
C. Sales commissions D. None of the above

42. Which of the system is not Team and group reward system?
A. Gain sharing B. Scanlon plan
C. Profit sharing plans D. Sales commissions

43. Sharing the cost savings that result from productivity improvements is,
A. Gain sharing B. Scanlon plan
C. Profit sharing plans D. Sales commissions

44. Similar to gain sharing, but the distribution of gains is tilted toward the employees and is spread across the organization

A. Gain sharing B. Scanlon plan
C. Profit sharing plans D. Sales commissions

45. Provide an organization wide incentive in the form of an annual bonus to all employees based on corporate profits
A. Gain sharing B. Scanlon plan
C. Profit sharing plans D. Sales commissions

46. Stock options allow executives to purchase company stock at a predetermined price.
A. True B. False
C. Policy D. None of the above

47. Pension plan in which all the funds for pension benefits are provided by the employer is,
A. Preplanned
B. Noncontributory plan
C. Both A and B
D. None of the above

48. Industrial Employment (Standing Orders) Act where passed by,
A. 1945 B. 1946
C. 1942 D. 1941

49. Income deferral benefit offered to a select group of management or highly compensated employees is,
A. Nonqualified deferred compensation plan
B. Qualified deferred compensation plan
C. Cannot describe
D. None of the above

50. A situation in which an individual is confronted by two or more incompatible demands is,
A. Individual conflict B. Role conflict
C. Both A and B D. None of the above

ANSWERS

1	2	3	4	5	6	7	8	9	10
A	B	C	B	B	A	A	A	C	B
11	**12**	**13**	**14**	**15**	**16**	**17**	**18**	**19**	**20**
A	A	A	A	D	A	D	B	A	B
21	**22**	**23**	**24**	**25**	**26**	**27**	**28**	**29**	**30**
A	B	A	A	C	B	D	A	C	A
31	**32**	**33**	**34**	**35**	**36**	**37**	**38**	**39**	**40**
C	A	B	A	B	A	D	A	A	A
41	**42**	**43**	**44**	**45**	**46**	**47**	**48**	**49**	**50**
C	D	A	B	C	A	B	B	A	B

❖_❖_❖

8

Labour Administration

LABOUR WELFARE: MEANING, DEFINITION, SCOPE

The term 'Labour Welfare' is very comprehensive and includes various types of actions undertaken for the economic, social, intellectual or moral benefit of the labour community. The actions are so varied that the concept of labour welfare may vary from country-to-country.

The term "welfare as applied to the industrial workers is one which must necessarily be of elastic nature to somewhat different interpretation from one country to another, according the different social customs, the degree of industrialization and the educational development of the worker". The labour welfare which is undertaken by an employer is, "to establish, within the existing industrial system, working and sometimes living and natural condition of his employees beyond what is required by law, the custom of industry and condition of the market. Labour welfare is stated as the measures for promoting the physical and general well-being of employees working in factories and other undertakings of industrial life.

The word 'Labour' means any productive activity. Thus in the wider sense the phrase, labour welfare means the adoption measures to promote the physical, social, psychological and general well-being of the working population. Welfare in any industry aims or should aim at improving the working and living conditions of workers and their families.

The term welfare is a desirable state of existence involving the physical, mental, moral and emotional well-being. All these four elements constitute the structure of welfare on which its totality is based.

Labour welfare has both positive and negative sides associated to it. On positive side, it deals with the provisions of opportunities which enable the worker and his family to lead a good life socially and personally, as well as help to adjust in the social transition in regards to his work life. On negative sides labour welfare functions in order to neutralize the beautiful effects of large scale industrialization and provides a counter-balance to the undesirable social consequences and the labour problems which have evolved in the process of this transition.

The concept of labour welfare, however, is flexible elastic and differs from time-to-time, region-to-region, industry-to-industry and country-to-country, depending upon the values system, level of education, social customs, degree of industrialization and the general standard of the socio-economic development of people. It is also related to the political environment of the country. It is moulded according to the age, group, sex, socio-cultural background, marital status, economic status and educational level of employees in the various industries. This nature of the concept of welfare makes it very difficult for us to give a precise, all inclusive single definition of the phrase.

The concept of labour welfare originated in the desire for a humanitarian approach to ameliorate

278

the sufferings of the working class. Later it became a utilitarian philosophy which worked as motivation force for the labour and for those who were interested in it.

Definitions

The Oxford Dictionary defines labour welfare as "efforts to make life worth living for worker". In Encyclopedia of Social Sciences, welfare is defined as "the voluntary efforts of the employers within the existing industrial system, working and sometimes living and cultural conditions of employees beyond what is required by law, the customs of the industry and the conditions of the market".

Yet another definition is, "Anything done for the comfort and improvement, intellectual and social, of the employees over and above the wage paid, which is not a necessity of the industry".

Labour welfare is also understood to mean "such services facilities and amenities, which may be established in, or in the vicinity of undertakings to enable persons employed there in to perform their work in healthy and congenial surroundings and to provide them with amenities conductive to good health and good morale".

A Resolution adopted by the International Labour Conference at its 39th Session in June 1956, has enumerated some of these services and amenities. These include,

(*i*) Feeding facilities in or near the undertaking,

(*ii*) Rest and recreation facilities, and

(*iii*) Transportation to and from work where ordinary transport is inadequate or impracticable.

Anyhow, labour welfare must necessarily be elastic, bearing a somewhat different interpretation in one country from the other. It is also felt that labour welfare "covers all the efforts which employers make for the benefit of their employees over and above the minimum standards of working conditions fixed by the Factory Act and over and above the provision of social legislation providing against accident, old age, unemployment and sickness".

Labour welfare refers to all those efforts of employers, trade unions, voluntary organizations and governmental agencies which help employees feel better and perform better.

Scope

It is slightly difficult to accurately lay down the scope of labour welfare work, because of the fact that labour class is composed of dynamic individuals with complex needs. Labour welfare work is increasing with changing opportunities and needs to meet varying environment along with the growing knowledge and experience of techniques. Ultimately the welfare officer includes those activities that would be encouraging to the well-being of the worker and his family. Here is the list follows related to the welfare program conducted both inside and outside the work place.

1. *Conditions of Work Environment*

   (*a*) The workshop sanitation and cleanliness must include the regulation of temperature, humidity, ventilation, lighting, elimination of dust, smoke, fumes and gases, convenience and comfort during work, operative postures, sitting arrangements etc., distribution of work hours and provision for rest times, meal time, breaks and workmen's safety measures.

   (*b*) The factory sanitation and cleanliness must consist of: provision of urinals, lavatories and bathing facilities; provisions of spittoons, water disposal, disposal of wastes and rubbish, general cleanliness, white-washing and repair of buildings and workshop; ingress, egress, passage and doors; and care of open spaces, gardens and roads.

   (*c*) Provision and care of drinking water.

   (*d*) Canteen services.

   (*e*) Management of workers'cloak rooms, rest rooms and library.

2. *Workers' Health Services*

   (*a*) Factory health centre: playgrounds; health education; medical examination of workers and health research.

(b) Factory dispensary and clinic for general treatment: treatment of individuals' diseases fatigue and treatment of accidents.

(c) Women and child welfare work, anti-natal and prenatal care; maternity aid; infant welfare; crèches; women's general education; health and family welfare.

(d) Workers' recreation facilities; playgrounds, outdoor life; athletics, gymnasium and women's recreation.

(e) Education; provision of reading rooms; libraries; circulating library; visual education; pictorial education; lecture programme; debating unions; study circles; education of workers' children nursery schools; primary schools; women's general education with emphasis on hygienic, sex life, family planning, child care, domestic economy and home handicrafts.

(f) Cultural activities include; musical evenings and circles; art circles; folk songs, the arts and stories; histrionics folk dancing and festival celebrations.

3. *Labour Welfare Programme*

These should cover, factory council consisting of representatives of labour and employers; workmen's arbitration and council, vocational and job adjustment, social welfare departments; co-operation with personnel administration, especially for case investigation, interview and vocational testing; employment, follow-up and research bureau.

4. *Labour's Economic Welfare Programme*

These should include, co-operatives or fair price shops for consumer necessities, especially grains, vegetables, milk, meat, oils and ghee, cloth and daily requirements, co-operative credit society, thrift schemes and saving bank, unemployment insurance, health insurance, employment bureau, profit sharing and bonus schemes and factory services.

5. *General Welfare Work*

This should relate to: housing and family care.

THEORIES, PRINCIPLES AND APPROACHES

Theories of Labour Welfare

Employee welfare refers to the benefits and attitudes held by agencies which provide welfare facilities. Some agencies provide welfare facilities inspired by religious faith, others as philanthropic duty and the likewise. Welfare facilities are not restricted to the workers alone. They have now been extended to the society in general. Labour welfare has been extended to include social welfare. By the way seven theories have constituted the conceptual framework of labour welfare, have also be outlined. They are:

1. The policy theory
2. The religious theory of labour welfare.
3. The philanthropic theory
4. The trusteeship theory
5. The placating theory
6. The public relations theory and
7. The functional theory of labour welfare.

1. *The policy theory:* This theory is based on the contention that a minimum standard of welfare is necessary for labourers. Here the assumption is that, without compulsion, periodical supervision and fear of punishment, employers will not provide even the minimum welfare facilities for workers. Apparently, this theory assumes that man is selfish and self-centered, and always tries to achieve his own ends, even at the cost of welfare of others. If wealth or authority or both help him to being an advantageous position he uses it for his own advantage, exploiting those who are under him. According to this theory, owners and managers of industrial undertakings get many opportunities for this kind of exploitation. The welfare state has therefore to steep into prevent this kind of exploitation and coerce industrialist to offer a minimum standard of welfare to their workers. Such interference is in the interest of the progress and welfare of the state as well. Laws are enacted to compel management's to provide

minimum wages, congenial working conditions, reasonable hours of work and social security. The policy theory leads to:

(*i*) The passing of laws relating to the provisions of minimum welfare for workers,

(*ii*) Periodical supervision to ascertain that these welfare measures are provided and implemented,

(*iii*) Punishment of employers who evade or disobey these laws.

In this theory, the emphasis is unfortunately on fear and not on the spirit of welfare which should be the guiding factor. There are some big employers who do not undertake welfare programs which are not required by law, even though they can easily do so. There are others who find loopholes in the legal requirements. Considering India the working conditions in many places are not at all up to the progress.

2. ***The religious theory of labour welfare:*** The basic aspects are:

(*a*) atonement   (*b*) investment

Many acts of man are related to religious sentiments and beliefs. These religious feelings sometimes prompt an employer to take up welfare activities in the expectation of future benefit either in this life or in some future life. According to this theory, any good work is considered as "an investment". Both the benefactor and the beneficiary are rewarded. Another aspect of the religious theory is the atonement aspect that is in a spirit of atonement for their sins. Thus the benevolent acts of welfare are treated either as an investment or atonement.

According to this theory, man is primarily concerned with his own welfare only and secondly he consider for the welfare of others. This theory is based on charity, cannot be rational and cannot be beneficial in the long run.

3. ***The philanthropic theory:*** This theory is based on mankind, in Greek *Philos* means loving and *anthropes* mean man. So philanthropic,

means "loving mankind". Man is believed to have an instinctive urge by which he strives to remove the suffering of others and promote their well-being. This drive may be rather powerful one and may impel him to perform noble scarifies. When some employers have compassion for their fellow men, they may undertake labour welfare movement that has happened in the early years of the Industrial Revolution with the support of such philanthropists as Robert Owen. In India, Mahatma Gandhi was one of the eminent philanthropists who strove for the welfare of labour.

This theory thus depends largely on man's love for others, and therefore cannot be universal or continuous. Irregular and occasional philanthropic acts of welfare may sometimes defeat the very purpose of welfare. All the same, the utilization of such sentiments on the part of employers and others has worked well for the time being at least.

4. ***The trusteeship theory:*** This is also called the paternalistic theory of labour welfare, according to which "the industrialist or employer holds the total industrial estate, properties and profits accruing from them in trust". It means that he uses it for himself, for the benefit of his workers and also for society workers are like minors, who are ignorant because of lack of education and are not able to look after their own interests. Employers therefore, have the moral responsibility to look after the interests of their wards, who are the workers. There is naturally no legal binding, but since it is a moral obligation, it is supposed to be no less affective. The main emphasis here is on the idea that employers should provide out of the funds under their control for the well-being of their workers. Mahatma Gandhi very strongly advocated this trusteeship theory.

Having labour welfare depends on the initiative of the top management. Since it has no legal sanction, its value is related to the moral conscience of the industrialist. Also, this theory treats, "workers as perpetual minors and industrialist as eternal guardians. The self reliant growth of the trade union movement is ignored in this theory; through it may create a basis of goodwill between labour and management.

5. *The placating theory:* This theory is based on the fact that labour groups are becoming demanding and militant and are more conscious of their rights and privilege than ever before. Their demand for higher wages and better standards cannot be ignored. According to this theory timely and periodical acts of labour welfare can appease the workers. They are some kind of pacifiers by way of friendly gesture.

Sincerity may lack in these programmes, though discontent can be bought off in this manner. Psychologically, this theory is unsound, though it has often been acted upon to secure the worker's co-operation.

6. *The public relations theory:* This theory provides the basis for an atmosphere of goodwill between labour and management and also between management and the public. Labour welfare programme, under this theory work as a sort of an advertisement and help an industrialist to build up good and healthy public relations. This theory is based on the assumption that the labour welfare movement may be utilized to improve relations between management and labour. An advertisement or exhibition and labour welfare programme many help an industrialist to project to the public a good image of his company. His sales as well as industrial relation may improve as a result of a two-fold benefit to the company.

But this kind of programme may also lack in sincerity and continuity. When such a programme loses its advertisement value, it may be neglected by the employers even though it is still useful for the employees. Here, welfare may trend to become a publicity stunt. Nevertheless, these programmes do improve industrial relations.

7. *The functional theory of labour welfare:* This is also called as efficiency theory. Here, welfare work is used a means to secure, preserve and develop the efficiency and productivity of labour. It is obvious that if an employer takes good care of his workers; they will tend to become more efficient and will thereby step up production. But all this will depend on a healthy collaboration between union and management and their mutual concern for the growth and development of industry. Higher production is of benefit for both management and their mutual concern for the growth and development of industry. Higher production is of benefit for both management and labour. The latter will get better wages and perhaps a share in the profits, which increases productivity. This theory is a reflection of contemporary support for labour welfare. It can work well if both the parties have an identical aim in mind that is higher production through better welfare. This will encourage labour's participation in welfare programmes.

In India it is said, the industrial system clings largely to the paternalistic approach. Some management, however, try to achieve results through police control. Either way, workers start expecting too much from employers, as a result of which employers provide welfare measures in a somewhat half-hearted manner. The trusteeship theory too can be applied suitably in Indian conditions, through in the longer run, it is better to act on the basis of the functional theory of labour welfare, for it works more effectively by reason of intelligent and willing participation of workers.

Principles of Labour Welfare

Labour welfare is dependent on certain basic principles, which must be kept in mind and properly followed to achieve a successful implementation of welfare programmes. These are:

(i) Principles of adequacy of wages
(ii) Principles of social responsibility of industry
(iii) Principles of re-personalization

(*iv*) Principles of totality of welfare

(*v*) Principles of co-ordination or integration

(*vi*) Principles of association or democratic values

(*vii*) Principles of responsibility

In brief the principles to be followed for successful implementation of any labour welfare program in an organization are:

(*i*) The labour welfare activities should pervade the entire hierarchy of an organization. Management should be welfare oriented at every level.

(*ii*) The employer should not bargain labour as a substitute for wages or monetary incentives. In other words, the workers have a right for adequate wages in addition to welfare measure.

(*iii*) There should be proper co-ordination, harmony and integration of all labour welfare services in an undertaking.

(*iv*) The labour welfare work of an organization must be administratively viable and essentially development oriented.

(*v*) The management should ensure co-operation and active participation of unions and workers in formulating and implementing labour welfare programmes.

(*vi*) There should be periodical assessment or evaluation of welfare measures and necessary timely improvements on the basis of feedback.

Approaches to labour welfare: The issues may be studied from different angles, such as:

1. The location, where these amenities are provided, within and outside the industrial undertakings;

2. The nature of amenities such as those concerned with "conditions of employment," and "living conditions of work people".

3. The welfare activities termed as 'statutory', 'voluntary' and 'mutual'.

4. The agency which provides these amenities.

5. On the basis of the location of welfare activities, labour welfare work has been classified into two specific categories, namely (*a*) intra-mural, (*b*) extra-mural.

STATUTORY AND NON-STATUTORY LABOUR WELFARE

1. Statutory Provisions: These are mandated by the Factories Act 1945, The Mines Act 1952, The Plantation Labour Act 1951 and some other Acts; of all these; the Factories Act is more important.

2. Non-statutory benefits: May also be called as voluntary benefits; include loans for house building, education of children, leave travel concession, fair price shop, loans for purchasing personal convergence and a host of other facilities.

INTRA-MURAL AND EXTRA-MURAL WELFARE

(*a*) Intra-mural activities consist of such welfare schemes provided within the factories as medical facilities, compensation for accidents, provisions of crèches and canteens, supply of drinking water, washing and bathing facilities, provision of safety measures such as fencing and covering of machines, good lay-out of the machinery and plant, sufficient lighting, first aid appliances, fire extinguishers: activities relating to improving conditions of employment, recruitment and discipline and provision of provident fund, pension and gratuity, maternity benefits etc.

(*b*) Extra-mural activities covers the services and facilities provided outside the factory such as housing accommodation, indoor and outdoor recreation facilities, amusement and sports, educational facilities for adults and children, provision of libraries and reading rooms.

AGENCIES OF LABOUR WELFARE: STATE, EMPLOYER, TRADE UNIONS

Welfare activities by State

Both the state Government as well central Government has enacted several laws from time to time. These laws are the Factories Act, 1948, the Mines Act 1952, the Plantation Labour Act 1957, the Bidi and Cigar workers (condition of employment) Act 1966, and the Contract Labour (Regulation and Abolition) Act 1970. Beyond the labour laws, the central government has been to constitute welfare funds for the benefit of the employees. The welfare activities covered by these funds include housing, medical, educational and recreational facilities for employees and their dependents.

Welfare activities by employer

The welfare activities established within the organization by the employers are; Latrines and urinal, washing and bathing facilities, crèches, rest shelters, arrangements for drinking water, health services, including occupational safety, arrangement for prevention of fatigue, administrative arrangements for the welfare of employees, uniform and protective clothing, shift allowances etc., welfare outside the establishment by the employer may extent to maternity benefit, social insurance measures, benevolent funds, medical facilities, educational facilities, housing facilities, recreation facilities, holiday homes, leave travel facilities, workers cooperatives, including consumers cooperative credit, thrift societies, vocational training and other welfare programmes for women, youth, and children also exists.

Welfare activities by trade unions

Labour unions have contributed their share for the betterment of the employees. Textile Labour Association of Ahmadabad and the Railway man's Union and Mazdoor Sabha of Kanpur, which have rendered invaluable services in the field of labour welfare. The welfare activities of the textile labour association, Ahmadabad are worth noting like,

1. Twenty five cultural and social centers
2. Schools for workers children, reading rooms, libraries, gymnasia
3. Dispensaries and maternity homes
4. A cooperative bank with which a number of housing societies consumers societies are affiliated.
5. Office offering legal help to members
6. Training programmes in the principles and practices of trade unionism.
7. A bi-weekly **the Mazdoor Sangh**.

Welfare activities by Voluntary agencies

Several voluntary social services, agencies have been doing useful labour welfare work made by the Bombay Social Service league, the Seva Sadan society, the Maternity and Infant welfare association, the YMCA the depressed classes' mission. Society and the women's institute of Bengal. The welfare activities of these organizations cover night schools, libraries and lectures, promotions of public health and organization of recreation and sports for the working class.

MULTIPLE CHOICE QUESTIONS

1. Pension plan in which the employer makes an annual payment to an employee's pension account is,
   A. Defined-contribution plan
   B. Gratuity
   C. Both A and B
   D. None of the above

2. A system by which qualified retirement plan participants become incrementally vested over a period of 5 to 15 years of service is,
   A. Voluntary retirement
   B. Graded vesting
   C. Both A and B
   D. None of the above

3. Fetal protection policies describes about the attempts to protect the fetus from workplace hazards is,
   A. Fact   B. Not a fact
   C. Partially fact   D. None of the above

4. Type of formula used to determine retirement plan payments based on the average earnings during a specified number of years is,

A. Lump sum amount
B. Final-pay formula
C. Both A and B
D. None of the above

5. A benefit designed to provide employees with an allotment of paid days off in addition to holidays, sick days or vacation days, which they can use to attend to personal matters is,
A. Over-time   B. Holiday camp
C. Personal days   D. None of the above

6. Clothing and other work accessories (i.e. safety glasses, hearing protection, etc.) designed to create a barrier against potential workplace hazards is,
A. Personal protective equipment
B. Employee dissatisfaction
C. Potential worker retaining
D. None of the above

7. A program which provides for retirement, disability and other related benefits for workers and their eligible dependents are,
A. Personnel security B. Social security
C. Self esteem   D. None of the above

8. A card displaying an individual's full legal name and social security number assigned to the individual is,
A. Personnel security card
B. Social security
C. Self esteem card
D. Social security card

9. Situation that exists when there is a substantial under-representation of protected-class members as a result of employment decisions that work to their disadvantage is,
A. Reserved class
B. Situation analysis
C. Environmental aspect
D. Disparate impact

10. Situation that exists when protected-class members are treated differently from others are,
A. Disparate impact
B. Disparate treatment
C. Reserved groups
D. None of the above

11. Perceived fairness in the distribution of outcomes are,
A. Domestic enquiry
B. Distributive justice
C. Justice
D. None of the above

12. Condition in which the physical well-being of people is protected is,
A. Safety
B. Environment
C. Individual behaviour
D. Group levels

13. Composed of workers from different levels and departments who are involved in safety planning and programs are,
A. Safety committees
B. Environment analysis
C. Individual behaviour
D. Group levels

14. An employee's right to receive present or future pension benefits, even if the employee does not remain in the service of the employer or the process by which a retirement benefit becomes non-forfeitable is,
A. Vesting
B. Employment right
C. Industrial democracy
D. None of the above

15. The law passed by congress in 1970 "to assure so far as possible every working man and woman in the nation safe and healthful working conditions and to preserve our human resources" is,
A. Occupational Safety and Health Act
B. National Labour Relations Act
C. Wagner Act
D. None of the above

16. The agency created within the Department of Labour to set safety and health standards for almost all workers in the United States is,
A. Occupational Safety and Health Act
B. Occupational Safety and Health Administration (OSHA)
C. Occupational Safety and Human Relation Act
D. None of the above

17. Summons informing employers and employees of the regulations and standards that have been violated in the workplace is,
    A. Employee references
    B. Notice board communication
    C. Citations
    D. None of the above

18. The mechanical and physical conditions that cause accidents is,
    A. Safe condition   B. Unsafe conditions
    C. Safety purpose   D. None of the above

19. Behaviour tendencies and undesirable attitudes that cause accidents is under,
    A. Safe condition   B. Unsafe Act
    C. Safety Act   D. None of the above

20. The total depletion of physical and mental resources caused by excessive striving to reach an unrealistic work-related goal is,
    A. Burnout   B. Unsafe conditions
    C. Lockout   D. None of the above

21. Preventive health programs offered by employers designed to improve the health and physical well-being of employees both on and off the job is
    A. Labour welfare   B. Factory wellness
    C. Wellness programs   D. All the above

22. A form of disciplinary action resulting in an employee being sent home without pay for a specified period of time (the Fair Labour Standards Act contains stricter rules relating to suspending salaried exempt employees without pay) is,
    A. Suspension   B. Withhold
    C. Both   D. None of the above

23. The process of preparing minorities for promotion into higher-level jobs, such as managerial positions are,
    A. Job structure   B. Job descriptions
    C. Upward mobility   D. All the above

24. Analysis in which economic or other statistical models are built to identify the costs and benefits associated with specific HR activities are,
    A. Labour output per unit
    B. Utility analysis

C. Equity theory
D. None of the above

25. Affirmative action plan term referring to the difference between the availability of members of a protected class and an organization's job group makeup, underutilization is having a smaller proportion of women or minorities than is indicated by their availabilities is termed as
    A. Performance appraisal system
    B. Identifying training needs
    C. Utilization
    D. None of the above

26. An analysis that identifies the number of protected class members employed and the types of jobs they hold in an organization is,
    A. Performance appraisal system
    B. Identifying training needs
    C. Utilization
    D. Utilization analysis

27. An audit and review of the services costs billed by health-care providers are,
    A. Performance appraisal system
    B. Identifying training needs
    C. Utilization
    D. Utilization review

28. Review and analysis of health care programs to determine cost control methods are,
    A. Chain management
    B. Informal review
    C. Stock verification
    D. Utilization management

29. Welfare Officers are to be appointed if Organization is engaging _____ or more employees.
    A. 500   B. 250
    C. 600   D. 750

30. A mediator should act as a neutral party is,
    A. True   B. False
    C. Must necessary   D. Not necessary

31. Practice of health care providers who seek to maximize reimbursement by coding a treated illness as more serious than presented is,
    A. Coding   B. Upcoding
    C. Representing   D. Participative

32. The seven 'S' is strategy, structure, system, staff, style, skills and super-ordinate goals of an organization.
   A. True
   B. False
   C. Both A and B
   D. None of the above

33. Individuals who pass on the benefits of their knowledge to other individuals who are usually younger and less experienced is,
   A. Mentors
   B. Mentees
   C. Guide
   D. All the above

34. The breakdown of a complex task into components so that individuals are responsible for a limited set of activities, instead of the task as a whole is,
   A. Fundamentals of management
   B. Division of work
   C. Organizing
   D. All the above

35. An organizational structure which is a combination of the functional and product types of organizations is,
   A. Line organization
   B. Staff organization
   C. Functional organization
   D. Matrix organization

36. A management style which focus on problems as they arise is,
   A. Line organization
   B. Staff organization
   C. Functional organization
   D. Management by crisis

37. The organizational system or subsystem whose function is to transform inputs into desired outputs is,
   A. Operations systems
   B. Functional conflict
   C. Managerial layout
   D. None of the above

38. The set of important understandings such as norms, values, attitudes, beliefs, shared by organizational members is termed as,
   A. Organizational policy
   B. Organizational structure
   C. Organizational design
   D. Organizational culture

39. The determination of the organizational structure that is most appropriate for the strategy, people, technology, task of the organization is,
   A. Organizational policy
   B. Organizational structure
   C. Organizational design
   D. Organizational culture

40. The ability to work with, communicate with, and motivate individuals to work in groups is,
   A. Human skill
   B. Technical skill
   C. Conceptual skill
   D. All the above

41. The ability to determine appropriate objectives doing the right things is
   A. Effectiveness
   B. Efficiency
   C. Both A and B
   D. None of the above

42. The ability to minimize the use of resources in achieving organizational objectives in common parlance,
   A. Smart work is efficiency
   B. Smart work is effectiveness
   C. Both A and B
   D. None of the above

43. The inherent responsibility of a business enterprise to its consumers, workers, shareholders and the community and the mutual responsibilities of these to one another is,
   A. Trusteeship approach
   B. Gandhian approach
   C. Both A and B
   D. None of the above

44. A formal group of employers set up to defend, represent, or advise affiliated employers and to strengthen their position in society at large with respect to labour maters as distinct from economic matters is,
   A. Employers' organization
   B. Organizational policy
   C. Organizational structure
   D. All the above

45. Voluntary organization of workers formed to promote and protect their interests through collective action is,
   A. Collective bargaining

B. Trade unions
C. Workers participation
D. None of the above

46. Trade unions are recognized by managements to identify a collective bargaining agent.
   A. True   B. False
   C. Myth   D. None of the above

47. The government that verifies the basis of membership is known as trade union recognition.
   A. True   B. False
   C. Myth   D. None of the above

48. The unions of workers organized in a single-sector industry, along occupational lines, or beyond the industry sector is,
   A. Occupational unions

B. General unions
C. Both A and B
D. None of the above

49. The unions of workers cutting across the boundaries of occupation or industry is,
   A. Occupational unions
   B. General unions
   C. Both A and B
   D. None of the above

50. The federations which group workers' unions vertically or horizontally with a view to coordinate them is,
   A. Territorial unions
   B. Occupational unions
   C. General unions
   D. None of the above

ANSWERS

1	2	3	4	5	6	7	8	9	10
A	B	A	B	C	A	B	D	D	B
11	**12**	**13**	**14**	**15**	**16**	**17**	**18**	**19**	**20**
B	A	A	A	A	B	C	B	B	A
21	**22**	**23**	**24**	**25**	**26**	**27**	**28**	**29**	**30**
C	A	C	B	C	D	D	D	A	D
31	**32**	**33**	**34**	**35**	**36**	**37**	**38**	**39**	**40**
B	A	A	A	D	D	A	D	C	A
41	**42**	**43**	**44**	**45**	**46**	**47**	**48**	**49**	**50**
A	A	C	A	B	A	A	A	B	A

❖—❖—❖

ARITHMETIC

1. NUMBERS

The development of the number system started with natural numbers. These are generally known as counting numbers.

Natural Numbers

Numbers which start from 1 are known as natural numbers. It is denoted by N. The smallest natural number is 1. It is written as,

$$N = \{1, 2, 3, ..., \infty\}$$

Whole Numbers

A number which starts from zero (0) is known as whole number. It is denoted by W. It is written as,

$$W = \{0, 1, 2, 3, ..., \infty\}$$

Integers

Natural numbers along with 0 and their negatives are known as integers. It is denoted by I. It is written as,

$$I = \{..., -4, -3, -2, -1, 0, 1, 2, 3, 4, ...\}$$

Even Numbers

A number which is divisible by 2 is known as even numbers.

Such as, 2, 4, 6, 10, 12, 128, 432 etc.

Odd Numbers

A number which is not divisible by 2 is known as odd numbers:

Such as, 1, 3, 5, 7, 9, 11, 13, 21, 29, 123 etc.

Prime Numbers

A number which is divided by itself is known as prime numbers. The smallest prime number is 2.

Such as, 2, 3, 5, 7, 11, 13, 17, 19, 23, ... etc.

Composite Numbers

A number which is divided by itself and others also is known as composite numbers. The smallest composite number is 4.

Such as, 4, 6, 8, 9, 10, 12, 14, 15, 16, 18, ... etc.

There are 25 prime numbers between 1 to 100.

Such as, 2, 3, 5, 7, 11, 13, 17, 19, 23, 29, 31, 37, 41, 43, 47, 53, 59, 61, 67, 71, 73, 79, 83, 89, 97.

Test, whether a given number is prime or composite: If we want to test any number more than 100, whether it is prime or not, take an integer larger than the approximate square root of that number. Let it be x. Test the divisibility of the given number by every prime number less than x. If it is not divisible by any of them, then it is prime; otherwise it is composite number.

EXAMPLE: Which of the following numbers are prime numbers?

   (i)   421   (ii) 671

SOLUTION:

(i) The square root of 421 is nearly 21. Prime numbers less than 21 are 2, 3, 5, 7, 11, 13, 17, 19. Clearly, 421 is not divisible by any of them. So, 421 is a prime number.

(ii) The square root of 671 is nearly 26. Prime numbers less than 26 are 2, 3, 5, 7, 11, 13, 17, 19, 23. Out of these, 671 is divisible by 11. So, 671 is not a prime number. Hence it is composite number.

The formulae given below are quite useful for quick multiplication:

  (i) $(a + b)^2 = a^2 + 2ab + b^2$

  (ii) $(a - b)^2 = a^2 - 2ab + b^2$

3

(iii) $a^2 - b^2 = (a + b)(a - b)$

(iv) $a^2 + b^2 = (a + b)^2 - 2ab$

(v) $(a + b)^3 = a^3 + b^3 + 3ab(a + b)$

(vi) $(a - b)^3 = a^3 - b^3 - 3ab(a - b)$

(vii) $a^3 + b^3 = (a + b)(a^2 - ab + b^2)$

(viii) $a^3 - b^3 = (a - b)(a^2 + ab + b^2)$

EXAMPLE: Simplify the following.

(i) $\dfrac{348 \times 348 \times 348 + 252 \times 252 \times 252}{348 \times 348 - 348 \times 252 + 252 \times 252}$

(ii) $\dfrac{261 \times 261 \times 261 - 77 \times 77 \times 77}{261 \times 261 + 261 \times 77 + 77 \times 77}$

SOLUTION:

(i) $\dfrac{348 \times 348 \times 348 + 252 \times 252 \times 252}{348 \times 348 - 348 \times 252 + 252 \times 252}$

Let $348 = a$

and $252 = b$

∴ Given expression is written as

$\dfrac{a \times a \times a + b \times b \times b}{a \times a - a \times b + b \times b} = \dfrac{a^3 + b^3}{a^2 - ab + b^2}$

$= \dfrac{(a + b)(a^2 - ab + b^2)}{(a^2 - ab + b^2)} = a + b$

$= 348 + 252 = 600.$

(ii) $\dfrac{261 \times 261 \times 261 - 77 \times 77 \times 77}{261 \times 261 + 261 \times 77 + 77 \times 77}$

Let $261 = a$

and $77 = b$

∴ $\dfrac{a^3 - b^3}{a^2 + ab + b^2} = \dfrac{(a - b)(a^2 + ab + b^2)}{(a^2 + ab + b^2)} = a - b$

∴ $261 - 77 = 184.$

If we divide a given number by another number, then

Dividend = (Divisor × Quotient) + Remainder

EXAMPLE: On dividing 18254 by a certain number, the quotient is 289 and the remainder is 47. Find the divisor.

SOLUTION: Here, Dividend = 18254

quotient = 289

remainder = 47

∴ Divisor $= \dfrac{\text{Dividend} - \text{Remainder}}{\text{Quotient}}$

$= \dfrac{18254 - 47}{289} = \dfrac{18207}{289} = 63$

Hence, divisor = 63.

EXAMPLE: What least number must be subtracted from 862 to get a number exactly divisible by 31?

SOLUTION: On dividing 862 by 31, the remainder obtained is 25.

Hence, the required number = 25.

MULTIPLE CHOICE QUESTIONS

1. The face value of 8 in the numeral 458926 is:
   A. 8000
   B. 8
   C. 1000
   D. 458000

2. $106 \times 106 + 94 \times 94 = x$, the value of x is:
   A. 21032
   B. 20032
   C. 23032
   D. 20072

3. If $m \times 48 = 173 \times 240$ then the value of m is:
   A. 545
   B. 685
   C. 865
   D. 495

4. $\left(1 - \dfrac{1}{3}\right)\left(1 - \dfrac{1}{4}\right)\left(1 - \dfrac{1}{5}\right)...\left(1 - \dfrac{1}{n}\right) = x$

   then the value of x is:

   A. $\dfrac{1}{n}$
   B. $\dfrac{2}{n}$
   C. $\dfrac{2(n - 1)}{n}$
   D. $\dfrac{2}{n(n + 1)}$

5. When simplified the product

   $\left(2 - \dfrac{1}{3}\right)\left(2 - \dfrac{3}{5}\right)\left(2 - \dfrac{5}{7}\right)...\left(2 - \dfrac{997}{999}\right)$ is

   equal to:

   A. $\dfrac{5}{999}$
   B. $\dfrac{1001}{999}$
   C. $\dfrac{1001}{3}$
   D. None of these

6. Which number should replace both the asterisks in $\left(\dfrac{*}{21}\right) \times \left(\dfrac{*}{189}\right) = 1$?

A. 21   B. 63

C. 3969   D. 147

7. In a division sum, the divisor is 12 times the quotient and 5 times the remainder. If the remainder be 48, then the dividend is:

A. 240   B. 576

C. 4800   D. 4848

8. What least number must be subtracted from 1294 so that the remainder when divided by 9, 11, 13 will leave in each case the same remainder 6?

A. 0   B. 1

C. 2   D. 3

9. If $\sqrt{\left(1+\dfrac{27}{169}\right)} = \left(1+\dfrac{x}{13}\right)$, then the value of x is:

A. 1   B. 3

C. 5   D. 7

10. If $\dfrac{x}{y} = \dfrac{3}{4}$, then the value of $\left(\dfrac{6}{7} + \dfrac{y-x}{y+x}\right)$ equals:

A. $\dfrac{5}{7}$ B. $1\dfrac{1}{7}$

C. 1   D. 2

11. The largest natural number by which the product of three consecutive even natural numbers is always divisible, is:

A. 16   B. 24

C. 48   D. 96

12. The least number of five digits which is exactly divisible by 12, 15 and 18 is:

A. 10080   B. 10800

C. 18000   D. 81000

13. The least number which when divided by 8, 9, 12, 16 and 20 leaves the same remainder 1 in each case is:

A. 712   B. 271

C. 721   D. 720

14. The value of 0.8693 + 0.092 + 0.87 + 0.4 equals:

A. 2.3213   B. 2.2331

C. 3.2313   D. 2.2313

15. The prime numbers between 1 to 50 are:

A. 8   B. 12

C. 15   D. 10

ANSWERS

1	2	3	4	5	6	7	8	9	10
B	D	C	B	C	B	D	B	A	C

11	12	13	14	15
C	A	C	D	C

EXPLANATORY ANSWERS

1. The face value of 8 in the numeral 458926 is 8.

2. $106 \times 106 + 94 \times 94 = x$

$\Rightarrow \qquad\qquad\qquad (106)^2 + (94)^2 = x$

$\Rightarrow \qquad\qquad (100+6)^2 + (100-6)^2 = x$

$\Rightarrow 10000 + 1200 + 36 + 10000 - 1200 + 36 = x$

$\Rightarrow \qquad\qquad\qquad\qquad\qquad 20072 = x$

$\Rightarrow \qquad\qquad\qquad x = 20072.$

3. $\because m = \dfrac{173 \times 240}{48} = 865.$

4. $\left(1-\dfrac{1}{3}\right)\left(1-\dfrac{1}{4}\right)\left(1-\dfrac{1}{5}\right)\ldots\left(1-\dfrac{1}{n}\right) = x$

$\because \qquad 1 - \dfrac{1}{3} = \dfrac{3-1}{3} = \dfrac{2}{3}$

$$1 - \frac{1}{4} = \frac{4-1}{4} = \frac{3}{4}$$

$$1 - \frac{1}{5} = \frac{5-1}{5} = \frac{4}{5}$$

$$\vdots$$

$$1 - \frac{1}{n} = \frac{n-1}{n}$$

$$\therefore \; \frac{2}{3} \times \frac{3}{4} \times \frac{4}{5} \times \dots \times \frac{n-2}{n-1} \times \frac{n-1}{n} = \frac{2}{n}$$

5. $\left(2 - \frac{1}{3}\right)\left(2 - \frac{3}{5}\right)\left(2 - \frac{5}{7}\right) \dots \left(2 - \frac{997}{999}\right)$

$$2 - \frac{1}{3} = \frac{6-1}{3} = \frac{5}{3}$$

$$2 - \frac{3}{5} = \frac{10-3}{5} = \frac{7}{5}$$

$$2 - \frac{5}{7} = \frac{14-5}{7} = \frac{9}{7}$$

$$2 - \frac{997}{999} = \frac{1998 - 997}{999} = \frac{1001}{999}$$

$$\therefore \; \frac{5}{3} \times \frac{7}{5} \times \frac{9}{7} \times \dots \times \frac{999}{997} \times \frac{1001}{999} = \frac{1001}{3}$$

6.

$$\frac{*}{21} \times \frac{*}{189} = 1$$

$$\frac{x^2}{21 \times 189} = 1$$

$$\Rightarrow \qquad x^2 = 21 \times 189 = 21 \times 21 \times 9$$

$$\Rightarrow \qquad x^2 = 21 \times 21 \times 3 \times 3$$

$$\Rightarrow \qquad x = 21 \times 3 = 63$$

7. Let quotient = Q and remainder = R
Then, divisor = 12Q = 5R
Now, R = 48
$\Rightarrow 12Q = 5 \times 48 \Rightarrow Q = 20$
$\therefore$ Dividend = $(20 \times 240 + 48) = 4848$

8. The number when divided by 9, 11, 13 leaving remainder 6 = (LCM of 9, 11, 13) + 6 = 1293
$\therefore$ Required number = (1294 − 1293) = 1

9.

$$\sqrt{\left(1 + \frac{27}{169}\right)} = \left(1 + \frac{x}{13}\right)$$

$$\Rightarrow \qquad \sqrt{\frac{169 + 27}{169}} = \frac{13 + x}{13}$$

$$\Rightarrow \qquad \sqrt{\frac{196}{169}} = \frac{x + 13}{13}$$

$$\Rightarrow \qquad \frac{14}{13} = \frac{x + 13}{13}$$

$$\Rightarrow \qquad x + 13 = 14$$

$$\Rightarrow \qquad x = 1$$

10. $\because \; \frac{x}{y} = \frac{3}{4}$ then,

$$\frac{6}{7} + \frac{y - x}{y + x} = \frac{6}{7} + \frac{\dfrac{y}{y} - \dfrac{x}{y}}{\dfrac{y}{y} + \dfrac{x}{y}}$$

[Divide numerator and denominator by y.]

$$= \frac{6}{7} + \frac{1 - \dfrac{3}{4}}{1 + \dfrac{3}{4}} = \frac{6}{7} + \frac{\dfrac{1}{4}}{\dfrac{7}{4}} = \frac{6}{7} + \frac{1}{7} = \frac{7}{7} = 1$$

11. It is $2 \times 4 \times 6 = 48$

12. Least number of 5 digits is 10000.
LCM of 12, 15, 18 is 180.
On dividing 10000 by 180, the remainder is 100.
$\therefore$ The least number = 10000 + (180 − 100)
$\qquad\qquad\qquad\qquad = 10080$.

13. Least number = (LCM of 8, 9, 12, 16, 20) + 1

2	8,	9,	12,	16,	20
2	4,	9,	6,	8,	10
2	2,	9,	3,	4,	5
3	1,	9,	3,	2,	5
	1,	3,	1,	2,	5

$\therefore$ LCM = $2^4 \times 3^2 \times 5 = 720$
Hence, least number = (720 + 1) = 721.

14.

$$
\begin{array}{r}
0.8693 \\
0.092 \\
0.87 \\
+ \; 0.4 \\
\hline
2.2313 \\
\hline
\end{array}
$$

$\therefore$ The value of $0.8693 + 0.092 + 0.87 + 0.4$
$\qquad\qquad\qquad\qquad\qquad = 2.2313$.

15. The prime numbers between 1 to 50 are 2, 3, 5, 7, 11, 13, 17, 19, 23, 29, 31, 37, 41, 43, 47.
Hence, there are 15 prime numbers between 1 to 50.

2. HCF AND LCM

FACTORS

The numbers are said to be factors of a given number when they exactly divide that number.

Example: Factors of 15 are 1, 3, 5 and 15 because each of these completely divides 15.

Highest Common Factor

The HCF of two or more than two numbers is the greatest number that divides each of them exactly. The highest common factor is also known as Greatest Common Divisor or Greatest Common Measure.

EXAMPLE: Let us consider two numbers 24 and 36. All possible factors of 24 are 1, 2, 3, 4, 6, 8, 12 and 24. All possible factors of 36 are 1, 2, 3, 4, 6, 9, 12, 18 and 36. The common factors of 24 and 36 are 1, 2, 3, 4, 6, 12. The greatest factor among these common factors is 12.

Hence, 12 is the HCF of 24 and 36.

EXAMPLE: Let us consider two numbers 18 and 30.

Now, $18 = 2 \times 3 \times 3$

and $30 = 2 \times 3 \times 5$

The factors common to the two numbers are 2 and 3. Hence the required HCF $= 2 \times 3 = 6$.

There are two methods of determining the HCF of two or more numbers.

(*i*) HCF by Factorization method
(*ii*) HCF by Division method.

HCF by Factorization Method

Express each one of the given number as the product of prime factors. Now choose common factors and take the product of these factors to obtain the required HCF.

EXAMPLE: Find the HCF of 126, 396 and 5400.

SOLUTION: $126 = 2 \times 3 \times 3 \times 7$

$396 = 2 \times 2 \times 3 \times 3 \times 11$

$5400 = 2 \times 2 \times 2 \times 3 \times 3 \times 3 \times 5 \times 5$

Common factors are 2, 3 and 3.

Hence, the HCF $= 2 \times 3 \times 3 = 18$.

EXAMPLE: Find the HCF of 1056, 1584 and 2178.

SOLUTION: $1056 = 2^5 \times 3 \times 11$

$1584 = 2^4 \times 3^2 \times 11$

and $2178 = 2 \times 3^2 \times 11^2$

Hence, HCF $= (2 \times 3 \times 11) = 66$.

HCF by Division Method

Suppose we have to find the HCF of two given numbers. Divide the larger number by the smaller one. Now, divide the divisor by the remainder. Repeat the process of dividing the preceding divisor by the remainder last obtained till zero is obtained as remainder. The last divisor is the required HCF.

Suppose we have to find the HCF of three numbers. Then HCF of [(HCF of any two numbers) and (the third number)] gives the HCF of three given numbers. Similarly, the HCF of more than three numbers may be obtained.

EXAMPLE: Find the HCF of 48, 168 and 324.

SOLUTION: Firstly, we find the HCF of 48 and 168.

```
     48) 1 6 8 (3
        – 1 4 4
          ‾‾‾‾‾‾‾
          2 4) 4 8 (2
               4 8
               ‾‾‾‾
                0
               ‾‾‾‾
```

Thus, HCF of 48 and 168 = 24.

Now, we find the HCF of 24 and 324.

24) 3 2 4 (13
$\underline{-\ 2\ 4}$
8 4
$\underline{-\ 7\ 2}$
1 2) 2 4 (2
2 4
$\underline{0}$

Thus, the HCF of 48, 168 and 324 is 12.

Lowest Common Multiple

The LCM of two or more numbers is the lowest or least number which is exactly divisible by each of them. In other words, it is the lowest number which contains each of them as a factor.

LCM by Factorization

Resolve each one of the given numbers into a product of prime factors. Then LCM is the product of highest powers of all the factors.

EXAMPLE: Find the LCM of 72, 189 and 1026.

SOLUTION: $72 = 2^3 \times 3^2$
$189 = 3^3 \times 7$
and $1026 = 2 \times 3^3 \times 19$
$\therefore$ $LCM = 2^3 \times 3^3 \times 7 \times 19$
$= 8 \times 27 \times 7 \times 19 = 28728$

EXAMPLE: Find the LCM of 12, 15, 20 and 54 by short cut method.

SOLUTION:

2	12,	15,	20,	54
2	6,	15,	10,	27
3	3,	15,	5,	27
5	1,	5,	5,	9
	1,	1,	1,	9

$\therefore$ $LCM = 2 \times 2 \times 3 \times 5 \times 9 = 540$

FORMULA

Product of two numbers = HCF × LCM.

$$LCM = \frac{Product\ of\ numbers}{HCF}$$

$$HCF = \frac{Product\ of\ numbers}{LCM}$$

$$First\ number = \frac{LCM \times HCF}{2nd\ number}$$

$$2nd\ number = \frac{LCM \times HCF}{First\ number}$$

HCF and LCM of Fractions

(i) $HCF = \dfrac{HCF\ of\ numerators}{LCM\ of\ denominators}$

(ii) $LCM = \dfrac{LCM\ of\ numerators}{HCF\ of\ denominators}$

EXAMPLE: Find the HCF and LCM of $\dfrac{3}{4}, \dfrac{6}{8}, \dfrac{15}{64}$ and $\dfrac{12}{32}$.

SOLUTION: $HCF = \dfrac{HCF\ of\ 3, 6, 15, 12}{LCM\ of\ 4, 8, 64, 32} = \dfrac{3}{64}$

$LCM = \dfrac{LCM\ of\ 3, 6, 15, 12}{HCF\ of\ 4, 8, 64, 32} = \dfrac{60}{4}$.

MULTIPLE CHOICE QUESTIONS

1. HCF of 1485 and 4356 is:
   A. 189   B. 89
   C. 99   D. 83

2. LCM of 18, 24, 42, 63 is:
   A. 302   B. 604
   C. 504   D. 404

3. Which of the following fractions is the greatest of all?
   $$\frac{7}{8}, \frac{6}{7}, \frac{4}{5}, \frac{5}{6}$$

   A. $\dfrac{6}{7}$ B. $\dfrac{4}{5}$

   C. $\dfrac{5}{6}$ D. $\dfrac{7}{8}$

4. Which of the following is in ascending order?

   A. $\dfrac{5}{7}, \dfrac{7}{8}, \dfrac{9}{11}$ B. $\dfrac{5}{7}, \dfrac{9}{11}, \dfrac{7}{8}$

   C. $\dfrac{7}{8}, \dfrac{5}{7}, \dfrac{9}{11}$ D. $\dfrac{9}{11}, \dfrac{7}{8}, \dfrac{5}{7}$

5. HCF of three numbers is 12. If they be in the ratio 1 : 2 : 3, the numbers are:
A. 12, 24, 36
B. 10, 20, 30
C. 5, 10, 15
D. 4, 8, 12

6. The largest natural number which exactly divides the product of any four consecutive natural numbers is:
A. 6
B. 12
C. 24
D. 120

7. The traffic lights at three different road crossings change after every 48 seconds, 72 seconds and 108 seconds respectively. If they all change simultaneously at 8 : 20 : 00 hrs; then they will again change simultaneously at:
A. 8 : 27 : 12 hrs
B. 8 : 27 : 24 hrs
C. 8 : 27 : 36 hrs
D. 8 : 27 : 48 hrs

8. The HCF of two numbers is 16 and their LCM is 160. If one of the number is 32, then the other number is:
A. 48
B. 80
C. 96
D. 112

9. The HCF of two numbers is 12 and their difference is also 12. The numbers are:
A. 66, 78
B. 70, 82
C. 94, 106
D. 84, 96

10. The largest number which exactly divides 210, 315, 147 and 161 is:
A. 3
B. 7
C. 21
D. 4410

11. The least perfect square number which is divisible by 3, 4, 5, 6 and 8 is:
A. 900
B. 1200
C. 2500
D. 3600

12. The smallest number which is divisible by 12, 15, 20 and is a perfect square, is:
A. 400
B. 900
C. 1600
D. 3600

13. The sum of two numbers is 216 and their HCF is 27. The numbers are:
A. 54, 162
B. 108, 108
C. 27, 189
D. None of these

14. The HCF and LCM of two numbers are 44 and 264 respectively. If the first number is divided by 2, the quotient is 44. The other number is:
A. 33
B. 66
C. 132
D. 264

15. The number of prime factors in $2^{222} \times 3^{333} \times 5^{555}$ is:
A. 3
B. 1107
C. 1110
D. 1272

16. The number of prime factors in the expression $(6)^{10} \times (7)^{17} \times (11)^{27}$ is:
A. 54
B. 64
C. 71
D. 81

17. Three measuring rods are 64 cm, 80 cm and 96 cm in length. The least length of cloth that can be measured exact number of times using any one of the above rod is:
A. 0.96 m
B. 19.20 m
C. 9.60 m
D. 96.00 m

18. The product of two numbers is 1600 and their HCF is 5. The LCM of the numbers is:
A. 320
B. 1605
C. 1595
D. 8000

19. About the number of pairs which have 16 as their HCF and 136 as their LCM, we can definitely say that:
A. Only one such pair exists
B. Only two such pairs exist
C. Many such pairs exist
D. No such pair exist

20. The total number of prime factors of the product $(8)^{20} \times (15)^{24} \times (7)^{15}$ is:
A. 59
B. 98
C. 123
D. 138

ANSWERS

1	2	3	4	5	6	7	8	9	10
C	C	D	B	A	C	A	B	D	B

11	12	13	14	15	16	17	18	19	20
D	D	C	C	C	B	C	A	D	C

EXPLANATORY ANSWERS

1. 1485) 4 3 5 6 (2
  2 9 7 0
  ‾‾‾‾‾‾‾
  1 3 8 6) 1 4 8 5 (1
      1 3 8 6
      ‾‾‾‾‾‾‾
      9 9) 1 3 8 6 (14
          9 9
          ‾‾‾
          3 9 6
          3 9 6
          ‾‾‾‾‾
            0

∴ HCF of 1485 and 4356 is 99.

2.

2	18,	24,	42,	63
3	9,	12,	21,	63
3	3,	4,	7,	21
7	1,	4,	7,	7
	1,	4,	1,	1

LCM of 18, 24, 42, 63 = $2 \times 3^2 \times 7 \times 4 = 504$.

3. $\dfrac{7}{8} = 0.875$, $\dfrac{6}{7} = 0.857$, $\dfrac{4}{5} = 0.8$

$\dfrac{5}{6} = 0.833$

Clearly, 0.875 is the greatest of all.

Hence, $\dfrac{7}{8}$ is the greatest of all.

4. $\dfrac{5}{7} = 0.714$, $\dfrac{7}{8} = 0.875$, $\dfrac{9}{11} = 0.818$

Now, $0.714 < 0.818 < 0.875$

Hence, $\dfrac{5}{7} < \dfrac{9}{11} < \dfrac{7}{8}$.

5. Let the numbers be x, $2x$ and $3x$.
Then, their HCF = x
According to the question, $x = 12$
∴ The numbers are 12, 24, 36.

6. $1 \times 2 \times 3 \times 4 = 24$
∴ Required number = 24.

7. LCM of 48, 72, 108 = 432
432 seconds = 7 min 12 seconds.
So, the next simultaneous change will take place at 8 : 27 : 12 hrs.

8. Other number = $\dfrac{\text{LCM} \times \text{HCF}}{\text{One number}} = \dfrac{160 \times 16}{32} = 80$
Hence, other number = 80.

9. 12 is not the HCF of given options A, B and C.
Hence, D is correct answer.
In 84, 96, 12 is HCF of 84 and 96
Difference of 96 − 84 = 12
So, required numbers are 84 and 96.

10. HCF of 210, 315, 147 and 161 = 7
Hence, the required number = 7.

11.

2	3,	4,	5,	6,	8
2	3,	2,	5,	3,	4
3	3,	1,	5,	3,	2
	1,	1,	5,	1,	2

LCM of 3, 4, 5, 6, 8 = $2 \times 2 \times 3 \times 5 \times 2$
Required number
= $(2 \times 2 \times 3 \times 3 \times 5 \times 5 \times 2 \times 2) = 3600$

12. LCM of 12, 15 and 20 = 60
Hence, required number = $60 \times 60 = 3600$.

13. HCF of 54, 162 = 54
HCF of 108, 108 = 108
HCF of 27, 189 = 27
Hence, required numbers are 27 and 189.

14. According to the question,
First number = $2 \times 44 = 88$
Other number
$= \dfrac{\text{LCM} \times \text{HCF}}{\text{First number}} = \dfrac{264 \times 44}{88} = 132$

15. The number of prime factors in the given product = $(222 + 333 + 555) = 1110$

16. 2, 3, 7, 11 are prime numbers in the given expression. The number of prime factors in the given expression $(10 + 10 + 17 + 27) = 64$

17. Required length = (LCM of 64, 80, 96) cm
= 960 cm = 9.60 m.

18. LCM = $\dfrac{\text{Product of numbers}}{\text{HCF}} = \dfrac{1600}{5} = 320$

19. HCF is always a factor of LCM. So no two numbers exist with HCF = 16 and LCM = 136.

20. Since 2, 3, 5, 7 are prime numbers and the given expression is $(2^3)^{20} \times (3 \times 5)^{24} \times (7)^{15}$
i.e. $2^{60} \times 3^{24} \times 5^{24} \times 7^{15}$, so the number of prime factors in the given expression
= $(60 + 24 + 24 + 15) = 123$

3. SIMPLIFICATION

Simplification means expressing in a simpler form. In order to simplify an expression we use the operations in the following order which is easily remembered as "BODMAS".

(*i*) Bracket (*ii*) Of (*iii*) Division (*iv*) Multiplication (*v*) Addition (*vi*) Subtraction.

'Of' means multiplication but it is operated even before division.

While removing brackets, first of all bar bracket '—' and after that small bracket '( )' is removed. Thereafter curley bracket '{ }' and at last square bracket '[ ]' is removed.

EXAMPLE: Simplify: $100 \div 25 \times 6 + 16 - 32$

SOLUTION: $100 \div 25 \times 6 + 16 - 32$
$$= 4 \times 6 + 16 - 32$$
$$= 24 + 16 - 32$$
$$= 40 - 32 = 8$$

EXAMPLE: Simplify: $54 + 24 \div 4 - 8 \times 5 + 4 \times 3$

SOLUTION: $54 + 24 \div 4 - 8 \times 5 + 4 \times 3$
$$= 54 + 6 - 40 + 12$$
$$= 72 - 40 = 32$$

EXAMPLE: Simplify: $10 - \left[6 - \left\{ 7 - \left(6 - \overline{8 - 5} \right) \right\} \right]$

SOLUTION: $10 - \left[6 - \left\{ 7 - \left(6 - 3 \right) \right\} \right]$
$$= 10 - [6 - \{7 - 3\}]$$
$$= 10 - [6 - 4] = 10 - 2 = 8.$$

EXAMPLE: Simplify: $\dfrac{12 \times 12 \times 12 - 1 \times 1 \times 1}{12 \times 12 + 12 \times 1 + 1 \times 1}$

SOLUTION: Let $a = 12$ and $b = 1$

$\therefore \quad \dfrac{a \times a \times a - b \times b \times b}{a \times a + a \times b + b \times b} = \dfrac{a^3 - b^3}{a^2 + ab + b^2}$

$$= \dfrac{(a - b)(a^2 + ab + b^2)}{(a^2 + ab + b^2)}$$

$$= a - b = 12 - 1 = 11$$

EXAMPLE: Simplify:

$$\dfrac{2.33 \times 2.33 \times 2.33 + 7.67 \times 7.67 \times 7.67}{2.33 \times 2.33 - 2.33 \times 7.67 + 7.67 \times 7.67}$$

SOLUTION: Let $a = 2.33$ and $b = 7.67$

$\dfrac{a^3 + b^3}{a^2 - ab + b^2} = \dfrac{(a + b)(a^2 - ab + b^2)}{(a^2 - ab + b^2)} = (a + b)$

$$= 2.33 + 7.67 = 10$$

MULTIPLE CHOICE QUESTIONS

1. $\dfrac{48 - 12 \times 3 + 9}{12 - 9 \div 3}$ equals:

   A. 3   B. 21

   C. $\dfrac{7}{3}$ D. $\dfrac{1}{3}$

2. $\dfrac{69 - 14 \times 3 + 2}{9 \times 5 - (5)^2}$ equals:

   A. 1.45   B. 2.75

   C. 26.5   D. 265

3. If $\dfrac{17.28 \div x}{3.6 \times 0.2} = 2$ then, the value of x is:

   A. 120   B. 1.20

   C. 12   D. 0.12

4. $171 \div 19 \times 9$ equals:

   A. 0   B. 1

   C. 18   D. 81

5. $3120 \div 26 + 13 \times 30$ equals:

   A. 2400   B. 3900

   C. 536   D. None of these

6. $\dfrac{31}{10} \times \dfrac{3}{10} + \dfrac{7}{5} \div 20$ equals:

   A. 0   B. 1

   C. 100   D. $\dfrac{107}{200}$

7. The simplification of $1 + \dfrac{1}{2 + \dfrac{1}{1 - \dfrac{1}{3}}}$ yields the

result:

   A. $\dfrac{2}{7}$ B. $\dfrac{7}{9}$

   C. $\dfrac{9}{7}$ D. $\dfrac{13}{7}$

8. The value of $1 + \dfrac{1}{4 \times 3} + \dfrac{1}{4 \times 3^2} + \dfrac{1}{4 \times 3^3}$ up to

four places of decimals is:

   A. 1.1202   B. 1.1203

   C. 1.1204   D. None of these

9. $\dfrac{\dfrac{1}{2} \div 4 + 20}{\dfrac{1}{2} \times 4 + 20}$ equals:

   A. $\dfrac{81}{88}$ B. $2\dfrac{3}{11}$

   C. $\dfrac{161}{176}$ D. 1

10. $3 \div \left[(8-5) \div \left\{ (4-2) \div \left(2 + \dfrac{8}{13} \right) \right\} \right]$ equals:

   A. $\dfrac{13}{17}$ B. $\dfrac{68}{13}$

   C. $\dfrac{17}{13}$ D. $\dfrac{13}{68}$

11. $10 - [9 - \{8 - (7-6)\}] - 5$ is equal to:

   A. -5 B. 1

   C. 3   D. 9

12. $\dfrac{\dfrac{1}{5} \div \dfrac{1}{5} \text{ of } \dfrac{1}{5}}{\dfrac{1}{5} \text{ of } \dfrac{1}{5} \div \dfrac{1}{5}}$ is equal to:

   A. 1   B. 5

   C. $\dfrac{1}{5}$ D. 25

13. The value of $1 + \dfrac{1}{1 + \dfrac{1}{1 + \dfrac{1}{9}}}$ is:

   A. $\dfrac{29}{19}$ B. $\dfrac{10}{19}$

   C. $\dfrac{29}{10}$ D. $\dfrac{10}{9}$

14. $\dfrac{3}{48}$ is what part of $\dfrac{1}{12}$?

   A. $\dfrac{3}{7}$ B. $\dfrac{1}{12}$

   C. $\dfrac{4}{3}$ D. None of these

15. How many $\dfrac{1}{8}$s are there in $37\dfrac{1}{2}$?

   A. 300   B. 400

   C. 500   D. None of these

ANSWERS

1	2	3	4	5	6	7	8	9	10
C	A	C	D	D	B	C	B	C	A

11	12	13	14	15
C	D	A	D	A

EXPLANATORY ANSWERS

1. $\dfrac{48-12\times3+9}{12-9\div3} = \dfrac{48-36+9}{12-3}$

$= \dfrac{57-36}{9} = \dfrac{21}{9} = \dfrac{7}{3}.$

2. $\dfrac{69-14\times3+2}{9\times5-5^2} = \dfrac{69-42+2}{45-25}$

$= \dfrac{71-42}{20} = \dfrac{29}{20} = 1.45.$

3. $17.28 \div x = 2 \times 3.6 \times 0.2$

$\Rightarrow \dfrac{17.28}{x} = 1.44 \Rightarrow 1.44\,x = 17.28$

$\Rightarrow x = \dfrac{17.28}{1.44} = \dfrac{1728}{144} = 12.$

4. $171 \div 19 \times 9 = 9 \times 9 = 81.$

5. $3120 \div 26 + 13 \times 30 = 120 + 390 = 510.$

6. $\dfrac{31}{10} \times \dfrac{3}{10} + \dfrac{7}{5} \div 20 = \dfrac{31}{10} \times \dfrac{3}{10} + \dfrac{7}{5} \times \dfrac{1}{20}$

$= \dfrac{93}{100} + \dfrac{7}{100} = \dfrac{93+7}{100} = \dfrac{100}{100} = 1$

7. $1 + \cfrac{1}{2 + \cfrac{1}{1 - \cfrac{1}{3}}} = 1 + \cfrac{1}{2 + \cfrac{1}{\cfrac{3-1}{3}}}$

$= 1 + \cfrac{1}{2 + \cfrac{1}{\cfrac{2}{3}}} = 1 + \cfrac{1}{2 + \cfrac{3}{2}} = 1 + \dfrac{1}{\dfrac{7}{2}} = 1 + \dfrac{2}{7} = \dfrac{9}{7}$

8. $1 + \dfrac{1}{4\times3} + \dfrac{1}{4\times3^2} + \dfrac{1}{4\times3^3}$

$= 1 + \dfrac{1}{12} + \dfrac{1}{36} + \dfrac{1}{108} = \dfrac{108+9+3+1}{108}$

$= \dfrac{121}{108} = 1.1203$

9. $\dfrac{\dfrac{1}{2} \div 4 + 20}{\dfrac{1}{2} \times 4 + 20} = \dfrac{\dfrac{1}{8} + 20}{2 + 20} = \dfrac{\dfrac{1+160}{8}}{22}$

$= \dfrac{161}{8\times22} = \dfrac{161}{176}$

10. $3 \div \left[(8-5) \div \left\{ (4-2) \div \left(2 + \dfrac{8}{13} \right) \right\} \right]$

$= 3 \div \left[3 \div \left\{ 2 \div \dfrac{34}{13} \right\} \right]$

$= 3 \div \left[3 \div \left\{ 2 \times \dfrac{13}{34} \right\} \right] = 3 \div \left[3 \div \dfrac{13}{17} \right]$

$= 3 \div \left[3 \times \dfrac{17}{13} \right] = 3 \div \dfrac{51}{13} = 3 \times \dfrac{13}{51} = \dfrac{13}{17}$

11. $10 - [9 - \{8 - (7 - 6)\}] - 5$

$= 10 - [9 - \{8 - 1\}] - 5$

$= 10 - [9 - 7] - 5 = 10 - 2 - 5 = 10 - 7 = 3$

12. $\dfrac{\dfrac{1}{5} \div \dfrac{1}{5} \text{ of } \dfrac{1}{5}}{\dfrac{1}{5} \text{ of } \dfrac{1}{5} \div \dfrac{1}{5}} = \dfrac{\dfrac{1}{5} \div \dfrac{1}{25}}{\dfrac{1}{25} \div \dfrac{1}{5}} = \dfrac{\dfrac{1}{5} \times \dfrac{25}{1}}{\dfrac{1}{25} \times \dfrac{5}{1}} = \dfrac{\dfrac{5}{1}}{\dfrac{1}{5}}$

$= \dfrac{5}{1} \times \dfrac{5}{1} = 25$

13. $1 + \cfrac{1}{1 + \cfrac{1}{1 + \cfrac{1}{9}}} = 1 + \cfrac{1}{1 + \cfrac{1}{\cfrac{10}{9}}} = 1 + \cfrac{1}{1 + \cfrac{9}{10}}$

$= 1 + \dfrac{1}{\dfrac{19}{10}} = 1 + \dfrac{10}{19} = \dfrac{29}{19}$

14. Let x of $\dfrac{1}{12} = \dfrac{3}{48}$

$\Rightarrow \dfrac{x}{12} = \dfrac{3}{48} \Rightarrow 48x = 36$

$\Rightarrow x = \dfrac{36}{48} = \dfrac{3}{4}.$

15. Let n times $\dfrac{1}{8} = 37\dfrac{1}{2}$

$\Rightarrow \dfrac{n}{8} = \dfrac{75}{2} \Rightarrow 2n = 8 \times 75$

$\Rightarrow n = \dfrac{8 \times 75}{2} = 4 \times 75 = 300.$

4. SURDS AND INDICES

SURDS

If 'a' is a rational number and n is a positive integer such that nth root of 'a', i.e., $a^{1/n}$ or $\sqrt[n]{a}$ is an irrational number, then $a^{1/n}$ is called a surd or radical.

In other words, an irrational root of a rational number is called a surd. The symbol '$\sqrt{\ }$' is known as surd sign or radical.

For example, $\sqrt{2} = 2^{1/2} = $ Square root of 2

$\sqrt[3]{5} = 5^{1/3} = $ Cube root of 5

Pure and Mixed Surds

Pure Surd: A surd which has unity only as rational factor, the other factor being irrational, is called a pure surd.

For example, $\sqrt{2}$, $\sqrt[3]{3}$, $\sqrt[5]{3}$ are pure surds.

Mixed Surd: A surd which has a rational factor other than unity, the other factor being irrational, is called a mixed surds.

For example, $2\sqrt{5}$ $3\sqrt[4]{7}$, $5\sqrt[3]{11}$ are mixed surds.

Rationalising Factor: When the product of two surds is a rational number, then each of them is called the rationalising factor (R.F.) of the other.

For example, $3\sqrt{5} \times \sqrt{5} = 3 \times 5 = 15$

$\therefore$ $\sqrt{5}$ is a rationalising factor of $3\sqrt{5}$.

Important Formulae Based on Surds

$\sqrt[n]{a} = a^{1/n}$ and it is called a surd of order n.

(i) $\sqrt[n]{a^n} = a$

(ii) $\sqrt[n]{ab} = \sqrt[n]{a}\,\sqrt[n]{b}$

(iii) $\sqrt{a} \times \sqrt{a} = a$

(iv) $\sqrt{a} \times \sqrt{b} = \sqrt{ab}$

(v) $\sqrt{a^2b} = a\sqrt{b}$

(vi) $\left(\sqrt{a} + \sqrt{b}\right)^2 = a + b + 2\sqrt{ab}$

(vii) $\left(\sqrt{a} - \sqrt{b}\right)^2 = a + b - 2\sqrt{ab}$

(viii) $\left(\sqrt{a} + \sqrt{b}\right)\left(\sqrt{a} - \sqrt{b}\right) = a - b$ where a and b are positive rational numbers.

INDICES

Let n be a positive integer and 'a' be a real number. The continued product of n factors each equal to a e.g., $a \times a \times a \times ... \times n$ times is written as a^n and is called "n^{th} power of a" or "a raised to the power n".

The expression a^n is termed as power function or simply power, a is called the base and n is called index or exponent of the power a^n.

For example, $2^2 = $ square of 2, $2^3 = $ cube of 2, etc.

Laws of Indices

(i) $a^m \times a^n = a^{m+n}$

(ii) $a^m \times a^n \times a^p \times ... = a^{m+n+p+...}$

(iii) $\dfrac{a^m}{a^n} = a^{m-n}$, if $m > n$

(iv) $\dfrac{a^m}{a^n} = \dfrac{1}{a^{n-m}}$, if $m < n$

(v) $(a^m)^n = a^{mn}$

(vi) $(ab)^n = a^n b^n$

(vii) $a^0 = 1$

(viii) If $a^m = a^n$ then $m = n$

(ix) If $a^m = b^m$ then $a = b$

(x) $\dfrac{a^m}{a^m} = a^{m-m} = a^0 = 1$

15

MULTIPLE CHOICE QUESTIONS

1. If the infinite series is $x = \sqrt{6 + \sqrt{6 + \sqrt{6 + \ldots}}}$ then the value of x is:

A. 2.5　　　　　　　　B. 3
C. 6　　　　　　　　　D. 8

2. If $\dfrac{9^n \cdot 3^2 \cdot 3^n - (27)^n}{3^{3m} \cdot 2^3} = \dfrac{1}{27}$, then the value of $(m - n)$ is:

A. 1　　　　　　　　　B. 2

C. $\sqrt{3}$　　　　　　　D. $\sqrt{\dfrac{2}{3}}$

3. If $x = \dfrac{\sqrt{5} + \sqrt{3}}{\sqrt{5} - \sqrt{3}}$ and $y = \dfrac{\sqrt{5} - \sqrt{3}}{\sqrt{5} + \sqrt{3}}$, then $(x + y)$ is equal to:

A. 8　　　　　　　　　B. 6

C. $2\sqrt{15}$　　　　　D. $2\left(\sqrt{5} + \sqrt{3}\right)$

4. $2^{x+1} + 2^{x+3} = 2560$, then x is equal to:

A. 12　　　　　　　　B. 11
C. 8　　　　　　　　　D. 6

5. If $\dfrac{5 + 2\sqrt{3}}{7 + 4\sqrt{3}} = a + b\sqrt{3}$, then b is equal to:

A. −6　　　　　　　　B. 6
C. −11　　　　　　　D. 11

6. If $\dfrac{(21)^{5.36}}{(21)^{3.47}} = (21)^x$, then the value of x is:

A. 8.88　　　　　　　B. 1.54
C. 9.32　　　　　　　D. 1.89

7. $\sqrt{24} + \sqrt{12}$ equal to:

A. $\sqrt{36}$　　　　　B. $2\sqrt{6} + 2\sqrt{3}$

C. $6\sqrt{2}$　　　　　D. $\sqrt{288}$

8. If $a^b = 64$, where a and b are positive integers then $(a - b)^{a+b-4}$ is:

A. 0　　　　　　　　　B. 1

C. 2　　　　　　　　　D. $\dfrac{1}{2}$

9. The value of $\dfrac{5^{10+n} \cdot 25^{3n-4}}{5^{7n}}$ is:

A. 5　　　　　　　　　B. 8
C. 25　　　　　　　　D. 16

10. $3^x - 3^{x-1} = 18$, then the value of x^x is:

A. 3　　　　　　　　　B. 8
C. 27　　　　　　　　D. 216

11. If $x = \sqrt{10 + \sqrt{25 + \sqrt{121}}}$, then x is equal to:

A. −2 only　　　　　B. 2 only
C. ±4　　　　　　　D. 4 only

12. If $a^x = b^y = c^z$ and $b^2 = ac$, then y is equal to:

A. $\dfrac{xz}{x + z}$　　　　B. $\dfrac{xz}{2(x - z)}$

C. $\dfrac{xz}{2(z - x)}$　　　D. $\dfrac{2xz}{x + z}$

13. $\dfrac{5^{n+3} - 6 \times 5^{n+1}}{9 \times 5^n - 5^n \times 2^2}$ is equal to:

A. 5　　　　　　　　　B. 19
C. 25　　　　　　　　D. 95

14. The value of $\left(\dfrac{x^a}{x^b}\right)^{(a+b)} \times \left(\dfrac{x^b}{x^c}\right)^{(b+c)} \times \left(\dfrac{x^c}{x^a}\right)^{(c+a)}$ is equal to:

A. 0　　　　　　　　　B. 2
C. 1　　　　　　　　　D. 3

15. If $\sqrt{3^n} = 729$, then the value of n is:

A. 12　　　　　　　　B. 8
C. 10　　　　　　　　D. 6

ANSWERS

1	2	3	4	5	6	7	8	9	10
B	A	A	C	A	D	B	B	C	C

11	12	13	14	15
D	D	B	C	A

EXPLANATORY ANSWERS

1. $x = \sqrt{6 + x}$

Squaring both sides

$$x^2 = 6 + x$$

$\Rightarrow \quad x^2 - x - 6 = 0$

$\Rightarrow \quad x^2 - 3x + 2x - 6 = 0$

$\Rightarrow \quad x(x - 3) + 2(x - 3) = 0$

$\Rightarrow \quad (x - 3)(x + 2) = 0$

$\Rightarrow \quad x = 3 \text{ or } x = -2$

But x cannot be -2.

Hence, the required value of x is 3.

2. $\dfrac{9^n \cdot 3^2 \cdot 3^n - (27)^n}{3^{3m} \cdot 2^3} = \dfrac{1}{27}$

$\Rightarrow \dfrac{3^{2n} \times 9 \times 3^n - 3^{3n}}{8 \times 3^{3m}} = \dfrac{1}{3^3}$

$\Rightarrow \dfrac{3^{3n}(9 - 1)}{8 \cdot 3^{3m}} = 3^{-3}$

$\Rightarrow \quad 3^{3n - 3m} = (3)^{-3}$

$\Rightarrow \quad 3m - 3n = 3$

$\Rightarrow \quad 3(m - n) = 3$

$\Rightarrow \quad m - n = \dfrac{3}{3} = 1$

3. $x = \dfrac{\sqrt{5} + \sqrt{3}}{\sqrt{5} - \sqrt{3}} \times \dfrac{\sqrt{5} + \sqrt{3}}{\sqrt{5} + \sqrt{3}} = \dfrac{\left(\sqrt{5} + \sqrt{3}\right)^2}{5 - 3}$

$\Rightarrow x = \dfrac{5 + 3 + 2\sqrt{15}}{2} = \dfrac{8 + 2\sqrt{15}}{2} = \dfrac{2\left(4 + \sqrt{15}\right)}{2}$

$\therefore \quad x = 4 + \sqrt{15}$

Again, $y = \dfrac{\sqrt{5} - \sqrt{3}}{\sqrt{5} + \sqrt{3}} \times \dfrac{\sqrt{5} - \sqrt{3}}{\sqrt{5} - \sqrt{3}}$

$= \dfrac{\left(\sqrt{5} - \sqrt{3}\right)^2}{5 - 3}$

$\Rightarrow \quad y = \dfrac{5 + 3 - 2\sqrt{15}}{2}$

$= \dfrac{8 - 2\sqrt{15}}{2} = \dfrac{2\left(4 - \sqrt{15}\right)}{2}$

$\Rightarrow \quad y = 4 - \sqrt{15}$

$\therefore \quad x + y = 4 + \sqrt{15} + 4 - \sqrt{15} = 8$

4. $2^{x+1} + 2^{x+3} = 2560$

$\Rightarrow \quad 2^x \times 2 + 2^x \times 2^3 = 2560$

$\Rightarrow \quad 2 \times 2^x + 8 \times 2^x = 2560$

$\Rightarrow \quad 2^x (2 + 8) = 2560$

$\Rightarrow \quad 2^x = 256 = 2^8$

$\Rightarrow \quad x = 8$

5. $\because \quad \dfrac{5 + 2\sqrt{3}}{7 + 4\sqrt{3}} = a + b\sqrt{3}$

$\dfrac{5 + 2\sqrt{3}}{7 + 4\sqrt{3}} \times \dfrac{7 - 4\sqrt{3}}{7 - 4\sqrt{3}} = \dfrac{35 - 20\sqrt{3} + 14\sqrt{3} - 24}{49 - 48}$

$= \dfrac{11 - 6\sqrt{3}}{1}$

Comparing then we get,

$a = 11, b = -6$

Hence, $b = -6$.

6. $\dfrac{(21)^{5.36}}{(21)^{3.47}} = (21)^x$

$\Rightarrow \quad (21)^{5.36 - 3.47} = (21)^x$

$\Rightarrow \quad x = 1.89$

7. $\sqrt{24} + \sqrt{12} = 2\sqrt{6} + 2\sqrt{3}$

8. $a^b = 64 = (4)^3 \Rightarrow a = 4, b = 3$

$\therefore (a - b)^{a+b-4} = (4 - 3)^{4+3-4} = (1)^3 = 1$

9. $\dfrac{5^{10+n} \cdot 25^{3n-4}}{5^{7n}} = \dfrac{5^{10} \times 5^n \times (5^2)^{3n-4}}{5^{7n}}$

$= \dfrac{5^{10} \times 5^n \times 5^{6n} \times 5^{-8}}{5^{7n}}$

$= \dfrac{5^{10-8} \times 5^{7n}}{5^{7n}} = 5^2 \times 5^{7n-7n}$

$= 25 \times 5^0 = 25 \times 1 = 25$

10. $3^x - 3^{x-1} = 18$

$\Rightarrow \quad 3^x - 3^x \times 3^{-1} = 18$

$\Rightarrow \quad 3^x \left(1 - \dfrac{1}{3}\right) = 18$

$\Rightarrow \quad 3^x \left(\dfrac{2}{3}\right) = 18$

$$\Rightarrow \qquad 3^x = \frac{18 \times 3}{2} = 27$$

$$\Rightarrow \qquad 3^x = (3)^3 \Rightarrow x = 3$$

$$\therefore \qquad x^x = (3)^3 = 27$$

11. $\qquad x = \sqrt{10 + \sqrt{25 + \sqrt{121}}}$

$$\Rightarrow \quad x = \sqrt{10 + \sqrt{25 + 11}}$$

$$\Rightarrow \quad x = \sqrt{10 + \sqrt{36}}$$

$$\Rightarrow \quad x = \sqrt{10 + 6} = \sqrt{16}$$

$$\Rightarrow \quad x = 4$$

12. Let $a^x = b^y = c^z = k$

then $a = k^{\frac{1}{x}}$, $b = k^{\frac{1}{y}}$, $c = k^{\frac{1}{z}}$

Now, $\qquad\qquad b^2 = ac$

$$\Rightarrow \qquad \left(k^{\frac{1}{y}}\right)^2 = k^{\frac{1}{x}} \cdot k^{\frac{1}{z}}$$

$$\Rightarrow \qquad k^{\frac{2}{y}} = k^{\frac{1}{x}+\frac{1}{z}}$$

$$\Rightarrow \qquad \frac{2}{y} = \frac{z+x}{xz}$$

$$\Rightarrow \qquad 2xz = y(x+z)$$

$$\Rightarrow \qquad y = \frac{2xz}{x+z}$$

13. $\dfrac{5^{n+3} - 6 \times 5^{n+1}}{9 \times 5^n - 5^n \times 2^2} = \dfrac{5^n \times 5^3 - 6 \times 5^n \times 5}{9 \times 5^n - 4 \times 5^n}$

$$= \frac{5^n(125-30)}{5^n(9-4)} = 5^0 \times \frac{95}{5}$$

$$= 1 \times 19 = 19.$$

14. $\left(\dfrac{x^a}{x^b}\right)^{(a+b)} \times \left(\dfrac{x^b}{x^c}\right)^{(b+c)} \times \left(\dfrac{x^c}{x^a}\right)^{(c+a)}$

$$= \left(x^{a-b}\right)^{(a+b)} \times \left(x^{b-c}\right)^{(b+c)} \times \left(x^{c-a}\right)^{c+a}$$

$$= x^{a^2-b^2} \times x^{b^2-c^2} \times x^{c^2-a^2}$$

$$= x^{a^2-b^2+b^2-c^2+c^2-a^2}$$

$$= x^0 = 1$$

15. $\qquad \sqrt{3^n} = 729 \Rightarrow 3^{n/2} = 3^6$

$$\Rightarrow \qquad \frac{n}{2} = 6$$

$$\Rightarrow \qquad n = 12.$$

5. RATIO AND PROPORTION

RATIO

When comparison is made by dividing one quantity by another of the same kind, the result is called ratio. If a and b are two numbers, ratio of a to b is denoted by $a : b$ or $\dfrac{a}{b}$. Here a is called first term and b is called the second term. The first term is also called antecedent and the second term is also called consequent.

EXAMPLE: The ratio $3 : 10$ represents $\dfrac{3}{10}$ with antecedent 3 and consequent 10.

The multiplication or division of each term of a ratio by a same non-zero number does not effect the ratio.

PROPORTION

Equality of two ratios is called proportion. If $a : b = c : d$, then a, b, c, d are called in proportion. In a proportion $a : b :: c : d$, then a and d are called extremes and b and c are called means.

Product of extremes = Product of means

Comparison of Ratio: Suppose $\dfrac{a}{b} > \dfrac{c}{d}$ then we say that $a : b > c : d$.

Compounded Ratio: The compound ratio of the ratios $a : b$, $c : d$ and $e : f$ is $ace : bdf$.

Duplicate Ratio: The duplicate ratio of $a : b$ is $a^2 : b^2$.

Triplicate Ratio: The triplicate ratio of $a : b$ is $a^3 : b^3$.

Sub-duplicate and Sub-triplicate ratios

The sub-duplicate and Sub-triplicate ratios of ratio $a : b$ are $a^{1/2} : b^{1/2}$ and $a^{1/3} : b^{1/3}$ respectively.

Mean Proportional: Mean proportional between a and b is $\sqrt{ab}$.

Third Proportional: The third proportional to a, b is the fourth proportional to a, b, b.

Fourth Proportional: If $a : b :: c : d$ is a proportion, then d is called the fourth proportional to a, b, c.

EXAMPLE: If $A : B = 3 : 4$ and $B : C = 8 : 9$ then find $A : C$.

SOLUTION: $A : B = 3 : 4 \quad \Rightarrow \quad \dfrac{A}{B} = \dfrac{3}{4}$

$\qquad\qquad B : C = 8 : 9 \quad \Rightarrow \quad \dfrac{B}{C} = \dfrac{8}{9}$

$\dfrac{A}{C} = \dfrac{A}{B} \times \dfrac{B}{C} = \dfrac{3}{4} \times \dfrac{8}{9} = \dfrac{2}{3}$

$\Rightarrow \qquad\qquad A : C = 2 : 3$

EXAMPLE: If 15% of A is the same as 20% of B, then find $A : B$.

SOLUTION: Given : 15% of A = 20% of B

$\Rightarrow \qquad \dfrac{15}{100} \times A = \dfrac{20}{100} \times B$

$\Rightarrow \qquad\qquad 3A = 4B$

$\Rightarrow \qquad\qquad \dfrac{A}{B} = \dfrac{4}{3}$

$\Rightarrow \qquad\qquad A : B = 4 : 3$

EXAMPLE: A stick 1.4 m long casts a shadow 1.3 m long at the same time when a pole casts a shadow 5.2 m long. Find the length of the pole.

SOLUTION: Clearly, more is the length of shadow, more is the length of the object.

Let the length of the pole be x metres.

Then, $1.3 : 5.2 : : 1.4 : x$

$\Rightarrow \qquad \dfrac{1.3}{5.2} = \dfrac{1.4}{x}$

$\Rightarrow \qquad \dfrac{1}{4} = \dfrac{1.4}{x}$

$\Rightarrow \qquad x = 1.4 \times 4 = 5.6$

Hence, the length of the pole is 5.6 m.

MULTIPLE CHOICE QUESTIONS

1. If $A : B = 2 : 3$ and $B : C = 4 : 5$, then $C : A$ is equal to:
   A. $15 : 8$
   B. $12 : 10$
   C. $8 : 5$
   D. $8 : 15$

2. If 10% of x is the same as 20% of y, then $x : y$ is equal to:
   A. $1 : 2$
   B. $2 : 1$
   C. $5 : 1$
   D. $10 : 1$

3. The mean proportional to $6 + \sqrt{27}$ and $6 - \sqrt{27}$ is:
   A. 3
   B. 9
   C. 10
   D. $\sqrt{10}$

4. If $x : y = 9 : 11$, the value of $\dfrac{5x + 3y}{3x + 5y}$ is:
   A. $45 : 55$
   B. $18 : 22$
   C. $37 : 41$
   D. $39 : 41$

5. If $a + b : b + c : c + a = 6 : 7 : 8$ and $a + b + c = 14$, then the value of c is:
   A. 14
   B. 7
   C. 8
   D. 6

6. Two numbers are in the ratio $2 : 3$. If 5 is added to each number, the ratio becomes $5 : 7$. The bigger number is:
   A. 30
   B. 40
   C. 60
   D. 20

7. What should be added to each of the numbers 12, 30, 40 and 86, so that they are in proportion?
   A. 6
   B. 4
   C. −6
   D. −4

8. The ratio of males and females of a village is $5 : 3$. If there are 800 males in the village, females are:
   A. 240
   B. 480
   C. 840
   D. 488

9. In a mixture of 60 litres, the ratio of ethanol to ether is $4 : 1$. How much ether must be added to the mixture to make this ratio $2 : 1$?
   A. 10 litres
   B. 12 litres
   C. 18 litres
   D. 24 litres

10. The proportion of zinc and copper in a brass piece is $4 : 5$. How much zinc will be there in 180 kg of such a piece?
    A. 40 kg
    B. 80 kg
    C. 100 kg
    D. 120 kg

11. The prices of a scooter and a television set are in the ratio $3 : 2$. If a scooter costs ₹ 6000 more than the television set, the price of the television set is:
    A. ₹ 18000
    B. ₹ 12000
    C. ₹ 10000
    D. ₹ 6000

12. The weight of a 13 metres long iron rod be 23.4 kg. The weight of 6 metres long of such rod will be:
    A. 7.2 kg
    B. 12.4 kg
    C. 10.8 kg
    D. 18 kg

13. The ratio between the ages of Gayatri and Savitri is $6 : 5$ and the sum of their ages is 44 years. The ratio of their ages after 8 years will be:
    A. $5 : 6$
    B. $7 : 8$
    C. $8 : 7$
    D. $14 : 13$

14. Two numbers are such that the ratio between them is $3 : 5$ but if each is increased by 10, the ratio between them becomes $5 : 7$. The numbers are:
    A. 3, 5
    B. 7, 9
    C. 13, 22
    D. 15, 25

15. In a factory the ratio of male workers to female workers was $5 : 3$. If the number of female workers was less by 40, the total number of workers in the factory was:
    A. 100
    B. 500
    C. 160
    D. 200

ANSWERS

1	2	3	4	5	6	7	8	9	10
A	B	A	D	D	A	A	B	B	B

11	12	13	14	15
B	C	C	D	C

EXPLANATORY ANSWERS

1. $\dfrac{A}{B} = \dfrac{2}{3}$ and $\dfrac{B}{C} = \dfrac{4}{5}$

$\Rightarrow \quad \dfrac{A}{B} \times \dfrac{B}{C} = \dfrac{2}{3} \times \dfrac{4}{5} \Rightarrow \dfrac{A}{C} = \dfrac{8}{15}$

$\Rightarrow \quad \dfrac{C}{A} = \dfrac{15}{8}$

Hence, $\quad C : A = 15 : 8$.

2. 10% of x = 20% of y

$\Rightarrow \quad \dfrac{10}{100}x = \dfrac{20}{100}y \quad \Rightarrow \dfrac{x}{10} = \dfrac{y}{5}$

$\Rightarrow \quad \dfrac{x}{y} = \dfrac{10}{5} \quad \Rightarrow x : y = 2 : 1$

3. Mean proportional $= \sqrt{\left(6 + \sqrt{27}\right)\left(6 - \sqrt{27}\right)}$

$= \sqrt{36 - 27} = \sqrt{9} = 3$

4. $\because \quad \dfrac{x}{y} = \dfrac{9}{11}$

$\dfrac{5x + 3y}{3x + 5y} = \dfrac{\dfrac{5x}{y} + \dfrac{3y}{y}}{\dfrac{3x}{y} + \dfrac{5y}{y}} = \dfrac{5\left(\dfrac{x}{y}\right) + 3}{3\left(\dfrac{x}{y}\right) + 5}$

$= \dfrac{5 \times \dfrac{9}{11} + 3}{3 \times \dfrac{9}{11} + 5} = \dfrac{\dfrac{45 + 33}{11}}{\dfrac{27 + 55}{11}} = \dfrac{78}{82} = \dfrac{39}{41}$

Hence, the value of $\dfrac{5x + 3y}{3x + 5y} = \dfrac{39}{41}$.

5. Given : $a + b = 6x$, $b + c = 7x$

and $\quad c + a = 8x$ ...(i)

and $\quad a + b + c = 14$ ...(ii)

Adding Eq. (i)

$a + b + b + c + c + a = 6x + 7x + 8x$

$\Rightarrow \quad 2(a + b + c) = 21x$

$\Rightarrow \quad 2 \times 14 = 21x$ [from Eq. (ii)]

$\Rightarrow \quad x = \dfrac{28}{21} = \dfrac{4}{3}$

$\therefore \quad a + b = 6x = 6 \times \dfrac{4}{3} = 8$

$\because \quad a + b + c = 14 \Rightarrow c = 14 - 8 = 6$

6. Let the two numbers are a and b

According to the question,

$\dfrac{a}{b} = \dfrac{2}{3} \Rightarrow 3a = 2b \Rightarrow b = \dfrac{3a}{2}$

Now, $\quad \dfrac{a + 5}{b + 5} = \dfrac{5}{7} \Rightarrow 7a + 35 = 5b + 25$

$\Rightarrow \quad 7a - 5b = -10$

$\Rightarrow \quad 7a - 5\left(\dfrac{3a}{2}\right) = -10$

$\Rightarrow \quad 14a - 15a = -20 \Rightarrow -a = -20$

$\Rightarrow \quad a = 20, b = 3 \times \dfrac{20}{2} = 30$

Hence, the bigger number is 30.

7. Let x be added to each of the numbers.

Then, $(12 + x) : (30 + x) :: (40 + x) : (86 + x)$

$\Rightarrow \quad \dfrac{12 + x}{30 + x} = \dfrac{40 + x}{86 + x}$

$\Rightarrow (12 + x)(86 + x) = (30 + x)(40 + x)$

$\Rightarrow 12 \times 86 + 12x + 86x + x^2$

$\qquad\qquad = 30 \times 40 + 30x + 40x + x^2$

$\Rightarrow \quad 1032 + 98x = 1200 + 70x$

$\Rightarrow \quad 28x = 168 \Rightarrow x = 6$

8. Ratio of Males : Females $= 5 : 3$

$\Rightarrow \quad \dfrac{800}{x} = \dfrac{5}{3} \Rightarrow 5x = 3 \times 800$

$\Rightarrow \quad x = \dfrac{3 \times 800}{5} = 3 \times 160 = 480$

Hence, number of females = 480.

9. Let ethanol = $4x$ and ether = $1x$

$4x + 1x = 60 \Rightarrow 5x = 60 \Rightarrow x = 12$

Quantity of ethanol = $12 \times 4 = 48$ litres

Quantity of ether = $1 \times 12 = 12$ litres

Let m litres of ether be added to mixture to get the desired ratio. Then,

$$\frac{48}{12 + m} = \frac{2}{1} \quad \Rightarrow \quad 24 + 2m = 48$$

$\Rightarrow \qquad 2m = 24 \quad \Rightarrow \qquad m = 12$

Hence, 12 litres of ether is to be added.

10. In 9 kg of brass, zinc = 4 kg

$\therefore$ In 180 kg of brass, zinc = $\dfrac{4}{9} \times 180 = 80$ kg.

11. Let the prices of a scooter and a television be ₹ $3x$ and $2x$ respectively.

According to the question,

$3x - 2x = 6000 \Rightarrow x = 6000$

$\therefore$ Price of a television = $2 \times 6000 = $ ₹ 12000.

12. Weight of 13 m long iron rod = 23.4 kg

Weight of 6 m long iron rod

$= \dfrac{23.4}{13} \times 6$ kg = $1.8 \times 6 = 10.8$ kg.

13. Let present age of Gayatri = $6x$ years and present age of Savitri = $5x$ years.

According to the question,

$\qquad 6x + 5x = 44 \Rightarrow 11x = 44 \Rightarrow x = 4$

Gayatri's age = $6 \times 4 = 24$ years

Savitri's age = $5 \times 4 = 20$ years

After 8 years their ages will be 32 years and 28 years.

Ratio of their ages after 8 years = $\dfrac{32}{28} = 8 : 7$.

14. Let numbers are x and y

$$\frac{x}{y} = \frac{3}{5}$$

$\Rightarrow \qquad\qquad 5x = 3y \Rightarrow x = \dfrac{3y}{5}$

According to the question,

$\qquad\qquad \dfrac{x + 10}{y + 10} = \dfrac{5}{7} \Rightarrow 7x + 70 = 5y + 50$

$\Rightarrow \qquad\quad 7x - 5y = -20$

$\Rightarrow \qquad 7\left(\dfrac{3y}{5}\right) - 5y = -20$

$\Rightarrow \qquad 21y - 25y = -100$

$\Rightarrow \qquad\qquad\quad 4y = 100 \Rightarrow y = 25$

$\therefore \qquad\qquad\quad x = \dfrac{3 \times 25}{5} = 15$

Hence, numbers are 15 and 25.

15. Let the number of male and female workers be $5x$ and $3x$ respectively.

According to the question,

$5x - 3x = 40 \Rightarrow 2x = 40 \Rightarrow x = 20$

$\therefore$ Number of male = $5 \times 20 = 100$

and number of female = $3 \times 20 = 60$

Hence, total number of workers = $100 + 60$ = 160.

6. PARTNERSHIP

Partnership is a form of association of two or more persons who contribute resources like money together in order to carry on a business. It may be of simple or compound type.

Simple partnership is one in which the capitals of the partners are invested for the same time. The profits or losses are divided among the partners in the ratio of their investments.

Compound partnership is one in which the capitals of the partners are invested for different periods. In such cases, equivalent capitals are calculated for each partner by multiplying their capital contributions with time. The profits or losses are then divided in the ratio of these equivalent capitals. Thus, the ratio of profits is directly proportional to both capital invested as well as time.

The partner who invests the money in the business as well as takes part in its management, is known as **Working partner**.

The partner who only invests the money in the business and does not work, is known as **Sleeping partner**.

A working partner gets either monthly payment or a share in the profit for his contribution in the management of the business. This payment is deducted from the total profit before its distribution.

EXAMPLE: A, B and C invest ₹ 15000, ₹ 20000 and ₹ 25000 respectively in a business. The profit earned is ₹ 1200. Find the share of each in the profit.

SOLUTION: This is a case of simple partnership
Ratio of investments,

$$\begin{array}{lcccc} & A & : B & : C \\ & = 15000 & : 20000 & : 25000 \\ & = 3 & : 4 & : 5 \end{array}$$

Sum of the ratios = 3 + 4 + 5 = 12

Share in the profit

$$\text{For A} = \frac{3}{12} \times 1200 = ₹\ 300$$

$$\text{For B} = \frac{4}{12} \times 1200 = ₹\ 400$$

$$\text{For C} = \frac{5}{12} \times 1200 = ₹\ 500$$

EXAMPLE: A and B are partners in a firm. A invests ₹ 15000 and B ₹ 25000. A is the working partner and gets 20% of the profit for his contribution in the management of the firm. B is the sleeping partner. If the profit is ₹ 475, find the share of each.

SOLUTION: First we have to deduct the payment to be made to A from the total profit for his contribution in the management of the firm.

20% of ₹ 475 = ₹ 95
Balance profit = 475 – 95 = ₹ 380

This has to be divided between A and B in the ratio of their investments *i.e.,* ₹ 15000 : ₹ 25000 = 3 : 5

$$\text{A's share} = ₹\ 380 \times \frac{3}{8} = ₹\ 142.5$$

$$\text{B's share} = ₹\ 380 \times \frac{5}{8} = ₹\ 237.5$$

Finally, A gets a total of (95 + 142.5) = ₹ 237.5 and B gets = ₹ 237.5

EXAMPLE: In a business A and B gained some amount in a certain ratio. B and C received the profit in the ratio as that of A and B. If B received ₹ 6400 and C received ₹ 10,000 then find the amount invested by B.

SOLUTION: Let the ratio of A's and B's profit be $\dfrac{a}{b}$.

Hence, the ratio of B's and C's profit = $\dfrac{a}{b}$

Thus, $\quad$ A : B : C = $a : b : \dfrac{b^2}{a}$

when A's profit, $\quad a = ₹\,6400$

and C's profit, $\quad \dfrac{b^2}{a} = ₹\,10,000$

$\Rightarrow \quad b^2 = 10,000 \times 6400 = 100 \times 100 \times 80 \times 80$

$\Rightarrow \quad b = 100 \times 80 = 8000$

Hence, the amount invested by B = ₹ 8000.

MULTIPLE CHOICE QUESTIONS

1. A, B and C share the profit in the ratio of 3 : 5 : 7. If the gain is ₹ 2040, then C's share is:
   A. ₹ 360
   B. ₹ 600
   C. ₹ 952
   D. ₹ 120

2. A, B and C started a business with ₹ 47000. A puts in ₹ 5000 more than B and B ₹ 3000 more than C. The share of A out of the profit of ₹ 14100 will be:
   A. ₹ 3600
   B. ₹ 4500
   C. ₹ 6000
   D. ₹ 6300

3. A starts a business with ₹ 5000. After 4 months B joins him with a sum of ₹ 4000. In the end of the year there is a profit of ₹ 8970. The share of A in the profit will be:
   A. ₹ 3120
   B. ₹ 4020
   C. ₹ 5850
   D. ₹ 6360

4. A, B, C are three partners in a business. The profit share of A is $\dfrac{3}{16}$ of the profit and B's share is $\dfrac{1}{4}$ of the profit. If C receives ₹ 243, then the amount received by B will be:
   A. ₹ 90
   B. ₹ 96
   C. ₹ 108
   D. ₹ 120

5. A, B and C share the profit in the ratio 2 : 3 : 7. If the average gain is ₹ 8000, then B's share is:
   A. ₹ 2000
   B. ₹ 1000
   C. ₹ 1500
   D. ₹ 3000

6. Ashok started a business investing ₹ 90,000. After 3 months Shabir joined him with a capital of ₹ 1,20,000. If at the end of one year the total profit made by them was ₹ 96,000, what will be the difference between their shares?
   A. ₹ 24000
   B. ₹ 8000
   C. ₹ 20000
   D. None of these

7. Mahesh received ₹ 6000 as his share out of the total profit of ₹ 9000 which he and Ram entered at the end of one year. If Mahesh invested ₹ 20,000 for 6 months, whereas Ram invested his amount for the whole year, what was the amount invested by Ram?
   A. ₹ 4000
   B. ₹ 5000
   C. ₹ 3000
   D. ₹ 6000

8. A and B started a business jointly. A's investment was thrice the investment of B and the period of his investment was two times the period of investment of B. If B received ₹ 40,000 as profit, then their total profit is:
   A. ₹ 2,40,000
   B. ₹ 28000
   C. ₹ 24000
   D. ₹ 2,80,000

9. Anil started a business investing ₹ 70,000. After 8 months Vimal joined him with a capital of ₹ 1,80,000. In what ratio should Anil and Vimal share the profit after two years?
   A. 8 : 7
   B. 7 : 5
   C. 7 : 6
   D. None of these

10. A, B and C starts a business. A invests ₹ 3,20,000 for four months. B invests ₹ 5,10,000 for three months and C invests ₹ 2,70,000 for five months. If at the end of year there is a profit of ₹ 1,24,800, then share of B is:
    A. ₹ 79000
    B. ₹ 49200
    C. ₹ 50000
    D. ₹ 45900

11. A, B and C contract a work for ₹ 550. Together A and B are to do $\dfrac{7}{11}$ of the work. The share of C should be:
    A. ₹ 400
    B. ₹ 300
    C. ₹ 200
    D. ₹ $183\dfrac{1}{3}$

12. Jagmohan, Rooplal and Pankaj rented a video cassette for one week at a rent of ₹ 350. If they use it for 6 hrs, 10 hrs and 12 hrs respectively, the rent to be paid by Pankaj is:
    A. ₹ 75
    B. ₹ 125
    C. ₹ 35
    D. ₹ 150

13. Manoj got ₹ 6000 as his share out of the total profit of ₹ 9000 which he and Ramesh earned at the end of one year. If Manoj invested ₹ 20,000 for 6 months, whereas Ramesh invested his amount for the whole year, the amount invested by Ramesh was:
   A. ₹ 60,000   B. ₹ 10,000
   C. ₹ 4000   D. ₹ 5000
14. A, B and C invest ₹ 2000, ₹ 3000 and ₹ 4000 in a business. After one year A removed his money, B and C continued the business for one more year. If the net profit after 2 years be ₹ 3200, then A's share in the profit is:
   A. ₹ 1000   B. ₹ 600
   C. ₹ 800   D. ₹ 400
15. A and B enter into partnership investing ₹ 12000 and ₹ 16000 respectively. After 8 months, C also joins the business with a capital of ₹ 15000. The share of C in a profit of ₹ 46500 after 2 years will be:
   A. ₹ 12000   B. ₹ 14400
   C. ₹ 19200   D. ₹ 21200

ANSWERS

1	2	3	4	5	6	7	8	9	10
C	C	C	C	A	D	B	D	D	D

11	12	13	14	15
C	D	D	D	A

EXPLANATORY ANSWERS

1. C's share $= \dfrac{7}{15} \times 2040 = ₹\,952$.

2. Let C's capital be ₹ x
   Then B's capital $= ₹\,(x + 3000)$
   and A's capital $= ₹\,(x + 3000 + 5000) = x + 8000$
   $\Rightarrow \quad x + (x + 3000) + (x + 8000) = 47000$
   $\Rightarrow \quad 3x + 11000 = 47000$
   $\Rightarrow \quad 3x = 47000 - 11000$
   $\qquad\qquad = 36000$
   $\Rightarrow \quad x = 12000$
   Thus, capital of A, B and C are ₹ 20000, ₹ 15000 and ₹ 12000 respectively.
   ∴ Profit sharing ratio $= 20 : 15 : 12$
   ∴ Profit of A $= \dfrac{20}{47} \times 14100 = ₹\,6000$

3. ₹ $5000 \times 12 = ₹\,60,000$ for A
   ₹ $4000 \times (12 - 4) = 4000 \times 8 = ₹\,32000$ for B
   Ratio of profit sharing $= 60000 : 32000$
   $\qquad\qquad\qquad\qquad = 60 : 32 = 15 : 8$
   ∴ Share of A in the profit $= \dfrac{15}{23} \times 8970$
   $\qquad\qquad\qquad = 15 \times 390 = ₹\,5850$

4. Let the profit be ₹ 1. Then,

   $A : B : C = \dfrac{3}{16} : \dfrac{1}{4} : \left[1 - \left(\dfrac{3}{16} + \dfrac{1}{4} \right) \right]$
   $= \dfrac{3}{16} : \dfrac{1}{4} : \dfrac{9}{16}$
   $= \dfrac{3}{16} : \dfrac{4}{16} : \dfrac{9}{16}$ $i.e.,\ 3 : 4 : 9$
   when C's share is ₹ 9, then B's share $= ₹\,4$
   when C's share is ₹ 243, then B's share
   $= \dfrac{4 \times 243}{9} = ₹\,108$

5. B's share $= \dfrac{3}{2 + 3 + 7} \times 8000$
   $= \dfrac{3 \times 8000}{12} = ₹\,2000$

6. The ratio of their investment
   $= 12 \times 90000 : (12 - 3) \times 120000$
   $= 12 \times 9 : 9 \times 12 = 1 : 1$
   Ashok's share $= \dfrac{1}{1 + 1} \times 96000 = ₹\,48000$
   Shabir's share $= \dfrac{1}{1 + 1} \times 96000 = ₹\,48000$

Difference between their shares
$$= ₹\,48000 - ₹\,48000 = 0.$$

7. The ratio of their profit
$$= ₹\,6000 : ₹\,(9000 - 6000)$$
$$= ₹\,6000 : ₹\,3000 = 2 : 1$$
Let $₹\,x$ be the amount invested by Ram.
The ratio of their profit = The ratio of their investment
$$\Rightarrow \qquad 2 : 1 = 6 \times 20000 : 12 \times x$$
$$\Rightarrow \qquad \frac{2}{1} = \frac{6 \times 20000}{12 \times x} \Rightarrow 2x = 10000$$
$$\Rightarrow \qquad x = 5000$$
∴ The investment of Ram is ₹ 5000.

8. Let $₹\,x$ be the investment of B and n years be the period of investment of B.
Given : A's investment $= 3 \times ₹\,x = ₹\,3x$
and period of investment of A $= 2n$ years
∴ The ratio of investment of A and B
$$= 2n \times 3x : n \times x$$
$$= 6nx : nx = 6 : 1$$
Let the total profit be $₹\,y$
Given B's share in profit $= ₹\,40,000$
$$\Rightarrow \frac{1}{6+1} \times y = ₹\,40,000 \Rightarrow y = ₹\,2,80,000$$
∴ Total profit is ₹ 2,80,000.

9. The ratio of Anil's and Vimal's share in the profit
= Ratio of their investments
$$= 24 \times 70000 : 16 \times 180000$$
$$= 24 \times 7 : 16 \times 18 = 7 : 12$$

10. The ratio of investments of A, B and C
$$= 4 \times 320000 : 3 \times 510000 : 5 \times 270000$$
$$= 4 \times 32 : 3 \times 51 : 5 \times 27$$
$$= 128 : 153 : 135$$
Total profit after 1 year $= ₹\,124800$
$$\text{Share of B} = ₹\,\frac{153}{128+153+135} \times 124800$$
$$= ₹\,\frac{153}{416} \times 124800 = ₹\,45900$$

11. C's share $= ₹\left(550 \times \dfrac{4}{11}\right) = ₹\,200$

12. Ratio of rents $= 6 : 10 : 12 = 3 : 5 : 6$
∴ Pankaj's share of rent $= ₹\left(350 \times \dfrac{6}{14}\right) = ₹\,150$

13. Let amount invested by Ramesh be $₹\,x$
∴ $20000 \times 6 : 12x = 6000 : 3000$
i.e., $\dfrac{12x}{120000} = \dfrac{3000}{6000}$ or $x = ₹\,5000$

14. Ratio of investments
$$= (2000 \times 1) : (3000 \times 2) : (4000 \times 2)$$
$$= 1 : 3 : 4$$
∴ A's share $= ₹\left(3200 \times \dfrac{1}{8}\right) = ₹\,400.$

15. Ratio of investments
$$= (12000 \times 24) : (16000 \times 24) : (15000 \times 16)$$
$$= 6 : 8 : 5$$
C's share of profit $= ₹\left(45600 \times \dfrac{5}{19}\right) = ₹\,12000$

7. AVERAGE

The sum of all the quantities of same kind divided by their number is called average (or mean) of those quantities.

FORMULAE

1. Average = $\left(\dfrac{\text{Sum of observations}}{\text{Number of observations}}\right)$

2. Sum of the first n natural numbers
    $$= 1 + 2 + 3 + ... + n = \frac{n(n+1)}{2}$$

3. Sum of the squares of the first n natural numbers
    $$= 1^2 + 2^2 + ... + n^2 = \frac{n(n+1)(2n+1)}{6}$$

4. Sum of the cubes of the first n natural numbers
    $$= 1^3 + 2^3 + ... + n^3 = \left\{\frac{n(n+1)}{2}\right\}^2$$

5. Sum of the first n odd numbers
    $$= 1 + 3 + 5 + ... + (2n-1) = n^2$$

6. Distance between two stations P and Q is x km. A person covers the journey from P to Q at 'a' km/hr and returns back to P with a uniform speed of 'b' km/hr. Then the average speed of the person during the whole journey
    $$= \frac{2ab}{a+b} \text{ km/hr.}$$

Different kinds of mean or average:
  (a) Arithmetic mean
  (b) Geometric mean
  (c) Harmonic mean

(a) **Arithmetic Mean:** It is most popularly used of all the averages. For example, average income, average profit, average mileage etc. As defined earlier, it is the sum total of all values of items divided by the total number of items. For detailed discussion we will confine ourselves to Arithmetic Mean only because this is the most relevant of all the average for us.

Let $x_1, x_2, x_3, ..., x_n$ be the n values of x.

Their average is denoted by $\bar{x}$ and given by

$$\bar{x} = \frac{\text{Sum of observations}}{\text{Total number of observations}}$$

or $\quad \bar{x} = \dfrac{x_1 + x_2 + x_3 + ... + x_n}{n}$

(b) **Geometric Mean :** For observations $x_1, x_2, x_3, ..., x_n$ the geometric mean denoted by G.M. is defined as:
$$\text{G.M.} = (x_1 . x_2 . x_3 ... x_n)^{1/n}$$

It is useful in calculating averages of ratios such as average population, growth rate, average percentage increase etc.

(c) **Harmonic Mean:** It is defined as
$$\text{H.M.} = \frac{n}{\dfrac{1}{x_1} + \dfrac{1}{x_2} + ... + \dfrac{1}{x_n}}.$$

EXAMPLE: Find the average of first ten prime numbers.

SOLUTION: First ten prime numbers are 2, 3, 5, 7, 11, 13, 17, 19, 23 and 29.

$$\therefore \text{ Average} = \frac{2+3+5+7+11+13+17+19+23+29}{10}$$

$$= \frac{129}{10} = 12.9$$

EXAMPLE: If x_1, x_2, x_3, x_4, x_5 are five consecutive odd numbers then find the average of these numbers.

SOLUTION: Since x_1 is the first odd number.

$$\therefore \quad x_2 = x_1 + 2$$
$$x_3 = x_2 + 2 = x_1 + 4$$
$$x_4 = x_3 + 2 = x_1 + 6$$
$$x_5 = x_4 + 2 = x_1 + 8$$

$$\therefore \text{ Average} = \frac{x_1 + x_1 + 2 + x_1 + 4 + x_1 + 6 + x_1 + 8}{5}$$

$$= \frac{5x_1 + 20}{5} = \frac{5(x_1 + 4)}{5} = x_1 + 4$$

EXAMPLE: If the average of four consecutive even numbers is 27, then find the largest of these numbers.

SOLUTION: Let x be the first even number in the series of four consecutive even numbers.

$$\therefore \quad 2^{nd} \text{ even number} = x + 2$$
$$3^{rd} \text{ even number} = x + 4$$
$$4^{th} \text{ even number} = x + 6$$

$$\text{Average} = \frac{x + x + 2 + x + 4 + x + 6}{4}$$

$$\Rightarrow \quad 27 = \frac{4x + 12}{4}$$

$$\Rightarrow \quad 4x + 12 = 27 \times 4 = 108$$
$$\Rightarrow \quad 4x = 96$$
$$\Rightarrow \quad x = 24$$

Largest number in this series is $x + 6$

i.e., $\quad 24 + 6 = 30$

EXAMPLE: The average of eight numbers is 14. The average of six of these numbers is 16. What is the average of the remaining two numbers?

SOLUTION: Sum of the eight numbers = $14 \times 8 = 112$

Sum of six of these eight numbers = $16 \times 6 = 96$

$\therefore$ Sum of the remaining two numbers = $112 - 96 = 16$

$\therefore$ Average of the remaining two numbers = $\dfrac{16}{2} = 8$

EXAMPLE: What is the average of first 30 multiples of 7?

SOLUTION: Required Average

$$= \frac{7 + 14 + 21 + \ldots + 210}{30}$$

$$= \frac{7(1 + 2 + 3 + \ldots + 30)}{30}$$

$$= \frac{7 \times 30(30 + 1)}{2 \times 30}$$

$$= \frac{7 \times 31}{2} = \frac{217}{2} = 108.5$$

EXAMPLE: The average of 11 results is 50. If the average of first six results is 49 and that of last six is 52, find the sixth result.

SOLUTION: Sum of 11 results = $11 \times 50 = 550$

Sum of first 6 results $6 \times 49 = 294$

Sum of last 6 results = $6 \times 52 = 312$

$\therefore \quad$ 6th result = $294 + 312 - 550$

$= 56$

EXAMPLE: The average age of three boys is 15 years. If their ages are in the ratio 3 : 5 : 7. What is the age of the youngest boy?

SOLUTION: Let the ages of the three boys be $3x$, $5x$ and $7x$.

$$\text{Average age} = \frac{3x + 5x + 7x}{3} = 5x$$

and $\quad 5x = 15 \Rightarrow x = 3$

The age of the youngest boy = $3x = 3 \times 3 = 9$ years.

EXAMPLE: The average of 100 observations is 45. It was later found that two observations 19 and 31 were incorrectly recorded as 91 and 13. Find the correct average.

SOLUTION: Sum of 100 observations

$$= 100 \times 45 = 4500$$

New sum of 100 observations

$$= 4500 + (19 + 31) - (91 + 13)$$
$$= 4500 + 50 - 104 = 4446$$

$$\text{Correct average} = \frac{4446}{100} = 44.46$$

MULTIPLE CHOICE QUESTIONS

1. The average of first five multiples of 3 is:
   A. 3 B. 9
   C. 12 D. 15
2. The average of 25 results is 18, that of first 12 is 14 and of the last 12 is 17. Thirteenth result is:
   A. 78 B. 85
   C. 28 D. 72
3. Out of three numbers, the first is twice the second and is half of the third. If the average of the three numbers is 56, the three numbers in order are:
   A. 48, 96, 24 B. 48, 24, 96
   C. 96, 24, 48 D. 96, 48, 24
4. The sum of three numbers is 98. If the ratio between first and second be 2 : 3 and that between second and third be 5 : 8, then the second number is:
   A. 30 B. 20
   C. 58 .D. 48
5. The average age of a committee of seven trustees is the same as it was 5 years ago; a young man having been substituted for one of them. The new man compared to the replaced old man, is younger in age by:
   A. 5 years B. 7 years
   C. 12 years D. 35 years
6. The average expenditure of a man for the first five months is ₹ 120 and for the next seven months is ₹ 130. His monthly average income if he saves ₹ 290 in that year, is:
   A. ₹ 160 B. ₹ 170
   C. ₹ 150 D. ₹ 140
7. The average salary of 20 workers in an office is ₹ 1900 per month. If the manager's salary is added, the average becomes ₹ 2000 per month. The manager's salary is:
   A. ₹ 24000 B. ₹ 25200
   C. ₹ 45600 D. None of these
8. The average temperature of first 3 days is 27°C and of the next 3 days is 29°C. If the average of the whole week is 28.5°C, the temperature of the last day is:
   A. 31.5°C B. 10.5°C
   C. 21°C D. 42°C

9. A cricketer scored 180 runs in the first test and 258 runs in the second. How many runs should he score in the third test so that his average score in the three tests would be 230 runs?
   A. 219 B. 242
   C. 334 D. None of these
10. The average of first five prime numbers is:
    A. 5.0 B. 5.2
    C. 5.6 D. 6.0
11. The average weight of 3 men A, B and C is 84 kg. Another man D joins the group and the average now becomes 80 kg. If another man E, whose weight is 3 kg more than that of D, replaces A, then average weight of B, C, D and E becomes 79 kg. The weight of A is:
    A. 70 kg B. 72 kg
    C. 75 kg D. 80 kg
12. The average age of A, B, C, D 5 years ago was 45 years. By including x, the present average of all the five is 49 years. The present age of x is:
    A. 64 years B. 48 years
    C. 45 years D. 40 years
13. The average height of 30 boys, out of a class of 50, is 160 cm. If the average height of the remaining boys is 165 cm, the average height of the whole class (in cm) is:
    A. 161 B. 162
    C. 163 D. 164
14. The average age of an adult class is 40 years. 12 new students with an average age of 32 years join the class, thereby decreasing the average of the class by 4 years. The original strength of the class was:
    A. 10 B. 11
    C. 12 D. 15
15. If a, b, c, d, e are five consecutive odd numbers, their average is:
    A. $5(a + 4)$ B. $\dfrac{abcde}{5}$
    C. $5(a + b + c + d + e)$ D. None of these
16. Of the three numbers, second is twice the first and is also thrice the third. If the average of the three numbers is 44, the largest number is:
    A. 24 B. 36
    C. 72 D. 108

17. The average of 50 numbers is 38. If two numbers namely, 45 and 55 are discarded, the average of remaining number is:

   A. 36.50   B. 37.00

   C. 37.50   D. 37.52

18. The average height of 30 girls out of a class of 40 is 160 cm and that of the remaining girls is 156 cm. The average height of the whole class is:

   A. 158 cm   B. 158.5 cm

   C. 159 cm   D. 159.5 cm

19. The average of n numbers is x. If 36 is subtracted from any two numbers each, then new average is $(x - 8)$. The value of n is:

   A. 6   B. 8

   C. 9   D. 72

20. The average salary of male employees in a firm is ₹ 520 and that of female employees is ₹ 420. The mean salary of all the employees is ₹ 500. The percentage of female employees is:

   A. 40%   B. 30%

   C. 25%   D. 20%

ANSWERS

1	2	3	4	5	6	7	8	9	10
B	A	B	A	D	C	D	A	D	C
11	**12**	**13**	**14**	**15**	**16**	**17**	**18**	**19**	**20**
C	C	B	C	D	C	C	C	C	D

EXPLANATORY ANSWERS

1. Average $= \dfrac{3(1+2+3+4+5)}{5} = \dfrac{(3 \times 15)}{5} = 9$

2. Thirteenth result

$= [(25 \times 18) - (12 \times 14 + 12 \times 17)]$

$= [450 - (168 + 204)]$

$= 450 - 372 = 78.$

3. Let the numbers be $2x$, x and $4x$.

   Average $= \dfrac{2x + x + 4x}{3} = \dfrac{7x}{3}$

According to the question,

$$\dfrac{7x}{3} = 56$$

$\Rightarrow \quad 7x = 3 \times 56$

$\Rightarrow \quad x = \dfrac{3 \times 56}{7} = 24$

Hence, the numbers in order are 48, 24 and 96.

4. Let the numbers be x, y, z, then

$x + y + z = 98$

$\dfrac{x}{y} = \dfrac{2}{3}$ and $\dfrac{y}{z} = \dfrac{5}{8}$

$\therefore \quad x = \dfrac{2y}{3}$ and $z = \dfrac{8y}{5}$

So, $\dfrac{2y}{3} + y + \dfrac{8y}{5} = 98$

$\Rightarrow \quad \dfrac{10y + 15y + 24y}{15} = 98$

$\Rightarrow \quad 49y = 15 \times 98$

$\Rightarrow \quad y = \dfrac{15 \times 98}{49} = 30$

5. During these five years, the total age would have increased by $(7 \times 5) = 35$ years.

But, it remains the same as it was 5 years ago.

$\therefore$ The new man is younger than the replaced old man by 35 years.

6. Total income for 12 months

$= ₹\ (120 \times 5 + 130 \times 7 + 290)$

$= ₹\ 1800$

Average monthly income $= ₹\ \dfrac{1800}{12} = ₹150$

7. Total salary of 20 workers

$= 20 \times 1900 = ₹\ 38000$

Total salary of 20 workers and manager

$= 21 \times 2000 = ₹\ 42000$

Monthly salary of the manager

$= 42000 - 38000 = ₹\ 4000.$

8. Total temperature of first 3 days

$= 27 \times 3 = 81°C$

Total temperature of next 3 days

$= 29 \times 3 = 87°C$

Total temperature of 7 days
$$= 28.5 \times 7 = 199.5°C$$
Temperature of the last day
$$= 199.5 - (81 + 87)$$
$$= 199.5 - 168 = 31.5°C$$

9. Let runs he should score in third test be x :

Then, $\dfrac{180 + 258 + x}{3} = 230$

$\Rightarrow \quad x = 690 - 438 = 252.$

10. Average $= \dfrac{2 + 3 + 5 + 7 + 11}{5} = \dfrac{28}{5} = 5.6.$

11. Weight of D $= (80 \times 4 - 84 \times 3)$ kg $= 68$ kg
Weight of E $= (68 + 3)$ kg $= 71$ kg
$(B + C + D + E)$'s weight $= (79 \times 4)$ kg $= 316$ kg
$\therefore$ $(B + C)$'s weight
$$= [316 - (68 + 71)] \text{ kg} = 177 \text{ kg}$$
Hence, A's weight
$$= [(84 \times 3) - 177]\text{kg} = 75 \text{ kg}$$

12. Total age of A, B, C and D 5 years ago
$= (45 \times 4)$ years $= 180$ years.
Total present age of A, B, C, D and x
$= (49 \times 5)$ years $= 245$ years.
Present age of A, B, C and D
$= (180 + 5 \times 4)$ years $= 200$ years.
$\therefore$ Present age of $x = 45$ years.

13. Total height of 30 boys $= 30 \times 160 = 4800$
Total height of 20 boys $= 20 \times 165 = 3300$
Total height of 50 boys $= 8100$

Average height of 50 boys $= \dfrac{8100}{50} = 162.$

14.
$$40x + 12 \times 32 = (12 + x) \times 36$$
$\Rightarrow \quad 40x + 384 = 432 + 36x$
$\Rightarrow \quad 4x = 432 - 384 = 48$

$\Rightarrow \quad x = \dfrac{48}{4} = 12$

Hence, the original strength of the class was 12.

15. Average $= \dfrac{a + a + 2 + a + 4 + a + 6 + a + 8}{5}$

$= \dfrac{5a + 20}{5} = \dfrac{5(a + 4)}{5} = a + 4$

16. Let the numbers be x, $2x$ and $\dfrac{2x}{3}$.

$$\text{Average} = \dfrac{x + 2x + \dfrac{2x}{3}}{3}$$

$\Rightarrow \qquad \dfrac{11x}{9} = 44$

$\Rightarrow \qquad x = \dfrac{44 \times 9}{11} = 36$

So, the numbers are 36, 72 and 24.
Hence, the largest one is 72.

17. Total of 50 numbers $= 50 \times 38 = 1900$

$$\text{Average of 48 numbers} = \dfrac{1900 - (45 + 55)}{48}$$

$$= \dfrac{1800}{48} = 37.50$$

18. The average of the whole class

$$= \dfrac{(30 \times 160 + 10 \times 156)}{40} = \dfrac{4800 + 1560}{40}$$

$$= \dfrac{6360}{40} = 159 \text{ cm}$$

19.
$$\dfrac{nx - 36 - 36}{n} = x - 8$$
$\Rightarrow \qquad nx - 72 = nx - 8n$
$\Rightarrow \qquad 8n = 72$
$\Rightarrow \qquad n = 9$

20. Let the total employees be 100.
n_1 = number of females = x
n_2 = number of males = $100 - x$

$$\bar{x} = \dfrac{n_1 \bar{x}_1 + n_2 \bar{x}_2}{n_1 + n_2}$$

$\Rightarrow \quad 500 = \dfrac{x \times 420 + (100 - x) \times 520}{100}$

$\Rightarrow \quad 500 = \dfrac{42x + 5200 - 52x}{10}$

$\Rightarrow 5000 = 5200 - 10x$
$\Rightarrow \quad 10x = 200$
$\Rightarrow \quad x = 20$ *i.e.,* 20%.

8. PROFIT AND LOSS

Cost Price (CP)

The price at which an article is purchased is called the cost price of the article.

Selling Price (SP)

The price at which an article is sold is called the selling price of the article.

Profit or Gain

If SP is greater than the CP, the seller is said to have a profit or gain.

Clearly,   Gain = SP – CP

Loss

If SP is less than CP, the seller is said to have a loss.

Clearly,   Loss = CP – SP

Profit or loss per cent is calculated on cost price.

$$\text{Profit \%} = \frac{\text{Profit}}{\text{CP}} \times 100$$

$$\text{Loss \%} = \frac{\text{Loss}}{\text{CP}} \times 100$$

$$\text{SP} = \frac{\text{CP} \times (100 + \text{Profit\%})}{100}, \text{ if there is gain}$$

$$\text{SP} = \frac{\text{CP} \times (100 - \text{Loss\%})}{100}, \text{ if there is loss}$$

$$\text{CP} = \text{SP} \times \left(\frac{100}{100 + \text{Profit\%}}\right), \text{ if there is gain}$$

$$\text{CP} = \text{SP} \times \left(\frac{100}{100 - \text{Loss\%}}\right), \text{ if there is loss}$$

If an article is sold at a gain of 20%,

then,   SP = (120% of CP)

If an article is sold at a loss of 20%,

then,   SP = (80% of CP)

Overheads

The expenses incurred on transportation, rent, personnel salary, maintenance, packaging, advertisements and the like are included under the general heading of overheads. These overhead and the profit when added to the cost price determine the selling price. If the overheads are not separately mentioned in the problem, we assume it to be zero or else these have been included in the cost price itself.

Discount

It is an offer made by the seller to the buyer for reduction in price to be paid. There are several cases where discounts are allowed. For instance, to dispose off old goods, to increase its market share when the customer is ready to pay the whole amount in cash instead of instalment and so on. It is subtracted from the original price and is usually expressed as per cent or a fraction of the marked price. The price obtained after deducting the discount from the original price is the selling price which the customer has to pay.

EXAMPLE: If an article is purchased for ₹ 570 and sold for ₹ 518.70, find the lost per cent.

SOLUTION: CP = ₹ 570

                  SP = ₹ 518.70

∴   Loss = CP – SP

            = 570 – 518.70 = ₹ 51.30

$$\text{Loss \%} = \frac{\text{Loss}}{\text{CP}} \times 100 = \frac{51.30}{570} \times 100$$

$$= \frac{5130}{570} = \frac{513}{57} = 9\%$$

EXAMPLE: A man buys a TV for ₹ 16,000. After two years he sells it for ₹ 12800. Find his loss per cent.

SOLUTION: Loss % = $\dfrac{\text{Loss}}{\text{CP}} \times 100$

$$= \dfrac{16000 - 12800}{16000} \times 100$$

$$= \dfrac{3200}{16000} \times 100 = 20\%$$

EXAMPLE: Mohan sells his watch at a loss of ₹ 500 for ₹ 1000. Find the cost price and loss per cent.

SOLUTION: CP = SP + Loss

$$= 1000 + 500 = ₹ 1500$$

Loss % = $\dfrac{\text{Loss}}{\text{CP}} \times 100 = \dfrac{500}{1500} \times 100$

$$= \dfrac{100}{3} = 33\dfrac{1}{3}\%$$

EXAMPLE: Ravi buys an article for ₹ 5000 and sells it at 20% gain. Find it selling price.

SOLUTION: Profit = 20% of CP $= \dfrac{20}{100} \times 5000$

$\Rightarrow$ Profit = ₹ 1000

SP = CP + Profit

$$= 5000 + 1000$$

$$= ₹ 6000$$

EXAMPLE: A man sells an article at 20% gain for ₹ 3600. Find its cost price.

SOLUTION: Let CP = ₹ 100

then SP = 100 + 20 = ₹ 120

When SP ₹ 120 then CP = ₹ 100

When SP ₹ 3600 then CP $= \dfrac{100}{120} \times 3600$

Hence CP = ₹ 3000

EXAMPLE: The cost price of 6 pens is equal to the selling price of 4 pens. Find the profit per cent.

SOLUTION: SP of 4 pens = CP of 6 pens

SP of 2 pens = CP of $\dfrac{6}{4} \times 2 = 3$ pens

Profit = CP of 3 pens

investment = CP of 6 pens

Profit % = $\dfrac{3}{6} \times 100 = 50\%$

Alternatively:

Let the CP of 1 pen be ₹ x.

$\therefore$ CP of 6 pens = ₹ $6x$

Also, SP of 4 pens = ₹ $6x$

$\therefore$ SP of 6 pens = $\dfrac{6x}{4} \times 6 = ₹ 9x$

Profit = SP – CP = $9x - 6x = 3x$

Profit % = $\dfrac{3x}{6x} \times 100 = 50\%$

EXAMPLE: If CP of 20 tables is equal to the SP of 25 tables. Find the loss percent.

SOLUTION: Let the CP of 1 table be ₹ x.

$\therefore$ CP of 20 tables = ₹ $20x$

Also, SP of 25 tables = ₹ $20x$

$\therefore$ SP of 20 tables = ₹ $\dfrac{20x}{25} \times 20 = ₹ 16x$

Loss = $20x - 16x = 4x$

Loss % = $\dfrac{\text{Loss}}{\text{CP}} \times 100$

$$= \dfrac{4x}{20x} \times 100 = 20\%$$

EXAMPLE: Ram sold a book at a profit of 6%. Had he sold it for ₹ 2 more he would have gained 10%. Find the cost price of the book.

SOLUTION: (10% – 6%) of CP = 4% of CP = ₹ 2

$\Rightarrow \qquad \dfrac{4}{100} \times \text{CP} = 2$

$\Rightarrow \qquad \text{CP} = \dfrac{200}{4} = ₹ 50$

EXAMPLE: An article is sold for ₹ 4600 at a gain of 15%. What would be the profit or loss per cent if it is sold for ₹ 3600?

SOLUTION: CP $= 4600 \times \dfrac{100}{115} = ₹ 4000$

Loss % = $\dfrac{4000 - 3600}{4000} \times 100 = 10\%$

MULTIPLE CHOICE QUESTIONS

1. A loss of 5% was suffered by selling a plot for ₹ 4085. The cost price of the plot was:
   A. ₹ 4350
   B. ₹ 4259.25
   C. ₹ 4200
   D. ₹ 4300

2. On selling an article for ₹ 240, a trader loses 4%. In order to gain 10%, he must sell that article for:
   A. ₹ 264.00
   B. ₹ 273.20
   C. ₹ 275.00
   D. ₹ 280.00

3. A man purchased a watch for ₹ 400 and sold it at a gain of 20% of the selling price. The selling price of the watch is:
   A. ₹ 300
   B. ₹ 320
   C. ₹ 440
   D. ₹ 500

4. If 5% more is gained by selling an article for ₹ 350 than by selling it for ₹ 340, the cost of the article is:
   A. ₹ 50
   B. ₹ 160
   C. ₹ 200
   D. ₹ 225

5. Profit after selling a commodity for ₹ 425 is same as loss after selling it for ₹ 355. The cost of the commodity is:
   A. ₹ 385
   B. ₹ 390
   C. ₹ 395
   D. ₹ 400

6. The cost price of an article, which on being sold at a gain of 12% yields ₹ 6 more than when it is sold at a loss of 12%, is:
   A. ₹ 30
   B. ₹ 25
   C. ₹ 20
   D. ₹ 24

7. The CP of an article which is sold at a loss of 25% for ₹150, is:
   A. ₹ 125
   B. ₹ 175
   C. ₹ 200
   D. ₹ 225

8. When the price of pressure cooker was increased by 15%, its sale fell down by 15%. The effect on the money receipt was:
   A. no effect
   B. 15% decrease
   C. 7.5% increase
   D. 2.25% decrease

9. A man sells 320 mangoes at the cost price of 400 mangoes. His gain per cent is:
   A. 10%
   B. 25%
   C. 15%
   D. 20%

10. By selling 12 oranges for one rupee a man loses 20%. How many for a rupee should he sell to get a gain of 20%?
    A. 5
    B. 8
    C. 10
    D. 15

11. A man sells a car to his friend at 10% loss. If the friend sells it for ₹ 54000 and gains 20%, the original CP of the car was:
    A. ₹ 25000
    B. ₹ 37500
    C. ₹ 50000
    D. ₹ 60000

12. The loss incurred on selling an article for ₹ 270 is as much as the profit made after selling it at 10% profit. The CP of the article is:
    A. ₹ 90
    B. ₹ 110
    C. ₹ 363
    D. ₹ 300

13. An item costing ₹ 200 is being sold at 10% loss. If the price is further reduced by 5%, the selling price will be:
    A. ₹ 179
    B. ₹ 175
    C. ₹ 171
    D. ₹ 170

14. A trader lists his articles 20% above CP and allows a discount of 10% on cash payment. His gain per cent is:
    A. 10%
    B. 6%
    C. 8%
    D. 5%

15. A discount series of 10%, 20% and 40% is equal to a single discount of:
    A. 50%
    B. 56.80%
    C. 70%
    D. 70.28%

ANSWERS

1	2	3	4	5	6	7	8	9	10
D	C	D	C	B	B	C	D	B	B

11	12	13	14	15
C	D	C	C	B

EXPLANATORY ANSWERS

1. Loss = 5%, SP = ₹ 4085

   Let CP = ₹ 100

∴   SP = ₹ 100 – 5 = ₹ 95

When SP ₹ 95 then CP = ₹ 100

When SP ₹ 4085 then CP = $\dfrac{100}{95} \times 4085$

        = 4300

Hence, the cost price of the plot was ₹ 4300.

2. Loss = 4%, SP = ₹ 240

Let CP = ₹ 100

∴ SP = 100 – 4 = 96

When SP ₹ 96 then CP = ₹ 100

When SP ₹ 240 then CP = $\dfrac{100}{96} \times 240$ = ₹ 250

Again 100 + 10 = 110

When CP 100 then SP = ₹ 110

When CP 250 then SP = $\dfrac{110}{100} \times 250$ = ₹ 275

3. Let SP = ₹ x

then, profit = $\dfrac{20}{100} \times x$ = ₹ $\dfrac{x}{5}$

CP = SP – profit = $x - \dfrac{x}{5}$ = ₹ $\dfrac{4x}{5}$

According to the question,

   $\dfrac{4x}{5} = 400$ ⇒ $4x = 2000$

⇒ $x = 500$

Hence, selling price of the watch = ₹ 500.

4. Let CP = ₹ x

Then, if SP = ₹350

Profit = SP – CP = ₹ $(350 - x)$

if SP = ₹ 340 then, profit = ₹ $(340 - x)$

∴ $(350 - x) - (340 - x) = \dfrac{5}{100}x$

⇒ $10 = \dfrac{5}{100}x$ ⇒ $x = 200$

Hence, the cost of the article = ₹ 200.

5. Let CP = ₹ x,

then, $425 - x = x - 355 \Rightarrow 2x = 780$

⇒ $x = 390$

Hence, the cost of commodity is ₹ 390.

6. Let CP of the article = ₹ x

Then, SP when profit is 12%

      = $\left(\dfrac{12x}{100} + x\right)$ = $\dfrac{112x}{100}$

∴ $\dfrac{112x}{100} - \dfrac{88x}{100} = 6$

⇒ $24x = 600$

⇒ $x = \dfrac{600}{24} = 25$

∴ CP of the article is ₹ 25.

7. $100 - 25 = 75$

When SP 75 then CP = ₹ 100

When SP 150 then CP = ₹ $\dfrac{100}{75} \times 150$ = ₹ 200

8. Let the original cost of each cooker be ₹ 1 and let the number sold originally be 100.

Total sale proceed = ₹ (100×1) = ₹ 100

New rate = (115% of ₹ 1) = ₹ 1.15

Number sold now = 85

∴ Sale proceed now = ₹(1.15×85) = ₹ 97.75

So, there is a decrease of 2.25% in the money receipt.

9. Let CP of each mango be ₹ 1.

Then, CP of 400 mangoes = ₹ 400

∴ CP of 320 mangoes = ₹ 320

  SP of 320 mangoes = ₹ 400

  Profit = 400 – 320 = ₹ 80

Profit% = $\dfrac{80}{320} \times 100$ = 25%

10. SP = ₹ 1, Loss = 20%

⇒ CP = $\left(\dfrac{100}{80} \times 1\right)$ ⇒ CP = ₹ $\dfrac{5}{4}$

Now, CP = ₹ $\dfrac{5}{4}$, gain, 20%

⇒ SP = $\dfrac{120}{100} \times \dfrac{5}{4}$ = ₹ $\dfrac{3}{2}$

For ₹ $\frac{3}{2}$, he must sell 12 oranges

For ₹ 1, he must sell $\left(12 \times \frac{2}{3}\right) = 8$ oranges.

11. SP = ₹ 54000 and gain earned = 20%

CP = ₹ $\left(\frac{100}{120} \times 54000\right)$ = ₹ 45000

Now, SP = ₹ 45000 and Loss = 10%

∴ CP = ₹ $\left(\frac{100}{90} \times 45000\right)$ = ₹ 50000

12. Let CP be ₹ x. Then,

$$x - 270 = 10\% \text{ of } x = \frac{x}{10}$$

$\Rightarrow \quad x - \frac{x}{10} = 270$

$\Rightarrow \qquad 9x = 10 \times 270$

$\Rightarrow \qquad x = \frac{10 \times 270}{9}$

$\Rightarrow \qquad x = 300$

∴ CP of the article is ₹ 300.

13. SP = 90% of ₹ 200 = ₹ 180

Further, SP = (95% of ₹180) = ₹ 171

14. Let CP = ₹ 100. Then, MP = ₹ 120.

SP = 90% of ₹ 120 = $\frac{90}{100} \times 120$ = ₹ 108

Profit = SP – CP = 108 – 100 = ₹ 8

Profit % = $\frac{\text{Profit}}{\text{CP}} \times 100 = \frac{8}{100} \times 100 = 8\%$

15. Let original price = ₹ 100

Price after 1st discount = ₹ 90

Price after 2nd discount

$$= ₹ \left(\frac{80}{100} \times 90\right) = ₹ 72$$

Price after 3rd discount

$$= ₹ \left(\frac{60}{100} \times 72\right) = ₹ 43.20$$

∴ Single discount = 100 – 43.20 = 56.8%.

9. SIMPLE AND COMPOUND INTEREST

In any money transaction there is a **lender** who gives money, and a **borrower** who receives money. The amount of loan borrowed, is called the principal (P). The borrower pays a certain amount for the use of this money. This is called **Interest (I)**. Interest is always calculated on the principal borrowed. The borrowing is for a specified **Time (t)** and on specified terms. The specified term is expressed as per cent of the principal and is called rate of interest.

The sum of the principal and the interest is called the **Amount (A)**. In general, the rate of interest may be yearly, half yearly, quarterly or monthly as mutually agreed upon by both parties at the time of transaction. Depending upon the period of rate of interest, time is expressed in multiples of this period.

Interest is of two kinds—**Simple Interest and compound Interest**. If the interest is calculated only, on a certain sum borrowed it is called Simple Interest.

The simple interest (SI) on a principal P at R% per annum for T years is given by:

$$SI = \frac{P \times R \times T}{100}$$

$$\therefore \quad P = \frac{SI \times 100}{R \times T}$$

$$\therefore \quad R = \frac{SI \times 100}{P \times T}$$

$$\therefore \quad T = \frac{SI \times 100}{P \times R}$$

Compound Interest differs from Simple Interest that in CI the interest for the future period is calculated not only on the principal but also on the interest earned until the previous period. Thus, the total interest earned in case of CI is not uniformly distributed over time units whereas in Simple Interest it is uniformly distributed. The interest due at the end of the first unit of time is added to the principal and the amount so obtained becomes the principal for the second unit. Similarly, the amount after the 2nd unit of time becomes the principal for the third unit of time and continues till the last unit of time.

The difference between the final amount (A) obtained at the last unit of time and the original principal is called the **Compound Interest**.

Important Relations

Principal = ₹ P (in rupees)

Rate = R % (in per cent per annum)

Time period = T years (in years)

Amount = ₹ A (in rupees)

I. When interest is compounded annually,

$$A = P\left[1 + \frac{R}{100}\right]^T$$

II. When interest is compounded half-yearly,

$$A = P\left[1 + \frac{R/2}{100}\right]^{2T} = P\left[1 + \frac{R}{200}\right]^{2T}$$

[R is divided by 2 and T is multiplied by 2.]

III. When interest is compounded quarterly,

$$A = P\left[1+\frac{R/4}{100}\right]^{4T} = P\left[1+\frac{R}{400}\right]^{4T}$$

[R is divided by 4 and T is multiplied by 4.]

IV. When interest is $R_1\%$ for first year, $R_2\%$ for 2nd year and $R_3\%$ for third year;

$$A = P\left[1+\frac{R_1}{100}\right]\left[1+\frac{R_2}{100}\right]\left[1+\frac{R_3}{100}\right]$$

V. $CI = A - P$

EXAMPLE: Find the simple interest on ₹ 1000 for 3 years at 10% p.a.

SOLUTION: $SI = \dfrac{P \times R \times T}{100} = \dfrac{1000 \times 10 \times 3}{100} = ₹\,300$

EXAMPLE: Find the amount of ₹ 600 in 4 years at 3% p.a.

SOLUTION: $SI = \dfrac{P \times R \times T}{100} = \dfrac{600 \times 3 \times 4}{100} = ₹\,72$

∴ Amount $= P + SI = 600 + 72 = ₹\,672$

EXAMPLE: In what time will ₹ 7000 give ₹ 3675 as interest at the rate of 7% p.a. simple interest?

SOLUTION: $T = \dfrac{SI \times 100}{P \times R} = \dfrac{3675 \times 100}{7000 \times 7}$

$$= \frac{15}{2} = 7\frac{1}{2} \text{ years.}$$

EXAMPLE: At what rate per annum will a sum of ₹ 5000 amount to ₹ 6000 in 4 years?

SOLUTION: $SI = A - P = 6000 - 5000 = ₹\,1000$

$$R = \frac{SI \times 100}{P \times T} = \frac{1000 \times 100}{5000 \times 4} = 5\%$$

EXAMPLE: In how many years will a sum of money double itself at 5% rate of interest?

SOLUTION: A sum doubles itself when amount of interest becomes equal to the principal

$$SI = P, R = 5\%$$

∴ $$T = \frac{100 \times P}{P \times 5} = 20 \text{ years}$$

EXAMPLE: A certain sum amounts to ₹ 115200 in 2 years and to ₹ 165888 in 4 years. Find the sum and rate per cent.

SOLUTION: Here, amount on ₹ 115200 for 2 years at CI is ₹ 165888

∴ $$115200\left(1+\frac{R}{100}\right)^2 = 165888$$

$$\left(1+\frac{R}{100}\right)^2 = \frac{165888}{115200} = 1.44$$

∴ $$1+\frac{R}{100} = 1.2$$

$$\frac{R}{100} = 1.2 - 1 = 0.2$$

⇒ $$R = 0.2 \times 100 = 20\%$$

Amount after 2 years is ₹ 115200

∴ $$P\left(1+\frac{20}{100}\right)^2 = 115200$$

⇒ $$P = \frac{115200}{\left(1+\dfrac{20}{100}\right)^2} = \frac{115200}{1.44} = 80000$$

∴ Principal = ₹ 80000

EXAMPLE: A sum of money doubles itself at CI in 15 years. In how many years will it become eight times?

SOLUTION: $$P\left(1+\frac{R}{100}\right)^{15} = 2P$$

⇒ $$\left(1+\frac{R}{100}\right)^{15} = 2$$

Let T be the required number of years that makes the principal 8 times of it.

∴ $$P\left(1+\frac{R}{100}\right)^{T} = 8P$$

⇒ $$\left(1+\frac{R}{100}\right)^{T} = 8 = (2)^3$$

⇒ $$\left(1+\frac{R}{100}\right)^{T} = \left[\left(1+\frac{R}{100}\right)^{15}\right]^3$$

⇒ $$\left(1+\frac{R}{100}\right)^{T} = \left(1+\frac{R}{100}\right)^{45}$$

⇒ $$T = 45 \text{ years}$$

Hence, required number of years is 45 years.

EXAMPLE: The difference between simple and compound interest on a sum of money at 5% p.a. for 2 years is ₹ 25. Find the sum.

SOLUTION: Let P = ₹ 100

$$SI = \frac{P \times R \times T}{100} = \frac{100 \times 5 \times 2}{100} = ₹ 10$$

$$A = P\left(1 + \frac{R}{100}\right)^T = 100\left(1 + \frac{5}{100}\right)^2$$

$$= \frac{100 \times 21 \times 21}{400} = ₹ \frac{441}{4}$$

$$CI = A - P = \frac{441}{4} - 100 = ₹ \frac{41}{4}$$

$$CI - SI = \frac{41}{4} - 10 = \frac{41 - 40}{4} = ₹ \frac{1}{4}$$

When difference ₹ $\frac{1}{4}$ then P = ₹ 100

When difference ₹ 25 then P = 100 × 4 × 25
$$= ₹ 10000$$

Hence, sum = ₹ 10000.

MULTIPLE CHOICE QUESTIONS

1. The simple interest on ₹ 500 for 6 years at 5% p.a. is:
   A. ₹ 250
   B. ₹ 150
   C. ₹ 140
   D. ₹ 120

2. A certain sum of money at SI amounts to ₹ 1012 in $2\frac{1}{2}$ years and to ₹ 1067.20 in 4 years. The rate of interest per annum is:
   A. 2.5%
   B. 3%
   C. 4%
   D. 5%

3. ₹ 1200 amounts to ₹ 1632 in 4 years at a certain rate of simple interest. If the rate of interest is increased by 1%, it would amount to how much?
   A. ₹ 1635
   B. ₹ 1644
   C. ₹ 1670
   D. ₹ 1680

4. A man will get ₹ 87 as simple interest on ₹ 725 at 4% per annum in:
   A. 3 years
   B. 3½ years
   C. 4 years
   D. 5 years

5. At simple interest, a sum doubles after 20 years. The rate of interest per annum is:
   A. 5%
   B. 10%
   C. 20%
   D. Data inadequate

6. A lent ₹ 600 to B for 2 years and ₹ 150 to C for 4 years and received altogether from both ₹ 90 as simple interest. The rate of interest is:
   A. 12%
   B. 10%
   C. 5%
   D. 4%

7. Interest on a certain sum of money for $2\frac{1}{3}$ years at $3\frac{3}{4}\%$ per annum is ₹ 210. The sum is:
   A. ₹ 2800
   B. ₹ 1580
   C. ₹ 2400
   D. None of these

8. A certain sum of money at simple interest amounts to ₹ 1260 in 2 years and to ₹ 1350 in 5 years. The rate per cent per annum is:
   A. 2.5%
   B. 3.75%
   C. 5%
   D. 7.5%

9. A sum of money doubles itself in 5 years. It will become 4 times itself in:
   A. 10 years
   B. 12 years
   C. 15 years
   D. 20 years

10. The simple interest on a sum of money will be ₹ 600 after 10 years. If the principal is trebled after 5 years, the total interest at the end of 10 years will be:
    A. ₹ 600
    B. ₹ 900
    C. ₹ 1200
    D. Data inadequate

11. ₹ 800 amounts to ₹ 920 in 3 years at simple interest. If the interest rate is increased by 3%, it would amount to how much?
    A. ₹ 1056
    B. ₹ 1112
    C. ₹ 1182
    D. ₹ 992

12. A sum of money at simple interest amounts to ₹ 2240 in 2 years and ₹ 2600 in 5 years. The sum is:
    A. ₹ 1880
    B. ₹ 2000
    C. ₹ 2120
    D. Data inadequate

13. If ₹ 7500 are borrowed at CI at the rate of 4% per annum, then after 2 years the amount to be paid is:
A. ₹ 8082
B. ₹ 7800
C. ₹ 8100
D. ₹ 8112

14. Simple interest on a sum at 4% per annum is ₹ 80 in 2 years. The compound interest on the

same sum for the same period is:
A. ₹ 81.60
B. ₹ 160
C. ₹ 1081.60
D. None of these

15. ₹ 800 at 5% per annum compound interest will amount to ₹ 882 in:
A. 1 year
B. 2 years
C. 3 years
D. 4 years

ANSWERS

1	2	3	4	5	6	7	8	9	10
B	C	D	A	A	C	C	A	C	C

11	12	13	14	15
D	B	D	A	B

EXPLANATORY ANSWERS

1. $SI = \dfrac{P \times R \times T}{100} = \dfrac{500 \times 5 \times 6}{100} = ₹\,150$

2. SI for $1\dfrac{1}{2}$ years $= 1067.20 - 1012 = ₹\,55.20$

SI for $2\dfrac{1}{2}$ years $= 55.20 \times \dfrac{2}{3} \times \dfrac{5}{2} = ₹\,92$

∴ Principal $= ₹\,(1012 - 92) = ₹\,920$

$R = \dfrac{SI \times 100}{P \times T} = \dfrac{92 \times 100 \times 2}{920 \times 5} = 4\%$

3. $R = \dfrac{SI \times 100}{P \times T} = \dfrac{432 \times 100}{1200 \times 4} = 9\%$

New rate $= (9 + 1)\% = 10\%$

$SI = \dfrac{P \times R \times T}{100} = \dfrac{1200 \times 10 \times 4}{100} = ₹\,480$

Amount $= P + SI = 1200 + 480 = ₹\,1680$

4. $T = \dfrac{SI \times 100}{P \times R} = \dfrac{87 \times 100}{725 \times 4} = 3$ years

5. Let P be ₹ x then A = ₹ $2x$

$SI = A - P = 2x - x = ₹\,x$

$R = \dfrac{SI \times 100}{P \times T} = \dfrac{x \times 100}{x \times 20} = 5\%$

6. $SI = \dfrac{P \times R \times T}{100} = \dfrac{600 \times R \times 2}{100} = 12R$

Again $SI = \dfrac{P \times R \times T}{100} = \dfrac{150 \times R \times 4}{100} = 6R$

Total SI $= 12R + 6R = 18R$

According to the question,

$18R = 90 \Rightarrow R = \dfrac{90}{18} = 5\%$

7. $T = 2\dfrac{1}{3} = \dfrac{7}{3}$ years,

$R = 3\dfrac{3}{4}\% = \dfrac{15}{4}\%$

$P = \dfrac{SI \times 100}{P \times T} = \dfrac{210 \times 100}{\dfrac{15}{4} \times \dfrac{7}{3}}$

$= \dfrac{210 \times 100 \times 4 \times 3}{15 \times 7} = ₹\,2400$

8. SI for 3 years $= ₹\,1350 - ₹\,1260 = ₹\,90$

SI for 1 year $= \dfrac{90}{3} = ₹\,30$

SI for 2 years $= ₹\,30 \times 2 = ₹\,60$

$P = A - SI = 1260 - 60 = ₹\,1200$

$R = \dfrac{SI \times 100}{P \times T} = \dfrac{60 \times 100}{1200 \times 2} = \dfrac{5}{2} = 2.5\%$

9. Let P be ₹ x, A = ₹ $2x$,

SI = $2x - x$ = ₹ x

$R = \dfrac{SI \times 100}{P \times T} = \dfrac{x \times 100}{x \times 5} = 20\%$

Again, P = ₹ x, A = $4x$,

SI = $4x - x = 3x$

$T = \dfrac{SI \times 100}{P \times R} = \dfrac{3x \times 100}{x \times 20} = 15$ years

10. Let P be ₹ x

SI = ₹ 600, T = 10 years.

$R = \dfrac{SI \times 100}{P \times T} = \dfrac{600 \times 100}{x \times 10} = \dfrac{6000}{x}\%$

SI for first 5 years = $\dfrac{x \times 5 \times 6000}{100 \times x}$ = ₹ 300

SI for last 5 years = $\dfrac{3x \times 5 \times 6000}{100 \times x}$ = ₹ 900

Total interest at the end of 10 years

= 900 + 300 = ₹ 1200.

11. P = ₹ 800, SI = 920 − 800 = ₹ 120

T = 3 years

$R = \dfrac{SI \times 100}{P \times T} = \dfrac{120 \times 100}{800 \times 3} = 5\%$

New rate = 8% (increase 3%)

$SI = \dfrac{P \times R \times T}{100} = \dfrac{800 \times 8 \times 3}{100} = ₹ 192$

∴ A = P + SI = 800 + 192 = ₹ 992.

12. SI for 3 years = 2600 − 2240 = ₹ 360

SI for 2 years = $\dfrac{360}{3} \times 2$ = ₹ 240

∴ Sum = 2240 − 240 = ₹ 2000

13. $A = P\left(1 + \dfrac{R}{100}\right)^{T} = 7500\left(1 + \dfrac{4}{100}\right)^{2}$

$= 7500 \times \dfrac{26}{25} \times \dfrac{26}{25} = ₹ 8112$

14. $P = \dfrac{SI \times 100}{T \times R} = \dfrac{80 \times 100}{4 \times 2} = ₹ 1000$

$A = P\left(1 + \dfrac{R}{100}\right)^{T} = 1000\left(1 + \dfrac{4}{100}\right)^{2}$

$= 1000 \times \dfrac{26}{25} \times \dfrac{26}{25} = 1081.60$

CI = A − P = 1081.60 − 1000 = ₹ 81.60

15. Let time = x years

$A = P\left(1 + \dfrac{R}{100}\right)^{T}$

$882 = 800\left(1 + \dfrac{5}{100}\right)^{x}$

$\Rightarrow \dfrac{882}{800} = \left(\dfrac{21}{20}\right)^{x}$

$\Rightarrow \left(\dfrac{21}{20}\right)^{2} = \left(\dfrac{21}{20}\right)^{x} \Rightarrow x = 2$

∴ Time = 2 years

10. TIME AND WORK

Performing or doing work of any amount involves efforts of person (S) over a period of time. Therefore, the number of persons (P), the quantity of work (W) and the period of time (T) are important variables in problems related to "Time and Work". Moreover time (T) taken to do a work depends not only on how many persons are employed to do it but also on how efficient they are. Efficiency here means rate of doing same work. This aspect comes into picture when the problem involves comparison of work done by different categories of persons. For instance, efficiencies of man, woman, boy, girl in general are different. Even efficiency of one man may not be same as that of other; but unless otherwise specifically stated in the problem, all men or women working in a group are assumed to do work with equal efficiency.

The problems on Time and Work can be solved by following two methods:

(i) Ratio and proportion method

(ii) Unitary method

(i) **Ratio and Proportion Method:** Since problems concerning to Time and Work have proportional relation, these can be solved by this method. We have tried to solve questions based on Time and Work in the chapter mentioned.

(ii) **Unitary Method:** This is a very simple and useful method. The term 'Unitary' is self-evident. In this method, we first proceed to reduce the problem to either work done by one person or work done in 1 day and so on as per the requirement of the problem. Let us try to understand it.

(a) If a man can do a piece of work in 10 days he will do $\frac{1}{10}$ of the work in 1 day. Conversely, if a man can do $\frac{1}{10}$ of the work in 1 day, he will do the work in 10 days.

(b) If the number of men engaged to do a piece of work be changed in the ratio 5 : 4, the time required for the work will be changed in the ratio 4 : 5.

(c) If A is x times as good a workman as B, then A will take $\frac{1}{x}$ of the time that B takes to do a certain work.

All the above points can be summarised into one and can be written in the following form:

If M_1 persons can do W_1 works in D_1 days and M_2 persons can do W_2 works in D_2 days then we have a very general formula in the relationship of

$$M_1 D_1 W_2 = M_2 D_2 W_1$$

The above relationship can be taken as a very basic and all-in-one formula we also derive:

(i) More men less days and conversely more days less men.

(ii) More men more work and conversely more work more men.

(iii) More days more work and conversely more work more days.

$$M_1 D_1 T_1 W_2 = M_2 D_2 T_2 W_1$$

EXAMPLE: 5 men can prepare 10 toys in 6 days working 6 hrs a day. How many days can 12 men prepare 16 toys working 8 hrs a day?

SOLUTION: $M_1 D_1 T_1 W_2 = M_2 D_2 T_2 W_1$

$$5 \times 6 \times 6 \times 16 = 12 \times D_2 \times 8 \times 10$$

$$D_2 = \frac{5 \times 6 \times 6 \times 16}{12 \times 8 \times 10} = 3 \text{ days.}$$

41

EXAMPLE: A can reap a field in 8 days, which B alone can reap in 12 days. In how many days, both together, can reap this field?

SOLUTION: A's 1 day's work $= \dfrac{1}{8}$

B's 1 day's work $= \dfrac{1}{12}$

$(A + B)$'s 1 day's work $= \left(\dfrac{1}{8} + \dfrac{1}{12}\right)$

$$= \dfrac{3 + 2}{24} = \dfrac{5}{24}$$

∴ Both together can reap the field in $\dfrac{24}{5}$ days

$$= 4\dfrac{4}{5} \text{ days.}$$

EXAMPLE: A and B together can do a piece of work in 12 days, B alone can finish it in 30 days. In how many days can A alone finish the work?

SOLUTION: $(A + B)$'s 1 day's work $= \dfrac{1}{12}$

B's 1 day's work $= \dfrac{1}{30}$

∴   A's 1 day's work $= \dfrac{1}{12} - \dfrac{1}{30}$

$$= \dfrac{5 - 2}{60} = \dfrac{3}{60} = \dfrac{1}{20}$$

Hence, A alone can finish the work in 20 days.

EXAMPLE: A and B can do a piece of work in 12 days, C and A in 20 days and B and C in 15 days. In how many days will they finish it together and separately?

SOLUTION: $(A + B)$'s 1 day's work $= \dfrac{1}{12}$

$(B + C)$'s 1 day's work $= \dfrac{1}{15}$

$(C + A)$'s 1 day's work $= \dfrac{1}{20}$

Adding, $2(A + B + C)$'s 1 day's work

$$= \left(\dfrac{1}{12} + \dfrac{1}{15} + \dfrac{1}{20}\right) = \dfrac{5 + 4 + 3}{60}$$

$$= \dfrac{12}{60} = \dfrac{1}{5}$$

or $(A + B + C)$'s 1 day's work $= \dfrac{1}{10}$

∴ A, B, C together can finish the work in 10 days.

Now, C's 1 day's work $= \dfrac{1}{10} - \dfrac{1}{12} = \dfrac{1}{60}$

∴ C alone can finish the work in 60 days.

Similarly B's 1 day's work $= \dfrac{1}{10} - \dfrac{1}{20} = \dfrac{1}{20}$

∴ B alone can finish the work in 20 days.

A's 1 day's work $= \dfrac{1}{10} - \dfrac{1}{15} = \dfrac{1}{30}$

∴ A alone can finish the work in 30 days.

EXAMPLE: A can do a piece of work in 25 days and B can finish it in 20 days. They work together for 5 days and then A goes away. In how many days will B finish the work?

SOLUTION: $(A + B)$'s 5 days work $= 5\left(\dfrac{1}{25} + \dfrac{1}{20}\right) = \dfrac{9}{20}$

Remaining work $= 1 - \dfrac{9}{20} = \dfrac{11}{20}$

Now, $\dfrac{1}{20}$ work is finished by B in 1 day

∴ $\dfrac{11}{20}$ work will be finished by B in $\left(\dfrac{20 \times 11}{20}\right)$

$= 11$ days.

EXAMPLE: A is thrice as good a workman as B and is therefore able to finish a piece of work in 60 days less than B. Find the time in which they can do it, working together.

SOLUTION: Ratio of work done by A and B in the same time $= 3 : 1$

Ratio of time taken by A and B $= 1 : 3$

Suppose B takes x days to finish a work

then, A takes $(x - 60)$ days

∴ $\dfrac{x - 60}{x} = \dfrac{1}{3}$ or $3(x - 60) = x \Rightarrow x = 90$

∴ B can finish the work in 90 days.

A can finish the work in $(90 - 60) = 30$ days

Both finish the work $= \left[\dfrac{1}{30} + \dfrac{1}{90} = \dfrac{2}{45}\right]$

$$= \dfrac{45}{2} = 22\dfrac{1}{2} \text{ days.}$$

EXAMPLE: A certain number of men complete a piece of work in 60 days. If there were 8 men more, the work could be finished in 10 days less. How many men were originally there?

SOLUTION: Let the original number of men be x.

Now, x men can finish the work in 60 days

and $(x + 8)$ men can finish it in $(60 - 10)$ i.e., 50 days.

$\therefore \qquad x + 8 : x :: 60 : 50$

$\Rightarrow \qquad \dfrac{x+8}{x} = \dfrac{60}{50} = \dfrac{6}{5}$

$\Rightarrow \qquad 6x = 5x + 40 \Rightarrow x = 40$

Hence, the original number of men = 40.

EXAMPLE: If 4 men or 6 boys can finish a piece of work in 20 days, in how many days can 6 men and 11 boys finish it?

SOLUTION: $\qquad 4$ men = 6 boys

$\therefore \qquad 6 \text{ men} = \dfrac{6}{4} \times 6 = \dfrac{36}{4} = 9 \text{ boys}$

$\qquad 6 \text{ men} + 11 \text{ boys} = 9 + 11 = 20 \text{ boys}$

Now, 6 boys can finish a work in 20 days.

$\qquad$ 1 boy can finish the same work in 6×20 days.

$\qquad 20 \text{ boys can finish the same work in } \dfrac{6 \times 20}{20}$

$\qquad\qquad\qquad\qquad\qquad\qquad = 6 \text{ days.}$

EXAMPLE: If 12 men can build a wall 360 m long in 54 days, how many days will it take to build a similar wall 160 m long, if 16 men working on it?

SOLUTION: 12 men can build 360 m long wall in 54 days.

1 man can build 360 m long wall in 54×12 days.

1 man can build 1 m long wall in $\dfrac{54 \times 12}{360}$ days

16 men can build 1 m long wall in $\dfrac{54 \times 12}{360 \times 16}$ days

16 men can build 160 m long wall in $\dfrac{54 \times 12 \times 160}{360 \times 16}$ days

$\qquad\qquad\qquad\qquad\qquad = 18 \text{ days.}$

EXAMPLE: If 3 persons weave 168 carpets in 7 days, how many carpets will 8 persons weave in 5 days?

SOLUTION: 3 persons can weave in 7 days 168 carpets

1 person can weave in 7 days = $\dfrac{168}{3}$ carpets

1 person can weave in 1 day = $\dfrac{168}{3 \times 7}$ carpets

8 persons can weave in 1 day = $\dfrac{168 \times 8}{3 \times 7}$ carpets

8 persons can weave in 5 days = $\dfrac{168 \times 8 \times 5}{3 \times 7}$ carpets

$\qquad\qquad\qquad\qquad\qquad = 320 \text{ carpets}$

EXAMPLE: Mukesh can do a job in 12 days while Manoj can do the same job in 15 days. They undertake to complete the job for ₹ 5400. What will be the share of each in the income?

SOLUTION: Mukesh's 1 day's work = $\dfrac{1}{12}$

Manoj's 1 day's work = $\dfrac{1}{15}$

Ratio of their 1 day's work = $\dfrac{1}{12} : \dfrac{1}{15} = 5 : 4$

$\therefore \qquad$ Mukesh's share = ₹$\dfrac{5}{9} \times 5400$ = ₹ 3000

Manoj's share = ₹$\dfrac{4}{9} \times 5400$ = ₹ 2400

MULTIPLE CHOICE QUESTIONS

1. A and B can together do a piece of work in 15 days. B alone can do it in 20 days. In how many days can A alone do it?
   A. 30 days
   B. 40 days
   C. 45 days
   D. 60 days

2. A can do a piece of work in 30 days while B can do it in 40 days. A and B working together can do it in:
   A. 70 days
   B. $42\dfrac{3}{4}$ days
   C. $27\dfrac{1}{7}$ days
   D. $17\dfrac{1}{7}$ days

3. A can do $\frac{1}{3}$ of the work in 5 days and B can do $\frac{2}{5}$ of the work in 10 days. In how many days both A and B together can do the work?

A. $7\frac{3}{4}$ days   B. $8\frac{4}{5}$ days

C. $9\frac{3}{8}$ days   D. 10 days

4. A, B and C can do a piece of work in 6, 12 and 24 days respectively. They altogether will complete the work in:

A. $3\frac{3}{7}$ days   B. $\frac{7}{24}$ days

C. $4\frac{4}{5}$ days   D. $\frac{5}{24}$ days

5. A, B and C contract a work for ₹ 550. Together A and B are to do $\frac{7}{11}$ of the work. The share of C should be:

A. ₹ $183\frac{1}{3}$ B. ₹ 200

C. ₹ 300   D. ₹ 400

6. A and B finish a job in 12 days while A, B and C can finish it in 8 days. C alone will finish the job in:

A. 20 days   B. 14 days
C. 24 days   D. 16 days

7. 12 men can complete a work in 8 days. Three days after they started the work, 3 more men joined them. In how many days will all of them together complete the remaining work?
A. 2   B. 4
C. 5   D. 6

8. Mahesh and Umesh can complete a work in 10 and 15 days respectively. Umesh starts the work and after 5 days Mahesh joins him. In all, the work would be completed in:
A. 9 days   B. 7 days
C. 11 days   D. None of these

9. Sunil completes a work in 4 days whereas Dinesh completes the work in 6 days. Ramesh works

$1\frac{1}{2}$ times as fast as Sunil. How many days it will take for the three together to complete the work?

A. $\frac{7}{12}$ B. $1\frac{5}{12}$

C. $1\frac{5}{7}$ D. None of these

10. A can complete a work in 6 days and B in 5 days. They work together, finish the job and receive ₹ 220 as wages. B's share should be:
A. ₹ 120   B. ₹ 110
C. ₹ 100   D. ₹ 90

11. 12 men and 8 children can finish a piece of work in 9 days. If each child takes twice the time taken by a man to finish the work, in how many days will 12 men finish the same work?
A. 8 days   B. 15 days
C. 9 days   D. 12 days

12. A, B and C together earn ₹ 150 per day while A and C together earn ₹ 94 and B and C together earn ₹ 76. The daily earning of C is:
A. ₹ 75   B. ₹ 56
C. ₹ 34   D. ₹ 20

13. If 5 men or 9 women can finish a piece of work in 19 days, 3 men and 6 women will do the same work in:
A. 10 days   B. 12 days
C. 13 days   D. 15 days

14. A can do a piece of work in 12 days. B is 60% more efficient than A. The number of days, it takes B to do the same piece of work, is:

A. $7\frac{1}{2}$ days   B. $6\frac{1}{4}$ days

C. 8 days   D. 6 days

15. A and B can do a piece of work in 45 and 40 days respectively. They began the work together, but A leaves after some days and B finished the remaining work in 23 days. After how many days did A leave?
A. 6 days   B. 8 days
C. 9 days   D. 12 days

ANSWERS

1	2	3	4	5	6	7	8	9	10
D	D	C	A	B	C	B	A	D	A
11	**12**	**13**	**14**	**15**					
D	D	D	A	C					

EXPLANATORY ANSWERS

1. $(A + B)$'s 1 day's work $= \dfrac{1}{15}$

B's 1 day's work $= \dfrac{1}{20}$

A's 1 day's work $= \dfrac{1}{15} - \dfrac{1}{20} = \dfrac{4-3}{60} = \dfrac{1}{60}$

$\therefore$ A can do this work alone in 60 days.

2. A's 1 day's work $= \dfrac{1}{30}$

B's 1 day's work $= \dfrac{1}{40}$

$(A + B)$'s 1 day's work

$$= \dfrac{1}{30} + \dfrac{1}{40} = \dfrac{4+3}{120} = \dfrac{7}{120}$$

$\therefore$ Both together will finish the work in $\dfrac{120}{7}$

$$= 17\dfrac{1}{7} \text{ days.}$$

3. $\dfrac{1}{3}$ of the work is done by A in 5 days.

$\therefore$ Whole work will be done by A in 3×5

$$= 15 \text{ days}$$

$\dfrac{2}{5}$ of the work is done by B in 10 days.

Whole work will be done by B in $\left(10 \times \dfrac{5}{2}\right)$

$$= 25 \text{ days}$$

$(A + B)$'s 1 day's work $= \dfrac{1}{15} + \dfrac{1}{25} = \dfrac{5+3}{75} = \dfrac{8}{75}$

$\therefore$ Both together can finish it in $\dfrac{75}{8} = 9\dfrac{3}{8}$ days.

4. A's 1 day's work $= \dfrac{1}{6}$

B's 1 day's work $= \dfrac{1}{12}$

C's 1 day's work $= \dfrac{1}{24}$

$(A + B + C)$'s 1 day's work $= \dfrac{1}{6} + \dfrac{1}{12} + \dfrac{1}{24}$

$$= \dfrac{4+2+1}{24} = \dfrac{7}{24}$$

$\therefore$ They all together will complete the work in

$\dfrac{24}{7}$ days $= 3\dfrac{3}{7}$ days

5. Work to be done by C $= \left(1 - \dfrac{7}{11}\right) = \dfrac{4}{11}$

$\therefore (A + B) : C = \dfrac{7}{11} : \dfrac{4}{11} = 7 : 4$

$\therefore$ C's share $= ₹\dfrac{4}{11} \times 550 = ₹\,200$

6. $(A + B)$'s 1 day's work $= \dfrac{1}{12}$

$(A + B + C)$'s 1 day's work $= \dfrac{1}{8}$

C's 1 day's work $= \dfrac{1}{8} - \dfrac{1}{12} = \dfrac{3-2}{24} = \dfrac{1}{24}$

Hence, C will complete the work in 24 days.

7. 1 man's 1 day's work $= \dfrac{1}{96}$

12 men's 3 day's work $= \dfrac{12}{96} \times 3 = \dfrac{3}{8}$

Remaining work = $\left(1 - \dfrac{3}{8}\right) = \dfrac{5}{8}$

15 men's 1 day's work = $\dfrac{15}{96}$

Now, $\dfrac{15}{96}$ work is done by them in 1 day

$\therefore$ $\dfrac{5}{8}$ work will be done by them in $\dfrac{96}{15} \times \dfrac{5}{8}$

$= 4$ days

8. Umesh's 5 day's work = $\dfrac{5}{15} = \dfrac{1}{3}$

Remaining work = $\left(1 - \dfrac{1}{3}\right) = \dfrac{2}{3}$

Now, $\left(\dfrac{1}{10} + \dfrac{1}{15}\right)$ work is done by A and B in 1 day.

$\therefore$ $\dfrac{2}{3}$ work will be done by A and B in $6 \times \dfrac{2}{3}$

$= 4$ days.

So, the work would be completed in $(5 + 4)$

$= 9$ days.

9. Time taken by Ramesh alone $= \dfrac{2}{3} \times 4 = \dfrac{8}{3}$ days

$\therefore$ Their 1 day's work $= \left(\dfrac{1}{4} + \dfrac{1}{6} + \dfrac{3}{8}\right)$

$= \dfrac{6 + 4 + 9}{24} = \dfrac{19}{24}$

So, together they can finish the work in $\dfrac{24}{19}$ days

$= 1\dfrac{5}{19}$ days.

10. Ratio of time taken by A and B = 6 : 5

Ratio of work done in same time = 5 : 6

So, the money is to be divided among A and B in the ratio 5 : 6.

$\therefore$ B's share $= ₹\dfrac{6}{11} \times 220 = ₹ 120$

11. 2 children = 1 man

$\therefore$ 8 children + 12 men = 4 + 12 = 16 men

Now, less men, more days

$12 : 16 : : 9 : x \Rightarrow \dfrac{12}{16} = \dfrac{9}{x} \Rightarrow x = 12$ days

12. B's daily earning $= ₹ (150 - 94) = ₹ 56$

A's daily earning $= ₹ (150 - 76) = ₹ 74$

C's daily earning $= ₹ [150 - (56 + 74)] = ₹ 20$

13. 5 men = 9 women $\Rightarrow$ 1 man $= \dfrac{9}{5}$ women

$\therefore$ 3 men + 6 women $= \left(3 \times \dfrac{9}{5} + 6\right) = \dfrac{57}{5}$ women

Now, 9 women can do the work in 19 days

$\therefore$ $\dfrac{57}{5}$ women can do it in $\dfrac{9 \times 19 \times 5}{57} = 15$ days

14. A's 1 day's work $= \dfrac{1}{12}$

B's 1 day's work $= \dfrac{1}{12} + 60\%$ of $\dfrac{1}{12} = \dfrac{2}{15}$

Hence, B can do the whole work in $\dfrac{15}{2}$

$= 7\dfrac{1}{2}$ days.

15. B's 23 day's work $= \dfrac{23}{40}$

Remaining work $= \left(1 - \dfrac{23}{40}\right) = \dfrac{17}{40}$

Now, (A + B)'s 1 day's work $= \left(\dfrac{1}{45} + \dfrac{1}{40}\right) = \dfrac{17}{360}$

$\dfrac{17}{360}$ work is done by A and B in 1 day

$\dfrac{17}{40}$ work is done by A and B in $\dfrac{360}{17} \times \dfrac{17}{40}$

$= 9$ days.

Hence, A left after 9 days.

11. AREA AND PERIMETER

The area of any figure is the amount of surface enclosed within its boundary lines. It is measured by the number of square metres or square centimetres or square inches (or some other units of square measure) it contains.

Perimeter

Perimeter of a geometrical figure is the total length of the sides enclosing the figure.

Triangle

A triangle is a plane figure bounded by three sides. It includes three angles. It is denoted by the symbol Δ. The sum of angles of a triangle is $180°$.

   (*i*) **Equilateral Triangle:** A triangle in which all sides are equal is called an equilateral triangle.
   (*ii*) **Isosceles Triangle:** A triangle in which two sides are equal is called an isosceles triangle.
   (*iii*) **Scalene Triangle:** A triangle in which all sides are different or unequal is called scalene triangle.
   (*iv*) **Right Angled Triangle:** A triangle having one of the angles equal to $90°$ is called a right angled triangle. The side opposite to the right angle of a triangle is called its hypotenuse.

Quadrilateral

A plane figure bounded by four straight lines is called a quadrilateral.

Various Types of Quadrilaterals:

   (*i*) **Rectangle:** A quadrilateral whose opposite sides are equal and all angles are at right angles. The diagonals of a rectangle are equal.
   (*ii*) **Square:** A rectangle having all sides are equal is called a square.

   (*iii*) **Parallelogram:** A quadrilateral whose opposite sides are equal and parallel is called parallelogram.
   (*iv*) **Rhombus:** A parallelogram having all the sides equal is called a rhombus. Diagonals of a rhombus are not equal and they bisect each other at right angles.
   (*v*) **Trapezium:** A quadrilateral having one pair of opposite sides parallel, is called a trapezium.

Circle

The path traced by a point which moves in such a way that its distance from a fixed point is always same, is called a circle. The fixed point is called its centre and fixed distance is called its radius. The length of the whole path of a circle is called its circumference.

   (*i*) **Arc:** Any part of the circumference of a circle is called an arc.
   (*ii*) **Chord:** The straight line joining the ends of an arc of a circle is called a chord.
   (*iii*) **Diameter:** The chord passing through the centre of a circle is called its diameter.
   The diameter of a circle divides the circle into two equal parts, each one of which is called a semi-circle.
   (*iv*) **Segment:** The area enclosed by an arc and a chord is called a segment.
   (*v*) **Sector:** The area bounded by an arc and two radii is called a sector.

Formulae for Area of Various Figures:

   (*i*) **Rectangle:**
   Area of rectangle $= l \times b$
   Perimeter of rectangle $= 2 (l + b)$.

(*ii*) **Square:**

Area of square = (side)²

Perimeter of square = 4 × side

Area of room = $l \times b$

Area of 4 walls of a room = $2(l + b) \times h$

(*iii*) **Parallelogram:**

Area of 11^{gm} = $b \times h$

Area of rhombus = $\dfrac{1}{2} \times d_1 \times d_2$.

(*iv*) **Trapezium:**

Area of trapezium = $\dfrac{1}{2}$ (sum of parallel sides)

× (distance between them)

(*v*) **Triangle:**

(*a*) Area of right triangle = $\dfrac{1}{2} \times b \times h$

(*b*) Area of equilateral triangle = $\dfrac{\sqrt{3}}{4} \times$ (side)²

(*c*) Area of scalene triangle

= $\sqrt{s(s-a)(s-b)(s-c)}$

where, $s = \dfrac{a+b+c}{2}$

(*vi*) **Circle:**

(*a*) Area of circle = πr^2

(*b*) Circumference of a circle = $2\pi r$

(*c*) Length of arc = $\dfrac{\theta}{360} \times 2\pi r$

(*d*) Area of sector = $\dfrac{\theta}{360} \times \pi r^2$

Polygon

A polygon is plane figure bounded by multiple number of sides. Normally, it is used for figures enclosed by more than four sides: *e.g.,* pentagon, hexagon, octagon etc.

Regular Polygon

It is a polygon whose all sides are equal.

For a regular polygon of *n* equal sides, its vertex angle θ is given by

$$\theta = \left(\frac{n-2}{n}\right) \times 180°$$

EXAMPLE: Find the area and perimeter of a rectangle whose length is 25 m and breadth is 15 m.

SOLUTION: Area of rectangle = $l \times b$

= 25 × 15 = 375 m²

Perimeter of rectangle = $2(l + b)$

= 2(25 + 15) = 80 m

EXAMPLE: Find the area of a rectangle whose one side is 6 m and the diagonal is 10 m.

SOLUTION: Another side of rectangle = $\sqrt{(10)^2 - (6)^2}$

= $\sqrt{100 - 36}$ = $\sqrt{64}$ = 8 m

Area of rectangle = $l \times b$ = 8 × 6 = 48 m²

EXAMPLE: Find area and perimeter of a square whose each side is 12 cm.

SOLUTION: Area of square = (side)² = (12)² = 144 cm²

Perimeter of square = 4 × side = 4 × 12 = 48 cm

EXAMPLE: Find the area of a parallelogram whose base is 35 m and altitude 18 m.

SOLUTION: Area of parallelogram = $b \times h$

= 35 × 18 = 630 m²

EXAMPLE: Find the area of a rhombus one side of which measures 20 cm and one diagonal 24 cm.

SOLUTION: Since the diagonals of a rhombus bisect at right angles, so one side and half of each of the diagonals form a right angled triangle. In this right angled triangle,

One side = 20 cm, another side = $\dfrac{24}{2}$ = 12 cm

Third side = $\sqrt{(20)^2 - (12)^2}$ = $\sqrt{400 - 144}$

= $\sqrt{256}$ = 16 cm

Hence other diagonal = 16 × 2 = 32 cm

Area of rhombus = $\dfrac{1}{2} \times d_1 \times d_2$

= $\dfrac{1}{2} \times 24 \times 32$ = 12 × 32

= 384 cm²

EXAMPLE: Find the area of an equilateral triangle each of whose sides measures 12 cm.

SOLUTION: Area of equilateral triangle

= $\dfrac{\sqrt{3}}{4}$ (side)² = $\dfrac{\sqrt{3}}{4} \times (12)^2$

$$= \frac{\sqrt{3}}{4} \times 144 = 36\sqrt{3} \text{ cm}^2$$

$$= 36 \times 1.73 = 62.28 \text{ cm}^2$$

EXAMPLE: Find the area of a triangle whose sides are 40 cm, 41 cm and 9 cm respectively.

SOLUTION: $\quad s = \dfrac{a+b+c}{2} = \dfrac{9+40+41}{2}$

$$= \frac{90}{2} = 45 \text{ cm}$$

Area of triangle $= \sqrt{s(s-a)(s-b)(s-c)}$

$$= \sqrt{45(45-9)(45-40)(45-41)}$$

$$= \sqrt{45 \times 36 \times 5 \times 4}$$

$$= \sqrt{225 \times 144}$$

$$= 15 \times 12 = 180 \text{ cm}^2$$

EXAMPLE: Find the circumference and the area of a circle of radius 3.5 cm.

SOLUTION: Circumference $= 2\pi r$

$$= 2 \times \frac{22}{7} \times 3.5 = 22 \text{ cm}$$

Area of circle $= \pi r^2 = \dfrac{22}{7} \times 3.5 \times 3.5$

$$= 38.5 \text{ cm}^2$$

EXAMPLE: In a circle of radius 35 cm, an arc subtends an angle of 72° at the centre. Find the length of the arc and the area of the sector.

SOLUTION: Length of arc $= \dfrac{\theta}{360} \times 2\pi r$

$$= \frac{72}{360} \times 2 \times \frac{22}{7} \times 35$$

$$= 44 \text{ cm}$$

Area of the sector $= \dfrac{\theta}{360} \times \pi r^2$

$$= \frac{72}{360} \times \frac{22}{7} \times 35 \times 35$$

$$= 770 \text{ cm}^2$$

EXAMPLE: Find the area of a trapezium whose parallel sides are 77 cm, 60 cm and the other sides are 25 cm and 26 cm.

SOLUTION:

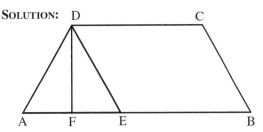

Let ABCD be the given trapezium in which AB = 77 cm, CD = 60 cm, BC = 25 cm, AD = 26 cm.

Draw DE ∥ BC and DF ⊥ AB

Now, $\qquad$ DE = BC = 25 cm

$$AE = AB - EB = AB - CD$$

$$= 77 - 60 = 17 \text{ cm}$$

In ΔDAE, $\quad s = \dfrac{17+25+26}{2} = \dfrac{68}{2} = 34 \text{ cm}$

Area of ΔDAE $= \sqrt{34(34-17)(34-25)(34-26)}$

$$= \sqrt{34 \times 17 \times 9 \times 8} = 204 \text{ cm}^2$$

Again area of ΔDAE $= \dfrac{1}{2} \times AE \times DF$

$$204 = \frac{1}{2} \times 17 \times DF$$

$\Rightarrow \qquad\qquad DF = \dfrac{2 \times 204}{17} = 24 \text{ cm}$

∴ Area of trapezium ABCD $= \dfrac{1}{2}(AB + CD) \times DF$

$$= \frac{1}{2}(77 + 60) \times 24$$

$$= \frac{1}{2} \times 137 \times 24$$

$$= 1644 \text{ cm}^2$$

EXAMPLE: A copper wire when bent in the form of a square, encloses an area of 484 cm². If the same wire is bent in the form of circle, find the area enclosed by it.

SOLUTION: Area of the square = 484 cm²

$$\text{Side} = \sqrt{484} = 22 \text{ cm}$$

Length of wire = Perimeter of square

$$= 4 \times \text{side} = 4 \times 22$$

$$= 88 \text{ cm}$$

Let r be the radius of the circle.

∴ Circumference of circle = Perimeter of square

∴ $2\pi r = 88 \Rightarrow r = \dfrac{88}{2\pi}$

$$= \dfrac{88 \times 7}{2 \times 22} = 14 \text{ cm}$$

Area of circle $= \pi r^2 = \dfrac{22}{7} \times 14 \times 14$

$$= 616 \text{ cm}^2$$

EXAMPLE: A bicycle wheel makes 5000 revolutions in moving 11 km. Find the diameter of the wheel.

SOLUTION: Distance covered by the wheel in 1 revolution

$$= \frac{\text{Distance covered}}{\text{Number of revolutions}} = \frac{11}{5000} \text{ km}$$

$$= \frac{11 \times 1000 \times 100}{5000} \text{ cm} = 220 \text{ cm}$$

∴ Circumference of the wheel = 220 cm

$$2\pi r = 220 \Rightarrow 2 \times \frac{22}{7} \times r = 220$$

$\Rightarrow$ $r = \dfrac{220 \times 7}{44} = 35 \text{ cm}$

Hence, diameter of the wheel = 35 × 2 = 70 cm

EXAMPLE: The perimeter of a square is 44 cm and circumference of a circle is 44 cm. Which area is greater and by how much?

SOLUTION: Side of square $= \dfrac{44}{4} = 11 \text{ cm}$

Area of square $= (11)^2 = 121 \text{ cm}^2$

Circumference of a circle $= 2\pi r$

$\Rightarrow$ $44 = 2 \times \dfrac{22}{7} \times r$

$\Rightarrow$ $r = \dfrac{44 \times 7}{44} = 7 \text{ cm}$

Area of circle $= \pi r^2$

$$= \frac{22}{7} \times 7 \times 7 = 154 \text{ cm}^2$$

Clearly, area of circle > area of square

Difference = 154 – 121 = 33 cm².

EXAMPLE: A sheet of paper is in the form of a rectangle ABCD in which AB = 40 cm and AD = 28 cm. A semi-circular portion with BC as diameter is cut off. Find the area of the remaining paper.

SOLUTION:

Area of ABCD = 40 × 28 = 1120 cm²

Area of semicircle $= \dfrac{1}{2}\pi r^2$

$$= \frac{1}{2} \times \frac{22}{7} \times 14 \times 14$$

$$= 22 \times 14 = 308 \text{ cm}^2$$

Area of the remaining paper = 1120 – 308 = 812 cm²

MULTIPLE CHOICE QUESTIONS

1. The length of a plot is four times its breadth. A playground measuring 1200 square metres occupies a third of the total area of the plot. What is the length of the plot, in metres?
   A. 20
   B. 30
   C. 60
   D. None of these

2. The width of a rectangular hall is $\dfrac{3}{4}$ of its length. If the area of the hall is 300 m², then the difference between its length and width is:
   A. 3 m
   B. 4 m
   C. 5 m
   D. 15 m

3. The length and breadth of a rectangular piece of land are in ratio of 5 : 3. The owner spent ₹ 3000 for surrounding it from all the sides at ₹ 7.50 per metre. The difference between its length and breadth is:
   A. 50 m
   B. 100 m
   C. 150 m
   D. 200 m

4. A room 8 m × 6 m is to be carpeted by a carpet 2 m wide. The length of carpet required is:

A. 12 m   B. 36 m
C. 24 m   D. 48 m

5. The length of a rectangle is increased by 60%. By what per cent would the width have to be decreased to maintain the same area?

A. $37\dfrac{1}{2}\%$ B. 60%

C. 75%   D. 120%

6. A man walked 20 m to cross a rectangular field diagonally. If the length of the field is 16 m, the breadth of the rectangle is:

A. 4 m
B. 16 m
C. 12 m
D. Cannot be determined

7. If the ratio of the areas of two squares is 9 : 1, the ratio of their perimeters is:

A. 9 : 1   B. 3 : 1
C. 3 : 4   D. 1 : 3

8. The perimeter of both, a square and a rectangle are each equal to 48 m and the difference between their areas is 4 m². The breadth of the rectangle is:

A. 10 m   B. 12 m
C. 14 m   D. None of these

9. Area of a square with side x is equal to the area of a triangle with base x. The altitude of the triangle is:

A. $\dfrac{x}{2}$ B. x

C. $2x$ D. $4x$

10. If only the length of the rectangular plot is reduced to $\dfrac{2}{3}$rd of its original length, the ratio of original area to reduced area is:

A. 2 : 3   B. 3 : 2
C. 1 : 2   D. None of these

11. If the radius of a circle be reduced by 50%, its area is reduced by:

A. 25%   B. 50%
C. 75%   D. 100%

12. The perimeter of a rhombus is 52 m while its longer diagonal is 24 m. Its other diagonal is:

A. 5 m   B. 10 m
C. 20 m   D. 28 m

13. The circumference of a circle is 352 m, then its area in m² is:

A. 9856   B. 8956
C. 6589   D. 5986

ANSWERS

1	2	3	4	5	6	7	8	9	10
D	C	A	C	A	C	B	A	C	B

11	12	13
C	B	A

EXPLANATORY ANSWERS

1. Area of the plot = 3 × 1200 = 3600 m²
Let breadth be x m. Then length = $4x$ m
According to the question,
$4x \times x = 3600 \Rightarrow x^2 = 900 \Rightarrow x = 30$
Hence, length of the plot = 4 × 30 = 120 m.

2. Let length be x m, then breadth = $\dfrac{3x}{4}$ m

Area of the hall = $x \times \dfrac{3x}{4} = \dfrac{3x^2}{4}$

According to the question,

$\dfrac{3x^2}{4} = 300 \Rightarrow x^2 = 400 \Rightarrow x = 20$

Length = 20 m and breadth = $\dfrac{3}{4} \times 20 = 15$ m

Difference = 20 – 15 = 5 m

3. Let length = $5x$ m and breadth = $3x$ m
Perimeter of rectangle = $2(5x + 3x) = 16x$ m

But perimeter = $\dfrac{\text{Total cost}}{\text{Rate}} = \dfrac{3000}{7.50} = 400$ m

Now, $\qquad 16x = 400 \Rightarrow x = 25$
$\qquad$ length $= 5x = 5 \times 25 = 125$ m
$\qquad$ breadth $= 3x = 25 \times 3 = 75$ m
$\qquad$ Difference $= 125 - 75 = 50$ m

4. Length of the carpet $= \dfrac{8 \times 6}{2} = 24$ m.

5. Initially, let length $= x$ and breadth $= y$
Let new breadth $= z$.

$\qquad$ Then new length $= \dfrac{160x}{100} = \dfrac{8x}{5}$

$\therefore \qquad \dfrac{8x}{5} \times z = xy \Rightarrow z = \dfrac{5y}{8}$

$\qquad$ Decrease in breadth $= \left(y - \dfrac{5y}{8}\right) = \dfrac{3y}{8}$

$\therefore$ Decrease per cent $= \dfrac{3y}{8} \times \dfrac{1}{y} \times 100$

$\qquad = \dfrac{75}{2} = 37.5\% =$

6. Breadth $= \sqrt{(20)^2 - (16)^2}$

$\qquad = \sqrt{400 - 256} = \sqrt{144} = 12$ m.

7. Let the areas of the squares be $(9x^2)$ m^2 and (x^2) m^2
Then, their sides are $3x$ m and x m respectively

Ratio of their perimeters $= \dfrac{12x}{4x} = 3 : 1$

8. Let length of rectangle $= x$ m
and breadth of rectangle $= y$ m
Also, let the side of the square be z m
According to the question,
$\qquad 2(x + y) = 4z = 48$
$\qquad x + y = 24$ and $z = 12$
Also, $\qquad z^2 - xy = 4$
$\Rightarrow \qquad (12)^2 - 4 = xy$
$\Rightarrow \qquad xy = 140$
$\because \qquad x + y = 24$ and $xy = 140$
$\qquad (x - y)^2 = (x + y)^2 - 4xy$
$\Rightarrow \qquad (x - y)^2 = (24)^2 - 4(140)$
$\Rightarrow \qquad (x - y)^2 = 576 - 560 = 16$
$\Rightarrow \qquad x - y = 4$

Now, $\qquad x + y = 24$
$\qquad\qquad x - y = 4$
Solving and get $x = 14$, $y = 10$
Hence, breadth of rectangle $= 10$ m.

9. According to the question,

$$x^2 = \dfrac{1}{2} \times x \times h$$

$\Rightarrow \qquad h = \dfrac{2x^2}{x} = 2x$

10. Let length $= x$ and breadth $= y$

New length $= \dfrac{2}{3}x$

$\therefore \dfrac{\text{Original area}}{\text{Reduced area}} = \dfrac{xy}{\dfrac{2}{3}xy} = \dfrac{3}{2} = 3 : 2$

11. Original area $= \pi r^2$, New area $= \pi\left(\dfrac{r}{2}\right)^2 = \dfrac{\pi r^2}{4}$

Reduction in area $= \pi r^2 - \dfrac{\pi r^2}{4} = \dfrac{3\pi r^2}{4}$

Reduction per cent $= \dfrac{3\pi r^2}{4} \times \dfrac{1}{\pi r^2} \times 100 = 75\%$

12. Side of rhombus $= \dfrac{52}{4} = 13$ m

In $\triangle ABM$,
$\qquad x^2 = (13)^2 - (12)^2$
$\qquad x^2 = 169 - 144$
$\qquad x^2 = 25$
$\Rightarrow \qquad x = 5$ m
$\therefore$ Another diagonal
$\qquad = 2 \times 5 = 10$ m

13. Circumference of a circle $= 2\pi r$

$\Rightarrow \qquad 352 = 2 \times \dfrac{22}{7} \times r$

$\Rightarrow \qquad r = \dfrac{352 \times 7}{44} = 56$ m

Area of circle $= \pi r^2 = \dfrac{22}{7} \times 56 \times 56$

$\qquad = 9856$ m^2

12. VOLUME AND SURFACE AREA

We know that every real object occupies some space. It is usually specified by its three dimensions—length, breadth and depth (or height or thickness). It may be a solid or a hollow object. In case of circular, cylindrical and spherical object the specifying dimensions may change to radius, angle etc. The amount of space occupied by the object is called its volume. Its unit of measurement is m^3, cm^3, (inches)^3 etc. The area of the surfaces (plane/curved) of the object is called its surface area.

A Cuboid and A Cube

The solid like wooden boxes, tea containers, match box etc. which have six faces, each of which is a rectangle, are called cuboids. It has 12 edges.

A cuboid in which every face is a square is called a cube. Length of each face of a cube is called its edge.

Prism

A right prism is a solid in which the two ends are congruent parallel figures and the side faces are rectangles. The total area of side faces of a prism is called the lateral surface of the prism.

Cylinder

The solid generated by the revolution of a rectangle about one of its sides as axis is called a cylinder.

Pyramid

A solid whose base is a plane rectilinear figure having the side faces as triangles meeting at a common vertex is called a pyramid. When the base of a pyramid is a triangle, the pyramid is called a tetrahedron.

Cone

The solid generated by the revolution of a right angled triangle about one of the sides containing the right angle as the axis is called a right circular cone.

The perpendicular distance from the vertex to the base is called the height of the cone and the length of slant face from vertex to the base is called the slant height of the cone.

Frustum

If a cone is cut by a plane parallel to the base so as to divide the cone into two parts, then the lower part is called the frustum of the cone.

Sphere

When a semicircle moves about its diameter, the solid generated is called a sphere.

Formulae

Cuboid:

Volume of cuboid = $l \times b \times h$ cubic units

Whole surface area = $2(lb + bh + hl)$ square units

Diagonal of cuboid = $\sqrt{l^2 + b^2 + h^2}$ units

Area of 4 walls of a room = $2(l + b) \times h$ square units

Cube:

Volume of cube = a^3 cubic units

Side of cube = $\sqrt[3]{\text{Volume}}$

Lateral surface area = $4a^2$ square units

Total surface area = $6a^2$ square units

Diagonal of the cube = $\left(\sqrt{3}\,a\right)$ units

Cylinder:

Volume of cylinder = $\pi r^2 h$ cubic units

Lateral surface area = $2\pi rh$ square units

Total surface area = $2\pi r(h + r)$ square units

Cone:

Volume of cone = $\dfrac{1}{3}\pi r^2 h$ cubic units

Lateral surface area = πrl square units

Total surface area = $\pi r(l + r)$ square units

Slant height (l) = $\sqrt{r^2 + h^2}$

Sphere:

Volume of sphere = $\dfrac{4}{3}\pi r^3$ cubic units

Surface area = $4\pi r^2$ square units

Hemisphere:

Volume = $\dfrac{2}{3}\pi r^3$ cubic units

Lateral surface area = $2\pi r^2$ square units

Total surface area = $3\pi r^2$ square units

Frustum:

Volume = $\dfrac{1}{3}\pi h(r_1^2 + r_1 r_2 + r_2^2)$ cubic units

Curved surface area = $\pi(r_1 + r_2) \times l$ square units

Total surface area = $\pi\left[r_1^2 + r_2^2 + (r_1 + r_2)l\right]$ square units

Pyramid:

Volume = $\dfrac{1}{2} \times$ (area of base) $\times$ height cubic units

EXAMPLE: The dimensions of a metallic cuboid are 100 cm $\times$ 80 cm $\times$ 64 cm. It is melted and recast into cube. Find the total surface area of the cube.

SOLUTION: Volume of cuboid = $l \times b \times h$

$= 100 \times 80 \times 64$

$= 512000$ cm^3

Volume of cube = a^3

According to the question,

$a^3 = 512000$

$\Rightarrow$ $a^3 = 8 \times 8 \times 8 \times 10 \times 10 \times 10$

$\Rightarrow$ $a = 8 \times 10 = 80$ cm

Total surface area of cube = $6a^2 = 6 \times 80 \times 80 = 38400$

Hence, total surface area of cube is 38400 cm^2.

EXAMPLE: Three cubes whose edges measure 3 cm, 4 cm and 5 cm respectively form a single cube. Find the total surface area of the new cube.

SOLUTION: Let the edge of new cube = x cm

$x^3 = 3^3 + 4^3 + 5^3$

$= 27 + 64 + 125 = 216$ cm^3

$\Rightarrow$ $x^3 = 6 \times 6 \times 6 \Rightarrow x = 6$ cm

Total surface area of cube = $6(x)^2 = 6 \times 6 \times 6 = 216$ cm^2

Hence, total surface area of new cube = 216 cm^2.

EXAMPLE: The capacity of a cylindrical tank is 6160 m^3. If the radius of its base is 14 m, find the depth of the tank.

SOLUTION: Volume of cylinder = $\pi r^2 h$

$\pi r^2 h = 6160$

$\Rightarrow$ $\dfrac{22}{7} \times 14 \times 14 \times h = 6160$

$\Rightarrow$ $h = \dfrac{6160}{44 \times 14} = 10$ m

Hence, depth of the tank is 10 m.

EXAMPLE: How many bullets can be made out of a lead cylinder 28 cm high and 6 cm radius, each bullet being 1.5 cm in diameter?

SOLUTION: Number of bullets

$= \dfrac{\text{Volume of cylinder}}{\text{Volume of 1 bullet}}$

$= \dfrac{\pi \times 6 \times 6 \times 28}{\dfrac{4}{3} \times \pi \times 0.75 \times 0.75 \times 0.75}$

$= \dfrac{6 \times 6 \times 28 \times 3}{4 \times \dfrac{3}{4} \times \dfrac{3}{4} \times \dfrac{3}{4}} = \dfrac{6 \times 6 \times 28 \times 4 \times 4 \times 3}{3 \times 3 \times 3}$

$= 1792$

EXAMPLE: A metal sphere of diameter 42 cm is dropped into a cylindrical vessel, which is partly filled with water. The diameter of the vessel is 1.68 metres. If the sphere is completely submerged, find by how much the surface of water will rise.

SOLUTION: Radius of the sphere = 21 cm

Volume of sphere = $\dfrac{4}{3}\pi r^3$

$= \dfrac{4}{3} \times \dfrac{22}{7} \times 21 \times 21 \times 21$

$= 38808$ cm^3

Volume of water displaced by sphere = 38808 cm^3
Let water rise by h cm.

Volume of cylinder = $\pi r^2 h$

$$\frac{22}{7} \times 84 \times 84 \times h = 38808$$

$\Rightarrow \quad h = \dfrac{38808 \times 7}{22 \times 84 \times 84} = \dfrac{7}{4} = 1.75 \text{ cm}$

EXAMPLE: A tent is in the form of a right circular cylinder surmounted by a cone. The diameter of cylinder is 24 m. The height of the cylindrical portion is 11 m while the vertex of the cone is 16 m above the ground. Find the area of the canvas required for the tent.

SOLUTION: Lateral surface area of cylinder = $2\pi rh$

$$= 2 \times \frac{22}{7} \times 12 \times 11 = \frac{5808}{7} \text{ m}^2$$

Height of cone = 16 – 11 = 5 m
Radius of cone = 12 m

Slant height $l = \sqrt{r^2 + h^2} = \sqrt{12^2 + 5^2}$

$$= \sqrt{169} = 13 \text{ m}$$

Lateral surface area of cone = πrl

$$= \frac{22}{7} \times 12 \times 13 = \frac{3432}{7} \text{ m}^2$$

Area of canvas $= \dfrac{5808}{7} + \dfrac{3432}{7}$

$$= \frac{9240}{7} = 1320 \text{ m}^2$$

EXAMPLE: The slant height of the frustum of a cone is 20 cm and the height of the frustum is 16 cm. The radius of the smaller circle is 8 cm. Find the volume and total surface area of the frustum.

SOLUTION: $l = \sqrt{h^2 + (R-r)^2} = \sqrt{16^2 + (R-8)^2}$

$\Rightarrow \qquad 20 = \sqrt{256 + R^2 - 16R + 64}$

$$= \sqrt{R^2 - 16R + 320}$$

$\Rightarrow R^2 - 16R + 320 = 400$

$\Rightarrow \quad R^2 - 16R - 80 = 0 \Rightarrow R = 20 \text{ cm}$

Volume of frustum $= \dfrac{1}{3}\pi h(R^2 + r^2 + Rr)$

$$= \frac{1}{3} \times \frac{22}{7} \times 16(400 + 64 + 160)$$

$$= \frac{73216}{7} \text{ cm}^3$$

Total surface area = $\pi(R^2 + r^2 + Rl + rl)$

$$= \frac{22}{7}(400 + 64 + 400 + 160)$$

$$= \frac{22}{7} \times 1024 = \frac{22528}{7}$$

$$= 3218.28 \text{ cm}^2$$

EXAMPLE: The length of a garden roller is 2 m and diameter is 1.4 m. How much area will it cover in 10 revolutions?

SOLUTION: Area covered

= Curved surface × no. of revolutions

= $2\pi rh \times 10$

$$= 2 \times \frac{22}{7} \times 0.7 \times 2 \times 10 = 88 \text{ m}^2$$

EXAMPLE: A cylinder is made by lead whose radius is 4 cm and height is 10 cm. By melting it how many spheres of radius 2 cm can be made?

SOLUTION: Given, radius of the cylinder = 4 cm
and height of the cylinder = 10 cm

$\therefore$ Volume of the cylinder = $\pi r^2 h = \pi(4)^2 \times 10$

$$= 160\pi \text{ cm}^3$$

Volume of sphere $= \dfrac{4}{3}\pi r^3 = \dfrac{4}{3}\pi(2)^3$

$$= \frac{32}{3}\pi \text{ cm}^3$$

$\therefore$ Number of spheres $= \dfrac{\text{Volume of cylinder}}{\text{Volume of one sphere}}$

$$= \frac{160\pi}{\dfrac{32}{3}\pi} = \frac{160 \times 3}{32} = 15$$

Hence, number of spheres that can be made are 15.

MULTIPLE CHOICE QUESTIONS

1. The surface area of a cube is 726 m^2. The volume of cube is:
   A. 1300 m^3 B. 1331 m^3
   C. 1452 m^3 D. 1542 m^3

2. Sum of the length, width and depth of a cuboid is s and its diagonal is d. Its surface area is:
   A. s^2 B. d^2
   C. $s^2 - d^2$ D. $s^2 + d^2$

3. A wooden box of dimensions 8 m × 7 m × 6 m is to carry rectangular boxes of dimensions 8 cm × 7 cm × 6 cm. The maximum number of boxes that can be carried in 1 wooden box is:
   A. 1200000   B. 1000000
   C. 9800000   D. 7500000

4. The length of the longest rod that can be placed in a room 30 m long, 24 m broad and 18 m high is:
   A. 30 m   B. $15\sqrt{2}$ m
   C. 60 m   D. $30\sqrt{2}$ m

5. If the volume of two cubes are in the ratio 8 : 1, the ratio of their edges is:
   A. 8 : 1   B. $2\sqrt{2} : 1$
   C. 2 : 1   D. None of these

6. A metal sheet 27 cm long 8 cm broad and 1 cm thick is melted into a cube. The difference between the surface areas of two solids will be:
   A. 284 cm^2 B. 296 cm^2
   C. 286 cm^2 D. 300 cm^2

7. If each edge of a cube is increased by 50%, the percentage increase in surface area is:
   A. 50%   B. 75%
   C. 100%   D. 125%

8. If a right circular cone of vertical height 24 cm has a volume of 1232 cm^3, then the area of its curved surface in cm^2 is:
   A. 1254   B. 704
   C. 550   D. 154

9. Two cubes have volumes in the ratio 1 : 27. The ratio of their surface areas is:
   A. 1 : 3   B. 1 : 8
   C. 1 : 9   D. 1 : 18

10. If the volumes of two cones are in the ratio 1 : 4 and their diameters are in the ratio 4 : 5, then the ratio of their heights is:
    A. 1 : 5   B. 5 : 4
    C. 5 : 16   D. 25 : 64

11. The radius of a wire is decreased to one-third. If volumes remains the same, length will increase:
    A. 1 time   B. 3 times
    C. 6 times   D. 9 times

12. A cylindrical piece of metal of radius 2 cm and height 6 cm is shaped into a cone of same radius. The height of cone is:
    A. 18 cm   B. 14 cm
    C. 12 cm   D. 8 cm

13. If 1 cubic cm of cast iron weight 21 g then the weight of a cast iron pipe of length 1 m with a bore of 3 cm and in which the thickness of the metal is 1 cm, is:
    A. 21 kg   B. 24.2 kg
    C. 26.4 kg   D. 18.6 kg

14. The number of solid spheres, each of diameter 6 cm, that could be moulded to form a solid metal cylinder of height 45 cm and diameter 4 cms, is:
    A. 3   B. 4
    C. 5   D. 6

15. A right cylinder and a right circular cone have the same radius and the same volume. The ratio of the height of the cylinder to that of the cone is:
    A. 3 : 5   B. 2 : 5
    C. 3 : 1   D. 1 : 3

ANSWERS

1	2	3	4	5	6	7	8	9	10
B	C	B	D	C	C	D	C	C	D

11	12	13	14	15
D	A	C	C	D

EXPLANATORY ANSWERS

1. Surface area of cube = $6a^2$

$6a^2 = 726 \Rightarrow a^2 = \dfrac{726}{6} = 121 \Rightarrow a = 11$ m

Volume of cube = $a^3 = 11 \times 11 \times 11 = 1331$ m^3

2. $\qquad l + b + h = s$

and $\sqrt{l^2 + b^2 + h^2} = d \Rightarrow l^2 + b^2 + h^2 = d^2$

$(l + b + h)^2 = s^2$

$\Rightarrow l^2 + b^2 + h^2 + 2(lb + bh + hl) = s^2$

$\Rightarrow \qquad d^2 + 2(lb + bh + hl) = s^2$

$\Rightarrow \qquad 2(lb + bh + hl) = s^2 - d^2$

$\therefore \qquad$ Surface area $= (s^2 - d^2)$.

3. Number of boxes = $\dfrac{800 \times 700 \times 600}{8 \times 7 \times 6} = 1000000$

4. Diagonal of cuboid = $\sqrt{l^2 + b^2 + h^2}$

$\therefore$ Length of longest rod = $\sqrt{30^2 + 24^2 + 18^2}$

$= \sqrt{900 + 576 + 324} = \sqrt{1800}$

$= \sqrt{30 \times 30 \times 2} = 30\sqrt{2}$ m

5. Let their volumes be $8x^3$ and x^3.

Then, their sides are $2x$ and x

$\therefore$ Ratio of their edges = 2 : 1

6. Volume of sheet = $27 \times 8 \times 1 = 216$ cm^3

Volume of cube formed = 216 cm^3

Side of cube = $\sqrt[3]{216} = 6$ cm

Surface area of cuboid = $2(lb + bh + hl)$

$= 2(27 \times 8 + 8 \times 1 + 1 \times 27) = 502$ cm^2

Surface area of cube = $6(\text{side})^2 = 6 \times 36 = 216$ cm^2

Difference in areas = $502 - 216 = 286$ cm^2

7. Let original length of cube = x

then, its surface area = $6x^2$

New edge = $\left(\dfrac{150}{100}x\right) = \dfrac{3}{2}x$

New surface area = $6 \times \left(\dfrac{3}{2}x\right)^2$

$= 6 \times \dfrac{9}{4}x^2 = \dfrac{27}{2}x^2$

Increase in surface area = $\left(\dfrac{27}{2} - 6\right)x^2 = \dfrac{15}{2}x^2$

$\therefore \qquad$ Increase % $= \dfrac{15x^2/2}{6x^2} \times 100$

$= \dfrac{15x^2}{12x^2} \times 100 = 125\%$

8. $\qquad$ Volume of cone = 1232

$\Rightarrow \qquad \dfrac{1}{3}\pi r^2 h = 1232$

$\Rightarrow \dfrac{1}{3} \times \dfrac{22}{7} \times r^2 \times 24 = 1232$

$\Rightarrow r^2 = \dfrac{3 \times 7 \times 1232}{22 \times 24} = 49 \Rightarrow r = 7$ cm

$\Rightarrow l = \sqrt{r^2 + h^2} = \sqrt{7^2 + 24^2} = \sqrt{625} = 25$ cm

Lateral surface area of cone = $\pi r l$

$= \dfrac{22}{7} \times 7 \times 25 = 22 \times 25 = 550$ cm^2

9. Let their volumes are x^3 and $27x^3$.

Then, their sides are x and $3x$.

Ratio of their surface areas = $\dfrac{6x^2}{6(3x)^2} = \dfrac{x^2}{9x^2}$

$= 1 : 9$

10. Let the diameters of the bases of the cones be $4r$ and $5r$. Let their heights be h and H.

then, $\qquad \dfrac{\dfrac{1}{3}\pi \times \left(\dfrac{4r}{2}\right)^2 \times h}{\dfrac{1}{3}\pi\left(\dfrac{5r}{2}\right)^2 \times H} = \dfrac{1}{4}$

$\Rightarrow \qquad \dfrac{16}{25} \times \dfrac{h}{H} = \dfrac{1}{4}$

$\Rightarrow \qquad \dfrac{h}{H} = \dfrac{25}{64}$

11. Let original radius = r

and original length = h

New radius = $\dfrac{1}{3}r$

Let new length = H

then, $\pi r^2 h = \pi\left(\dfrac{1}{3}r\right)^2 \times H = \dfrac{\pi r^2 H}{9}$

$\therefore$ H = $9h$

Thus length becomes 9 times.

12. Volume of cone = Volume of cylinder

$$\dfrac{1}{3}\pi r^2 h = \pi r^2 h$$

$\Rightarrow$ $\dfrac{1}{3}\times\dfrac{22}{7}\times 2\times 2\times h = \dfrac{22}{7}\times 2\times 2\times 6$

$\Rightarrow$ $\dfrac{h}{3} = 6 \Rightarrow h = 18$ cm

$\therefore$ Height of cone = 18 cm

13. Diameter = 3 cm, h = 1 m = 100 cm

$\therefore$ Radius = $\dfrac{3}{2}$ cm = 1.5 cm

thickness = 1 cm

$\therefore$ R = 1.5 + 1 = 2.5 cm

r = 1.5 cm

Volume of metal = $\pi(R^2 - r^2) \times h$

$= \pi[(2.5)^2 - (1.5)^2] \times 100$

$= \pi[4] \times 100 = \pi \times 400$ cm^3

$\because$ 1 cm^3 = 21 g

$\therefore$ $\pi \times 400$ cm^3 = $21 \times \pi \times 400$ g

$= 21 \times \dfrac{22}{7} \times \dfrac{400}{1000}$ kg

$= 26.4$ kg

14. Number of spheres = $\dfrac{\text{Volume of cylinder}}{\text{Volume of sphere}}$

$= \dfrac{\pi \times 2 \times 2 \times 45}{\dfrac{4}{3}\pi \times (3)^3} = \dfrac{4 \times 45 \times 3}{4 \times 27} = 5$

15. Volume of cylinder = Volume of cone

$$\pi r^2 h = \dfrac{1}{3}\pi r^2 H$$

$\Rightarrow$ $3h = H \Rightarrow \dfrac{h}{H} = \dfrac{1}{3}$

13. DATA INTERPRETATION

The collection of figures and facts in every field is called the statistical data. There are three types of statistical data.

(a) **Primary data:** The data collected by the investigator or the statistician to be used or integrated himself are called primary data. It is more reliable and relevant because it is collected by the investigator himself for the first time for his study.

(b) **Secondary data:** The data which are collected originally by someone else and used and interpreted by others for statistical analysis are called secondary data.

(c) **Grouped data:** When primary data is arranged in classes or groups to bring out certain sailent feature of the data is called grouped data.

Graphical Representation of Data

A graph is a visual form for presentation of data, highlighting their basic facts and relationship.

The word graph, chart and diagram are used interchangeably for the pictorial representation of data. However, the visual form made by using rectangular coordinate system is called a graph. In general, the other pictorial representation in which the coordinate system is not used are called diagrams or charts.

Variate: The quantity that we measure from observation-to-observation is called a variate.

Class-Interval: Every data is generally divided into small group using some interval is said to be in class-interval, *e.g.,* 0–5, 5–10, 10–15 etc.

Class-Size: The difference between the true upper limit and true lower limit of a class gives the size of a class-interval, *e.g.,* class-size of the class-interval 0–5 is 5.

Mid Value: The variable value which is mid-way between the lower and upper limit of a class is called its mid-value, *e.g.,* mid-value of class-interval 0–5 is $\dfrac{0+5}{2}$ = 2.5.

Frequency: The number of observations corresponding to particular class is said to be the frequency of that class, *e.g.,* frequency of the interval 5–10 is 6. It means 6 persons have got 5 or more articles but less than 10.

Cumulative Frequency: The sum of the preceding frequencies is called cumulative frequency. Last frequency of cumulative frequency column is equal to the sum of the frequencies.

Class Limit: Every interval has two limits. Lower number of the interval is called lower limit while upper number of the interval is called upper limit, *e.g.,* in class-interval 0–5, 0 is lower limit while 5 is the upper limit.

Histogram

A statistical graph that represents by the height of a rectangular column the number of times that each class of result occurs in a sample or experiment, *e.g.,* the following table represents the number of matured persons in age group (15–20) in a city.

Age Group	Number of persons
15–20	200
20–25	350
25–30	475
30–35	600
35–40	750
40–45	900
45–50	100

Then the histogram of the data is given below:

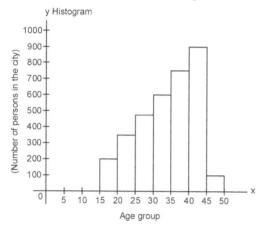

Bar Chart

A graph consisting of bars whose lengths are proportional to quantities in a set of data. It can be used when one axis cannot have a numerical scale, *e.g.,* to show how many different columns of flowers grow from a packet of mixed seeds, *e.g.,*

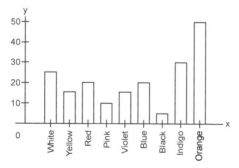

Pie Chart

A diagram in which proportions are illustrated as sectors of a circle. The relative area of the sectors representing the different proportions, *e.g.,* if out of 100 military personnels 25 personnels use tank, 30 personnels use warship, 40 personnels use aircraft and rest of them use rifles. Then pie-chart of the above data is

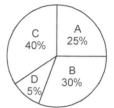

A uses tank $= \dfrac{25}{100} \times 360 = 90°$

B uses warship $= \dfrac{30}{100} \times 360 = 108°$

C uses aircraft $= \dfrac{40}{100} \times 360 = 144°$

D uses rifles $= \dfrac{5}{100} \times 360 = 18°$

EXAMPLE: Find out the marks obtained in different subjects from the following pie-diagram, if the total marks be 540.

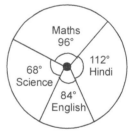

SOLUTION: Sum of the angles at the centre of circle $= 360°$

Total marks $= 540$

$\therefore$ Marks obtained in Hindi $= \dfrac{112}{360} \times 540 = 168$

Marks obtained in English $= \dfrac{84}{360} \times 540 = 126$

Marks obtained in Science $= \dfrac{68}{360} \times 540 = 102$

Marks obtained in Maths $= \dfrac{96}{360} \times 540 = 144$

MULTIPLE CHOICE QUESTIONS

Directions (Qs. 1 to 5): *Answers the questions on the basis of the following table:*

Assume all colleges sent equal number of candidates in all subjects for the examination.

Percentage of results for Subjects

College	Maths	Physics	Chemistry	Zoology	Botany
A	52	65	62	47	40
B	47	62	52	35	38
C	53	70	46	54	39
D	35	72	58	62	57

1. Taking all the colleges into account which subject has shown highest percentage result?
   A. Chemistry
   B. Maths
   C. Zoology
   D. Physics

2. Taking the performance in all the subjects into account which college has shown highest level of percentage results?
   A. D   B. A
   C. B   D. C

3. Seeing the performance of all the four colleges together which combination of groups has shown lowest level of percentage results?
   A. Zoology and Botany
   B. Physics and Chemistry
   C. Maths and Physics
   D. Chemistry and Botany

4. Taking all the colleges into account which subject has shown lowest percentage result?
   A. Maths
   B. Physics
   C. Chemistry
   D. Botany

5. Taking the performance in all subjects into account which college has shown lowest level?
   A. A   B. B
   C. C   D. D

Directions (Qs. 6 to 10): *These questions refer to the following circle graph showing the expenditure distribution of a certain family. The family spends ₹6500 per month.*

Expenditure Distribution of a Certain Family

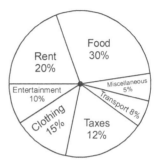

6. How much it spends on food per month?
   A. ₹ 1950
   B. ₹ 2950
   C. ₹ 4850
   D. ₹ 850

7. How much are its annual taxes?
   A. ₹ 6500   B. ₹ 9360
   C. ₹ 8900   D. ₹ 9500

8. How many degrees should there be in the central angle showing clothing, taxes and transportation combined?
   A. 100   B. 115
   C. 118   D. 126

9. How much more money per month is spent by the family on food as compared to the rent?
   A. ₹ 650   B. ₹ 750
   C. ₹ 550   D. ₹ 850

10. If the expenditure budget of the family is raised to ₹ 8000 per month and distribution on various items remain the same, then the monthly expenses on both, the entertainment and the transport, will be:
    A. ₹ 1700
    B. ₹ 1650
    C. ₹ 1440
    D. ₹ 1320

Directions (Qs. 11 to 15): *Study the following graph carefully and answer the following questions.*

Demand and Production of Colour TV sets of Five Companies for October 1988

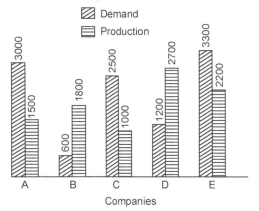

11. What is the ratio of companies having more demand than production of those having more production than demand?

A. 2 : 3   B. 4 : 1

C. 2 : 2   D. 3 : 2

12. What is the difference between average demand and average production of the five companies taken together?

A. 1400   B. 400

C. 280   D. 138

13. The production of Company 'D' is approximately how many times that of the production of the Company A?

A. 1.8   B. 4.5

C. 2.5   D. 4.9

14. The demand for Company 'B' is approximately what per cent of the demand for Company 'C'?

A. 4%   B. 24%

C. 20%   D. 60%

15. If Company A desires to meet the demand by purchasing surplus TV sets from a single company, which one of the following companies can meet the need adequately?

A. B   B. C

C. D   D. None of these

Directions (Qs. 16 to 20): *Study the following graph to answer the given questions.*

Per cent profit earned by two companies over the given years

$$\% \text{ Profit} = \frac{\text{Income} - \text{Expenditure}}{\text{Expenditure}} \times 100$$

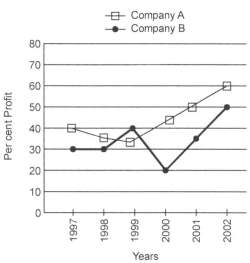

16. If the expenditure of Company B in 2000 was ₹ 200 crores, what was its income?

A. ₹ 240 crores   B. ₹ 220 crores

C. ₹ 160 crores   D. ₹ 180 crores

17. If the income of Company A in 2002 was ₹ 600 crores, what was its expenditure?

A. ₹ 360 crores   B. ₹ 480 crores

C. ₹ 375 crores   D. ₹ 320 crores

18. If the income of Company B in 1998 was ₹ 200 crores, what was its profit in 1999?

A. ₹ 21.5 crores

B. ₹ 153 crores

C. ₹ 46.15 crores

D. Cannot be determined

19. If the incomes of the two companies in 1998 were equal, what was the ratio of their expenditure?

A. 1 : 2   B. 26 : 27

C. 4 : 5   D. 100 : 67

20. What is the per cent increase in per cent profit for Company B from year 2000 to 2001?

A. 75   B. 175

C. 160   D. 150

ANSWERS

1	2	3	4	5	6	7	8	9	10
D	A	A	D	B	A	B	D	A	C
11	**12**	**13**	**14**	**15**	**16**	**17**	**18**	**19**	**20**
D	C	A	B	C	A	C	D	B	A

EXPLANATORY ANSWERS

1. Maths   : 52 + 47 + 53 + 35 = 187
   Physics   : 65 + 62 + 70 + 72 = 269
   Chemistry : 62 + 52 + 46 + 58 = 218
   Zoology   : 47 + 35 + 54 + 62 = 198
   Botany   : 40 + 38 + 39 + 57 = 174
   Clearly, Physics has shown highest percentage result.

2. A : 52 + 65 + 62 + 47 + 40 = 266
   B : 47 + 62 + 52 + 35 + 38 = 234
   C : 53 + 70 + 46 + 54 + 39 = 262
   D : 35 + 72 + 58 + 62 + 57 = 284
   Clearly, college D has shown highest level of percentage result.

3. Zoology and Botany of groups has shown lowest level of percentage result.

4. Total marks of Botany = 174 which shows lowest percentage result.

5. College B has shown lowest level because its total percentage result in all five subjects is 234 which is lowest.

6. Food 30% of ₹ 6500 = $\dfrac{30}{100} \times 6500$ = ₹ 1950

7. Taxes = 12% of ₹ 6500
   $= \dfrac{12}{100} \times 6500$ = ₹ 780/month
   = ₹ 780 × 12 = ₹ 9360/year
   ∴ Annual taxes = ₹ 9360

8. Clothing, taxes and transportation combined are 35%.
   Now,   100% = 360°
   $35\% = \dfrac{360°}{100} \times 35 = 126°$

9. 10% of ₹ 6500 = $\dfrac{10}{100} \times 6500$ = ₹ 650/month

10. 18% of ₹ 8000 = $\dfrac{18}{100} \times 8000$ = ₹ 1440

11. The companies having more demand than production are A, C and E *i.e.* their number is 3. The companies having more production than demand are B and D *i.e.* their number is 2.
   So, the required ratio is 3 : 2.

12. Average demand
   $= \dfrac{1}{5}(3000 + 600 + 2500 + 1200 + 3300)$
   $= \dfrac{10600}{5} = 2120$
   Average production
   $= \dfrac{1500 + 1800 + 1000 + 2700 + 2200}{5}$
   $= \dfrac{9200}{5} = 1840$
   ∴ Difference between average demand and average production = 2120 – 1840 = 280

13. Let   K(1500) = 2700
   $\Rightarrow$ $K = \dfrac{2700}{1500} = \dfrac{9}{5} = 1.8.$

14. Let x% of (demand for C) = (demand for B)
   $\Rightarrow$ $\dfrac{x}{100} \times 2500 = 600$
   $\Rightarrow$ $x = \dfrac{600 \times 100}{2500} = 24\%$

15. Since Company D produces highest number of TV sets and Company A desires to meet the demand by purchasing surplus TV sets from a single Company.
   Clearly, D can meet the demand of A.
   ∴ Correct answer is C.

16. Let the income be ₹ x crores

$$\therefore \qquad 20 = \frac{x - 200}{200} \times 100$$

$$\Rightarrow \qquad 40 = x - 200$$

$$\Rightarrow \qquad x = 240$$

$\therefore$ Income = ₹ 240 crores

17. The income of Company A in 2002

$$= ₹ 600 \text{ crores}$$

% Profit = 60

Let the expenditure be ₹ x crores.

$$\therefore \qquad 60 = \frac{600 - x}{x} \times 100$$

$$\Rightarrow \qquad x = \frac{600 - x}{60} \times 100$$

$$\Rightarrow \qquad x = \frac{(600 - x)5}{3}$$

$$\Rightarrow \qquad 3x = 3000 - 5x$$

$$\Rightarrow \qquad 8x = 3000$$

$$\Rightarrow \qquad x = \frac{3000}{8} = 375$$

Hence, expenditure = ₹ 375 crores.

18. It cannot be determined as Income and Expenditure of respective year is not known.

19. Let their equal incomes be ₹ 1 crore. Also, let expenditure of Company A be ₹ E_1 crores and that of Company B be ₹ E_2 crores.

Now, $\qquad 35 = \frac{1 - E_1}{E_1} \times 100$

$$35 E_1 = 100 - 100 E_1$$

$$135 E_1 = 100 \qquad\qquad ...(i)$$

Similarly $\qquad 30 = \frac{1 - E_2}{E_2} \times 100$

$$130 E_2 = 100 \qquad\qquad ...(ii)$$

From (i) and (ii)

$$135 E_1 = 130 E_2$$

$$\Rightarrow \qquad \frac{E_1}{E_2} = \frac{130}{135} = \frac{26}{27}$$

$$\therefore \qquad E_1 : E_2 = 26 : 27$$

20. Required percentage $= \dfrac{35 - 20}{20} \times 100$

$$= \frac{15}{20} \times 100 = 75.$$

General English

Comprehension Passages

Comprehension is a very important part of General English paper. The questions on comprehension lay particular stress on understanding a given passage. You are required to read a passage and answer a few questions based on it. Various comprehension questions are set solely with the objectives named below:

1. To test your ability to detect the central idea or the focal point in the given passage.
2. To test your ability to understand and interpret the given passage.
3. To judge your capability to pick out the various arguments put forward by the writer for or against something.
4. To test your accuracy and richness of vocabulary.
5. To test your academic ability to understand the implied and the clearly and fully expressed ideas of the writer of the passage.
6. To test, occasionally, your power of appreciating critically the views contained in the given passage.

While answering comprehension questions, you must comply with the following important points:

1. First, read the whole passage attentively, carefully and quickly.
2. Read it for the second time, slowly but steadily.
3. Work out the probable meaning of new words, from the context in which they have been used.
4. Underline and look for transitional words and phrases as an aid to comprehension.
5. The process of elimination should be used while selecting the correct answer.
6. Recheck your answers before marking in the answersheet.

Multiple Choice Questions

PASSAGE-1

Internet banking is the term used for new age banking system. Internet banking is also called as online banking and it is an outgrowth of PC banking. Internet banking uses the internet as the delivery channel by which to conduct banking activity, for example, transferring funds, paying bills, viewing checking and savings account balances, paying mortgages and purchasing financial instruments and certificates of deposits. Internet banking is a result of explored possibility to use internet application in one of the various domains of commerce. It is difficult to infer whether the internet tool has been applied for convenience of bankers or for the customers' convenience. But ultimately it contributes in increasing the efficiency of the banking operation as well providing more convenience to customers. Without even interacting with the bankers, customers *transact* from one corner of the country to another corner.

There are many advantages of online Banking. It is convenient, it isn't bound by operational timings, there are no geographical barriers and the services can be offered at a *minuscule* cost. Electronic banking has experienced explosive growth and has transformed traditional practices in banking.

Private Banks in India were the first to implement internet banking services in the banking industry. Private Banks, due to late entry into the industry, understood that the establishing network in remote corners of the country is a very difficult task. It was clear to them that the only way to stay connected to the customers at any place and at any time is through Internet applications. They took the Internet applications as a weapon of competitive advantage to corner the great *monoliths* like State Bank of India, Indian Bank etc. Private Banks are pioneer in India to explore the *versatility* of Internet applications in delivering services to customers.

Several studies have attempted to assess the relative importance of B2B and B2C business domains. There is wide difference in estimates of volume of business transacted over Internet and its components under B2C and B2B. However, most studies agree that volume of transactions in B2B domain far exceeds that in B2C. This is the expected result. There is also a growing opinion that the future of e-business lies in B2B domain, as compared to B2C. This has several reasons, like low penetration of PCs to households, low bandwidth availability etc., in a large part of the world. The success of B2C ventures depends to a large extent on the shopping habits of people in different parts of the world. A survey sponsored jointly by Confederation of Indian Industries and Infrastructure Leasing and Financial Services on e-commerce in India in 2010 the following observations. 62% of PC owners and 75% of PC non-owners but who have access to Internet would not buy through the net, as they were not sure of the product offered. The same study estimated the size of B2B business in India by the year 2011 to be varying between ₹ 1250 billion to ₹ 1500 billion. In a recent study done by Arthur Anderson, it has been estimated that 84% of total e-business revenue is generated from B2B segment and the growth prospects in this segment are substantial. It has estimated the revenues to be anywhere between US $ 8.1 trillion to over US $ 21 trillion within the next three years (2014).

1. Which bank(s) is/are pioneer in India to explore the versatility of Internet banking in serving customers?
   A. State Bank of India
   B. Indian Bank
   C. Public Sector Banks
   D. Private Banks
   E. None of these

2. Which of the following is not an advantage of online banking?
   A. It is convenient.
   B. It is bound by operational timings.
   C. The services can be offered at a minimum cost.
   D. There is no geographical barrier.
   E. None of these

3. What percentage of PC non-owners but who have access to Internet would not prefer to buy through the net, as they are not sure of the product offered?
   A. 75%   B. 62%
   C. 84%   D. 76%
   E. None of these

4. Which type of activities are performed by Internet banking?
   A. Paying bills
   B. Transferring funds
   C. Paying mortgages
   D. Purchasing financial instruments and certificates of deposits
   E. All of these

5. What estimate was made by Confederation of Indian Industries regarding the size of B2B business in India by the year 2011?
   A. Between ₹ 250 billion to ₹ 500 billion
   B. Between ₹ 1250 billion to ₹ 1500 billion
   C. Between ₹ 850 billion to ₹ 1050 billion
   D. Between $ 8.7 trillion to $ 21 trillion
   E. None of these

Directions (Qs. 6 to 8) : *Choose the word which is MOST SIMILAR in meaning to the word printed in BOLD as used in the passage.*

6. VERSATILITY
   A. multi-utility   B. vesicle
   C. dullness   D. necessity
   E. meanness

7. MONOLITHS
   A. large blocks of stone
   B. large organisations
   C. monopoly
   D. dwarfs
   E. niche

8. TRANSACT
   A. do business   B. tranquillize
   C. transcend   D. exceed
   E. transfer

Directions (Qs. 9 & 10) : *Choose the word which is MOST OPPOSITE in meaning to the word printed in BOLD as used in the passage.*

9. SUBSTANTIAL
   A. meagre   B. considerable
   C. large   D. submissive
   E. sufficient

10. MINUSCULE
   A. small   B. minimum
   C. minute   D. large
   E. maximum

PASSAGE-2

One could, in theory, conceive of a country "specialising" entirely in agriculture and obtaining all its industrial requirements from abroad. But it could never become a high income country simply because technologically developed agriculture could never absorb more than a fraction of the working population on the available land. Though in all underdeveloped countries the greater part of the working population is "occupied" in agriculture, most of this represents disguised unemployment; a rural community maintains all its members and expects everyone to share in the work. Much of the greater part of this labour could be withdrawn from agricultrue if alternative employment opportunities were available without any *adverse* effect, and probably with a beneficial effect, on total agricultural output. For the relief of the pressure of labour on the land is itself a most potent factor in *inducing* improvements in technology which raise yields per acre, as well as the yield per man. These improvements normally require an increase in the

capital employed on the land; but the savings necessary for the increase in capital are themselves a by-product of reduced population pressure. The reduction in the agricultural population, and the increased use of capital in agriculture are thus different aspects of the same process. As there are fewer mouths to feed, the "agricultural surplus" rises (the excess of agricultural production over the self-consumption of the farming population). The rise in the "surplus" enables the farmers to plough back a higher proportion of their output—in the form of better tools, improved seeds, fertilisers, etc., and such improvements tend to both "labour saving" and "land saving"; they *diminish* the labour requirements at the same time as they increase the yield of the land.

1. According to the passage, it is theoretically possible to think of country
   A. advanced both in agriculture and industry
   B. specialised in industry but not in agriculture
   C. backward both in agriculture and industry
   D. specialised in agriculture but not in industry
   E. borrowing all its requirements from abroad

2. What, according to the passage, will be the achievement of inducing improvement in technology?
   A. Higher specialisation in agriculture
   B. Better employment opportunities
   C. Beneficial effects on quality of life of people
   D. Relieving the pressure of employment in industry
   E. None of these

3. What could be done, according to the passage, to induce improvement in agricultural technology?
   A. Import of better agricultural technology
   B. Providing better weather forecasts
   C. To relieve pressure of labour on land
   D. Providing irrigation facilities
   E. None of these

4. According to the passage, in underdeveloped countries
   A. agriculture is in a primitive stage
   B. per acre yield is very high
   C. land is available in plenty

D. alternative employment opportunities will have adverse effect on the lives of people

E. significant proportion of working population works in agriculture

5. Why, according to the passage, a country specialised in agriculture only cannot become a high income country?
   A. It simply cannot borrow all its industrial requirements from abroad
   B. It can absorb only a fraction of its working population
   C. Agriculture needs huge investments and infrastructural facilities
   D. Technological advancements in agriculture has limitations
   E. None of these

6. Which of the following statements is TRUE in the context of the passage?
   A. Underdeveloped countries are rapidly growing industrially
   B. Technologically developed agriculture solves all the problems of unemployment
   C. Relief of the pressure of labour on land raises yields per acre
   D. Yield per acre and yield per man are unrelated
   E. Surplus in agriculture is spent for domestic purposes

7. Which of the following statements is NOT TRUE in the context of the passage?
   A. Theoretically there could be a country specialised entirely in agriculture
   B. Capital is required to increase the per acre yield of the land
   C. Agriculture surplus will rise if there are fewer mouths to feed
   D. Technologically developed agriculture will absorb most of the working population on the available land
   E. A rural community maintains all its members and expects everyone to share in the work

8. Which of the following is most OPPOSITE in meaning of the work ADVERSE as used in the passage?

A. Negative   B. Facilitating
C. Supplementary   D. Derogative
E. Decorative

9. Which of the following is most nearly the SAME in meaning as the word INDUCING as used in the passage?
   A. Causing   B. Augmenting
   C. Reducing   D. Developing
   E. Increasing

10. Which of the following is most nearly the SAME in meaning as the word DIMINISH as used in the passage?
    A. Reduce   B, Shorten
    C. Prohibit   D. Increase
    E. Worsen

PASSAGE-3

Morning and afternoon, all the young girls and maidens used to *gather* around the village well with their water pots. There they exchanged pleasantries, chatted and discussed. Lakshmi was the prettiest girl at the well. But, she was an orphan.

One day, a well-built man came to Lakshmi's house. He brought with him the richest clothes and jewels as presents for her, "I am your dead father's brother," he told the astonished girl. "You have not seen me before because I have been staying abroad. You must come and live with me now." Lakshmi believed his sweet words and in a short time, locked up her little house and set out with the man.

But a terrible surprise was in store for poor Lakshmi when she got to her new-found uncle's home. The man locked her in a room. "I am not your uncle, but a robber. And I am going to marry you," he told her. Lakshmi howled and wept when she heard this. Saying he would be back in a day or two after making arrangements for the wedding, the man went away. Lakshmi continued sobbing for a while and then stopped. "I must think of a plan to escape," she told herself. Lakshmi guessed that the robber would try to enter her room. So she kept near her bed a sharp knife which she could find in the room.

One night the robber did enter her room but Lakshmi did not make any sound. She just kept a tight hold of the knife and pretended to be sound asleep. When the robber was near her bed, she stood up suddenly, brandishing the knife. The robber was taken aback and with a loud cry, he ran out. Lakshmi *gave chase* and he climbed up the nearest tall tree. Lakshmi then gathered some dry figs and sticks around the foot of the tree and set them on fire. On seeing the rising flames, the robber gave a mighty yell and jumped down. But it was such a long way to the ground that he broke a couple of bones and was unable to move away from the place he fell.

In the mean time, the police was informed by someone about the robber. Very soon they reached the spot and arrested the robber. The people who had gathered at the spot were all praise for Lakshmi's courage and presence of mind,

1. The reason given by the man for his inability to meet Lakshmi was that
   A. he had not known earlier where she lived
   B. he was not friendly terms with her father
   C. he was living in a foreign country
   D. he was not sure whether she would recognise him
   E. he was staying in another village, far away from her place

2. Why did Lakshmi go with the man?
   A. She was convinced that the man was her uncle
   B. She wanted to accompany him and then get him arrested by the police
   C. She intended to teach him a good lesson
   D. She wanted the man to marry her
   E. She felt it necessary to verify his claim by accompanying him

3. Why did the robber run out of the room?
   A. He was stabbed by Lakshmi
   B. He got scared of the rising flames
   C. Lakshmi told him to go out as fast as possible
   D. He was afraid that Lakshmi would strike him with the knife
   E. He ran out to catch hold of Lakshmi and bring her back

4. How was the robber injured?
   A. Lakshmi stabbed him with the sharp knife
   B. He fell down accidently while climbing the tree
   C. He was beaten by Lakshmi and his bones were broken
   D. He jumped down from the tree to save his life
   E. He got burnt in the rising flames

5. *"But a terrible surprise was in store ..... uncle's home."* What is the "terrible surprise" that is being referred to?
   A. The man told her that her father was dead
   B. The man refused to marry her
   C. The man took away her ornaments and locked her in a room
   D. The man told her that he was her real uncle
   E. The man turned out to be a robber interested in marrying her

6. Where did the robber apparently go after locking up Lakshmi?
   A. He went to her house to loot all the things
   B. He went out to bring a sharp knife
   C. He went away to bring clothes and jewels for her
   D. He went away to make preparations for his marriage
   E. He went out to bring the priest for performing the wedding ceremony

7. Which of the following is most nearly the SAME in meaning as the phrase, GAVE CHASE as used in the passage?
   A. escaped   B. continued
   C. followed   D. prevented
   E. raced

8. Which of the following is TRUE in the context of the passage?
   A. Lakshmi told the robber to climb up the tall tree
   B. At night, the robber entered Lakshmi's room with a knife
   C. Lakshmi had no near relatives and she stayed alone
   D. The robber started running after jumping from the tree
   E. The people who had gathered at the spot set fire to the tree

9. Which of the following is most OPPOSITE in meaning of the word GATHER as used in the passage?
   A. Collect
   B. Reduce
   C. Distribute
   D. Break
   E. Disperse

10. Which of the following statements is NOT TRUE in the context of the passage?
    A. The police was summoned by Lakshmi herself
    B. The well-built man was not the real brother of Lakshmi's father
    C. When the robber entered the room at night, Lakshmi was awake
    D. Lakshmi used to go to the village well to collect water
    E. Lakshmi's guess regarding the robber turned out to be correct

PASSAGE-4

Progress in life depends a good deal on crossing one threshold after another. Some time ago, a man watched his little nephew try to write his name. It was hardwork, very hardwork. The little boy had arrived at an effort threshold. Today he writes his name with comparative ease. No new threshold confronts him. This is the way with all of us. As soon as we cross one threshold, as soon as we conquer one difficulty, a new difficulty appears, or should appear. Some people make the mistake of steering clear of thresholds. Anything that requires genuine thinking and use of energy they avoid. They prefer to stay in a rut where thresholds are not met. Probably, they have been at their job a number of years. Things are easy for them. They make no effort to seek out new obstacles to overcome. Real progress stops under such circumstances.

Some middle-aged and elderly people greatly enrich their lives by continuing to cross thresholds. One man went into an entirely new business when he was past middle life and made success of it, De Morgan didn't start to write novels until he was past sixty. Psychologists have discovered that man can continue to learn throughout his life. And it is undoubtedly better to try and fail than not to try at

all. There one can be placed in the category of the Swiss mountaineer of whom it was said, *"He died climbing"*. When a new difficulty arises to obstruct your path, do not complain. Accept the challenge. Determine to cross this threshold as you have crossed numerous other thresholds in your past. In the words of a poet, do not rest but strive *to pass from dream to grander dream.*

1. What obstructs real progress in life?
   A. Remaining at one and the same post
   B. Avoiding the thinking and energy
   C. Shunning every work
   D. Stopping education
   E. Worrying about the future

2. What does progress in life depend upon?
   A. Good habits
   B. Hardwork
   C. Overcoming one difficulty after another
   D. Spirit of service and cooperation
   E. None of these

3. What does *He died climbing* signify?
   A. He died when he was climbing the hill
   B. He died before getting at the top
   C. He strove hard till the last moment of life
   D. He climbed the hill and then died
   E. He found it difficult to climb

4. What does *to pass from dream to grander dream* mean?
   A. Always having greater and greater aspiration in life
   B. Seeing one good dream and then greater aspiration in life
   C. Making plan after plan
   D. Seeing one dream after the other
   E. None of these

5. What did the man entering a new business past middle life do of his business?
   A. He miserably failed in it
   B. He achieved partial success
   C. He dropped the business after sometime
   D. He achieved good success in it
   E. He started writing novels

6. How can you accomplish the most difficult tasks?

A. By mobilizing all possible resources
B. By avoiding all obstacles
C. By sticking to hardwork
D. By getting other people to do your work for you
E. By doing it bit by bit and persisting in the effort

7. What does De Morgan's life teach?
   A. That it is futile to learn many things
   B. That one is never old in case he has vigour
   C. That it is never too late to learn
   D. That creative writing can be made even late in life
   E. None of these

8. How do middle-aged and elderly people add brilliance to their lives?
   A. By overcoming difficulty one after another
   B. By getting sycophants to surround them
   C. By making fine speeches
   D. By acquiring resourcefulness
   E. None of these

9. What should we do when a new difficulty obstructs our path?
   A. Run away from it
   B. Be bold and face it
   C. Manoeuvre to get it removed
   D. Enlist other people's help to get it over
   E. None of these

10. When did De Morgan start to write novels?
    A. When he was sixty years old
    B. When he was below sixty
    C. When he studied psychology
    D. When he was a student
    E. None of these

PASSAGE-5

In terms of the total energy consumed by different sectors, the largest consumer is understandably the industrial sector, which accounts for nearly half the total energy used in the country today. This is followed by the transport sector which consumes about 25%, the household sector (about 14%) and the agricultural sector (about 9%). This last sector has shown considerable increase in energy use over the last four decades. Among the primary fuels, the relative proportion of coal has dropped from nearly 80% to 40% and that of oil has gone up from 17% to 44% over the same period.

Total energy consumption in India today is equivalent to 291 million tons of oil of which 26% comes from wood. On a per capita basis it works out to about one litre of oil per day, which is extremely low by international standards. The future energy demand depends upon the level of development envisaged and also on the sections of people to be affected by it.

The energy disparity between the urban and the rural population is at present *as wide as* between nations on a *worldwide scale.* There is apparently a greater need to provide energy in the rural areas and to improve the efficiency of energy use than merely to increase the national figures for energy consumption limiting its use to those who are getting the bulk share already.

With the projected rate of population growth, improving upon the per capita energy consumption is a Herculean task as our coal reserves and the capacity to import oil cannot be increased beyond a point. *There is clearly no escape* from the utilisation of renewable energy sources in a big way if the gap between the desired levels of energy supply and available resources has to be kept at the minimum.

1. The author is laying greater emphasis on which of the following?
   (*a*) Efficient use of energy
   (*b*) Increasing national indices for energy consumption
   (*c*) Controlling population growth
   A. Only (*a*)   B. Only (*b*)
   C. Only (*c*)   D. All the three
   E. Both (*b*) and (*c*)

2. The author feels that increasing per capita use of energy is
   A. rather difficult, but not impossible
   B. not easy, but certainly achievable
   C. not at all desirable
   D. a matter of great difficulty
   E. a routine matter

3. According to the passage, the energy requirement of the future will be decided on the basis of which of the following?
   (a) Total energy already consumed by us in the past
   (b) Level of development of oil industry
   (c) Profile of the affected people
   A. Only (a)   B. Only (b)
   C. Only (c)   D. Both (a) and (b)
   E. Both (b) and (c)

4. Which of the following shows correctly the different sectors consuming energy arranged in ascending order?
   A. Agriculture, transport, household, industrial
   B. Agriculture, household, transport, industrial
   C. Industrial, transport, household, agriculture
   D. Industrial, household, agriculture, transport
   E. None of these

5. Which of the following has been suggested by the author as the best possible solution to overcome energy crisis?
   A. Importing large quantities of coal
   B. Exploration of oil reserves
   C. Reducing share of bulk users
   D. Maximisation of renewable sources
   E. Reducing the energy disparity between urban and rural areas

6. Which of the following styles has been adopted by the author?
   A. Unsubstantiated arguments and views
   B. Data based, but coloured by socialism
   C. Highly subjective with bias for rural people
   D. Objective, descriptive, lacking clarity
   E. Data based, objective, positive, solution oriented

7. Which of the following has been mentioned as a major hurdle in enhancing per capita consumption of energy in India?
   A. Present level of development in India
   B. Increased use of energy in agriculture sector
   C. Disparity in use of energy in rural and urban areas
   D. International norm of 1 litre of oil per day per person
   E. None of these

8. Which of the following statements is TRUE in the context of the passage?
   A. The household sector has shown considerable increase in energy use
   B. Use of oil has increased from 40% to 80%
   C. Industrial sector uses 50% of total energy used in India
   D. Energy consumption in India is 26% of world consumption
   E. Import of oil to the extent required is quite possible

9. *The energy disparity ..... as wide as ..... worldwide scale*, the first sentence of third paragraph means
   A. disparity in urban and rural is observed in all nations
   B. in no other nation such disparity is observed
   C. developed countries consume more energy than developing countries
   D. worldwide scale is different for rural and urban areas
   E. None of these

10. *There is clearly no escape .....* means.....
   A. there is a way out, but it is ambiguous
   B. there is a problem, but without solution
   C. there is also no solution to this
   D. there is hardly any alternative except
   E. there is more than one way

PASSAGE-6

Peace and order are necessary, not just in our own country but also at the international level, if we are to secure national progress and development. The different countries in the world are coming closer today due to faster means of transport and communication. Economically, they are becoming increasingly interdependent. If peace is disturbed in one part of the world, it has adverse effects in other parts of the world as well. Nuclear weapons have already threatened the world with nuclear war. If the conflicts between different nations are not settled in time, they might *culminate* in a nuclear war destroying the whole world. It is therefore, in our own interest that the world is free of conflicts. If at all there are any, they must be settled promptly and peace should be restored. That is why we have declared the establishment of international peace and understanding as an objective of our foreign policy.

We need the help and cooperation of other countries for our scientific, industrial and economic development, especially in those fields where we have yet to achieve self-sufficiency. We obtain the latest machinery, technology and financial aid from the developed countries. On our part we too offer help to the under-developed countries. We are keen on maintaining friendly relations with other countries. Such friendly relations *foster* international understanding.

We have always exerted ourselves to see that the disputes arising between the different nations are settled through peaceful negotiations. We play an active role in the United Nations, the South Asian Association for Regional Cooperation, the Commonwealth of Nations and other such international organisations. We make it a point to participate in the international conferences on issues like energy crisis, environmental imbalance, nuclear arms race etc. We always offer a helping hand to other nations affected by natural calamities such as famines, earthquakes, floods and so on. We strive to maintain peaceful and friendly relations with our neighbouring countries. *Why do we do all this!* We sincerely believe that conflicts in today's world should be minimised, making way for better cooperation among the nations. If this is achieved, human resources will no longer be wasted in things like war or aggression. There will be no destruction of wealth. We believe that, in a peaceful world, there will be greater scope for the economic and cultural development of countries.

1. According to the passage, maintaining friendly relations with other countries facilitate
   A. developing international understanding
   B. exchange of scientists and technologists
   C. strategic planning in defence matters
   D. import and export of several vital commodities
   E. None of these

2. If conflicts between nations do not cease
   A. international bodies will have to take up these issues

   B. international understanding will not be fostered
   C. nuclear war will destroy the whole world
   D. the means of transport and communication will be disrupted

3. Which of the following is obtained by us from the developed countries, according to the passage?
   A. Fertilisers   B. Foodgrains
   C. Leather Products   D. Technology
   E. Crude Oil

4. Which of the following according to the passage, is facilitating the process of different countries coming together?
   A. Emerging world order
   B. Asian Association for Regional Cooperation
   C. Our participation in international conferences
   D. Need for self-sufficiency
   E. Faster means of transport and communication

5. Minimising the conflicts and making way for better cooperation among the nations will result in
   A. useful and purposive utilisation of human resources
   B. better utilisation of means of transport and communication
   C. culmination of nuclear war destroying the world
   D. keenness on maintaining friendly relations with other countries
   E. preservation of our national unity and integrity

6. Which of the following statements is NOT TRUE in the context of the passage?
   A. International conflicts must be settled promptly
   B. We try to maintain friendly relations with our neighbours
   C. We participate in many international conferences
   D. Friendly relations with other countries foster international understanding

E. Each country can be considered isolated and insulated from the effects of other countries

7. Which of the following words is largely SIMILAR in meaning of the word CULMINATE as used in the passage?
A. Reach the highest point
B. Stretch to the maximum
C. Absolute standards
D. Total destruction
E. Coming of age

8. Which of the following words is MOST OPPOSITE in meaning of the word FOSTER as used in the passage?
A. Advocate   B. Hinder
C. Obviate   D. Facilitate
E. Jettison

9. The question "Why do we do all this" is asked in the passage in which of the following contexts?
A. We always offer a helping hand to other nations in improving their technology
B. We endeavour to maintain peaceful and friendly relations with our neighbours
C. We obtain the latest machinery, technology and financial aid from the developed countries
D. We have shaped our foreign policy in a balanced and purposeful manner
E. None of these

10. Does any of the following sentences contain any idea expressed in the passage?
A. We have to make conscious efforts to preserve our national unity
B. Our country is huge in size and population where many languages are spoken
C. We have adopted the objective of democracy in the interest of overall development of our country
D. Citizens must be well-informed about public issues in order to participate meaningfully in public
E. None of these statements contain any idea expressed in the passage

PASSAGE-7

There is a fairly universal sentiment that the use of nuclear weapon is clearly contrary to morality and that its production does not go far enough. These activities are not only opposed to morality but also to law and if the legal objection can be added to the moral, the argument against the use and the manufacture of these weapons will considerably be reinforced. Now the time is ripe to evaluate the responsibility of scientists who knowingly use their expertise for the construction of such weapons which has *deleterious* effect on mankind.

To this must be added the fact that more than 50 per cent of the skilled scientific manpower in the world is how engaged in the armaments industry. How appropriate it is that all this valuable skill should be *devoted* to the manufacture of weapons of death in a world of poverty is a question that must touch the scientific conscience.

A meeting of biologists on the Long-Term Worldwide Biological Consequences of Nuclear War added frightening dimensions to those forecasts. Its report suggested that the long biological effects resulting from climatic changes may at least be as serious as the immediate ones.

Subfreezing temperatures, low light levels and high dose of ionizing and ultraviolet radiation extending for many months, after a large-scale nuclear war, could destroy the biological support systems of civilization, at least in the Northern Hemisphere. Productivity in natural and agricultural ecosystems could be severely restricted for a year or more. Post-war survivors would face starvation as well as freezing conditions in the dark and be exposed to near-lethal dose of radiation. If, as now seems possible, the Southern Hemisphere were affected also, global disruption of the biosphere could ensue. In any event, there would be severe consequences, even in the areas not affected directly, because of the interdependence of the world economy. In either case the extinction of a large fraction of the earth's animals, plants, and microorganism seems possible. The population size of Homo Sapiens conceivably could be reduced to pre-historic levels or below and extinction of the human species itself cannot be excluded.

1. The author's most important objective of writing the above passage seems to
   A. highlight the use of nuclear weapons as an effective population control measure
   B. illustrate the devastating effects of use of nuclear weapons on mankind
   C. duly highlight the supremacy of the nations which possess nuclear weapons
   D. summarise the long biological effects of use of nuclear weapons
   E. explain scientifically the climatic changes resulting from use of nuclear weapons

2. The scientists possessing expertise in manufacturing destructive weapons are
   A. very few in number
   B. irresponsible and incompetent
   C. more than half of the total number
   D. engaged in the armaments industry against their desire
   E. not conscious of the repercussions of their actions

3. According to the passage, the argument against the use and manufacture of nuclear weapons
   A. does not stand the test of legality
   B. possess legal strength although it does not have moral standing
   C. is acceptable only on moral grounds
   D. becomes stronger if legal and moral considerations are combined
   E. None of these

4. Which of the following is one of the consequences of Nuclear War?
   A. Fertility of land will last only for a year or so
   B. Post-war survivors being very few will have abundant food
   C. Lights would be cooler and more comfortable
   D. Southern hemisphere would remain quite safe in the post-war period
   E. None of these

5. Choose the word which is MOST OPPOSITE in meaning of the word DELETERIOUS as used in the passage.

A. Beneficial   B. Harmful
C. Irreparable   D. Non-cognizable
E. Revolutionary

6. The author of the passage seems to be of the view that
   A. utilization of scientific skills in manufacture of weapons is appropriate
   B. the evaluation of the scientists' expertise show their incompetence
   C. manufacture of weapons of death would help eradication of poverty
   D. spending money on manufacture of weapons may be justifiable subject to the availability of funds
   E. utilization of valuable knowledge for manufacture of lethal weapons is inhuman

7. Which of the following BEST EXPLAINS the word DEVOTED as used in the passage?
   A. dedicated for a good cause
   B. utilized for betterment
   C. abused for destruction
   D. underutilized
   E. overutilized

8. It appears from the passage that the use of nuclear weapons is considered against morality by
   A. only such of those nations who cannot afford to manufacture weapons
   B. almost all the nations of the world
   C. only the superpowers who can afford to manufacture and sell weapons
   D. a minority group of scientists who have the necessary skill and competence
   E. most of the scientists who devote their valuable skills to manufacture nuclear weapons

9. Which of the following statement(s) *(a)*, *(b)* and/ or *(c)* is/are definitely true in the context of the passage?
   (a) Living organisms in the areas which are not directly affected by the consequences of nuclear war would also suffer
   (b) There is a likelihood of extinction of the human species as a consequence of nuclear war

(c) The post-war survivors would be exposed to the risk of near-lethal radiation
A. Only *(a)*   B. Only *(b)*
C. Only *(c)*   D. Only *(a)* and *(b)*
E. All the three

10. The biological consequences of nuclear war as given in the passage include all the following except
A. fall in temperature below zero degree celsius
B. ultraviolet radiation
C. high dose of ionizing
D. low light levels
E. None of these

PASSAGE-8

Mahatma Gandhi has repeatedly called himself a truthseeker and has learned, in the course of his search, that truth is a condition of being, not a quality outside of oneself or a moral acquisition, that it is of the very essence of the divine in man. Though he saw deceit and falsehood all around him and knew that it was accepted as the standard of life by people occupying positions of authority and influence, he was never afterwards tempted to *yield to* it even when to have done so would have brought advantage and no condemnation.

For healing he always had a great love and some aptitude and when at the age of seventeen *his family in conclave* suggested his going to England to study law, he *begged* to be allowed to study medicine instead. This, however, was not permitted and law was chosen for him. But, the love of healing remained, and though he could not study in the *orthodox* schools of medicine, he *gratified* his desire by studying various forms of nature-cure treatment and by experimenting with these on his person and on his friends and relatives. Some of these experiments produced remarkable results possibly not only due to the treatment but also to his devoted and instinctive nursing.

1. On whom did Gandhiji practice nature-cure?
A. On sick patients in hospitals
B. On people occupying positions of authority and influence
C. Those who were in great need of the treatment

D. Those who were not cured by other medicines
E. None of these

2. Gandhiji studied law mainly because
A. he wanted to be an eminent lawyer
B. he wanted to go to England
C. his family thrust upon him the study of law
D. he knew he can make a good career in legal profession
E. he wanted to serve people by solving their legal problems

3. What was Gandhiji's idea of truth?
A. It should be assimilated as a personal quality
B. It should be observed with a healing touch
C. It should not be followed with an idea of sacrifice
D. It should be searched in the world around you
E. None of these

4. Mahatma Gandhi described himself as a man:
A. in search of divine qualities
B. who would like to serve people
C. who would like to set standard of life
D. who would not compromise on his principles
E. None of these

5. Choose the word that is MOST OPPOSITE in meaning of the word BEGGED as used in the passage.
A. Demanded   B. Appealed
C. Suggested   D. Requested
E. Protested

6. Choose the word which is MOST OPPOSITE in meaning of the word ORTHODOX as used in the passage.
A. Backward   B. Non-conventional
C. Unpopular   D. Modern
E. Customary

7. What temptation did Gandhiji always resist?
A. Getting attracted towards wordly comforts
B. Ignoring the dictates of elderly people
C. Healing the wound of other
D. Following deceit and falsehood
E. None of these

8. What was probably the real cause of Gandhiji's success in nature-cure?
   A. His detailed study of various medicinal systems
   B. His confidence and desire to help people
   C. His skills and aptitude in nursing
   D. His experiments in search of truth
   E. None of these

9. What did Mahatma Gandhi learn in the course of his search?
   A. Being truthful is a divine blessing
   B. Truth is synonymous with one's existence
   C. People are full of deceit and falsehood
   D. Truth is a quality outside of oneself
   E. None of these

10. What did Gandhiji see around him?
    A. Sick and unhealthy people
    B. People accepting proper standard of life
    C. People suffering from poverty and disease
    D. People not having love and aptitude for healing
    E. Dishonesty and untruthfulness

11. Explain the meaning of expression 'his family in conclave' as used in the passage.
    A. Members of the family and relatives
    B. Figurehead of the family
    C. Private meeting of the family
    D. Family meeting for celebrating Gandhiji's seventeenth birthday
    E. None of these

12. Choose the word that is most nearly the SAME in meaning as the word GRATIFIED as used in the passage.
    A. Purified   B. Satisfied
    C. Nurtured   D. Glorified
    E. Projected

13. Choose the word which is most nearly the SAME in meaning as the word YIELD as used in the passage.
    A. Surrender   B. Provoke
    C. Confine   D. Adapt
    E. Adhere

14. Which of the following statements is NOT TRUE in the context of the passage?

A. Gandhiji did many experiments in the area of nature-cure
B. Gandhiji did not study medicine in the orthodox school
C. Studying law was Gandhiji's first love
D. Truthfulness is the condition of being
E. Gandhiji was always a truthseeker

15. Which of the following statement(s) is/are true in the context of the passage?
    (a) Gandhiji had a love and aptitude for nursing
    (b) Gandhiji experimented nature-cure on himself
    (c) Gandhiji encouraged deceit and psychofancy
    A. Only (a)   B. (a) and (c)
    C. Only (c)   D. (a) and (b)
    E. Only (b)

PASSAGE-9

Believe it or not, once a wonderful plate made of gold fell from heaven into the court of a temple at Banares. On the plate these words were inscribed: "A gift from Heaven to him who loves best." The priest at once made a proclamation that everyday, all those who would like to claim the plate should *assemble* at the temple to have their kind deeds *judged*.

Everyday for a whole year all kinds of holy men, hermits, scholars and nobles came and related to the priests their deeds of charity. The priests heard their claims. At last they decided that the one who seemed to be the greatest lover of mankind was a rich man who had every year given all his wealth to the-poor. So they gave him the plate of gold. But when he took it in his hand, it *turned* to worthless lead. When he dropped it in his amazement on to the floor, it became gold again.

For another year claimants came and the priests presented the heavenly gift three times. But the same thing happened, showing that Heaven did not consider these men *worthy* of the gift.

Meanwhile a large number of beggars came and lay about the temple gate, hoping that the claimants who came would give them alms to prove they were worthy of the golden plate. It was a good thing for the beggars because the pilgrims gave them money but showed no sympathy, nor even a look of pity.

At last a peasant who had heard nothing about the plate of gold came near the temple. He was so *touched* by the sight of the miserable beggars that he wept. When he saw a poor blind and maimed wretch at the temple gate, he knelt at his side and *comforted* him with kind words. When this peasant went inside the temple, he was shocked to find it full of men boasting of their kind deeds and quarrelling with the priests. The priest who held the golden plate in his hand saw the peasant standing there and beckoned to him to know what he wanted. The peasant went near the priest and knowing nothing about the plate, accidentally touched it. At once it shone out with three times its former splendour and the priest said: "Son, the gift is yours, for you are the one who loves best."

1. The gift from Heaven was meant for those who
   A. were scholars
   B. were highly religious and loved God best
   C. gave money to the poor
   D. loved others in the best way
   E. were poor peasants

2. What did the peasant see inside the temple?
   A. Miserable beggars and blind men
   B. Priests quarrelling among themselves
   C. People speaking high of their kind deeds and fighting with the priests
   D. The golden plate being converted to worthless lead
   E. None of these

3. For which of the following was the proclamation made by the priest?
   A. To find the richest person in the town
   B. To find the rightful owner of the plate
   C. To judge the worth of the golden plate
   D. To judge his own deeds with the help of the people

4. What happened to the plate when it was touched by the peasant?

   A. It started glowing with greater splendour
   B. It changed from gold to lead
   C. It became heavier and fell on the ground
   D. It turned into gold
   E. Not mentioned in the passage

5. The rich man dropped the golden plate to the floor as he was
   A. not intersted in possessing it
   B. afraid of holding it
   C. curious to know about its purity
   D. surprised to see it turning to lead
   E. the rightful owner of the plate

6. Why did the beggars stay near the temple gate? They
   A. wanted to prove their claim on the golden plate
   B. had come to pray in the temple
   C. knew that the visitors would give them alms
   D. wanted to seek the sympathy of the peasant
   E. wanted to have a glimpse of the golden plate

7. The priests could decide on the rightful owner of the plate when the peasant
   A. met with an accident
   B. entered the temple and stood there
   C. put forward his claim on the heavenly gift
   D. touched the plate unknowingly
   E. comforted the poor blind man with kind words

8. Which of the following statements is TRUE in the context of the passage?
   A. The rich man did not turn out to be the greatest lover of humanity
   B. The peasant touched the plate to know whether he was its rightful owner
   C. The priest told the peasant to narrate his kind deeds
   D. The plate shone out in splendour when the peasant dropped it on the floor
   E. The peasant went near the priest to ask for the golden plate

9. What made the peasant weep?
   A. The quarrel between the priests and some people

B. The greediness of the rich people

C. The boastful crowd inside the temple

D. The pitiable condition of the beggars

E. None of the above

Directions (Qs. 10 to 12): *Choose the word which is most nearly the SAME in meaning as the word given in BOLD as used in the passage.*

10. TURNED
    A. bent   B. moved
    C. changed   D. revolved
    E. fell

11. WORTHY
    A. useful   B. promising
    C. successful   D. necessary
    E. deserving

12. JUDGED
    A. ordered   B. justified
    C. announced   D. explainded
    E. assessed

Directions (Qs. 13 to 15): *Choose the word which is most OPPOSITE in meaning of the word given in BOLD as used in the passage.*

13. COMFORTED
    A. consoled   B. ignored
    C. advised   D. scolded
    E. controlled

14. ASSEMBLE
    A. distribute   B. gather
    C. partition   D. disperse
    E. dismantle

15. TOUCHED
    A. moved   B. indifferent
    C. disconnected   D. excited
    E. arrogant

PASSAGE-10

A struggle for power began with Bimbisara and Ajatshatru of the Kingdom of Magadha. In the 4th century BC, the Nandas came to power, with their capital at Pataliputra. The latter were replaced by the Mauryas at the close of the same century. This came about partly as a result of Alexander's invasion and the decline of Iranian strength in India.

Chandragupta Maurya took advantage of the unsettled conditions and with the help of his adviser Kautilya, built the first great empire in India. Under him and his two great successors, Bindusara and Ashoka, almost the whole of India, with the exception of the farthest south, was unified into one empire.

Many important developments took place in the social, economic and cultural life of the Indian people in this period—322 to 184 BC. Particularly important was the spread of Buddhism, which had been introduced earlier.

The decline of the Mauryan Empire after the rule of Ashoka was followed by a long period of new invasions and the formation of small states. Of the foreign invasions, the first was that of the Greeks who were the rulers of Bactria. They conquered the Punjab and parts of Sind and their contact had a lasting influence on the culture of India. Gandhara style of art emerged and flourished. The greatest Greek ruler in India was Menander (Milinda) in the 2nd century BC, who became a Buddhist.

The Greek invasion was followed by that of the Sakas. The Sakas displaced the Greek in Bactria and spread their power in Western India. One of the Saka kings was Rudradaman who, as the name suggests, was a devotee of Siva. He was responsible for important irrigation works in Saurashtra. The Sakas, like other invaders, became a part of Indian life and played an important role in the development of Indian Culture. Another group of invaders from Central Asia was that of the Kushanas early in the first century AD. The greatest of the Kushana rulers was Kanishka who, according to some historians, started the Saka Era in AD 78. Kanishka ruled his vast empire in India and Central Asia from Purushapura (modern Peshwar) for 40 years. Kanishka's empire brought to India the cultural tradition of Iran, Greece and Rome. It also provided a stimulus to trade between India and other parts of the world Kanishka patronised the Mahayan form of Buddhism. It spread to Central Asia during this period and from there to China, Korea and Japan. The Kushana Empire declined in the third century AD.

1. A suitable title for the above passage is
   A. Alexander's invasion of India
   B. Kanishka, the great Kushana ruler
   C. Development of India's Culture
   D. India—the Period of Empires
   E. None of these

2. The Kingdom of Magadha was ruled by the Nandas about
   A. 2000 years ago
   B. 2400 years ago
   C. 2800 years ago
   D. over 3000 years ago
   E. None of these

3. The successors of the Nandas, whose capital was at Pataliputra, were the
   A. Greeks   B. Iranians
   C. Mauryas   D. Sakas
   E. None of these

4. The cultural traditions of Iran, Greece and Rome came to India during the rule of
   A. Ashoka   B. Kanishka
   C. Menander   D. Rudradaman
   E. None of these

5. Who, amongst the following, had their capital at Purushapura (modern Peshawar)?
   A. The Mauryans   B. The Nandas
   C. The Kushanas   D. The Sakas
   E. None of these

6. The Saka Era is believed to have been established by
   A. the Kushanas
   B. Milinda, the Greek ruler
   C. the Nandas
   D. The Sakas
   E. None of these

7. All of the following were foreign invaders of India, except
   A. the Greeks   B. the Kushanas
   C. the Mauryas   D. the Sakas
   E. None of these

8. The greatest Greek ruler in India was
   A. Ajatshatru   B. Bimbisara
   C. Bindusara   D. Milinda
   E. None of these

9. Who were the founders of the first great unified empire in India?
   A. The Mauryans   B. The Nandas
   C. The Kushanas   D. The Sakas
   E. None of these

10. Which particularly important development took place in India between 322 to 184 BC?
   A. The rulers of Bactria invaded India
   B. Buddhism spread far and wide
   C. The Sakas displaced the Greeks
   D. Gandhara style of art attained its zenith
   E. None of these

ANSWERS

PASSAGE-1

1	2	3	4	5	6	7	8	9	10
D	B	A	E	B	A	B	A	A	D

PASSAGE-2

1	2	3	4	5	6	7	8	9	10
D	E	C	E	B	C	D	B	B	A

PASSAGE-3

1	2	3	4	5	6	7	8	9	10
C	A	D	D	E	D	C	C	E	A

PASSAGE-4

1	2	3	4	5	6	7	8	9	10
A	C	C	A	D	E	B	A	B	E

PASSAGE-5

1	2	3	4	5	6	7	8	9	10
A	D	E	B	D	E	E	C	C	D

PASSAGE-6

1	2	3	4	5	6	7	8	9	10
A	C	D	E	A	E	A	B	B	E

PASSAGE-7

1	2	3	4	5	6	7	8	9	10
B	C	D	A	A	E	C	B	E	E

PASSAGE-8

1	2	3	4	5	6	7	8	9	10
E	C	A	A	E	B	D	C	B	E

11	12	13	14	15
C	B	A	C	D

PASSAGE-9

1	2	3	4	5	6	7	8	9	10
D	C	B	A	D	C	D	A	D	C

11	12	13	14	15
E	E	D	D	B

PASSAGE-10

1	2	3	4	5	6	7	8	9	10
C	D	C	B	C	A	C	D	A	B

Synonyms & Antonyms

There are thousands of words in English language. No one can remember their meanings easily but with regular practice one can memorise most of them. A number of words with their Synonyms and Antonyms are compiled here. Try to learn as many as you can and answer the questions thereafter.

Words	Synonyms	Antonyms
Abandon	Cease, Forsake	Continue
Abhor	Hate, Loathe, Detest	Like, Love
Abiding	Enduring, Durable	Fleeting
Able	Proficient, Competent	Incompetent, Unfit
Ability	Skill, Power	Disability, Inability
Abortive	Fruitless, Futile	Fruitful, Successful
Abolish	Destroy, Undo	Restore, Revive
Abridge	Shorten, Curtail	Lengthen, Expand
Absolve	Forgive, Pardon, Excuse	Condemn
Accelerate	Hasten	Retard
Accord	Agreement, Harmony	Discord, Disagreement
Accumulate	Collect, Store, Amass	Distribute, Scatter
Adamant	Hard, Inflexible	Flexible
Adversity	Misfortune, Distress	Prosperity
Adept	Expert, Skillful	Inexpert, Unskillful
Aggravate	Heighten, Intensify	Quell, Suppress
Agile	Nimble	Clumsy, Undeft
Alert	Vigilant	Heedless
Allay	Calm, Soothe, Assuage	Arouse
Ameliorate	Improve, Advance, Amend	Worsen, Deteriorate
Ambiguous	Vague, Unclear	Clear
Amiable	Lovable, Agreeable	Disagreeable
Annihilate	Destroy	Create
Arduous	Hard, Strenuous	Easy

Words	Synonyms	Antonyms
Attacks	Assault	Defend
Audacity	Boldness	Cowardice
Auspicious	Favourable, Propitious, Lucky	Ominous, Inauspicious, Unlucky
Austere	Harsh, Severe, Rigorous	Easy-going
Authentic	True, Genuine	Spurious, False
Avarice	Greed	Generosity
Averse	Unwilling, Loath, Disinclined	Willing, Inclined
Aversion	Hostility, Hatred	Affinity, Liking
Base	Low, Mean, Ignoble	Noble, Exalted
Boisterous	Noisy, Stormy	Calm, Quiet
Brave	Courageous, Daring, Bold, Plucky	Cowardly, Dastardly, Timid
Brief	Short, Concise, Laconic	Lengthy, Diffuse
Bright	Vivid, Radiant	Dull, Dark
Brutal	Savage, Cruel	Humane, Kindly
Callous	Hard, Cruel, Indifferent	Soft, Tender, Concerned
Cautious	Careful, Wary	Rash, Reckless, Foolhardy
Censure (*n*)	Blame, Condemnation	Praise
Censure (*vb*)	Blame, Condemn	Praise, Commend
Circumscribed	Restricted, Confined, Limited	Unconfined, Unrestricted
Civil	Polite, Courteous, Gracious, Urbane	Rude, Uncivil, Impolite, Ungracious
Coerce	Compel, Force	Volunteer
Compassionate	Pitiful, Sympathetic, Merciful	Unsympathetic, Merciless, Cruel
Compress	Condense, Abbreviate	Expand, Lengthen
Conspicuous	Noticeable, Manifest	Inconspicuous
Constant	Steady, Steadfast, Uniform	Inconstant, Variable
Cordial	Friendly, Warm, Hearty	Cold, Unfriendly
Covert	Hidden, Secret	Overt, Open
Cruel	Savage, Ruthless, Vicious	Kind, Gentle, Benevolent
Cursory	Rapid, Superficial	Thorough, Exhaustive, Intensive
Credible	Believable, Probable, Plausible	Incredible, Unbelievable, Fantastic
Crafty	Cunning, Sly	Artless, Simple, Ingenuous
Costly	Expensive, Dear	Cheap, Inexpensive
Confidence	Trust, Reliance	Distrust, Doubt
Death	Decease, Demise	Existence, Life
Dearth	Scarcity, Lack, Want, Paucity, Shortage	Plenty, Abundance
Decay	Dissolution, Decline, Decomposition, Disintegration	Regeneration

Words	Synonyms	Antonyms
Deference	Respect, Reverence	Disrespect, Irreverence
Deficient	Lacking, Inadequate	Complete, Sufficient
Desolate	Lonely, Deserted	Crowded, Occupied
Destitute	Wanting, Needy	Rich, Affluent
Diligence	Industry, Perseverance	Idleness
Disgrace	Dishonour, Discredit	Honour, Credit
Dwindle	Decrease, Shrink	Grow, Increase
Earthly	Terrestrial, Mundane	Celestial, Heavenly, Unearthly
Eligible	Qualified, Suitable	Ineligible, Unsuitable
Emancipate	Liberate, Free	Enslave
Excited	Impassioned, Stimulated	Composed, Cool, Impassive
Extraordinary	Uncommon, Remarkable, Marvellous	Commonplace, Ordinary
Extravagant	Lavish, Prodigal, Wastrel, Spendthrift	Thrifty, Economical, Frugal
Fabricate	Construct, Make	Destroy
Fabulous	Fictitious, Mythical	Actual, Real
False	Untrue, Mendacious	True, Genuine
Famous	Well-known, Renowned	Obscure, Unknown
Fantastic	Fanciful, Imaginative, Visionary	Practical, Down to earth
Fearful	Nervous, Anxious, Afraid, Scared	Fearless, Dauntless
Felicity	Happiness	Sorrow
Gaiety	Joyousness, Hilarity	Mourning, Dullness
Garrulous	Talkative, Loquacious	Taciturn, Silent, Reserved
Generous	Liberal, Magnanimous	Stingy, Miserly
Gigantic	Huge, Colossal	Minute, Small
Graphic	Vivid, Pictorial, Meaningful	Vague
Guest	Visitor	Host
Guile	Fraud, Trickery	Artlessness, Ingenuousness
Gratitude	Gratefulness	Ingratitude, Ungratefulness
Gratuitous	Voluntary, Spontaneous, Unwarranted	Involuntary, Forced
Hamper	Hinder, Obstruct	Facilitate, Ease
Haughty	Arrogant, Proud	Humble, Modest
Hazardous	Dangerous, Perilous	Safe, Secure Protected
Headstrong	Obstinate, Stubborn	Weak-willed, Flexible

Words	Synonyms	Antonyms
Hope	Belief, Conviction, Expectation	Despair, Hopelessness
Improvident	Prodigal, Carelessness	Provident, Economical
Incessant	Unceasing, Continuous	Discontinuous
Indolent	Slothful, Lethargic	Active, Energetic
Joy	Delight, Pleasure	Sadness, Gloom
Jolly	Jovial, Merry	Gloomy, Sad
Judicious	Discreet, Prudent	Indiscreet, Injudicious
Knowledge	Enlightenment, Learning	Ignorance, Stupidity
Laborious	Industrious, Assiduous	Slothful, Lazy
Laxity	Slackness, Looseness	Firmness
Lenient	Mild, Forbearing	Strict, Stern
Lethal	Deadly, Fatal, Mortal	Life-giving, Vital, Vivifying
Liberal	Generous, Tolerant	Intolerant, Illiberal
Liberty	Freedom, Independence	Slavery, Bondage
Lively	Animated, Active	Dull, Listless
Loyal	Faithful, Devoted	Treacherous, Disloyal, Unfaithful
Lucky	Fortunate	Unlucky, Unfortunate
Lucrative	Profitable	Unprofitable
Magnanimous	Generous, Largehearted	Ungenerous, Stingy
Malady	Illness, Ailment	Health
Manifest	Noticeable, Obvious	Obscure, Puzzling
Meagre	Small	Plentiful, Large
Mean	Low, Abject	Noble, Exalted
Mendacious	False, Untruthful	Truthful
Misery	Sorrow, Distress	Happiness, Joy
Morbid	Sick, Diseased	Healthy
Mournful	Sorrowful, Sad	Joyful, Happy
Negligent	Careless, Heedless	Careful
Notorious	Infamous, Disreputable	Reputable
Obedient	Submissive, Compliant, Docile	Disobedient, Recalcitrant, Wayward
Obsolete	Antiquated, Out-of-Date	Current, Modern
Opportune	Timely, Seasonable	Inopportune
Opulence	Wealth, Riches	Penury, Poverty
Onerous	Heavy, Burdensome	Light, Easy
Palatable	Tasty, Delicious	Unpalatable
Pathetic	Touching	Joyous, Cheery
Persuade	Urge, Induce	Dissuade
Praise (*vb*)	Applaud, Eulogise	Condemn

Words	Synonyms	Antonyms
Praise (*n*)	Applause, Eulogy	Condemnation
Precarious	Risky, Uncertain	Safe, Certain
Pretence	Pretext, Excuse	Candour, Frankness
Propagate	Breed, Circulate	Terminate, Restrict
Quaint	Odd, Singular	Usual, Ordinary
Quell	Suppress, Subdue	Agitate, Arouse
Rare	Uncommon, Scarce	Common, Ordinary
Refined	Polished, Elegant	Crude, Coarse
Remote	Distant	Near, Close
Renown	Fame, Reputation	Infamy, Notoriety
Rigid	Stiff, Unyielding	Flexible, Yielding
Remorseful	Regretful, Repentant	Unrepentant
Rebellion	Revolt, Mutiny, Insurgency	Loyalty
Scared	Holy, Consecrated	Profane, Unholy
Sane	Sensible, Sound	Insane
Scold	Chide, Rebuke	Praise
Serious	Grave, Earnest	Frivolous
Shy	Bashful	Bold, Impudent
Simple	Plain, Artless	Complex, Cunning, Shrewd
Solitary	Single, Lonely, Secluded	Numerous, Multitude
Shallow	Superficial	Deep
Solace	Comfort, Relief	Discomfort, Grief
Spurious	Sham, False	Genuine, Authentic
Stagnant	Still, Motionless	Moving
Surplus	Excess	Deficit, Shortage
Tame	Gentle, Mild, Domesticated	Savage, Wild
Teacher	Instructor, Educator	Student, Pupil
Tedious	Wearisome, Monotonous	Agreeable, Lively
Temporal	Worldly, Secular	Spiritual
Temperate	Moderate	Immoderate, Intemperate
Tortuous	Winding, Circuitous	Straight, Direct
Tough	Hard, Strong	Tender, Soft, Flexible
Transient	Temporary, Fleeting	Lasting, Durable, Permanent
Trusworthy	Reliable	Unreliable, Untrustworthy
Tranquil	Calm	Agitated
Ugly	Unsightly, Repulsive	Beautiful, Attractive
Useful	Advantageous, Serviceable	Useless
Vehemence	Passion, Force	Apathy, Indifference

Words	Synonyms	Antonyms
Vindictive	Revengeful	Forgiving
Wholesome	Healthy	Unwholesome, Morbid, Unhealthy, Diseased
Wicked	Evil, Impious	Pious, Good
Wise	Sagacious, Erudite	Foolish, Stupid
Wrath	Anger, Fury, Rage	Love, Peace, Calm
Wreck	Ruin, Destroy	Create, Construct
Yield	Surrender, Submit	Resist, Revolt
Yielding	Submissive, Supple	Inflexible, Intractable
Yoke	Oppression, Bondage	Freedom
Zeal	Passion, Fervour	Apathy, Indifference
Zest	Relish, Enthusiasm	Distaste, Disrelish

Multiple Choice Questions

Directions (Qs. 1 to 100): *In the following questions choose the words which best expresses the MEANING of the given words.*

1. INDICT
   A. Condemn
   B. Reprimand
   C. Accuse
   D. Allege
   E. Trap

2. SCINTILLATING
   A. Smouldering
   B. Glittering
   C. Touching
   D. Warming
   E. Glowing

3. REFECTORY
   A. Restaurant
   B. Parlour
   C. Living Room
   D. Dining Room
   E. Factory

4. DISTINCTION
   A. Diffusion
   B. Disagreement
   C. Difference
   D. Degree
   E. Honour

5. IMPROVEMENT
   A. Advancement
   B. Betterment
   C. Promotion
   D. Preference
   E. Enhance

6. ADVERSITY
   A. Failure
   B. Helplessness
   C. Misfortune
   D. Crisis
   E. Negativity

7. TURN UP
   A. Land up
   B. Show up
   C. Crop up
   D. Come up
   E. Rotate

8. DEIFY
   A. Flatter
   B. Challenge
   C. Worship
   D. Face
   E. Obstruct

9. ERROR
   A. Misadventure
   B. Misgiving
   C. Ambiguity
   D. Blunder
   E. Flaw

10. SHALLOW
    A. Artificial
    B. Superficial
    C. Foolish
    D. Worthless
    E. Deep

11. MASSACRE
    A. Murder
    B. Stab
    C. Assassinate
    D. Slaughter
    E. Shoot

12. COMBAT
    A. Conflict
    B. Quarrel
    C. Feud
    D. Fight
    E. Jostle

13. VORACIOUS
- A. Wild
- B. Hungry
- C. Angry
- D. Quick
- E. Beautiful

14. IMPROMPTU
- A. Offhand
- B. Unimportant
- C. Unreal
- D. Effective
- E. Punctual

15. RABBLE
- A. Mob
- B. Noise
- C. Roar
- D. Rubbish
- E. Erase

16. TEPID
- A. Hot
- B. Warm
- C. Cold
- D. Boiling
- E. Sticky

17. MAYHEM
- A. Jubilation
- B. Havoc
- C. Excitement
- D. Defeat
- E. Movement

18. TIMID
- A. Fast
- B. Slow
- C. Medium
- D. Shy
- E. Rapid

19. CANTANKEROUS
- A. Quarrelsome
- B. Rash
- C. Disrepectful
- D. Noisy
- E. Obese

20. PRECARIOUS
- A. Cautious
- B. Critical
- C. Perilous
- D. Brittle
- E. Sharp

21. TACITURNITY
- A. Dumbness
- B. Changeableness
- C. Hesitation
- D. Reserveness
- E. Preserve

22. INEBRIATED
- A. Dreamy
- B. Stupefied
- C. Unsteady
- D. Drunken
- E. Broken

23. HARBINGER
- A. Massenger
- B. Steward
- C. Forerunner
- D. Pilot
- E. Performer

24. INTIMIDATE
- A. To hint
- B. Frighten
- C. Bluff
- D. Harass
- E. Inform

25. IRONIC
- A. Inflexible
- B. Bitter
- C. Good-natured
- D. Disguisedly sarcastic
- E. Hard

26. STRINGENT
- A. Tense
- B. Stringy
- C. Strict
- D. Causing to shrink
- E. Liberal

27. ECSTATIC
- A. Animated
- B. Bewildered
- C. Enraptured
- D. Erratic
- E. Gloomy

28. COMMENSURATE
- A. Measurable
- B. Proportionate
- C. Beginning
- D. Appropriate
- E. Finish

29. DESTITUTION
- A. Humility
- B. Moderation
- C. Poverty
- D. Beggary
- E. Orphanage

30. ASCEND
- A. Leap
- B. Grow
- C. Deviate
- D. Mount
- E. Invite

31. UNCOUTH
- A. Ungraceful
- B. Rough
- C. Slovenly
- D. Dirty
- E. Gracious

32. LYNCH
- A. Hang
- B. Madden
- C. Kill
- D. Shoot
- E. Start

33. LAUD
- A. Lord
- B. Eulogy
- C. Praise
- D. Extort
- E. Clap

34. CORRESPONDENCE
- A. Agreements
- B. Contracts
- C. Documents
- D. Letters
- E. News

35. VENUE
- A. Place
- B. Agenda
- C. Time
- D. Duration
- E. Ceremony

36. STERILE
- A. Barren
- B. Arid
- C. Childless
- D. Dry
- E. Fertile

37. SYNOPSIS
- A. Index
- B. Mixture
- C. Summary
- D. Puzzle
- E. End

38. GERMANE
- A. Responsible
- B. Logical
- C. Possible
- D. Relevant
- E. Foreigner

39. PONDER
- A. Think
- B. Evaluate
- C. Anticipate
- D. Increase
- E. Sprinkle

40. CANNY
- A. Obstinate
- B. Handsome
- C. Clever
- D. Stout
- E. Container

41. ABUNDANT
- A. Ripe
- B. Cheap
- C. Plenty
- D. Absent
- E. Closed

42. CONSEQUENCES
- A. Results
- B. Conclusions
- C. Difficulties
- D. Applications
- E. Series

43. SHIVER
- A. Shake
- B. Rock
- C. Tremble
- D. Move
- E. Cry

44. DILIGENT
- A. Progressive
- B. Brilliant
- C. Inventive
- D. Hard-working
- E. Masculine

45. DISTANT
- A. Far
- B. Removed
- C. Reserved
- D. Separate
- E. Unreachable

46. FORAY
- A. Excursion
- B. Contest
- C. Ranger
- D. Intuition
- E. Light

47. FRUGALITY
- A. Foolishness
- B. Extremity
- C. Enthusiasm
- D. Economy
- E. Weakness

48. GARNISH
- A. Paint
- B. Garner
- C. Adorn
- D. Abuse
- E. Attract

49. VIGOUR
- A. Strength
- B. Boldness
- C. Warmth
- D. Enthusiasm
- E. Vitality

50. CANDID
- A. Apparent
- B. Explicit
- C. Frank
- D. Bright
- E. Sweet

51. BRIEF
- A. Limited
- B. Small
- C. Little
- D. Short
- E. Compress

52. GARRULITY
- A. Credulity
- B. Senility
- C. Loquaciousness
- D. Speciousness
- E. Misery

53. FURORE
- A. Excitement
- B. Worry
- C. Flux
- D. Anteroom
- E. Noise

54. NEUTRAL
- A. Unbiased
- B. Non-aligned
- C. Undecided
- D. Indifferent
- E. Unmoved

55. LAMENT
- A. Regret
- B. Comment
- C. Condone
- D. Console
- E. Sadden

56. MASTERLY
  A. Crafty   B. Skillful
  C. Meaningful   D. Cruel
  E. Rightfully

57. MOROSE
  A. Annoyed   B. Gloomy
  C. Moody   D. Displeased
  E. Happy

58. BARE
  A. Uncovered   B. Tolerate
  C. Clear   D. Neat
  E. Least

59. FEEBLE
  A. Weak   B. Vain
  C. Arrogant   D. Sick
  E. Sleek

60. PRESTIGE
  A. Influence   B. Quality
  C. Name   D. Wealth
  E. Strength

61. WARRIOR
  A. Soldier   B. Sailor
  C. Pirate   D. Spy
  E. Juggler

62. ENTIRE
  A. Part   B. Quarter
  C. Whole   D. Half
  E. Tiring

63. RESCUE
  A. Command   B. Help
  C. Defence   D. Safety
  E. Problem

64. INFREQUENT
  A. Never   B. Usual
  C. Rare   D. Sometimes
  E. Often

65. WRETCHED
  A. Poor   B. Foolish
  C. Insane   D. Strained
  E. Broken

66. DIVERSION
  A. Amusement   B. Distortion
  C. Deviation   D. Bylane
  E. Subway

67. AWAKENED
  A. Enlightened   B. Realised
  C. Shook   D. Waken
  E. Walking

68. HESITATED
  A. Stopped   B. Paused
  C. Slowed   D. Postponed
  E. Obstructed

69. PIOUS
  A. Pure   B. Pretentious
  C. Clean   D. Devout
  E. Thirsty

70. TORTURE
  A. Torment   B. Chastisement
  C. Harassment   D. Terror
  E. Beat

71. ATTEMPT
  A. Serve   B. Explore
  C. Try   D. Explain
  E. Chance

72. RESTRAINT
  A. Hindrance   B. Repression
  C. Obstacle   D. Restriction
  E. Tolerance

73. CHASTE
  A. Honest   B. Dignified
  C. Virtuous   D. Noble
  E. Truthful

74. INSOMNIA
  A. Lethargy   B. Sleeplessness
  C. Drunkenness   D. Unconsciousness
  E. Blindness

75. TRANSIENT
  A. Transparent   B. Fleeting
  C. Feeble   D. Fanciful
  E. Flowing

76. MANDACIOUS
  A. Full of confidence   B. False
  C. Encouraging   D. Provocative
  E. Thinkable

77. VORACIOUS
  A. Truthful   B. Gluttonous
  C. Funny   D. Venturous
  E. Fearful

78. CONNOISSEUR
    A. Ignorant   B. Lover of art
    C. Interpreter   D. Delinquent
    E. Officer

79. REPERCUSSION
    A. Clever reply   B. Recollection
    C. Remuneration   D. Reaction
    E. Discussion

80. REPEAL
    A. Sanction   B. Perpetuate
    C. Pass   D. Cancel
    E. Appeal

81. INFAMY
    A. Dishonour   B. Glory
    C. Integrity   D. Reputation
    E. Beauty

82. FAKE
    A. Original   B. Imitation
    C. Trustworthy   D. Loyal
    E. Lie

83. DEBACLE
    A. Collapse   B. Decline
    C. Defeat   D. Disgrace
    E. Mistake

84. ADMONISH
    A. Punish   B. Curse
    C. Dismiss   D. Reprimand
    E. Admit

85. EMBEZZLE
    A. Misappropriate   B. Balance
    C. Remunerate   D. Clear
    E. Mix

86. CORPULENT
    A. Lean   B. Gaunt
    C. Emaciated   D. Obese
    E. Corrupt

87. AUGUST
    A. Common   B. Ridiculous
    C. Dignified   D. Petty
    E. Month

88. STRINGENT
    A. Dry   B. Strained
    C. Rigorous   D. Shrill
    E. Thready

89. INSOLVENT
    A. Poor   B. Bankrupt
    C. Penniless   D. Broke
    E. Unsoluble

90. EXTRICATE
    A. Pull   B. Free
    C. Tie   D. Complicate
    E. Expel

91. INEXPLICABLE
    A. Confusing
    B. Unaccountable
    C. Chaotic
    D. Unconnected
    E. Undesired

92. GRATIFY
    A. Appreciate   B. Frank
    C. Indulge   D. Pacify
    E. Regard

93. ALERT
    A. Energetic   B. Observant
    C. Intelligent   D. Watchful
    E. Smart

94. UNTIE
    A. Unfold   B. Unchain
    C. Undo   D. Unhinge
    E. Free

95. OBJECT
    A. Challenge   B. Disapprove
    C. Deny   D. Disobey
    E. Refuse

96. BROWSE
    A. Heal   B. Deceive
    C. Examine   D. Strike
    E. Vision

97. SALACITY
    A. Bliss   B. Depression
    C. Indecency   D. Recession
    E. Urban

98. ZANY
    A. Clown   B. Pet
    C. Thief   D. Magician
    E. Virtuous

99. WARY
- A. Sad
- B. Vigilant
- C. Distorted
- D. Tired
- E. Different

100. RECKLESS
- A. Courageous
- B. Rash
- C. Bold
- D. Daring
- E. Disorganised

Directions (Qs. 101 to 200): *In the following questions choose the word which is the exact OPPOSITE of the given words.*

101. DEAR
- A. Priceless
- B. Free
- C. Worthless
- D. Cheap
- E. Expensive

102. FLAGITIOUS
- A. Innocent
- B. Vapid
- C. Ignorant
- D. Frivolous
- E. Stupid

103. LIABILITY
- A. Property
- B. Assets
- C. Debt
- D. Treasure
- E. Responsibilty

104. VIRTUOUS
- A. Wicked
- B. Corrupt
- C. Vicious
- D. Scandalous
- E. Dishonest

105. ENCOURAGE
- A. Dampen
- B. Disapprove
- C. Discourage
- D. Warn
- E. Land

106. MORTAL
- A. Divine
- B. Immortal
- C. Spiritual
- D. Eternal
- E. Strong

107. LEND
- A. Borrow
- B. Cheat
- C. Pawn
- D. Hire
- E. Ask

108. COMIC
- A. Emotional
- B. Tragic
- C. Fearful
- D. Painful
- E. Adult

109. ADDITION
- A. Division
- B. Enumeration
- C. Subtraction
- D. Multiplication
- E. Minus

110. MINOR
- A. Big
- B. Major
- C. Tall
- D. Heavy
- E. Adult

111. REPEL
- A. Attend
- B. Concentrate
- C. Continue
- D. Attract
- E. Expel

112. ARTIFICIAL
- A. Red
- B. Natural
- C. Truthful
- D. Solid
- E. Superficial

113. CAPACIOUS
- A. Limited
- B. Caring
- C. Foolish
- D. Changeable
- E. Spacious

114. PROVOCATION
- A. Vocation
- B. Pacification
- C. Peace
- D. Destruction
- E. Convocation

115. METICULOUS
- A. Mutual
- B. Shaggy
- C. Meretricious
- D. Slovenly
- E. Ridiculous

116. ABLE
- A. Disable
- B. Inable
- C. Unable
- D. Misable
- E. Probable

117. COMFORT
- A. Uncomfort
- B. Miscomfort
- C. Discomfort
- D. Uneasy
- E. Luxury

118. GAIN
- A. Loose
- B. Fall
- C. Lost
- D. Lose
- E. Again

119. SYNTHETIC
- A. Affable
- B. Natural
- C. Plastic
- D. Cosmetic
- E. Pathetic

120. ACQUITTED
   A. Freed
   B. Burdened
   C. Convicted
   D. Entrusted
   E. Predicted

121. STRINGENT
   A. General
   B. Vehement
   C. Lenient
   D. Magnanimous
   E. Astringent

122. FLIMSY
   A. Frail
   B. Filthy
   C. Firm
   D. Flippant
   E. Fat

123. BUSY
   A. Occupied
   B. Engrossed
   C. Relaxed
   D. Engaged
   E. Free

124. ADAPTABLE
   A. Adoptable
   B. Flexible
   C. Yielding
   D. Rigid
   E. Solid

125. LOVE
   A. Villainy
   B. Hatred
   C. Compulsion
   D. Force
   E. Fight

126. BALANCE
   A. Disbalance
   B. Misbalance
   C. Debalance
   D. Imbalance
   E. Unbalance

127. RELINQUISH
   A. Abdicate
   B. Renounce
   C. Possess
   D. Deny
   E. Occupy

128. MOUNTAIN
   A. Plain
   B. Plateau
   C. Precipice
   D. Valley
   E. Ocean

129. FICKLE
   A. Courageous
   B. Sincere
   C. Steadfast
   D. Humble
   E. Strong

130. PERENNIAL
   A. Frequent
   B. Regular
   C. Lasting
   D. Rare
   E. Often

131. RARELY
   A. Hardly
   B. Definitely
   C. Frequently
   D. Periodically
   E. Barely

132. STARTLED
   A. Amused
   B. Relaxed
   C. Endless
   D. Astonished
   E. Finished

133. ADHERENT
   A. Detractor
   B. Enemy
   C. Alien
   D. Rival
   E. Follower

134. QUIESCENT
   A. Indifferent
   B. Troublesome
   C. Weak
   D. Unconcerned
   E. Silent

135. CONDENSE
   A. Expand
   B. Distribute
   C. Interpret
   D. Lengthen
   E. Lighten

136. BENIGN
   A. Malevolent
   B. Soft
   C. Friendly
   D. Unwise
   E. Kind

137. OBSCURE
   A. Implicit
   B. Obnoxious
   C. Explicit
   D. Pedantic
   E. Incurable

138. HYPOCRITICAL
   A. Gentle
   B. Sincere
   C. Amiable
   D. Dependable
   E. Critical

139. EVASIVE
   A. Free
   B. Honest
   C. Liberal
   D. Frank
   E. Invasive

140. INDUSTRIOUS
   A. Indifferent
   B. Indolent
   C. Casual
   D. Passive
   E. Serving

141. EXTRICATE
   A. Manifest
   B. Palpable
   C. Release
   D. Entangle
   E. Intricate

142. LUCID
  A. Glory
  B. Noisy
  C. Obscure
  D. Distinct
  E. Clear

143. INSIPID
  A. Tasty
  B. Stupid
  C. Discreet
  D. Feast
  E. Flavoured

144. OBEYING
  A. Ordering
  B. Following
  C. Refusing
  D. Contradicting
  E. Insulting

145. VICTORIOUS
  A. Defeated
  B. Annexed
  C. Destroyed
  D. Vanquished
  E. Triumphant

146. COMMISSIONED
  A. Started
  B. Closed
  C. Finished
  D. Terminated
  E. Salaried

147. VANITY
  A. Pride
  B. Humility
  C. Conceit
  D. Ostentious
  E. Grace

148. ZENITH
  A. Acme
  B. Top
  C. Nadir
  D. Pinnacle
  E. Core

149. TANGIBLE
  A. Ethereal
  B. Concrete
  C. Actual
  D. Solid
  E. Delicious

150. REPRESS
  A. Inhibit
  B. Liberate
  C. Curb
  D. Quell
  E. Suppress

151. EPILOGUE
  A. Dialogue
  B. Prelude
  C. Post script
  D. Epigram
  E. Monologue

152. FRAUDULENT
  A. Candid
  B. Direct
  C. Forthright
  D. Genuine
  E. Real

153. LOQUACIOUS
  A. Reticent
  B. Talkative
  C. Garrulous
  D. Verbose
  E. Verbatim

154. NIGGARDLY
  A. Frugal
  B. Thrifty
  C. Stingy
  D. Generous
  E. Mean

155. PERTINENT
  A. Irrational
  B. Irregular
  C. Insistent
  D. Irrelevant
  E. Inconsistent

156. FAINT-HEARTED
  A. Warm-hearted
  B. Full-blooded
  C. Hot-blooded
  D. Stout-hearted
  E. Kind-hearted

157. VIOLENT
  A. Humble
  B. Harmless
  C. Gentle
  D. Tame
  E. Pet

158. STATIONARY
  A. Active
  B. Mobile
  C. Rapid
  D. Busy
  E. Unfixed

159. HONORARY
  A. Dishonourable
  B. Reputed
  C. Paid
  D. Official
  E. Obligatory

160. COMMON
  A. Rare
  B. Small
  C. Petty
  D. Poor
  E. General

161. FRUGAL
  A. Copious
  B. Extravagant
  C. Generous
  D. Ostentatious
  E. Thrifty

162. MALICIOUS
  A. Kind
  B. Boastful
  C. Generous
  D. Indifferent
  E. Harmful

163. FAMILIAR
  A. Unpleasant
  B. Dangerous
  C. Friendly
  D. Strange
  E. Known

164. PRELIMINARY
- A. Final
- B. First
- C. Secondary
- D. Initial
- E. Main

165. DOUBTFUL
- A. Famous
- B. Certain
- C. Fixed
- D. Important
- E. Vague

166. REMISS
- A. Forgetful
- B. Watchful
- C. Dutiful
- D. Harmful
- E. Break

167. INDISCREET
- A. Reliable
- B. Honest
- C. Prudent
- D. Stupid
- E. Credible

168. FRESH
- A. Faulty
- B. Sluggish
- C. Disgraceful
- D. Stale
- E. Old

169. ANNOY
- A. Praise
- B. Rejoice
- C. Please
- D. Reward
- E. Happy

170. TRANSPARENT
- A. Semi-transparent
- B. Muddy
- C. Opaque
- D. Dark
- E. Clear

171. REVEALED
- A. Denied
- B. Concealed
- C. Ignored
- D. Overlooked
- E. Appealed

172. EXTRAVAGANCE
- A. Luxury
- B. Poverty
- C. Economy
- D. Cheapness
- E. Vengeance

173. CROWDED
- A. Busy
- B. Congested
- C. Quiet
- D. Deserted
- E. Empty

174. SHRINK
- A. Contract
- B. Spoil
- C. Expand
- D. Stretch
- E. Droop

175. ENMITY
- A. Important
- B. Unnecessary
- C. Friendship
- D. Likeness
- E. Infamy

176. EXODUS
- A. Influx
- B. Home-coming
- C. Return
- D. Restoration
- E. Entry

177. CULPABLE
- A. Defendable
- B. Blameless
- C. Careless
- D. Irresponsible
- E. Bailable

178. SUBSERVIENT
- A. Aggressive
- B. Straightforward
- C. Dignified
- D. Supercilious
- E. Submissive

179. AWARE
- A. Uncertain
- B. Ignorant
- C. Sure
- D. Doubtful
- E. Beware

180. GRACEFUL
- A. Rough
- B. Expert
- C. Miserable
- D. Awkward
- E. Beautiful

181. AUTONOMY
- A. Slavery
- B. Subordination
- C. Dependence
- D. Submissiveness
- E. Democracy

182. NADIR
- A. Modernity
- B. Zenith
- C. Liberty
- D. Progress
- E. Horizon

183. CONCEDE
- A. Object
- B. Refuse
- C. Grant
- D. Accede
- E. Exceed

184. SUPPRESS
- A. Encourage
- B. Grow
- C. Praise
- D. Permit
- E. Swell

185. FAMOUS
- A. Disgraced
- B. Notorious
- C. Evil
- D. Popular
- E. Ugly

186. EXPAND
    A. Contract   B. Condense
    C. Congest   D. Conclude
    E. Compact

187. ARROGANT
    A. Polite   B. Cowardly
    C. Meek   D. Gentlemanly
    E. Vibrant

188. ENORMOUS
    A. Soft   B. Average
    C. Tiny   D. Weak
    E. Gigantic

189. URBANE
    A. Illiterate   B. Backward
    C. Discourteous   D. Orthodox
    E. Villager

190. HOSTILITY
    A. Courtesy   B. Hospitality
    C. Relationship   D. Friendliness
    E. Casualty

191. BELITTLE
    A. Praise   B. Flatter
    C. Exaggerate   D. Adore
    E. Decry

192. HAPLESS
    A. Cheerful   B. Consistent
    C. Fortunate   D. Shapely
    E. Hopeful

193. HAPHAZARD
    A. Fortuitous   B. Indifferent
    C. Deliberate   D. Accidental
    E. Random

194. GREGARIOUS
    A. Antisocial   B. Glorious
    C. Horrendous   D. Similar
    E. Affable

195. VALUABLE
    A. Invaluable   B. Worthless
    C. Inferior   D. Lowly
    E. Worthy

196. ABSOLUTE
    A. Deficient   B. Faulty
    C. Limited   D. Scarce
    E. Whole

197. CONFESS
    A. Deny   B. Refuse
    C. Contest   D. Contend
    E. Profess

198. GULLIBLE
    A. Incredulous   B. Fickle
    C. Easy   D. Stylish
    E. Credulous

199. HIRSUTE
    A. Scaly   B. Bald
    C. Erudite   D. Quiet
    E. Hairy

200. HINDRANCE
    A. Aid   B. Persuasion
    C. Cooperation   D. Agreement
    E. Encumbrance

ANSWERS

1	2	3	4	5	6	7	8	9	10
C	B	D	C	B	C	B	C	D	B
11	12	13	14	15	16	17	18	19	20
D	D	B	A	A	B	B	D	A	B
21	22	23	24	25	26	27	28	29	30
D	D	C	B	D	C	C	B	C	D
31	32	33	34	35	36	37	38	39	40
A	C	C	D	A	A	C	D	A	C
41	42	43	44	45	46	47	48	49	50
C	A	C	D	A	A	D	C	A	C
51	52	53	54	55	56	57	58	59	60
D	C	A	A	A	B	B	A	A	C

61	62	63	64	65	66	67	68	69	70
A	C	B	D	A	C	D	B	A	A
71	72	73	74	75	76	77	78	79	80
C	D	C	B	B	B	B	B	D	D
81	82	83	84	85	86	87	88	89	90
A	B	A	D	A	D	C	C	B	B
91	92	93	94	95	96	97	98	99	100
B	D	D	C	B	C	C	A	B	B
101	102	103	104	105	106	107	108	109	110
D	A	B	C	C	B	A	B	C	B
111	112	113	114	115	116	17	18	19	20
D	B	A	B	D	C	C	D	B	C
121	122	123	124	125	126	127	128	129	130
C	C	C	D	B	D	C	D	C	D
131	132	133	134	135	136	137	138	139	140
D	B	B	A	C	A	C	B	B	B
141	142	143	144	145	146	147	148	149	150
D	C	A	A	A	D	B	C	A	B
151	152	153	154	155	156	157	158	159	160
B	D	A	D	D	D	C	B	C	A
161	162	163	164	165	166	167	168	169	170
B	C	D	A	B	C	C	D	C	C
171	172	173	174	175	176	177	178	179	180
B	C	D	D	C	A	A	C	B	D
181	182	183	184	185	186	187	188	189	190
C	B	B	B	B	B	A	C	C	D
191	192	193	194	195	196	197	198	199	200
C	C	C	A	B	C	A	A	B	A

Fill in the Blanks

Fill in the blanks is such an exercise that starts with the primary education and continues at the highest level of examinations. One must practise it regularly to score well in competitive exams.

Multiple Choice Questions

Directions: *Pick out the most effective word(s) from the given words to fill in the blanks to make the sentence meaningfully complete.*

1. Leadership defines what the future should look like and ..... people with that vision.
   A. aligns   B. develops
   C. trains   D. encourages
   E. transforms

2. We upset ourselves by responding in an ..... manner to someone else's actions.
   A. unabashed   B. irrational
   C. arduous   D. arguable
   E. invalid

3. Nothing probably has more contributed to ..... the poverty and backwardness of India than the want of good roads.
   A. alleviate   B. circumvent
   C. perpetuate   D. accelerate
   E. accentuate

4. The main objective of this dedicated institution is to ..... poverty.
   A. enhance   B. magnify
   C. manifest   D. entertain
   E. alleviate

5. He feels that the ..... of his achievements goes to his father.
   A. reward   B. compensation

C. attribute   D. credit
E. gist

6. Both the brothers are equally handsome but the elder ..... the two is more intelligent.
   A. among   B. than
   C. of   D. in
   E. between

7. ..... being a handicapped person, he is very co-operative and self-reliant.
   A. Because   B. Although
   C. Since   D. Basically
   E. Despite

8. The employees were unhappy because their salary was not increased .....
   A. marginally   B. abruptly
   C. substantially   D. superfluously
   E. negligibly

9. No sooner did the bell ring, ... the actor started singing.
   A. when   B. than
   C. after   D. before
   E. through

10. Unfavourable weather conditions can ..... illness.
    A. cure   B. detect
    C. treat   D. enhance
    E. diagnose

11. They demanded a lot of things, but he cannot ..... to grant them for want of funds.
A. afford   B. decide
C. permit   D. buy
E. expect

12. The little child was so excited that he could not ..... the burning candle.
A. threw   B. thrown
C. drift   D. lights
E. throw

13. Though the brothers are twins, they look .....
A. alike   B. handsome
C. indifferent   D. identical
E. different

14. If I ..... realized it, I would not have acted on his advice.
A. was   B. had
C. were   D. have
E. being

15. Why don't you ..... your work in advance before commencing it.
A. start   B. complete
C. finish   D. plan
E. execute

16. The manager is to help his subordinates ..... their potential in their present as well as in their future assignment.
A. respect   B. train
C. delegate   D. judge
E. realise

17. All the employees in the company are entitled ..... reimbursement of medical expenses.
A. of   B. for
C. on   D. to
E. with

18. It is ..... in pursuit of these very objectives that our Government has made some basic changes in our economic policies.
A. greatly   B. constantly
C. clearly   D. largely
E. precisely

19. The Management of so many projects and of different nature ..... no common capacity and vigour.
A. demands   B. require

C. permits   D. urge
E. offers

20. He could ..... a lot of money in such a short time by using his intelligence and working hard.
A. spend   B. spoil
C. exchange   D. accumulate
E. pay

21. With his ..... income, he finds it difficult to live a comfortable life.
A. brief   B. sufficient
C. meagre   D. huge
E. adequate

22. The child broke ..... from his mother and ran towards the painting.
A. away   B. after
C. down   D. with
E. heavily

23. His interest in the study of human behaviour is indeed very .....
A. broad   B. strong
C. vast   D. large
E. deep

24. Finally, the thief ..... that he had stolen the ornaments.
A. argued   B. decided
C. appealed   D. admitted
E. obeyed

25. Since there was no evidence to prove him ..... he was acquitted.
A. innocent   B. offence
C. guilty   D. honest
E. accused

26. Marketing is one area in which our country has been particularly ..... and new strategies need to be evolved to strengthen it.
A. efficient   B. deficient
C. strongest   D. overemphasised
E. powerful

27. There is no doubt that one has to keep ..... with the changing times.
A. himself   B. tuning
C. pace   D. oneself
E. aside

28. The poor ones continue to ..... out a living inspite of economic liberalisation in that country.
    A. eke   B. go
    C. manage   D. bring
    E. find

29. ..... eye witnesses, the news reporter gave a graphic description of how the fire broke.
    A. Reporting   B. Seeing
    C. Examining   D. Quoting
    E. Observing

30. Before getting elected, he was ..... to the welfare of the people.
    A. devoted   B. attended
    C. focussed   D. neglected
    E. concentrated

31. The union leader was very critical ..... the attitude of the management.
    A. for   B. at
    C. on   D. against
    E. of

32. The passengers and crew members of the aeroplane had a ..... escape when it was taking off from the runway.
    A. little   B. narrow
    C. brief   D. large
    E. better

33. Eight scientists have ..... the national awards for outstanding contribution and dedication to the profession.
    A. picked   B. conferred
    C. bagged   D. discovered
    E. bestowed

34. There has been a ..... lack of efficiency in all the crucial areas of the working of Public Sector Undertakings.
    A. conspicuous B. stimulative
    C. insignificant D. surprising
    E. positive

35. Rohan is too ..... as far as his food habits are concerned.
    A. curious   B. enjoyable
    C. interesting D. involved
    E. fastidious

36. Some people ..... themselves into believing that they are indispensable to the organisation they work for.
    A. force   B. delude
    C. denigrate   D. fool
    E. keep

37. Arpan had to drop his plan of going to picnic as he had certain ..... to take of during that period.
    A. transactions B. preparations
    C. commitments D. urgencies
    E. observations

38. No country can ..... to practise a constant, rigid foreign policy in view of the world power dynamics.
    A. envisage   B. anticipate
    C. afford   D. visualise
    E. obliviate

39. After a recent mild paralytic attack his movements are ..... restricted; otherwise he is still very active.
    A. not   B. entirely
    C. slightly   D. nowhere
    E. frequently

40. ..... he woke up, he saw that his bag was stolen.
    A. If   B. When
    C. Where   D. So
    E. Neither

41. I am going to Bhopal today and plan to ..... by tomorrow evening.
    A. returning   B. returned
    C. have returned D. be returning
    E. return

42. Since the priest did not arrive in time, the ceremony was ..... late.
    A. begins   B. begun
    C. began   D. beginning
    E. begin

43. He succeeded in getting possession ..... his land after a long court case.
    A. to   B. against
    C. of   D. with
    E. for

44. The villagers have not ..... over the shock of losing everything in the earthquake.
A. got   B. made
C. forgotten   D. freed
E. felt

45. Ajay is the ..... head of the family and commands a lot of respect from the family members.
A. solely   B. strongest
C. undisputed   D. full
E. controversial

46. The blood donation camp was organised ..... the Naval Youth Club.
A. to   B. by
C. from   D. with
E. along

47. Last year the performance of this production unit was ..... .
A. tall   B. staggered
C. fantastic   D. below
E. upwards

48. We all must ..... that people are the most important assets of any organisation.
A. find   B. look
C. realise   D. involve
E. dispel

49. Since Vivek stays far away from our place, we do not meet each other ..... .
A. rarely   B. shortly
C. timely   D. frequently
E. momentarily

50. The lights ..... just as we sat down to watch the movie on television.
A. went off   B. shut out
C. put out   D. blew down
E. gave off

51. To ..... yourself from ..... wear warm clothes.
A. save, heat   B. suffer, cold
C. prevent, ice   D. protect, cold
E. prohibit, heat

52. He is ..... to ..... any kind of work with due sincerity.
A. determined, undertake
B. found, perform
C. eager, avoid

D. willing, ignore
E. reluctant, entrust

53. They wanted to ..... all these books, but they could not find ..... time to do so.
A. buy, some   B. read, sufficient
C. dispose, some   D. pursue, necessary
E. cover, almost

54. They started their ..... branch in this city today; their other ..... branches are in the next by-lane.
A. first, new   B. first, old
C. second, old   D. third, two
E. new, several

55. Due to ..... rainfall this year, there will be ..... cut in water supply.
A. meagre, least
B. abundant, considerable
C. enough, substantial
D. surplus, abundant
E. sufficient, no

56. The judge ..... him because he was found ..... on the basis of the evidence.
A. acquitted, criminal
B. punished, guilty
C. sentenced, innocent
D. suspended, involved
E. pardoned, innocent

57. The speaker's ..... over his subject was seen through his ..... discourse.
A. mastery, fluent
B. efficiency, thorough
C. lethargy, dull
D. grip, boring
E. skill, pleasant

58. Workers in earlier days were ..... because of which the industries ..... a lot.
A. honest, lost
B. rich, flourished
C. autocrats, developed
D. inefficient, suffered
E. idle, prospered

59. A close ..... of the bill shows that the provisions are ..... and there is a need to add certain crucial elements to them.

A. examination, sufficient
B. observation, helpful
C. scrutiny, inadequate
D. file, numerous
E. account, excellent

60. His ..... speech has seriously ..... the young minds.
A. audacious, delighted
B. maiden, flattered
C. humorous, damaged
D. irresponsible, misled
E. eccentric, questioned

61. On ..... of the enquiry, if it is found that the ..... are true, the enquiry officer will report the matter to the higher authority.
A. demand, findings
B. completion, allegations
C. instituting, charges
D. withdrawal, inferences
E. establishment, results

62. After the present tax holiday period ....., the power cost to users may become ..... .
A. starts, unreasonable
B. sets, perishable
C. ends, less
D. enhances, negligible
E. ends, intolerable

63. A good teacher-student relationship helps create a ..... and peaceful atmosphere where there is no room for any ..... of educational activity.
A. harmonious, interruption
B. congenial, development
C. quiet, confusion
D. cordial, education
E. delightful, exaggeration

64. No self-made person would ever like to ..... to any ..... .
A. take, task
B. yield, cause
C. submit, dimension
D. surrender, proposal
E. succumb, pressure

65. Though I had behaved with him very ....., he was ....., enough to forgive me.

A. nicely, unkind
B. rudely, indecent
C. nastily, reluctant
D. impolitely, kind
E. politely, generous

66. We cannot ..... up with your requirements for want of ..... facilities.
A. put, urgent
B. take, expert
C. cope, infrastructural
D. end, ancillary
E. give, deployable

67. He is too ..... to tolerate ..... .
A. humble, lethargy   B. impatient, delay
C. fast, speed   D. wicked, vices
E. lazy, sluggishness

68. The flood ..... in the State ..... to 261 with four more deaths reported today.
A. water, rose   B. level, aroused
C. toll, mounted   D. destruction, spread
E. catchment, increased

69. Right from the earliest ages, India's ..... developed a sense of unity and ..... among its people.
A. people, diversity
B. rulers, commitment
C. culture, commonness
D. population, diversification
E. heritage, disparity

70. ....., there is a widespread ..... among the educated youth which makes them increasingly alienated.
A. Luckily, dedication
B. Co-incidentally, feeling
C. Obviously, enthusiasm
D. Unfortunately, frustration
E. Nevertheless, optimism

71. The problem of ..... another war has assumed great urgency because of the ..... of nuclear weapons.
A. fighting, destruction
B. preventing, invention
C. precipitating, disarmament
D. stopping, need
E. winning, growth

72. In many countries, ... development arising out of fast technological ..... has led to some problems.
  A. meagre, inventions
  B. cultural, practices
  C. agricultural, development
  D. optimum, intervention
  E. excessive, progress

73. Shyness is ..... through abnormal behaviour in various ..... .
  A. manifested, ways
  B. removed, people
  C. shown, kinds
  D. developed, things
  E. enhanced, aspects

74. In that country, bureaucracy is ..... as a group of men and women that had arrogated to itself power ..... responsibility.
  A. perceived, without
  B. believed, within
  C. held, into
  D. known, unto
  E. allowed, for

75. The employees of the factory owing ..... to the workers union have ..... of an agitation from next week in support of their demands.
  A. allegiance, warned
  B. respect, called
  C. shelter, started
  D. pressure, proposal
  E. assurance, sought

76. Yesterday, around 400 huts were ..... in a major fire which ..... the slum area.
  A. burn. hit   B. gutted, engulfed
  C. fired, took   D. burning, blazed
  E. demolished, entered

77. As a ..... of Chetan's rude behaviour he was ..... a memo by his boss.
  A. sequel, issued
  B. part, delivered
  C. consequence, given
  D. punishment, rewarded
  E. reaction, presented

78. Deepak has ..... some unfinished work to ..... up before he can go home.
  A. yet, get   B. since, come
  C. still, clear   D. let, take
  E. set, give

79. After careful ..... the thief ..... that he has committed the crime.
  A. investigation, refused
  B. questioning, divulged
  C. consideration, felt
  D. action, agreed
  E. finding, insisted

80. The mining activity comes under the ..... of the forest conservation act and we must ..... that the law is followed strictly.
  A. debate, see   B. course, observe
  C. control, insist   D. purview, ensure
  E. limits, stipulate

81. All the teachers ..... that Arpita would stand at the top in the examination, she ..... short of their expectation.
  A. thought, fell   B. expected, ran
  C. presumed, failed   D. dreamt, achieved
  E. started, reached

82. In a ..... decision the government has announced that elementary education for children in the age group of six to fourteen would be ..... a fundamental right.
  A. historical, obtained
  B. landmark, deplore
  C. clear, absolved
  D. significant, made
  E. rush, given

83. The researcher ..... information about the number of villages in each state which are ..... as problem villages to be covered by National Drinking Water Mission.
  A. invested, found
  B. got, designed
  C. collected, identified
  D. investigated, imagined
  E. knows, gathered

84. The rules of the institute ..... that employees should not undertake any outside ..... work without seeking written permission of the institute.
  A. conclude, devoted
  B. strengthen, assignment
  C. allow, important
  D. stipulate, remunerative
  E. direct, extra

85. The television boom might not ..... newspaper readership but magazines which are not leaders in their segment might ..... .
A. link, close
B. effect, prosper
C. reduce, encourage
D. attract, continue
E. affect, suffer

86. The other servants had to ..... since Appu alone ..... all the food.
A. leave, prepared   B. eat, cooked
C. wait, spoiled   D. cook, wasted
E. starve, consumed

87. If you do not ..... all your monthly expenses would ..... your income.
A. spend, gain   B. save, outwit
C. economise, exceed   D. think, swallow
E. realise, enhance

88. Ankur ..... me coming to his table, he smiled and ..... me a chair.
A. looked, gave   B. welcomed, took
C. saw, offered   D. found, signalled
E. met, sat

89. The counter clerk was very busy and ..... not pay any ..... to my request.
A. did, attention   B. had, cash
C. could, respect   D. can, help
E. certainly, acceptance

90. The speech ..... with subtle threats has resulted in ..... tension in the sensitive areas of the city.
A. full, escalating
B. started, reduced
C. followed, continuous
D. replete, increased
E. forced, dissolving

91. The State Government employees ..... threatened to launch an indefinite strike from next month to ..... their demands.
A. have, press   B. did, get
C. were, meet   D. nearly, fulfil
E. has, press

92. Virat ..... another feather ..... his cap by his wonderful preformance in the one day match.
A. created, by   B. took, in
C. captured from   D. kept, in
E. added, to

93. We are ..... to have him ..... here to make this function a great success.
A. happy, arrive   B. wonderful, again
C. sure, come   D. pleased, over
E. proud, leave

94. The charges made in the system were so ..... that they didn't require any ..... .
A. marginal, expenses
B. big, time
C. obvious, modifications
D. certain, expertise
E. genuine, intelligence

95. The police ..... any attempt of arson by ..... at the trouble spot quite in time.
A. predisposed, visiting
B. preempted, arriving
C. made, encircling
D. thwarted, presenting
E. squashed, surrounding

96. It is ..... for every tax-payer to ..... the tax returns to the Income Tax Department.
A. binding, pay   B. possible, remit
C. worthwhile, evade   D. obligatory, submit
E. necessary, lodge

97. ..... by long queues and bad weather the voters ..... their way to polling stations any way they could.
A. Undaunted, made
B. Worried, lost
C. Encouraged, prepared
D. Going, dropped
E. Satisfied, turned

98. The Chief Minister ..... the House that ..... action would be taken against all those found involved in corruption.
A. instructed, preventive
B. called, strict
C. assured, stringent
D. reiterated, strictly
E. informed, constructive

99. In his ..... he followed the ..... course.
A. ignorance, wrong
B. bewilderment, appropriate
C. hurry, diversified
D. agony, funny
E. predicament, proper

43

100. He is usually ..... but today he appears rather ..... .
A. tense, restless
B. quiet, calm
C. happy, humorous
D. strict, unwell
E. calm, distrubed

ANSWERS

1	2	3	4	5	6	7	8	9	10
D	B	D	E	D	C	E	C	B	D
11	12	13	14	15	16	17	18	19	20
A	E	E	B	D	E	D	E	A	D
21	22	23	24	25	26	27	28	29	30
C	A	E	D	C	B	C	A	D	A
31	32	33	34	35	36	37	38	39	40
E	B	C	A	E	B	C	C	C	B
41	42	43	44	45	46	47	48	49	50
E	B	C	A	C	B	C	C	D	A
51	52	53	54	55	56	57	58	59	60
D	A	B	D	E	B	A	D	C	D
61	62	63	64	65	66	67	68	69	70
B	E	A	E	D	C	B	C	C	D
71	72	73	74	75	76	77	78	79	80
B	E	B	A	A	B	A	C	B	D
81	82	83	84	85	86	87	88	89	90
A	D	C	D	E	E	C	C	A	D
91	92	93	94	95	96	97	98	99	100
A	E	D	C	B	D	A	C	A	E

Spotting Errors

The most common errors in English are of spellings, grammar and usage of words. By regular practice, the errors can be easily spotted and minimised. Read the following sentences and learn to spot the errors. Test your learning in the exercise that follows.

Common Errors with Nouns and Noun-Phrases

Incorrect	Correct
1. I have bought new *furnitures.*	I have bought new *furniture.*
2. The wages of sin *are* death.	The wages of sin *is* death.
3. She told these *news* to her mother.	She told her mother this *news.*
4. He took *troubles* to do his work.	He took *trouble* (or pains) over his work.
5. The *cattles* were grazing.	The *cattle* were grazing.
6. He showered *many abuses* on me.	He showered *much abuse* on me.
7. I spent the holidays with my *family members.*	I spent the holidays with my *family.*
8. There is no *place* in this compartment.	There is no *room* in this compartment.
9. Write this new *poetry* in your *copy.*	Write this new *poem* in your *note-book.*
10. He took *insult* at this.	He took *offence* at this.
11. Put your *sign* here.	Put your *signatures* here.
12. She is my *cousin sister.*	She is my *cousin.*
13. *Sunil's* my *neighbour's* house was burgled.	*Sunil* my *neighbour's* house was burgled.
14. I lost a *ten-rupees* note.	I lost *a ten-rupee* note.
15. Road closed for *repair.*	Road closed for *repairs.*
16. His house is out of *repairs.*	His house is out of *repair.*
17. What is the *reason* of an earthquake?	What is the *cause* of an earthquake?
18. This building is made of *stones.*	This building is made of *stone.*
19. I disapprove of *these kinds* of games.	I disapprove of *this kind* of games.
20. Veena's and Sheela's father is ill.	Veena and Sheela's father is ill.
21. His *son-in-laws* are doctors.	His *sons-in-law* are doctors.
22. *Alms* is given to the *poor.*	*Alms* are given to the poor.
23. He always keeps his words.	He always keeps his *word.*
24. I carried the *luggages.*	I carried the *luggage.*
25. *Two-third* of the work is left.	*Two-thirds* of the work is left.

44

Common Errors with Pronouns

Incorrect	Correct
1. Both did not go.	Neither went.
2. We all did not go.	None of us went.
3. Each of these boys play.	Each of these boys plays.
4. Whoever does best he will get a prize.	Whoever does best will get a prize.
5. One should not waste his time.	A man should not waste his time.
6. I and she are sisters.	She and I are sisters.
7. He is wiser than me.	He is wiser than I.
8. Between you and I, Anil is not to be trusted.	Between you and me, Anil is not to be trusted.
9. Nobody was there but I.	Nobody was there but me.
10. Who is there ? It is me.	Who is there ? It is I.
11. Only he and me can use this card.	Only he and I can use this card.
12. Let you and I go now.	Let you and me go now.
13. Everyone got one's pay.	Everyone got his pay.
14. Everyone is frightened when they see a tiger.	Everyone is frightened when he sees a tiger.
15. These two friends are fond of one another.	These two friends are fond of each other.
16. I did not like him coming at that hour.	I did not like his coming at that hour.
17. Who do you think I met?	Whom do you think I met?
18. You should avail this opportunity.	You should avail yourself this opportunity.
19. When you have read these books, please return the same to me.	When you have read the books, please return them to me.
20. They that are humble need fear no fall.	Those that are humble need fear no fall.

Common Errors with Adjectives

Incorrect	Correct
1. These all oranges are good.	All these oranges are good.
2. He held the book in the both hands.	He held the book in both hands.
3. Both men have not come.	Neither man has come.
4. That man should do some or other work.	That man should do some work or other.
5. He is elder than I.	He is older than I.
6. Shakespeare is greater than any other poets.	Shakespeare is greater than any other poet.
7. He is a coward man.	He is a cowardly man.
8. Many villagers cannot write his own name.	Many villagers cannot write their own name.
9. Each of us loves our home.	Each of us loves his home.
10. Much efforts bring their reward.	Much effort brings its reward.
11. He found hundred rupees.	He found a hundred rupees.
12. He had leave of four days.	He had four days leave.

Incorrect	Correct
13. This is a worth seeing sight.	This is a sight worth seeing.
14. He will spend his future life here.	He will spend the rest of his life here.
15. There is a best teacher in that class.	There is a very good teacher in that class.
16. Of the two plans this is the best.	Of the two plans this is the better.
17. He is becoming strong every day.	He is becoming stronger every day.
18. He is worst than I.	He is worse than I.
19. Jaipur is hot than Delhi.	Jaipur is hotter than Delhi.
20. In our library the number of books is less.	In our library the number of books is small.

Common Errors with Verbs

Incorrect	Correct
1. He asked had we taken our luggage.	He asked if we had taken our luggage.
2. She asked what are you doing.	She asked what we were doing.
3. Rama asked to Anil why he is angry.	Rama asked Anil why he was angry.
4. He does not care for his money.	He does not take care of his money.
5. He does not care for his work.	He takes no care over his work.
6. No one cared for him after his mother died.	No one took care of him after his mother died.
7. He got angry before I said a word.	He got angry before I had said a word.
8. I met a man who was my tutor 20 years ago.	I met a man who had been my tutor twenty years ago.
9. I had been for walking yesterday.	I went for a walk yesterday.
10. If I shall do this I shall be wrong.	If I do this I shall be wrong.
11. I have left trekking.	I have given up trekking.
12. I came to know as to how he did this.	I learnt how he did this.
13. I came to know why he was sad.	I found out why he was sad.
14. He knows to swim.	He knows how to swim.
15. The criminal's head was cut.	The criminal's head was cut off.
16. I said to him to go.	I told him to go.
17. I told the teacher to excuse me.	I asked the teacher to excuse me.
18. He is troubling me.	He is giving me trouble.
19. I have got a hurt on my leg.	I have hurt my leg.
20. She gave a speech.	She made a speech.

Common Errors in Subject-Verb Agreement

Incorrect	Correct
1. The owners of this factory *is* very rich.	The owners of this factory *are* very rich.
2. The pleasures of nature that one can experience at Shimla *is* beyond description.	The pleasures of nature that one can experience at Shimla *are* beyond description.

Incorrect	*Correct*
3. There *is* no street lights in our colony.	There *are* no street lights in our colony.
4. He and I *am* entrusted with the job.	He and I *are* entrusted with the job.
5. Rice and curry *are* his favourite dish.	Rice and curry *is* his favourite dish.
6. The honour and glory of our country *are* at stake.	The honour and glory of our country *is* at stake.
7. Time and tide *waits* for none.	Time and tide *wait* for none.
8. All the passengers with the driver *was* killed.	All the passengers, with the driver, *were* killed.
9. The teacher, with her students, *were* going out.	The teacher, with her students, *was* going out.
10. I as well as they *am* tired.	I as well as they *are* tired.
11. Not only the soldiers but their captain also *were* captured.	Not only the soldiers but their captain also *was* captured.
12. Neither you nor I *were* selected.	Neither you nor I *was* selected.
13. Either of these two applicants *are* fit for the job but neither want to accept it.	Either of these two applicants *is* fit for the job but neither wants to accept it.
14. One of these students are sure to stand first.	One of these students *is* sure to stand first.
15. Everyone of these workers want a raise.	Everyone of these workers *wants* a raise.
16. None of these letters has been answered so far.	None of these letters *have* been answered so far.
17. None of the girls were present at the party.	None of the girls *was* present at the party.
18. Many a battle were fought on Indian soil.	Many a battle *was* fought on Indian soil.
19. A lot of work remain to be done.	A lot of work *remains* to be done.
20. The majority of these girls likes music.	The majority of these girls *like* music.

Common Errors in the Use of Modals/Auxiliary Verbs

Incorrect	*Correct*
1. When I shall see him I shall tell him this.	When I *see* him, I shall tell him this.
2. If I should do wrong, he would punish me.	If I *did* wrong, he would punish me.
3. Until he will have confessed his fault, he will be kept in prison.	Until he *has* confessed his fault, he will be kept in prison.
4. She will obey me.	She *shall* obey me.
5. You would work hard.	You *should* work hard.
6. You shall find him in the garden.	You *will* find him in the garden.
7. He must have died of exposure, but we cannot be certain.	He *might* have died of exposure, but we cannot be certain.
8. You might not show disrespect to your elders.	You *must* not show disrespect to your elders.
9. You may take exercise in order to maintain good health.	You *must* take exercise in order to maintain good health.
10. He must be a crook for all we know.	He *may* be a crook for all we know.

Common Errors in the Use of Adverbs

Incorrect	Correct
1. He is very much angry.	He is *very* angry.
2. She was very good enough to help me.	She was *good enough* to help me.
3. She runs much fast.	She runs *very* fast.
4. She runs very faster than Seema.	She runs *much* faster than Seema.
5. It is bitter cold today.	It is *bitterly* cold today.
6. He is a much learned man.	He is a very learned man.
7. She is thinking very hardly.	She is thinking very hard.
8. To tell in brief the film was boring.	*In short* the film was boring.
9. He told the story in details.	He told the story *in detail.*
10. I did it anyhow.	I *managed to do* it somehow.
11. Aeroplanes reach Europe soon.	Aeroplanes reach Europe quickly.
12. Before long there were dinosaurs on the earth.	*Long ago,* there were dinosaurs on the earth.
13. This book is too interesting.	This book is *very* interesting.
14. He lives miserly.	He lives in *a miserly* way.
15. Just I had gone when she came.	I had just gone when she came.
16. He sings good.	He sings *well.*
17. He sings good than I.	He sings *better* than I.
18. Really speaking it is cold.	*As a matter of fact* it is cold.
19. He is enough tall to reach the ceiling.	He is *tall enough* to reach the ceiling.
20. He went directly to his college.	He went *direct* to his college.

Common Errors in the Use of Conjunctions

Incorrect	Correct
1. As he is fat so he runs slowly.	As he is fat *he* runs slowly.
2. If he is fat then he will run slowly.	If he is fat, he will run slowly.
3. Though he is fat still he runs fast.	Though he is fat, *he runs* fast.
4. *As* I pulled the trigger at the sametime he shook my arm.	As I pulled the trigger, he shook my arm.
5. No sooner I had spoken than he left.	No sooner *had* I spoken than he left.
6. Not only he will go, but also he will stay there.	Not only *will he* go, but he *will also* stay there.
7. Neither he comes nor he writes.	Neither *does he* come nor *does he* write.
8. Scarcely he entered the room than the telephone rang.	Scarcely *had* he entered the room *when the* telephone rang.
9. Hardly she had left the house than it began to rain.	Hardly *had she* left the house *when* it began to rain.
10. He is the fastest runner and he comes last.	He is the fastest runner *but* he comes last.
11. She is as innocent as if she looks.	She is as innocent as she looks.
12. Until he does not try he must be punished.	He must be punished unless he tries.
13. I want to know as to why you are late.	I want to know why you are late.

Incorrect	*Correct*
14. I am fond of Chinese food as for example sweet and sour prawns.	I am fond of Chinese food, for example, sweet and sour prawns.
15. He was angry therefore I ran away.	He was angry so I ran away.
16. I was trying to work, at that time he was disturbing me.	While I was trying to work, he was disturbing me.
17. Supposing if he is late, what will happen?	Supposing he is late (or if he is late) what will happen?
18. He asked me that why I was late.	He asked me why I was late.
19. Let us catch a taxi lest we should not get late.	Let us catch a taxi lest we should get late.
20. She dresses herself like the teacher does.	She dresses herself as the teacher does.
21. Wait while I come.	Wait *until* (or *till)* I come.
22. Until, there is corruption in India, there can be little progress.	*As long* as there is corruption in India there can be little progress.
23. I have never told a lie nor cheated anybody.	I have never told a lie *nor have I* cheated anybody.
24. Both Mohan as well as Arun are responsible for this action.	Both Mohan *and* Arun are responsible for this action.
25. Hindus and Muslims both are to blame for the riots.	*Both Hindus* and Muslims are to blame for the riots.

Common Errors in the Use of Prepositions

Incorrect	*Correct*
1. I will not listen him.	I will not listen *to* him.
2. Copy this word by word.	Copy this word *for* word.
3. He enquired from her where she lived.	He enquired *of* her where she lived.
4. Sign here with ink.	Sign here *in* ink.
5. Has she come in train or by foot?	Has she come *by* train or *on* foot?
6. She said this at his face.	She said this *to* his face.
7. Open the book on page one.	Open the book *at* page one.
8. I was invited for lunch.	I was *invited to* lunch.
9. I am ill since three months.	I have been *ill for* three months.
10. This paper is inferior than that.	This paper is inferior *to* that.
11. This resembles to that.	This *resembles* that.
12. My brother is superior than you in strength.	My brother is superior *to* you in strength.
13. He wrote me.	He wrote *to* me.
14. I shall explain them this.	I shall explain this *to* them.
15. Send this letter on my address.	Send this letter *to* my address.
16. He suggested me this.	He suggested this *to* me.
17. He goes *on his* work.	He goes *to his* work.
18. He *reached to* Nagpur.	He *reached* Nagpur.
19. He told *to me* to go.	He told *me* to go.
20. The term begins *from* July 1st.	The term begins *on* July 1st.

Miscellaneous Errors

Incorrect	Correct
1. Many *homes* are lying vacant.	Many *houses* are lying vacant.
2. It is cool in the *shadow* of the tree.	It is cool in the *shade* of the tree.
3. She *keeps* good health.	She *enjoys* good health.
4. My leg is *paining*.	*I am feeling pain* in my leg.
5. *See* this word in the dictionary.	*Look up* this word in the dictionary.
6. The train will arrive *just now*.	The train will arrive *shortly*.
7. They are *pulling* on well.	They are *getting* on well.
8. The river has *over flown* its bank.	The river has *over flown* its banks.
9. He was appointed *on* the post.	He was appointed *to* the post.
10. Last but not *the least,* we have to discuss the problem of over population.	Last but not *least,* we have to discuss the problem of over population.
11. *Cities* after *cities* fell.	*City* after *city* fell.
12. What is the use Munir going there?	What is the use of Munir going there?
13. He *did many mischief.*	He *made much mischief.*
14. It is exact five *in* my watch.	It is exact five *by* my watch.
15. I will dine with them on *next Sunday.*	I will dine with them *Sunday next.*
16. Misfortunes when faced bravely and *manly* become less troublesome.	Misfortunes when faced bravely and *manfully* become less troublesome.
17. I am *laid down* with fever.	I am *laid up* with fever.
18. He is habituated to smoking.	He is *addicted* to smoking.
19. *According to my opinion* he is right.	*In my opinion* (or according *to me*) he is right.
20. Could you please *open* this knot?	Could you please *untie* this knot?

Multiple Choice Questions

Directions: *In each question below, a sentence is broken into four parts which are marked as (A), (B), (C) and (D). One of them may be grammatically or structurally wrong in the context of the sentence. The letter of that word is the answer. If there is no error, your answer will be (E), i.e., 'No error'. (Ignore the errors of punctuation, if any).*

1. (A) There is just not enough/(B) timing in my job to sit around/(C) talking about how we feel/(D) about each other./(E) No error.

2. (A) Reasonable ambition, if supported/(B) at persistent efforts,/(C) is likely to yield/(D) the desired results./(E) No error.

3. (A) Even after worked in the office/(B) for as many as fifteen years,/(C) he still does not understand/(D) the basic objectives of the work./(E) No error.

4. (A) Why some people don't get/(B) what they deserve/(C) and why others get what they don't deserve/(D) is a matter decided by luck./(E) No error.

5. (A) the five-member committee were/(B) of the view that the present service conditions/(C) of the employees of this company/(D) are quite good./(E) No error.

6. (A) If you would have/(B) gone to his house/(C) before 10 a.m., you would have/(D) got his autograph./(E) No error.

7. (A) His speech was/(B) judged by many/(C) as one of the most important speech/(D) given in the function./(E) No error.

8. (A) I am contacting you/(B) sometime in next week/(C) to explain to you/(D) my problem in detail./(E) No error.

9. (A) Whatever he was/(B) today is only because/(C) of his mother who/(D) was a renowned scientist./(E) No error.

10. (A) The Head of the Department along with his colleagues/(B) are coming to attend/(C) the conference which is/(D) scheduled this afternoon./(E) No error.

11. (A) One of the most effective/(B) solutions is that/(C) she should work on Sunday/(D) and complete the assignment./(E) No error.

12. (A) He had to/(B) seek legal help in/(C) order for settling/(D) the dispute./(E) No error.

13. (A) Since I had been gone/(B) through the book/(C) long back, I could/(D) not remember the contents./(E) No error.

14. (A) We have to take/(B) him to the hospital yesterday/(C) because he was/(D) suffering from fever./(E) No error.

15. (A) The interviewer asked the actress/(B) how could she/(C) manage to attain fame/(D) in a short period./(E) No error.

16. (A) The Head of the Department/(B) advised all the staff/(C) to not to/(D) indulge in gossip./(E) No error.

17. (A) I shall be able/(B) to complete the work in/(C) stipulated time provide/(D) you do not disturb me./(E) No error.

18. (A) Having learn my lessons/(B) I was very careful/(C) in dealing with him/(D) in front of his room-mate./(E) No error.

19. (A) In spite of his/(B) being a Quiz Master/(C) show was/(D) a big flop./(E) No error.

20. (A) No sooner the/(B) clock strike six than/(C) all the employees/(D) rushed out of office./(E) No error.

21. (A) He could not/(B) decide as to which/(C) course he should do/(D) after obtaining his Degree./(E) No error.

22. (A) One of the objective/(B) of the meeting which/(C) was held today was to/(D) elect new office-bearers./(E) No error.

23. (A) She would have/(B) surely got the job/(C) if she would have/(D) attended the interview./(E) No error.

24. (A) When the national/(B) anthem was being/(C) sung, everyone were/(D) standing in silence./(E) No error.

25. (A) She herself wash/(B) all the clothes and/(C) never gives them/(D) to the laundry./(E) No error.

26. (A) But for your/(B) kind help this/(C) task could not/(D) have been completed./(E) No error.

27. (A) Since it was a memory test/(B) the students were instructed/(C) to learn the/(D) passage with heart./(E) No error.

28. (A) So longer as/(B) you are honest/(C) and forthright I will/(D) support you in this task./(E) No error.

29. (A) The customer scarcely had/(B) enough money to pay/(C) to the cashier/(D) at the cash counter./(E) No error.

30. (A) Neither the earthquake/(B) nor the subsequent fire/(C) was able to dampen/(D) the spirit of the residents./(E) No error.

31. (A) Not one of the children/(B) has ever sang/(C) on any occasion/(D) in public before./(E) No error.

32. (A) If the by-stander had not been/(B) familiar with first-aid techniques,/(C) the driver which had met/(D) with the accident would have died./(E) No error.

33. (A) Even after requesting/(B) him, he did not/(C) tell us that how/(D) he solved the problem/(E) No error.

34. (A) We never thought/(B) that he is/(C) oldest than the other/(D) players in the team./(E) No error.

35. (A) No sooner did he/(B) got up from bed/(C) than he was sent/(D) to the dairy./(E) No error.

36. (A) By arresting the local criminals/(B) and encouraging good people/(C) we can end/(D) hostilities of that area./(E) No error.

37. (A) The apparently obvious solutions/(B) to most of his problems/(C) were overlook by/(D) many of his friends./(E) No error.

38. (A) In spite of the difficulties/(B) on the way,/(C) they enjoyed their/(D) trip to Gangotri./(E) No error.

39. (A) We decided not tell to/(B) the patient about/(C) the disease he was/(D) suffering from./(E) No error.

40. (A) The principals of equal justice/(B) for all is one of/(C) the cornerstones of our/(D) democratic way of life./(E) No error.

41. (A) The Trust has succeeded/(B) admirably in raising/(C) money for/(D) its future programmes./(E) No error.

42. (A) Honesty, integrity and being intelligent/(B) are the qualities which/(C) we look for when/(D) we interview applicants./(E) No error.

43. (A) In order to save petrol,/(B) motorists must have to/(C) be very cautious/(D) while driving along the highways./(E) No error.

44. (A) The committee is thankful to you/(B) for preparing not only the main report/(C) but also for preparing/(D) the agenda notes and minutes./(E) No error.

45. (A) All of you will agree with me/(B) that no problem faced by our society/(C) is as grave and intractable/(D) as this problem is/(E) No error.

46. (A) I would have lost/(B) my luggage and other belongings/(C) if I would have left the compartment/(D) and gone out to fetch drinking water./(E) No error.

47. (A) He did not like/(B) leaving his old parents alone in the house/(C) but he had no alternative/(D) as he has to go out to work./(E) No error.

48. (A) I was being astonished/(B) when I heard that/(C) he had left the country/(D) without informing anyone of us./(E) No error.

49. (A) According to one survey/(B) only those forests which were/(C) not under village management/(D) succumbed from fires recently./(E) No error.

50. (A) We can not handle/(B) this complicated case today/(C) unless full details are not given/(D) to us by now./(E) No error.

51. (A) We will pack not only/(B) the material properly/(C) but will also deliver it/(D) to your valued customers./(E) No error.

52. (A) While he was away/(B) on a long official tour/(C) his office receive an important letter/(D) which was marked 'Urgent'./(E) No error.

53. (A) We now look forward for/(B) some great achievements/(C) which to some extent/(D) can restore the country's prestige once again./(E) No error.

54. (A) Mahatma Gandhi did not solve/(B) all the problems of the future/(C) but he did solve/(D) problems of his own age./(E) No error.

55. (A) No country can long endure/(B) if its foundations/(C) were not laid deep/(D) in the material prosperity./(E) No error.

56. (A) Though he suffered of fever,/(B) he attended office/(C) and completed all the pending/(D) work by sitting late./(E) No error.

57. (A) As always have been said,/(B) parents should not/(C) impose their desires/(D) on their wards./(E) No error.

58. (A) Being a very fast worker,/(B) he is always liking/(C) by all his colleagues./(D) and superiors too./(E) No error.

59. (A) We fail to understand/(B) why do most educated people/(C) lose their temper even/(D) without any apparent reason./(E) No error.

60. (A) You may not always/(B) get whatever you deserve/(C) but that does not belittle/(D) the importance for your work./(E) No error.

61. (A) On resuming his duty,/(B) he asked his superiors/(C) that whether he would be/(D) permitted to leave early./(E) No error.

62. (A) We don't deny/(B) your right to know/(C) whatever happened while/(D) you were not in the office./(E) No error.

63. (A) He loved his mentor immensely/(B) and gave him fullest loyalty,/(C) yet he had his own/(D) independent way of thinking./(E) No error.

64. (A) We have done everything/(B) that could be done/(C) to avert the storm/(D) which is now coming on./(E) No error.

65. (A) Our school is making/(B) every possible effort/(C) to provide best facilities/(D) and personal attention for each child./(E) No error.

66. (A) They have been/(B) struggling with the management/(C) from the past five years/(D) but their demands are not considered./(E) No error.

67. (A) When I stood up spontaneously/(B) and questioned the speaker;/(C) someone commented that/(D) it was a boldly step./(E) No error.

68. (A) Their only demand/(B) for additional wages were/(C) considered sympathetically/(D) by the progressive management./(E) No error.

69. (A) He has been undergoing/(B) the special training course/(C) which each of the employees/(D) is required to./(E) No error.

70. (A) You must had/(B) a kind and gentle heart/(C) if you want/(D) to be a successful doctor./(E) No error.

71. (A) If you cannot/(B) sympathy with the poor,/(C) how will you be/(D) able to do social work?/(E) No error.

72. (A) He loosened his temper/(B) whenever he knows/(C) things do not take place/(D) as per his planning./(E) No error.

73. (A) They wanted money/(B) to purchase certain things/(C) for themselves and/(D) for donated to their colleagues./(E) No error.

74. (A) As the ticket was/(B) firm affixed/(C) on the envelope, he/(D) could not remove it./(E) No error.

75. (A) I asked him/(B) whom he thought/(C) would be able to/(D) get the first prize./(E) No error.

76. (A) He was too/(B) irritated to/(C) concentrate on his work/(D) for a long time./(E) No error.

77. (A) Both the brothers are/(B) so good-natured that/(C) they look at their/(D) old and aged parents very well./(E) No error.

78. (A) The observers felt that/(B) the stronger team had to face/(C) defeat because the players/(D) didn't play wholehearted./(E) No error.

79. (A) Every animal in the zoo/(B) is fed regularly/(C) and attended to/(D) very promptly./(E) No error.

80. (A) How you eat/(B) is as important/(C) as what/(D) you eat./(E) No error.

81. (A) All his relatives/(B) expect his daughter/(C) have gone on/(D) a month's vacation tour./(E) No error.

82. (A) All renew licences/(B) may be collected from/(C) the cashier's counter after/(D) paying the fees./(E) No error.

83. (A) We are happy/(B) to know that/(C) the project completed/(D) strictly as per the schedule./(E) No error.

84. (A) They would not/(B) have able to plan/(C) the details of the job,/(D) if you had no cooperated./(E) No error.

85. (A) Very few employees./(B) in our company are/(C) so dedicated as/(D) he will./(E) No error.

86. (A) He won the case as/(B) he argued very forcefully and/(C) in such the intelligent way/(D) that the judge changed his opinion./(E) No error.

87. (A) The basket of apples/(B) sent by the gardener/(C) contained a number of/(D) green mangoes also./(E) No error.

88. (A) In the absence of/(B) clear instructions/(C) one cannot be expected/(D) to be functioned effectively./(E) No error.

89. (A) They could have/(B) helped him/(C) had they approached by him./(D) for help well in advance./(E) No error.

90. (A) He has in/(B) his possession a/(C) price collection of very old coins,/(D) and some ancient paintings./(E) No error.

91. (A) Everyone is/(B) impress by/(C) his zeal/(D) and enthusiasm./(E) No error.

92. (A) The patient recover/(B) so fast that/(C) the expert doctors/(D) also were surprised/(E) No error.

93. (A) His father told me/(B) that though his son had/(C) worked very hard,/(D) but he had failed to make any mark in the examination./(E) No error.

94. (A) We must go/(B) and congratulate him for/(C) his brilliant/(D) performance./(E) No error.

95. (A) He deserted the path of honour/(B) in order to/(C) satisfy his ambition/(D) and then went down his doom very quickly./(E) No error.

96. (A) At last the rain ceased/(B) and the sky was/(C) cleared by clouds/(D) and lightening./(E) No error.

97. (A) He said that/(B) he had a difference/(C) with/(D) the chairman at his statement./(E) No error.

98. (A) The future is/(B) yet to come/(C) but you have a/(D) right to shape it./(E) No error.

99. (A) We have keep/(B) our promise and/(C) you can expect/(D) a lot from us in future./(E) No error.

100. (A) He has collected/(B) all the necessary documents/(C) and have written a good paper/(D) for this conference./(E) No error.

ANSWERS

1	2	3	4	5	6	7	8	9	10
B	B	A	A	A	A	C	B	A	B
11	**12**	**13**	**14**	**15**	**16**	**17**	**18**	**19**	**20**
E	C	A	A	B	C	C	A	C	A
21	**22**	**23**	**24**	**25**	**26**	**27**	**28**	**29**	**30**
E	A	C	C	A	E	D	A	A	C
31	**32**	**33**	**34**	**35**	**36**	**37**	**38**	**39**	**40**
B	C	C	C	B	C	C	E	A	A
41	**42**	**43**	**44**	**45**	**46**	**47**	**48**	**49**	**50**
E	A	B	C	B	C	D	A	D	C
51	**52**	**53**	**54**	**55**	**56**	**57**	**58**	**59**	**60**
A	C	A	B	C	A	A	B	B	D
61	**62**	**63**	**64**	**65**	**66**	**67**	**68**	**69**	**70**
C	E	D	A	D	C	D	B	D	A
71	**72**	**73**	**74**	**75**	**76**	**77**	**78**	**79**	**80**
B	A	D	B	B	E	C	D	C	E
81	**82**	**83**	**84**	**85**	**86**	**87**	**88**	**89**	**90**
C	A	C	B	D	C	E	D	C	C
91	**92**	**93**	**94**	**95**	**96**	**97**	**98**	**99**	**100**
B	A	D	B	D	C	D	A	A	C

5

Sentence Correction

A sentence will convey its true meaning and make the right impact if it is written in a grammatically correct way. One must learn the general rules of grammar and practise well to improve one's English regularly. Try your skills in this exercise.

Multiple Choice Questions

Directions: *Which of the phrases given below each sentence should replace the phrase printed in **bold** type to make the sentence grammatically correct? If the sentence is correct as it is, mark 'E' as the answer.*

1. The research study is an eye-opener and **attempts to acquaint** us with the problems of the poor nations.
   A. attempted to acquaint
   B. attempts at acquainting
   C. attempt to acquaint
   D. attempting to acquaint
   E. No correction required

2. The man who has committed such a serious crime must **get the mostly severe** punishment.
   A. be getting the mostly severely
   B. get the most severe
   C. have got the most severely
   D. have been getting the severemost
   E. No correction required

3. Acquisition of certain specific skills **can be facilitated from** general awareness, education and exposure to novel situations.
   A. can be facilitated by
   B. may facilitate through
   C. can be felicitated with
   D. may be felicitated with

E. No correction required

4. He confidently asked the crowd if they thought he was right and the crowd shouted **that they did.**
   A. that he did
   B. that they had
   C. that he is
   D. that he didn't
   E. No correction required

5. If he has to spend five hours in the queue, it **was really a wastage.**
   A. is a really wastage
   B. is real a wastage
   C. has really a wastage
   D. is really a wastage
   E. No correction required

6. Why **did you not threw** the bag away?
   A. did you not throw
   B. had you not threw
   C. did you not thrown
   D. you did not thrown
   E. No correction required

7. They **are not beware of** all the facts
   A. are not aware for
   B. are not aware of
   C. are not to be aware
   D. must not to be aware for
   E. No correction required

55

8. **If I would have** realised the nature of the job earlier, I would not have accepted it.
A. If I have had
B. In case I would have
C. Had I been
D. Had I
E. No correction required

9. The moment they saw me, they **were delight**
A. had delighted
B. were delighted
C. are delighted
D. have been delighted
E. No correction required

10. The small child does whatever his father **was done.**
A. has done   B. did
C. does   D. had done
E. No correction required

11. It was unanimously resolved that the parties **should unitedly undertook** launching of popular programmes.
A. should be united undertook
B. should be unitedly undertaken
C. should be unitedly undertake
D. should unitedly undertake
E. No correction required

12. One of my drawbacks is that **I do not have to** tolerance of ambiguity.
A. do not have   B. cannot have to
C. am not   D. did not have to
E. No correction required

13. They **should have calmly thought of** the advantages that would accrue to them.
A. should have been calm in thinking about
B. should be calmly thought of
C. shall have to calmly thought of
D. should have calmly think of
E. No correction required

14. Their earnings are such that they find it difficult **to make both ends to meet**.
A. to making both ends meet
B. to make both ends for meeting
C. to make both ends meet
D. for making both ends to meet
E. No correction required

15. They **were all shocked at** his failure in the competition.
A. were shocked at all
B. had all shocked at
C. had all shocked by
D. had been all shocked on
E. No correction required

16. He is too impatient **for tolerating** any delay.
A. to tolerate   B. to tolerating
C. at tolerating   D. with tolerating
E. No correction required

17. Why **should the candidates be** afraid of English Language is not clear.
A. the candidates should be
B. do the candidates be
C. should be the candidates
D. are the candidates
E. No correction required

18. Rohan is **as tall if not,** taller than Arpan.
A. not as tall but   B. not so tall but as
C. as tall as, if not   D. as if not
E. No correction required

19. The easiest **of the thing to do** is to ask the address to the shopkeeper.
A. of the things to do
B. among the things did
C. of the thing to be done
D. of all the things done
E. No correction required

20. The player was asked **that why he had not** attended the prayer.
A. why had he not
B. that why had he not
C. why he was not
D. is hesitated to listen to
E. No correction required

21. He **hesitated to listen to** what his brother was saying.
A. listened to hesitate
B. hesitated listen to
C. hesitates to listening
D. is hesitated to listen to
E. No correction required

22. Hardly **does the sun rise** when the stars disappeared.
A. have the sun rose
B. had the sun risen
C. did the sun rose
D. the sun rose
E. No correction required

23. The police has **so far succeeded in recovering** only a part of the stolen property.
A. thus far succeeded for recovery
B. so far succeed in the recovery of
C. as far as succeeded in recovery of
D. so far succeed to recover
E. No correction required

24. **What happens to** all those travellers on the ship was not known?
A. What happened of
B. That is what happens to
C. What is that happens to
D. What happened to
E. No correction required

25. Because of his ill health, the doctor has advised him **not to refrain** from smoking.
A. to not refrain from
B. to resort to
C. to refrain from
D. to be refrained from
E. No correction required

26. The courts **are actively to safeguard** the interests and the rights of the poor.
A. are actively to safeguarding
B. have been actively safeguarding
C. have to active in safeguarding
D. are actively in safeguarding
E. No correction required

27. He is a singer of repute, but his **yesterday's performance was** quite disappointing.
A. performances for yesterday were
B. yesterday performance was
C. yesterday performances were
D. performances about yesterday were
E. No correction required

28. **Despite of their** differences on matters of principles, they all agree on the demand of hike in salary.
A. Despite their
B. Despite of the
C. Despite for their
D. Despite off their

29. The orator **had been left** the auditorium before the audience stood up.
A. had been leaving
B. was left
C. left
D. would leave
E. No correction required

30. This is one of the most important **inventions of this century**.
A. invention of this century
B. invention of these centuries
C. inventions of centuries
D. inventions of the centuries
E. No correction required

31. Can you tell me **why did you not speak** the truth?
A. why did not you speak
B. that why did you not speak
C. why you did not speak
D. why did you not spoke
E. No correction required

32. The chemist **hadn't hardly any of those kind** of medicines.
A. had hardly any of those kinds
B. had hardly not any of those kind
C. had scarcely any of those kind
D. had hardly any of those kind
E. No correction required

33. She cooks, washes dishes, does her homework and **then relaxing.**
A. relaxing then
B. then is relaxing
C. relaxing is then
D. then relaxes
E. No correction required

34. Anyone interested in the use of computers can learn much if **you have access** to a personal computer.
A. they have access
B. access can be available
C. he or she has access
D. one of them have access
E. No correction required

35. **By such time** you finish that chapter, I will write a letter.
A. The time when
B. By the time
C. By that time
D. The time
E. No correction required

36. **Had I realised** how close I was to the edge of the valley, I would not have carried the bags there.
A. Had I been realised
B. If I would have realised
C. When I realised
D. Had I had realised
E. No correction required

37. Later he became unpopular because he tried **to lord it on** his followers.
A. to lord it for   B. to lord over
C. to lord it over   D. to lord it over on
E. No correction required

38. **The long or short of it** is that I do not want to deal with that new firm.
A. The long and short of it
B. The long and short for it
C. The long or short for it
D. The short and long of it
E. No correction required

39. The people generally try to **curry favour** with the corrupt but influential person.
A. cook favour   B. seek favour
C. extract favour   D. display favour
E. No correction required

40. My hair **stood off ends** when I saw the horrible sight.
A. stood at ends   B. stood on ends
C. stood to ends   D. stands on ends
E. No correction required

41. "Friends and comrades, the light has gone **away from** our lives and there is darkness everywhere."
A. off   B. out of
C. out from   D. out off
E. No correction required

42. We **can not always convey** ourselves in simple sentences.
A. cannot always convey
B. can not always express
C. cannot always express
D. can not always communicate
E. No correction required

43. **Shapes** of gods and goddesses are worshipped by people.
A. Images   B. Reflections
C. Clay shapes   D. Clay toys
E. No correction required

44. The crops are dying; **it must not had** rained.
A. must had not
B. must not be
C. must not have
D. must not have been
E. No correction required

45. It is always better to make people realise the importance of discipline than to **impose them on it.**
A. impose it with them
B. impose them with it
C. imposing them on it
D. impose it on them
E. No correction required

46. The performance of our players was rather **worst than I had expected.**
A. bad as I had expected
B. worse than I had expected
C. worse than expectation
D. worst than was expected
E. No correction required

47. For some days the new professor lectured **above the heads of** his pupils.
A. over the head of
B. over the heads of
C. on the heads of
D. through the heads of
E. No correction required

48. For many centuries in Indian history there was no city so famous **like** the city of Ujjain.
A. as   B. such as
C. likewise   D. so like
E. No correction required

49. Making friends is more rewarding than **to make enemies**.
A. to be unsociable   B. to be sociable
C. being unsociable   D. making enemies
E. No correction required

50. You need not come unless you want to.
   A. You don't need to come unless you want to
   B. You come only when you want to
   C. You come unless you don't want to
   D. You needn't come until you don't want to
   E. No correction required

51. The drama had many scenes which were so humorous that it was **hardly possible to keep** a straight face.
   A. hardly possible for keeping
   B. hardly impossible keeping
   C. hardly impossible to keep
   D. hardly possible keeping
   E. No correction required

52. The moment the manager came to know of the fradulent action of his assistant, he **order immediately dismissed him**.
   A. immediately ordered his dismissed
   B. ordered his immediate dismissal
   C. immediately order dismissal of his
   D. ordered for immediately dismissal him
   E. No correction required

53. We met him immediately after the session in which he **had been given** a nice speech.
   A. would be giving
   B. has been given
   C. will have given
   D. had given
   E. No correction required

54. The world has seen **small** real attempt at population and resource planning.
   A. few   B. little
   C. less   D. a few
   E. No correction required

55. One of the most significant **phenomenons** of our time has been the development of the cinema.
   A. phenomenon   B. phenomena
   C. character   D. symptom
   E. No correction required

56. It was until many years later that Gandhi became a rebel against authority.

   A. It was not until many years
   B. It was till many years
   C. It was not many years
   D. Until it was many years
   E. No correction required

57. There are not many men who are so famous that they are frequently referred to by their **short names** only.
   A. initials   B. signatures
   C. pictures   D. middle names
   E. No correction required

58. Though we **have kept in mind to try and maintain** most facilities, we would like to request you to kindly bear with us any inconvenience that may be caused.
   A. must keep in mind to try and maintain
   B. have kept in mind trying and maintain
   C. would keep in mind to try and maintain
   D. should have kept in mind to try and to maintain
   E. No correction required

59. The tea-estate administration is **in such mess there** is no leader to set the things right.
   A. in such a mess here
   B. in a such mess that here
   C. in such a mess that there
   D. with such a mess that there
   E. No correction required

60. My doctor knew that I would eventually recover and do the kind of work **I would be doing** before.
   A. would have been doing
   B. would have done
   C. had been done
   D. had been doing
   E. No correction required

61. If you are thinking about investigation overseas, **isn't it makes** sense to find an experience guide?
   A. it is not making
   B. doesn't it make
   C. does it make
   D. is it making
   E. No correction required

62. The **crime has growth rapidly** in Russia since the disintegration of the communist system.
A. rapid crime has grown
B. crime has grown rapid
C. crimes grow rapidly
D. crimes have been rapidly grown
E. No correction required

63. Technology **must use to feed** the forces of change.
A. must be used to feed
B. must have been using to feed
C. must use having fed
D. must be using to feed
E. No correction required

64. In addition **to enhanced their reputations** through strategic use of philanthropy, companies are sponsoring social initiatives to open new markets.
A. of enhancing their reputations
B. to having enhance their reputation
C. to enhancing their reputation
D. to have their reputation enhancing
E. No correction required

65. They failed **in their attempt to repair** the demolished portion of the building.
A. for their attempt to repair
B. in their attempting to repair
C. with their attempt to repair
D. in their attempt for repairs
E. No correction required

66. We don't know **how did the thief made** an escape.
A. how the thief did make
B. how the thief does make
C. how the thief made
D. how was the thief made
E. No correction required

67. They have a scheme of rewarding **the best of the performers** every year.
A. a best performer
B. the best among the performer
C. a best among performers
D. the best of the performer
E. No correction required

68. No sooner **do the bells ring** than the curtain rose.
A. did the bell ring
B. did the bells ring
C. had the bell rang
D. had the bell rung
E. No correction required

69. Most of the Indian workers are **as healthy as, if not healthier** than, the British workers.
A. as if healthy as and not healthier
B. healthier but not as healthy
C. as healthy, if not healthier
D. so healthy, if not healthier
E. No correction required

70. He admired the speed with which he completed the work and **appreciating the method adopted** by him.
A. appreciate the method being adopted
B. appreciated the method adopted
C. appreciate the method of adoption
D. appreciated the adopting method
E. No correction required

71. The population of Tokyo is **greater than that of any other** town in the world.
A. greatest among any other
B. greater than all other
C. greater than those of any other
D. greater than any other
E. No correction required

72. They examined both the samples very carefully but failed to detect **any difference** in them.
A. some difference in
B. some difference between
C. any difference between
D. any difference among
E. No correction required

73. Tax evaders **should heavily fined** as they do it intentionally.
A. should be heavy fined
B. should have heavily fined
C. shall have heavy fine
D. should be heavily fined
E. No correction required

74. He never **has and ever will take** such strong measures.
A. had taken nor will ever take
B. had taken and will ever take
C. has and never will take
D. had and ever will take
E. No correction required

75. The intruder stood quietly **for few moments**.
A. for few time
B. for the few moments
C. for moments
D. for a few moments
E. No correction required

76. He **should not had** done it.
A. had not   B. should had not
C. should not have   D. should have
E. No correction required

77. The meeting was **attended to by all** the invitees.
A. all attended to by
B. attended by all
C. fully attended to by
D. like attending to all
E. No correction required

78. I have got some tea, but I do not have **a sugar**.
A. some   B. got
C. more   D. any
E. No correction required

79. I need not offer any explanation regarding this incident—my behaviour **is speaking itself**.
A. will speak to itself
B. speaks for itself
C. has been speaking
D. speaks about itself
E. No correction required

80. Ankur has the guts **to rise from** the occasion and come out successfully.
A. in rising from
B. to raise with
C. to rise against
D. to rise to
E. No correction required

81. Mary unnecessarily **picked up** a quarrel with Rosy and left the party hurriedly.
A. has picked up
B. picked on
C. picked
D. picking up
E. No correction required

82. The train will leave at 8.30 p.m., we **have been** ready by 7.30 p.m. so that we can reach the station in time.
A. were   B. must be
C. are   D. should have
E. No correction required

83. He dislikes the word dislike, **isn't he**?
A. didn't he   B. doesn't he
C. hasn't he   D. does he
E. No correction required

84. The prosecution failed **in** establish in every case today.
A. to   B. on
C. as   D. upon
E. No correction required

85. We were still standing in the queue when the **film was beginning**.
A. film began
B. film had begun
C. beginning of the film was over
D. film begins
E. No correction required

86. **I earnestly believe that** you will visit our relatives during your forthcoming trip to Mumbai.
A. had hardly believe that
B. sincerely would believe
C. certainly believing that
D. could not believe
E. No correction required

87. We must **take it granted** that she will not come for today's function.
A. take it for granted
B. taking it granted
C. took it as granted
D. have it granted
E. No correction required

88. He has received no other message than an urgent telegram **asking him to rush his village** immediately.
   A. asked him to rush his village
   B. asking him to have rush his village
   C. asking him to rush to his village
   D. asking him rushing at his village
   E. No correction required

89. They continued to work in the field **despite of the heavy rains**.
   A. even though there is heavy rain
   B. although heavily rains
   C. in spite the heavy rains
   D. even though it rained heavily
   E. No correction required

90. **Had you been told** me about your problem, I would have helped you.
   A. If you would have told
   B. Had you have told
   C. had you told
   D. If you have told
   E. No correction required

91. They felt humiliated because they realised that they **had cheated**.
   A. have been cheated
   B. had been cheated
   C. had been cheating
   D. were to be cheated
   E. No correction required

92. He found the gold coin **as he cleans** the floor.
   A. as he had cleaned
   B. while he cleans
   C. which he is cleaning
   D. while cleaning
   E. No correction required

93. Because of his mastery in this field, his suggestions **are wide accepted**.
   A. are widely accepted
   B. are wide acceptance
   C. have widely accepted
   D. have been wide accepted
   E. No correction required

94. The man to **who I sold** my house was a cheat.
   A. to whom I sell
   B. to who I sell
   C. who was sold to
   D. to whom I sold
   E. No correction required

95. **If I was you,** I would not have joined the party.
   A. If I am you
   B. If I be you
   C. As you
   D. Were I you
   E. No correction required

96. You will be late if you **do not leave** now.
   A. did not leave
   B. left
   C. will not leave
   D. do not happen to leave
   E. No correction required

97. All the allegations **levelled against** him were found to be baseless.
   A. level against
   B. level with
   C. levelling with
   D. levelled for
   E. No correction required

98. What **does agonise me most** is not this criticism, but the trivial reason behind it.
   A. most agonising me
   B. agonises me most
   C. agonising me most
   D. I most agonised
   E. No correction required

99. The accused now flatly denies **have admitted** his guilt in his first statement.
   A. having admitted
   B. had admitted
   C. have been admitting
   D. has admitting
   E. No correction required

100. We demonstrated to them how we **were prepared** the artistic patterns.
   A. are prepared
   B. have prepared
   C. are preparing
   D. had prepared
   E. No correction required

ANSWERS

1	2	3	4	5	6	7	8	9	10
B	B	A	E	D	A	B	D	B	C
11	**12**	**13**	**14**	**15**	**16**	**17**	**18**	**19**	**20**
D	A	E	C	E	A	A	C	A	D
21	**22**	**23**	**24**	**25**	**26**	**27**	**28**	**29**	**30**
E	B	E	D	C	B	E	A	C	E
31	**32**	**33**	**34**	**35**	**36**	**37**	**38**	**39**	**40**
C	A	D	C	B	E	C	A	E	B
41	**42**	**43**	**44**	**45**	**46**	**47**	**48**	**49**	**50**
B	C	A	C	D	B	B	A	D	A
51	**52**	**53**	**54**	**55**	**56**	**57**	**58**	**59**	**60**
E	B	D	B	B	A	A	E	C	D
61	**62**	**63**	**64**	**65**	**66**	**67**	**68**	**69**	**70**
B	B	A	C	E	C	E	B	E	B
71	**72**	**73**	**74**	**75**	**76**	**77**	**78**	**79**	**80**
E	C	D	A	D	C	B	D	B	D
81	**82**	**83**	**84**	**85**	**86**	**87**	**88**	**89**	**90**
C	B	B	A	B	E	A	C	D	C
91	**92**	**93**	**94**	**95**	**96**	**97**	**98**	**99**	**100**
B	D	A	D	D	E	E	B	A	D

6

Cloze Test

A cloze test is a procedure in which you are asked to supply words which have been removed from a passage. It is meant to test your ability to comprehend text. Try and practise it to master it in this exercise.

Multiple Choice Questions

Directions: *In the following passages there are some blanks, each of which has been numbered. These numbers are also printed below the passages and against each five words are suggested, one of which fits the blank appropriately. Find out the appropriate word in each case.*

PASSAGE-1

Mobile banking (M banking) involves the use of a mobile phone or any other mobile device to ...(1)... financial transactions linked to a client's account. M banking is new in most countries and most mobile payment models even in developed countries, to date operate on a ...(2)... scale. A mobile network offers a ...(3)... available technology platform onto which other services can be provided at low cost with effective results. For example, M banking services which use ...(4)... such as SMS can be carried at a cost of less than one US cent per message. The low cost of using existing infrastructure makes such services more ...(5)... to use by customers with lower purchasing power and opens up access to services which did not reach them earlier due to ...(6)... cost of service delivery. Although M banking is one aspect in the wider ...(7)... of e-banking there are reasons to single it out for focus-especially because there are a lot more people with mobile phones than

bank accounts in India.

M banking could provide a ...(8)... solution to bring more "unbanked" people to the financial mainstream. Without traditional credit, individuals are ...(9)... to exploitation by abusive lenders offering very high interest rates on short term loans. Also of considerable importance are public safety implications for the unbanked—they are often victims of crime because many operate on a cash only basis and end up carrying significant amounts of cash on their ...(10)... or store cash in their homes.

1. A. Disburse   B. Undertake
   C. Subscribe   D. Lure
   E. Amass

2. A. Full   B. Voluminous
   C. Substantial   D. Limited
   E. Rapid

3. A. Readily   B. Tangible
   C. Routinely   D. Securely
   E. Unique

4. A. Process   B. Waves
   C. Deliveries   D. Connection
   E. Channels

5. A. Valuable   B. Answerable
   C. Amenable   D. Exposed
   E. Responsible

64

6. A. Waning   B. Stable
   C. Proportionate   D. Marginal
   E. High

7. A. Archive   B. Domain
   C. Purpose   D. Component
   E. Aspect

8. A. Law abiding   B. Tried
   C. Reassuring   D. Cost effective
   E. Stopgap

9. A. Inclined   B. Immune
   C. Vulnerable   D. Surrendered
   E. Pressured

10. A. Person   B. Own
    C. Relatives   D. Purses
    E. Self

PASSAGE-2

The world economy is in recession—the deepest and the most widespread ...(1)... the 1930s. There are ...(2)... of ...(3)... in the industrial countries, but most serious economic ...(4)... anticipate that rates of growth and levels of economic activity will remain low.

In all that has been written about world ...(5)..., the ...(6)... have been overwhelmingly and narrowly economic. Few have ...(7)... the human consequences in more than a superficial manner. Not a single international study has ...(8)... the recession's ...(9)... on the most vulnerable half of the world's population—the children.

The need for ...(10)... clearly the ...(11)... between world economic conditions and child welfare has thus become even more urgent in the last few years. The worldscale of current child distress also makes it artificial to restrict the analysis of causes to the ...(12)... level.

1. A. in   B. for
   C. by   D. before
   E. since

2. A. risks   B. glimmers
   C. studies   D. tips
   E. histories

3. A. development   B. downfall
   C. recovery   D. slackness
   E. impact

4. A. analysts   B. journalists
   C. surveys   D. findings
   E. students

5. A. development   B. economy
   C. wars   D. recession
   E. conflicts

6. A. emphasis   B. aims
   C. glimpses   D. suppositions
   E. preoccupations

7. A. delved   B. taught
   C. propagated   D. investigated
   E. manifested

8. A. understood   B. analysed
   C. highlighted   D. prepared
   E. planned

9. A. analysis   B. undercurrents
   C. impact   D. overtures
   E. study

10. A. chalking out   B. curbing
    C. bringing out   D. implementing
    E. propagating

11. A. linkages   B. fallouts
    C. dependence   D. contrasts
    E. similarities

12. A. international   B. political
    C. low   D. national
    E. highest

PASSAGE-3

Nowadays, under the ...(1)... system of education, however good it may be, when a young man comes out of the University, there seems to be this ...(2)... in him that the higher the standard of living rises, the less should a man work. Thus, mathematically higher the standard of living, according to this misconceived notion, the less the ...(3)... . Ultimately, what should be the highest standard of living then? ...(4)... work! This leads to an unhealthy ...(5)... among the workers. A typist who types over twenty letters a day asks his ...(6)... how many letters he had typed that day. The latter ...(7)... "fifteen". The former thinks, "Tomorrow I should type only fifteen or even ...(8)... . This tendency is quite ...(9)..., and may ultimately lead to ...(10)... . Even one's family life may be affected adversely due to such tendency.

1. A. developed   B. extinct
   C. outdated   D. proposed
   E. modern
2. A. anxiety   B. misconception
   C. realisation   D. worry
   E. apprehension
3. A. salary   B. comfort
   C. work   D. energy
   E. time
4. A. Minimum   B. Maximum
   C. Less   D. No
   E. Ample
5. A. competition   B. dispute
   C. delay   D. jealousy
   E. ambition
6. A. employee   B. subordinate
   C. boss   D. client
   E. colleague
7. A. suggests   B. remembers
   C. replies   D. types
   E. all
8. A. less   B. all
   C. more   D. few
   E. some
9. A. discouraging B. heartening
   C. healthy   D. unfortunate
   E. unnatural
10. A. evil   B. retardation
    C. progress   D. denial
    E. complexity

PASSAGE-4

Four cases of burglary have been ...(1)... with the arrest of one ...(2)... criminal. The police have ...(3)... gold and silver jewellery from him. The police increased their public contacts with the residents of the area after following a spate of burglaries. They held corner meetings to ...(4)... the residents on steps to ...(5)... prevention. They were ...(6)... to inform their neighbours if they had to ...(7)... their houses unattended. Consequently, some ...(8)... of the locality observed one ...(9)... leaving an empty house. He was ...(10)... and a case was registered.

1. A. connected   B. adjusted
   C. solved   D. deferred
   E. dealt
2. A. notorious   B. more
   C. thief   D. imprisoned
   E. extremely
3. A. withdrawn   B. amassed
   C. sold   D. recovered
   E. stolen
4. A. harass   B. arrest
   C. probe   D. threaten
   E. educate
5. A. loss   B. crime
   C. its   D. burglar
   E. their
6. A. required   B. forbidden
   C. instructed   D. entrusted
   E. forced
7. A. paint   B. sell
   C. protect   D. leave
   E. build
8. A. criminals   B. neighbours
   C. burglars   D. pedestrians
   E. residents
9. A. stranger   B. resident
   C. neighbour   D. entrant
   E. alien
10. A. misled   B. apprehended
    C. neglected   D. boycotted
    E. informed

PASSAGE-5

...(1)... change is the ...(2)... of the day, a proper orientation to ...(3)... with the change becomes a natural necessity ...(4)... assured organisational stability. In this ...(5)... of organisational change and survival, the author brings in the concept of 'praxis', ...(6)... it as the dynamo of change and uses it for ...(7)... a conceptual and methodological ...(8)... for the identification of training needs. Training, ...(9)... perceived as only one of the many elements in the organisational reflection process, is believed to stand ...(10)... as the means for relevant learning.

1. A. Few   B. Many
   C. No   D. If
   E. Why

2. A. order   B. scope
   C. large   D. direction
   E. result
3. A. assist   B. renew
   C. become   D. try
   E. cope
4. A. in   B. for
   C. from   D. which
   E. but
5. A. end   B. decision
   C. context   D. scope
   E. focus
6. A. describes   B. throws
   C. rejects   D. leaves
   E. derives
7. A. neglecting   B. developing
   C. calculating   D. experiencing
   E. diluting
8. A. routine   B. idea
   C. book   D. follow up
   E. framework
9. A. be   B. may
   C. though   D. gets
   E. as
10. A. in   B. against
   C. through   D. out
   E. with

PASSAGE-6

Each year, middle class Indian children ...(1)... hundreds of crores of rupees in pocket money and ...(2)... a heavy burden on parental ...(3)... . Like adults, these kids have ...(4)... connected with budgeting and saving money. Unfortunately, basic money ...(5)... is ...(6)... taught in schools. At home, very few parents ...(7)... money matters with their children. Kids who ...(8)... about money ...(9)... have been found to be way ahead of their peers. Indeed, learning to ...(10)... with money properly fosters discipline, good work habits and self-respect.

1. A. spend   B. steal
   C. save   D. give
   E. invest
2. A. move   B. take
   C. risk   D. put
   E. lift

3. A. promises   B. payments
   C. demands   D. attitudes
   E. incomes
4. A. expenses   B. experience
   C. problems   D. guidance
   E. necessities
5. A. availability   B. inflation
   C. economics   D. problem
   E. management
6. A. carefully   B. rarely
   C. generally   D. always
   E. thoroughly
7. A. discuss   B. understand
   C. teach   D. reveal
   E. advise
8. A. quarrel   B. ask
   C. learn   D. waste
   E. spend
9. A. slowly   B. early
   C. timely   D. lately
   E. regularly
10. A. decide   B. earn
   C. control   D. deal
   E. pay

PASSAGE-7

Architecture is a unique ...(1)... of art and science that has ...(2)... out of man's primary need for shelter. It is concerned with the design and ...(3)... of buildings in their sociological, technological and environmental context. This field is not only ...(4)...but also provide the ...(5)... of designing and building pleasing and ...(6)... refined structures to serve various needs. ...(7)... the fairly large number of practising architects, the countrywide ...(8)... in building activity offers scope for more. And though the initial earnings in the field are relatively ...(9)... what you make thereafter will depend entirely on your ...(10)... .

1. A. procedure   B. process
   C. portion   D. blend
   E. subject
2. A. drifted   B. fizzled
   C. contrived   D. earned
   E. arisen

3. A. painting   B. construction
   C. decoration   D. repairing
   E. appearance
4. A. fatiguing   B. strenuous
   C. encouraging   D. vast
   E. rewarding
5. A. satisfaction   B. facility
   C. infrastructure   D. amenities
   E. decorum
6. A. practically   B. ideologically
   C. aesthetically   D. principally
   E. readily
7. A. Considering   B. Having
   C. Assuming   D. Regarding
   E. Despite
8. A. variation   B. slack
   C. lethargy   D. spurt
   E. deterioration
9. A. escalating   B. modest
   C. unpredictable   D. negligible
   E. exorbitant
10. A. ambition   B. appearance
    C. expectation   D. experience
    E. need

PASSAGE-8

Without science there is no future for any society. Even with science, ...(1)... it is controlled by some spiritual impulses, there is also no future. One great thing about science is that it does not accept anything on mere ...(2)... . Everything has to be ...(3)... beyond any doubt. All acceptance comes after experiement which has no room for any ...(4)... . This is the reason ...(5)... development of science and technology has revolutionised human life all over the world. There are very few spheres of human activity which have not experienced the ...(6)... of such development. However, despite its manifold ...(7)... science has not been ...(8)... to solve any of man's moral or spiritual problems. Society is still ...(9)... in the dark to find out what its future will be. The need, therefore, is to make science ...(10)... for the ultimate truth.

1. A. unless   B. without
   C. if   D. before
   E. because

2. A. principles   B. conjecture
   C. experiment   D. research
   E. experience
3. A. accepted   B. demonstrated
   C. proved   D. performed
   E. understood
4. A. precision   B. exactness
   C. confirmation   D. speculation
   E. apprehension
5. A. for   B. how
   C. that   D. about
   E. why
6. A. impact   B. futility
   C. causes   D. problems
   E. nature
7. A. limitations   B. benefits
   C. shortcomings   D. researches
   E. inventions
8. A. employed   B. developed
   C. able   D. entrusted
   E. taught
9. A. engulfed   B. lost
   C. enlightening   D. investigating
   E. groping
10. A. useful   B. worthy
    C. ready   D. search
    E. fit

PASSAGE-9

Faced with an ...(1)... number and variety of products on the market, managers are finding it more difficult to ...(2)... demand and plan production and order ...(3)... . As a result ...(4)... forecasts are increasing and, along with them, the costs of those errors. Many managers today, ...(5)... speed is the ...(6)..., have turned to one or another popular production scheduling system. But these tools tackle only part of the problem. ...(7)... really needed is a way to ...(8)... forecasts and simultaneously redesign planning processes to ...(9)... the impact of ...(10)... forecasts.

1. A. exact   B. equal
   C. optimum   D. eccentric
   E. unprecedented
2. A. meet   B. predict
   C. ignore   D. accept
   E. register

3. A. immediately   B. quickly
   C. accordingly   D. positively
   E. spontaneously
4. A. inaccurate   B. buoyant
   C. frequent   D. inadequate
   E. exorbitant
5. A. consider   B. neglecting
   C. visualising   D. believing
   E. notwithstanding
6. A. problem   B. answer
   C. source   D. outcome
   E. lacuna
7. A. What's   B. That's
   C. One   D. Managers
   E. Companies
8. A. ignore   B. obtain
   C. vitiate   D. negate
   E. improve
9. A. rationalise   B. substantiate
   C. minimise   D. counter
   E. tolerate
10. A. dangerous   B. absolute
    C. unpredicted   D. erroneous
    E. popular

PASSAGE-10

In view of the ...(1)... demand for personnel with commerce background, in the post-liberalisation period, courses in commerce have ...(2)... the attention of students and parents. There is growing ...(3)... for these courses not only in schools but also in colleges. But the ...(4)... of commerce education in schools leaves ...(5)... to be desired. Its popularity, importance and quality, to a large extent, depends much on the teaching methodology being ...(6)... in schools. Of course, the ...(7)... review and ...(8)... of syllabic also ...(9).... But this aspect is ...(10)... taken care of suitably, by the concerned organisations.

1. A. exaggerated   B. unreasonable
   C. tremendous   D. increasing
   E. diminishing
2. A. distorted   B. ameliorated
   C. attracted   D. weighed
   E. encouraged
3. A. demand   B. contempt
   C. dissatisfaction   D. commotion
   E. urgency
4. A. awareness   B. intricacy
   C. status   D. necessity
   E. quality
5. A. scope   B. much
   C. short   D. everything
   E. nothing
6. A. abandoned   B. practised
   C. contemplated   D. assimilated
   E. taught
7. A. unscrupulous   B. partial
   C. expert   D. general
   E. periodical
8. A. discussions   B. perusal
   C. reduction   D. updating
   E. formulation
9. A. matters   B. flourishes
   C. desires   D. encompasses
   E. needs
10. A. duly   B. seldom
    C. being   D. often
    E. never

ANSWERS

PASSAGE-1

1	2	3	4	5	6	7	8	9	10
B	D	D	A	D	E	B	D	C	A

PASSAGE-2

1	2	3	4	5	6	7	8	9	10
E	A	D	A	B	B	A	B	C	C

11	12
D	D

PASSAGE-3

1	2	3	4	5	6	7	8	9	10
E	B	C	D	E	C	C	A	A	B

PASSAGE-4

1	2	3	4	5	6	7	8	9	10
C	A	D	E	B	A	D	E	A	B

PASSAGE-5

1	2	3	4	5	6	7	8	9	10
D	A	E	B	C	A	B	E	C	D

PASSAGE-6

1	2	3	4	5	6	7	8	9	10
A	D	E	C	E	B	A	C	C	D

PASSAGE-7

1	2	3	4	5	6	7	8	9	10
D	E	B	D	C	C	E	D	B	D

PASSAGE-8

1	2	3	4	5	6	7	8	9	10
A	B	C	D	E	A	B	C	E	E

PASSAGE-9

1	2	3	4	5	6	7	8	9	10
E	B	C	A	D	B	A	E	C	E

PASSAGE-10

1	2	3	4	5	6	7	8	9	10
D	C	A	E	B	B	E	D	A	A

Idioms & Phrases

An idiom is a group of words established by usage having a meaning different from individual words.

A phrase is a small group of words standing together as an idiomatic expression.

Learn and practise as may as you can and test your knowledge in the exercise that follows.

Idioms and Idiomatic Phrases

+ **ABC** (basic principles)
  I do not know the ABC of photography.

+ **At one's beck and call** (ready to obey)
  He had a dozen men at his beck and call.

+ **At sixes and sevens** (in disorder)
  The drawing room articles were lying at sixes and sevens on the floor.

+ **A wet blanket** (a discouraging person)
  Don't allow him to accompany you to the hunting trip, he is a wet blanket.

+ **A big gun** (an important person)
  Mr Tata is a big gun in our city.

+ **At a stone's throw** (at a short distance from)
  My school is at a stone's throw from my house.

+ **A man of word** (a person who keeps his promise)
  Mr Modi is a man of word.

+ **A man of a few words** (a remarkable person)
  Gandhiji was a man of a few words.

+ **At arm's length** (to keep away)
  We should always keep bad boys at arm's length

+ **A bolt from the blue** (a sudden and unexpected event)
  The news of my friend's death came to me like a bolt from the blue.

+ **A man of letters** (a scholar)
  Radha Krishnan was a man of letters.

+ **A hard nut to crack.** (a puzzling problem)
  To get a win over American basket ball team is a hard nut to crack for India.

+ **A yeoman's service** (service which is beneficial to the human beings)
  He did yeoman's service through his life.

+ **A snake in the grass** (a hidden foe)
  Beware of him because he seems to be a snake in the grass.

+ **Acid test** (hard test)
  The election will be an acid test for the ruling party.

+ **A wolf in sheep's clothing** (a hypocrite)
  You should not keep company with him because he is a wolf in sheep's clothing.

+ **At the eleventh hour** (at the last moment)
  The war was about to start but fortunately at the eleventh hour a messenger came to the PM with a message of peace.

+ **A great card** (an important person)
  Mr Rajan is a great card in the ministry of finance.

+ **A fool of the first water** (one completely foolish)
  Being a fool of the first water he could not solve even the simplest sum.

+ **A bone of contention** (to be the cause of quarrel)
  Kashmir is the bone of contention between India and Pakistan.

+ **A green hand** (not very much experienced)
  We shall pay a little to a green hand.

+ **All in all** (completely)
  Rajesh is all in all in this office.

71

+ **A bed of roses** (a comfort)
Life is not a bed of roses.

+ **An apple of discord** (to be the cause of)
Kashmir is an apple of discord between India and Pakistan.

+ **A white elephant** (of no use)
This sort of glib talker always proves a white elephant in the end.

+ **A red letter day** (an important day)
15th August is a red letter day for the Indians.

+ **By hook or by crook** (by any means fair or foul)
You must complete this job by hook or by crook.

+ **Black sheep** (a traitor)
Later on the person proved a black sheep.

+ **By dint of** (by means of)
By dint of hard work, she earned a lot of money.

+ **Break ones back** (to work hard to get something)
He broke his back to earn his livelihood.

+ **Break the back of** (accomplish the hardest part of a certain job)
There is nothing to be worried about as we've already broken the back of the problem.

+ **Beat about the bush** (to go on talking on some worthless topic)
Stop this beating about the bush, come to the main task.

+ **Beyond one's means** (beyond one's budget)
He is living beyond his means, therefore, he is sure to get ruined.

+ **Cut loose** (keep away)
India should cut loose from bad politics.

+ **Chips of the same block** (having the same taste)
They are the chips of the same block.

+ **Cut-throat competition** (a stiff competition)
There is a cut-throat competition among the publishers in the market.

+ **Come what may** (no matter what happens)
I'll do it, come what may.

+ **Drop someone a line** (send a letter, etc.)
Please drop me a line of your well-being.

+ **Dull the edge of** (reduce the intensity of)
Take this pill and it will dull the edge of pain.

+ **From hand to mouth** (without any saving)
The poor factory worker is living from hand to mouth.

+ **Fair and square** (clean)
One must be fair and square in one's dealing.

+ **Hard of hearing** (somewhat deaf)
She is a bit hard of hearing.

+ **In the good books of** (be good in one's mind)
Jack is in the good books of his teachers.

+ **In black and white** (in written)
Don't give him anything in black and white.

+ **In cold blood** (mercilessly)
The old woman was murdered in cold blood.

+ **In a crack** (all of a sudden or rapidly)
The thief left the place in a crack.

+ **In full swing** (in full force)
The studies of the students are going on in full swing.

+ **In the twinkling of an eye** (quickly)
The monkey ate up grams in the twinkling of an eye.

+ **Keep the ball rolling** (to maintain the progress of some activity)
After the death of his father he had to take the charge of his office to keep the ball rolling.

+ **Neck and neck** (even)
There is a neck and neck fight between the two boxers.

+ **Once in a blue moon** (seldom)
She visits her brother once in a blue moon.

+ **Slow and steady** (slowly but continually)
Slow and steady wins the race.

+ **To cut a sorry figure** (present oneself in a bad way)
She cut a sorry figure on the stage.

+ **To give a red carpet reception** (to give a warm welcome)
The PM was given a red carpet reception in America.

+ **To dance one's tune** (to follow someone submissively)
He always dances to his brother's tune.

+ **To turn a deaf ear to** (to disregard)
She turned a deaf ear to her parents' advice.

+ **To call a spade a spade** (to speak the truth)
Gandhiji always called a spade a spade.

+ **To bring to book** (to scold)
The naughty boy was brought to book by the teacher.

+ **To cut short** (to reduce)
Smoking will cut short your life.

+ **To grease the palm of** (to bribe)
Rohit greased the palm of the clerk and got the file moved.

+ **Through thick and thin.** (under all circumstances)
We'll stand by you through thick and thin.

+ **To die by inches** (to die a painful death)
The old man died by inches.

+ **To eat one's words** (to retract one's statement)
You'll have to eat your words because you have spoken without thinking.

+ **To burn the midnight oil** (to work hard)
You'll have to burn the midnight oil if you want to get good marks.

+ **To poke one's nose into** (to meddle with)
It is bad to poke your nose into others' affair.

+ **To fall flat** (to have no effect)
His father's advice fell flat on him.

+ **To make a clean breast of** (to confess)
He made a clean breast of his involvement in the bomb blast.

+ **To get the better of** (overcome)
Anger got the better of him.

+ **To break somebody's back** (to give too much work to him to do)
She broke his back by giving him so much hard work to do.

+ **Throw cold water on** (to discourage)
She tried to throw cold water on his plan but he was well-determined.

+ **The long and short of** (in brief)
The long and short of his lecture is that we should live like brothers.

+ **To burn one's fingers** (to get oneself in trouble)
You have burnt your fingers by speaking against him.

+ **To turn over a new leaf** (to change the course of life)
He has turned over a new leaf in his life.

+ **To have one's own axe to grind** (to have vested interest)
He has his own axe to grind in this matter.

+ **To take to one's heels** (to run away)
The thief took to his heels as soon as he saw the policeman.

+ **To move heaven and earth** (to make too much effort)
The young man moved heaven and earth to find a job.

+ **To be caught red handed** (to be caught at the time of committing a crime)
The clerk was caught red handed when he was accepting bribe from Mr ABC.

+ **To receive with open arms** (to give a warm welcome)
The new president of the club was received with open arms by the members.

+ **To be born with a silver spoon in one's mouth** (to be born in a rich family)
Mr. J. L. Nehru was born with a silver spoon in his mouth.

+ **To come to light** (to be known)
A new disease has recently come to light.

+ **To be the apple of one's eye** (be very dear)
He is the apple of his parent's eye.

+ **To make fun of** (laugh at)
The children made fun of the waiter in the hotel.

+ **To let the cat out of the bag** (to divulge secret)
It was I who let the cat out of the bag by telling the real matter.

+ **To open a new chapter** (to start some habit, etc.)
By quitting drinking, you've opened a new chapter in your life.

+ **To make the flesh creep** (to terrify)
The story made my flesh creep.

+ **To lose ground** (to retreat)
After fighting for some time the Pakistani army began to lose ground.

- **To bring to book** (to punish)
  The student was brought to book by the teacher.
- **To show a clean pair of heels** (to run away)
  The thief showed a clean pair of heels as soon as he saw the policeman approaching.
- **To gain ground** (to be established)
  He gained ground in India in a few years.
- **To get wind of** (to get information)
  I got wind of his secret plans.
- **Under a cloud** (be in trouble or in a state of disgrace or suspicion)
  His company seemed to be under a cloud as it had no funds to pay the wages to the workers.

Verbal Phrases

- **Act upon** (to follow)
  I acted upon my father's advice.
- **Act upto** (to perform within limits)
  He acted upto his conscience.
- **Act beyond** (to perform crossing limits)
  We should not act beyond our capacity.
- **Act for** (to perform in place of someone else)
  The vice principal acted for the principal.
- **Back up** (to make a queue)
  The vehicles began to back up.
- **Back down** (withdraw claim in the presence of opposition)
  The leader backed down from his previous statement.
- **Back off** (draw back some plan or action)
  They backed off from building a flyover.
- **Back out** (withdraw from a promise, etc.)
  The government backed out of its promise.
- **Break down** (stop working) My car broke down on the highway.
- **Break into** (enter in certain premises by breaking the door, etc.)
  Last night a thief broke into my neighbour's.
- **Break off** (to detach by breaking)
  The branch broke off from the tree.
- **Break out** (spread)
  Cholera has broken out in the town.

- **Break out of** (escape from)
  A prisoner broke out of the prison last night.
- **Break up** (disperse)
  The cloud of fog began to break up as the sun rose.
- **Break something up** (cause something to break into small pieces)
  She broke up the chocolate to distribute it among the children.
- **Break with** (cut off connection after quarrelling with someone)
  He has broken with his brother.
- **Call on** (pay a visit to somebody)
  I'll call on Mohan's today.
- **Call out** (to start)
  The workers have called out a strike.
- **Call off** (to stop the strike etc.)
  The workers have called off the strike.
- **Call at** (to visit someone's house)
  I called at his house yesterday.
- **Call in** (send for)
  Please call in the doctor.
- **Carry on** (continue)
  Please carry on your work.
- **Carry something out** (perform a task)
  Our company is carrying out a big deal with a foreign company.
- **Carry something over** (postpone)
  The fancy dress competition had to be carried over till Monday)
- **Carry someone off** (kill somebody)
  Cancer carried her off on the day of her 20th birthday.
- **Come of age** (get established)
  As our company has come of age, so, there is no problem in selling our goods.
- **Come of** (belong to)
  She comes of a royal family.
- **Come over** (surmount)
  We at last came over all our problems.
- **Come off** (to take place)
  The marriage of my brother comes off in the next month.

+ **Come round** (agree)
At last he came round to my views.

+ **Come under** (fall in the category of)
All these animals come under the same species.

+ **Come down with** (suffer from)
She came down with whopping cough.

+ **Come from** (be the native of)
She came from London.

+ **Come about** (happen)
The explosion came about when the worker struck the match to light a cigarette.

+ **Cut off** (die)
The cricketer is cut off in the prime of his life.

+ **Cut down** (reduce)
The prices of consumer goods should be cut down.

+ **Cut someone out** (exclude someone)
His father cut him out of his will.

+ **Fall in**
She fell in love with the prince.

+ **Fall down** (fail)
The deal fell down for lack of transparency.

+ **Fall out** (quarrel)
She fell out with his elder brother.

+ **Fall through** (fail)
The project fell through for lack of funds.

+ **Get away** (escape)
She got away with her life.

+ **Get by** (to accomplish something with great difficulty)
She is not rich. She has just enough to get by.

+ **Get on** (perform)
How are you getting on with your studies?

+ **Get out** (become known)
The news got out that the PM was paying a visit to Russia.

+ **Get over** (overcome)
At last I got over all obstacles.

+ **Get up** (rise)
When do you get up in the morning?

+ **Give up** (stop)
He gave up smoking.

+ **Give out** (emit)
Garlic gives out a pungent smell.

+ **Give in** (collapse)
The bridge gave in under the heavy load.

+ **Give away** (distribute)
The Principal gave away the prizes.

+ **Give out** (announce)
It was given out that the President of India would visit the place soon.

+ **Go off** (explode)
The gun went off suddenly.

+ **Go on** (continue)
She went on about how she flew the aeroplane.

+ **Go through** (examine)
I'll go through this book later on.

+ **Go up** (be built)
The construction of the house is going up.

+ **Grind on** (continue for a long time in a tedious way)
The discussion over political issues ground on.

+ **Grind something out** (produce something a tedious way)
She will grind some more short stories.

+ **Look out** (be careful)
Look out! there is a snake.

+ **Look down upon** (hate)
We should not look down upon the poor.

+ **Look at** (watch)
Look at the blackboard.

+ **Look after** (take care of)
We ought to look after our old parents.

+ **Look into** (investigate)
The new police inspector will look into the matter.

+ **Look up** (rise)
The prices of consumer goods are looking up.

+ **Look back** (think of the past)
It made her feel disolate when she looked back on things of the past.

+ **Make up** (to fulfil)
I'll make up my deficiency in Mathematics.

+ **Make out** (understand)
I could not make out what she said.

+ **Make up one' mind** (to resolve)
I have made up my mind to settle in the USA.

+ **Make off** (leave hurriedly)
She made off without informing anybody.

+ **Make something over** (transfer)
She should make her property over to her sons.

+ **Make over** (hand over)
He made over the charge of the file to Mr Robert.

+ **Pull back** (retreat)
The government has pulled back from its previous policy.

+ **Pull something down** (demolish)
The authorities concerned pulled down a few building which were illegally built on government land.

+ **Pull out** (pluck)
The child pulled out a few petals of the flower.

+ **Pull through** (recover)
The patient will pull through.

+ **Push on** (continue a journey)
It was getting darker but we pushed on.

+ **Push at** (exert force)
He pushed at the bell, but it did not ring.

+ **Push for** (demand persistently)
The workers have been pushing for the installation of new machines for five years.

+ **Put out** (extinguish)
She put out the light.

+ **Put on** (wear)
He put on an overcoat.

+ **Put off** (postpone)
The plan had to be put off.

+ **Put by** (spare something for future)
We must put by some money for future.

+ **Put up with** (stay)
Your aunt is out of town for a couple of days, you may put up with us till she comes.

+ **Put something down** (record something)
She put a new idea down on the paper.

+ **Take after** (resemble)
He takes after his father.

+ **Take off** (remove)
He took off his shoes.

+ **Take something out** (obtain)
You may take out some money from Rohit if you want to purchase this car.

+ **Take to** (fall into the habit of)
He took to gambling.

+ **Turn something down** (reject something)
The judge turned down his appeal.

+ **Turn on** (attack)
The thief turned on him with a knife.

Multiple Choice Questions

Directions: *Some idioms/phrases are given below with their probable meanings. Select the options with their correct meanings.*

1. **Carry out**
   A. To take from one place to another
   B. To continue
   C. To obey
   D. To make efforts
   E. None of these

2. **In the same boat**
   A. A worn out choice
   B. Indifferent
   C. In identical circumstances
   D. Carry off

E. None of these

3. **In one's good book**
   A. A costly book
   B. A priceless treasure
   C. In one's favour
   D. An enchanting beauty
   E. None of these

4. **Keep a straight face**
   A. To do make up
   B. To change clothes
   C. Assume responsibility
   D. To remain serious
   E. None of these

5. **To be above board**
   A. To have a good height
   B. To be honest in any business deal
   C. To have no debts
   D. To try to be beautiful
   E. None of these

6. **On the face of it**
   A. To agree   B. From an action
   C. More than enough D. Apparently
   E. None of these

7. **Let the bygones be bygones**
   A. In one's favour   B. To pretend
   C. To forget the past D. Other choice
   E. None of these

8. **To split hairs**
   A. Major distinctions
   B. Hair with two ends
   C. To make minute distinction
   D. Without distinction
   E. None of these

9. **Bread and butter**
   A. Both bread and butter
   B. Something essential
   C. Livelihood
   D. Relevant things
   E. None of these

10. **To bell the cat**
    A. To catch a cat and tie a bell round its neck
    B. To make an effort
    C. To be quick
    D. To face a risk
    E. None of these

11. **Hard and fast**
    A. Strict   B. Solid
    C. Fast moving   D. Some hard surface
    E. None of these

12. **Part and parcel**
    A. The part of a parcel
    B. An essential part
    C. A missing parcel
    D. Some part of a machine sent by parcel
    E. None of these

13. **Null and void**
    A. Something invalid
    B. Something that can be avoided
    C. Something that can be nullified

    D. Something evil
    E. None of these

14. **To make clean breast of**
    A. To gain prominence
    B. To praise oneself
    C. To confess without reserve
    D. To destroy before it blooms
    E. None of these

15. **Trump card**
    A. A powerful means of achieving an object
    B. Resourcefulness
    C. The best gamble to attain success
    D. A travel card
    E. None of these

16. **Tall talk**
    A. A discussion continued for a long time
    B. A high sounding talk
    C. A meaningful talk
    D. A useless talk
    E. None of these

17. **Small talk**
    A. Gossip
    B. A discussion carried on for a long time
    C. A brief discussion
    D. A talk of small children
    E. None of these

18. **Throw out of gear**
    A. To replace   B. Hinder, disturb
    C. To decide   D. Take up tune
    E. None of these

19. **To and fro**
    A. Back and forth   B. Puzzled
    C. Amazed   D. Reprove
    E. None of these

20. **To bell the cat**
    A. To do an easy job
    B. To be indifferent to
    C. To undertake a difficult job
    D. To clarify
    E. None of these

21. **To be under cloud**
    A. Puzzle
    B. Enjoy the favour
    C. Talk thoughtlessly
    D. To be under suspicion
    E. None of these

22. A labour of love
A. A tragic end
B. A funny thing
C. Not fruitful
D. Work done without payment
E. None of these

23. Follow suit
A. Follow an example   B. Wear a new dress
C. Irrelevant   D. A gay person
E. None of these

24. Foul play
A. Bad intentions
B. A play not well acted
C. A play not liked by the audience
D. A foul scored at play
E. None of these

25. To pick holes
A. To find some reason to quarrel
B. To destroy something
C. To criticise someone
D. To cut some part of an item
E. None of these

26. To smell a rat
A. To see signs of plague epidemic
B. To get bad smell of a dead rat
C. To suspect foul dealings
D. To be in a bad mood
E. None of these

27. To put a spoke in one's wheel
A. To encourage
B. Act without restraint
C. Risk something
D. To obstruct one's progress
E. None of these

28. To pull one's leg
A. To give up   B. Take care of
C. To befool   D. To know
E. None of these

29. To play with fire
A. Grasp the truth
B. To handle something dangerous
C. To ridicule
D. To flee away
E. None of these

30. To reckon with
A. Take up time
B. Make an inventory

C. To deal with
D. Submit to punishment
E. None of these

31. To run short
A. Talk until one is tired at
B. Apply to oneself
C. To get rid of
D. To have or be too little
E. None of these

32. A man of letters
A. A postman   B. A learned man
C. A hypocrite   D. An ignorant man
E. None of these

33. A maiden speech
A. A speech made in the parliament
B. A speech made before unmarried girls
C. A speech made by a political leader
D. A speech made for the first time
E. None of these

34. Order of the day
A. An order passed on a particular day
B. A current law
C. Something common or general
D. A major order of court
E. None of these

35. To end in smoke
A. To make completely understand
B. To ruin oneself
C. To excite great applause
D. To die smoking
E. None of these

36. To give vent to
A. To allow to flow forth
B. To prove a failure
C. To amass wealth
D. To evade
E. None of these

37. To eat humble pie
A. To apologise or confess
B. To order
C. To flatter
D. To get a small share
E. None of these

38. A black sheep
A. An unlucky person
B. A negro
C. An ugly person

D. A man in animal skin

E. None of these

39. To catch a tartar
- A. To trap wanted criminal with great difficulty
- B. To catch a dangerous person
- C. To meet with disaster
- D. To deal with a person who is more than one's watch
- E. None of these

40. Sit on fence
- A. To remain neutral
- B. To show contempt
- C. To enjoy the surroundings
- D. To become fond of
- E. None of these

41. Pay off old scores
- A. To repay the debt   B. To have revenge
- C. To invite   D. Secretly
- E. None of these

42. Turn turtle
- A. To cheat
- B. To be lopsided
- C. To frustrate
- D. To dance to the tune
- E. None of these

43. Wash one's hands of
- A. To refuse   B. To assist
- C. To abuse   D. To refuse to be
- E. None of these

44. Under duress
- A. Under compulsion
- B. Willing
- C. To elicit information

D. To demand

E. None of these

45. To turn the tables
- A. To ruin someone
- B. To turn the situation to one's own side
- C. To reverse the situation
- D. To move from one point to another
- E. None of these

46. On the cards
- A. Possibly   B. Probably
- C. Openly   D. Likely

47. To leave someone in the lurch
- A. To come to compromise with someone
- B. Constant source of annoyance to someone
- C. To put someone at ease
- D. To desert someone in his difficulties
- E. None of these

48. To play second fiddle
- A. To be happy, cheerful and healthy
- B. To reduce importance of one's senior
- C. To support the role and view of another person
- D. To do backseat driving
- E. None of these

49. To yearn for
- A. To weep for   B. To remember
- C. To admire   D. To long for intensely
- E. None of these

50. Call off
- A. To finish   B. To withdraw
- C. To postpone   D. To cry
- E. None of these

ANSWERS

1	2	3	4	5	6	7	8	9	10
C	C	C	D	B	D	C	C	C	D
11	**12**	**13**	**14**	**15**	**16**	**17**	**18**	**19**	**20**
A	B	A	C	C	B	A	B	A	C
21	**22**	**23**	**24**	**25**	**26**	**27**	**28**	**29**	**30**
D	D	A	A	C	C	D	C	B	C
31	**32**	**33**	**34**	**35**	**36**	**37**	**38**	**39**	**40**
D	B	D	C	D	A	A	D	B	A
41	**42**	**43**	**44**	**45**	**46**	**47**	**48**	**49**	**50**
B	B	D	A	C	D	D	C	D	B

Reordering Sentences

A paragraph is formed from sentences, it will convey its true meaning and purpose only when the sentences are arranged in a proper manner. One must try and practise it regularly to score well. Test your skills in this exercise.

Multiple Choice Questions

Directions (Qs. 1 to 60): *Each of these questions sets has a group of sentences marked with numbers. Rearrange them in proper sequence to form a meaningful paragraph and answer the questions given below each set.*

SET-1

1. After examining him, the doctor smiled at him mischievously and took out a syringe.
2. Thinking that he was really sick, his father summoned the family doctor.
3. That day, Banku wanted to take a day off from school.
4. Immediately, Banku jumped up from his bed and swore that he was fine.
5. Therefore; he pretended to be sick and remained in bed.

1. Which sentence should come **fourth** in the pargaraph?
A. 1   B. 2
C. 3   D. 4
E. 5

2. Which sentence should come **last** in the paragraph?
A. 1   B. 2
C. 3   D. 4
E. 5

3. Which sentence should come **first** in the paragraph?
A. 1   B. 2
C. 3   D. 4
E. 5

4. Which sentence should come **third** in the paragraph?
A. 1   B. 2
C. 3   D. 4
E. 5

5. Which sentence should come **second** in the paragraph?
A. 1   B. 2
C. 3   D. 4
E. 5

SET-2

1. In his literary work he spoke of that province of human life which mere intellect does not speak.
2. He has also given innocent joy to many children by his stories like 'Kabuliwalah'.
3. Thsese songs are sung not only in Bengal but all over the country.
4. Rabindranath's great works sprang from intensity of vision and feelings.
5. He sang of beauty and heroism, nobility and charm.

6. Which sentence should come **third** in the sequence?
A. 1 B. 2
C. 3 D. 4
E. 5

7. Which sentence should come **fourth** in the sequence?
A. 1 B. 2
C. 3 D. 4
E. 5

8. Which sentence should come **second** in the sequence?
A. 1 B. 2
C. 3 D. 4
E. 5

9. Which sentence should come **first** in the sequence?
A. 1 B. 2
C. 3 D. 4
E. 5

10. Which sentence should come **fifth** in the sequence?
A. 1 B. 2
C. 3 D. 4
E. 5

SET-3

1. I reached office at 11 o'clock after sending the money.
2. Some money had to be sent to my parents.
3. After that, I spent almost an hour at the post office.
4. Therefore, I went to the bank to withdraw some money.
5. However, I had no money with me.

11. Which statement should come **first** in the paragraph?
A. 1 B. 2
C. 3 D. 4
E. 5

12. Which statement should come **second** in the paragraph?
A. 1 B. 2
C. 3 D. 4
E. 5

13. Which statement should come **third** in the paragraph?
A. 1 B. 2
C. 3 D. 4
E. 5

14. Which statement should come **fourth** in the paragraph?
A. 1 B. 2
C. 3 D. 4
E. 5

15. Which statement should come **fifth** in the paragraph?
A. 1 B. 2
C. 3 D. 4
E. 5

SET-4

1. In fact, it prevents us from helping children to analyse conflict, to learn to cope with it and counter it.
2. Children have always known that there is conflict in the adult world.
3. However, the make-believe world that nineteenth century rationally imposed on childhood in Europe and which we impose in an institutionalised manner through our modern education system can hardly be described as related in this regard.
4. We may therefore conclude that conflict in an institutionalised manner is not a matter of faith in children's capacities, rather, it is a lack of faith in ourselves as adults.
5. Further, psychologists tell us and story tellers have always known that the child's desire to search for order and coherence gathers strength from the knowledge of conflict.

16. Which of the following should be the **last** sentence in the paragraph?
A. 1 B. 2
C. 3 D. 4
E. 5

17. Which of the following should be the **first** sentence in the paragraph?
A. 1 B. 2
C. 3 D. 4
E. 5

18. Which of the following should be the **fourth** sentence in the paragraph?
A. 1   B. 2
C. 3   D. 4
E. 5

19. Which of the following should be the **third** sentence in the paragraph?
A. 1   B. 2
C. 3   D. 4
E. 5

20. Which of the following should be the **second** sentence in the paragraph?
A. 1   B. 2
C. 3   D. 4
E. 5

SET-5

1. A case in point is the programme involving the Sardar Sarovar Dam which would displace about 2,00,000 people.
2. Critics decry the fact that a major development institution appears to absorb more capital than it distributes to borrowers.
3. For all its faults critics however, concede that the bank remains a relatively efficient instrument for distribution of development-aid money.
4. One of the key complaints focuses on this non-profit bank's recent "profitability".
5. Although the lives of millions of people around the globe have been improved by the bank's activities, it is now under fire.
6. The bank is also being blamed for large-scale involuntary resettlement to make way for dams and other construction projects.

21. Which sentence should come **third** in the paragraph?
A. 2   B. 5
C. 1   D. 4
E. 6

22. Which sentence should come **fourth** in the paragraph?
A. 6   B. 3
C. 5   D. 2
E. 1

23. Which sentence should come **first** in the paragraph?
A. 4   B. 6
C. 3   D. 2
E. 5

24. Which sentence should come **second** in the paragraph?
A. 3   B. 1
C. 4   D. 6
E. 5

25. Which sentence should come **last** (*i.e.* **sixth**) in the paragraph?
A. 5   B. 4
C. 2   D. 1
E. 3

SET-6

1. Akash was shocked when he realised that the leg had lost sensation.
2. When he tried to get up, he felt his left leg was very heavy.
3. He had to lie down hopelessly, till he saw a flashlight.
4. It was an odd night time and hence nobody heard his voice.
5. Due to sudden sprain Akash fell down.
6. Nervous with this realisation, he called out for help.

26. Which of the following should be the **third** sentence?
A. 1   B. 2
C. 3   D. 4
E. 5

27. Which of the following should be the **sixth (last)** sentence?
A. 6   B. 5
C. 4   D. 3
E. 2

28. Which of the following should be the **first** sentence?
A. 1   B. 2
C. 3   D. 4
E. 5

29. Which of the following should be the **second** sentence?

A. 1   B. 2
C. 3   D. 4
E. 5

30. Which of the following should be the **fourth** sentence?
A. 1   B. 2
C. 6   D. 4
E. 5

SET-7

1. The history of mankind is full of such fightings between communities, nation and people.
2. From the primitive weapons of warfare, man has advanced to the modern nuclear weapons.
3. Ever since the dawn of civilisation man has been fighting with man.
4. A modern war is scientific in character, but the effect is the same wiping human existence out of this earth.
5. The only difference now seems to be in the efficiency of the instruments used for killing each other.

31. Which of the following should be the **fifth (last)** sentence?
A. 1   B. 2
C. 3   D. 4
E. 5

32. Which of the following should be the **fourth** sentence?
A. 1   B. 2
C. 3   D. 4
E. 5

33. Which of the following should be the **first** sentence?
A. 1   B. 2
C. 3   D. 4
E. 5

34. Which of the following should be the **second** sentence?
A. 1   B. 2
C. 3   D. 4
E. 5

35. Which of the following should be the **third** sentence?
A. 1   B. 2
C. 3   D. 4
E. 5

SET-8

1. Its current was very powerful and could take away big tree trunks.
2. There were some children, playing on the bank of the waterway.
3. In the forest of Bharatpur, there is a big lake.
4. The excess water started flowing forcefully through the waterway.
5. Once there was a very heavy rain because of which the lake started overflowing.
6. A poor man noticed it and rushed to save them.

36. Which of the following should be the **first** sentence?
A. 6   B. 5
C. 4   D. 3
E. 2

37. Which of the following should be the **third** sentence?
A. 6   B. 5
C. 4   D. 3
E. 2

38. Which of the following should be the **sixth (last)** sentence?
A. 6   B. 5
C. 4   D. 3
E. 2

39. Which of the following should be the **fourth** sentence?
A. 5   B. 4
C. 3   D. 2
E. 1

40. Which of the following should be the **second** sentence?
A. 6   B. 5
C. 4   D. 3
E. 2

SET-9

1. The means and methods they employ to deal with public pressures are also different.
2. They will make no move unless the gallery is packed.
3. The poorest are over-hesitant, evasive and preoccupied with their relationships with others.

4. Enormous difference is generally observed in the ways in which various public officials respond to public pressures.

5. The best possess understanding of the forces that must be taken into account, determination not to be swerved from the path of public interest.

6. They confront all embarrasments with a stale general formula.

41. Which of the following should be the **third** sentence?
A. 1   B. 2
C. 3   D. 4
E. 5

42. Which of the following should be the **sixth (last)** sentence?
A. 2   B. 3
C. 4   D. 5
E. 6

43. Which of the following should be the **first** sentence?
A. 6   B. 5
C. 4   D. 3
E. 2

44. Which of the following should be the **second** sentence?
A. 1   B. 2
C. 3   D. 4
E. 5

45. Which of the following should be the **fourth** sentence?
A. 2   B. 3
C. 4   D. 5
E. 6

SET-10

1. A taxi was summoned and Raju was taken to Lifeline Hospital.
2. While hurrying home from school.
3. Since they did not succeed, they decided to take him to a hospital.
4. When Raju opened his eyes, he found himself surrounded by doctors and nurses.
5. Some people rushed towards him and tried to bring him to his senses.
6. He was thrown a couple of feet away and lost consciousness.

46. Which sentence should come **third** in the paragraph?
A. 6   B. 2
C. 5   D. 1
E. 4

47. Which sentence should come **fourth** in the paragraph?
A. 3   B. 5
C. 6   D. 2
E. 1

48. Which sentence should come **first** in the paragraph?
A. 4   B. 6
C. 2   D. 5
E. 3

49. Which sentence should come **last** (*i.e.,* **sixth**) in the paragraph?
A. 2   B. 3
C. 1   D. 4
E. 5

50. Which sentence should come **second** in the paragraph?
A. 5   B. 1
C. 4   D. 3
E. 6

SET-11

1. But by then it was too late to correct things.
2. It is impossible to steer such a large project to success without planning.
3. He had to stand by and watch helplessly.
4. The whole scheme was destined, to fail from the beginning.
5. Bhaskar started realising this only towards the end.

51. Which sentence should come **first** in the paragraph
A. 1   B. 2
C. 3   D. 4
E. 5

52. Which sentence should come **third** in the paragraph?
A. 1   B. 2
C. 3   D. 4
E. 5

53. Which sentence should come **last** in the paragraph?

A. 1   B. 2
C. 3   D. 4
E. 5

54. Which sentence should come **second** in the paragraph?

A. 1   B. 2
C. 3   D. 4
E. 5

55. Which sentence should come **fourth** in the paragraph?

A. 1   B. 2
C. 3   D. 4
E. 5

SET-12

1. John did not have the money to buy the beautiful clip.
2. After a while, Jane explained to John that she had sold her hair to buy a gold chain for his watch.
3. As it was Christmas, John wanted to give Jane a surprise present.
4. When Jane saw it, she felt like crying.
5. He decided to present her a clip made of ivory for her long flowing hair.

6. He, therefore, sold off his watch and brought home the present.

56. Which of the sentences should come **last** in the paragraph?

A. 5   B. 4
C. 1   D. 3
E. 2

57. Which of the sentences should come **first** in the paragraph?

A. 3   B. 6
C. 2   D. 5
E. 4

58. Which of the sentences should come **second** in the paragraph?

A. 6   B. 1
C. 5   D. 4
E. 3

59. Which of the sentences should come **third** in the paragraph?

A. 4   B. 5
C. 6   D. 2
E. 1

60. Which of the sentences should come **fourth** in the paragraph?

A. 1   B. 2
C. 3   D. 6
E. 5

ANSWERS

1	2	3	4	5	6	7	8	9	10
A	D	C	B	E	B	E	A	D	C
11	**12**	**13**	**14**	**15**	**16**	**17**	**18**	**19**	**20**
B	E	D	C	A	D	B	C	A	E
21	**22**	**23**	**24**	**25**	**26**	**27**	**28**	**29**	**30**
B	A	D	C	E	A	D	E	B	C
31	**32**	**33**	**34**	**35**	**36**	**37**	**38**	**39**	**40**
E	D	C	A	B	D	C	A	D	B
41	**42**	**43**	**44**	**45**	**46**	**47**	**48**	**49**	**50**
C	E	C	A	D	C	A	C	D	E
51	**52**	**53**	**54**	**55**	**56**	**57**	**58**	**59**	**60**
D	E	C	B	A	E	A	C	E	D

Spelling Errors

The most common errors in English are of spellings of words. Even the most learned men are sometimes confused about the correct spellings of some words. One must keep and use a dictionary religiously. Never ignore and let pass a new word casually.

A number of question to test your knowledge of spellings are compiled here. Try to solve as many as you can.

Multiple Choice Questions

Directions: *Find the correctly spelt word out of the four options in each question. If none of the words is correctly spelt, mark 'E' as your answer.*

1. A. Accompalish   B. Ackmplesh
   C. Acomplush   D. Accomplish
   E. None of these

2. A. Acommodation   B. Acomodation
   C. Accomodation   D. Accommodation
   E. None of these

3. A. Astonished   B. Astronished
   C. Astoneshed   D. Asstonished
   E. None of these

4. A. Benefeted   B. Benefitted
   C. Benifited   D. Benefited
   E. None of these

5. A. Belligerent   B. Beligirent
   C. Belligarant   D. Belligerrent
   E. None of these

6. A. Chancelery   B. Chancellery
   C. Chancellary   D. Chancelary
   E. None of these

7. A. Discriminate   B. Discremineta
   C. Discrimenate   D. Discriminat

   E. None of these

8. A. Damage   B. Dammage
   C. Damaige   D. Dammege
   E. None of these

9. A. Efficiant   B. Effecient
   C. Efficient   D. Eficient
   E. None of these

10. A. Extravagant   B. Extreragent
    C. Extreregant   D. Extravegent
    E. None of these

11. A. Efflorascence   B. Eflorescene
    C. Effllorescence   D. Efflorescence
    E. None of these

12. A. Equinimity   B. Equanimmity
    C. Equannimity   D. Equanimity
    E. None of these

13. A. Farmament   B. Farmement
    C. Fermament   D. Fremament
    E. None of these

14. A. Grieff   B. Grief
    C. Grieef   D. Grrief
    E. None of these

15. A. Guarantee   B. Garuntee
    C. Guaruntee   D. Gaurantee
    E. None of these

16. A. Hypocritical   B. Hypocretical
    C. Hypocriticel   D. Hypocirticel
    E. None of these

17. A. Humurous   B. Humorous
    C. Humoreus   D. Humorrous
    E. None of these

18. A. Itenerary   B. Itinarery
    C. Itinarary   D. Itinerary
    E. None of these

19. A. Indipenseble   B. Indispansible
    C. Indispensable   D. Indipensable
    E. None of these

20. A. Imprecticability   B. Impracticebility
    C. Impracticibility   D. Impracticability
    E. None of these

21. A. Incradulous   B. Incredulous
    C. Incridulous   D. Incredalous
    E. None of these

22. A. Juddicious   B. Judiceous
    C. Judicious   D. Judiceus
    E. None of these

23. A. Kleptomonia   B. Kleptemonia
    C. Kleptomania   D. Klaptomania
    E. None of these

24. A. Lackdaisical   B. Lackadaisical
    C. Lckadaisicle   D. Lackadisical
    E. None of these

25. A. Licentious   B. Licontious
    C. Licenttious   D. Licientious
    E. None of these

26. A. Meddicine   B. Medicine
    C. Medicene   D. Medicinne
    E. None of these

27. A. Meritricious   B. Merefrecious
    C. Meretricious   D. Merritricious
    E. None of these

28. A. Missunderstood   B. Miesunderstood
    C. Misunderstood   D. Misunderstod
    E. None of these

29. A. Occurad   B. Occurred
    C. Ocurred   D. Occured
    E. None of these

30. A. Osttentatious   B. Ostentetious
    C. Ostentatious   D. Ostenttatious
    E. None of these

31. A. Obnosious   B. Obnoxeous
    C. Obnoxious   D. Obnoseous
    E. None of these

32. A. Omenous   B. Ominous
    C. Ommineous   D. Omineous
    E. None of these

33. A. Pecification   B. Pacification
    C. Pecifacation   D. Pecefication
    E. None of these

34. A. Prograssive   B. Progressive
    C. Progresive   D. Prograsive
    E. None of these

35. A. Pasiveness   B. Passiveness
    C. Passeveniss   D. Passivines
    E. None of these

36. A. Polyendry   B. Poliendry
    C. Pollyendry   D. Polyandry
    E. None of these

37. A. Puerille   B. Puerrile
    C. Puerile   D. Purrile
    E. None of these

38. A. Pesanger   B. Passenger
    C. Pessenger   D. Pasanger
    E. None of these

39. A. Querrelsome   B. Quarrelsame
    C. Quarrelsome   D. Querralsome
    E. None of these

40. A. Rigourous   B. Rigerous
    C. Rigorous   D. Regerous
    E. None of these

41. A. Survellance   B. Surveilance
    C. Surveillance   D. Survaillance
    E. None of these

42. A. Schedule   B. Schdule
    C. Schedale   D. Schedeule
    E. None of these

43. A. Sepalchrle   B. Sepalchral
    C. Sepulchrle   D. Sepulchral
    E. None of these

44. A. Sympathetic   B. Smypathetic
    C. Sympothetic   D. Sympethetic
    E. None of these

45. A. Sincerely   B. Sencerely
    C. Sincerelly   D. Sincerrely
    E. None of these

46. A. Satellite   B. Sattellite
    C. Satelite   D. Sattelite
    E. None of these

47. A. Teracherous   B. Treacherous
    C. Treacheraus   D. Treachereans
    E. None of these

48. A. Uncivilized   B. Uncevilized
    C. Uncivillized   D. Uncevelized
    E. None of these

49. A. Vainglorious   B. Vaniglorious
    C. Vaniglerious   D. Vaingloreus
    E. None of these

50. A. Vulnarable   B. Valnerable
    C. Velnerable   D. Vulnerable
    E. None of these

51. A. Valuptuous   B. Volluptous
    C. Voluptuous   D. Volupttuous
    E. None of these

52. A. Veneration   B. Venration
    C. Venneration   D. Venerration
    E. None of these

53. A. Tacciturnity   B. Taciturnity
    C. Taciturrnity   D. Tacitturnity
    E. None of these

54. A. Tranquilitty   B. Tranquility
    C. Trenquility   D. Tranquillity
    E. None of these

55. A. Tranquil   B. Trenquil
    C. Tranquel   D. Trinquil
    E. None of these

56. A. Neggardly   B. Nigardly
    C. Niggerdly   D. Niggardly
    E. None of these

57. A. Quadruplets   B. Quedruplets
    C. Quadroplets   D. Quadruplats
    E. None of these

58. A. Schezophrenia   B. Schizaphrenia
    C. Schizophrenia   D. Schizophrania
    E. None of these

59. A. Transperency   B. Transparency
    C. Transpirency   D. Tranporency
    E. None of these

60. A. Superanuation   B. Superennuation
    C. Superannuation   D. Superannuetion
    E. None of these

ANSWERS

1	2	3	4	5	6	7	8	9	10
D	D	A	B	A	C	A	A	C	A
11	12	13	14	15	16	17	18	19	20
D	D	C	B	A	A	B	D	C	D
21	22	23	24	25	26	27	28	29	30
B	C	C	B	A	B	C	C	B	C
31	32	33	34	35	36	37	38	39	40
C	B	B	B	B	D	C	B	C	C
41	42	43	44	45	46	47	48	49	50
C	A	D	A	A	A	B	A	A	D
51	52	53	54	55	56	57	58	59	60
C	A	B	B	A	D	A	C	B	C

REASONING ABILITY

Series

LETTER SERIES

In letter series, the letters follow a definite order. The given series of letters can be in natural order or in reverse order or combination of both. The letters may be skipped or repeated or consecutive. The given series may be single or may comprise two different series merged at alternate positions. While attempting questions on letter series one should note the pattern of alphabet series.

Alphabets in natural series

A B C D E F G H I J K L M N O P Q R S T U V W X Y Z
1st   5th   10th   15th   20th   25th

are:

Alphabets in reverse series

Z Y X W V U T S R Q P O N M L K J I H G F E D C B A
1st   5th   10th   15th   20th   25th

Note: On reaching Z, the series restarts from A and on reaching A, it restarts from Z.

Example

1. A Z B Y C ?
  A. D
  B. X
  C. U
  D. E

Ans.: (B) There are two alternate series.
  Series I : A B C (Consecutive letters in natural series)
  Series II : Z Y X (Consecutive letters in reverse series)

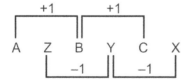

REPEAT SERIES

In this type of series small letters of the alphabet are used to make a set of letters which are repeated. The candidate has to find the set of letters which will fit the blanks left in the given series in such a manner that one section of the series is further repeated in the same manner.

Example

2. Which of the following groups of letters will complete the given series?

ba-b-aab-a-b

  A. baab   B. abba
  C. abaa   D. babb

Ans.: (B) The series is baab, baab, baab. Here the section 'baab' is repeated in the series. Solving steps : The candidate has to look for clues to solve such series pattern. 'aab' in the series indicates that 'b' in this series is preceded by two 'a' so, the first blank and the last blank will be filled by 'a'. Now the first set is formed, *i.e.*, 'baab' in the beginning. This set is repeated, so the second and third blanks will have 'b' filling them.

NUMBER SERIES

In this type of series, the set of given numbers in a series are related to one another in a particular pattern or manner. The relationship between the numbers may be (i) consecutive odd/even numbers; (ii) consecutive prime numbers; (iii) squares/cubes of some numbers with/without variation of addition or subtraction of some number; (iv) sum/product/difference of preceding numbers; (v) addition/subtraction/multiplication/division by some number; and (vi) many more combinations of the relationships given above.

Example

3. Complete the given series. 2, 14, 98, 686, ?
- A. 1976
- B. 2548
- C. 980
- D. 4802

Ans.: (D) The numbers are multiplied by 7 to obtain the next numbers.

The given series may also comprise of two alternate series merged as one.

MIXED SERIES

Mixed series comprises of the combinations of letters and numbers. In this type of series, the letters and numbers may have a common sequence pattern or may have separate sequence patterns.

Example

4. What should come in the place of question mark in the following letter-number combination?

F6, H8, J10, L12, ?

- A. N15
- B. O14
- C. N14
- D. O13

Ans.: (C) The letters are moved two steps forward and the number indicates the position of the letter in the alphabet series.

EXERCISE

Directions (Qs. 1 to 8): *In each of the following series determine the order of the letters. Then from the given options select the one which will complete the given series.*

1. GH, JL, NQ, SW, YD, ?
- A. EJ
- B. FJ
- C. EL
- D. FL

2. AI, BJ, CK, ?
- A. DL
- B. DM
- C. GH
- D. LM

3. b e d f ? h j ? l
- A. i m
- B. m i
- C. i n
- D. j m

4. ADVENTURE, DVENTURE, DVENTUR, ?, VENTU
- A. DVENT
- B. VENTURE
- C. VENTUR
- D. DVENTU
- E. None of these

5. PERPENDICULAR, ERPENDICULA, RPENDICUL, ?
- A. PENDICUL
- B. PENDIC
- C. ENDIC
- D. ENDICU
- E. None of these

6. ATTRIBUTION, TTRIBUTIO, RIBUTIO, IBUTI, ?
- A. IBU
- B. UT
- C. UTI
- D. BUT
- E. None of these

7. M, N, O, L, R, I, V, ?
- A. A
- B. E
- C. F
- D. H
- E. Z

8. A, CD, GHI, ?, UVWXY
- A. LMNO
- B. MNO
- C. MNOP
- D. NOPQ

Directions (Qs. 9 to 15): *Which letter(s) in each of the following series is wrong or is misfit in the series?*

9. Z A W B X C
- A. D
- B. C
- C. X
- D. W

10. M L O N Q P T R
- A. T
- B. O
- C. Q
- D. L

11. D K R Y F L
A. L
B. D
C. R
D. Y

12. L N Q T W Z C F
A. C
B. Q
C. L
D. F

13. XW, DC, CB, NM, PQ, QP
A. NM
B. CB
C. PQ
D. XW

14. B E I N S A I
A. A
B. E
C. S
D. I

15. Z T P K H F
A. Z
B. P
C. T
D. F

Directions (Qs. Nos. 16 to 20): *In each of the following letter series, some of the letters are missing which are given in that order as one of the alternatives below it. Choose the correct alternative.*

16. ba _ cb _ b _ bab _
A. acbb
B. bacc
C. bcaa
D. cabb

17. c _ bba _ cab _ ac _ ab _ ac
A. abebe
B. acbcb
C. babec
D. bcacb

18. ab _ _ baa _ _ ab _
A. aaaaa
B. aabaa
C. aabab
D. baabb

19. _ bc _ ca _ aba _ c _ ca
A. abcbb
B. bbbec
C. bacba
D. abbec

20. ab _ aa _ bbb _ aaa _ bbba
A. abba
B. baab
C. aaab
D. abab

Directions (Qs. 21 to 25): *Choose the correct alternative that will continue the same pattern and replace the question mark in the given series.*

21. 3, 9, 27, 81, 243, ?
A. 486
B. 729
C. 972
D. 359

22. 1, 6, 12, 19, 27 ?
A. 38
B. 35
C. 36
D. 54

23. 125, 80, 45, 20, ?
A. 5
B. 8
C. 10
D. 12

24. 120, 99, 80, 63, 48, ?
A. 35
B. 38
C. 39
D. 40

25. 589654237, 89654237, 8965423, 965423, ?
A. 58965
B. 65423
C. 89654
D. 96542

Directions (Qs. 26–33): *In each series given below, what would come in place of the question-mark?*

26. 2B, 4C, 8E, 14H, ?
A. 20L
B. 22L
C. 21I
D. 16K

27. C(1)L, F(4)O, I(9)R, L(16)U, ?
A. P(27)W
B. N(24)Y
C. M(23)X
D. O(25)X

28. 3F, 6G, 11I, 18L, ?
A. 27P
B. 21O
C. 27Q
D. 25N

29. W(1)A, X(4)Z, Y9Y, ?, A(25)W
A. X(11)Z
B. Z(21)A
C. Z(16)X
D. Z(14)X

30. 81Y, 27S, 9N, 3J, ?
A. 0H
B. IG
C. 0F
D. IE

31. E5, K11, Q17, ?
A. X20
B. Y24
C. V22
D. W25

32. D2, I3, N6, S18, ?
A. V72
B. W36
C. Y90
D. X108

33. 3J, 6M, 12L, ?, 48N
A. 24O
B. 8M
C. 26M
D. 22O

Directions (Qs. Nos. 34 and 35) : *Which of the following does not fit in the letter number series given below?*

34. G4T, J10R, M20P, P43N, S90L
A. J10R
B. S90L
C. M20P
D. G4T

35. B0R, G3U, E3P, J7S, H9N
A. E3P
B. J7S
C. H9N
D. G3U

ANSWERS

1	2	3	4	5	6	7	8	9	10
D	A	A	C	E	C	B	C	D	A
11	12	13	14	15	16	17	18	19	20
A	C	C	C	B	B	B	B	A	B
21	22	23	24	25	26	27	28	29	30
B	C	A	A	D	B	D	A	C	B
31	32	33	34	35					
C	D	A	A	B					

EXPLANATORY ANSWERS

1. 1st letter:

$$G \xrightarrow{+3} J \xrightarrow{+4} N \xrightarrow{+5} S \xrightarrow{+6} Y \xrightarrow{+7} (F)$$

2nd letter:

$$H \xrightarrow{+4} L \xrightarrow{+5} Q \xrightarrow{+6} W \xrightarrow{+7} D \xrightarrow{+8} (L)$$

2. 1st letter: $A \xrightarrow{+1} B \xrightarrow{+1} C \xrightarrow{+1} (D)$

2nd letter: $I \xrightarrow{+1} J \xrightarrow{+1} K \xrightarrow{+1} (L)$

3. The series may be divided into groups as shown: b e d / f ? h / j ? l

Clearly in the first group, the second and third letters are respectively three and two steps ahead of the first letter. A similar pattern would follow in the second and third groups.

4. One letter from the beginning and one from the end of a term are removed, one by one, in alternate steps.

5. Each term of the series is obtained by removing two letters from the preceding term one from the beginning and one from the end. So, the missing term is PENDICU.

6. In the first step, one letter from the beginning and one from the end of a term are removed to give the next term. In the second step, two letters from the beginning of a term are removed. These two steps are repeated alternately.

7. The given sequence is a combination of two series: I. M, O, R, V and II. N, L, I, ?

The pattern in I is: $M \xrightarrow{+2} O \xrightarrow{+3} R \xrightarrow{+4} V$

The pattern in II is: $N \xrightarrow{-2} L \xrightarrow{-3} I \xrightarrow{-4} (E)$

8. Each term consists of consecutive letters in order. The number of letters in the terms goes on increasing by one at each step. Also, there is a gap of one letter between the last letter of the first term and the first letter of the second term; a gap of two letters between the last letter of the second term and the first letter of the third term; and so on. So, there should be a gap of three letters between the last letter of the third term and the first letter of the desired term.

9. There are two alternate series I. Z, Y, X and II. A, B, C

The pattern in I is : $Z \xrightarrow{-1} (Y) \xrightarrow{-1} X$

The pattern in II is : $A \xrightarrow{+1} B \xrightarrow{+1} C$

10. Two consecutive letters are written backwards.

ML ON OP SR (←)

S should be in place of T.

11. The pattern in this series is moving the letters seven steps forward.

D K R Y F (M), +7 +7 +7 +7 +7

M should be in place of L.

12. The pattern in the series is +3

K should be in place of L.

13. The series is made with any two consecutive letters written backwards.

XW DC CB NM QP
← ← ← ← ←

Q should come before P in the series.

14. The difference between the letters is increased by one at each step.

B E I N ⓣ A I
+3 +4 +5 +6 +7 +8

T should be in place of S.

15. The difference between the letters is decreased by one at each step.

Z T O K H F
-6 -5 -4 -3 -2

O should be in place of P.

16. The series is babc/babc/babc. Thus, the pattern 'babc' is repeated.

17. The series is cabbac/cabbac/cabbac. Thus, the pattern 'cabbac' is repeated.

18. The series is aba/aba/aba/aba. Thus, the pattern 'aba' is repeated.

19. The series is abc/bca/cab/abc/bca. Thus, the letters change places in a cyclic order.

20. The series is abb/aaabbb/aaaabbbb/a. Thus, the letters are repeated twice, then thrice, then four times and so on.

21. The numbers in the series are multiplied by 3 to get the next numbers.

22. The difference between the numbers in the series increases by 1, after beginning from 5,

i.e., 1 6 12 19 27 36
+5 +6 +7 +8 +9

23. The pattern is –45, –35, –25, ...
So, missing term = 20 – 15 = 5.

24. The pattern is –21, –19, –17, –15,.....
So, missing term = 48 – 13 = 35.

25. The digits are removed one-by-one from the beginning and the end in order alternately, so as to obtain the subsequent terms of the series.

26. The sequence of numbers is +2, +4, +6, +8 and sequence of letters is +1, +2, +3, +4.

27. The corresponding letters are moved 3 steps forward and the sequence of numbers is +3, +5, +7, +9.

28. The sequence of numbers is +3, +5, +7, +9 and the letters are moved 1, 2, 3, 4 steps forward.

29. The letters on the left are in reverse series, the letters on the right are in natural series, and the numbers are squares of numbers in natural order starting from 1.

30. The numbers are divided by 3 at each step and the letters are moved 6, 5, 4, 3 steps backward.

31. The series comprises of random letters and numbers indicate the position of the letter in alphabet series.

32. The letters are moved five steps forward and every third number is the product of two preceding numbers.

33. Every number is double the previous number and the sequence of letters is +3, –1 (3 steps forward, 1 step backward) which is repeated.

34. The letters on the left are moved 3 steps forward, the letters on the right are moved 2 steps backward and the sequence of numbers is (4 × 2) +1, (9 × 2) +2, (20 × 2) +3, (43 × 2) +4. So, J9R should be in place of J10R.

35. The sequence of letters on the left is +5, –2 (5 steps forward, 2 steps backward) which is repeated, the sequence of letters on the right is +3, –5 (3 steps forward, 5 steps backward) which is repeated, and the numbers are the sum of two preceeding numbers. So, J6S should be in place of J7S.

❀ ❀ ❀

2 Coding-Decoding

Coding is a secretive language which is used to change the representation of the actual term/word/value. This coded language can be framed by

(*i*) moving the letters one or more steps forward or backward;

(*ii*) substituting numbers for letters and vice-versa;

(*iii*) writing the letters of the given word in reverse order in part or in whole; and

(*iv*) replacing the letters in their natural series by the same positioned letters in their reverse series.

Alphabet in natural series are :

A̲ B C D E̲ F G H I J̲ K L M N O̲ P Q R S T̲ U V W X Y̲ Z
1st   5th   10th   15th   20th   25th

Alphabet in reverse series are :

Z̲ Y X W V̲ U T S R Q̲ P O N M L̲ K J I H G̲ F E D C B̲ A
1st   5th   10th   15th   20th   25th

> **Note :** On reaching Z, the series restarts from A and on reaching A, it restarts from Z

Example

1. If FACE is coded as GBDF, then BADE will be coded as :

A. CBEF   B. CEBF

C. CFBE   D. CBFE

Ans.: (A) The word is coded by moving the letters one step forward

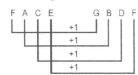

Similarly,

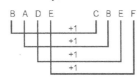

2. In a certain code 'ra mei ket' means 'he is rich'; 'rui pha jeu' means 'run for money'; and 'pha rui ket' means 'money for rich'. Which of the following is the code for 'rich'?

A. ra   B. pha

C. ket   D. jeu

Ans.: (C) The given information is :

Code	Sentence
1. ra mei ket	he is rich
2. rui pha jeu	run for money
3. pha rui ket	money for rich

After comparing codes and sentences 1 and 3, it is clear that word 'rich' is common and so is the code 'ket'.

3. If 'banana' is called 'jelly', 'jelly' is called 'green', 'green' is called 'apple'. 'apple' is called 'mango', what is the colour of leaf?

A. green B.   mango

C. apple D.   banana

Ans.: (C) Leaf is green in colour and according to the codes in the question 'green' is called 'apple'.

In another form of coding, the Digits and its coded Letters or vice versa are already given. One has to find out the answers to the given questions just by tallying the given codes.

EXERCISE

Directions (Qs. Nos. 1 to 8): *In the following questions select the right option which indicates the correct code for the word or letter given in the question.*

1. If PHILOSOPHY is coded as HPLISOPOYH, ornamental will be coded as :
   A. ROANEMNTLA   B. ONRAMNEALT
   C. ROANEMTNLA   D. ROANEMNATL

2. If OPFGBCST stands for NEAR, in the same manner IJVWHI will stand for :
   A. HAG   B. HUG
   C. HUT   D. KEG

3. If m is coded as g, g as o, a as *i* and *i* as y, then 'imagination' will be written as :
   A. ygagynatyin   B. ygioynityog
   C. ygioynityon   D. ygioyintyon

4. If OUT is coded as 152120, IN will be coded as :
   A. 1015   B. 819
   C. 1813   D. 914

5. If BAD is coded as 7. HIS as 9, LOW will be coded as :
   A. 50   B. 8
   C. 23   D. 5

6. In a certain code ABCD is written as 2468 and EFGH as 1357. How will CAGE be written in that code?
   A. 6453   B. 6251
   C. 6521   D. 6215

7. If HARD is coded as 1357 and SOFT as 2468, what will 21448 stand for?
   A. SHAFT   B. SHORT
   C. SHOOT   D. SHART

8. If FACE is coded as 6135, BIG as 297, HAD as 814 and BADGE as 21475, then what is the code for 'A'?
   A. 3   B. 1
   C. 2   D. 4

Directions (Qs. 9 to 13): *In the following questions study the coded patterns and then select the right option from the given alternatives.*

9. In a certain language, A. 'FOR' stands for 'old is gold'; B. 'ROT' stands for 'gold is pure'; C. 'ROM' stands for 'gold is costly'. How will 'pure old gold is costly' be written?
   A. TFROM   B. FOTRM
   C. FTORM   D. TOMRF

10. In a certain code '643' means 'she is beautiful', '593' means 'he is handsome', and '567' means 'handsome meets beautiful'. What number will indicate the word 'meets'?
    A. 5   B. 3
    C. 7   D. 6

11. In a certain code language, A. 'pic vic nic' stands for 'winter is cold'; B. 'to nic re' for 'summer is hot'; C. 're pic boo' for 'winter and summer' and D. 'vic tho pa' for nights are cold'. Which of the following word is the code for 'summer'?
    A. nic   B. boo
    C. to   D. re

12. In a certain language 'mu mit es' means 'who is she' and 'elb mu es' means 'where is she'. What is the code for 'where' in this language?
    A. es   B. elb
    C. mu   D. mit

13. In a certain code language 'roi ja kyo twa' means ' Moody is writing letters', 'pok ju ja twa' means 'Woody is writing cards', 'trn kyo pos un' means 'they are writing letters', and 'koi rus pok' means 'gifts and cards'. What is the code word for 'Moody'?
    A. ja   B. twa
    C. roi   D. kyo

Directions (Qs. 14 to 18): *Read the given coded information and choose the correct answer from the given options.*

14. If 'red' is called 'air', 'air' is called 'black', 'black' is called 'sky', 'sky' is called 'blue', 'blue' is called 'wind' and 'wind' is called 'white', where to birds fly?
    A. air   B. sky
    C. blue   D. wind
    E. black

15. If 'green' is called 'pink', 'pink' is called 'blue', 'blue' is called 'purple', 'purple' is called 'white', 'white' is called 'orange' and 'orange' is called 'peach', what is the colour of snow?
- A. peach
- B. orange
- C. purple
- D. blue
- E. white

16. If 'colour' is called 'blue', 'blue' is called 'light', 'light' is called 'showy', 'showy' is called 'dark' and 'dark' is called 'colour', what is the colour of ink?
- A. blue
- B. showy
- C. dark
- D. colour
- E. light

17. If 'yellow', is called 'pale', 'pale' is called 'blue', 'blue' is called 'orange', 'orange' is called 'dull', 'dull' is called 'green' and 'green' is called 'yellow' , what is the colour of grass in a lawn?
- A. pale
- B. yellow
- C. blue
- D. green
- E. orange

18. If 'black' is called 'pink', 'pink' is called 'blue', 'blue' is called 'brown', 'brown' is called 'orange', 'orange' is called 'violet', 'violet' is called 'red' and 'red' is called 'black', what is the colour of blood?
- A. black
- B. brown
- C. pink
- D. orange
- E. red

Directions (Qs 19 to 23): *The following questions are based on the code pattern given below :*

Letters : T R A H U X C I B L
Numbers : 3 0 1 7 4 9 6 8 2 5

Which of the given options has the correct coded form of the given letters?

19. RACIXT
- A. 016823
- B. 016873
- C. 016843
- D. 016893

20. BUHLAI
- A. 247018
- B. 247508
- C. 247538
- D. 247518

21. LBIHAR
- A. 528471
- B. 528710
- C. 528947
- D. 528103

22. UBAXTC
- A. 421736
- B. 421956
- C. 421936
- D. 421906

23. HULBRT
- A. 745203
- B. 723045
- C. 752340
- D. 732145

ANSWERS

1	2	3	4	5	6	7	8	9	10
C	B	C	D	D	B	B	B	A	C
11	12	13	14	15	16	17	18	19	20
D	B	C	C	B	E	B	A	D	D
21	22	23							
B	C	A							

EXPLANATORY ANSWERS

1. The places of two consecutive letters in the word are interchanged to form the coded word.

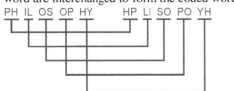

Similarly,

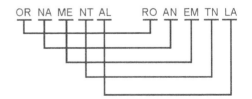

2. The manner of decoding is

↓ OP ↓ FG ↓ BC ↓ ST → codes

N   E   A   R   → given word

The letters preceeding two consecutive letters in the alphabetical series are picked to depict the words.

Similarly,

↓ IJ ↓ VW ↓ HI → given codes

H   U   G → answer word

3. Alphabet whose codes are given

m → g
g → o
a → i
i → y

All other alphabet will remain unchanged so, 'imagination' will be coded as :

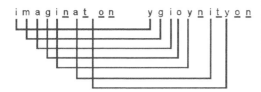

4. The coded number signifies the position of the alphabet in its natural alphabetical series (ABCD...)

O   U   T → OUT

15th 21st 20th→ 152120

Similarly,

I   N → IN

9th   14th → 914

5. The coded number is the sum of number digits signifying the position of the alphabet in the natural order.

B   A   D
↓   ↓   ↓
2nd   1st   4th

i.e., 2 + 1 + 4 = 7

Similarly,

H   I   S
↓   ↓   ↓
8th   9th   19th

i.e., 8 + 9 + 19 = 36, further 3 + 6 = 9

Also,

L   O   W
↓   ↓   ↓
12th   15th   23rd

i.e., 12 + 15 + 23 = 50,

further, 5 + 0 = 5

6. The letters of the given groups are coded by numbers and the word CAGE is formed by letters from the given words. So, to find the answer, select the respective numbers.

A   B   C   D   E   F   G   H → letters

2   4   6   8   1   3   5   7 → codes

So,

C   A   G   E → letters

6   2   5   1 → answer codes

7. The numbers represent letters and to find the answer, select the respective letters.

1   3   5   7   2   4   6   8 → codes

H   A   R   D   S   O   F   T → letters

So,

2   1   4   4   8 → codes

S   H   O   O   T → answer letters

8. The letter 'A' is present in three words and so is the number '1' in all the three words.

FACE   HAD   BADGE

6135   814   21475

9.   *Code*   *Sentence*

1.   F O R   old is gold

2.   R O T   gold is pure

3.   R O M   gold is costly

Therefore,

F stands   for old
O stands   for is
R stands   for gold
T stands   for pure
M stands   for costly

So, 'pure old gold is costly' will be written as 'TFROM'.

10. *Code*   *Sentence*

1. 643   she is beautiful
2. 593   he is handsome
3. 567   handsome meets beautiful

From 3rd code and its sentence, neither number '7' nor the word 'meets' is repeated.

11. *Code*   *Sentence*

1. pic vic nic   winter is cold
2. to nic re   summer is hot
3. re pic boo   winter and summer
4. vic tho pa   nights are cold

The word 'summer' is common in 2nd and 3rd sentences and so is the code 're'

12. *Code*   *Sentence*

1. mu mite es   who is she

2. **elb** mu es   **where** is she

The code words 'mu' and 'es' are repeated in Ist sentence. The only code left is 'elb' which means 'where'

13. *Code Sentence*

1. **roi** *ja kyo twa*   **Moody** is *writing letters*
2. pok ju *ja twa*   Woody is *writing* cards
3. trn *kyo* pos un   they are writing *letters*
4. koi rus pok   gifts and cards

'Moody' is in 1st sentence only. The code words 'ja' and 'twa' are repeated in 2nd sentence and 'kyo' in 3rd sentence. Only code 'roi' remains which stands for 'Moody'.

14. Birds fly in the 'sky' and 'sky' is called 'blue'.

15. Colour of snow is 'white' and 'white' is called 'orange'.

16. Colour of ink is 'blue' and 'blue' is called 'light'.

17. The colour of grass in a lawn is 'green' and 'green' is called 'yellow'.

18. Colour of blood is 'red' and 'red' is called 'black'.

3   Symbol Substitution

Questions in these category are easy to attempt. Candidates must be quick in substituting symbols and calculations. The common pattern of questions asked are given below.

Example

1. If '+' stands for '×'; '×' stands for '÷'; '÷' stands for '–' and '–' stands for '+' then
   $2 - 8 \times 2 + 6 \div 7 = ?$
   A. 32   B. 19
   C. 23   D. 9
   E. 15

Ans. After substituting the symbols in the given expression the new expression will be :
   $2 + 8 \div 2 \times 6 - 7$
   The solving steps will be :
   $2 + 4 \times 6 - 7$
   $2 + 24 - 7$
   $26 - 7 = 19$

2. If   ▲ stands for '+'
     ■ stands for '–'
     ● stands for '÷'
     ✳ stands for '×' then
   13 ▲ 5 ✳ 20 ● 10 ■ 9 = ?
   A. 26   B. 37
   C. 14   D. 55
   E. 20

Ans. After substituting the symbols the new expression will be :
   $13 + 5 \times 20 \div 10 - 9$
   The solving steps will be :
   $13 + 5 \times 2 - 9$
   $13 + 10 - 9$
   $23 - 9 = 14$

EXERCISE

1. If × stand for addition, ÷ stands for subtraction, + stands for multiplication and – stands for division, then $(20 \times 6 \div 6 \times 4)$ is equal to
   A. 5   B. 24
   C. 25   D. 80
   E. None of these

2. If "+" means "×"; "÷" means "–"; "×"means "÷" and "–" means "+", what will be the value of the following expression?
   $4 + 11 \div 5 - 50 = ?$
   A. 79   B. – 11
   C. 91   D. – 48.5
   E. None of these

3. If P = 6, J = 4, L = 8, M = 24, then which of the given values can replace the question mark (?) in the following?
   $M \times J \div L + J = ?$
   A. 8   B. 36
   C. 52   D. 0
   E. 16

4. If A + B > C + D, B + E = 2 C and C + D > B + E, it necessarily follows that
   A. A > C   B. A + B > 2D
   C. A + B > 2C   D. A + B > 2E
   E. D + B < 2C

5. If A + D > C + E, C + D = 2B and B + E > C + D, it necessarily follows that
   A. A + D > B + E
   B. A + D > B + C
   C. A + B > 2D
   D. B + D > C + E
   E. A + D < B + C

6. What will be the correct mathematical signs that can be inserted in the following equation?
9 . . . 8 . . . 8 . . . 4 . . . 9 = 65
A. − + × ÷
B. ÷ × + −
C. ÷ + × −
D. × + ÷ −
E. + × ÷ −

7. If "÷" means "+"; "−" means "÷"; "×"means "−" and "+" means "×", then
32 ÷ 8 − 4 × 12 + 4 = ?
A. 40
B. 1/12
C. 16
D. 12
E. None of these

8. If "x" stands for "+"; "y" stands for "−"; "z"stands for "÷" and "w" stands for "×", then
10w 2x 5y 5 = ?
A. 15
B. 12

C. 20
D. 10
E. 25

9. If "−" stands for "×"; "×" stands for "+"; "+"stands for "÷" and "÷" stands for "−", then what will be the value of the following equation?
8 − 4 + 16 × 8 − 10 = ?
A. 54
B. 82
C. 15
D. 10
E. 110

10. If Δ denotes =; + denotes >, − denotes <, □ denotes ≠, × denotes > and ÷ denotes < then
a + b − c denotes
A. b Δ c □ a
B. b □ a ÷ c
C. a ÷ b × c
D. b − a + c
E. none of these

ANSWERS

1	2	3	4	5	6	7	8	9	10
B	E	E	C	B	D	E	C	B	D

EXPLANATORY ANSWERS

1. 20 + 6 − 6 + 4 = 24
2. 4 × 11 − 5 + 50
44 − 5 + 50 = 89
3. 24 × 4 ÷ 8 + 4
12 + 4 = 16
4. A + B > C + D > B + E or 2 C
∴ A + B > 2C
5. 1. A + D > C + E
2. B + E > C + D or 2 B
Since, the relation between 1 and 2 is not clear it is however certain that A + D > B + C (combination with C is < A + D).
6. A. 9 − 8 + 8 × 4 ÷ 9 = 65
(8 × 4 ÷ 9 gives the result in fractions. So, there is no need for further calculation as the result 65 is a whole number.)
B. 9 ÷ 8 × 8 + 4 − 9 = 65
9 + 4 − 9 ie 4 = 65

C. 9 ÷ 8 + 8 × 4 − 9 = 65
(9 ÷ 8 gives the result in fraction)
D. 9 × 8 + 8 ÷ 4 − 9 = 65
72 + 2 − 9 ie 65 = 65
E. 9 + 8 × 8 ÷ 4 − 9
9 + 16 − 9 ie 16 = 65
7. 32 + 8 ÷ 4 − 12 × 4
32 + 2 − 48 = − 14
8. 10 × 2 + 5 − 5
20 + 5 − 5 = 20
9. 8 × 4 ÷ 16 + 8 × 10
2 + 80 = 82
10. What is given is a > b < c
The equations are :
A. b = c ≠ a   which is wrong
B. b ≠ a < c   which is wrong
C. a < b > c   which is wrong
D. b < a > c   which is correct
Therefore, 'd' is the answer.

❀ ❀ ❀

Blood Relation

Coded relationships problem involves interpreting a given relationship—string which is coded in a particular way and then matching it with the relationship mentioned in the questions. The process of decoding each and every relation and then interpreting from the given relationship—string the final relationship is a cumbersome process and doing it for all the choices makes it very time consuming. However systematic representation and some clever common sense observations may give a speedy solution.

BLOOD RELATIONSHIPS

While attempting questions on blood relations, one should be clear of all the relation patterns that can exist between any two individuals. Very well-known relations are:

Mother	Father	Son
Daughter	Brother	Sister
Niece	Nephew	Uncle
Aunt	Husband	Wife
Grandmother	Grandfather	Grandson
Granddaughter	Brother-in-law	Sister-in-law
Father-in-law	Mother-in-law	Son-in-law
Daughter-in-law	Cousin	

The patterns of some relationships which help in solving questions in these tests are :

Father's or Mother's Father	– Grandfather (Paternal or Maternal)
Father's or Mother's Mother	– Grandmother (Paternal or Maternal)
Father's or Mother's Son	– Brother
Father's or Mother's Daughter	– Sister
Father's Brother	– Paternal Uncle
Father's Sister	– Paternal Aunt
Mother's Brother	– Maternal Uncle
Mother's Sister	– Maternal Aunt

Uncle or Aunt's Son or Daughter	– Cousin
Son's Wife	– Daughter-in-law
Daughter's Husband	– Son-in-law
Husband's or Wife's Brother	– Brother-in-law
Husband's or Wife's Sister	– Sister-in-law
Brother's Wife	– Sister-in-law
Sister's Husband	– Brother-in-law
Brother's Son	– Nephew
Brother's Daughter	– Niece

Example

1. R is the daughter of Q. M is the sister of B, who is the son of Q. How is M related to R?
   A. Cousin   B. Niece
   C. Sister   D. Aunt
   E. None of these

Ans. C. B is the son of Q and R is the daughter of Q. This means M is sister of B and R.

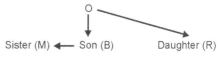

2. M is father of N. L is brother of M. P is mother of L. How is N related to P?
   A. Grandson
   B. Nephew
   C. Granddaughter
   D. Can't be determined
   E. None of these

Ans. D. P is mother of L and M. N is child of M. Therefore, N is grandson or granddaughter of P.

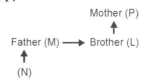

EXERCISE

1. Introducing a boy, a girl said, "He is the son of the daughter of the father of my uncle." How is the boy related to the girl?
   A. Brother   B. Nephew
   C. Uncle   D. Son-in-law

2. Pointing to a photograph of a boy Suresh said, "He is the son of the only son of my mother." How is Suresh related to that boy?
   A. Brother   B. Uncle
   C. Cousin   D. Father

3. If A + B means A is the brother of B; A – B means A is the sister of B and A × B means A is the father of B. Which of the following means that C is the son of M?
   A. M – N × C + F   B. F – C + N × M
   C. N + M – F × C   D. M × N – C + F

4. If A is the brother of B; B is the sister of C; and C is the father of D, how D is related to A?
   A. Brother
   B. Sister
   C. Nephew
   D. Cannot be determined

5. If A + B means A is the mother of B; A – B means A is the brother of B; A % B means A is the father of B and A × B means A is the sister of B, which of the following shows that P is the maternal uncle of Q?
   A. Q – N + M × P   B. P + S × N – Q
   C. P – M + N × Q   D. Q – S % P

6. Pointing to a photograph Lata says, "He is the son of the only son of my grandfather." How is the man in the photograph related to Lata?
   A. Brother   B. Uncle
   C. Cousin   D. Data is inadequate

7. If D is the brother of B, how B is related to C? To answer this question which of the statements is/are necessary?
   1. The son of D is the grandson of C.
   2. B is the sister of D.
   A. Only 1

   B. Only 2
   C. Either 1 or 2
   D. 1 and 2 both are required

8. Pointing to a photograph. Balram said, "He is the son of the only daughter of the father of my brother." How Balram is related to the man in the photograph?
   A. Nephew   B. Brother
   C. Father   D. Maternal Uncle

9. Pointing to a woman, Abhay said, "Her granddaughter is the only daughter of my brother." How is the woman related to Abhay?
   A. Sister   B. Grandmother
   C. Mother-in-law   D. Mother

10. If A + B means A is the sister of B; A × B means A is the wife of B, A % B means A is the father of B and A – B means A is the brother of B. Which of the following means T is the daughter of P?
    A. P × Q % R + S – T
    B. P × Q % R – T + S
    C. P × Q % R + T – S
    D. P × Q % R + S + T

11. Deepak said to Naresh, "That boy playing with the football is the younger of the two brothers of the daughter of my father's wife." How is the boy playing football related to Deepak?
    A. Son   B. Brother
    C. Cousin   D. Brother-in-law

12. Reena who is the sister-in-law of Ashok, is the daughter-in-law of Kalyani. Dheeraj is the father of Suresh who is the only brother of Ashok. How Kalyani is related to Ashok?
    A. Mother-in-law   B. Aunt
    C. Wife   D. None of these

13. A and B are children of M. Who is the father of A? To answer this question which of the statements 1 and 2 is necessary?
    1. C is the brother of A and the son of E.
    2. F is the mother B.
    A. Only 1   B. Only 2
    C. Either 1 or 2   D. 1 and 2 both

14. Anil said, "This girl is the wife of the grandson of my mother". How is Anil related to the girl?
  A. Brother
  B. Grandfather
  C. Husband
  D. Father-in-law

15. Pointing towards a man, a woman said, "His mother is the only daughter of my mother." How is the woman related to the man?
  A. Mother   B. Grandmother
  C. Sister   D. Daughter

16. If P $ Q means P is the brother of Q; P # Q means P is the mother of Q; P * Q means P is the daughter of Q in A # B $ C * D, who is the father?
  A. D
  B. B
  C. C
  D. Data is inadequate

17. Introducing Shalu, Aamir says, "She is the wife of only nephew of only brother of my mother." How Shalu is related to Aamir?
  A. Wife
  B. Sister
  C. Sister-in-law
  D. Data is inadequate

Directions (Qs. Nos. 18 and 19): *Read the following information to answer the questions:*
  A + B means A is the father of B
  A − B means A is the sister of B
  A × B means A is the husband of B
  A % B means A is the wife of B

18. Which of the following means 'T is the nephew of Q'?
  A. Q × R − S + T
  B. Q + R % S + T
  C. Q − R % S + T
  D. None of these

19. Which of the following means S is granddaughter of R?
  A. R + P % Q + S
  B. K % R + P × Q − L + S
  C. K % R + P % Q + S − L
  D. K % R + P % Q + S + L

20. If 'A + B' means 'A is brother of B', 'A − B' means 'A is sister of B', 'A × B' means 'A is wife of B' and 'A % B' means 'A is father of B', then which of the following indicates 'S is the son of P'?
  A. P × Q % R + S − T
  B. P × Q % S − R + T
  C. P × Q % R − T + S
  D. P × Q % R − S + T

ANSWERS

1	2	3	4	5	6	7	8	9	10
A	D	D	D	C	A	D	D	D	B

11	12	13	14	15	16	17	18	19	20
B	D	B	D	A	A	A	D	C	D

EXPLANATORY ANSWERS

1.

The father of the boy's uncle → the grandfather of the boy and daughter of the grandfather → sister of father.

2.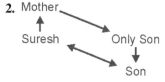

The boy in the photograph is the only son of the son of Suresh's mother *i.e.*, the son of Suresh. Hence, Suresh is the father of boy.

3.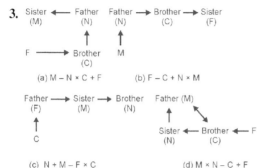

(a) M – N × C + F   (b) F – C + N × M

(c) N + M – F × C   (d) M × N – C + F

M × N → M is the father of N
N – C → N is the sister of C
and C + F → C is the brother of F.
Hence, M is the father of C or C is the son of M.

4. Father (C) ⟶ Sister (B) ⟶ Brother (A)
⬆
D

If D is Male, the answer is Nephew.
If D is Female, the answer is Niece.
As the sex of D is not known, hence, the relation between D and A cannot be determined.
Note: Niece - A daughter of one's brother or sister, or of one's brother-in-law or sister-in-law.
Nephew - A son of one's brother or sister, or of one's brother-in-law or sister-in-law.

5.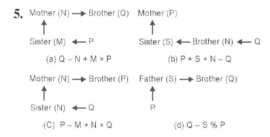

(a) Q – N + M × P   (b) P + S × N – Q

(C) P – M + N × Q   (d) Q – S % P

6.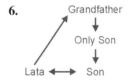

The man in the photograph is the son of the only son of Lata's grandfather *i.e.*, the man is the son of Lata's father. Hence, the man is the brother of Lata.

7.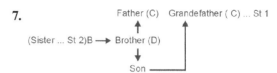

Given: D is the brother of B.
From statement 1, we can detect that D is son of C (son of D is the grandson of C).
From statement 2, we can detect that B is 'Female' (sister of D).
Therefore, B is daughter of C.

8.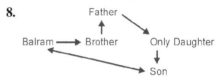

The man in the photograph is the son of the sister of Balram. Hence, Balram is the maternal uncle of the man in the photograph.

9.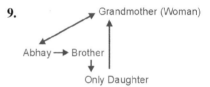

Daughter of Abhay's brother → niece of Abhay. Thus the granddaughter of the woman is Abhay's niece. Hence, the woman is the mother of Abhay.

10. We can note that sex of last person in each option will be unknown. Since T should be daughter of P so T will be definitely female in correct option. So options A and D are straightaway ruled out. Also in the correct option only '+' or '×' will follow T as T is definitely a female so option C is also ruled out.

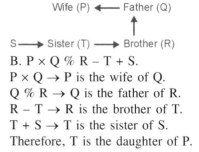

B. P × Q % R – T + S.
P × Q → P is the wife of Q.
Q % R → Q is the father of R.
R – T → R is the brother of T.
T + S → T is the sister of S.
Therefore, T is the daughter of P.

11.

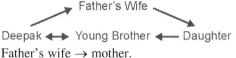

Father's wife → mother.

Hence, the daughter of the mother means sister and sister's younger brother means brother. Therefore, the boy is the brother of Deepak.

12.

Ashok is the only brother of Suresh and Reena is the sister-in-law of Ashok. Hence, Reena is the wife of Suresh. Kalyani is the mother-in-law of Reena. Kalyani is the mother of Ashok.

13.

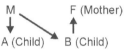

From main st. & st. 1

M   F (Mother)
↓   ↗ ↑
A (Child)   B (Child)

From main st. & st. 2

A and B are children of M. From 1, C is the brother B and son of E. Since, the sex of M and E are not known. Hence 1 is not sufficient to answer the question.

From 2. F is the mother of B. Hence, F is also the mother of A. Hence M is the father of A. Thus, 2 is sufficient to answer the question.

14.

The girl is the wife of grandson of Anil's mother *i.e.*, the girl is the wife of son of Anil. Hence, Anil is the father-in-law of the girl.

15.

Mother
↑   ↘
Woman   Only Daughter
     ↘
        Son (Man)

Only daughter of my mother → myself.

Hence, the woman is the mother of the man.

16.

Mother (A)   D
↑   ↑
Brother (B) ← Daughter (C)

A is the mother of B, B is the brother of C and C is the daughter of D. Hence, D is the father.

17. Mother ⟶ Only Brother

Brother of mother means maternal uncle. Hence only nephew of Aamir's maternal uncle means Aamir himself. Therefore Shalu is the wife of Aamir.

18. Since 'T is the nephew of Q' so 'T' must be a male but sex of 'T' cannot be established in any of the option.

19. Choice A, B is not correct as sex of S is not known. D is ruled out because S is a male here. Representation for choice C is as follows:

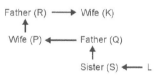

So, S is granddaughter of R is correct here.

20. As 'S' is female in option A and B, both are rejected directly. The sex of 'S' in option C is not known, hence it is also eliminated. Now, check option D.

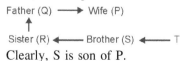

Clearly, S is son of P.

❀ ❀ ❀

5 Direction Sense

In these type of tests, the directions in questions needs to be perceived, Such questions are based on the direction chart.

N = North, S = South, E = East, W = West

The sense of the different directions are guided by the left and righ turns or angular turns.

Example

1. Shobha was facing East. She walked 20 metres. Turning left she moved 15 metres and then turning right moved 25 metres. Finally, she turned right and moved 15 metres more. How far is she from her starting point?

(a) 25 metres
(b) 35 metres
(c) 50 metres
(d) 45 metres

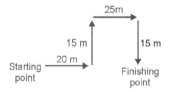

Ans.: Shobha turns left after walking 20 metres towards East. Now she walks 15 metres towards North. She turns right towards East again and walks 25 metres further. Finally turning right towards South, she walks 15 metres. The distance moved towards North and towards South is same, i.e., 15 metres. So, Shobha is 20 + 25 metres = 45 metres away from her starting point.

EXERCISE

1. One morning Urmilla and Vishal were talking to each other face to face at a crossing. If Vishal's shadow was exactly to the left of Urmilla, which direction was Urmilla facing?
   A. East   B. West
   C. North   D. South

2. If South-East becomes North, North-East becomes West and so on. What will West become?
   A. North - East   B. North - West
   C. South - East   D. South - West

3. Ravi put his timepiece on the table in such a way that at 6 P.M. hour hand points to North. In which direction the minute hand will point at 9.15 P.M. ?

   A. South - East   B. South
   C. North   D. West

4. Rakesh walked 20 m towards north. Then he turned right and walks 30 m. Then he turns right and walks 35 m. Then he turns left and walks 15 m. Finally he turns left and walks 15 m. In which direction and how many metres is he from the starting position?
   A. 15 m West   B. 30 m East
   C. 30 m West   D. 45 m East

5. Starting from the point X, John walked 15 m towards west. He turned left and walked 20 m. He then turned left and walked 15 m. After this he turned to his right and walked 12 m.

How far and in which directions is now John from X?

A. 32 m, South   B. 47 m, East
C. 42 m, North   D. 27 m, South

6. Suman is 40 metres South – West of Ashok, Prakash is 40 metres South – East of Ashok. Prakash is in which direction of Suman?

A. South   B. West
C. East   D. North – East

7. Vijayan started walking towards South. After walking 15 metres he turned to the left and walked 15 metres. He again turned to his left and walked 15 metres. How far is he from his original position and in which direction?

A. 15 metres, North
B. 15 metres, East
C. 30 metres, South
D. 15 metres, West

Directions (8 to 10): *Each of the following questions is based on the following information:*
1. P # Q means B is at 1 metre to the right of P.
2. P $ Q means B is at 1 metre to the North of P.
3. P * Q means B is at 1 metre to the left of P.
4. P @ Q means B is at 1 metre to the south of P.
5. In each question first person from the left is facing North.

8. According to X @ B * P, P is in which direction with respect to X?

A. North   B. South
C. North - East   D. South-West

9. According to M # N $ T, T is in which direction with respect to M?

A. North-West   B. North-East
C. South-West   D. South-East

10. According to P # R $ A * U, in which direction is U with respect to P?

A. East   B. West
C. North   D. South

Directions (Qs. 11 to 15): *P, Q, R and S are standing on four corners of a square piece of plot as shown in the given figure. They start moving, and the movements are explained in each of the questions. Read the question and select the right alternative.*

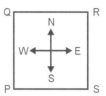

11. P, Q , R and S walk diagonally to opposite corners and from there Q and R walk one and a half sides anti-clockwise while P and S walk one side clockwise along the sides. Where is S now?

A. At the North – West corner
B. At the North -East
C. At the South – West corner
D. None of these

12. Q travelled straight to R, a distance of 10 m. He turned right and walked 7 m towards S, again he turned right and walked 8 m, and then finally turned right and walked 7m. How far is he from his original position?

A. 7 m   B. 8 m
C. 2m   D. 3m

13. From the original position, S starts crossing the field diagonally. After walking half the distance he turns right; walks some distance and turns left. Which direction is S facing now?

A. South - East   B. North - West
C. South - West   D. North

14. P and S walk one and a half length of the side clockwise and anti-clockwise respectively. Which one of the following statements is true?

A. P is at midpoint between Q and R and S at the corner originally occupied by P
B. P and S are both at the midpoint between R and S
C. P and S are both at the midpoint between Q and R.
D. S is at midpoint between Q and R and P is at the midpoint between original side of R and S

15. P, Q, R and S walk one and a half sides clockwise. Who is on the left of Q if he is facing West?

A. P   B. R
C. S   D. No one

ANSWERS

1	2	3	4	5	6	7	8	9	10
C	C	D	D	A	C	B	D	B	C

11	12	13	14	15
B	C	B	C	B

EXPLANATORY ANSWERS

1.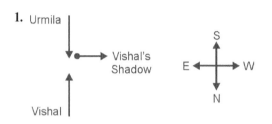

2.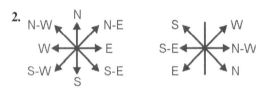

It is clear from the diagrams that new name of West will become South-East.

3.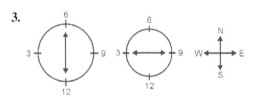

At 9.15 P.M., the minute hand will point towards west.

4.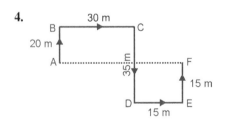

Required distance = AF = 30 + 15 = 45 m. From the above figure, F is in East direction from A. So the answer is '45 m East'.

5.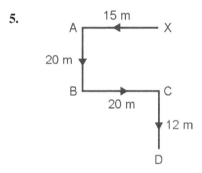

Required distance = 20 + 12 = 32 m South.

6.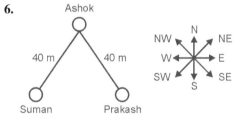

7.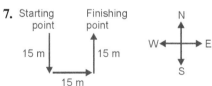

8. According to X @ B * Y

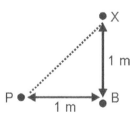

Hence, P is in South-West of X.

9. According to M # N $ T

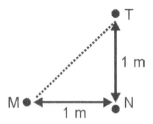

Hence, T is in the North-East of M.

10. According to P # R $ A * U

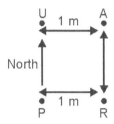

Hence, U is in North direction with respect to P.

11.

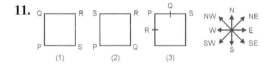

(1)   (2)   (3)

12. (10 m – 8 m = 2 m)

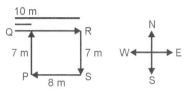

13.

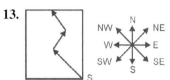

14. The movements are :

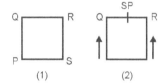

(1)   (2)

15.

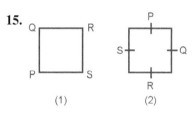

(1)   (2)

In these questions, a series of interlinked information or data is given. Quantitatively analysis of given information or data provides certain conclusions.

In Statement Analysis (Problem Solving) questions, all given information has to be interpreted and arranged step-by-step. One should be careful that no given data is left incorporated. A brief glimpse to all questions asked on given data is helpful in preparing the solution format.

Directions: *Read the following information carefully and answer the questions given below:*

In a family of six persons—A, B, C, D, E and F—there are three males and three females. There are two married couples and two persons are unmarried. Each one of them reads different newspapers, viz. Times of India, Indian Express, Hindustan Times, Financial Times, Navbharat Times and Business Standard. E, who reads Indian Express, is mother-in-law of A, who is wife of C. D is the father of F and he does not read Times of India or Business Standard. B reads Navbharat Times and is the sister of F, who reads Hindustan Times. C does not read Business Standard.

1. Who among the following reads the Times of India?
   A. C   B. D
   C. A   D. Data inadequate
   E. None of these

2. How is F related to E?
   A. Daughter   B. Brother
   C. Son   D. Data inadequate
   E. None of these

3. Which of the following is one of the married couples?
   A. D-B   B. D-E
   C. B-F   D. E-F
   E. None of these

4. Which of the following newspapers is read by 'A'?
   A. Times of India   B. Navbharat Times
   C. Financial Times   D. Data inadequate
   E. None of these

5. How many sons does E have?
   A. Four   B. Three
   C. Two   D. One
   E. None of these

Following is the detail presentation of mental approach for solution of the given problem. In practice these questions are solved briefly.

E, who reads Indian Express, is mother-in-law of A, who is the wife of C

Person	Newspaper read	Sex	Information/Reasons
A		Fe	A-C Couple
B			
C		M	A is the wife of C
D			
E	I.E	Fe	mother-in-law of A
F			

D is the father of F and he does not read TOI or B.S

Person	Newspaper read	Sex	Information/Reasons
A		Fe	A-C Couple
B			
C		M	A is the wife of C
D	H.T or F.T or N.T	M	father of F, (TOI, B.S,I.E- not)
E	I.E	Fe	mother-in-law of A

As there are two married couples. This implies that D and E are couples. B reads N.T and is the sister of F, who reads H.T. C does not read B.S

Person	Newspaper read	Sex	Information/Reasons
A	B.S	Fe	A-C Couple
B	N.T	Fe	Sister of F
C	TOI	M	B.S -no
D	F.T	M	father of F
E	I.E	Fe	D-E, Couple
F	H.T	M	There are 3 males- 3 females

E is mother in law of A and A is wife of C implies C is Son of E. D is father of F and D-E are couples implies F is Son of E.

1. A **2.** C **3.** B **4.** E **5.** C

EXERCISE

Directions (Qs. Nos. 1 to 4): *Read the following information carefully and answer the questions given below:*

1. There are five types of cards viz. A, B, C, D and E. There are three cards of each type. These are to be inserted in envelopes of three colours—red, yellow and brown. There are five envelopes of each colour.
2. B, D and E type cards are to be inserted in red envelopes; A, B and C type cards are to be inserted in yellow envelopes; and C, D and E type cards are to be inserted in brown envelopes.
3. Two cards each of B and D type are inserted in red envelopes.

1. How many cards of E type are inserted in brown envelopes?
A. Nil   B. One
C. Two   D. Three
E. Data inadequate

2. Which of the following combinations of the type of cards and the number of cards is **definitely correct** in respect of yellow-coloured envelopes?
A. A-2, B-1, C-2   B. B-1, C-2, D-2
C. A-2, E-1, D-2   D. A-3, B-1, C-1
E. None of these

3. Which of the following combinations of types of cards and the number of cards and colour of envelope is **definitely correct**?
A. C-2, D-1, E-2, Brown
B. C-1, D-2, E-2, Brown
C. B-2, D-2, A-1, Red
D. A-2, B-2, C-1, Yellow
E. None of these

4. Which of the following combinations of colour of the envelope and the number of cards is **definitely correct** in respect of E type cards?

A. Red-2, Brown-1
B. Red-1, Yellow-2
C. Red-2, Yellow-1
D. Yellow-1, Brown-2
E. None of these

Directions (Qs. Nos. 5 to 7): *Read the following information carefully and answer the questions given below:*

Six persons A, B, C, D, E and F took up a job with a firm in a week from Monday to Saturday. Each of them joined for different posts on different days. The posts were of–Clerk, Officer, Technician, Manager, Supervisor, and Sales Executive, though not respectively. F joined as a Manager on the first day. B joined as a Supervisor but neither on Wednesday nor Friday. D joined as a Technician on Thursday. Officer joined the firm on Wednesday. E joined as a clerk on Tuesday. A joined as a Sales Executive.

5. Who joined the firm on Wednesday?
A. B
B. C
C. B or C
D. Data inadequate
E. None of these

6. Who was the last person to join the firm?
A. E
B. F
C. A
D. B
E. None of these

7. On which of the following days did the Sales Executive join?
A. Tuesday
B. Thursday
C. Saturday
D. Wednesday
E. None of these

Directions (Qs. Nos. 8 to 11): *Read the following information carefully and answer the questions given below:*

(a) An examination board has organised examination for ten s ubjects viz. A, B, C, D, E, F, G, H, I and J on six days of the week with a holiday on Sunday, not having more than two papers on any of the days.

(b) Exam begins on Wednesday with subject F.

(c) D is accompained by some other subject but not on Thursday. A and G are on the same day immediately after holiday.

(d) There is only one paper on last day and Saturday. B is immediately followed by H, which is immediately followed by I.

(e) C is on Saturday. H is not on the same day as J.

8. Examination for which of the following pairs of subjects is on Thursday?
A. HE
B. DB
C. FD
D. Data inadequate
E. None of these

9. Examination for which of the following subjects is on the next day of D?
A. B
(2) C
C. I
D. H
E. None of these

10. Examination for which of the following subjects is on the last day?
A. B
B. E
C. J
D. Data inadequate
E. None of these

11. Examination for subject F is on the same day as which of the following subjects?
A. E
(2) D
C. I
D. B
E. None of these

Directions (Qs. Nos. 12 to 16): *Study the following information to answer the given questions:*

P, Q, R, S, T, V, W and Z are travelling to three destinations Delhi, Chennai and Hyderabad in three different vehicles Honda City, Swift D'Zire and Ford Ikon. There are three females among them one in each car. There are atleast two persons in each car. R is not travelling with Q and W. T , a male, is travelling with only Z and they are not travelling to Chennai. P is travelling in Honda City to Hyderabad. S is sister of P and travels by Ford Ikon. V and R travel together. W does not travel to Chennai.

12. Who is travelling with W?
A. Only Q
B. Only P
C. Both P and Q
D. Cannot be determined
E. None of these

13. Members in which of the following combinations are travelling in Honda City?
    A. PRS   B. PQW
    C. PWS   D. Data inadequate
    E. None of these

14. In which car are four members travelling?
    A. None
    B. Honda City
    C. Swift D'zire
    D. Ford Ikon
    E. Honda City or Ford Ikon

15. Which of the following combinations represents the three female members?
    A. QSZ
    B. WSZ
    C. PSZ
    D. Cannot be determined
    E. None of these

16. Members in which car are travelling To Chennai?
    A. Honda City
    B. Swift D'Zire
    C. Ford Ikon
    D. Either Swift D'Zire or Ford Ikon
    E. None of the above

Directions (Qs. 17-23): *Each problem consists of three statements. Based on the first two statements, the third statement may be true, false, or uncertain.*

17. (i) Tanya is older than Easha.
    (ii) Celina is older than Tanya.
    (iii) Easha is older than Celina.

    If the first two statements are true, the third statement is
    A. True   B. False
    C. Uncertain   D. None of these

18. (i) Blueberries cost more than strawberries.
    (ii) Blueberries cost less than raspberries.
    (iii) Raspberries cost more than both straw-berries and blueberries.

    If the first two statements are true, the third statement is
    A. True   B. False
    C. Uncertain   D. None of these

19. (i) Maria runs faster than Gail.
    (ii) Lily runs faster than Maria.
    (iii) Gail runs faster than Lily.

    If the first two statements are true, the third statement is
    A. True   B. False
    C. Uncertain   D. None of these

20. (i) A fruit basket contains more apples than mangoes.
    (ii) There are more mangoes in the basket than there are oranges.
    (iii) The basket contains more apples than oranges.

    If the first two statements are true, the third statement is
    A. True   B. False
    C. Uncertain   D. None of these

21. (i) Jullie is younger than Katrina.
    (ii) Maya was born after Jullie.
    (iii) Katrina is older than Maya.

    If the first two statements are true, the third statement is
    A. True   B. False
    C. Uncertain   D. None of these

22. (i) The temperature on Monday was lower than on Tuesday.
    (ii) The temperature on Wednesday was lower than on Tuesday.
    (iii) The temperature on Monday was higher than on Wednesday.

    If the first two statements are true, the third statement is
    A. True   B. False
    C. Uncertain   D. None of these

23. (i) All Lamels are Signots with buttons.
    (ii) No blue Signots have buttons.
    (iii) No Lamels are blue.

    If the first two statements are true, the third statement is
    A. True
    B. False
    C. Uncertain
    D. None of these

ANSWERS

1	2	3	4	5	6	7	8	9	10
C	D	A	E	B	D	E	A	B	C

11	12	13	14	15	16	17	18	19	20
D	C	B	A	D	C	B	A	B	C

21	22	23
A	C	A

EXPLANATORY ANSWERS

Solution (1-4): From (2), Out of fifteen cards nine cards will be inserted as following:

Red envelope	Yellow envelope	Brown envelope
B	A	C
D	B	D
E	C	E

From (3) and using the above table, we get

Red envelope	Yellow envelope	Brown envelope
B(2)	A	C
D(2)	B(1)	D(1)
E(1)	C	E(2)

The digits in brackets shows the no. of cards. Now, From (1), it is clear that each colour of envelope contains five cards, so there are two cards of C-type in brown envelope. Hence the remaining one card of C-type is in yellow envelope. Hence all the three A-type are in yellow envelope.

4. Brown-2, Red-1.

Solution (5-7): Summarising the given information in tabular form, we get

Person	Posts	Days
F	Manager	Monday
B	Supervisor	*Saturday*
D	Technician	Thursday
C	Officer	Wednesday
E	Clerk	Tuesday
A	Sales Executive	*Friday*

The places of italized letter/words is the last left one and can be filled easily by fulfilling all other given conditions.

Solution (8-11):

Wed	Thu	Fri	Sat	Sun	Mon	Tue
F, B	H, E	I, D	C	Hol	A, G	J

12-16: T(m) Z(f) Swift D'Zire Delhi
QWP Honda City Hyderabad
V(m)R(m)S(f) Ford Ikon Chennai.

17. Because the first two statements are true, Easha is the youngest of the three, so the third statement must be false.

18. Because the first two statements are true, raspberries are the most expensive of the three.

19. We know from the first two statements that Lily runs fastest. Therefore, the third statement must be false.

20. There are fewer oranges than either apples or mangoes, so the statement is true. (another approach)
   1. A fruit basket contains more apples than mangoes = App > Mang.
   2. There are more mangoes in the basket than there are oranges = Mang > Org
   Now, Combine the above two results: App > Mang > Org.
   3. The basket contains more apples than oranges (App > ... > Org) = Yes.
   Therefore, the given 3rd statement is true.

21. Jullie is younger than Katrina and older than Maya, so Maya must be younger than Katrina.

22. We know from the first two statements that Tuesday had the highest temperature, but we cannot know whether Monday's temperature was higher than Tuesday's.

23. We know that there are Signots with buttons, or Lamels, and that there are blue Signots, which have no buttons. Therefore, Lamels do not have buttons and cannot be blue.

❈ ❈ ❈

Sitting arrangement around circle: Nowadays in some competitive exams problems based on sitting arrangement around circle is frequently asked. These questions appear very simple but are not a cakewalk and are often solved wrongly. Main confusing point is deciding between left hand side and right hand side of a person when all persons are sitting around a circle facing centre. Because the left hand side of a person in lower semicircle is right hand side of a person in upper semicircle. This confusion is not met when these problems are solved by numbered line method. In numbered line method all members are first placed on a numbered line numbered up to total number of persons starting from one. For extreme end members line is assumed to be continued with other extreme member as immediate neighbour. Right hand side or left hand side confusion is by passed in this method. Following solved problems will make the method very clear.

Example

Directions (Qs. Nos. 1 to 6): *Study the following information carefully and answer the questions given below:*

P, Q, R, S, T, V, W and Z are sitting around a circle facing at the centre. R is fourth to the left of P who is second to the right of S. V is fourth to the right of S. Q is fourth to the left of W who is not an immediate neighbour of P or S. Z is not an immediate neighbour of R.

1. Who is to the immediate right of V?
   A. R   B. W
   C. Z   D. Data inadequate
   E. None of these

2. Who is to the immediate right of R?
   A. T   B. S
   C. W   D. Data inadequate
   E. None of these

3. Who is second to the left of Z?
   A. Q   B. V
   C. S   D. W
   E. None of these

4. In which of the following pairs is the first person sitting to the immediate right of the second person?
   A. VW   B. RT
   C. WR   D. QP
   E. ZP

5. Which of the following pairs are the immediate neighbours of Z?
   A. WQ   B. VQ
   C. WP   D. VP
   E. None of these

6. Who is third to the right of R?
   A. P   B. S
   C. Q   D. Data inadequate
   E. None of these

Solution (1-6):

(a) R is fourth to the left of P who is second to the right of S.
(b) V is fourth to the right of S.
(c) Q is fourh to the left of W who is not an immediate neighbour of P or S.
(d) Z is not an immediate neighbour of R.

```
                        _____ V .... (b)
     R      S|        P, ...(a)
     1.....2....3.....4.....5.....6.....7.....8
                               Z .... (d)
     ( c)... Q                         W
     _____
     R   T   S   Q   P   Z   V   W
     1.....2....3.....4.....5.....6.....7.....8
```

1. B   2. A   3. A   4. E   5. D   6. C

EXERCISE

Directions (Qs. Nos. 1 to 5): *Study the following information carefully and answer the questions given below:*

M, P, J, B, R, T and F are sitting around a circle facing at the centre. B is third to the left of J who is second to the left of M. P is third to the left of B and second to the right of R. T is not an immediate neighbour of M.

1. Who is fourth to the right of M?
   A. B
   B. T
   C. J
   D. Data inadequate
   E. None of these

2. Who is second to the left of T?
   A. F
   B. M
   C. P
   D. J
   E. Data inadequate

3. In which of the following pairs the second person is sitting to the immediate right of the first person?
   A. JR
   B. PJ
   C. TR
   D. MP
   E. None of these

4. What is F's position with respect to R?
   A. Third to the left
   B. Fourth to the right
   C. Third to the right
   D. Both A and B
   E. None of these

5. Who is third to the right of B?
   A. R
   B. J
   C. M
   D. Data inadequate
   E. None of these

Directions (Qs. Nos. 6 to 10): *Study the following information to answer the given questions:*

Representatives from eight different Banks viz. A, B, C, D, E, F, G and H are sitting around a circular table facing the centre but not necessarily in the same order. Each one of them is from a different Bank viz. UCO Bank, Oriental Bank of Commerce, Bank of Maharashtra, Canara Bank, Syndicate Bank, Punjab National Bank, Bank of India and Dena Bank. F sits second to right of the representative from Canara Bank. Representative from Bank of India is an immediate neighbour of the representative from Canara Bank. Two people sit between the representative of Bank of India and B. C and E are immediate neighbours of each other. Neither C nor E is an immediate neighbour of either B or the representative from Canara Bank. Representative from Bank of Maharashtra sits second to right of D. D is neither the representative of Canara Bank nor Bank of India. G and the representative from UCO Bank are immediate neighbours of each other. B is not the representative of UCO Bank. Only one person sits between C and the representative from Oriental Bank of Commerce. H sits third to left of the representative from Dena Bank. Representative from Punjab National Bank sits second to left of the representative from Syndicate Bank.

6. Who amongst the following sit exactly between B and the representative from Bank of India?
   A. A and the representative from UCO Bank
   B. F and G
   C. H and the representative from Bank of Maharashtra
   D. H and G
   E. Representatives from Syndicate Bank and Oriental Bank of Commerce

7. Who amongst the following is the representative from Oriental Bank of Commerce?
   A. A
   B. C
   C. H
   D. G
   E. E

8. Four of the following five are alike in a certain way based on the given arrangement and thus form a group. Which is the one that does not belong to that group?
   A. H – UCO Bank
   B. A – Canara Bank
   C. D – Bank of Maharashtra
   D. E – Syndicate Bank
   E. F – Punjab National Bank

9. Who amongst the following sits second to left of B?
   A. C
   B. H
   C. The representative from Canara Bank
   D. The representative from Punjab National Bank
   E. G

10. Which of the following is true with respect to the given sitting arrangement?
    A. B is the representative from Bank of Maharashtra
    B. C sits second to right of H
    C. The representative from Dena Bank sits to the immediate left of the representative from UCO Bank
    D. A sits second to right of the representative from Bank of India
    E. The representatives from Bank of Maharashtra and Syndicate Bank are immediate neighbours of each other

Directions (Qs. Nos. 11 to 14): *Six friends P, Q, R, S, T and U are sitting around the hexagonal table each at one corner and are facing the centre of the hexagonal. P is second to the left of U. Q is neighbour of R and S. T is second to the left of S.*

11. Which one is sitting opposite to P?
    A. R   B. Q
    C. T   D. S

12. Who is the fourth person to the left of Q?
    A. P
    B. U
    C. R
    D. Data inadequate

13. Which of the following are the neighbours of P?
    A. U and P
    B. T and R
    C. U and R
    D. Data inadequate

14. Which one is sitting opposite to T?
    A. R
    B. Q
    C. Cannot be determined
    D. S

Direction (Qs. Nos. 15 and 16): *Five girls are sitting on a bench to be photographed. Seema is to the left of Rani and to the right of Bindu. Mary is to the right of Rani. Reeta is between Rani and Mary.*

15. Who is sitting immediate right to Reeta?
    A. Bindu   B. Rani
    C. Mary   D. Seema

16. Who is in the middle of the photograph?
    A. Seema   B. Rani
    C. Reeta   D. Seema

Directions (Qs. Nos. 17 to 20) : *In a class there are seven students (including boys and girls) A, B, C, D, E, F and G. They sit on three benches I, II and III. Such that at least two students on each bench and at least one girl on each bench. C who is a girl student, does not sit with A, E and D. F a boy student sits with only B. A boyfriend of D sits on the bench I with his best friends. G sits on the bench III. E is the brother of C.*

17. How many girls are there out of these 7 students?
    A. 3   B. 3 or 4
    C. 4   D. Data inadequate

18. Which of the following is the group of girls?
    A. BAC   B. BFC
    C. BCD   D. CDF

19. Who sits with C?
    A. B   B. D
    C. G   D. E

20. On which bench there are three students?
    A. Bench I   B. Bench II
    C. Bench III   D. Bench I or II

Directions (Qs. Nos. 21 to 25): *In an Exhibition seven cars of different companies—Tata, Ambassador, Fiat, Maruti, Mercedes, Bedford and Fargo are standing facing to east in the following order.*
   I. Tata is next to right of Fargo.
   II. Fargo is fourth to the right of Fiat.
   III. Maruti car is between Ambassador and Bedford.
   IV. Fiat which is third to the left of Ambassador, is at one end.

21. Which of the cars are on both the sides of Tata car?
  A. Ambassador and Maruti
  B. Maruti and Fiat
  C. Fargo and Mercedes
  D. Ambassador and Fargo

22. Which of the following statement is correct?
  A. Maruti is next left of Ambassador.
  B. Bedford is next left of Fiat.
  C. Bedford is at one end.
  D. Fiat is next second to the right of Maruti.

23. Which one of the following statements is correct?
  A. Fargo car is in between Ambassador and Fiat.

  B. Tata is next left to Mercedes car.
  C. Fargo is next right of Tata.
  D. Maruti is fourth right of Mercedes.

24. Which of the following groups of cars is to the right of Ambassador?
  A. Tata, Fargo and Maruti
  B. Mercedes, Tata and Fargo
  C. Maruti, Bedford and Fiat
  D. Bedford, Tata and Fargo

25. Which one of the following is the correct position of Mercedes?
  A. Next to the left of Tata
  B. Next to the left of Bedford
  C. Fourth to the right of Maruti
  D. Fourth to the right of Maruti

ANSWERS

1	2	3	4	5	6	7	8	9	10
E	A	C	D	B	C	E	B	D	E
11	**12**	**13**	**14**	**15**	**16**	**17**	**18**	**19**	**20**
D	A	B	B	C	B	A	C	C	A
21	**22**	**23**	**24**	**25**					
C	A	B	B	D					

EXPLANATORY ANSWERS

1-5: (a) B is third to the left of J who is second to the left of M.
  (b) P is third to the left of B and second to the right of R.
  (c) T is not an immediate neighbour of M.

6-10:

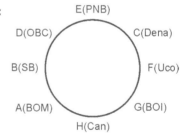

11-14:

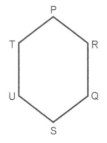

15-16:

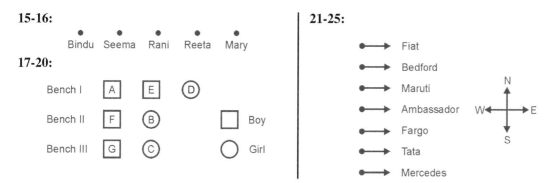

•   •   •   •   •
Bindu Seema Rani   Reeta   Mary

17-20:

Bench I   [A] [E] (D)

Bench II   [F] (B)   [ ] Boy

Bench III [G] (C)   ( ) Girl

21-25:

•——▶ Fiat

•——▶ Bedford

•——▶ Maruti

•——▶ Ambassador

•——▶ Fargo

•——▶ Tata

•——▶ Mercedes

N
W ◀——▶ E
S

❀ ❀ ❀

In these questions, all one have to do is to analyse the given data and see if the answer to the problem can be given by all the data provided or by few of the data provided or cannot be answered with the data provided. Sometimes questions are qualitative in nature, wherein one has to apply his own value-judgement in order to reach a conclusion.

Example

Directions: *In the question below consists of a question and two or three statements given below it. You have to decide whether the data provided in the statements are sufficient to answer the question.*

EXERCISE

Directions (Qs. Nos. 1 to 30): *In each of the questions below consists of a question and two statements numbered I and II given below it. You have to decide whether the data provided in the statements are sufficient to answer the question. Read both the statements and* give answer:

A. If the data in statement I alone are sufficient to answer the question, while the data in statement II alone are not sufficient to answer the question.

B. If the data in statement II alone are sufficient to answer the question, while the data in statement I alone are not sufficient to answer the question.

C. If the data either in statement I alone or in statement II alone are sufficient to answer the question.

D. If the data given in both statements I and II together are not sufficient to answer the question and

2. Who is the North-East of R?
   1. S is to the South-East of N, who is to the South-West of P, who is to the North of Q.
   2. T is to the North-West of Q, who is to the South of P.
   3. R, who is to the North of S, is midway between N and Q, N being to the West of R.
   A. All 1, 2, 3 together are required
   B. Only 1 and 3 together are sufficient
   C. Only 2 and 3 together are sufficient
   D. Either 1 and 3 together or 2 and 3 together are sufficient
   E. None of these

Ans. D

E. If the data in both statements I and II together are necessary to answer the question.

1. The last Sunday of March, 2006 fell on which date?
   Statements:
   I. The first Sunday of that month fell on 5th.
   II. The last day of that month was Friday.

2. In which year was Raju born?
   Statements:
   I. Raju at present is 25 years younger to his mother.
   II. Raju's brother, who was born in 1964, is 35 years younger to his mother.

3. How many children does M have?
   Statements:
   I. H is the only daughter of X who is wife of M.
   II. K and J are brothers of M.

4. How much was the total sale of the company?
Statements:
  I. The company sold 8000 units of product A each costing ₹ 25.
  II. This company has no other product line.

5. What will be the total weight of 10 rods, each of the same weight?
Statements:
  I. One-fourth of the weight of each rod is 5 kg.
  II. The total weight of three rods is 20 kilograms more than the total weight of two rods.

6. How is J related to Y?
Statements:
  I. Y and Z are children of D who is wife of J.
  II. R's sister J is married to Y's father.

7. How is T related to F?
Statements:
  I. R's sister J has married T's brother L, who is the only son of his parents.
  II. F is the only daughter of L and J.

8. What is the code for 'sky' in the code language?
Statements:
  I. In the code language, 'sky is clear' is written as 'de ra fa'.
  II. In the same code language, 'make it clear' is written as 'de ga jo'.

9. How is J related to P?
Statements:
  I. M is brother of P and T is sister of P.
  II. P's mother is married to J's husband who has one son and two daughters.

10. How many children are there between P and V in a row of children?
Statements:
  I. P is fifteenth from the left in the row.
  II. V is exactly in the middle and there are ten children towards his right.

11. B is the brother of A. How is A related to B?
Statements:
  I. A is the sister of C.
  II. E is the husband of A.

12. Who is to the immediate right of P among five persons P, Q, R, S and T facing North?
Statements:
  I. R is third to the left of Q and P is second to the right of R.
  II. Q is to the immediate left of T who is second to the right of P.

13. How is X related to Y?
Statements:
  I. Y says, "I have only one brother".
  II. X says, "I have only one sister".

14. How many children are there in the row of children facing North?
Statements:
  I. Vibha who is fifth from the left end is eighth to the left of Ashish who is twelfth from the right end.
  II. Rohit is fifth to the left of Nisha who is seventh from the right end and eighteenth from the left end.

15. How is Tannu related to the man in the photograph?
Statements:
  I. Man in the photograph is the only son of Tannu's grandfather.
  II. The man in the photograph has no brothers or sisters and his father is Tannu's grandfather.

16. On which day of the week was birthday of Salim?
Statements:
  I. Salim celebrated his birthday the very next day on which Arun celebrated his birthday.
  II. The sister of Salim was born on the third day of the week and two days after Salim was born.

17. How many doctors are practicing in this town?
Statements:
  I. There is one doctor per seven hundred residents.
  II. There are 16 wards with each ward having as many doctors as the number of wards.

18. How many pages of book C did Robert read on Sunday?
Statements:
   I. The book has 300 pages out of which two-thirds were read by him before Sunday.
   II. Robert read the last 40 pages of the book on the morning of Monday.

19. Among F, V, B, E and C, who is the third from the top when arranged in the descending order of their weights?
Statements:
   I. B is heavier than F and C and is less heavier than V who is not the heaviest.
   II. C is heavier than only F.

20. On a T.V. channel, four films A, B, C and D were screened, one on each day, on four consecutive days but not necessarily in that order. On which day was the film C screened?
Statements:
   I. The first film was screened on 23rd, Tuesday and was followed by film D.
   II. Film A was not screened on 25th and one serial was screened between films A and B.

21. Which word in the code language means 'flower'?
Statements:
   I. 'de fu la pane' means 'rose flower is beautiful' and 'la quiz' means 'beautiful tree'.
   II. 'de la chin' means 'red rose flower' and 'pa chin' means 'red tea'.

22. Who is C's partner in a game of cards involving four players A, B, C and D?
Statements:
   I. D is sitting opposite to A.
   II. B is sitting right of A and left of D.

23. How many students in a class play football?
Statements:
   I. Only boys play football.
   II. There are forty boys and thirty girls in the class.

24. Can Ramesh retire from office X in January 2020, with full pension benefits?
Statements:
   I. Ramesh will complete 30 years of service in office X in April 2014 and desires to retire.
   II. As per office X rules, an employee has to complete minimum 30 years of service and attain age of 60. Ramesh has 3 years to complete age of 60.

25. On which date in August was Kunal born?
Statements:
   I. Kunal's mother remembers that Kunal was born before nineteenth but after fifteenth.
   II. Kunal's brother remembers that Kunal was born before seventeenth but after twelfth.

26. Madan is elder than Kamal and Sharad is younger than Alok. Who among them is the youngest?
Statements:
   I. Sharad is younger than Madan.
   II. Alok is younger than Kamal.

27. What is the code for 'or' in the code language?
Statements:
   I. 'nik sa te' means 'right or wrong', 'ro da nik' means 'he is right' and 'fe te ro' means 'that is wrong'.
   II. 'pa nik la' means 'that right man', 'sa ne pa' means 'this or that' and 'ne ka re' means 'tell this there'.

28. What is Gagan's age?
Statements:
   I. Gagan, Vimal and Kusum are all of the same age.
   II. Total age of Vimal, Kusum and Anil is 32 years and Anil is as old as Vimal and Kusum together.

29. How much money do Vivek and Sunny have together?
Statements:
   I. Sunny has 20 rupees less than what Tarun has.
   II. Vivek has 30 rupees more than what Tarun has.

30. Who among P, Q, R, S and T is the lightest?
Statements:
   I. R is heavier than Q and T but lighter than S.
   II. S is not the heaviest.

ANSWERS

1	2	3	4	5	6	7	8	9	10
C	E	D	E	C	C	E	D	B	E
11	**12**	**13**	**14**	**15**	**16**	**17**	**18**	**19**	**20**
C	C	D	C	C	B	B	E	A	E
21	**22**	**23**	**24**	**25**	**26**	**27**	**28**	**29**	**30**
D	C	D	E	E	B	C	E	D	D

EXPLANATORY ANSWERS

1. From I, we conclude that 5th, 12th, 19th and 26th of March, 2006 were Sundays.
   So, the last Sunday fell on 26th.
   From II, we conclude that 31st March, 2006 was Friday. Thus, 26th March, 2006 was the last Sunday of the month.

2. From both I and II, we find that Raju is (35 – 25) = 10 years older than his brother, who was born in 1964. So, Raju was born in 1954.

3. From I, we conclude that H is the only daughter of M. But this does not indicate that M has no son. The information given in II is immaterial.

4. From I, total sale of product A = ₹ (8000 × 25) = ₹ 200000.
   From II, we know that the company deals only in product A.
   This implies that sale of product A is the total sale of the company, which is ₹ 200000.

5. From I, we conclude that weight of each rod
   = (4 × 5) kg = 20 kg.
   So, total weight of 10 rods = (20 × 10) kg
   = 200 kg.
   From II, we conclude that:
   Weight of each rod = (weight of 3 rods) – (weight of 2 rods) = 20 kg.
   So, total weight of 10 rods = (20 × 10) kg
   = 200 kg.

6. From I, we conclude that Y is the child of D who is wife of J i.e. J is Y's father.
   From II, J is married to Y's father. This implies that J is Y's mother.

7. From I, we know that L is T's brother and J's husband. Since L is the only son of his parents, T is L's sister.
   From II, we know that F is L's daughter. Thus, from I and II, we conclude that T is the sister of F's father i.e. T is F's aunt.

8. The only word common to I and II is 'clear' and as such, only the code for 'clear' can be ascertained from the given information.

9. From II, we know that P's mother is married to J's husband, which means that J is P's mother.

10. From II, V being in the middle, there are 10 children to his right as well as to his left. So, V is 11th from the left. From I, P is 15th from the left. Thus, from both I and II, we conclude that there are 3 children between P and V.

11. B is A's brother means A is either brother or sister of B. Now, each one of I and II individually indicates that A is a female, which means that A is B's sister.

12. From I, we have the order: R, –, P, Q.
    From II, we have the order: P, Q, T. Clearly, each one of the above two orders indicates that Q is to the immediate right of P.

13. The statements in I and II do not provide any clue regarding relation between X and Y.

14. Since 8th to the left of 12th from the right is 20th from the right, so from I, we know that Vibha is 5th from left and 20th from right i.e. there are 4 children to the left and 19 to the right of Vibha.

So, there are (4 + 1 + 19) *i.e.* 24 children in the row.

From II, Nisha is 7th from right and 18th from left end of the row.

So, there are (6 + 1 + 17) = 24 children in the row.

15. From I, we conclude that the man is the only son of Tannu's grandfather *i.e.* he is Tannu's father or Tannu is the man's daughter.

From II, we conclude that the man's father is Tannu's grandfather. Since the man has no brothers or sisters, so he is Tannu's father or Tannu is the man's daughter.

16. I does not mention the day of the week on the birthday of either Arun or Salim. According to II, Salim's sister was born on Wednesday and Salim was born two days before Wednesday *i.e.* on Monday.

17. From I, total number of doctors in town = (1/700 × N), where N = total number of residents in town. But, the value of N is not known.

From II, total number of doctors in town
= (Number of wards in town) × (Number of doctors in each ward)
= 16 × 16 = 256.

18. From I and II, we find that Robert read (300 × 2/3) *i.e.* 200 pages before Sunday and the last 40 pages on Monday. This means that he read [300 – (200 + 40)] *i.e.* 60 pages on Sunday.

19. From I, we have: B > F, B > C, V > B. Thus, V is heavier than each one of B, F and C. But V is not the heaviest. So, E is the heaviest.

Thus, we have the order:
E > V > B > T > C or E > V > B > C > F.
Clearly, B is third from the top.

20. From I, we know that the films were screened on 23rd, 24th, 25th and 26th. Clearly, D was screened second *i.e.* on 24th, Wednesday.

From II, we know that one film was screened between A and B.

So, A and B were screened first and third, *i.e.*

on 23rd and 25th. But, A was not screened on 25th.

So, A was screened on 23rd and B on 25th. Thus, C was screened on 26th, Friday.

21. From the given two statements in I, the code for the only common word 'beautiful' can be determined.

From the given two statements in II, the code for the only common word 'red' can be determined.

In I and II, the common words are 'rose and 'flower' and the common code words are 'de' and 'la'. So, the code for 'flower' is either 'de' or 'la'.

22. Clearly, each of the given statements shows that B is sitting opposite to C or B is the partner of C.

23. It is not mentioned whether all the boys or a proportion of them play football.

24. Clearly, the facts given in I and II contain two conditions to be fulfilled to get retirement and also indicate that Ramesh fulfils only one condition out of them.

25. From I, we conclude that Kunal was born on any one of the dates among 16th, 17th and 18th.

From II, we conclude that Kunal was born on any one of the dates among 13th, 14th, 15th and 16th.

Thus, from both I and II, we conclude that Kunal was born on 16th August.

26. As given, we have: M > K, A > S.
From II, K > A.
Thus, we have: M > K > A > S.

So, Sharad is the youngest. From I, M > S. Thus, we have: M > K > A > S or M > A > K > S or M > A > S > K.

27. I. In 'right or wrong' and 'he is right', the common word is 'right' and the common code word is 'nik'. So 'nik' means 'right'. In 'right or wrong' and 'that is wrong', the common word is 'wrong' and the common code word is 'te'. So, 'te' means 'wrong'. Thus, in 'right or wrong', 'sa' is the code for 'or'. II. In 'that right man' and 'this or that', the common word is 'that' and the common code word is 'pa'. So, 'pa' means 'that'. In 'this or that' and 'tell this there', the common word is 'this' and the common code word is 'ne'. So, 'ne' means 'this'. Thus, in 'this or that', 'sa' is the code for 'or'.

28. As given in I and II, we have: G = V = K, V + K + A = 32 and A = V + K.
Putting V + K = A in V + K + A = 32, we have: 2A = 32 or A = 16.
Thus, V + K = 16 and V = K. So, V = K = 8.
Thus, G = 8.

29. From I, we have: S = T – 20.
From II, we have: V = T + 30.
Thus, from both I and II, we have:
V + S = (T + 30) + (T – 20) = (2 T + 10).
So, to get the required amount, we need to know the amount that Tarun has.

30. From I, we have: R > Q, R > T, S > R *i.e.*
S > R > Q > T or S > R > T > Q.
From II, S is not the heaviest. So, P is the heaviest.
Thus, we have: P > S > R > Q > T or P > S > R > T > Q.
Hence, either T or Q is the lightest.

9 \ Coded Inequalities

To solve coded inequalities problem one's primarily task is to combine (visualise) two or more inequalities in to one combined notation.

Rule-Carry one directional lightest inequality to deduce conclusion from combined inequality Whenever inequalities are combined together in one combined notation writing common terms only once then conclusion will follow between any two terms if and only if all the inequalities between these two terms points in one same direction and conclusion will carry lightest ('<' is lighter than '≤' and '>'is lighter than '≥') inequality sign present between these two terms.

Basics of above rule

1. Two inequalities can be combined if and only if they have a common term.
2. Two inequalities can be combined (to give valid conclusion) if and only if the common term is greater than (or 'greater than or equal to') one and less than (or 'less than or equal to') the other.
3. The conclusion –inequality will have an '≥' sign (or a '≤' sign) if and only if both the signs in the combined inequality were '≥'(or '≤',as the case may be).

(EXERCISE)

Directions (Qs. Nos. 1 to 6): *In the following questions, the symbols @, ©, •, % and $ are used with the following meaning as illustrated below:*

'P © Q' means 'P is neither greater than nor smaller than Q'.

'P @ Q' means 'P is smaller than Q'.

'P $ Q' means 'P is greater than Q'.

'P • Q' means 'P is either smaller than or equal to Q'.

'P % Q' means 'P is either greater than or equal to Q'.

Now in each of the following questions assuming the given statements to be true, find which of the two conclusions I and II given below them is/are Definitely true?

Give answer :
- A. if only conclusion I is true
- B. if only conclusion II is true
- C. if either conclusion I or II is true
- D. if neither conclusion I nor II is true
- E. if both conclusions I and II are true

1. **Statements:** J $ N, N % F, F • D
   Conclusions: I. F @ J   II. D % N

2. **Statements:** J % N, N © D, D @ K
   Conclusions : I. D © J   II. D @ J

3. **Statements:** R © M, M @ V, V $ F
   Conclusions: I. F @ M   II. V $ R

4. **Statements:** N @ K, K • F, F $ W
   Conclusions: I. F % N   II. W @ K

5. **Statements:** B •K, K $ R, R % E
   Conclusions: I. E @ K   II. E @ B

6. **Statements:** M• T, T @ R, R © K
   Conclusions: I. K $ T   II. R % M

Directions (Qs. Nos. 7 to 11): *In the following questions, the symbols @, ©, %, $ and β are used with the following meaning as illustrated below:*

'P © Q' means 'P is smaller than Q'.

'P @ Q' means 'P is either smaller than or equal to Q'.

'P % Q' means 'P is greater than Q'.

'P $ Q' means 'P is either greater than or equal to Q'.

'P β Q' means 'P is equal to Q'.

Now in each of the following questions

assuming the given statements to be true, find which of the two conclusions I and II given below them is/are Definitely true?

Give answer:

A. if only conclusion I is true

B. if only conclusion II is true

C. if either conclusion I or II is true

D. if neither conclusion I nor II is true

E. if both conclusions I and II are true

7. **Statements:** B © T, T β M, M % F
   Conclusions: I. B © M   II. B © F

8. **Statements:** M β R, R % T, T $ K
   Conclusions: I. K @ M   II. K © M

9. **Statements:** W © D, D @ H, H β N
   Conclusions: I. N $ D   II. W © N

10. **Statements:** W @ D, D $ R, R © K
    Conclusions: I. R β W   II. R % W

11. **Statements :** F $ J, J % V, V © N
    Conclusions: I. N $ F   II. N % J

Directions (Qs. Nos. 12 to 16): *In the following questions, certain symbols have been used to indicate relationships between elements as follows:*
A % B means A is neither smaller than nor greater than B.
A $ B means A is greater than B.
A & B means A is either greater than or equal to B.
A @ B means A is smaller than B.
A # B means A is either smaller than or equal to B.

In each question, three statements showing relationships have been given, which are followed by two conclusions I and II. Assuming that the given statements are true, find out which conclusion(s) is/are definitely true.

Mark answer :

A. if only conclusion I is true

B. if only conclusion II is true

C. if either conclusion I or II is true

D. if neither conclusion I nor II is true

E. if both conclusions I and II are true

12. **Statements:** P & Q, Q $ R, Q % S
    Conclusions: I. P @ S   II. R @ P

13. **Statements:** F & G, G % H, H $ K
    Conclusions: I. H @ F   II. F % H

14. **Statements:** T # V, V $ X, X & Y
    Conclusions: I. V $ Y   II. X # T

15. **Statements:** C % E, E # W, W @ Z
    Conclusions: I. W & C   II. C @ Z

16. **Statements :** L # M, M @ N, N $ P
    Conclusions: I. L # N   II. M & P

Directions (Qs. Nos. 17 to 22): *In the following questions, the symbols @, ©, %, $ and ? are used with the following meaning as illustrated below :*
'P © Q' means 'P is either smaller than or equal to Q.
'P Ω Q' means 'P is either greater than or equal to Q'.
'P % Q' means 'P is smaller than Q'.
'P $ Q' means 'P is greater than Q'.
'P @ Q' means 'P is equal to Q'

Now in each of the following questions assuming the given statements to be true, find which of the two conclusions I and II given below them is/are Definitely true?

Give answer:

A. if only conclusion I is true

B. if only conclusion II is true

C. if either conclusion I or II is true

D. if neither conclusion I nor II is true

E. if both conclusions I and II are true

17. **Statements:** M % T, T $ K, K © D
    Conclusions: I. T $ D   II. D $ M

18. **Statements:** F @ B, B % N, N $ H
    Conclusions: I. N $ F   II. H $ F

19. **Statements:** R Ω M, M @ K, K © J
    Conclusions: I. J $ M   II. J @ M

20. **Statements:** B $ N, N Ω R, R @ K
    Conclusions: I. K © N   II. B $ K

21. **Statements:** J © K, K $ N, N Ω D
    Conclusions: I. J % N   II. D % K

22. **Statements:** R @ D, D © M, M $ T
    Conclusions: I. T % D   II. M Ω R

Directions (Qs. Nos. 23 to 27): *In the following questions, the symbols $, •, %, Ω and @ are used with the following meaning as illustrated below :*
'P • Q' means ' P is neither greater than nor equal to Q'.
'P @ Q' means ' P is neither smaller than nor equal to Q,.
'P Ω Q' means ' P is not greater than Q'.
'P % Q' means 'P is not smaller than Q'.
'P $ Q' means 'P is neither greater than nor smaller than Q'.

Now in each of the following questions assuming the given statements to be true, find which of the two conclusions I and II given below them is/are Definitely true?

Give answer:

A. if only conclusion I is true
B. if only conclusion II is true
C. if either conclusion I or II is true
D. if neither conclusion I nor II is true
E. if both conclusions I and II are true

23. Statements: R % W, W @ F, F $ Z
Conclusions: I. F • R II. Z • W

24. Statements: B @ K, K % J, J • M
Conclusions: I. J • B II. M @ B

25. Statements: D $ T, T Ω H, H @ N
Conclusions: I. H $ D II. H @ D

26. Statements: H Ω N, N • K, K Ω D
Conclusions: I. D @ N II. H • K

27. Statements : W % E, E @ K, K $ J
Conclusions: I. J Ω E II. W % K

Directions (Qs. Nos. 28 to 30): *Read the information/statement given in each question carefully and answer the questions.*

28. Which of the following expressions will be true if the expression' $A > B \geq C < D$ is definitely true?

A. $A > D$ B. $C \leq A$
C. $D > B$ D. $D \geq A$
E. None is true

29. Which of the following expressions will not be true if the expression ' $F \leq G = H < K$' is definitely true?

A. $K \geq F$ B. $H \geq F$
C. $G < K$ D. $F < K$
E. None of these

30. In which of the following expressions will the expression '$P < Q$' be definitely true?

A. $P \geq R > N = Q$ B. $Q < R \geq N > P$
C. $P < R \leq Q > N$ D. $P \geq N \geq M > Q$
E. None is true

ANSWERS

21	22	23	24	25	26	27	28	29	30
A	C	B	D	A	A	A	B	E	D
31	32	33	34	35	36	37	38	39	40
D	B	C	A	E	D	D	A	C	E
41	42	43	44	45	46	47	48	49	50
D	B	E	A	C	E	D	E	A	C

EXPLANATORY ANSWERS

(1-6): © → = • → ≤ @ → < $ → > % → ≥

1. $J $ N → J > N$, $N \% F → N \geq F$,
$F • D → F \leq D$
Therefore, $J > N \geq F \leq D$
Conclusions:
I. $F @ J → F < J$: True
II. $D \% N → D \geq N$: False

2. $J \% N → J \geq N$, $N © D → N = D$,
$D @ K → D < K$
Therefore, $J \geq N = D < K$
Conclusions:
I. $D © J → D = J$: False
II. $D @ J → D < J$: False
Either I or II is true

3. $R © M → R = M$, $M @ V → M < V$,
$V $ F → V > F$
Therefore, $R = M < V > F$
Conclusions:
I. $F @ M → F < M$: False
II. $V $ R → V > R$: True

4. $N @ K → N < K$,
$K • F → K \leq F$,
$F $ W → F > W$
Therefore, $N < K \leq F > W$
Conclusions:
I. $F \% N → F \geq N$: False
II. $W @ K → W < K$: False

5. B • K → B ≤ K,
   K $ R → K > R,
   R % E → R ≥ E
   Therefore, B ≤ K > R ≥ E
   Conclusions:
   I. E @ K → E < K : True
   II. E @ B → E < B : False

6. M • T → M ≤ T,
   T @ R → T < R,
   R © K → R = K
   Therefore, M ≤ T < R = K
   Conclusions:
   I. K $ T → K > T : True
   II. R % M → R ≥ M : False

(7- 11): © → < @ → ≤ % → > $ → ≥ β → =

7. B © T → B < T,
   T β M → T = M,
   M % F → M > F
   Therefore, B < T = M > F
   Conclusions:
   I. B © M → B < M : True
   II. B © F → B < F : False

8. M β R → M = R,
   R % T → R > T,
   T $ K → T ≥ K
   Therefore, M = R > T ≥ K
   Conclusions:
   I. K @ M → K ≤ M : False
   II. K © M → K < M : True

9. W © D → W < D,
   D @ H → D ≤ H,
   H β N → H = N
   Therefore, W< D ≤ H = N
   Conclusions:
   I. N $ D → N ≥ D : True
   II. W © N → W < N : True

10. W @ D → W ≤ D,
    D $ R → D ≥ R,
    R © K → R < K
    Therefore, W ≤ D ≥ R < K
    Conclusions:
    I. R β W → R = W : False
    II. R % W → R > W : False

11. F $ J → F ≥ J,
    J % V → J > V,
    V © N → V < N
    Therefore, F ≥ J > V< N
    Conclusions:
    I. N $ F → N ≥ F : False
    II. N % J → N > J : False

(12- 16): A % B → A = B, A $ B → A > B, A & B → A ≥ B, A @ B → A < B, A # B → A ≤ B

12. P & Q → P ≥ Q,
    Q $ R → Q > R,
    Q % S → Q = S
    Therefore, P ≥ Q = S > R
    Conclusions:
    I. P @ S → P < S : False
    II. R @ P → R < P : True

13. F & G → F ≥ G,
    G % H → G = H,
    H $ K → H > K
    Therefore, F ≥ G = H > K
    Conclusions:
    I. H @ F → H < F : False
    II. F % H → F = H : False
    H is either smaller than or equal to F.

14. T # V → T ≤ V,
    V $ X → V > X,
    X & Y → X ≥ Y
    Therefore, T ≤ V > X ≥ Y
    Conclusions:
    I. V $ Y → V > Y : True
    II. X # T → X ≤ T : False

15. C % E → C = E,
    E # W → E ≤ W,
    W @ Z → W < Z
    Therefore, C = E ≤ W < Z
    Conclusions:
    I. W & C → W ≥ C : True
    II. C @ Z → C < Z : True

16. L # M → L ≤ M,   M @ N → M < N,
    N $ P → N > P
    Therefore, L ≤ M < N > P
    Conclusions:
    I. L # N → L ≤ N : False
    II. M & P → M ≥ P : False

(17-22): @ → =, © → ≤, % → <, \$ → >, Ω → ≥

17. M % T → M < T,
    T \$ K → T > K,
    K © D → K ≤ D
    Therefore, M < T > K ≤ D
    Conclusions:
    I. T \$ D → T > D : False
    II. D \$ M → D > M : False

18. F @ B → F = B,
    B % N → B < N,
    N \$ H → N > H
    Therefore, F = B < N > H
    Conclusions:
    I. N \$ F → N > F : True
    II. H \$ F → H > F : False

19. R Ω M → R ≥ M,
    M @ K → M = K,
    K © J → K ≤ J
    Therefore, R ≥ M = K ≤ J
    Conclusions:
    I. J \$ M → J > M : False
    II. J @ M → J = M : False
    J is either greater than M or equal to M.

20. B \$ N → B > N,
    N Ω R → N ≥ R,
    R @ K → R = K
    Therefore, B > N ≥ R = K
    Conclusions:
    I. K © N → K ≤ N : True
    II. B \$ K → B > K : True

21. J © K → J ≤ K,
    K \$ N → K > N,
    N Ω D → N ≥ D
    Therefore, J ≤ K > N ≥ D
    Conclusions:
    I. J % N → J < N : False
    II. D % K → D < K: False

22. R @ D → R = D, D © M → D ≤ M,
    M \$ T → M > T
    Therefore, R = D ≤ M > T
    Conclusions:
    I. T % D → T < D : False
    II. M Ω R → M ≥ R : True

(23 – 27): • → <, @ → >, Ω → ≤, % → ≥, \$ → =

23. **Statements:** R % W → R ≥ W,
    W @ F → W > F,
    F \$ Z → F = Z
    Therefore, R ≥ W > F = Z
    Conclusions:
    I. F • R → F < R : True
    II. Z • W → Z < W: True

24. **Statements:** B @ K → B > K,
    K % J → K ≥ J,
    J • M → J < M
    Therefore,   B > K ≥ J < M
    Conclusions:
    I. J • B → J < B : True
    II. M @ B → M > B : False

25. **Statements:** D \$ T → D = T,
    T Ω H → T ≤ H,
    H @ N → H > N
    Therefore, D = T ≤ H > N
    Conclusions:
    I. H \$ D → H = D : False
    II. H @ D → H > D: False
    H is greater than or equal to D.
    So either I or II is true

26. **Statements:** H Ω N → H ≤ N,
    N • K → N < K,
    K Ω D → K ≤ D
    Therefore, H ≤ N < K ≤ D
    Conclusions:
    I. D @ N → D > N : True
    II. H • K → H < K : True

27. **Statements:** W % E → W ≥ E,
    E @ K → E > K,
    K \$ J → K = J
    Therefore, W ≥ E > K = J
    Conclusions:
    I. J Ω E → J ≤ E : False
    II. W % K → W ≥ K : False

28. A > B ≥ C < D None is true.

29. F ≤ G = H < K, we have K > F.
    Therefore, K ≥ F is not true.

30. In P < R ≤ Q > N , P < Q is true.

❀ ❀ ❀

In input-output problems one is asked to imagine that there is some computer or a word-processing machine and it performs some operation on a given input. These operations are performed repeatedly as per a pre-fixed pattern and subsequently one has different output in different steps. One's primarily job is to deduce the rule followed by computer/ machine in arranging numbers and words. One should analyze final arranged step while deducing rule applied.

Example

Directions (Qs. Nos. 1 to 4): *Study the following information to answer the given questions:*
A word rearrangement machine when given an input line of words, rearranges them, following a particular rule, in each step. The following is an illustration of input and the steps of rearrangement.
Input: over you pat me crow easy to.
Steps: (I) pat over you crow easy to me
(II) crow pat over you to me easy
(III) over crow pat to me easy you
(IV) to over crow pat easy you me, and so on.

As per the rule followed in the above steps, find out the appropriate step for the given input in the following questions.

1. If step V of an input is 'put down col in as much sa', what would be the VIIIth step?
   A. down in put much sa as col
   B. in put down col much sa as
   C. much in put down sa as col
   D. col put down as much sa in
   E. None of these

Ans. E. The steps followed are :
   Step V : put down col in as much sa
   Step VI : in put down col much sa as
   Step VII : down in put much sa as col
   Step VIII : much down in put as col sa

2. **Input:** but calm free are so not eat. Which of the following will be the IIIrd step for this input?
   A. so free but calm eat are not
   B. but calm are free not so eat
   C. are but calm free not eat so
   D. but so free eat are not calm
   E. None of these

Ans. D. The step followed are :
   Input : but calm free are so not eat
   Step I : free but calm so not eat are
   Step II : so free but calm eat are not
   Step III : but so free eat are not calm

3. **Input :** rim bye eat klin fe to low. Which of the following steps would be 'fe low rim to bye klin eat'?
   A. VIth   B. Vth
   C. IVth   D. IIIrd
   E. None of these

Ans. B. The step followed are :
   Input : rim bye eat klin fe to low
   Step I : eat rim bye fe to low klin
   Step II : fe eat rim bye low klin to
   Step III : rim fe eat low klin to bye
   Step IV : low rim fe eat to bye klin
   Step V : fe low rim to bye klin eat

4. If step II of an input is 'ge su he for game free but', what would be the step VI?
   A. ge for but free he game su
   B. for free ge game su he but
   C. free ge for but game su he
   D. he ge su but game free for
   E. None of these

Ans. E. The step followed are :
   Step II : ge su he for game free but
   Step III : he ge su game free but for
   Step IV : game he ge su but for free
   Step V : ge game he but for free su
   Step VI : but ge game he free su for

EXERCISE

Directions (Qs. Nos. 1 to 5): *Study the following information carefully and answer the questions given below:*

When an input line of words is given to a word arrangement machine, it rearranges them following a particular rule in each step.

Input: car some pour tie more tin bee goat
Step I : goat car some pour tie more tin bee
Step II : goat more car some pour tie tin bee
Step III : goat more pour car some tie tin bee
Step IV : goat more pour some car tie tin bee
Step V : goat more pour some bee car tie tin
and step V is the last output.

1. If the 3rd step of an input is:
   bend take vide nut zeal pot car tin.
   Which of the following will be the last step?
   A. 6th
   B. 5th
   C. 7th
   D. 4th
   E. None of these

2. If the 2nd step of an input is:
   coat some for die song kill bit son.
   Which is certainly the input?
   A. for come die song kill coat bit son
   B. for die come song kill coat bit son
   C. for die song come kill coat bit son
   D. Can't be determined
   E. None of these

3. **Input :** door site may for you mean now goal
   Which of the following is the 3rd step of the above input?
   A. door goal mean site for may now you
   B. door goal mean site may for you now
   C. door site goal mean may for you now
   D. Can't be determined
   E. None of these

4. **Input:** mute deal sit cut coat day long for
   Which of the following will be the 4th step?
   A. coat deal mute sit cut day long for
   B. coat deal long mute sit cut day for
   C. coat deal long mute cut sit day for
   D. coat deal long mute cut day for sit
   E. None of these

5. **Input :** ask not feel task opt sale dark den
   Which of the following will be the last step?
   A. 5th
   B. 6th
   C. 4th
   D. 7th
   E. None of these

Directions (Qs. Nos. 6 to 10): *Study the following information to answer the questions given below:*

A number arrangement machine when given an input of numbers, rearranges them following a particular rule in each step. The following is an illustration of input and steps of rearrangement.

Input: 48 245 182 26 99 542 378 297
Step I   542 48 245 182 26 99 378 297
Step II 542 26 48 245 182 99 378 297
Step III 542 26 378 48 245 182 99 297
Step IV 542 26 378 48 297 245 182 99
Step V   542 26 378 48 297 99 245 182

This is the final arrangement and step V is the last step for this input.

6. What will be the fourth step for an input whose second step is given below?
   Step II: 765 42 183 289 542 65 110 350
   A. 765 42 542 350 183 289 65 110
   B. 765 42 542 65 110 183 289 350
   C. 765 42 542 65 183 289 110 350
   D. Cannot be determined
   E. None of these

7. What should be the third step of the following input?
   Input: 239 123 58 361 495 37
   A. 495 37 361 123 239 58
   B. 495 37 58 361 123 239
   C. 495 37 58 123 361 239
   D. 495 37 361 239 123 58
   E. None of these

8. How many steps will be required to get the final output from the following input?
   Input: 39 88 162 450 386 72 29
   A. Two
   B. Three
   C. Four
   D. Six
   E. None of these

9. What should be the last step of the following input?
Input: 158 279 348 28 326 236
A. 348 28 326 158 279 236
B. 348 28 326 236 158 279
C. 348 28 236 158 279 326
D. 348 28 158 326 236 279
E. None of these

10. If the first step of an input is "785 198 32 426 373 96 49", then which of the following steps will be "785 32 426 49 198 373 96"?
A. Third   B. Fourth
C. Fifth   D. Second
E. None of these

Directions (Qs. Nos. 11 to 15): *A word-number arrangement machine, when given an input as a set of words and numbers, rearranges them following a particular rule and generates stepwise outputs till the rearrangement is complete following that rule.*

Followings is an illustration of input and steps of rearrangement till the last step.
Input: pour ask   57   dear   39   fight   17   28
Step I :   ask pour 57   dear   39   fight   17   28
Step II : ask   57   pour dear 39   fight   17   28
Step III : ask   57   dear pour 39   fight   17   28
Step IV : ask   57   dear   39   pour fight 17   28
Step V :   ask   57   dear   39   fight pour 17   28
Step VI : ask   57   dear   39   fight   28   pour   17
and Step VI is the last output.

As per the rule followed in the above steps find out the answer to each of the following questions:

11. If step II of an input is "cut 97 38 end for 29 46 down", which of the following will be the last step?
A. Fifth   B. Fourth
C. Sixth 4   D. Seventh
E. None of these

12. If the 4th step of an input is "ago 85 elite 79 exile fat 26 41", which of the following will definitely be the 2nd step of the input?
A. ago 85   79   elite fat   41   26   exile
B. ago 85   exile elite 41   26   fat   79
C. ago 85   26   exile 41   elite 79   fat
D. Cannot be determined
E. None of these

13. If the 1st step of an input is "car 17 vas tiger 92 87 like 52", which of the following will be the 4th step?
A. car 92 like 87 tiger 52 17 vas
B. car 92 like 87 17 vas tiger 52
C. car 92 like 87 tiger 17 vas 52
D. car 92 like 17 vas tiger 87 52
E. None of these

14. **Input:** zeal for 49 31 high 22 track 12
Which of the following will be the 3rd step?
A. for 49   high   31   track   22   zeal   12
B. for 49   high   31   zeal   22   track 12
C. for 49   high zeal   31   22   track 12
D. for 49   high   31   track zeal   22   12
E. None of these

15. **Input :** 19 feat 34 28 dog bag take 43
Which of the following steps would be "bag 43 dog 19 feat 34 28 take"?
A. Second
B. Fourth
C. First
D. Cannot be determined
E. None of these

Directions (Qs. Nos. 16 to 20): *A word-number arrangement machine, when given an input as a set of words and numbers, rearranges them following a particular rule and generates stepwise outputs till the rearrangement is complete following that rule.*

Followings is an illustration of input and steps of rearrangement till the last step.
Input: sine 88 71 cos theta 14 56 gamma delta 26
Step I: cos sine 71 theta 14 56 gamma delta 26 88
Step II: delta cos sine theta 14 56 gamma 26 88 71
Step III: gamma delta cos sine theta 14 26 88 71 56
Step IV: sine gamma delta cos theta 14 88 71 56 26
Step V: theta sine gamma delta cos 88 71 56 26 14

And Step V is the last Step of the arrangement of the above input as the intended arrangement is obtained.

As per the rules followed in the above steps, find out in each of the following questions the appropriate steps for the given input, Input for the questions

Input : for 52 all 96 25 jam road 15 hut 73 bus stop 38 46

(all numbers are in two digits)

16. Which word/number would be at the 6th position from the left in Step V?
A. 25
B. stop
C. jam
D. all
E. road

17. Which of the following would be the Step III?
A. hut for bus all 25 jam road 15 stop 38 96 73 52 46
B. for us all 25 jam road 15 hut 38 stop 96 46 73 52
C. hut for bus all jam road 15 stop 38 96 73 52 46 25
D. for bus all 25 jam road 15 hut stop 38 46 96 73 52
E. None of the above

18. Which word/number would be at the 8th position from the right in Step IV?
A. 15
B. road
C. hut
D. jam
E. stop

19. Which of the following would be Step VII?
A. stop road jam hut for bus all 15 96 73 52 46 38 25
B. road jam hut for bus all stop 15 25 38 46 52 73 96
C. stop road jam hut for bus all 96 73 52 46 38 25 15
D. jam hut for bus all 25 road stop 15 96 73 52 46 38
E. There will be no such step as the arrangement gets established at Step VI

20. Which step number would be the following output?
bus all for 52 25 jam road 15 hut stop 38 46 96 73
A. There will be no such step
B. III
C. II
D. V
E. VI

Directions (Qs 21 to 24.): *A word-number arrangement machine, when given an input as a set of words and numbers, rearranges them following a particular rule and generates stepwise outputs till the rearrangement is complete following that rule.*

Input : tall 48 13 rise alt 99 76 32 wise jar high 28 56 barn

Followings is an illustration of input and steps of rearrangement till the last step.

Input : tall 48 13 rise alt 99 76 32 wise jar high 28 56 barn

Step I: 13 tall 48 rise 99 76 32 wise jar high 28 56 barn alt

Step II: 28 13 tall 48 rise 99 76 32 wise jar high 56 alt barn

Step III: 32 28 13 tall 48 rise 99 76 wise jar 56 alt barn high

Step IV: 48 32 28 13 tall rise 99 76 wise 56 alt barn high jar

Step V: 56 48 32 28 13 tall 99 76 wise alt barn high jar rise

Step VI: 76 56 48 32 28 13 99 wise alt barn high jar rise tall

Step VII: 99 76 56 48 32 28 13 alt barn high jar rise tall wise

Step VII is the last step of the above input, as desired arrangement is obtained.

As per the rules followed in the above steps, find out in each of the following questions the appropriate steps for the given input.

Input: 84 why sit 14 32 not best ink feet 51 27 vain 68 92 (All the numbers are two digit numbers)

21. Which step number is the following output?
32 27 14 84 why sit not 51 vain 92 68 feet best ink
A. Step V
B. Step VI
C. Step IV
D. Step III
E. There is no such step

22. Which word/number would be at 5th position from the right in Step V?
A. 14
B. 92
C. feet
D. best
E. why

23. How many elements (words or numbers) are there between 'feet' and '32' as they appear in the last step of the output?

A. One B. Three
C. Four D. Five
E. Seven

24. Which of the following represents the position of 'why' in the fourth step?
A. Eighth from the left
B. Fifth from the right
C. Sixth from the left
D. Fifth from the left
E. Seventh from the left

Directions (Qs. Nos. 25 to 30): *A word-number arrangement machine, when given an input as a set of words and numbers, rearranges them following a particular rule and generates stepwise outputs till the rearrangement is complete following that rule.*

Followings is an illustration of input and steps of rearrangement till the last step.

Input : rose girl 13 petal 16 go 35 ate 71 wild 22 87

Step I : go rose girl 13 petal 16 35 ate 71 wild 22 87

Step II : go 13 rose girl petal 16 35 ate 71 wild 22 87

Step III : go 13 ate rose girl petal 16 35 71 wild 22 87

Step IV : go 13 ate 16 rose girl petal 35 71 wild 22 87

Step V : go 13 ate 16 girl rose petal 35 71 wild 22 87

Step VI : go 13 ate 16 girl 22 rose petal 35 71 wild 87

Step VII: go 13 ate 16 girl 22 rose 35 petal 71 wild 87

Step VIII: go 13 ate 16 girl 22 rose 35 wild petal 71 87

Step IX : go 13 ate 16 girl 22 rose 35 wild 71 petal 87

and Step IX is the last step of the rearrangement.

25. Input: man 79 over 63 like 43 joy 15 never climbed 21 56
How many steps will be required to complete the arrangement?

A. Eight B. Nine
C. Ten D. Eleven
E. None of these

26. Step II of an input: to 13 world news 73 29 win 52.
How many more steps will be required to complete the arrangement?
A. Six B. Four
C. Five D. Two
E. None of these

27. Input : no 11 19 94 join for 81 style 37 matched.
Which of the following steps will be the last?
A. VI B. VII
C. VIII D. IX
E. None of these

28. Step III of an input is : we 12 you 19 meet 17 discuss 15 result 16.
Which of the following will be step II?
A. we 12 you 17 meet 19 discuss 15 result 16
B. we 12 17 you meet 19 discuss 15 result 16
C. we 12 you 15 17 meet 19 discuss result 16
D. Cannot be determined
E. None of these

29. Which of the following cannot be definitely Step V of an input?
A. be 13 did 27 eye 43 soon 34 39 wonder
B. be 13 did 27 eye 43 soon 39 34 wonder
C. be 13 did 27 soon 43 eye 39 wonder 34
D. Cannot be determined
E. None of these

30. If two given inputs gives identically same output, which of the following is definitely true?
A. Both require same number of steps for final arrangement.
B. Two inputs are identically same
C. Both contains same elements which may or may not be in same sequence
D. 2nd last step for both arrangements will be same
E. None of these

ANSWERS

1	2	3	4	5	6	7	8	9	10
B	D	E	C	A	C	D	E	A	B
11	12	13	14	15	16	17	18	19	20
A	D	B	C	E	A	D	B	C	A
21	22	23	24	25	26	27	28	29	30
E	D	B	C	C	B	A	D	C	C

EXPLANATORY ANSWERS

Solution (1 to 5): Following rule is followed here: Words are arranged according to their no. of letters. Words with largest no. of letters are arranged first. If two words have equal no. of letters then the word which comes first in English Dictionary is arranged first. In each step only one word is arranged and the rest shift one position rightwards. The process goes on until all the words are arranged.

1.
Step III: bend take vide nut zeal pot car tin
⑥ 4 ⑥ 5 ⑥
Step III : bend take vide nut zeal pot car tin
Step IV : bend take vide zeal nut pot car tin
Step V : bend take vide zeal car nut pot tin

2. Previous step can't be determined

3.
Input: door site may for you mean now goal
① ③ 3 2 1
Input : door site may for you mean now goal
Step I : door goal site may for you mean now
Step II : door goal mean site may for you now
Step III : door goal mean site for may you now

4.
Input: mute deal sit cut coat day long for
④ 2 4 1 3
Input: mute deal sit cut coat day long for
Step I: coat mute deal sit cut day long for
Step II: coat deal mute sit cut day long for
Step III: coat deal long mute sit cut day for
Step IV: coat deal long mute cut sit day for

5.
Input: ask not feel task opt sale dark den
⑤ ⑥ 2 4 ⑥ 3 4 5

Input : ask not feel task opt sale dark den
Step I : dark ask not feel task opt sale den
Step II : dark feel ask not task opt sale den
Step III : dark feel sale ask not task opt den
Step IV : dark feel sale task ask not opt den
Step V : dark feel sale task den ask not opt

Solution(6 to 10): On observing last step it is clear that there are two alternating series of numbers: one in descending order and the other in ascending order. When we reach step 1 through input, we find that the largest no. becomes the first and remaining numbers shift rightward. In the next step, the smallest no. becomes the second and the rest shift rightward. These two steps continue alternately until the two alternate series are formed.

6.
Step II: 765 42 183 289 542 65 110 350
3 4
Step II : 765 42 183 289 542 65 110 350
Step III : 765 42 542 183 289 65 110 350
Step IV : 765 42 542 65 183 289 110 350

7.
Input: 239 123 58 361 495 37
3 1 2
Input: 239 123 58 361 495 37
Step I : 495 239 123 58 361 37
Step II : 495 37 239 123 58 361
Step III : 495 37 361 239 123 58

8.
Input: 39 88 162 450 386 72 29
④ 4 1 3 5 2
Input: 39 88 162 450 386 72 29
Step I : 450 39 88 162 386 72 29

Step II : 450   29   39   88   162 386 72
Step III : 450   29 386 39   88 162 72
Step IV : 450   29 386 39 162   88 72
Step V : 450   29 386 39 162   72 88

9.

Input: 158 279 348 28 326 236
         ④   4   1   2   3

Last step can be known directly.

10.

Step I : 785 198 32 426 373 96 49
         1   2   3   4

Step I : 785 198 32 426 373 96 49
Step II : 785 32 198 426 373 96 49
Step III : 785 32 426 198 373 96 49
Step IV : 785 32 426 49 198 373 96

Solution (11 to 15): Following rule is followed here: Words are arranged in alphabetical order and nos. are arranged in decreasing order alternately. In output the word, which comes first in dictionary, comes to the first place and the rest shift one place rightwards. In the next step, the largest no. comes to the second place and the rest shift one place rightwards. These two steps occur alternately until the last step is obtained.

11.

Step II : <u>cut</u> <u>97</u> 38 end for 29 46 down
      ⑥   5   ⑥ ⑥   4   3

Step II : cut 97 38 end for 29 46 down
Step III : cut 97 down 38 end for 29 46
Step IV : cut 97 down 46 38 end for 29
Step V : cut 97 down 46 end 38 for 29

13.

Step I : <u>car</u> 17 vas tiger 92   87 like 52
                    2   4   3

Step I : car 17 vas tiger 92   87 like 52
Step II : car 92 17 vas tiger 87 like 52
Step III : car 92 like 17 vas tiger 87 52
Step IV : car 92 like 87 17 vas tiger 52

14.

Input: zeal for 49 31 high 22 track 12
             1   2   3

Step I: for zeal 49 31 high 22 track 12
Step II: for 49 zeal 31 high 22 track 12
Step III: for 49 high zeal 31 22 track 12

15.

Input : 19 feat 34 28 dog bag take 43
                 3   1   2

Input : 19 feat 34 28 dog bag take 43
Step I : bag 19 feat 34 28 dog take 43
Step II : bag 43 19 feat 34 28 dog take
Step III : bag 43 dog 19 feat 34 28 take

Solution (16 to 20) : Here in Step I word which come first in dictionary takes first position from left and rest elements shifts one position rightwards and in the same step largest number takes first position from right and other elements shifts one step leftwards. In next step, same methodology is applied to only unarranged ones. Process continues until all words are arranged fzrom left to right in reverse dictionary order and numbers are arranged in increasing sequence from right to left.

Input: sine 88 71 cos theta 14 56 gamma delta 26
       4 1B 2B 1   5   5B 3B   3   2   4B

Here, to get final arrangement sequence will be : 5 4 3 2 1 1B 2B 3B 4B 5B

(Note here first unnumbered from left or right will not be circled as no element could arrive at arranged position)

Input: for 52 all 96 25 jam road 15 hut 73 bus stop 38 46
       3 3B 1 1B 6B 5   6 7B 4 2B 2   7 5B 4B

Input : for 52 all 96 25 jam road 15 hut 73 bus stop 38 46

Step I : all for 52 25 jam road 15 hut 73 bus stop 38 46 96

Step II : bus all for 52 25 jam road 15 hut stop 38 46 96 73

Step III : for bus all 25 jam road 15 hut stop 38 46 96 73 52

Step IV : hut for bus all 25 jam road 15 stop 38 96 73 52 46

Step V : jam hut for bus all 25 road 15 stop 96 73 52 46 38

Step VI : road jam hut for bus all 15 stop 96 73 52 46 38 25

Step VII : stop road jam hut for bus all 96 73 52 46 38 25 15

Solution (21 to 24) : Here in Step I smallest number takes first position from left and rest elements shifts one position rightwards and in the same step word which comes first in dictionary takes first position from right and rest elements shifts one position leftwards. In next step, same methodology is applied to only unarranged ones. Process continues until all numbers are arranged in decreasing sequence from left to right and all words are arranged in reverse dictionary order from right to left.

Input: 8 4 why sit 14 32 not best ink feet 51 27vain 68 92
6 7B 5B 1 3 4B 1B 3B 2B 4 2 6B 5 7

Here, to get final arrangement sequence will be:

7 6 5 4 3 2 1 1B 2B 3B 4B 5B 6B 7B

(Note here first unnumbered from left or right will not be circled as no element could arrive at arranged position)

Input : 84 why sit 14 32 not best ink feet 51 27 vain 68 92

Step I : 14 84 why sit 32 not best ink feet 51 27 vain 68 92 best

Step II : 27 14 84 why sit 32 not ink 51 vain 68 92 best feet

Step III : 32 27 14 84 why sit not 51 vain 68 92 best feet ink

Step IV : 51 32 27 14 84 why sit vain 68 92 best feet ink not

Step V : 68 51 32 27 14 84 why vain 92 best feet ink not sit

Step VI : 84 68 51 32 27 14 why 92 best feet ink not sit vain

Step VII : 92 84 68 51 32 27 14 best feet ink not sit vain why

Solution (25 to 30) : Here numbers and words are arranged alternately. Numbers are arranged in increasing order while words are arranged in decreasing order of their dictionary placements. If a number or word is already arranged, then next member is arranged in the same step.

25.

Input : man   79 over63 like 43 joy 15   never climbed21 56
③   6 9 4 5 1 2 8   10 3 7

Input : man 79 over 63 like 43 joy 15 never climbed 21 56

Step I : joy man 79 over 63 like 43 15 never climbed 21 56

Step II : joy 15 man 79 over 63 like 43 never climbed 21 56

Step III : joy 15 man 21 79 over 63 like 43 never climbed 56

Step IV : joy 15 man 21 like 79 over 63 43 never climbed 56

Step V : joy 15 man 21 like 43 79 over 63 never climbed 56

Step VI : joy 15 man 21 like 43 over 79 63 never climbed 56

Step VII : joy 15 man 21 like 43 over 56 79 63 never climbed

Step VIII : joy 15 man 21 like 43 over 56 never 79 63 climbed

Step IX : joy 15 man 21 like 43 over 56 never 63 79 climbed

Step X : joy 15 man 21 like 43 over 56 never 63 climbed 79

26.

Step II: <u>to 13</u> world news 73 29 win 52
⑦   5 ⑦ 4 3 6

Step II: to 13 world news   73   29   win 52

Step III : to 13 win world news 73   29   52

Step IV : to 13 win   29 world news 73   52

Step V : to 13 win   29 news world 73   52

Step VI : to 13 win   29 news 52 world 73

This is the final arrangement.

27.

Input : no 11 19 94 join for 81 style 37 matched
① ① ② ⑦ 2 1 5 4 3   6

Input : no 11 19 94 join for 81 style 37 matched

Step I : no 11 for 19 94 join 81 style 37 matched

Step II : no 11 for 19 join 94 81 style 37 matched

Step III : no 11 for 19 join 37 94 81 style matched

Step IV : no 11 for 19 join 37 style 94 81 matched

Step V : no 11 for 19 join 37 style 81 94 matched

Step VI : no 11 for 19 join 37 style 81 matched 94

This is the final arrangement.

28. Previous steps cannot be determined.

29. Step V of any input should have at least five elements arranged.

❀ ❀ ❀

Drawing Inference

In evaluating inferences problems a passage is followed by some inferences and the job is to decide whether a given inference follows or not in the context of the given passage. The most vital aspect of this question is intensity of probability of a particular inference. Some of the inferences can be easily and quickly judged because they are directly based on the facts given in the passage. But in some cases, an inference is indirect. Here the interference appears to be overlapping *i.e.* one may be confused between definitely true or probably true, probably true or data inadequate, data

inadequate or probably false and probably false or data inadequate

The inference can

(1) directly follow from the passage

(2) be inferred from the passage

(3) be inferred with the help of some key words.

While evaluating inferences, first of all check whether it can be evaluated with the help of the passage directly. Check if the given inference is directly supported (or contradicted) by something in the passage. More or less direct inference is a restatement of something already stated in the passage.

EXERCISE

Directions (Qs. 1 to 20): *Below are given some passages followed by several possible inferences which can be drawn from the facts stated in the passage. You have to examine each inference separately in the context of the passage and decide upon its degree of truth or falsity.*

Mark answer

A. if the inference is definitely true, *i.e.* properly follows from the statement of facts given.

B. if the inference is probably true, though not 'definitely true' in the light of facts given.

C. if the data are inadequate, *i.e.* from the facts given you cannot say whether the inference is likely to be true or false.

D. if the inference is probably false, *i.e.* though not 'definitely false' in the light of the facts given.

E. if the inference is 'definitely false', *i.e.* it cannot possibly be drawn from the facts given or it contradicts the given facts.

PASSAGE 1

The immediate challenge is on the food front. Shortfalls in production have been allowed to affect

supplies and hence prices. The government is planning to focus on investment in irrigation and strategy. It appears that the Green Revolution instruments to encourage farmers to invest are no longer effective. The Green Revolution strategy was based on the state taking out the risk of collapse in prices. Farmers were offered remunerative prices and a guaranteed procurement of their produce in case the open market could not absorb it. Farmers could then borrow from banks, acquire the Green Revolution Technology and produce as much as they could. The pressure on the food subsidy was manageable as long as there was a food shortage. Prices in the open market then tended to be above the procurement prices. But with the food surpluses the situation has changed. The situation was unsustainable not merely because of the magnitude of this subsidy. It was also inefficient. It meant farmers were being led to produce crops based just on the prices Government fixed and not in relation to any legal demand. In these circumstances, the Government was reluctant to keep increasing procurement prices at the pace that used to be the norm in earlier years.

1. The Government is planning to make crucial changes in the Green Revolution strategies.

2. The Government is no longer in a position to provide subsidy to farmers.

3. As the open market prices are lower, all the burden of procurement of crops is on the Government.

4. Demand is much higher than the quantity of crops produced by the farmers.

5. The farmers tend to produce the crops as per their convenience and not constant with the demand.

PASSAGE 2

Long term economic progress comes mainly from the invention and spread of improved technologies. The scientific revolution was made possible by the printing press, the industrial revolution by the steam engine and India's escape from famine by increased farm yields the so called 'Green Revolution'. Right now rich countries are changing the world's climate by emitting billions of tones of carbon dioxide each year from the use of coal, oil and natural gas. In future years, China and India will make massive contributions to increase carbon dioxide in the atmosphere. Yet no country rich or poor, is keen to cut its energy use, owing to concern that to do so would threaten jobs, incomes and economic growth. New technologies will provide a key part of the solution. Already, 'hybrid' automobiles, which combine gasoline and battery power, can roughly double fuel efficiency cutting carbon dioxide emission by half. Similarly, engineers have developed ways to capture the carbon dioxide that results from burning coal in power plants and store it safely underground. The new technology called "carbon capture and sequestration" can cut 80%, of the carbon dioxide emitted during the production of electricity.

6. It may not be practically possible to switch over to the new hybrid technologies from the present ones.

7. In the forthcoming years, India and China are going to be at the top of the list of world's developed countries.

8. The more developed is a country; less is the contribution to increase in air pollution.

9. The new technologies can control emission of carbon dioxide caused only during electricity generation.

10. The developing countries in the world are trying to evolve new technologies to reduce the emission of carbon dioxide.

PASSAGE 3

In the overall economy of India, agriculture is the largest sector of economic activity. It plays a crucial role in the country's economic development by providing food to its people and raw materials to industry. It accounts for the largest share to the national income. The share of the various agricultural commodities, animal husbandry and ancillary activities has been more than 40 per cent since independence. During the decade of the fifties, it actually contributed about half of the national output.

11. Agriculture is the mainstay of Indian economy.

12. The contribution of agricultural sector has decreased in recent years.

13. Agriculture is the only source of income in India.

14. The contribution of agriculture to Indian economy rose substantially after independence.

15. Agriculture contributes to national income more than all other activities put together.

PASSAGE 4

Gujarat has hardly 8.5 per cent of its total area under forest. Of this a considerable portion is covered by wild grass and marshes. Denuded of thick forests, fauna have disappeared from many places. Mandvi, for instance, had its share of panthers once. The state government has imposed a total ban on cutting of trees for five years from this year. The imminent destruction of over 40000 hectares of forest land by the Narmada project has led to nationwide strong protest.

16. People in Gujarat are quite conscious of the need of conservation of forests.

17. There is thick forest in 8.5 per cent of the total area of Gujarat.

18. Gujarat is the first state in India to impose a total ban on cutting of trees.

19. A dam on the Narmada river is planned.

20. Once there was thick forest in Mandvi.

ANSWERS

1	2	3	4	5	6	7	8	9	10
A	B	E	E	E	E	E	E	E	A

11	12	13	14	15	16	17	18	19	20
A	C	E	A	A	A	E	C	A	A

SOME SELECTED EXPLANATORY ANSWERS

6. A new technology is developed in view of its viability and acceptance. So, the inference is false.

7. A developed country does not emit huge quantity of carbon dioxide.

9. It is clear from the passage that the technologies are being developed to decrease the emission of carbon dioxide from automobiles as well as from the production of electricity.

❀ ❀ ❀

Syllogism

Syllogism was introduced by Aristotle (a reasoning consisting two premises and a conclusion). Aristotle gives the following definition of syllogism in his fundamental treatise Organon.

"A syllogism is discourse, in which, certain things being stated, something other than what is stated follows of necessity from their being so". Things that have stated are known as premises and the one that follows from the premises is known as the conclusion of the syllogism.

A categorical syllogism is a type of argument with two premises and one conclusion. Each of these three propositions is one of four forms of categorical proposition.

Type	Form	Example
A	All S are P	All monkeys are mammals
E	No S is P	No monkeys are birds
I	Some S are P	Some philosophers are logicians
O	Some S are not P	Some logicians are not philosophers

These four type of proposition are called A, E, I and O type propositions, the variables S and P are place-holders for terms which represent out a class or category of thing, hence the name "categorical" proposition.

Example

Directions (Qs. 1 to 3): *Below are given three or four statements followed by three or four conclusions. You have to take the given statements to be true even if they appear to be at variance with commonly known facts, and then decide which of the conclusions logically follow(s) from the given statements. For each question, mark out an appropriate answer choice that you think is correct.*

1. **Statements:**   **Solution:**
    (*a*) All locks are keys   (*a*) LL – K
    (*b*) All keys are bats   (*b*) KK – B
    (*c*) Some clocks are bats   (*c*) C – B

    Conclusions:
    1. Some bats are locks.   1. B – L
    2. Some clocks are keys.   2. C – K ×
    3. All keys are locks.   3. KK – LL ×
    A. Only 1 and 2 follow
    B. Only 2 and 3 follow
    C. Only 1 follows
    D. Only 2 follows
    E. 1, 2 and 3 follow
    C. Only 1 follows

2. **Statements:**   **Solution:**
    (*a*) Some cups are pots   (*a*) C – P
    (*b*) All pots are tubes   (*b*) PP – T
    (*c*) All cups are bottles   (*c*) CC – B

    Conclusions:
    1. Some bottles are tubes. 1. B – T
    2. Some pots are bottles   2. P – B
    3. Some tubes are cups   3. T – C
    A. Only 1 and 2 follow
    B. Only 2 and 3 follow
    C. Only 1 and 3 follow
    D. 1, 2 and 3 follow
    E. None follows
    D. 1, 2 and 3 follow

3. **Statements:**   **Solution:**
    (*a*) All papers are books.   PP – B
    (*b*) All bags are books.   BaBa – B
    (*c*) Some purses are bags   Pu – Ba

    Conclusions:
    1. Some papers are bags.   P – Ba ×
    2. Some books are papers. B – P
    3. Some books are purses. B – Pu
    A. Only 1 follow
    B. Only 2 and 3 follow
    C. Only 1 and 3 follow
    D. Only 1 and 2 follow
    E. 1, 2 and 3 follow
    D. Only 2 and 3 follow

EXERCISE

Directions (Qs. Nos. 1 to 10): *In each question below are given two statements followed by two conclusions numbered I and II. You have to take the given two statements to be true even if they seem to be at variance from commonly known facts. Read the conclusion and then decide which of the given conclusions logically follows from the two given statements, disregarding commonly known facts.*

Give answer:
A. If only conclusion I follows
B. If only conclusion II follows
C. If either I or II follows
D. If neither I nor II follows and
E. If both I and II follow.

1. Statements: I. All tables are chalks.
  II. All chalks are chairs.

  Conclusions: I. All chairs are tables.
   II. All tables are chairs.

2. Statements: I. Some radios are stones.
  II. All stones are rods.

3. Statements: I. Some birds are flowers.
  II. Some flowers are books.

  Conclusions: I. Some birds are books.
   II. No book is a flower.

4. Statements: I. Some cows are jackals.
  II. No fox is a cow.

  Conclusions: I. Some jackals are foxes.
   II. Some jackals are not foxes.

5. Statements: I. Only cats are animals.
  II. No dog is an animal.
  Conclusions: I. Some cats are not dogs.
   II. Some dogs are cats.

6. Statements : I. All shoes are carpets.
  II. No carpet is a pullover.
  Conclusions: I. No shoes are pullovers.
   II. All carpets are shoes.

7. Statements: I. No window is a wall.
  II. No wall is a door.
  Conclusions: I. No window is a door.
   II. No door is a window.

8. Statements: I. All players are tall.
  II. Johan is tall.
  Conclusions: I. Johan is a player.
   II. Johan is not a player.

9. Statements: I. All dogs are wolves.
  II. Some wolves are tigers.
  Conclusions: I. Some dogs are tigers.
   II. Tigers which are wolves are not dogs.

10. Statements: I. All cars fly.
  II. Some cycles fly.
  Conclusions: I. All cars are cycles.
   II. Some cycles do not fly.

Directions (Qs. Nos. 11 to 20): *In each question below are given three statements followed by two conclusions numbered I and II. You have to take the given two statements to be true even if they seem to be at variance from commonly known facts. Read the conclusion and then decide which of the given conclusions logically follows from the two given statements, disregarding commonly known facts.*

Give answer:
A. If only conclusion I follows
B. If only conclusion II follows
C. If either I or II follows
D. If neither I nor II follows and
E. If both I and II follow.

11. Statements: I. Some spoons are pots.
  II. All pots are cups.
  III. Some cups are cards.

  Conclusions: I. Some cards are spoons.
   II. Some cups are spoons.

12. Statements: I. Some keys are locks.
  II. Some locks are doors.
  III. Some doors are windows.

  Conclusions: I. Some windows are locks.
   II. Some doors are keys.

13. Statements: I. Some boys are flowers.
  II. All flowers are jungles.
  III. All jungles are houses

Conclusions: I. Some houses are flowers.
II. Some houses are boys.

14. Statements: I. All bottles are tanks.
II. All tanks are drums.
III. All drums are pipes.

Conclusions: I. Some pipes are tanks.
II. Some drums are bottles.

15. Statements: I. All sticks are brushes.
II. No brush is a fruit.
III. Some fruits are trees.

Conclusions: I. Some trees are sticks.
II. No tree is stick.

16. Statements: I. Some shirts are pants.
II. All pants are clothes.
III. Some clothes are napkins.

Conclusions: I. Some napkins are shirts.
II. Some clothes are shirts.

17. Statements: I. All packets are tents.
II. All tents are houses.
III. Some boxes are houses.

Conclusions: I. Some houses are packets.
II. Some boxes are tents.

18. Statements: I. Some nuts are bolts.
II. Some bolts are hammers.
III. Some hammers are nails.

Conclusions: I. Some nails are bolts.
II. No nail is a bolt.

19. Statements: I. All windows are doors.
II. No door is mountain.
III. Some mountains are roads.

Conclusions: I. Some roads are windows.
II. Some roads are doors.

20. Statements: I. Some phones are bangles.
II. Some bangles are rings.
III. All rings are sticks.

Conclusions: I. Some rings are phones.
II. Some sticks are bangles.

Directions (Qs. Nos. 21 to 25): *In each question below are given four statements followed by four conclusions numbered I, II, III and IV. You have to take the given two statements to be true even if*

they seem to be at variance from commonly known facts. Read the conclusion and then decide which of the given conclusions logically follows from the two given statements, disregarding commonly known facts.

21. Statements: I. All silver are metals.
II. All metals are steel.
III. Some steel are stones.
IV. All stones are stands.

Conclusions: I. Some stands are metals.
II. Some stones are silver.
III. Some stands are steel.
IV. Some stones are steel.

A. Only conclusions III and IV follow
B. Only conclusion I follows
C. Only conclusion II follows
D. Only conclusion III follows
E. None of these

22. Statements: I. All chairs are tables.
II. All tables are songs.
III. Some songs are rhythms.
IV. Some rhythms are pillows.

Conclusions: I. Some tables are chairs.
II. All tables are rhythms.
III. All chairs are songs.
IV. Some pillows are songs.

A. Only conclusions I and III follow
B. Only conclusions I and IV follow
C. Only conclusion I follows
D. Only conclusion III follows
E. None of these

23. Statements: I. Some mobiles are pens.
II. Some pens are covers.
III. Some covers are plates.
IV. All plates are papers.

Conclusions: I. All mobiles are covers.
II. Some pens are papers.
III. All plates are pens.
IV. Some papers are mobiles.

A. Only conclusion I follows
B. Only conclusion II follows
C. Only conclusions I and IV follow
D. Only conclusions II and IV follow
E. None follows

24. Statements:
  I. All shoes are tables.
  II. Some tables are lanes.
  III. All caps are lanes.
  IV. Some lanes are row.

Conclusions:
  I. Some tables are rows.
  II. Some tables are shoes.
  III. Some rows are caps.
  IV. Some lanes are shoes.

A. Only conclusions I and II follow
B. Only conclusion II follows
C. Only conclusion III follows
D. Only conclusion I either or conclusion IV follows
E. None of these

25. Statements:
  I. Some symbols are numbers.
  II. Some numbers are letters.
  III. All alphabets are symbols.
  IV. All pianos are letters.

Conclusions:
  I. Some symbols are letters.
  II. Some numbers are pianos.
  III. No letter is symbol.
  IV. Some symbols are alphabets.

A. Only conclusion I follows
B. Only conclusion II follows
C. Only conclusions III and IV follow
D. Only conclusion IV follows
E. Only either I or III and IV follow

ANSWERS

1	2	3	4	5	6	7	8	9	10
B	E	D	B	A	A	D	C	D	D
11	**12**	**13**	**14**	**15**	**16**	**17**	**18**	**19**	**20**
B	D	E	E	C	B	A	C	D	B
21	**22**	**23**	**24**	**25**					
A	A	E	B	E					

EXPLANATORY ANSWERS

1. [A + A = A, All tables are chairs]

2. [I + A = I, Some radios are rods. Also, some radios are stones *conversion* Some stones are radios.]

3. [I + I = no conclusion]

4. [Change order of the statements to align. Now, No fox is a cow + Some cows are jackals = E + I = O*, Some jackals are not foxes.]

5. [Change order first. Now, No dog is an animal + Only cats are animals *implies* No dog is an animal + All animals are cats = E + A = O*, Some cats are not dogs.]

6. [A + E = E]

7. [E + E = no conclusion]

8. [Align: Johan is tall + Some tall are players = A + I = no conclusion. But, Johan should either be a player or a non-player. Hence either of the two choices follows.

9. [A + I = no conclusion]

10. [After alignment, All cars fly + Some fly are cycles = no conclusion]

11. [Some spoons are *pots,* + *All pots* are cups. I + A = I type of conclusion "Some spoons are cups". Conclusion II is converse of it.]

12. [All the three premises are I type. No conclusion follows from two I premises.]

13. Some boys are *flowers.* + *All flowers* are jungles. I + A = I type conclusion, "Some boys are jungles". Some boys are flowers + *All jungles* are houses.

I + A = I type conclusion, "Some boys are houses". Conclusion II is converse of it.

14. All bottles are tanks. + All tanks are drums. A + A = A – type of conclusion *i.e.* "all bottles are drums'. Conclusion II is converse of it. All tanks are drums + All drums are pipes A + A implies A-type of conclusion "All tanks are pipes". Conclusion I is converse of it.

15. All sticks are brushes + No brush is fruit. *i.e.* A + E = E type of conclusion. "No stick is fruit". No brush is fruit + Some fruits are trees. *i.e.* E + I = O*,"Some trees are not brushes". Conclusions I and II forms a complementary pair. Therefore, either I or II follows.

16. Some shirts are pants + All pants are clothes = Some shirts are clothes. Conclusion II is converse of it.

17. All packets are tents + All tents are houses = All packets are houses. Conclusion I is the converse of it.

18. All the three premises are particular affirmative. No conclusion can be reached from two particular premises (I type).

19. All windows are doors + No door is mountain = No window is mountain. No door is mountain + Some mountains are roads = Some roads are not doors.

20. Some bangles are rings + All rings are sticks = Some bangles are sticks. Conclusion II is converse of the third premise.

21. All silver are metals + All metals are steel = All silver are steel. Some steel are stones + All stones are stands = Some steel are stands conversion Conclusion III. Conclusion IV is converse of the third premise.

22. All chairs are tables + All tables are songs = All chairs are songs (Conclusion III) Conclusion I is converse of first premise.

23. Some covers are plates + All plates are papers = Some covers are papers.

24. All shoes are tables + Some tables are lanes = no conclusion.

Conclusion II is the converse of the first premise.

25. All alphabets are symbols + Some symbols are numbers = no conclusion.

Conclusion IV follows from the conversion of the third premise. Conclusion I and III form complementary pair.

Cause & Effect

In these questions, the job is to determine whether a given event is the cause or the effect of some other event. Events do not just happen without any cause behind them. These causes are the conditions under which these events (or results or effects) happen. Cause is an event which leads to a said effect and this fact is either scientifically proven or logically expected. An immediate cause means a cause that immediately precedes the effect and a principal cause means a cause that immediately precedes the effect and a principal cause means a cause that was the most important reason behind the effect. Obviously cause must occur before the effect, we can merely look at the given two events first and by analyzing the time of occurrence, we can find which event can't be a cause.

Example

Directions (Qs. Nos. 1-4): *In each of the following questions, two statements numbered I and II are given. There may be cause and effect relationship between the two statements. These two statements may be the effect of the same cause or independent causes. These statements may be independent causes without having any relationship. Read both the statements in each question and mark your answer as*

A. If statement I is the cause and statement II is its effect;
B. If statement II is the cause and statement I is its effect;
C. If both the statements I and II are independent causes;
D. If both the statements I and II are effects of independent causes; and
E. If both the statements I and II are effects of some common cause.

1. **Statements:**
   I. Police had resorted to lathi-charge to disperse the unruly mob from the civic headquarters.
   II. The civic administration has recently hiked the property tax of the residential buildings by about 30 per cent.

Ans. D: Both the statements I and II are the effects of independent causes.

2. **Statements:**
   I. The government has allowed private airline companies in India to operate to overseas destinations.
   II. The national air carrier has increased its flights to overseas destinations.

Ans. A: Since the Government has allowed private airline companies in India to operate to overseas, so the national air carrier has increased its flights to overseas destinations.

3. **Statements:**
   I. Many people visited the religious place during the week-end.
   II. Few people visited the religious place during the week days.

Ans. E: Both the statements I and II are the effects of some common cause.

4. **Statements:**
   I. The performance of Indian sports persons in the recently held Olympics could not reach the level of expectation the country had on them.
   II. The performance of Indian sports person in the last Asian games was far better than any previous games.

Ans. E: Both the statements are effects of some common cause.

EXERCISE

Directions (Qs. Nos. 1 to 12): *In each of the following questions, two statements numbered I and II are given. There may be cause and effect relationship between the two statements. These two statements may be the effect of the same cause or independent causes. These statements may be independent causes without having any relationship. Read both the statements in each question and mark your answer as*

   A. If statement I is the cause and statement II is its effect;

   B. If statement II is the cause and statement I is its effect;

   C. If both the statements I and II are independent causes;

   D. If both the statements I and II are effects of independent causes; and

   E. If both the statements I and II are effects of some common cause.

1. Statements:
   I. The prices of petrol and diesel in the domestic market have remained unchanged for the past few months.
   II. The crude oil prices in the international market have gone up substantially in the last few months.

2. Statements:
   I. India has surpassed the value of tea exports this year over all the earlier years due to an increase in demand for quality tea in the European market.
   II. There is an increase in demand of coffee in the domestic market during the last two years.

3. Statements:
   I. The government has recently fixed the fees for professional courses offered by the unaided institutions which are much lower than the fees charged last year.
   II. The parents of the aspiring students launched a severe agitation last year protesting against the high fees charged by the unaided institutions.

4. Statements:
   I. The Reserve Bank of India has recently put restrictions on few small banks in the country.
   II. The small banks in the private and co-operative sector in India are not in a position to withstand the competitions of the bigger in the public sector.

5. Statements:
   I. All the schools in the area had to be kept closed for most part of the week.
   II. Many parents have withdrawn their children from the local schools.

6. Statements:
   I. There is unprecedented increase in the number of young unemployed in comparison to the previous year.
   II. A large number of candidates submitted applications against an advertisement for the post of manager issued by a bank.

7. Statements:
   I. The school authority has asked the X Std. students to attend special classes to be conducted on Sundays.
   II. The parents of the X Std. students have withdrawn their wards from attending private tuitions conducted on Sundays.

8. Statements:
   I. Majority of the students in the college expressed their opinion against the college authority's decision to break away from the university and become autonomous.
   II. The university authorities have expressed their inability to provide grants to its constituent colleges.

9. Statements:
   I. The police authority has recently caught a group of house breakers.
   II. The citizens group in the locality have started night vigil in the area.

10. **Statements:**
    I. The Government has imported large quantities of sugar as per trade agreement with other countries.
    II. The prices of sugar in the domestic market have fallen sharply in the recent months.

11. **Statements:**
    I. It is the aim of the city's civic authority to get the air pollution reduced by 20% in the next two months.

II. The number of asthma cases in the city is constantly increasing.

12. **Statements:**
    I. The private medical colleges have increased the tuition fees in the current year by 200 per cent over the last year's fees to meet the expenses.
    II. The Government medical colleges have not increased their fees in spite of price escalation.

ANSWERS

1	2	3	4	5	6	7	8	9	10
D	C	B	B	D	A	A	B	E	A

11	12
B	C

EXPLANATORY ANSWERS

1. The prices of petrol and diesel being stagnant in the domestic market and the increase in the same in the international market must be backed by independent causes.

2. The two statements discuss two separate statistical and generalised results.

3. The parents' protest against high fees being charged by the institutions led the government to interfere and fix the fees at a more affordable level.

4. The inability of the small banks to compete with the bigger ones shall not ensure security and good service to the customers, which is an essential concomitant that has to be looked into by the Reserve Bank. I seems to be a remedial step for the same.

5. Closing the schools for a week and the parents withdrawing their wards from the local schools are independent issues, which must have been triggered by different individual causes.

6. An increase in the number of unemployed youth is bound to draw in huge crowds for a single vacancy.

7. It seems quite evident that the parents have instructed their wards to abstain from private tuitions on Sundays and attend special classes organised by the school.

8. Clearly, the university's decision to refuse grant to the colleges must have triggered the college authority to become autonomous.

9. Both the statements are clearly backed by a common cause, which is clearly an increase in the number of thefts in the locality.

10. Since the Government has imported large quantities of sugar as per trade agreement with other countries, therefore, the prices of the sugar in the domestic market have fallen sharply in the recent months.

11. The increase in number of asthma cases must have alerted the authorities to take action to control air pollution that triggers the disease.

12. The increase in the fees of the private colleges and there being no increase in the same in Government colleges seem to be policy matters undertaken by the individual decisive boards at the two levels.

In these questions, a situation is presented and some courses of action are suggested in the context of that situation. Job is to determine which of them should be followed. Such questions tests one's ability to judge a problem correctly, to determine the root cause of the problem and then to prescribe a suitable course of action.

Basically there are two broad types of patterns in such questions, it is a 'problem-solution' or 'fact-follow-up action' type.

To solve questions on 'course of action' first of all, determine whether it is a 'problem-solution' or 'fact-follow-up action' type.

Example

Directions (Qs. Nos. 1 and 2): *In each question given below a statement is followed by three courses of action denoted 1, 2 and 3. A course of action is a step or administrative decision to be taken for improvement, follow-up for further action in regard to the problem, policy etc. on the basis of the information given in the statement. You have to assume everything in the statement to be true, then decide which of the three given/suggested courses of action logically follows for pursuing and decide the answer.*

1. **Statement:** The chairman of the car company announced in the meeting that all trial of its first product of the new car model 'M' are over and company plans to launch its car in the market after six months.

   Courses of action:
   1. The network of dealers is to be finalised and all legal, financial and other matters in this connection will have to be finalised shortly.
   2. The company will have to make plan for product other than car.
   3. Material, managerial and other resources will have to be in fine tune to maintain production schedule.

   A. 1 and 3 only   B. Only 1
   C. All the three   D. Only 2
   E. None of these

Ans. A: After trials, the best availability of material, managerial and other resources is necessary to maintain production schedule. Hence 3 follows. As stated 'model M is its first product', so it is necessary to finalise the network of dealers and all matters regarding the sale of the product. Hence 1 follows. 2 has no connection with the statement.

2. **Statement:** The Company 'X' has rejected first lot of valves supplied by company"Y' and has cancelled its entire huge order quoting use of inferior-quality material and poor crafts-manship.

   Courses of action:
   1. The Company 'Y' needs to investigate functioning of its purchase, production and quality control departments.
   2. The Company 'Y' should inspect all the valves rejected by Company 'X'.
   3. The Company 'Y' should inform Company 'X' that steps have been taken for improvement and renegotiate schedule of supply.

   A. Only 1 and 2   B. Only 2
   C. All 1, 2 and 3   D. 2 and either 1 or 3
   E. None of these

Ans. 3: As stated 'rejection due to inferior-quality material and poor craftsmanship', since purchase deptt is responsible for purchasing the inferior quality material and for improper inspection. Hence investigation is compulsory for all the departments. Hence 1 follows. 2 follows because claim of company 'X' may not be true. 3 follows because relationships with a previous client should always be kept out.

EXERCISE

Directions (Qs. Nos. 1 to 15): *In each question below is given a statement followed by two courses of action numbered I and II. You have to assume everything in the statement to be true and on the basis of the information given in the statement, decide which of the suggested courses of action logically follow(s) for pursuing.*

A. If only I follows
B. If only II follows
C. If either I or II follows
D. If neither I nor II follows
E. If both I and II follow

1. **Statement:** Severe drought is reported to have set in several parts of the state.
   Courses of Action:
   I. Government should immediately make arrangement for providing financial assistance to those affected.
   II. Food, water and fodder should immediately be sent to all these areas to save the people and cattle.

2. **Statement:** A large number of people in ward J of the city are diagnosed to be suffering from a fatal dengue type fever.
   Courses of Action:
   I. The city municipal authority should take immediate steps to carry out extensive fumigation in ward J.
   II. The people in the area should be advised to take steps to avoid mosquito bites.

3. **Statement:** Since its launching in 2001, Kingfisher Airlines has so far accumulated losses amounting to ₹ 8000 crore.
   Courses of Action:
   I. Kingfisher Airlines should be directed to reduce wasteful expenditure and to increase passenger fare.
   II. An amount of about ₹ 300 crore should be provided to Kingfisher Airlines to make the airliner economically viable.

4. **Statement:** Exporters in the town are alleging that commercial banks are violating a Reserve Bank of India directive to operate a post shipment export credit denominated in foreign currency at international rates from March this year.

Courses of Action:
I. The officers concerned in the commercial banks are to be suspended.
II. The RBI should be asked to stop giving such directives to commercial banks.

5. **Statement:** A large number of people suffer illness every year due to drinking polluted water during the rainy season.
   Courses of Action:
   I. The government should make adequate arrangements to provide safe drinking water to all its citizens.
   II. The people should be educated about the dangers of drinking polluted water.

6. **Statement:** Most of those who study in premier government engineering colleges in India migrate to developed nations for better prospects in their professional pursuits.
   Courses of Action:
   I. All the students joining these colleges should be asked to sign a bond at the time of admission to the effect that they will remain in India at least for ten years after they complete education.
   II. All those students who desire to settle in the developed nations should be asked to pay entire cost of their education which the government subsidies.

7. **Statement:** As stated in the last census report the female to male ratio is alarmingly low in most of the states.
   Courses of Action:
   I. The government should conduct another census to verify the results.
   II. The government should immediately issue orders to all the departments to encourage people to improve the ratio.

8. **Statement:** The retired Professors of the S Institute should also be invited to deliberate on restructuring of the organization, as their contribution may be beneficial to the Institute.
   Courses of Action:
   I. Management may seek opinion of the employees before calling retired professors.

II. Management should involve experienced people for the systematic restructuring of the organization.

9. **Statement:** Three districts in State F have been experiencing severe drought for the last four years resulting into exodus of people from these districts.
Courses of Action:
   I. The government should immediately start food for work programme in these districts to put a halt to the exodus.
   II. The government should make sincere efforts to provide drinking/potable water to these districts.

10. **Statement:** The sale of a particular product has gone down considerably causing great concern to the company.
Courses of Action:
   I. The company should make a proper study of rival products in the market.
   II. The price of the product should be reduced and quality improved.

11. **Statement:** A recent study revals that children below five die in the cities of the developing countries mainly from diarrhoea and parasitic intestinal worms.
Courses of Action:
   I. Governments of the developing countries should take adequate measures to improve the hygienic conditions in the cities.
   II. Children below five years in the cities of the developing countries need to be kept under periodic medical check-up.

12. **Statement:** A recent survey shows that the teachers are still not familiarised with the need, importance and meaning of population education in the higher education system. They are not even clearly aware about their role and responsibilities in the population education programme.

Courses of Action:
   I. Population education programme should be included in the college curriculum.
   II. Orientation programme should be conducted for teachers on population education.

13. **Statement:** STAR TV is concerned about the quality of its programmes particularly in view of stiff competition it is facing from SAB and other satellite TV channels and is contemplating various measures to attract talent for its programmes.
Courses of Action:
   I. In an effort to attract talent, the STAR TV should revise its fee structure for the artists.
   II. The fee structure should not be revised until other electronic media also revise it.

14. **Statement:** The Asian Development Bank has approved a $285 million loan to finance a project to construct coal ports by Coal India Limited in Kerala.
Courses of Action:
   I. India should use financial assistance from other international financial organisations to develop such ports in other places.
   II. India should not seek such financial assistance from the international financial agencies.

15. **Statement:** The Rabi crops have been affected by the insects for consecutive three years in the district and the farmers on average harvested less than fifty percent of produce during these years.
Courses of Action:
   I. The farmers should seek measures to control the attack of insects to protect their crops next year.
   II. The Government should increase the support price of Rabi crops considerably to protect the economic interests of farmers.

ANSWERS

1	2	3	4	5	6	7	8	9	10
B	E	A	D	E	B	B	B	E	A

11	12	13	14	15
E	B	A	A	E

EXPLANATORY ANSWERS

1. In the break-out of a natural calamity, the basic duty of the government becomes to provide the basic amenities essential to save the lives of people and cattle. Providing financial assistance to all would put undue burden on the country's resources. So, only II follows.

2. Clearly, prevention from mosquitoes and elimination of mosquitoes are two ways to prevent dengue. So, both the courses follow.

3. Clearly, for better economic gain, losses should be reduced and income increased. So, only course I follows.

4. The statement mentions that the commercial banks violate a directive issued by the RBI. The remedy is only to make the banks implement the Act. So, none of the courses follows.

5. The situation demands creating awareness among people about the dangers of drinking polluted water so that they themselves refrain from the same, and at the same time taking steps to provide safe drinking water. So, both the courses follow.

6. Clearly, no student can be bound to live and work in the country against his wish. So, I does not follow. However, it is quite right to recover the extra benefits awarded to students if they do not serve their own country. So, II follows.

7. A census is always conducted with the utmost precision, leaving negligible chances of differences. So, I does not follow. Further, the ratio can be improved by creating awareness among the masses and abolishing female foeticide. Thus, only course II follows.

8. The statement stresses that the contribution of retired Professors shall be beneficial. This means that these people's experience regarding working of the organisation is helpful. So, only course II follows.

9. The exodus can be checked by providing the people conditions conducive to living. So, both the courses follow.

10. Clearly, a study of rival products in the market will help assess the cause for the lowering down of sales and then a suitable action can be taken. Thus, I follows. The second course may not be implementable.

11. Clearly, the two diseases mentioned are caused by unhygienic conditions. So, improving the hygienic conditions will check the spread of disease. Also, periodic medical check-up will help timely detection of the disease and hence a proper treatment. So, both I and II follow.

12. The statement stresses on teachers' lack of awareness and knowledge in population education and as such the best remedy would be to guide them in this field through orientation programmes. So, only course II follows.

13. Revised its fee structure for artists will attract talent and enchance quality of STAR TV programmes. It cannot wait till other media take action. So, only course I follows.

14. Clearly, such projects will provide employment and shall be an asset and a source of income to the country later on. So, course I shall follows. Course II will slowdown country's economic growth.

15. Clearly, the problem demands taking extra care and adequate precautions to protect crops from insects and extending help to farmers to prevent them from incurring huge losses. Thus, both the courses follow.

15\ Distinguishing Argument

Arguments are the fundamentals unit of logic. An argument contains two explict constituents: supporting premises and conclusion. Some supporting premises make strong arguments while some make weak arguments. The question statement is (usually) in the form of a suggested course of action. Followed by the statement are two arguments, one argument advocates the suggested course of action by stating out the positive features or positive results of that action and the other argues against the suggested course of action by stating out the negative features or harmful results of that action.

To determine forcefulness of argument it should be preliminary screened first to reject an argument on the basis of preliminary observations. An argument can be rejected if it is ambiguous or if it is 'half-hearted' or if it is too simple to be acceptable or if it is in the form of a question. If a argument is not rejected in preliminary screening then argument is subjected to three steps to ascertain its strength.

Thus, solution consists of four stages: 1. Preliminary screening 2. Check, whether the result really follows or not 3. Check, whether the result really desirable or not (or harmful, in case of negative arguments)? 4. Check, whether the argument and the suggested course of action are properly related or not?

If an argument passes all the four checks, it is a strong argument, otherwise it is weak.

Example

Directions (Qs. Nos. 1 and 2): *In making decisions about important questions, it is desirable to be able to distinguish between "strong" arguments and "weak" arguments insofar as they relate to the question. "Strong" arguments are those which are both important and directly related to the question. "Weak" arguments are those which are of minor importance and also may not be directly related to the question or may be related to a trivial aspect of the question.*

Instructions: Each statement below is followed by two arguments denoted by I and II. you have to decide which of the arguments is a "strong" argument and which is a "weak" argument.

Give answer:

   A. if only argument I is "strong".
   B. if only argument II is "strong".
   C. if either I or II is "strong".
   D. if neither I nor II is "strong".
   E. if both I and II are "strong".

1. **Statement:** Should one close relative of a retiring government employee be given a job in government services in India?

   Arguments:

   I. Yes, where else relative get a job like this?
   II. No, it will close doors of government service to competent and needy youth.

Ans. B: I is weak because that relative may not be suitable for the job. II is strong. As the seats will be filled by close relatives of retiring government employees, deserving and other needy youths won't get entry for government services.

2. **Statement:** Should purchase of gold by individuals be restricted in India to improve its foreign exchange position?

Arguments:

I. Yes, interference on customer's right and freedom is desirable.

II. No, business interest has to be guarded first.

Ans. D: I is weak because such interference is not desirable in a democracy. II is weak because it gives priority to business interest on foreign exchange position, which is undesirable.

EXERCISE

Directions (Qs. 1 to 10): *Each question given below consists of a statement, followed by two arguments numbered I and II. You have to decide which of the arguments is a 'strong' argument and which is a 'weak' argument.*

1. **Statement:** Should there be a restriction on the migration of people from one state to another state in India?
   Arguments:
   I. No. Any Indian citizen has a basic right to stay at any place of his/her choice and hence they cannot be stopped.
   II. Yes. This is the way to effect an equitable distribution of resources across the states in India.

2. **Statement:** Should there be a complete ban on use of all types of chemical pesticides in India?
   Arguments:
   I. No. The pests will destroy all the crops and the farmers will have nothing to harvest.
   II. Yes. The chemical pesticides used in agriculture pollute the water underground and this has become a serious health hazard.

3. **Statement:** Should officers accepting bribe be punished?
   Arguments:
   I. No. Certain circumstances may have compelled them to take bribe.
   II. Yes. They should do the job they are entrusted with, honestly.

4. **Statement:** Should cutting of trees be banned altogether?
   Arguments:
   I. Yes. It is very much necessary to do so to restore ecological balance.

   II. No. A total ban would harm timber based industries.

5. **Statement:** Should all refugees, who make unauthorized entry into a country, be forced to go back to their homeland?
   Arguments:
   I. Yes. They make their colonies and occupy a lot of land.
   II. No. They leave their homes because of hunger or some terror and on human grounds, should not be forced to go back.

6. **Statement:** Should all the practising doctors be brought under Government control so that they get salary from the Government and treat patients free of cost?
   Arguments:
   I. No. How can any country do such an undemocratic thing?
   II. Yes. Despite many problems, it will certainly help minimize, if not eradicate, unethical medical practices.

7. **Statement:** Should there be a ban on product advertising?
   Arguments:
   I. No. It is an age of advertising. Unless your advertisement is better than your other competitors, the product will not be sold.
   II. Yes. The money spent on advertising is very huge and it inflates the cost of the product.

8. **Statement:** Are nuclear families better than joint families?
   Arguments:
   I. No. Joint families ensure security and also reduce the burden of work.
   II. Yes. Nuclear families ensure greater freedom.

9. **Statement:** Should there be compulsory medical examination of both the man and the woman before they marry each other?

Arguments:
  I. No. This is an intrusion to the privacy of an individual and hence cannot be tolerated.
  II. Yes. This will substantially reduce the risk of giving birth to children with serious ailments.

10. **Statement:** Should government stop spending huge amounts of money on international sports?

Arguments:
  I. Yes. This money can be utilized for upliftment of the poor.
  II. No. Sports persons will be frustrated and will not get international exposure.

ANSWERS

1	2	3	4	5	6	7	8	9	10
A	E	B	E	B	B	E	E	B	B

EXPLANATORY ANSWERS

1. Clearly, argument I holds strong, while argument II is vague.

2. Obviously, pesticides are meant to prevent the crops from harmful pests. But at the same time, they get washed away with water and contaminate the groundwater. Thus, both the arguments hold strong.

3. Obviously, officers are paid duly for the jobs they do. So, they must do it honestly. Thus, argument II alone holds.

4. Definitely, trees play a vital role in maintaining ecological balance and so must be preserved. So, argument I holds. Also, trees form the basic source of timber and a complete ban on cutting of trees would harm timber based industries. So, only a controlled cutting of trees should be allowed and the loss replenished by planting more trees. So, argument II is also valid.

5. Obviously, refugees are people forced out of their homeland by some misery and need shelter desperately. So, argument II holds. Argument I against the statement is vague.

6. A doctor treating a patient individually can mislead the patient into wrong and unnecessary treatment for his personal gain. So, argument II holds strong. Also, a policy benefiting common people cannot be termed 'undemocratic'. So, I is vague.

7. Obviously, it is the advertisement which makes the customer aware of the qualities of the product and leads him to buy it. So, argument I is valid. But at the same time, advertising nowadays has become a costly affair and the expenses on it add to the price of the product. So, argument II also holds strong.

8. Obviously, with so many people around in a joint family, there is more security. Also, work is shared. So, argument I holds. In nuclear families, there are lesser number of people and so lesser responsibilities and more freedom. Thus, II also holds.

9. Definitely, such a step would help to prevent the growth of diseases like AIDS. So, only argument II is strong.

10. Obviously, spending money on sports should not be avoided merely because it can be spent on socio-economic problems. So, argument I does not hold. Also, if the expenses on sports are curtailed, the sports persons would face lack of facilities and training and our country will lag behind in the international sports competitions. So, II holds.

❀ ❀ ❀

16 Drawing Conclusions

In this reasoning pattern, a statement is given followed by two conclusions. The statement is to be taken as the fact. Then based on it one has to decide which of the conclusion(s) definitely follows or does not follow from the given statement.

Example

In the questions below the answer is given as:
  A. If only conclusion I follows
  B. If only conclusion II follows
  C. If either I or II follows
  D. If neither I nor II follows and
  E. If both I and II follow.

1. **Statement:** It is said that teachers should not go on strike. Why should they not? Strike is an inherent right.

   Conclusions:
   I. Teachers cannot get justice unless they go on strike.
   II. Every teacher should go on strike.

Ans. A: Only conclusion I follows from the given statements, *i.e.*, as an inherent right the teachers can get justice in appropriate cases if they go on strike. Conclusion II does not follow.

2. **Statement:** The government of country 'X' has recently announced several concessions and offered attractive package tours for foreign visitors.

   Conclusions:
   I. Now, more numbers of foreign tourists will visit the country.
   II. The government of country 'X' seems to be serious in attracting foreign tourists.

Ans. E: Concessions and attractive package tours will encourage tourists and country 'X' has taken the step only because it seems to be serious about foreign visitors. So both conclusion I and conclusion II follow from the given statement.

EXERCISE

Directions (Qs. Nos. 1 to 10): *In each question below is given a statement followed by two conclusions numbered I and II. You have to assume everything in the statement to be true, then consider the two conclusions together and decide which of them logically follows beyond a reasonable doubt from the information given in the statement*

  Give answer:
  A. If only conclusion I follows
  B. If only conclusion II follows
  C. If either I or II follows
  D. If neither I nor II follows and
  E. If both I and II follow.

1. **Statement:** In a one day cricket match, the total runs made by a team were 200. Out of these 160 runs were made by spinners.

   Conclusions:
   I. 80% of the team consists of spinners.
   II. The opening batsmen were spinners.

2. **Statement:** The old order changed yielding place to new.

   Conclusions:
   I. Change is the law of nature.
   II. Discard old ideas because they are old.

71

3. **Statement:** Government has spoiled many top ranking financial institutions by appointing bureaucrats as Directors of these institutions.

   Conclusions:
   I. Government should appoint Directors of the financial institutes taking into consideration the expertise of the person in the area of finance.
   II. The Director of the financial institute should have expertise commensurate with the financial work carried out by the institute.

4. **Statement:** Population increase coupled with depleting resources is going to be the scenario of many developing countries in days to come.

   Conclusions:
   I. The population of developing countries will not continue to increase in future.
   II. It will be very difficult for the governments of developing countries to provide its people decent quality of life.

5. **Statement:** Prime age school-going children in urban India have now become avid as well as more regular viewers of television, even in households without a TV. As a result, there has been an alarming decline in the extent of readership of newspapers.

   Conclusions:
   I. Method of increasing the readership of newspapers should be devised.
   II. A team of experts should be sent to other countries to study the impact of TV. On the readership of newspapers.

6. **Statement:** The Government run company had asked its employees to declare their income and assets but it has been strongly resisted by employees union and no employee is going to declare his income.

   Conclusions:
   I. The employees of this company do not seem to have any additional undisclosed income besides their salary.
   II. The employees union wants all senior officers to declare their income first.

7. **Statement:** The distance of 900 km by road between Bombay and Jafra will be reduced to 280 km by sea. This will lead to a saving of ₹ 7.92 crores per annum on fuel.

   Conclusions:
   I. Transportation by sea is cheaper than that by road.
   II. Fuel must be saved to the greatest extent.

8. **Statement:** The manager humiliated Sachin in the presence of his colleagues.

   Conclusion:
   I. The manager did not like Sachin.
   II. Sachin was not popular with his colleagues.

9. **Statements:** Nation X faced growing international opposition for its decision to explode eight nuclear weapons at its test site.

   Conclusions:
   I. The citizens of the nation favoured the decision.
   II. Some powerful countries do not want other nations to become as powerful as they are.

10. **Statement:** National Aluminium Company has moved India from a position of shortage to self-sufficiency in the metal.

    Conclusions:
    I. Previously, India had to import aluminium.
    II. With this speed, it can soon become a foreign exchange earner.

ANSWERS

1	2	3	4	5	6	7	8	9	10
D	A	E	B	D	D	B	D	D	E

EXPLANATORY ANSWERS

1. According to the statement, 80% of the total runs were made by spinners. So, I does not follow. Nothing about the opening batsmen is mentioned in the statement. So, II also does not follow.

2. Clearly, I directly follows from the given statement. Also, it is mentioned that old ideas are replaced by new ones, as thinking changes with the progressing time. So, II does not follow.

3. According to the statement, Government has spoiled financial institutions by appointing bureaucrats as Directors. This means that only those persons should be appointed as Directors who are experts in finance and are acquainted with the financial work of the institute. So, both I and II follow.

4. The fact given in I is quite contrary to the given statement. So, I does not follow. II mentions the direct implications of the state discussed in the statement. Thus, II follows.

5. The statement concentrates on the increasing viewership of TV. and does not stress either on increasing the readership of newspapers or making studies regarding the same. So, neither I nor II follows.

6. Nothing about the details of the employees' income or the cause of their refusal to declare their income and assets, can be deduced from the given statement. So, neither I nor II follows.

7. According to the statement, sea transport is cheaper than road transport in the case of route from Bombay to Jafra, not in all the cases. So, conclusion I does not follow. The statement stresses on the saving of fuel. So, conclusion II follows.

8. The manager might have humiliated Sachin not because of his dislike but on account of certain negligence or mistake on his part. So, I does not follow. Also, nothing about Sachin's rapport with his colleagues can be deduced from the statement. So, II also does not follow.

9. Neither the citizens response to the decision nor the reason for opposition by other nations can be deduced from the statement. So, neither I nor II follows.

10. According to the statement, National Aluminium Company has moved India from a position of shortage in the past to self-sufficiency in the present. This means that previously, India had to import aluminium. So, I follows. Also, it can be deduced that if production increases at the same rate, India can export it in future. So, II also follows.

17 | Statement Assumptions

The mental recognition of cause-and-effect relationship is called reasoning. It may be the prediction of an event from an observed cause or the inference of a cause from an observed event. Logical reasoning is a process of passing from the known to the unknown. It is the process of deriving a logical inference from a hypothesis through reasoning.

Argumentation is fundamental to all logic. In logic, we advocate a certain point of view with the help of some evidences and certain assumptions. The whole thing is known as "argumentation". An argument contains two explicit constituents: supporting premises and conclusion. There is also an implict (hidden) constituent called assumption. Conclusion is arrived at with the help of one or more than one statement, which may be called premise or proposition. In an argument, the number of premises can be more than one and it is not necessary that every argument have an assumption *i.e.* if an argument is complete in itself and does not have the hidden links, it will not have any assumptions. An assumption is something which is assumed, supposed and taken for granted.

Example

Directions: *In each question below is given a statement followed by two assumptions numbered 1 and 2. An assumption is something supposed or taken for granted. You have to consider the statement and the following assumptions and to decide which of the assumptions is implict in the statement.*

Give answer

  A. if only assumption 1 is implict.
  B. if only assumption 2 is implict.
  C. if either 1 or 2 is implict.
  D. if neither 1 nor 2 is implict.
  E. if both 1 and 2 are implict.

1. Statement: The 'X' group of employees' association have opposed Voluntary Retirement Scheme to the employees of some organisations.
Assumptions:
1. Only those employees who are not efficient may opt for the scheme.
2. The response of the employees may be lukewarm towards the scheme and it may not the benefit the organisation to the desired level.

Ans. A: The employees association is generally concerned with the welfare of employees and not with benefit of the organisation, hence 2 is not implict. 1 is not related with the statement.
    Alter: If assumptions 1 and 2 are considered wrong then too main statement is valid one so none of them follows.

2. Statement: In view of the statement on the ongoing strike of work by the employees, the government has agreed to work out an effective social security programme.
Assumptions:
1. The striking employees may not be satisfied with the announcement and continue the agitation.
2. The striking employees may withdraw their agitation with immediate effect and start working.

Ans. B: Assuming 2 only, the government has agreed to work out an effective social security programme.
    Alter: If 1 is considered correct than the main statement is absurd so 1 does not follow. Main statement is meaningful only when 2 is considered correct, so 2 follows.

EXERCISE

Directions (Qs. Nos. 1-10): *In each question below is given a statement followed by two assumptions numbered I and II. You have to consider the statement and the following assumptions and decide which of the assumptions is implicit in the statement.*

Give answer

A. if only assumption I is implict.
B. if only assumption II is implict.
C. if either I or II is implict.
D. if neither I nor II is implict.
E. if both I and II are implict.

1. **Statement:** Many historians have done more harm than good by distorting truth.
   Assumptions:
   I. People believe what is reported by the historians.
   II. Historians are seldom expected to depict the truth.

2. **Statement:** "As there is a great demand, every person seeking tickets of the programme will be given only five tickets."
   Assumptions:
   I. The organizers are not keen on selling the tickets.
   II. No one is interested in getting more than five tickets.

3. **Statement:** "Computer education should start at schools itself."
   Assumptions:
   I. Learning computers is easy.
   II. Computer educated is hardly unemployed.

4. **Statement:** "The programme will start at 6 p.m. but you can come there up to 7 p.m. or so and still there is no problem."
   Assumptions:
   I. The programme will continue even after 7 p.m.
   II. The programme may not even start by that time.

5. **Statement:** The organization should promote employees on the basis of merit alone and not on the basis of length of service or seniority.
   Assumptions:
   I. Length of service or seniority do not alone reflect merit of an employee.
   II. It is possible to determine and measure merit of an employee.

6. **Statement:** The higher echelons of any organization are expected to be models of observational learning and should not be considered as merely sources of reward and punishments.
   Assumptions:
   I. Employees are likely to be sensitive enough to learn by observing the behaviour of their bosses.
   II. Normally bosses are considered as sources of reward and punishment.

7. **Statement:** "If you want to give any advertisement, give it in the newspaper X." — A tells B.
   Assumptions:
   I. B wants to publicise his products.
   II. Newspaper X has a wide circulation.

8. **Statement:** Kundan left for Delhi on Tuesday by train to attend a function to be held on Friday at his uncle's house in Delhi.
   Assumptions:
   I. Kundan may reach Delhi on Wednesday.
   II. Kundan may reach Delhi before Friday.

9. **Statement:** "Get rid of your past for future, get our new generation fridge at a discount in exchange of old".—An advertisement.
   Assumptions:
   I. The sales of the new fridge may increase in the coming months.
   II. People prefer to exchange future with past.

10. **Statement:** "Ensure a good night's sleeps for your family with safe and effective X mosquito coil."—An advertisement.
    Assumptions:
    I. X mosquito coil is better than any other mosquito coil.
    II. A good night's sleep is desirable.

ANSWERS

1	2	3	4	5	6	7	8	9	10
A	D	A	A	E	E	B	B	E	B

EXPLANATORY ANSWERS

1. The view that historians have done harm by distorting truth means that people believe what is reported by the historians. So, I is implicit. II does not follow from the statement and so is not implicit.

2. Clearly, the organizers are adopting this policy not to reduce the sale but to cope up with great demand so that maximum can get the ticket. So, I is not implicit. Also, due to great demand, the maximum number of tickets one person can get has been reduced to five. So, II is also not implicit.

3. Computer education can be started at the school level only if it is easy. So, I is implicit. Statement does not talk about the link between jobs and computer education. So, II is not implicit.

4. The statement tells that there is no problem if one comes up to 7 p.m. also. This means that the programme will continue even after 7 p.m. So, I is implicit. Also, it is clearly mentioned that the programme will start at 6 p.m. So, II is not implicit.

5. The statement advocates to award promotion to a person who has been displaying remarkable talent and performing extraordinarily for the organization rather than the one who has been working steadily for the organization since long. Thus, length of service does not alone prove a man worthy. His talent and his performance are the criteria to be considered. So, both I and II are implicit.

6. The statement advises people not to consider their bosses as mere 'instruments' to control and assess their acts, but as 'models' to imitate in their working. So, both I and II are implicit.

7. The statement speaks for any advertisement and it may not be restricted to promotion of products only. So I is not implicit. It is advised that advertisements be given in newspaper X. This means that X will help advertise better *i.e.*, it has wider circulation. So, II is implicit.

8. Clearly, it cannot be deduced as to which day Kundan would reach Delhi. But Kundan has left for Delhi to attend a function to be held on Friday. So, he must have planned his journey to reach Delhi before Friday. Thus, only II is implicit.

9. Obviously, the scheme is aimed to encourage those owning an old fridge to go for a new one at a reasonable price without the hassles of disposing off the old one. So, I is implicit. An advertisement highlights that which appeals to masses and which customers desire for. So, II is also implicit.

10. The statement mentions the good qualities of X coil but this does not necessitate it is the best. So, I is not implicit. Besides, an advertisement highlights the feature which is desirable by customers and can lure them. So, II is implicit.

The questions related to problems on cubes and dice are aimed to check the imaginative power of the candidate. The candidate must have the ability to visualise quickly in three-dimensional object for what is asked of it. To attempt such questions some basic facts should be kept in mind and the visualisation ability should be combined with fast and accurate calculations.

Cube

- Cube has six faces/sides and eight corners.
- Problems are based on the same or different coloured faces.
- Dice has six faces/sides.
- Problems are based only on the value occurring on the six faces.
- Problems are based on cutting the squares into specified number of smaller equal parts.

Dice

Diagrammatically, the explanation of a cube which is painted green on all sides can be understood easily taking one side of the cube.

a	b	a
b	c	b
a	b	a

This cube is divided into $3 \times 3 \times 3 = 27$ equal small cubes.

There are four corner pieces 'a', so 4×2, *i.e.*, 8 pieces will be painted on 3 sides.

There are four middle pieces 'b', so 4×3, *i.e.*, 12 pieces will be painted on 2 sides

There is one middle piece 'c', so 1×6, *i.e.*, 6 pieces will be painted only on 1 side.

There will be one piece right in the centre of this cube, *i.e.*, piece will not have paint at all.

So, this cube has $8 + 12 + 6 + 1$, *i.e.*, 27 smaller cubes.

EXERCISE

1. Two positions of a dice are shown below. When there are two circles at the bottom, the number of circles at the top will be :

A. 5
B. 2
C. 3
D. 6
E. None of these

2. Two positions of a dice are shown below. When 4 is at the bottom, what number will be on the top?

A. 1
B. 2
C. 5
D. 6
E. None of these

3. A cube is painted red on two adjacent faces and on one opposite face, yellow on two adjacent faces and green on the remaining face. It is then cut into 64 equal cubes. How many cubes have only one red and one green face?

A. 4   B. 8
C. 12   D. 16
E. None of these

4. A cube, on whose sides letters have been written, is shown below in different positions as can be seen from different directions. Find the missing letter?

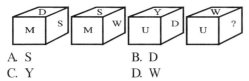

A. S   B. D
C. Y   D. W
E. None of these

5. In a dice a, b, c and d, are written on the adjacent faces, in a clockwise order and e and f at the top and bottom. When c is at the top, what will be at the bottom?

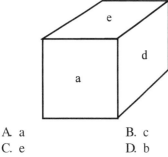

A. a   B. c
C. e   D. b
E. None of these

6. The number of cubes arranged one over the other in this figure will be :

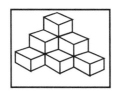

A. 8   B. 6
C. 5   D. 10
E. None of these

7. Two positions of a dice are shown below. When 2 is at the bottom, which number will be at the top?

A. 1   B. 2
C. 3   D. 4
E. None of these

8. The sides of a cube are painted in different colours. Black side is opposite to red. White side is between black and red. Green side is adjacent to grey and blue side is adjacent to green. What colour will be on the side opposite to the white side of the cube?

A. Blue   B. Green
C. Grey   D. Data is insufficient
E. None of these

9. A cube is painted black on two adjacent faces and on one opposite face, red on two opposite faces and green on the remaining face. If it is cut into 64 equal cubes, then how many cubes will have only one black coloured face?

A. 32   B. 16
C. 12   D. 8
E. None of these

10. Six sides of a cube are coloured in the following manner

If blue and orange are opposite and red is on the top, which colour will be at the bottom?

A. Orange   B. Purple
C. Black   D. Yellow
E. None of these

11. A toy cube is painted orange on all sides. It is cut into 64 smaller cubes of equal size. How many smaller cubes are not painted at all?

A. 4   B. 8
C. 16   D. 20
E. None of these

Directions (Qs. 12-13) : *A die is thrown 4 times and its four different positions are given below :*

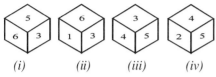

(i)   (ii)   (iii)   (iv)

12. Find the number on the face opposite the face showing 3.
    A. 2   B. 1
    C. 5   D. 4
    E. None of these

13. Find the number on the face opposite the face showing 6.
    A. 5   B. 3
    C. 4   D. 1
    E. None of these

Directions (Qs. 14 to 16): *Study the information given below :*

The six faces of a cube are coloured black, brown, green, red, white and blue.
(*i*) Red is opposite of black
(*ii*) Green is between red and black
(*iii*) Blue is adjacent to white
(*iv*) Brown is adjacent to blue
(*v*) Red is at the bottom

14. Which colour is opposite of brown?
    A. White   B. Red
    C. Green   D. Blue
    E. None of these

15. Which of the following can be deduced from (*i*) and (*v*)?
    A. Black is on the top
    B. Blue is on the top
    C. Brown is on the top
    D. Brown is opposite of black
    E. None of these

16. The four adjacent colours are :
    A. black, blue, brown, red
    B. black, blue, brown, white
    C. black, blue, red, white
    D. black, blue, red, white
    E. None of these

Directions (Qs. 17 to 19): *In each question below a dice has been marked with some letters or nu-*

merals and placed in three different positions. Answer the questions that follow :

17. Which letter is opposite to Q?

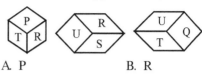

    A. P   B. R
    C. S   D. T
    E. None of these

18. Which letter/numeral is opposite to 3?

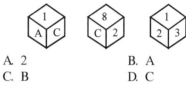

    A. 2   B. A
    C. B   D. C
    E. None of these

19. If one of the 3 visible faces of the cube is hidden, which letter is opposite to O?

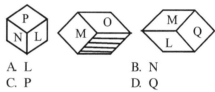

    A. L   B. N
    C. P   D. Q
    E. None of these

Directions (Qs. 20 to 22): *Given below are the three positions of the same dice. Answer the questions that follow :*

20. What is the number on the face opposite of face 2?
    A. 1
    B. 6
    C. 5
    D. Cannot be determined
    E. None of these

21. In the third position of the dice which number lies on the face on the bottom?
    A. 2   B. 3
    C. 4   D. 5
    E. None of these

22. When value 5 is on the face on the top, which value lies on the face on the bottom?
A. 3   B. 4
C. 1   D. 2
E. None of these

Directions (Qs. 23 to 25): *A solid cube with each side 3 cm has been painted red, blue and green on pairs of opposite faces. It is then cut into small cubes with each side 1 cm. Answer the questions that follow :*

23. How many cubes have one face painted red and one face painted green?
A. 12   B. 8
C. 6   D. 14
E. None of these

24. How many cubes have only one face painted?
A. 6   B. 4
C. 12   D. 9
E. None of these

25. How many cubes are painted blue on one face and either red or green on another face?
A. 4   B. 6
C. 8   D. 12
E. None of these

Directions (Qs. 26 to 29): *The questions are based on the following statement :*

A cube is painted red on two adjacent faces, yellow on two opposite faces and green on the remaining faces. It is cut into 64 smaller cubes of equal size.

26. How many cubes are painted on two faces only and that too with the same colour?
A. 0   B. 4
C. 8   D. 16
E. None of these

27. How many cubes have three faces painted?
A. 4   B. 8
C. 16   D. 32
E. None of these

28. How many cubes are painted on one face only and are yellow?
A. 32   B. 16
C. 8   D. 4
E. None of these

29. How many cubes are painted on all faces?
A. 0   B. 4
C. 8   D. 64
E. None of these

ANSWERS

1	2	3	4	5	6	7	8	9	10
A	A	B	C	A	D	D	B	C	D
11	12	13	14	15	16	17	18	19	20
B	A	C	A	A	D	B	D	A	B
21	22	23	24	25	26	27	28	29	
C	A	A	A	C	B	B	C	A	

SOME SELECTED EXPLANATORY ANSWERS

1. After observing the views of the same dice, the faces that can be clearly understood to be the opposites are :
2 – 5, 4 – 3 and 1 – 6.

3.
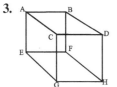

The red sides are EGAC, ABCD and BDFH.
The yellow sides are ABEF and EFGH
The green side is CDGH.

Sides GC, CD and DH are adjacent to red sides and side GH is adjacent to yellow side.

So, only 8 cubes will have one side red and one green.

4. The letters on the top and bottom sides are W and D respectively and the letters on the sides are U, Y, M and S clockwise.

5. The two positions of dice will be :

and the opposite sides will be a – c, b – d.

6.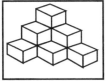

There are three columns containing 1 cube each. There are two columns containing 2 cubes each. There is one column containing 3 cubes. So, the total number of cubes is : $(3 \times 1) + (2 \times 2) + (1 \times 3)$, i.e., $3 + 4 + 3 = 10$.

9.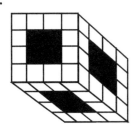

Three faces of the cube are painted black and the rest are in different colours. If this cube is cut into 64 equal cubes, then only the 4 cubes in centre of one face will come out with only one black coloured face. So, the total number of one black coloured face small cubes will be $4 \times 3 = 12$.

10.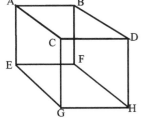

If side ABCD is red; then ABEF will be white; and ACEG will be blue. If side BDFH is orange (opposite to blue); then CDGH will be black; and EFGH will be yellow (opposite to red and at the bottom).

11. The smaller 64 pieces will be cut in the manner that :
1. 8 pieces will be painted on 3 sides,
2. 24 pieces on 2 sides.
3. 24 pieces on 1 side, and
4. 8 will not have paint at all.
Diagrammatically, the explanation taking one side of the cube will be :

a	b	b	a
b	c	c	b
b	c	c	b
a	b	b	a

1. 'a' are the corner pieces [$4 \times 2 = 8$]
2. 'b' are the centre pieces of the cornered sides [$8 \times 3 = 24$]
3. 'c' are the centre pieces [$4 \times 6 = 24$]
4. Remaining interior pieces
   = $64 - (8 + 24 + 24)$
   = $64 - 56 = 8$.

12. From figures (i), (ii) and (iii) it is clear that the faces adjacent to 3 have numbers 6, 5, 1 and 4. So, the number on face opposite of face 3 will be 2.

13. From figures (i), (iii) and (iv) it is clear that the faces adjacent to 5 have numbers 6, 3, 4 and 2. So, the number on face opposite of face 5 is 1. In earlier question the face opposite 3 was 2. Now the opposite faces are 3 – 2, 5 – 1 and 4 – 6.

14. A, 15. A, 16. D :

According to the given information the two positions of the cube will be :

The whole cube will be :

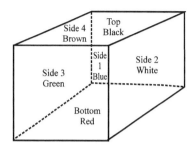

The colours on opposite faces will be : Red—Black, Green—Blue and Brown—White.

20. B, 21. C,   22. A,

The following observations can be made from the three positions of the same dice.

(i) Letters adjacent to 5 are 4, 2, 6 and 1. So, 3 is opposite 5.

(ii) Letters adjacent to 6 are 5, 4, 1 and necessarily 4. So, 2 is opposite 6.

(iii) When opposite numbers are 3–5 and 2–6 then 1 and 4 must be opposites.

23. A, 24. A,   25. C :

The whole cube is :

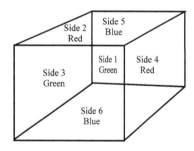

The divided cube is :

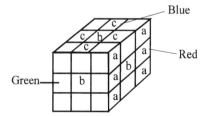

'a'— 12 cubes (6 each on opposite sides) have one face painted red and the other painted green.

'b'— 6 cubes (1 on each side) have only one face painted).

'c'— 8 cubes (4 each on opposite side) have one face painted blue and either red or green on the other.

26. B, 27. B,   28. C,   29. A :

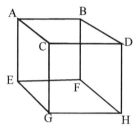

Red faces are ABCD and ABEF
Yellow faces are ACEG and BDFH
Green faces are EFGH and CDGH.

Note that Red and Green colours are on two adjacent faces. So, 2 corner cubical pieces of Red and 2 of Green (i.e., total 4 cubes) will be painted on two faces only and that too with the same colour.

All the corners pieces of the cube will have three faces painted, i.e., 8 cubes.

Yellow sides are on the opposites. Diagrammatically, the explanation taking one side will be :

a	b	b	a
b	c	c	b
b	c	c	b
a	b	b	a

'c' are the centered pieces and are painted on one face only in yellow. So, 4 × 2 (sides) i.e., 8 cubes will have one side painted and in yellow.

Also, note that when a painted cube is cut into smaller cubes like this, not all pieces are coloured. The maximum number of sides painted in a small cube will be 3. No cube will be painted on all faces.

19 | Figure Series

In this form of non-verbal series, which are the most common, four or five consecutive problem figures form a definite sequence and one is required to select the one figure from the given set of Answer Figures that will continue the same sequence.

One has to try different set of moves, changes, replacements, rotations, repetitions and a lot more variations to arrive at the logical pattern making the series. Practising alone will sharpen one's skill of solving such sequences.

Example

1. Problem Figures   **Answer Figures**

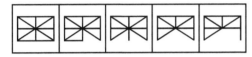

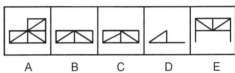

Answer E : Problem Figures consist of a rectangle divided into sections. At each step one of the lines is removed. First from the right, then left and then the centre. To continue this pattern, a right diagonal line is removed. In the answer figure a left diagonal line should be removed. Answer Figure 'E' continues the series.

EXERCISE

Directions : *Each of the following questions consist of problem figures followed by answer figures. Select a figure from amongst the answer figures which will continue the same series or pattern as established by the problem figures.*

1. Problem Figures

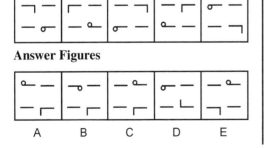

Answer Figures

2. Problem Figures

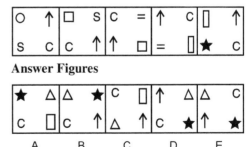

Answer Figures

3. Problem Figures

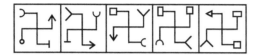

Answer Figures

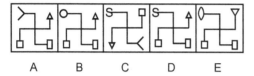

    A   B   C   D   E

4. Problem Figures

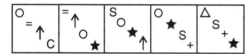

Answer Figures

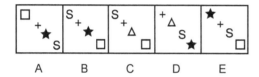

    A   B   C   D   E

5. Problem Figures

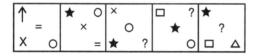

Answer Figures

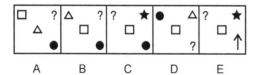

    A   B   C   D   E

6. Problem Figures

Answer Figures

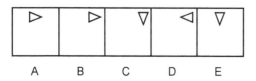

    A   B   C   D   E

7. Problem Figures

Answer Figures

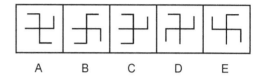

    A   B   C   D   E

8. Problem Figures

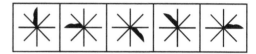

Answer Figures

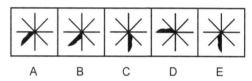

    A   B   C   D   E

9. Problem Figures

Answer Figures

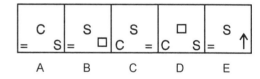

    A   B   C   D   E

10. Problem Figures

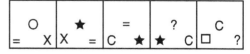

Answer Figures

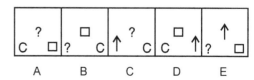

    A   B   C   D   E

11. Problem Figures

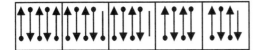

Answer Figures

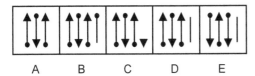

A   B   C   D   E

12. Problem Figures

Answer Figures

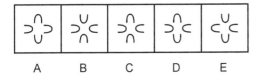

A   B   C   D   E

13. Problem Figures

Answer Figures

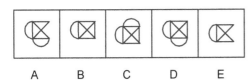

A   B   C   D   E

14. Problem Figures

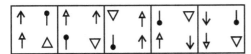

Answer Figures

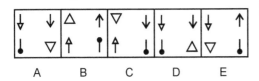

A   B   C   D   E

15. Problem Figures

Answer Figures

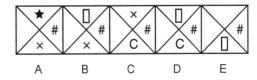

A   B   C   D   E

16. Problem Figures

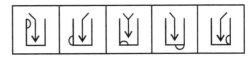

Answer Figures

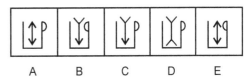

A   B   C   D   E

17. Problem Figures

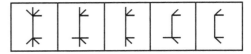

Answer Figures

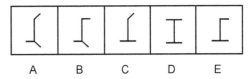

A   B   C   D   E

18. Problem Figures

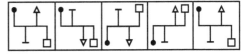

Answer Figures

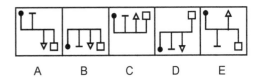

A   B   C   D   E

19. Problem Figures

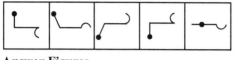

Answer Figures

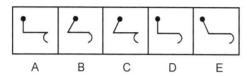

A   B   C   D   E

20. Problem Figures

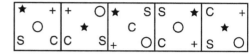

Answer Figures

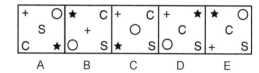

A   B   C   D   E

ANSWERS

1	2	3	4	5	6	7	8	9	10
A	B	D	C	D	B	A	E	B	E
11	**12**	**13**	**14**	**15**	**16**	**17**	**18**	**19**	**20**
D	C	A	D	B	C	E	A	B	D

SOME SELECTED EXPLANATORY ANSWERS

1. In alternate figures the four elements are moved clockwise.

3. The shape is turned 90° clockwise and the element attached to its top left side is replaced by an entirely new element.

6. The triangle is moved half and one steps anticlockwise alternately and turned 90° anticlockwise at each step.

7. In alternate figures the design is turned 90° clockwise.

8. The number of spikes the shade is moved anticlockwise, is increased by one at each step and the placement of the shade is same in alternate figures.

11. Starting from the extreme right element, at a time one part is removed in a set order. Answer Figure D continues the series.

12. Clockwise, starting from the left first one 'u' shape and then two 'u' shapes are turned by 180°. Option C fits the series.

13. Without lifting the pen one part is added to the figure at each step.

16. In alternate figures the semicircle is moved one step clockwise. The three stages of the arrow are repeated from the fourth figure.

18. First the two middle elements are turned to the other side of the horizontal line, then the two corner elements are turned. Also note, this series is repeated from the fifth figure.

20. Starting from the two bottom elements, anticlockwise, their places are interchanged, while the places of other three elements are changed one step anticlockwise.

20 | Analogies or Relationships

Analogy is a process of reasoning between two parallel cases. It relates to agreement or correspon-dence in certain respects between two things. It is a process whereby the underlying relationship that exists between two figures, designs or patterns is determined. Under the process, one has to discover the features common to the two figures or designs. This common feature is a model or base. The question seeks solution on the basis of this model or base.

EXERCISE

Directions : *The second figure in the first unit of the Problem Figures bears a certain relationship to the first figure. Similarly, one of the figures in the Answer Figures bears the same relationship to the first figure in the second unit of the Problem Figures. Locate the figure which would fit the question mark.*

1. Problem Figures

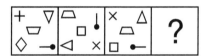

Answer Figures

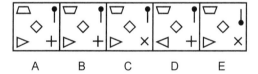

A   B   C   D   E

2. Problem Figures

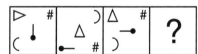

Answer Figures

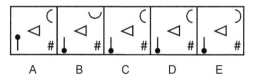

A   B   C   D   E

3. Problem Figures

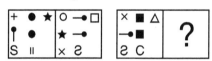

Answer Figures

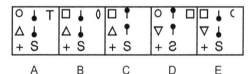

A   B   C   D   E

4. Problem Figures

Answer Figures

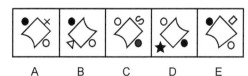

A   B   C   D   E

5. Problem Figures

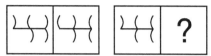

Answer Figures

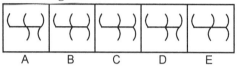

6. Problem Figures

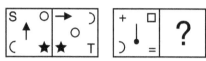

Answer Figures

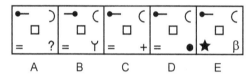

7. Problem Figures

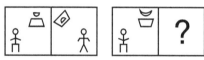

Answer Figures

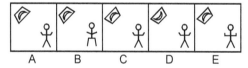

8. Problem Figures

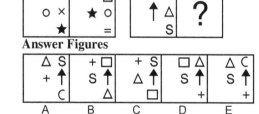

9. Problem Figures

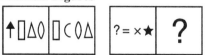

Answer Figures

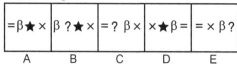

10. Problem Figures

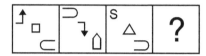

Answer Figures

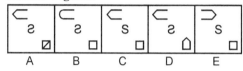

11. Problem Figures

Answer Figures

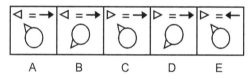

12. Problem Figures

Answer Figures

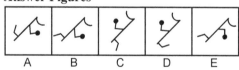

13. Problem Figures

Answer Figures

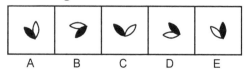

14. Problem Figures   **15. Problem Figures**

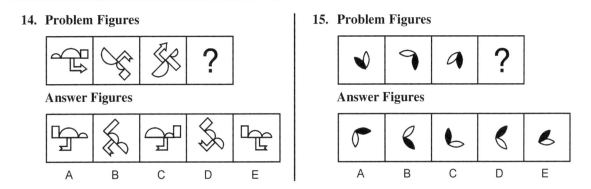

Answer Figures   **Answer Figures**

Directions (Q. 16–20): *In each of the following questions, a related pair of figures is followed by five numbered pairs of figures. Select the pair that has a relationship* **similar** *to that in the unnumbered pair.*

Problem Figure   **Answer Figures**

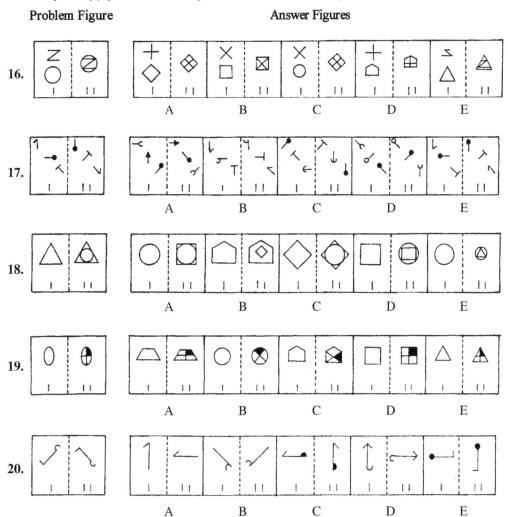

ANSWERS

1	2	3	4	5	6	7	8	9	10
B	C	B	A	E	D	A	E	A	B

11	12	13	14	15	16	17	18	19	20
B	B	A	E	D	B	A	E	D	E

SOME SELECTED EXPLANATORY ANSWERS

2. The element in the top left corner is turned 90° anticlockwise and moved to the centre, the element in the centre is turned 90° clockwise and moved to the bottom left corner position, the element in the bottom left corner is laterally inverted and moved to the top right corner position, and the element in the top right corner is laterally inverted and moved to the bottom right corner position.

4. The first figure is turned 135° clockwise, the inner element is moved out towards the base, the blank circle is shaded and a circle is added on its opposite side to get the second figure.

5. All arcs in the first figure except the left are below the line segment are turned to the other side to get the second figure.

7. The human sketch is moved to the right side and its hands and legs are extended and shortened respectively in a particular manner. The other two elements are turned upside down, the smaller one is enclosed within the larger one and then the two together are moved to the left and rotated 45° anticlockwise.

9. The left most element is made new and then the two corner elements are moved inbetween the two middle elements.

11. The triangle inside the circle is moved one and a half steps clockwise and turned outside. The elements on the side arc moved one step anticlockwise, the arrow and the triangle are

turned 90° clockwise, and 90° anticlockwise respectively.

12. The first figure is turned 90° anticlockwise, one arc is turned to the other side to be in front of the line with a dot to get the second figure.

13. The petals in first figure are turned 135° anticlockwise to get the second figure.

14. Of the three elements the right most element is moved to the left, the design is turned 135° anticlockwise, the arrow is turned to the other side and the lines making the arrowhead are turned inwards.

15. The blank and shaded petals in first figure are turned 90° and 135° anticlockwise respectively to get the second figure.

16. The uppermost design enters into innerside side of the lower design from Ist figure to the IInd figure.

17. In element I to II upper left design comes at lower right rotating 135° C.W. Middle design goes to upper left and rotates 90° CW. While lower right design goes to middle and it also rotates 90° C.W. The same changes occur in option A.

18. In element I to II and ellipse is put in the triangle. Similarly in option E a triangle is put in the ellipse.

19. From first figure to IInd figure, design is divided into four equal parts and right side of the upper portion becomes shaded.

20. From Ist figure to IInd figure, design is reversed after moving 90° anticlockwise direction.

❀ ❀ ❀

21 Classification or Odd-One Out

Classification means arranging the given content in groups or classes having qualities of same kind. In classification type questions, the figures or items are sorted out in groups on the basis of their similarities in qualities in shapes, size, pattern, structure, genus, order, species, grade, style, constituents and other specifications, and thus the answer is found out.

Example

Which one of the following figures is different from the rest. Spot the figure.

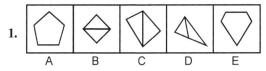

1.

A   B   C   D   E

Answer D : Figures A, B, C and E are made of 5 straight lines, while D has only four straight lines. Thus A, B, C and E have a common characteristic (they have 5 straight lines each), but D does not have this characteristic. Therefore, D is different from the other four figures.

EXERCISE

Directions : *In each of the following questions one of the figures is different from the rest. Spot the figure.*

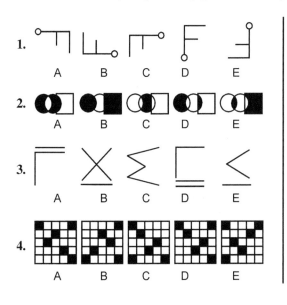

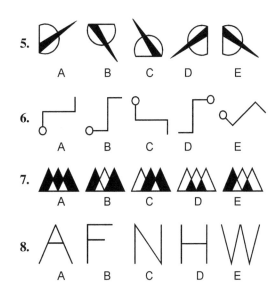

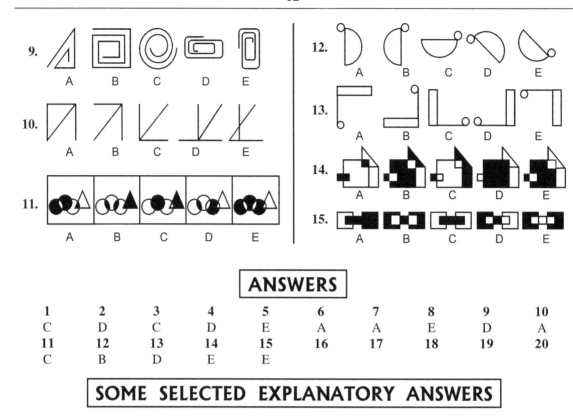

9. A B C D E

10. A B C D E

11. A B C D E

12. A B C D E

13. A B C D E

14. A B C D E

15. A B C D E

ANSWERS

1	2	3	4	5	6	7	8	9	10
C	D	C	D	E	A	A	E	D	A
11	**12**	**13**	**14**	**15**	**16**	**17**	**18**	**19**	**20**
C	B	D	E	E					

SOME SELECTED EXPLANATORY ANSWERS

1. All other figures are identical. The two line segments are to the left of the line with a circle in this option.

2. Figures A and E and figures B and C form opposite pairs. Only figure D is left single.

3. All other figures are Roman Numerals rotated 90° anticlockwise.

4. All other figures have identical squares shaded. In this option one shaded square is on the diagonally opposite corner.

5. All other figures are identical. In this option the shaded part is rising from the left of the base.

6. In all other figures the line segment with the circle is to the right of the straight line. In this option it is on the left side.

7. In all other figures only two sections are shaded.

8. All other figures are made of three straight lines.

9. In all other figures the line forming the pattern is drawn clockwise from outside to inside.

10. All other figures contain three straight lines.

11. Figures A and D and figures B and E are matched opposite pairs. Only figure C is left single.

12. All other figures can be rotated into each other.

13. In all other figures the line with the circle is to the right side at the rectangle base.

14. Only this figure has two segments shaded, all others have three.

15. This is the only figure with a white/blank middle square.

❀ ❀ ❀

CPSIA information can be obtained
at www.ICGtesting.com
Printed in the USA
VHW101159031220
2964LV00040B/1142